A PASSION FOR PLANTS

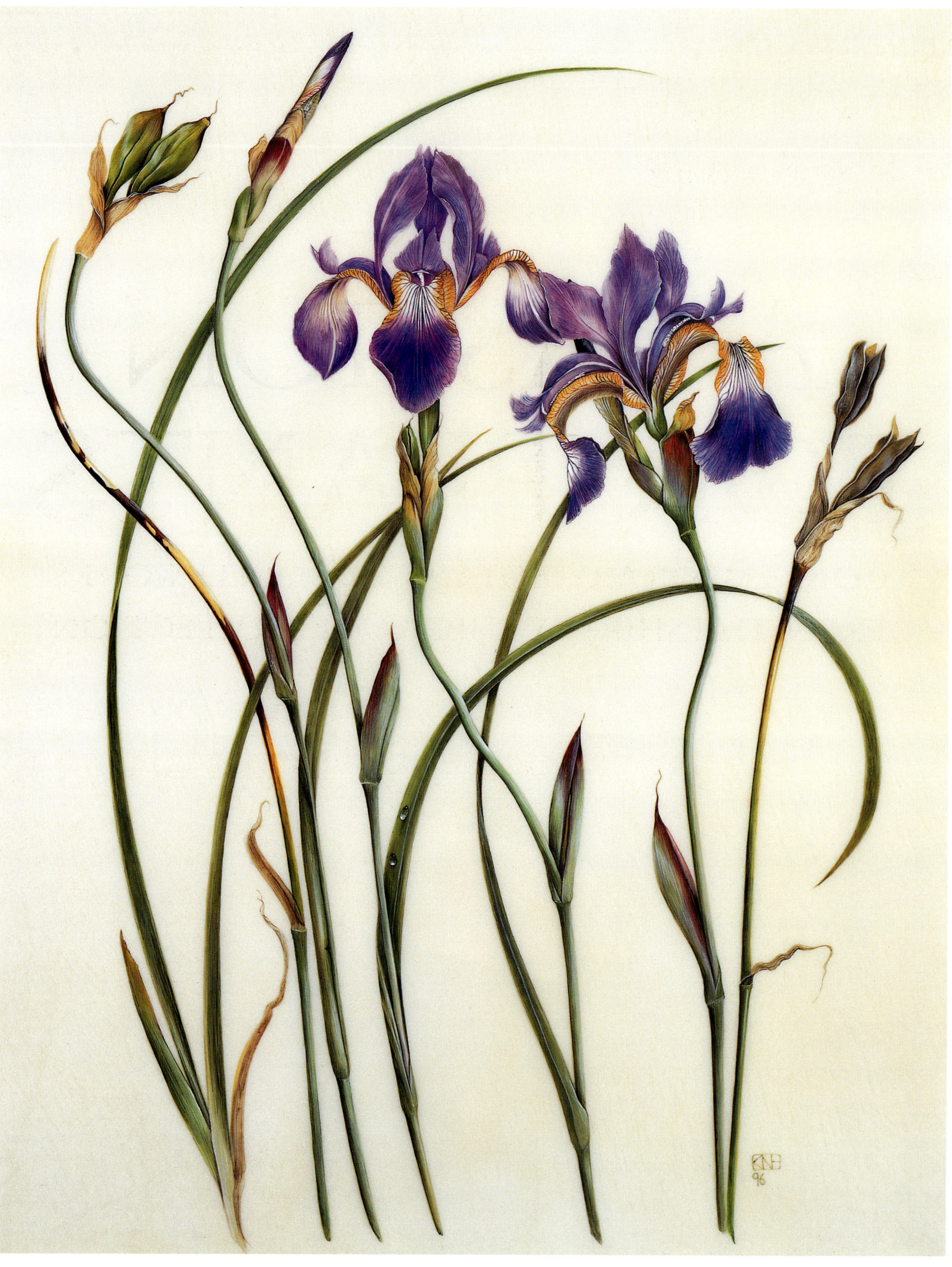

A PASSION FOR PLANTS

CONTEMPORARY BOTANICAL MASTERWORKS FROM THE SHIRLEY SHERWOOD COLLECTION

BY SHIRLEY SHERWOOD

CASSELL&CO

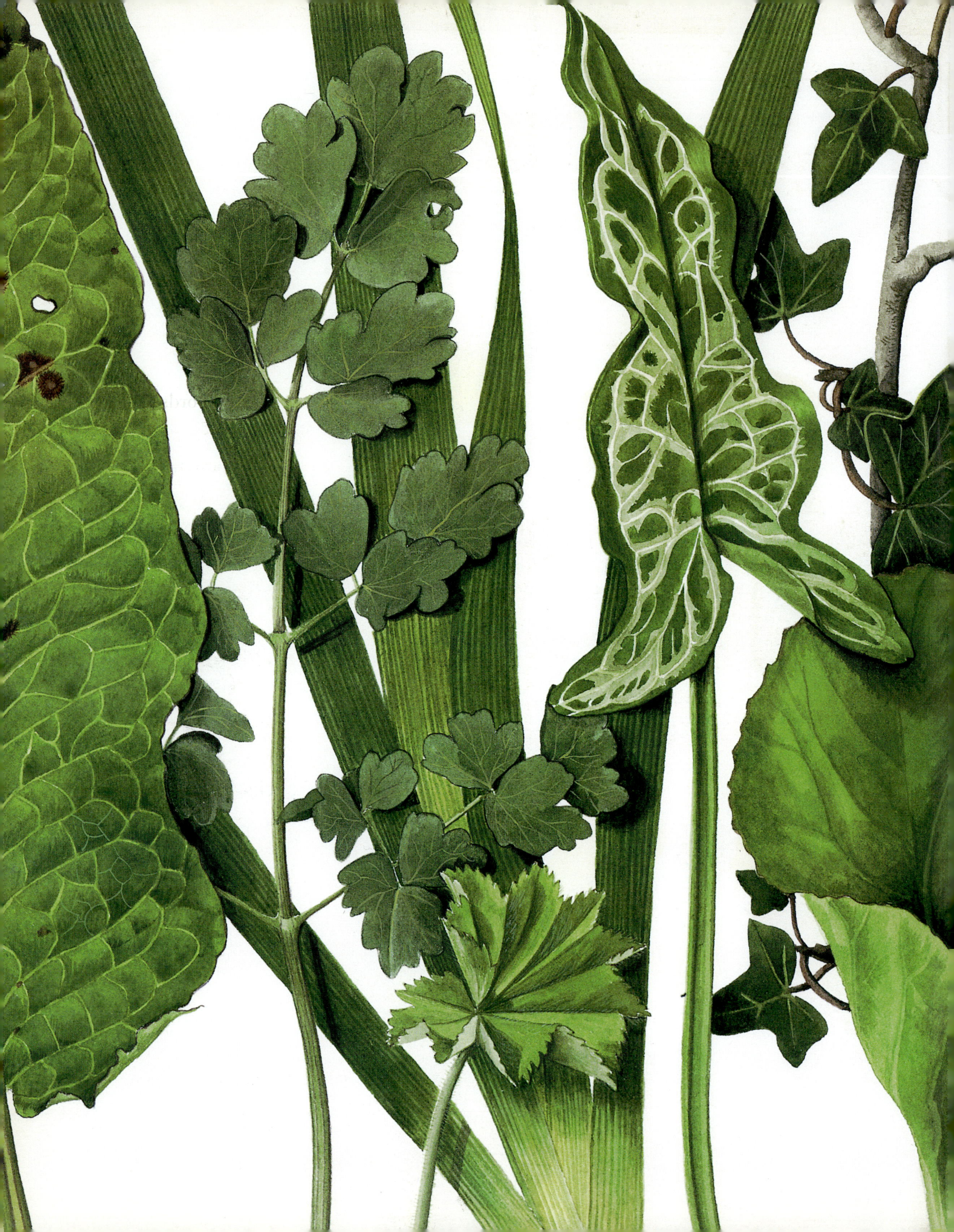

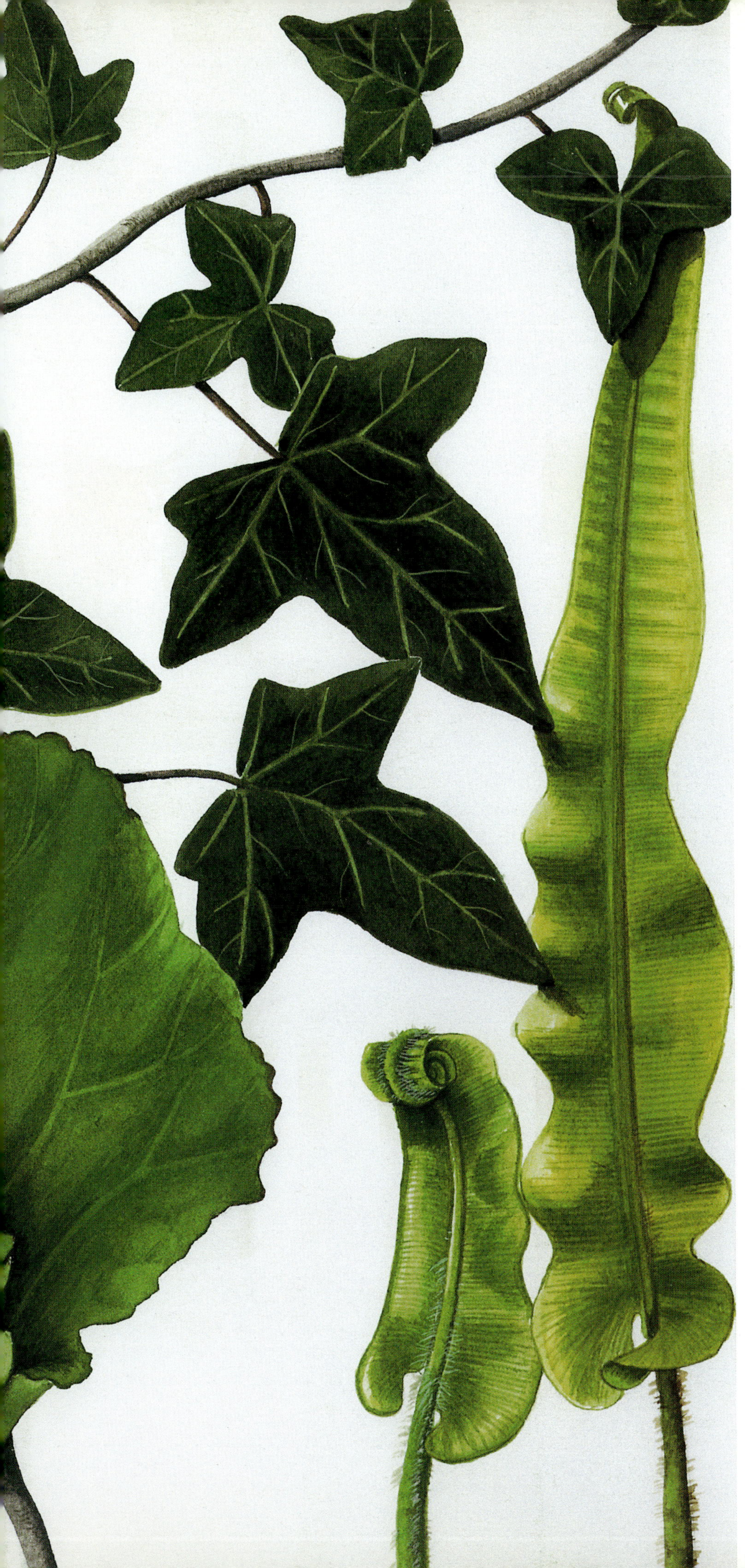

Contents

(Left) Green Leaves by Susan Ogilvy (detail from painting which appears on page 162)
(Title page) Siberian Flag: *Iris siberica* by Celia Hegedus (painting appears on page 103)

Exhibition Venues

1996
Kew Gardens Gallery
Royal Botanic Gardens, Kew, Richmond, Surrey, England

The Hunt Insitute for Botanical Documentation
Carnegie Mellon University, Pittsburgh, Pennsylvania, United States

1997
Gibbes Gallery
Charleston, South Carolina, United States

New Orleans Museum of Art
New Orleans, Louisiana, United States

Wave Hill
at the National Arts Club, 15 Gramercy Park South, New York, New York, United States

Museum of Modern Art
National Galleries of Scotland, Edinburgh, Scotland

1998
S. H. Ervin Gallery
Sydney, Australia

Yasuda Kasai Museum of Art
Tokyo, Japan

Kirstenbosch National Botanical Gardens
Cape Town, South Africa

1999
Millesgarden Museum
Stockholm, Sweden

2000
Dixon Gallery & Gardens
Memphis, Tennessee, United States

Forthcoming Exhibitions

2001
Marciana Library
Venice, Italy

2002
Ashmolean Museum
Oxford, England

Forewords

Dr Shirley Sherwood is on my list of originals. Single-handed she has acted as a catalyst, signalling and at the same time, encouraging a worldwide revival in the art of botanical painting. Artists around the globe have been made aware that they are not solitary exponents of a dying genre but members of a community which has achieved a remarkable renaissance. It is one thing, however, for that to happen but it is quite another for that fact to be presented and promoted to a far wider public.

And that is where Dr Sherwood's contribution has been singular. She has not only been an avid collector of work by its finest exponents but a passionate believer in promoting their work through exhibitions, publications, events and courses. In this book she has the boldness to place the work of today side by side with that of the acclaimed geniuses of the past. The achievements of these old masters was driven on by the renaissance rediscovery of the natural world and by the influx of new plants from the voyages of discovery. As a consequence, their works combine scientific exactitude with a constant amazement of creation. The result is an intensity of vision which still holds us today. Can we say the same of the work of our own age? I leave that to the reader to decide. But there is much to be said for the fact that the present renaissance is also a reflection of just such an intensity of vision, albeit a different one. No longer, or rarely, are these of the wonder of discovery. Rather they are passionate delineations of the beauties of the natural world under threat. Earlier artists took up their brushes to record what had not been seen before. So often now it is a case of recording what may never be seen again, if the rape of the natural world through global pollution is allowed to continue.

Roy Strong

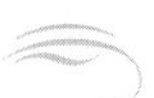

Since publication in 1996 of Dr Shirley Sherwood's immensely successful book, *Contemporary Botanical Artists: The Shirley Sherwood Collection*, her superb collection has been exhibited in the UK, the United States, Australia, Japan, South Africa and Sweden, and throughout the world she has organised classes on botanical art taught by noted artists. Now this more comprehensive book emphasises the renaissance of botanical art today – the theme of her forthcoming exhibition at the Ashmolean Museum at Oxford University. Dr Sherwood's efforts have set the highest standards for artists and collectors alike, and have introduced many thousands of gallery-goers to her passion, and mine. Certainly Dr Sherwood's name is at the forefront of this welcome resurgence of botanical art.

James J. White
Curator of Art and Principal Research Scholar
Hunt Insitute for Botanical Documentation
Carnegie Mellon University, Pittsburgh, Pennsylvania

PAUL JONES (1921–97)
Sunflower
Signed Paul Jones '78
Acrylic on paper 700 × 510 mm
Original in Shirley Sherwood Collection

Introduction

Early in the 1990s when I started collecting contemporary botanical art I soon realised that there was a wealth of wonderful painters, unheralded and almost unrecognised by much of the artistic and scientific community. Most of the art lovers I spoke to thought that botanical art only existed in the past and were amazed at my enthusiasm for today's work. During the last ten years I have seen this revival become a renaissance and I believe that the work currently being done by artists all over the world can be compared with that of the greatest botanical painters of the past. The sub-title of this book, *Contemporary Botanical Masterworks*, makes a claim for contemporary artists, which I hope to justify by presenting works from the past and present side by side.

Botanical art has been described as the meeting place between the arts and the sciences, and perhaps because of my training as a scientist, its rigour and precision appeal to me as well as its beauty. I have enjoyed collecting the whole gamut of works from precise line drawings to dramatic and romantic portrayals of plants. Each acquisition has a disciplined underpinning of botanical correctness, the 'bones' that come from intense observation, married to a wealth of background knowledge. Artists usually fall in love with the plant they are drawing and this shows in their work.

I have collected almost all the modern works illustrated here since the end of 1995, when I finished my book *Contemporary Botanical Artists: the Shirley Sherwood Collection*. There have been several printings, amounting to over 35,000 copies, an encouraging number for a 'niche' book, and it has become the key handbook for today's artists as well

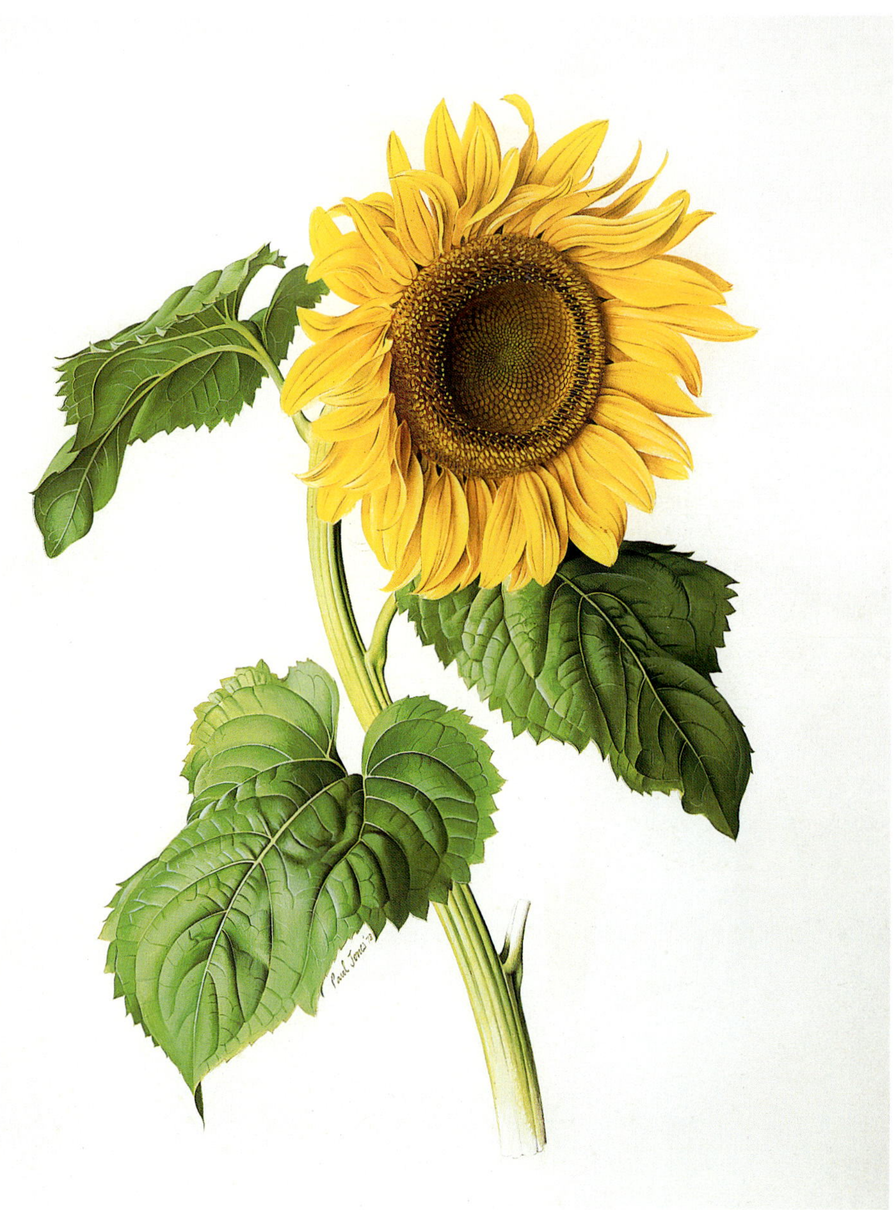

ALEXANDER MARSHAL (*c.* 1620–82)
Sunflower and a liver-coloured dog
Watercolour on paper 460 × 333 mm
Original in the *Florilegium of Alexander Marshal* at Windsor Castle.

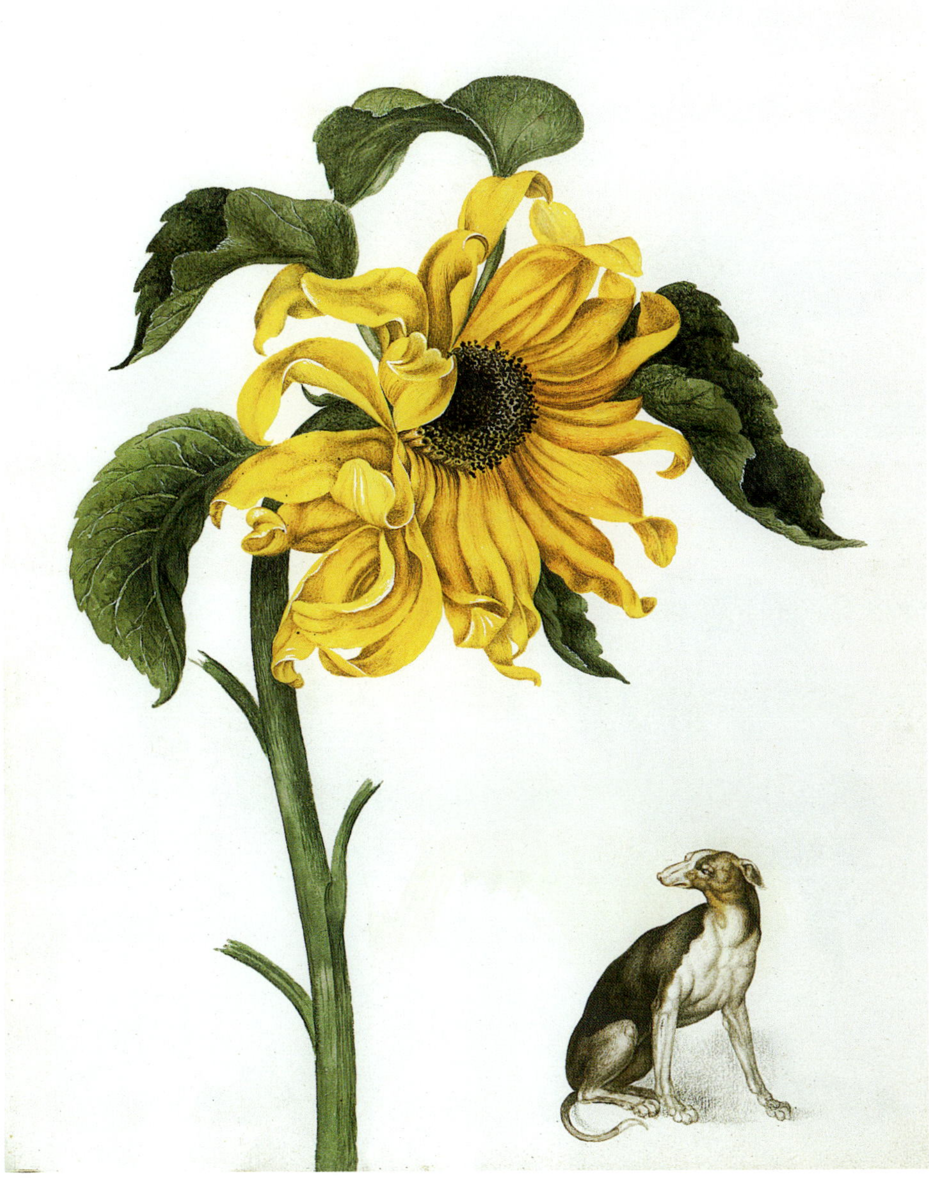

as a standard reference book in libraries. By now my collection has grown to more than 400 works, executed by 180 artists from over twenty countries – so it is by no means insular. There are far more women than men painting in this area, in a ratio of three to one, probably because it is still hard to make a living as a self-supporting artist. There are many new artists coming into the field and I have acquired works from fifty-five of them, which are shown here for the first time, as well as additional works from a number of artists that I had collected previously in the period 1990–95. I have met nearly all of them and many keep in touch with me on a regular basis. All but three of the artists were alive when I acquired their paintings, but sadly a few have died since.

I only have space here to chose ten paintings of 'Old Masters', some of which have not been widely published before, and I have matched them against ten paintings of 'New Masters' from my collection. It has been an exciting and a difficult choice, as there are so many competing drawings and so many wonderful 'matches' of old and new. After much agonising I decided that my 'big four' artists from the first Golden Age are Georg Dionysius Ehret (1708–70), Francis Bauer (1758–1840) and his

I chose this matching pair of new and old sunflower studies as both artists, although separated by 300 years, have responded with equal vigour and skill to the subject. Marshal's Florilegium (*near left*) is a collection of delightful seasonal pages executed in the 1600s but has only just been published. Australian Paul Jones (*far left*), one of the most celebrated contemporary botanical artists, is renowned today for his superb flower portraits and his exquisite camellias.

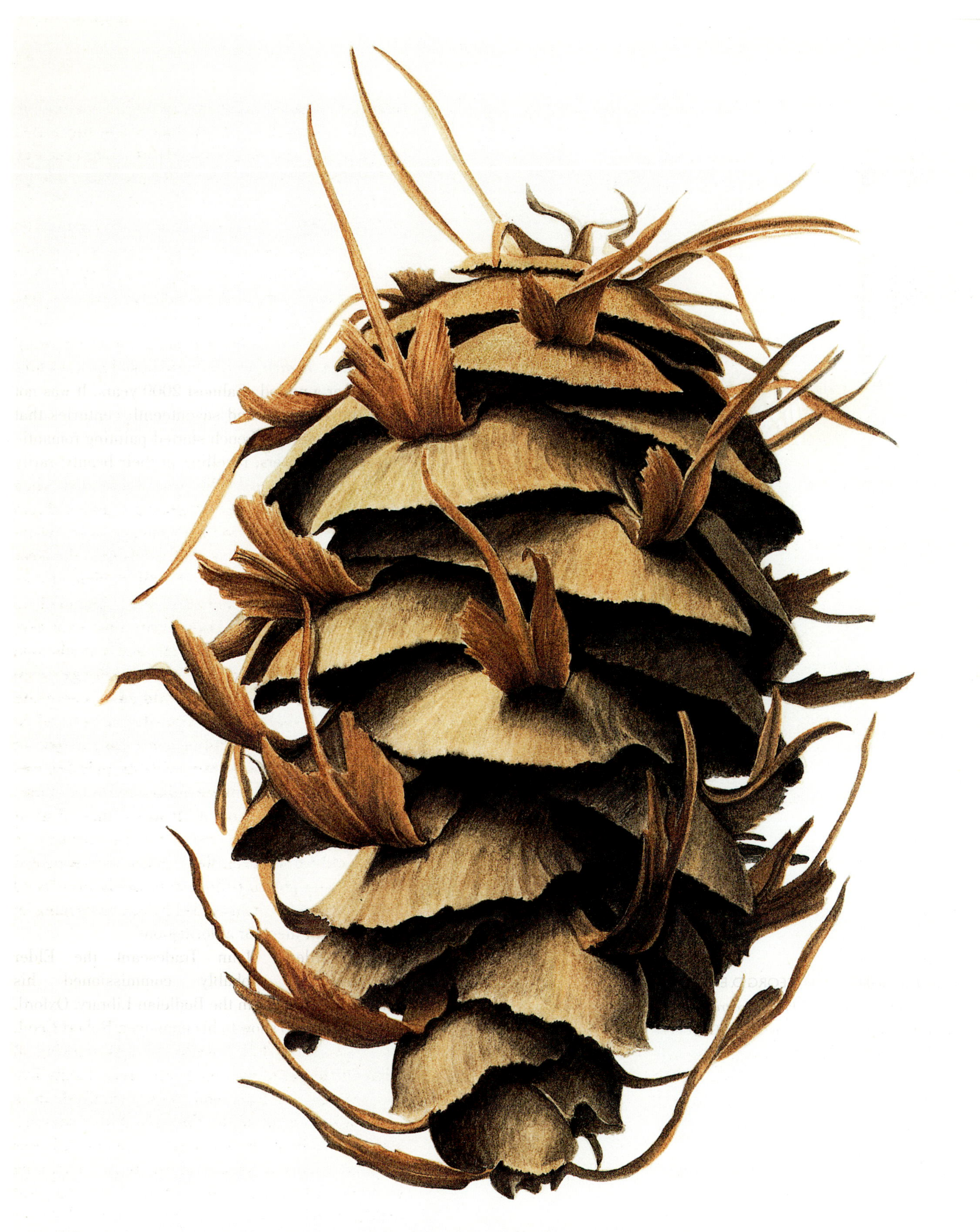
Pseudotsuga menziesii x 2½
with acknowledgements to Professor William Harlow
1993

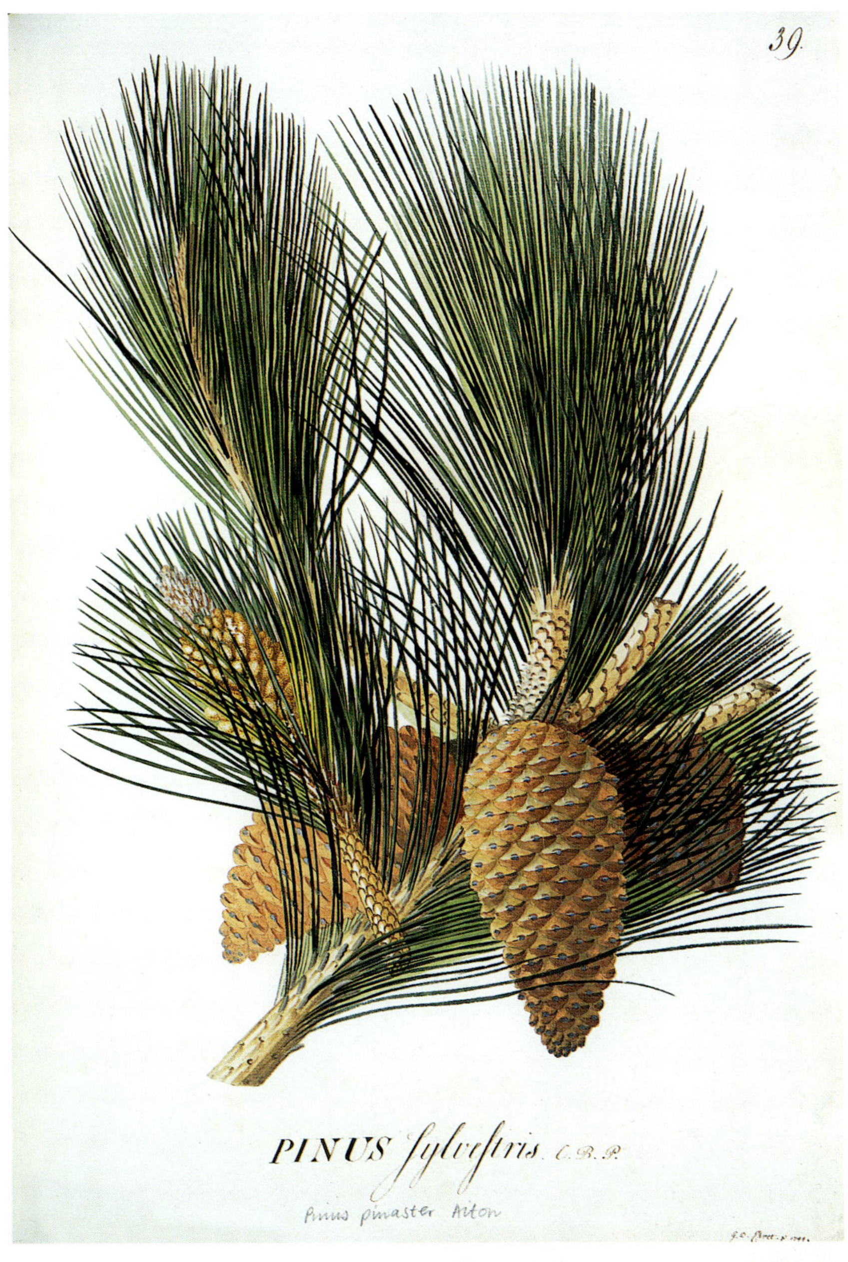

Ehret was one of the world's greatest botanical artists and his masterly study of this pine (*above*) contrasts well with Brigid Edwards' modern, enlarged and dramatic cone (*left*). She is perhaps the most outstanding and successful of today's exponents in this expanding field, exhibiting in the UK and the United States. Contemporary artists Ann Farrer and Kate Nessler have also painted conifers with a skill to rival that of Ehret.

GEORG D. EHRET (1708–70)
Pinus sylvestris
Signed G. D. Ehret 1744
Watercolour on paper
526 × 363 mm
Original in the Natural History Museum, London

BRIGID EDWARDS (1940–)
Douglas Fir: *Pseudotsuga menziesii* × 2½
Watercolour over pencil on vellum 250 × 180 mm
Original in Shirley Sherwood Collection

brother Ferdinand (1760–1826) and Pierre-Joseph Redouté (1759–1840). These four are distinguished by the beauty and skill of their work, their accuracy and their incredible industry. I have also added a newly published work by Alexander Marshal (*c.* 1620–82) kept in the library at Windsor Castle. The rest of this book belongs to the contemporary artists I have collected since the beginning of 1996; their work will reinforce my claim for today's renaissance.

Most of the earliest botanical studies were focused on the medicinal use of plants. Dioscorides' *De Materia Medica* was an herbal used as a doctor's guide over a period of almost 2000 years. It was not until the sixteenth and seventeenth centuries that the Dutch and the French started painting romantic still-lifes of flowers, revelling in their beauty, rarity and lustrous colours. This was the period when hundreds of new species were being introduced into Europe. Ambassadors to the Ottoman Empire would send home bulbs, rhizomes and seeds from the Near East; when these were successfully cultivated they caused great excitement and were included in painted flower pieces. At the same time explorers were bringing back strange plants and animals from all over the world. Coconuts and ostrich eggs were so treasured they were made into silver-encrusted goblets, and shells were exquisitely displayed in cabinets of curiosities. Tulipomania was raging over Europe and a contemporary still-life painting was hardly to be found without tulips and other introduced and valued 'exotica'. It was a time of great intellectual excitement and of intense curiosity in the natural world, when the wealthy, well-educated person would grow a collection of newly introduced plants and have them recorded by commissioning an artist to paint them for a florilegium.

The gardener John Tradescant the Elder (*c.*1570–1638) probably commissioned his 'Orchard', now kept in the Bodleian Library, Oxford, as a catalogue to show to his employer, Robert Cecil, first Earl of Hatfield, while he was working at Hatfield House. It comprises two folios of sixty-five watercolours of fruit and nuts, arranged in a sequence of availability throughout the seasons. Designed to be used as a 'planting planner', it was probably executed by several artists in a charming but very naive style. Tradescant was himself a great collector and his son John Tradescant the Younger (1608–62) went on three expeditions to Virginia, bringing back a variety of unusual treasures. The Tradescant collection of curiosities became the first museum in England, commonly known as 'The Ark'.

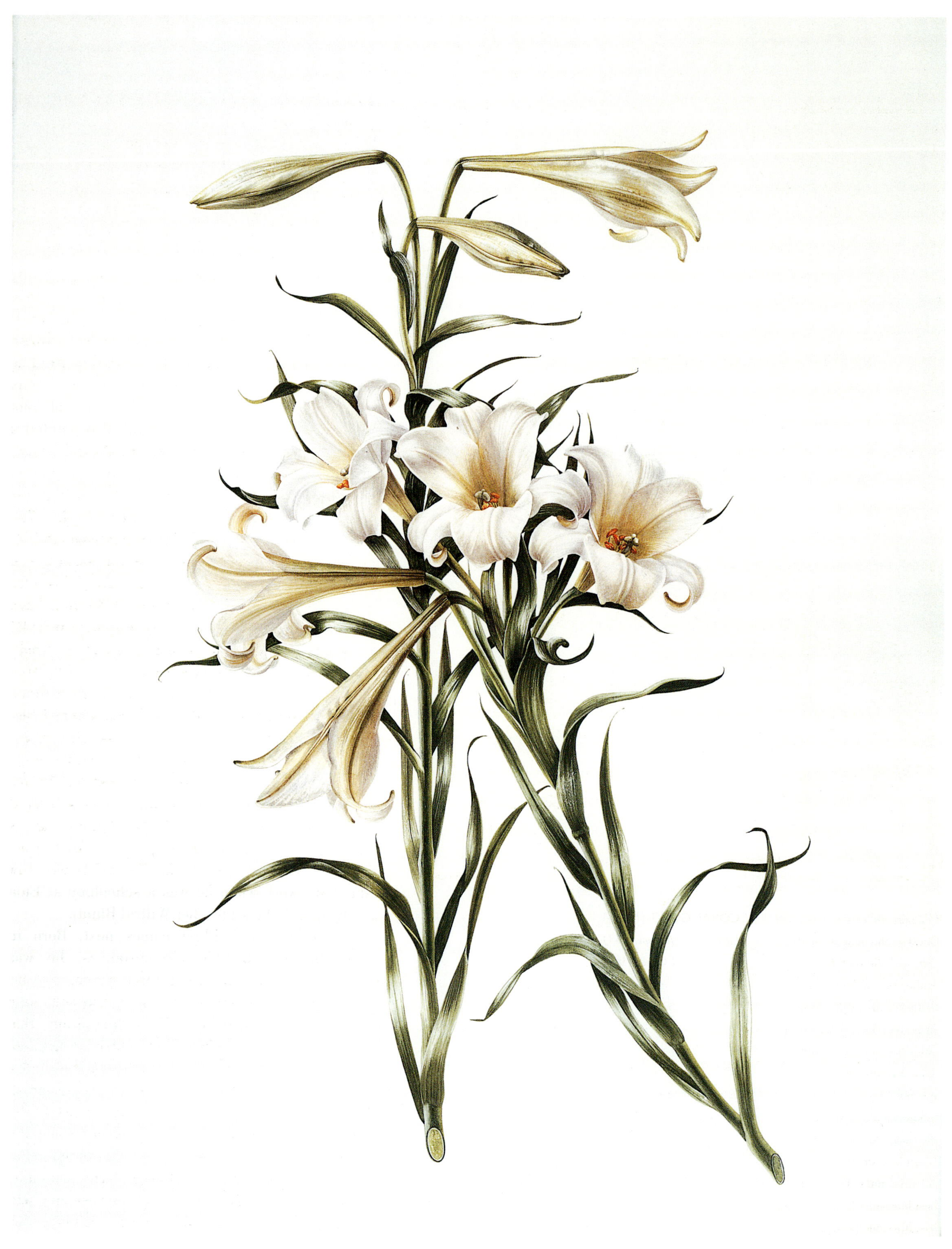

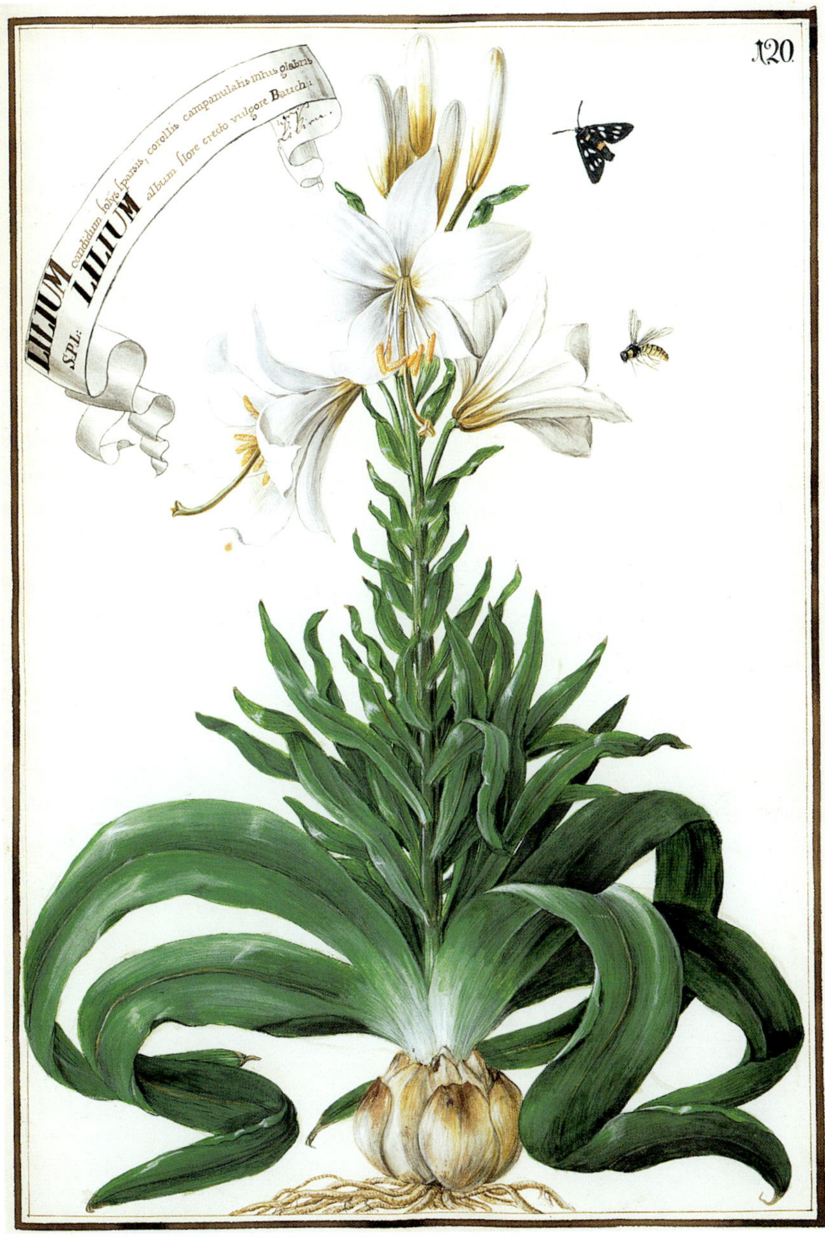

Compare the elegance of Coral Guest's contemporary study (*left*) with the youthful exuberance of the Bauer brothers's lily (*above*). Their early work has only just been published, although painted more than two centuries ago. It is not known which of the brothers painted this portrait in the Codex Liechtenstein. Coral Guest is a superb water-colourist and gifted teacher, best known for her paintings of iris, lilies and peonies.

CORAL GUEST (1955–)
Lilium longiflorum 'Ice Queen'
Signed Coral Guest 1995
Watercolour on paper
760 × 570 mm. Original in Shirley Sherwood Collection

FRANCIS BAUER (1758–1840) & FERDINAND BAUER (1760–1826)
Lilium candidum. Painted *c.* 1778. Watercolour on paper
522 × 377 mm
Original in the *Codex Liechtenstein*, Vaduz

This collection was eventually acquired by Elias Ashmole and became part of the Ashmolean Museum which he founded in Oxford.

John Tradescant the Younger lived in South Lambeth and in 1641 the artist Alexander Marshal (*c.* 1620–82) came to live with him. During the 1640s Marshal executed a florilegium on vellum of the plants in Tradescant's garden which he completed in 1650 and which has now sadly disappeared. It is possible that at the same time Marshal painted the border surrounding the posthumous painting of John Tradescant the Elder which is now in the Ashmolean; the central portrait is attributed to Cornelius de Neve. The border is a mix of tulips, shells, grapes and bunches of root vegetables painted in oil. Marshal also painted a florilegium for himself which, thankfully, did survive and is now held at Windsor Castle Library as part of the Royal Collection. Prudence Reith-Ross has just written a wonderfully illustrated book, *The Florilegium of Alexander Marshal* (published 2000).

He painted some 650 individual flowers, arranged seasonally, and was known for mixing his own colours. One of the artists in my collection, Luca Palermo, spent some time at Windsor in 1984 undertaking a detailed investigation of Marshal's Florilegium. Luca, too, now makes many of his own colours which he uses for working on vellum. Marshal's work has a skill and delicacy that I find particularly appealing and so I have chosen his painting of a sunflower as one of my examples of the work of early masters of botanical painting. As this work was first published in Reith-Ross's book it cannot have been 'copied' by today's artists (although I suppose it is possible that Rory McEwen, might be one of the few artists who saw Marshal's work when he was a schoolboy at Eton studying with the art teacher Wilfrid Blunt).

Georg Dionysius Ehret comes next. Born in Heidelberg in humble circumstances, he was apprenticed as a gardener and was noticed by Carl Wilhelm, the Margrave of Baden-Durlach, who made a collection of over 6000 illustrations that Ehret made of his garden. Ehret's outstanding talent was also recognised by Jakob Trew (1695–1769) a Nuremberg physician and passionate botanist. Eventually Ehret travelled to England, met Philip Miller and Sir Hans Sloane and became a popular figure, teaching his aristocratic patrons whilst painting in their great gardens. Ehret preferred vellum to paper and body-colour to transparent watercolour. The huge body of work which he produced is mainly

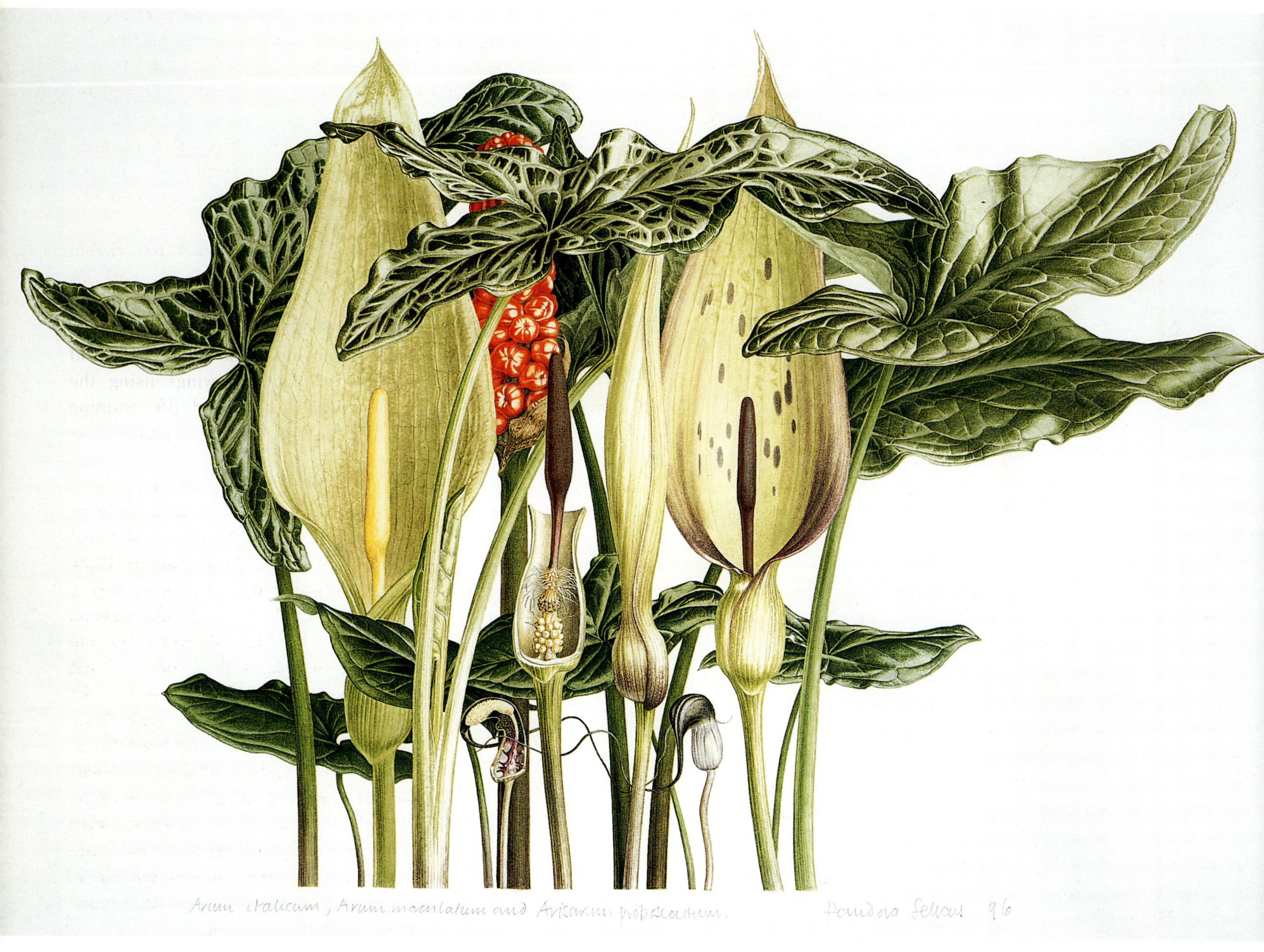

PANDORA SELLARS (1936–)
Arum italicum, Arum maculatum & Arisarum proboscideum
Named and signed Pandora Sellars '96
Watercolour on paper
350 × 470 mm
Original in Shirley Sherwood Collection

held in museums and most remains unpublished. His work has a combination of strength and sensibility and he truly deserves his increasing recognition as one of the greatest botanical artists.

Over a century after Marshal, Prince Joseph Fürst of Liechtenstein (1726–81) cultivated elaborate gardens at Feldsberg, Lower Austria. His court painter, Lukas Bauer, died leaving three talented young boys – Joseph, Francis and Ferdinand – who were taken under the wing of Father Nobert Boccius and engaged to paint specimens for a new florilegium. These watercolours on paper, mostly executed by Francis and Ferdinand Bauer, were bound together in fourteen volumes and became the *Codex Liechtenstein*. Just recently Prince Philipp of

Liechtenstein organised the publication of eighty-eight of these lovely studies in *A Garden for Eternity*, with a commentary by H. Walter Lack. It is a beautiful book containing many fresh and delightful paintings by two of the greatest botanical painters of all time. I thought it would be interesting to compare some of these newly published works of the teenaged Bauer brothers with recent work by modern masters.

Both Francis and Ferdinand had remarkable careers in botanical art after their early work for Nobert Boccius. Francis lived most of his life at Kew and was buried in St Mary's churchyard there in 1840. Renowned for his work on orchids and heathers and his exquisite drawings using the microscope, he spent a contented life painting specimens sent to the famous botanical garden from all over the world.

His brother Ferdinand had a much more adventurous time. He was recommended to John Sibthorp, Sherardian Professor of Botany at Oxford, and joined him on his first journey to the Levant in 1786, painting plants from southern Italy, Greece, Turkey and the islands of the eastern Mediterranean. Ferdinand worked up his sketches and notes into superb portraits of the plants they collected and those original paintings are now conserved in the Department of Plant Sciences, Oxford (called the Botany Department, when I took my degree there). His studies were eventually published as *Flora Graeca* (1806–40) and there are still two sets of the ten published volumes held at Oxford. (It was such a costly venture that only twenty-five sets were printed.) Sibthorp died before it was published, having succumbed to tuberculosis after his second journey to the eastern Mediterranean.

Some years later, in 1800, Ferdinand joined another expedition, this time financed by Sir Joseph Banks. Led by Matthew Flinders, Bauer set sail as official artist with the explorers who were eventually to circumnavigate Australia, proving it was an island-continent. His beautiful drawings of many previously unrecorded species are now kept at the Natural History Museum, London. These include wallabies, frilly sea horses, Australian parrots and a wealth of new plants. I saw these original paintings when a number were shown for the first time in Sydney in 1998.

While Ehret and Francis Bauer mostly worked in England, Pierre-Joseph Redouté made his name in France. Redouté arrived in Paris from the Belgian Ardennes, and at twenty-three met Charles Louis

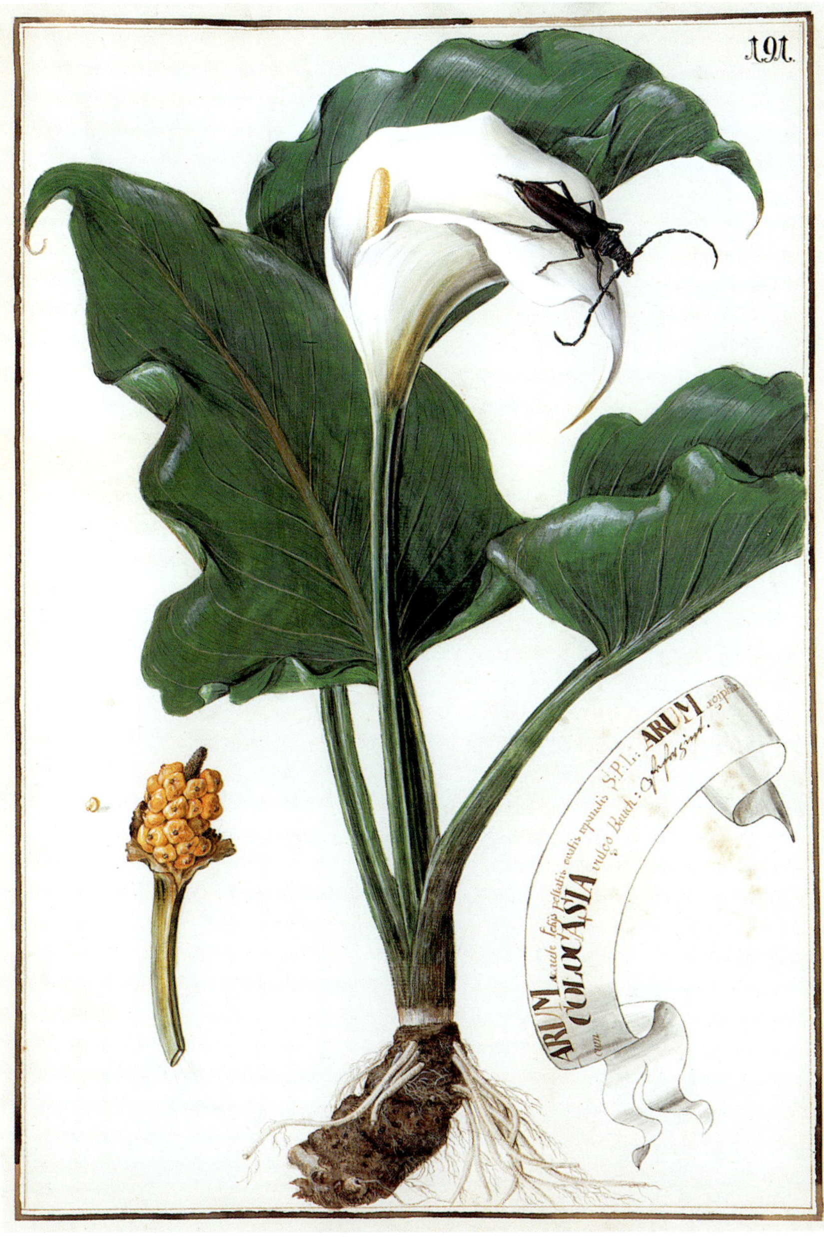

Celebrated for her masterly compositions and subtle colour, Pandora Sellars' highly individual style (*left*) contrasts with the lively rendering by the young Bauers at the beginning of their careers (*above*). Pandora Sellars is particularly well known for her studies of arums and orchids, and she must be considered one of the most important botanical artists of all time. She transcends the scientific plant study to paint true works of art.

BAUER BROTHERS
(1758–1840) & (1760–1826)
Zantedeschia aethiopica
Painted *c.* 1778
Watercolour on paper
522 × 377 mm
Original in the *Codex Liechtenstein*, Vaduz

l'Héritier de Brutelle who became both his botanical teacher and his patron. In 1800, Redouté was commissioned by the Empress Joséphine to record her plant collection at Malmaison, her estate some ten miles outside Paris. His watercolours of Joséphine's plants were published in two books: Ventenat's *Jardin de la Malmaison* (1803–4) in which 120 were reproduced as stipple-engravings, and Bonpland's *Descriptions des Plantes Rares Cultivées à Malmaison et à Navarre* (1812–17) with fifty-four of the sixty-four plates by Redouté. Later he painted 468 watercolours on vellum for *Les Liliacées*, which, despite the title, includes many plants besides lilies. *Les Roses* contains probably the most widely reproduced botanical images which today can be found on everything from boxes of toilet tissues to prints for the walls of hotel corridors.

His work is exquisite and he is without doubt the most famous of all botanical artists, but I must echo Wilfrid Blunt who said, 'A certain artificiality, a certain Empire elegance, is apparent in all Redouté's work'.

I am always being asked 'who is the best botanical artist today?', but I feel that there are just too many good artists to give one person that specific accolade. When I wrote *Contemporary Botanical Artists: the Shirley Sherwood Collection*, a book solely devoted to 113 of today's artists, I could not answer that question, and since then even more artists have appeared on the scene, some who have long worked in obscurity and others who have leapt, seemingly fully formed, onto the public stage. Nearly every week since the book was published, I have been contacted by aspiring artists stimulated by my book or excited by the exhibitions I have organised around the world to show these paintings to a wider audience.

Even if I cannot answer the question 'who is the best?' I do think it is possible to speculate on who has been the most influential. I believe that there have been two main forces at work, fuelling the new renaissance of botanical art and that these have been spearheaded by certain artists who have influenced and drawn in others by their example.

Margaret Mee (1909–88) is a prime example of a leader of the green revolution, alerting the world to the destruction and exploitation of the Amazonian rainforest. A veteran of many solo expeditions into the Amazon, through her paintings of endangered species she succeeded in setting off alarm bells, not only in Brazil but also world-wide. Some of her later paintings are of plants pictured against their forest backgrounds, emphasising how they grew and flourished in their local environment which was at risk from indiscriminate 'slash and burn' farming, logging or surface gold mining. She was passionately involved in her crusade and I think this comes through in her painting: they are not dry, tight illustrations, but beautifully designed plant portraits of great quality and faithful to botanical detail. The paintings shown at her important exhibition at Kew in 1988 have since been circulating the United States in a travelling exhibition. Margaret Mee's life and work have inspired many artists and ecologists, particularly in Brazil, but also further afield, through the activities of the Margaret Mee Foundation which helps facilitate the exchange of artists and scientists between Brazil and Kew. Now,

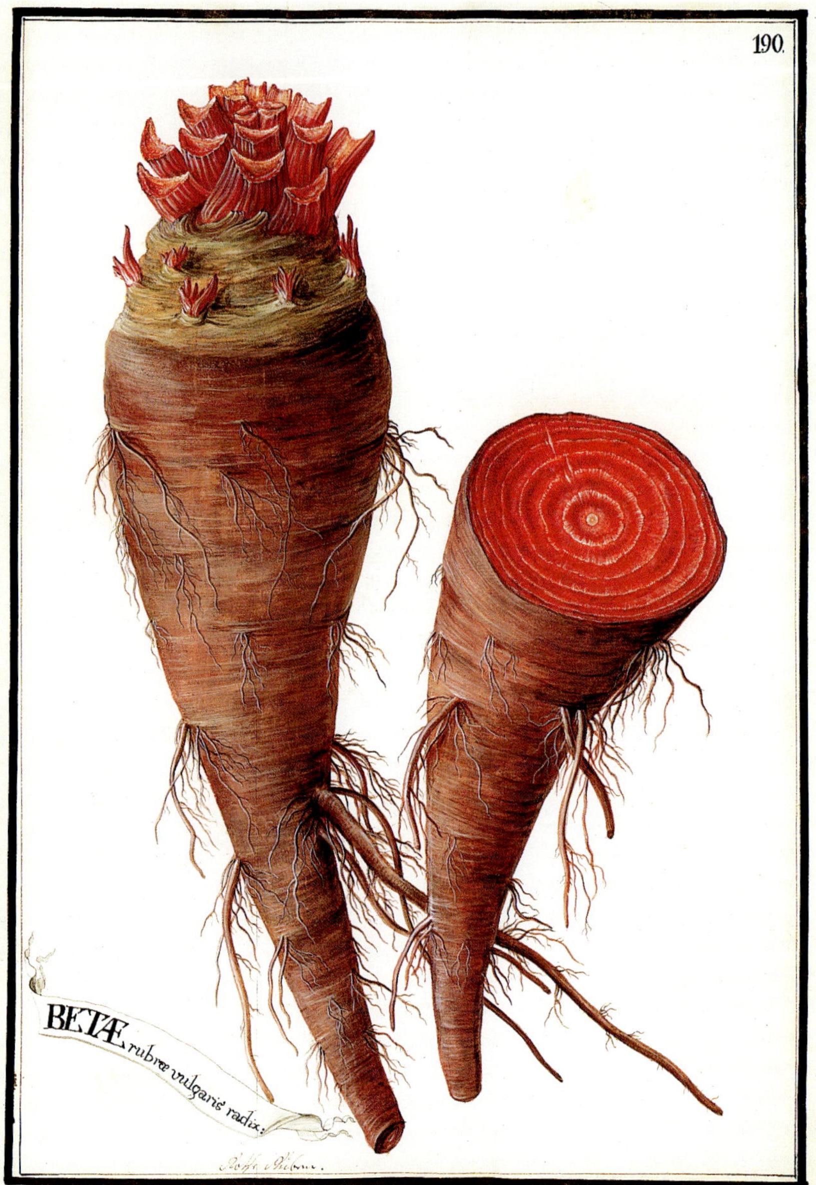

BAUER BROTHERS
Beta vulgaris
Painted *c.* 1779
Watercolour on paper
522 × 377 mm
Original in the *Codex Liechtenstein*, Vaduz

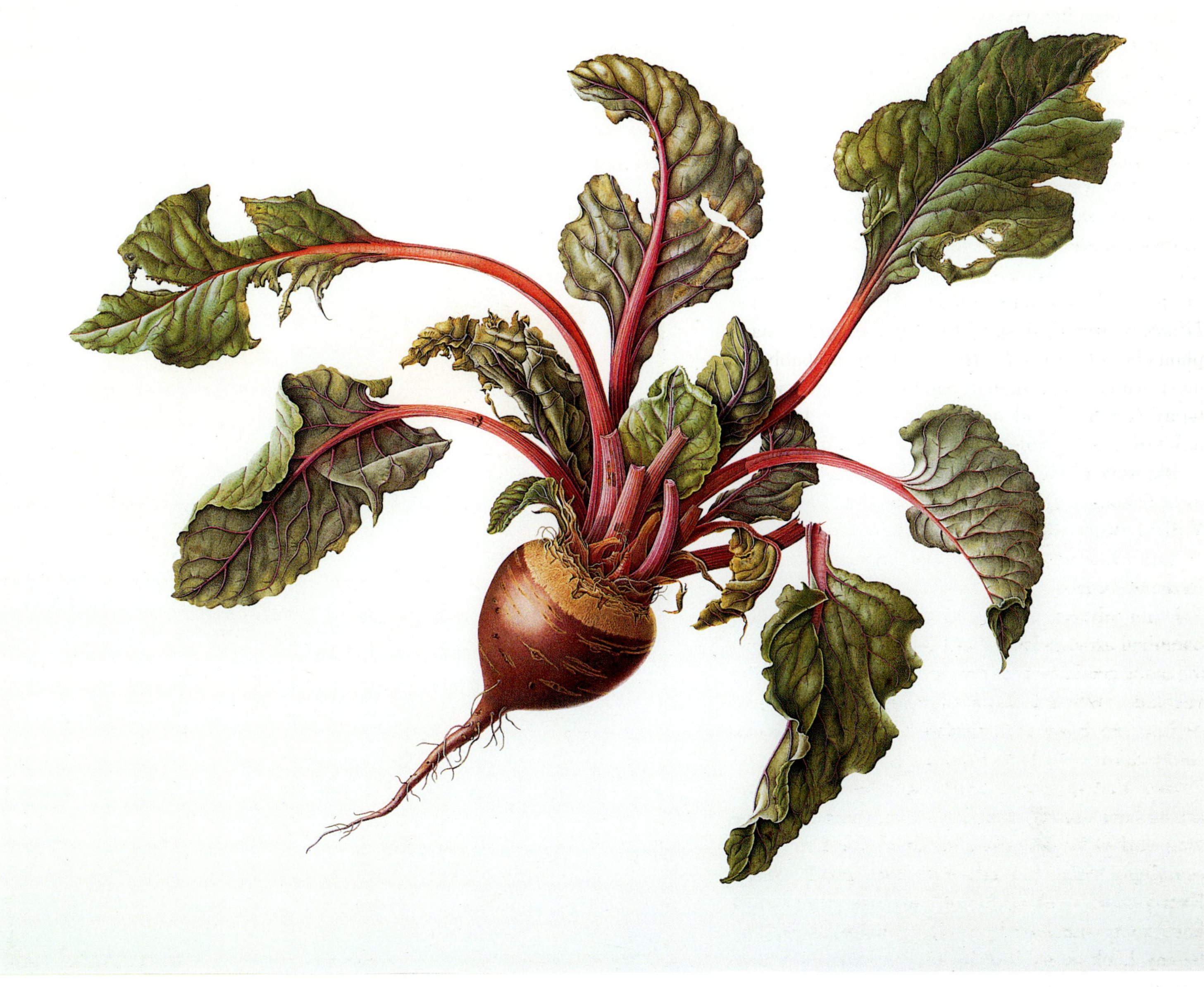

The young Bauer brothers' robust, sliced beetroot (*left*) is an appropriate match for Susannah Blaxill's renowned study, one of the most exciting vegetable portraits of today (*above*). Her wonderfully detailed, dramatic picture appeared on the front page of the *New York Times* arts section whilst on exhibition in that city.

SUSANNAH BLAXILL (1954–)
Beetroot
Artist's stamp, undated
Watercolour on paper
480 × 640 mm
Original in Shirley Sherwood Collection

all over the world there are other artists recording endangered natural communities, anxious to capture, at least in paint, some precious images of plants that may soon vanish together with their threatened habitats. Margaret Mee has become an icon to the environmentalists.

Another force at work in the resurgence of botanical art can be exemplified by the Scottish artist Rory McEwen (1932–82). By coincidence his work was also shown in an exhibition in 1988 and many of the artists in my collection went to see both his retrospective show at the Serpentine Gallery, London and the Margaret Mee exhibition at Kew. McEwen's approach was quite different from Margaret Mee's depiction of the exotic and sometimes endangered plants of Brazil. He aspired to be a modern artist, while drawing on the subjects that were favourites of artists in the past such as roses, auriculas and tulips, carnations and fritillaries. He also painted dead and crumpled leaves as if conscious of his own mortality.

Twentieth-century art has become more and more abstract and yet there are many artists who still want to paint in a realistic way. It is increasingly difficult to obtain formal teaching as a representational artist and many people turn to flower painting as a way of training themselves for other things. Accurate observation and capturing a likeness have been scorned by the art schools until recently, and yet many artists would like to have that basic knowledge, even if they eventually move into more abstract fields. Consequently, private classes for botanical art and for life studies are filled with refugees from art schools which may lack the staff capable of teaching classical drawing and painting. When the American Academy of Arts started in New York as a school for graduate art students who wanted to draw from the model, the directors found it very difficult to find teachers for what was once one of the prime functions of an art school, namely to teach life studies and the nude.

There was also a turning point in the 1980s when a number of well-established artists turned to botanical painting; suddenly it became respectable to paint flowers. Artists like Rory McEwen made people take a different view of what had been considered an almost effeminate subject. As a consequence of his retrospective exhibition at the Serpentine Gallery, several artists were inspired and felt sufficiently confident to start painting flowers seriously. Of course this was not the only trigger but it influenced a number of artists in my collection

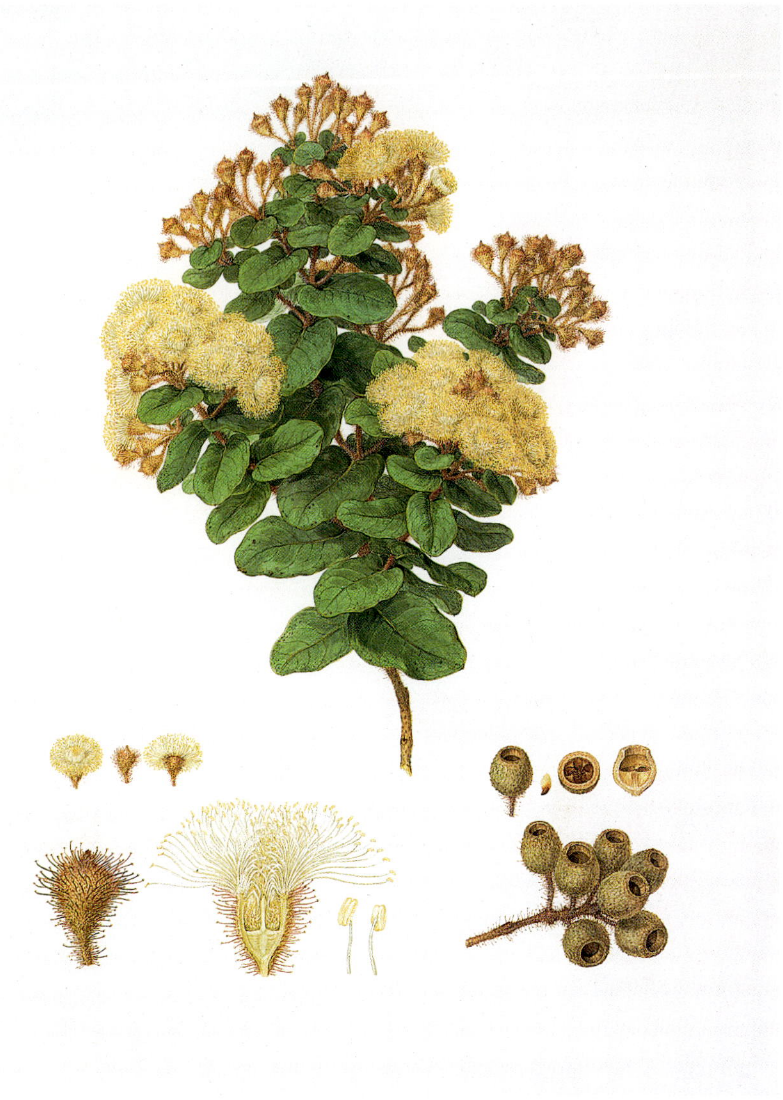

FERDINAND BAUER (1760–1826)
Corymbia setosa
Collected 1802, drawn 1803–12. *The Australian Paintings of Ferdinand Bauer*, plate 57
Watercolour on paper
524 × 357 mm
Original in the Natural History Museum, London

JENNY PHILLIPS (1949–)
Corymbia ficifolia
Signed Jenny K. Phillips 1998
Watercolour on vellum
530 × 390 mm
Original in Shirley Sherwood Collection

I asked Jenny Phillips to do a painting in the style of the superlative artist, Ferdinand Bauer, so that we could make a direct comparison of techniques. We had both seen an exhibition in Sydney of his Australian studies from the Flinders Expedition of 1802–3 (*above*). This portrait of a pink gum (*right*) is Jenny's answer to the challenge. She is the most influential of today's flourishing school of Australian botanical artists and an extraordinarily gifted teacher.

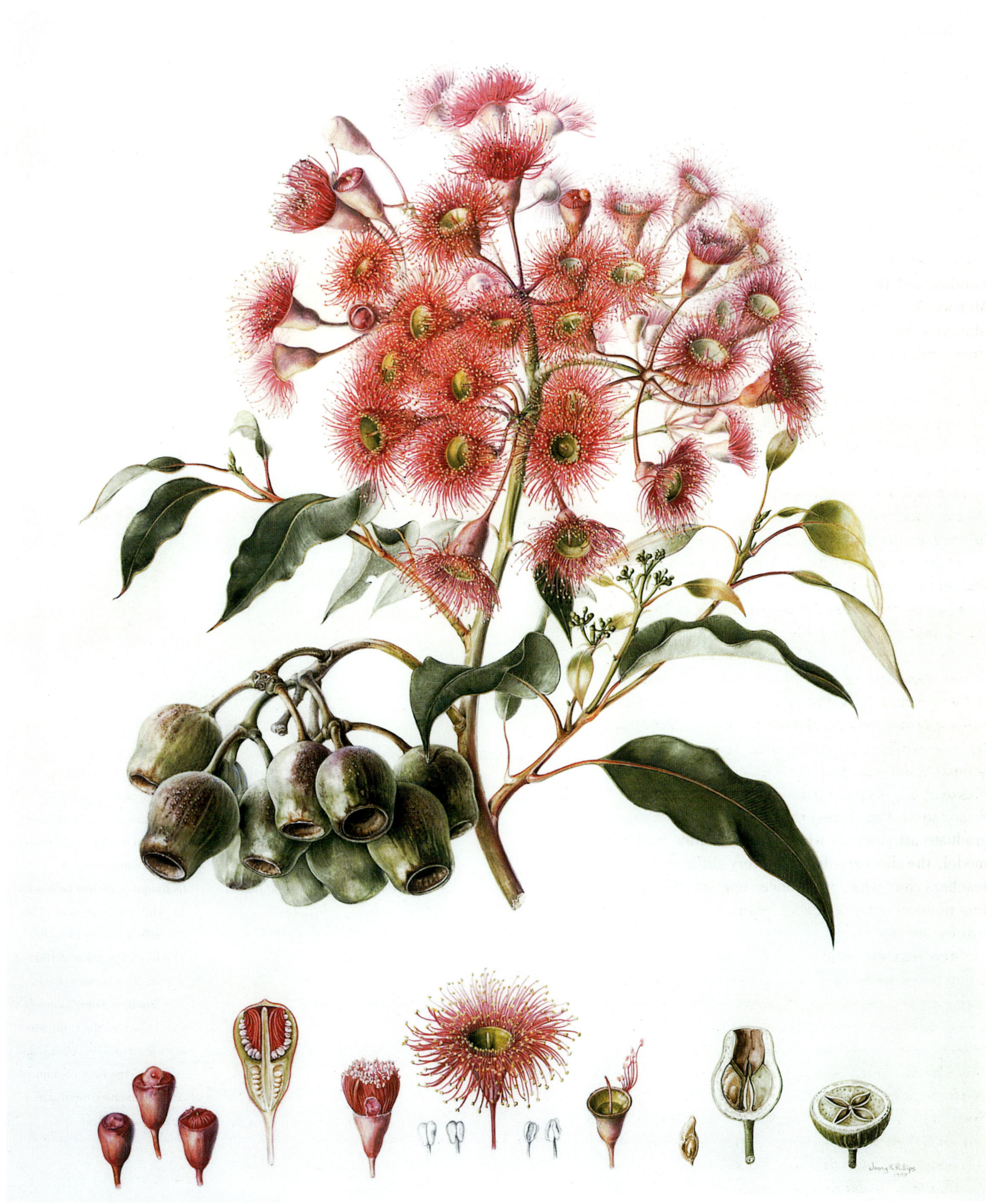
Jenny K. Phillips

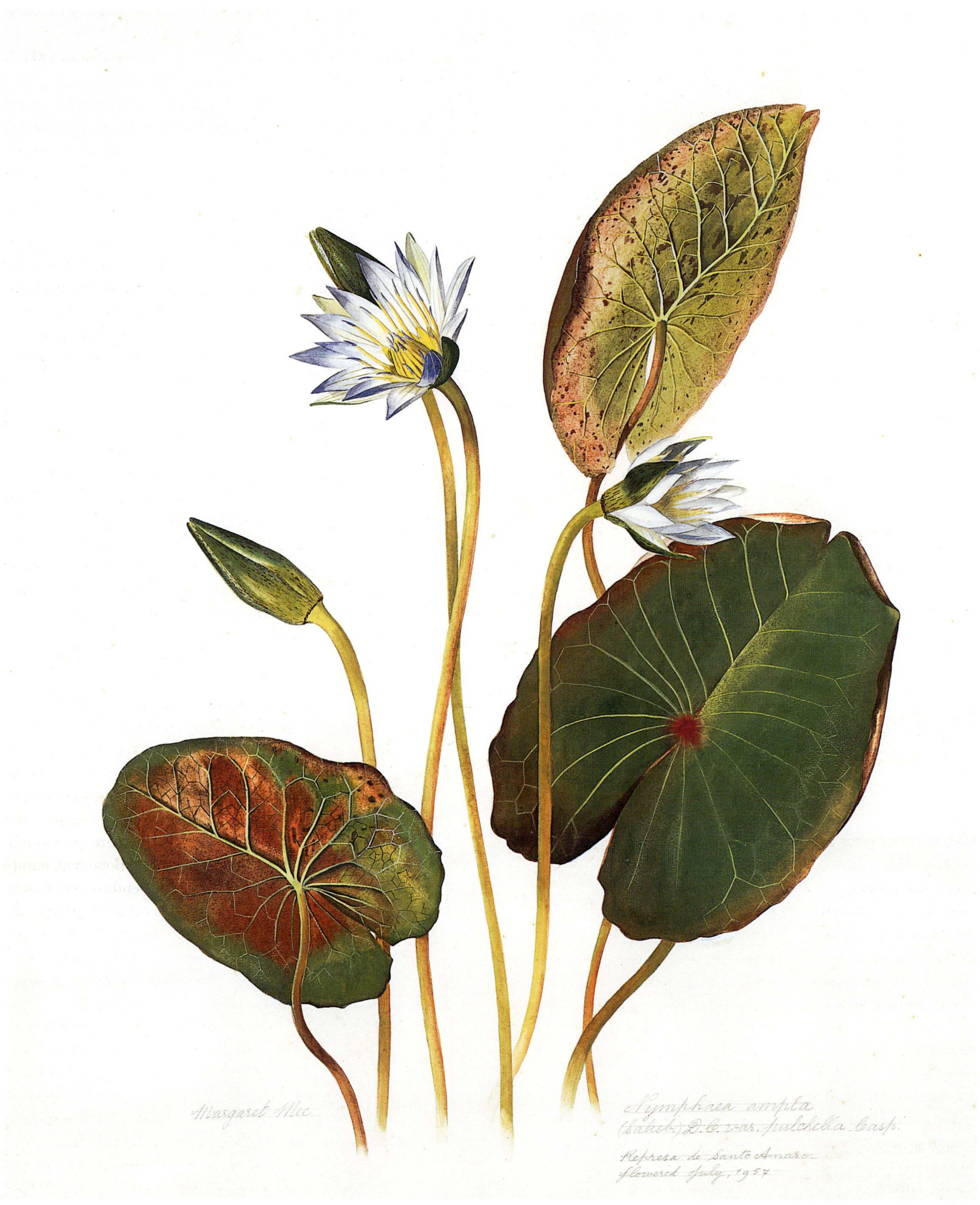
Margaret Mee
Nymphaea ampla
(Salisb.) D.C. var. pulchella Casp.
Represa de Santo Amaro
flowered July, 1957

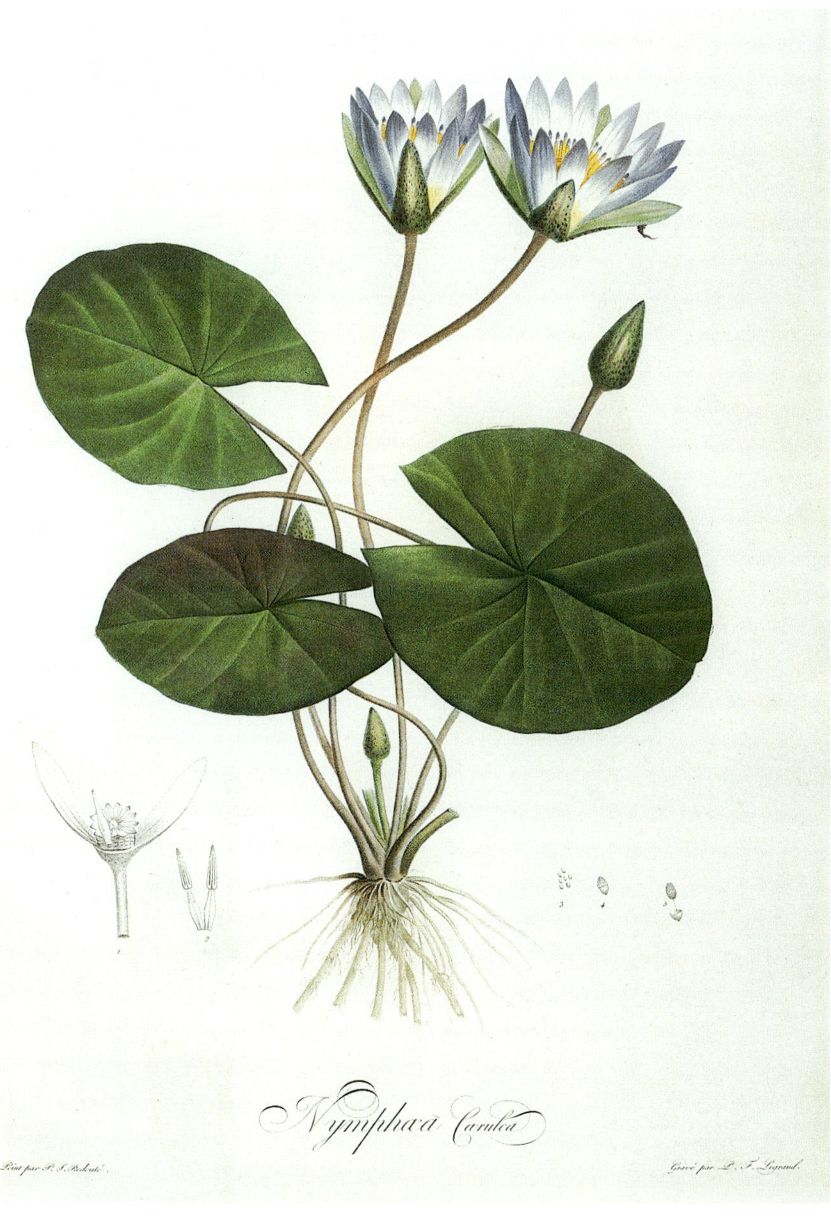

MARGARET MEE (1909–88)
Nymphaea ampla. Signed Margaret Mee (undated) *Nymphaea ampla* (Salisb.) D.C. var. *pulchella* Casp. flowered July 1957. Watercolour on paper 630 × 460 mm. Original in Shirley Sherwood Collection

PIERRE-JOSEPH REDOUTÉ (1759–1840)
Nymphaea caerulea. Signed P. J. Redouté. Hand-coloured engraving on paper 335 × 235 mm. From his *Choix des plus belles fleurs* (1828).

Artist-explorer Margaret Mee was one of Brazil's most prominent 'green' advocates, triggering interest in saving the rainforest and encouraging others to follow her lead. She painted her water lily in the Amazon after collecting it in 1957 (*left*). Redouté, the most well-known of all botanical artists, painted his blue water lily (*above*) after it was introduced to France in the eighteenth century. His is a more superficial study, beautiful but unnaturally perfect.

such as Coral Guest and Brigid Edwards. In quite distinctly different ways Rory McEwen and Margaret Mee became the advance guard of today's botanical artists.

Another reason why botanical art has come to the forefront recently is the enormous increased interest in gardening. It is simply amazing how many people visit gardening centres, swap plants and belong to gardening societies and clubs. There are gardening programmes on every television channel. This renewed interest is particularly noticeable in Britain where I have seen great changes in the last twenty years, although I see it in my travels around the world as well. Attractive planting is no longer the preserve of the rich and wealthy dilettante, but is to be seen in small London plots, on New York roof tops, in the 'greening' of Singapore and even in the deliberate planting and seeding of wildflowers along the verges of super highways in Europe and the United States. Institutions are starting to create florilegia once again (Prince Charles has just started a florilegium at Highgrove), groups of artists work on environmental studies together and specialist gardeners commission portraits of their favourite plants, or start painting themselves. I have commissioned Pandora Sellars, Coral Guest, Annie Farrer and Jo Hague to paint special plants that grow in my garden or orangery.

All this activity has meant that there are huge numbers of people painting plants and this has given rise to some outstanding artists who can certainly be comfortable when compared with those of the past. The standard of painting has certainly risen during the ten years that I have been collecting. It has been interesting to see the effect of my first book in this area because it seems to have pulled together many artists who were previously unaware of each other's existence. Botanical painting is an isolated activity, but the enthusiasm that is generated by the occasional meeting of artists can be felt on occasions like the openings of exhibitions, meetings at botanical artists' societies and master classes. This excitement can be harnessed to some very worthwhile projects.

One of the best examples of this is the Chelsea Physic Garden Florilegium Society which was started in 1995. The Chelsea Physic Garden itself was founded in 1693 by the Worshipful Society of Apothecaries in London to teach the therapeutic properties of plants and to exchange plants and knowledge with other botanical gardens around the world. Its most famous gardener was Philip Miller

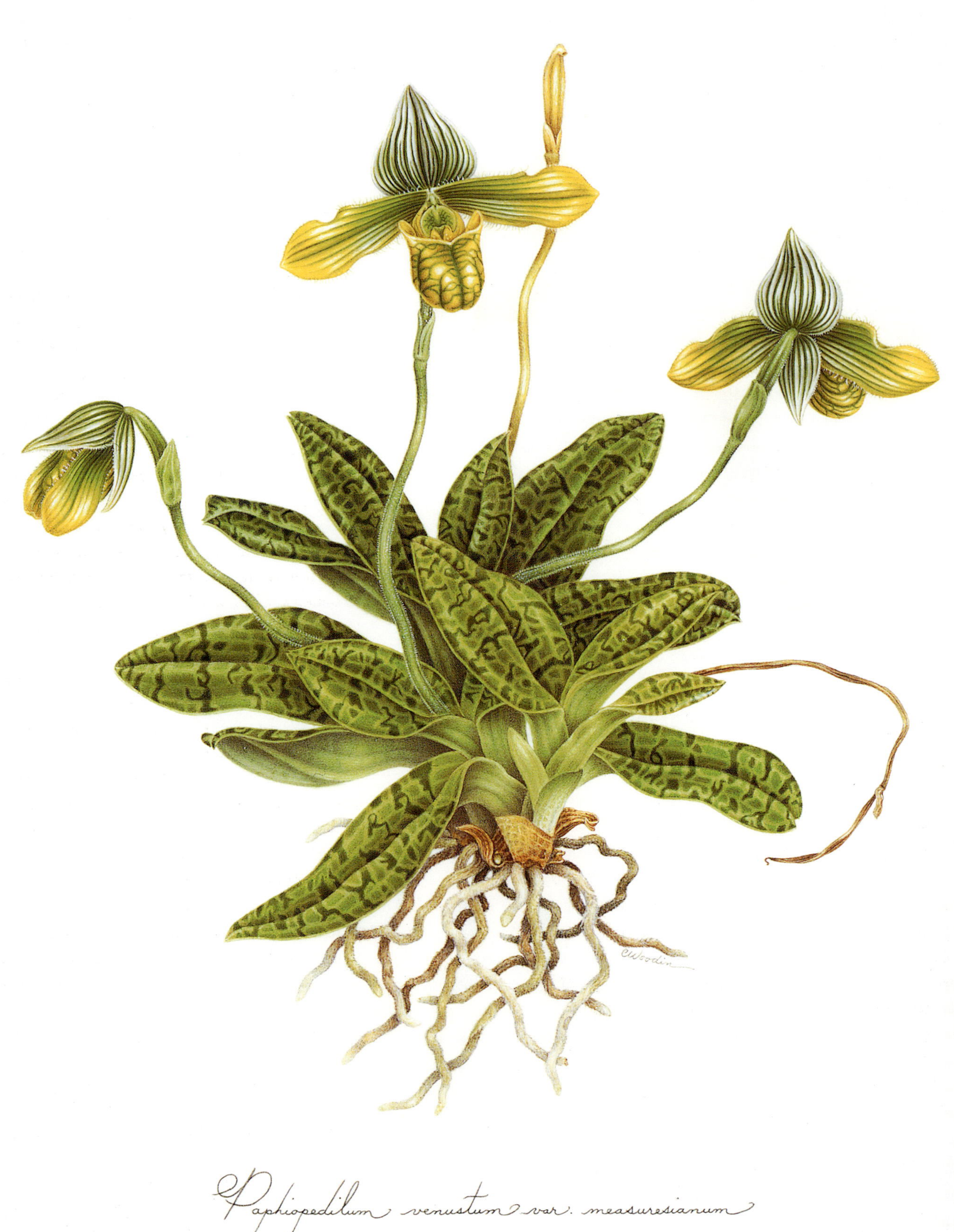

Paphiopedilum venustum var. measuresianum

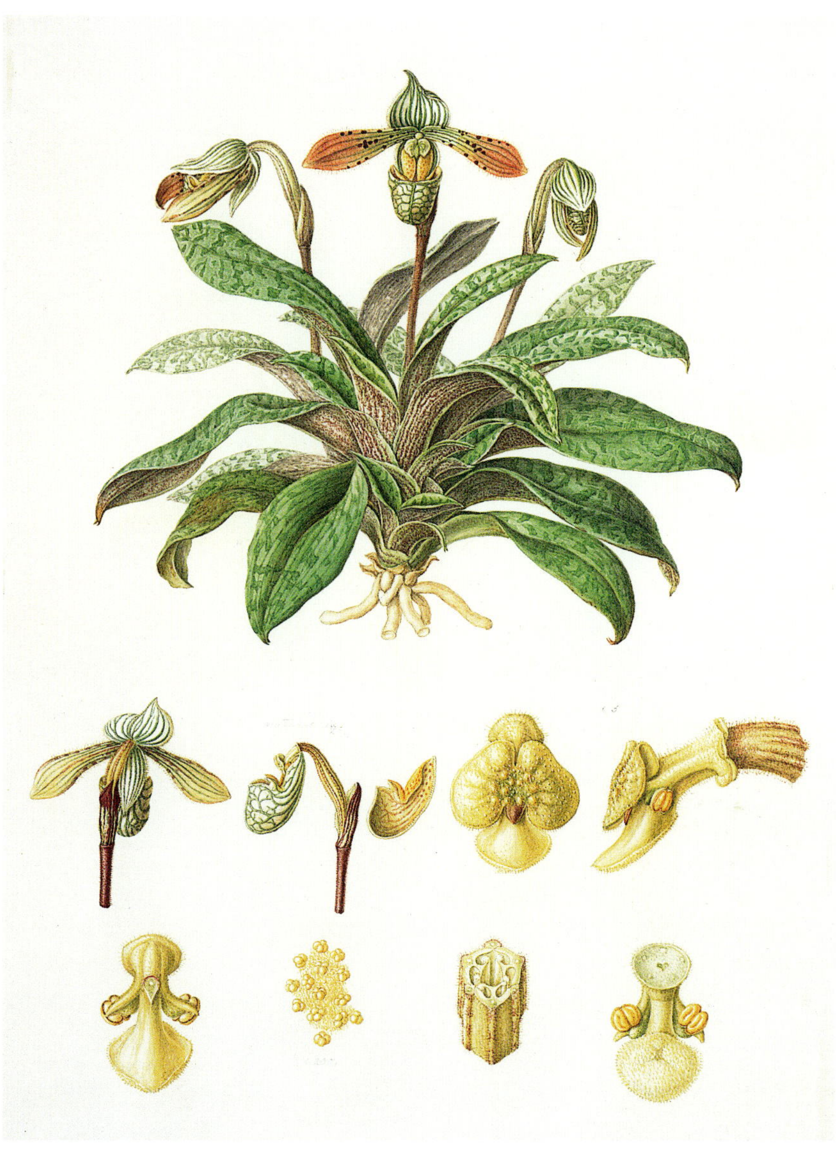

CAROL WOODIN (1956–)
Paphiopedilum venustum var. *measuresianum*
Signed C. Woodin
Watercolour on vellum
400 × 330 mm
Original in Shirley Sherwood Collection

FRANCIS BAUER (1758–1840)
Cypripedium venustum (now *Paphiopedilum venustum*)
Watercolour on paper
486 × 316 mm
Original in the Natural History Museum, London

Francis Bauer is considered one of the greatest botanical artists of all time and is most celebrated for his paintings of orchids cultivated at Kew, where he worked most of his life (*above*). Carol Woodin's recent portrait of an albino variant of the same orchid (*left*) shows subtle colour differences of the flower and spectacularly mottled leaves. Her intense work on vellum has a glowing translucency. She is one of the most outstanding of the new wave of American artists.

(appointed 1722) who for fifty years received and grew plants from all over the world, introduced new species and employed some of the best botanical artists to record them.

The Chelsea Physic Garden is home to the English Gardening School, formed in the 1980s by Rosemary Alexander. Founded to teach garden design, the school has developed into one of the mainsprings of botanical art and illustration in the UK, taught by the inspired teacher Anne-Marie Evans. Once a month sixty members of the Florilegium Society meet to illustrate the plants still cultivated in the garden, work which is becoming an important record of the collection grown there, with over 140 paintings donated to the Garden's Library. I gave a talk to the Society, as part of their lecture series and was delighted to have such an enthusiastic and knowledgeable audience. Their recent project has been to paint introductions by Philip Miller which are still growing in the garden today.

The Chelsea Garden Florilegium Society works so well because artists enjoy an occasional 'day out', meeting with other kindred spirits, and the gift of one painting a year by each society member is not too onerous. It is satisfying for members to feel that their work will be held in a respected archive, for a genuinely useful purpose.

When I started talking about my collection in the mid-1990s, I very quickly realised that my audience was quite astonished at the beauty and variety of my paintings. I was often asked about classes and felt that my exhibitions would make a wonderful teaching tool. So when parts of my collection were shown in Charleston, South Carolina and New Orleans, historic cities where my husband's company also has Orient-Express hotels, I felt it might be worthwhile to set up master classes, using our hotels as a base. Starting with Katie Lee as teacher, the classes became a huge success. I led groups through the exhibitions and organised large rooms where the class could have their easels and tables set up with good lighting and interesting subject matter. Since then the programme in Orient-Express hotels has grown, with classes in the Observatory, Sydney; the Mount Nelson, Cape Town; the Westcliff, Johannesburg; the Cipriani Hotel, Venice and Reid's Palace, Madeira. Several experienced teachers have taught in the different venues. As the programme expanded I asked Coral Guest, Siriol Sherlock, Jenny Phillips and Margaret Saul to join in. Between 1996 and 2000 we have organised thirty-four classes, sometimes with the students living in the hotel, others with the students coming in on a daily basis, generally with no more than fifteen students in each group. For those who do not know the area we organise an interesting programme of local visits, sometimes including outside work. Two of the teachers, Siriol Sherlock and Coral Guest, have recently written excellent and well-received books on botanical art. Our latest innovation is to start a 'Safari Sketchbook' which Katie Lee teaches in the three Orient-Express 'Gametracker' camps in Botswana. The first one was a huge success, filmed by CNN, and appeared world-wide on their travel programme.

There is a range of other classes available world-wide, mostly started during the last decade. Australia has several centres, the best-known run by Jenny Phillips in Melbourne and Margaret Saul in Brisbane. Katie Lee has taught at the New York Botanical Gardens and there are numerous other classes in the United States, as detailed in the newsletters of the American Society of Botanical Artists. There are classes in Rome taught by Luca Palermo, classes in Brazil taught by Margaret Mee scholars returning from Kew, and new groups are flourishing in South Africa. In England Anne-Marie Evans's year-long courses at London's English Gardening School have been an inspiration to many excellent artists in this book, while Coral Guest, Annie Farrer and Christabel King all teach at Kew. Besides the London-based groups there are now courses for diplomas elsewhere in the UK – indeed many institutions, both old and new, are becoming involved in botanical art classes.

Following a recent article about my collection in the German Architectural Digest *Architektur & Wohnen*, I received an amazing amount of correspondence, asking about exhibitions, books, galleries and classes. As my collection has been shown around the world it has engendered an astonishing degree of publicity for the artists. There have been articles in the major English titles but also in the *New York Times*, the *Wall Street Journal* (asking if this is the time to invest in botanical art) and the South African dailies. I have thick scrapbooks, filled with cuttings from newspapers and magazines, the longest from a beautifully illustrated eighteen-page article in the Japanese equivalent of *Vogue*. Sometimes an exhibition has struck such a local chord that organisations of botanical artists have been formed as a result. This has happened in Sydney and Canberra, in South Africa and in the United States. Japanese botanical artists were

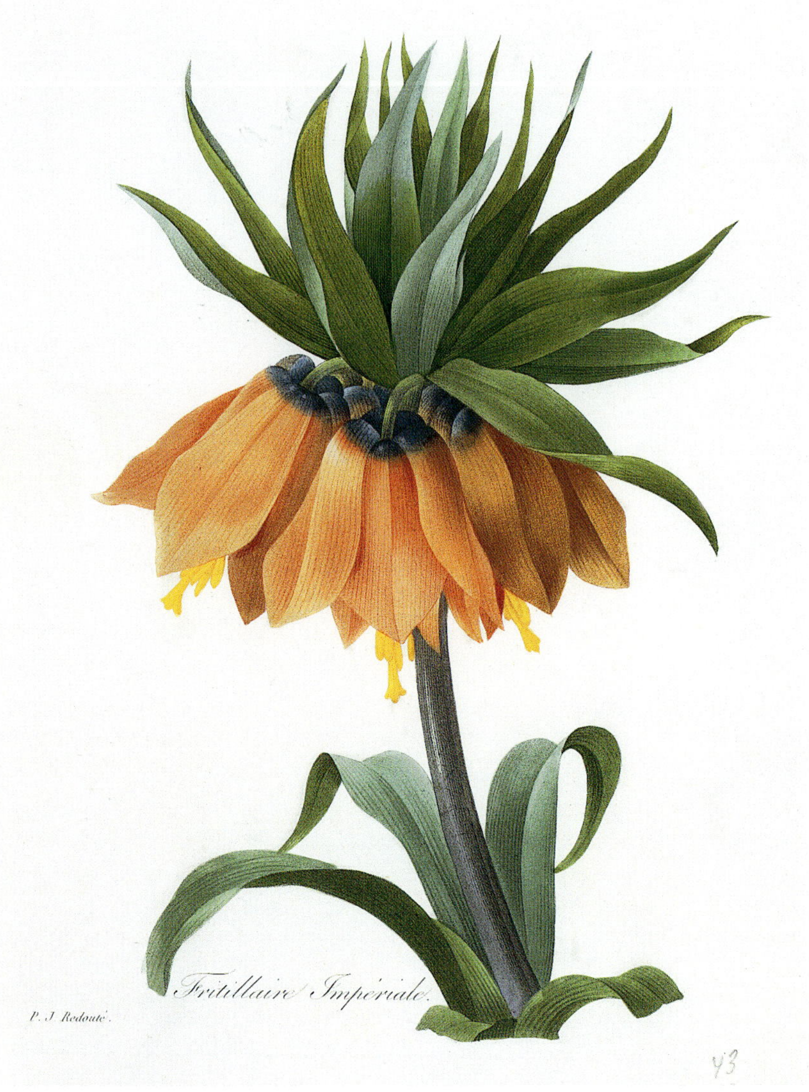

Separated by two centuries, Redouté (*above*) and McEwen were both outstanding botanical artists of their times. McEwen's superb fritillary (*right*) is one of the best examples of contemporary flower portraiture. He has been one of the foremost artists of the renaissance of botanical art, encouraging artists as well as scientists into the field.

PIERRE-JOSEPH REDOUTÉ (1759–1840)
Fritillaire impériale: *Fritillaria imperialis*
Signed P. J. Redouté pinx.
Hand-coloured engraving on paper 514 × 345 mm
From P. J. Redouté *Les Liliacées*

RORY McEWEN (1932–82)
Crown Imperial: *Fritillaria imperialis*
Signed Rory McEwen 1965
Watercolour on vellum
780 × 565 mm
Original in Shirley Sherwood Collection

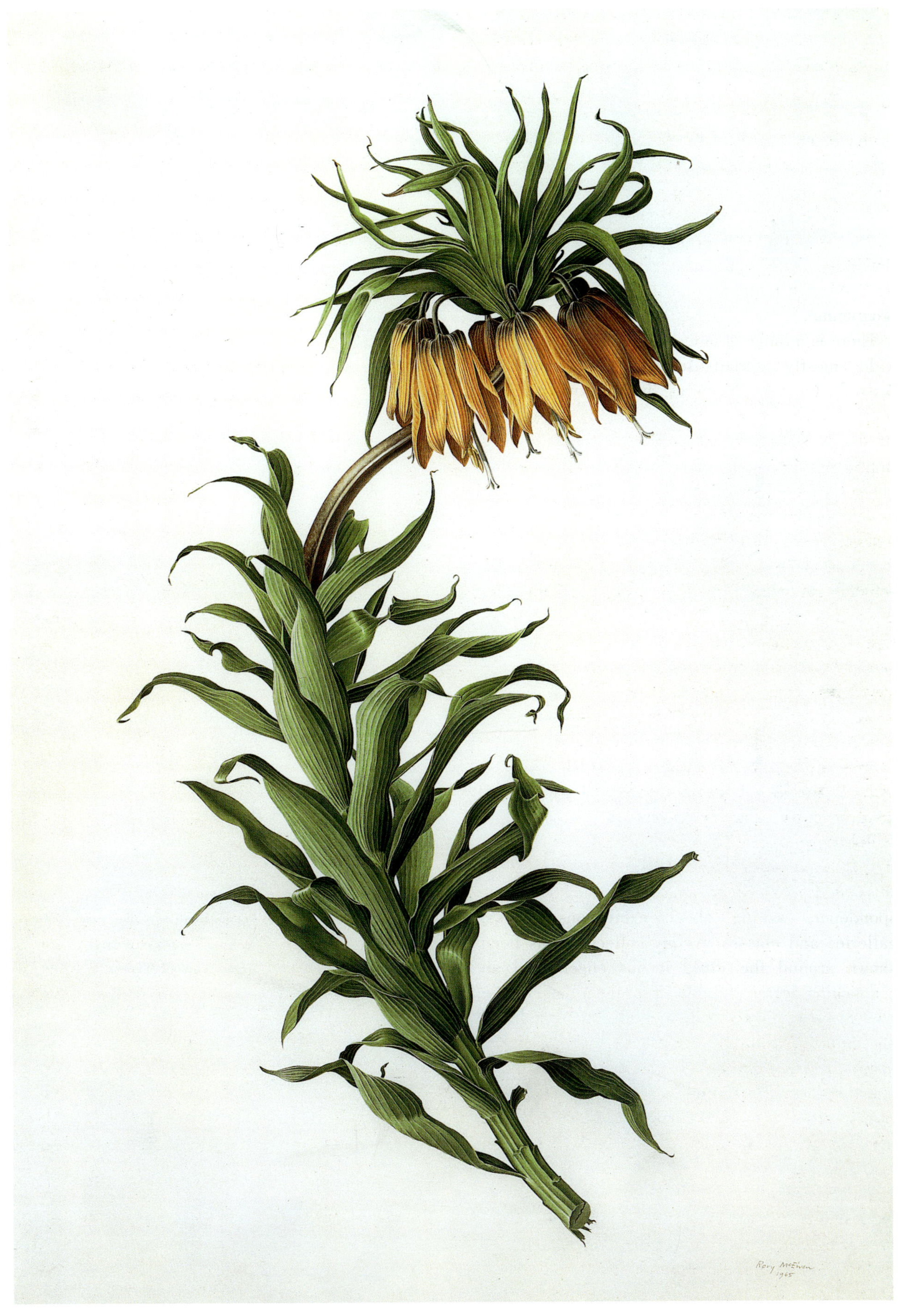
Rory McEwen
1965

stimulated by the show in Tokyo and I have already been asked to lend paintings there again. This was the first big show ever held in Japan (of 150 contemporary paintings) at the elegant Yasuda Kasai Gallery which was visited by over 40,000 people.

Over the last few years I have urged institutions in London to collect more contemporary work. There is an unrivalled collection of botanical artists' work from the past housed at Kew, in the Natural History Museum, the Victoria & Albert Museum and in the Lindley Library of the Royal Horticultural Society (RHS), sometimes as original paintings and drawings, often in wonderful books. These are not easily accessible to the general public although the situation is slowly improving with some good recent exhibitions at the Natural History Museum. At last the Lindley Library has been adding more vigorously to its contemporary collection, sometimes by purchasing work on exhibition at the RHS shows, occasionally by commissioning some of today's most important artists. Much has been achieved on a tiny budget, with many splendid new paintings being added to the Library in the last two years. The Library is currently undergoing renovation and when it re-opens there will an area where some of its treasures from both past and present can be exhibited more frequently.

For many years, the RHS has mounted four shows of artists' work a year. A range of medals is awarded and work can be sold after the judging. Even though the required eight drawings are only hung for two days they are nevertheless seen by a great number of people attending the plant displays. Over the several years that I have been a judge, I have watched the standard improve. A gold medal is highly prized and mentioned prominently in any botanical artist's *résumé*. Since my exhibitions abroad there are more people sending in work from overseas. Many of the artists in my collection have been awarded medals at these shows at some time in their careers.

Kew started to exhibit in the 1990s with a series of splendid, exciting exhibitions in its Kew Gardens Gallery. Initiated by Dr Brinsley Burbidge in the late 1980s, it was one of the most significant triggers of the recent renaissance, showing the work of Margaret Mee, Pandora Sellars, Coral Guest, Brigid Edwards, Jo Hague and many more. Kew was where I made my very first purchase, a spectacular painting by Pandora Sellars of the orchid *Laelia tenebrosa* in a dramatic backdrop of tropical foliage, which Brinsley Burbidge categorised as 'Botanical Theatre'. I bought a number of paintings there in the

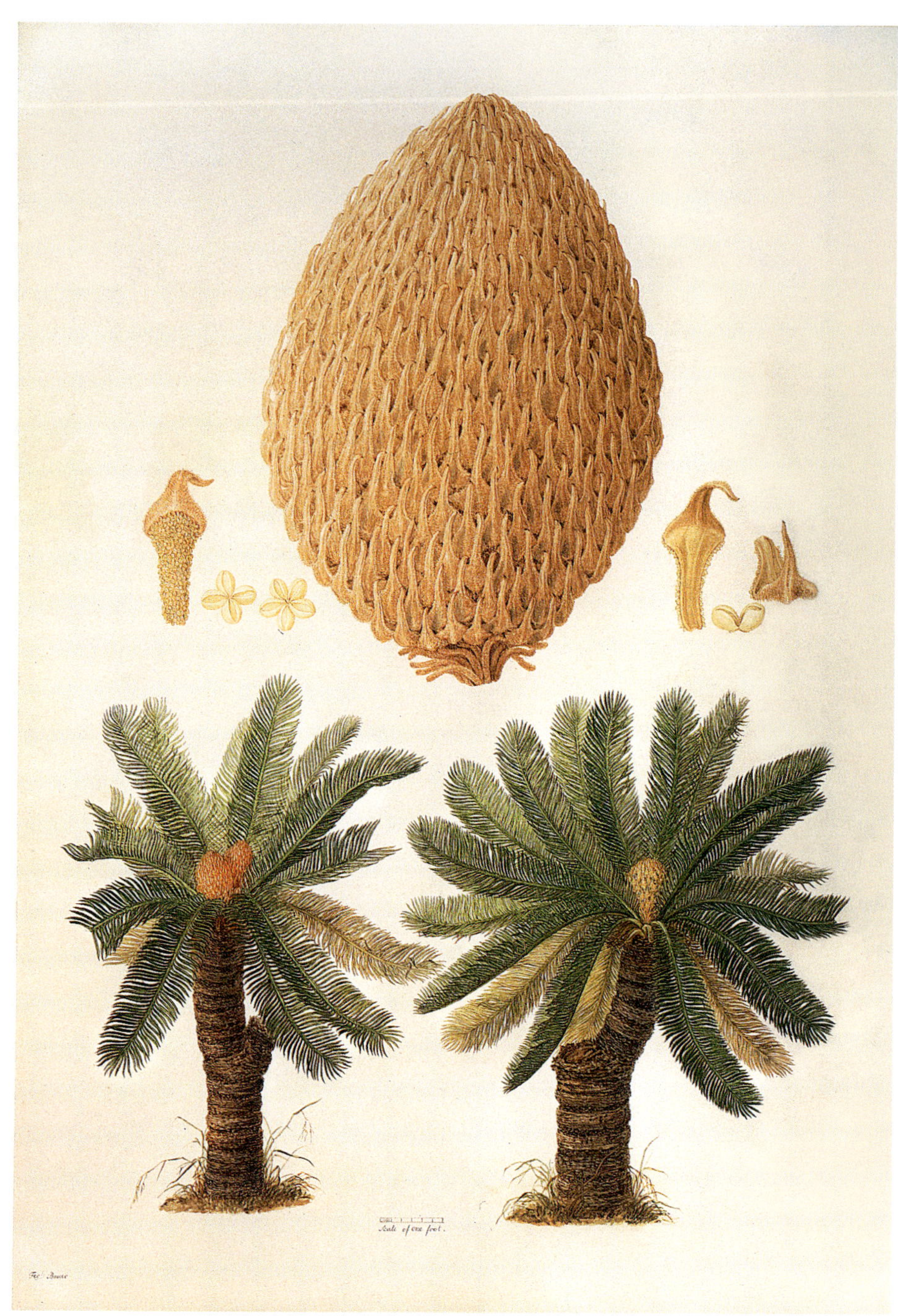

Ferdinand Bauer was the first to record many indigenous plants (*above*) when he joined Matthew Flinders on his circumnavigation of Australia in 1802–3. Leslie Berge was inspired to paint cycads by a recent visit to South Africa. Berge interprets the cluster of golden cones (*right*) with a vigour that gives the stylised portait an extraordinary drama.

FERDINAND BAUER
(1760–1826)
Cycad: Ricketty Bush *Cycas media* (male)
Signed Fer. Bauer, collected 1802, drawn 1803–12
Watercolour on paper
525 × 358 mm
The Australian Paintings of Ferdinand Bauer, plate 157
Original in the Natural History Museum, London

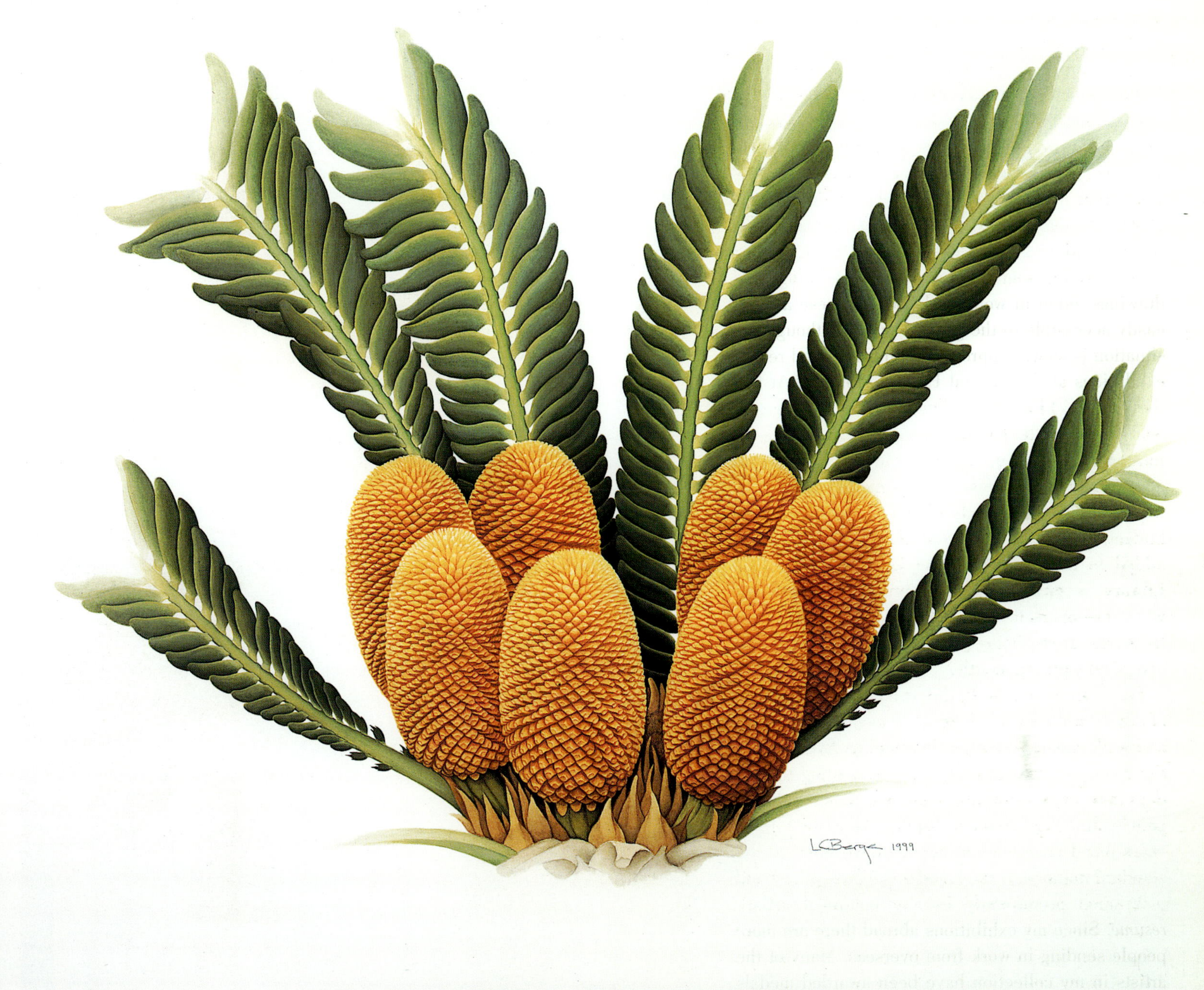

LESLIE C. BERGE
(1959–)
Cycad: Male Cones of
Encephalartos woodii
Signed L. C. Berge
1999
Watercolour on paper
570 × 760 mm
Original in Shirley
Sherwood Collection

early 1990s and eventually Kew became the venue for the first exhibition of my collection for four months in the spring of 1996. It proved a very successful show, beautifully hung by Laura Giuffrida, and seen by an audience of over 20,000 people. With the encouragement of Professor Gren Lucas 4000 copies of my book *Contemporary Botanical Artists: the Shirley Sherwood Collection*, which had just been published in association with Kew, were sold as the exhibition catalogue, to both artists and visitors during this time. During most of the ten years I was a trustee for the Kew Foundation (which raises money for Kew projects) the gallery was a real force in the botanical art world, putting on some splendid exhibitions and encouraging both artists and collectors in the field.

The Hunt Institute for Botanical Documentation on the Carnegie Mellon University campus in Pittsburgh has performed a very important role in encouraging botanical art in the United States. Based on Rachel Hunt's superb library, it has become one of the vital institutions promoting today's artists. Every few years James White, the Curator of Art, organises an international exhibition of about seventy-five new artists who show one, or occasionally, two works in the beautiful wood-panelled gallery. Artists come from all over the world to enjoy the openings. When I started collecting I bought all the earlier catalogues, which proved an invaluable source of information on my travels, as the artists' addresses are included as well as useful biographies.

Because I have been building up my own collection, rather than advising an academic institution, I do not have to find reasons for acquiring a particular artist's work. I am not sure if my taste has changed since I started but perhaps now I do pay more attention to 'wall-appeal'. Seeing my paintings hung by different curators in galleries ranging from the predominantly scientific such as Kew, the Hunt Institute, Pittsburgh and Kirstenbosch Botanical Gardens, Cape Town to the definitely artistic *milieu* of the Museum of Modern Art, National Galleries of Scotland, the Yasuda Kasai Gallery, Tokyo or the Dixon Gallery and Gardens, Memphis has made me look at them differently. These exhibitions have given me surprise after surprise, as each curator will chose a different selection of paintings to emphasise, changing the positioning of paintings and the way in which the works are lit. Sometimes there are groupings of different artists or subjects which would never have occurred to me.

I am particularly pleased to have experienced such a wide range of venues because their audiences are also likely to be varied and because, collectively, they straddle the arts-science 'divide'. There has always been a 'two cultures' element in Britain, far more so than in the United States or in mainland Europe. British critics can be quite disparaging, while those elsewhere are surprised and delighted by what they see. Despite its popular appeal – indeed perhaps because of it – there have always been those who dismiss botanical art as 'mere illustration'. When I was young, sometimes even botanists themselves held these artists in low regard. Artists were expected to know their place at the back of the herbarium and rarely had their names mentioned in the scientific papers that they illustrated. But at last most botanical institutions are realising that their skilled artists have had years of training and often spend months of labour to produce those definitive plant portraits (which can record more comprehensively than any photograph) and value them accordingly.

I have especially enjoyed trying to make good 'matches' of the work of old masters and that of today's artists and have had a wonderful time foraging in London's great libraries with their wealth of unpublished material. I hope to make good 'matches' in my next show as well, which will be in a new gallery at the Ashmolean Museum, Oxford. But some contemporary artists are going much further than echoing the triumphs of the past. They are painting new interpretations of familiar subjects, so that I will never be able to see a humble beetroot again without thinking of Susannah Blaxill's amazing portrait. Cycads have taken on a new dimension since Leslie Berge so boldly interpreted them and Pandora Sellars' exquisite compositions are, indeed, 'botanical theatre' of the most subtle kind. Rory McEwen's paintings are the very essence of their subject, a distillation of beauty suspended in space, while Brigid Edwards has already been recognised as a painter of the most potent images which have an arresting yet subtle impact. There are a number of artists who have taken what I shall describe as 'botanical flower painting' into new realms of excellence, like Coral Guest and Paul Jones, while Mariko Imai has, with her combination of sensitivity and vigour, set fresh goals for Japanese artists.

All these artists are looking at their subjects with a new vision, drawing new interpretations and setting new standards. In my last book I mentioned the hapless critic who claimed that botanical art was dead – nothing could be further from the truth with so many serious, gifted and passionate artists working today in so many places around the world.

There are now more galleries showing botanical art, more institutions encouraging artists by buying their work, more classes and more people collecting. The whole area has expanded in the last ten years almost beyond recognition. In many ways I feel that my 'mission' to make the contemporary botanical artist more accepted and recognised has been achieved and I am certain that the renaissance is continuing at this very moment. Long may this new 'Golden Age' of botanical art last.

The Artists

THE SHIRLEY SHERWOOD COLLECTION

WORKS ACQUIRED 1996–2000

Fay Anderson

BORN LAHORE, PAKISTAN 1931

I first bought a painting of the Jersey Lily from Fay Anderson in 1994. She has expended a great deal of industry and skill in illustrating numerous publications of South African plants. The most recent major book is *Gladiolus of South Africa* by Goldblatt and Manning which appeared in 1998. This imposing volume with innumerable plates by Fay Anderson was given to me as a 'thank-you' present by Professor Brian Huntley, Chief Executive of the National Botanical Institute, Kirstenbosch, when I opened an exhibition of my collection in their new conference centre in September 1998.

At that time Fay came to see me in Cape Town and told me that her house had burnt down about a year before. She had lost many paintings, although thankfully much must have been published. She wanted me to have an example of *Nivenia stokoei* which she particularly treasured as she felt she had got the very difficult blue of the petals exactly right. Apparently this colour is not easy to capture as this rare plant's flowers photograph pink (like the flowers of the morning glory 'Heavenly Blue' which reproduce quite mauve on film). It is a member of the woody *Iridaceae* which grows from a woody base with brittle stems and fans of stiff bright green leaves. The nine species of *Nivenia* grow in very limited areas of the South Western Cape mountains. They vary in height from 20 cm to 2 metres and all have brilliant sky-blue flowers like *Nivenia stokoei.*

Fay Anderson told me that *Nivenia stokoei* is a wonderful sight growing on white sand, surrounded by ericas and proteas and can be found flowering in February and March in the Highlands Forest Reserve near Houw Hoek, Betty's Bay, where she collected it. Luckily the flowers last well in water, with buds opening over a ten-day period, which makes the task of a botanical artist easier.

She has recently painted a new species, *Lachenalia valeria,* which appears in the June 2000 edition of the journal *Flowering Plants of Africa*, and is described by Duncan Grant. South Africa is an amazing place to study plants as new species seem to appear every year, especially after fire has swept through the fynbos, triggering the germination of long-dormant seeds. Indeed, one of the few consolations of the ferocious fires that swept through part of the Cape's forests early in 2000 may be a regeneration of some interesting plants during the next spring when a wealth of bulbs is expected to bloom.

Another of Fay Anderson's recent projects has been the painting of *Agapanthus* and *Moraea* for plates commissioned for the newly redecorated Blue Train that runs between South Africa and Zimbabwe. In 1998 she was awarded the South African Association of Botanical Artists' Certificate of Merit for her outstanding contribution to botany.

NIVENIA STOKOEI
Signed Fay Anderson
(undated)
Acquired from the artist 1998
Watercolour on paper
370 × 275 mm

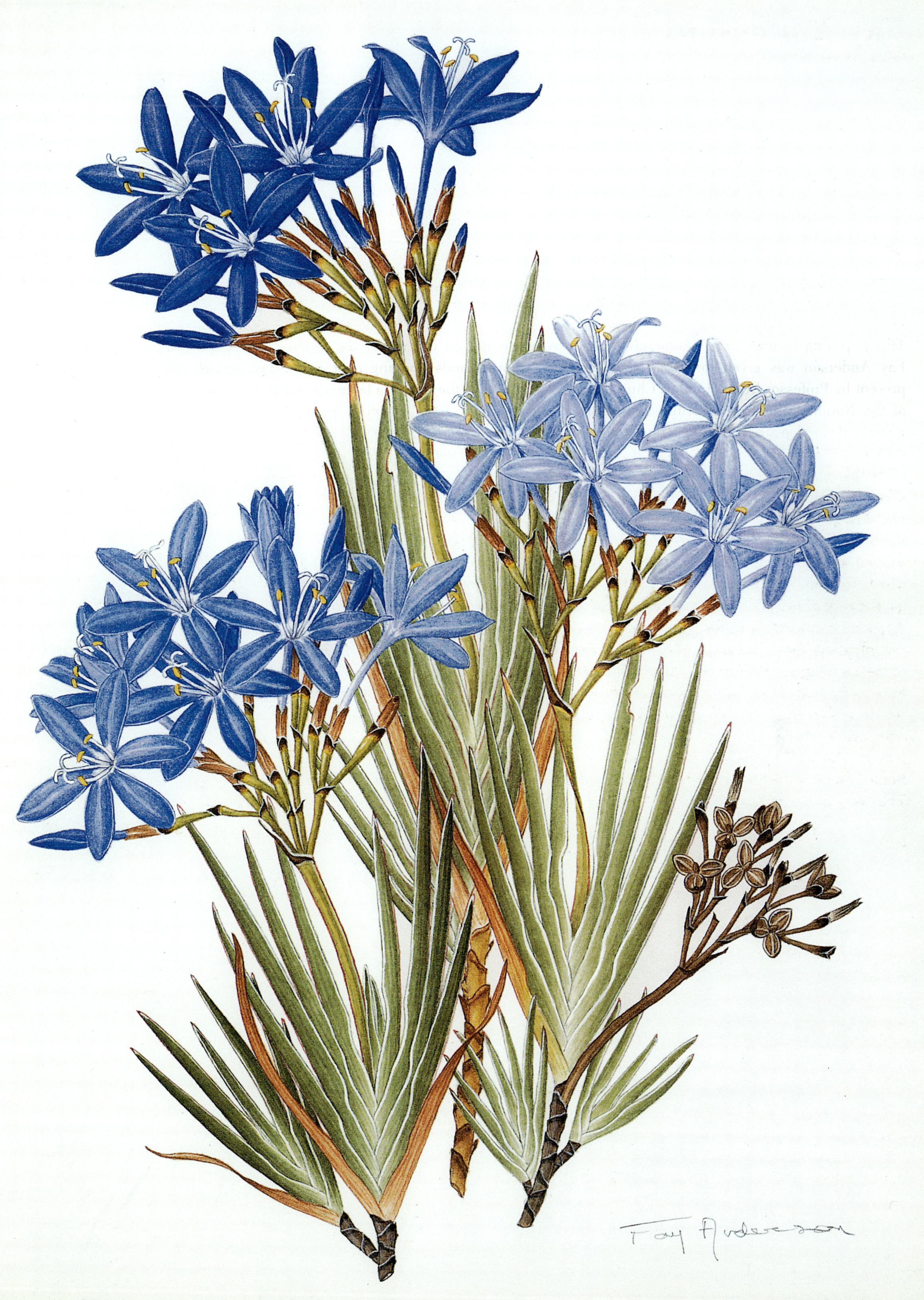
Fay Anderson

Francesca Anderson

Born Washington DC, USA 1946

Francesca Anderson lives in Brooklyn, New York and mainly works high up in her roof-top studio there, although she also spends some time at her farm out on the end of Long Island, in what has recently become her own nature reserve. Much of her energy over the last few years has been directed to developing a home and garden on a promontory washed by the sea.

She has a most distinctive style, always working in pen and ink. She has had many solo exhibitions all over the United States and has prepared the plates for two books with Michael Balick, an ethnobotanist, on the palms of Belize and on Ayurvedic herbs (both still unpublished). She has been awarded two gold medals at the RHS – one for a series of drawings of amaryllis (1995) and the other for a series of brassicas (1998).

Her work is always full of movement and she chooses large subjects which swirl across her pages. In 1996 I bought a series of six large sunflowers and a huge four-part study of an orchid cactus from her. I decided to hang the four sheets of the cactus in one enormous frame and it proved a real challenge to my framer and mounter. It is placed far up on the wall on my country house staircase, but has come down for exhibitions in New Orleans, the Museum of Modern Art, National Galleries of Scotland, Sydney and the Yasuda Kasai Gallery, Tokyo.

My sunflower series No. 1, dated 1988, is one of her very earliest botanical drawings. Up until then she had drawn nudes and painted landscapes. She prefers to work on a series of ten or more similar subjects like her amaryllis, brassicas, poisonous plants, vegetables and bulbs. She wrote to me:

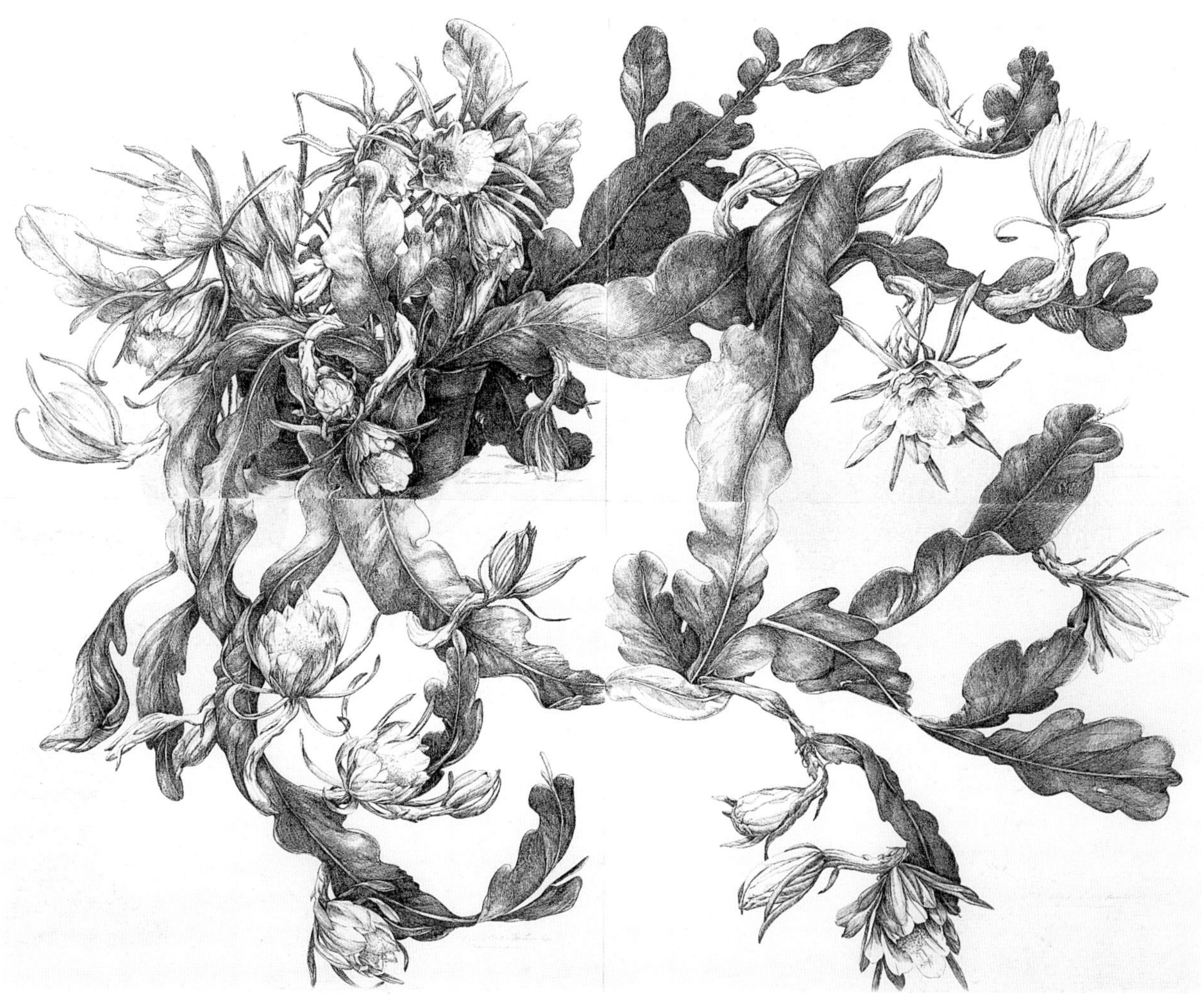

ORCHID CACTUS: *EPIPHYLLUM OXYPETALUM*
Signed Orchid Cactus Francesca Anderson 1993
Acquired from the artist 1996
Pen & ink 1160 × 1460 mm (4 parts each 580 × 730 mm)

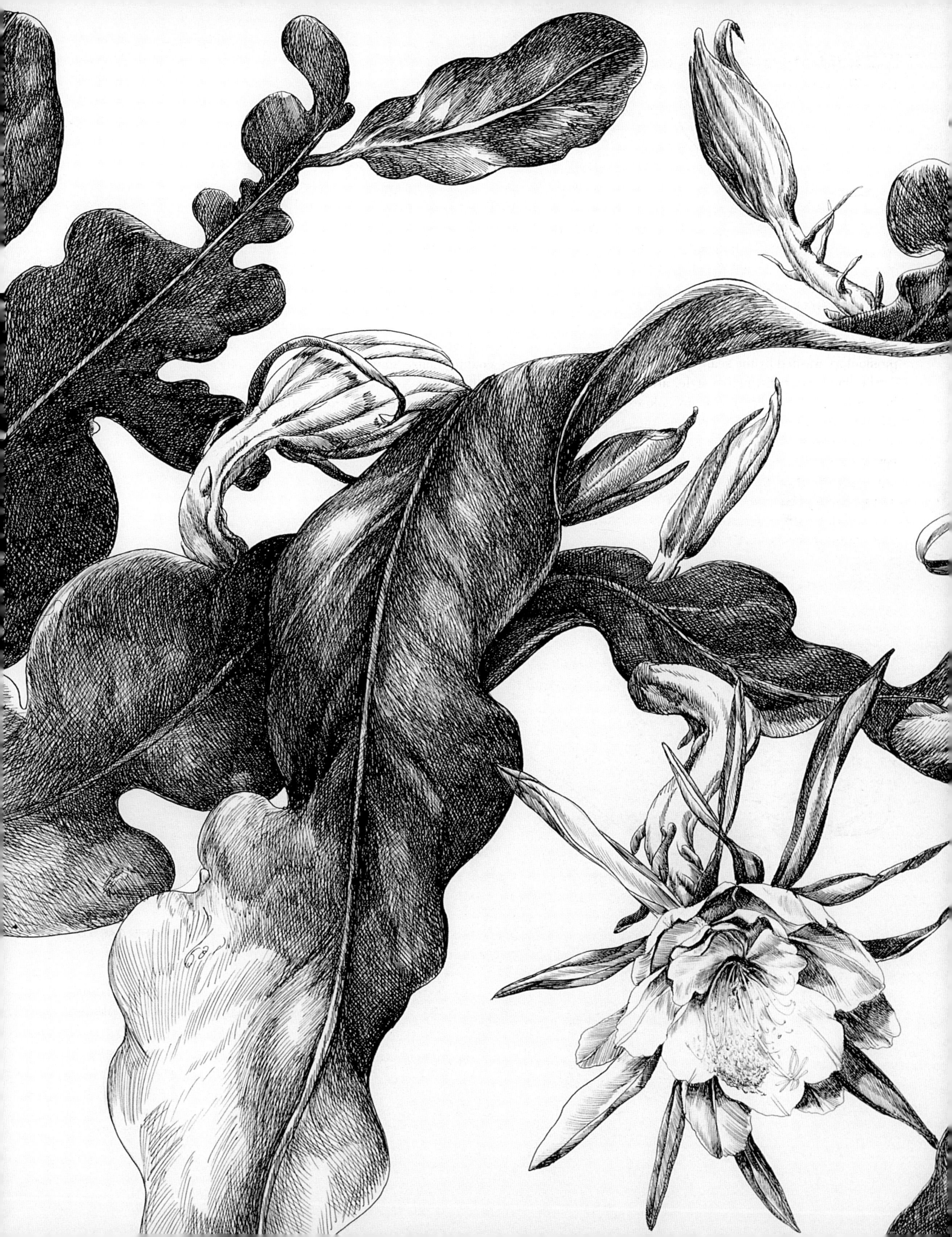

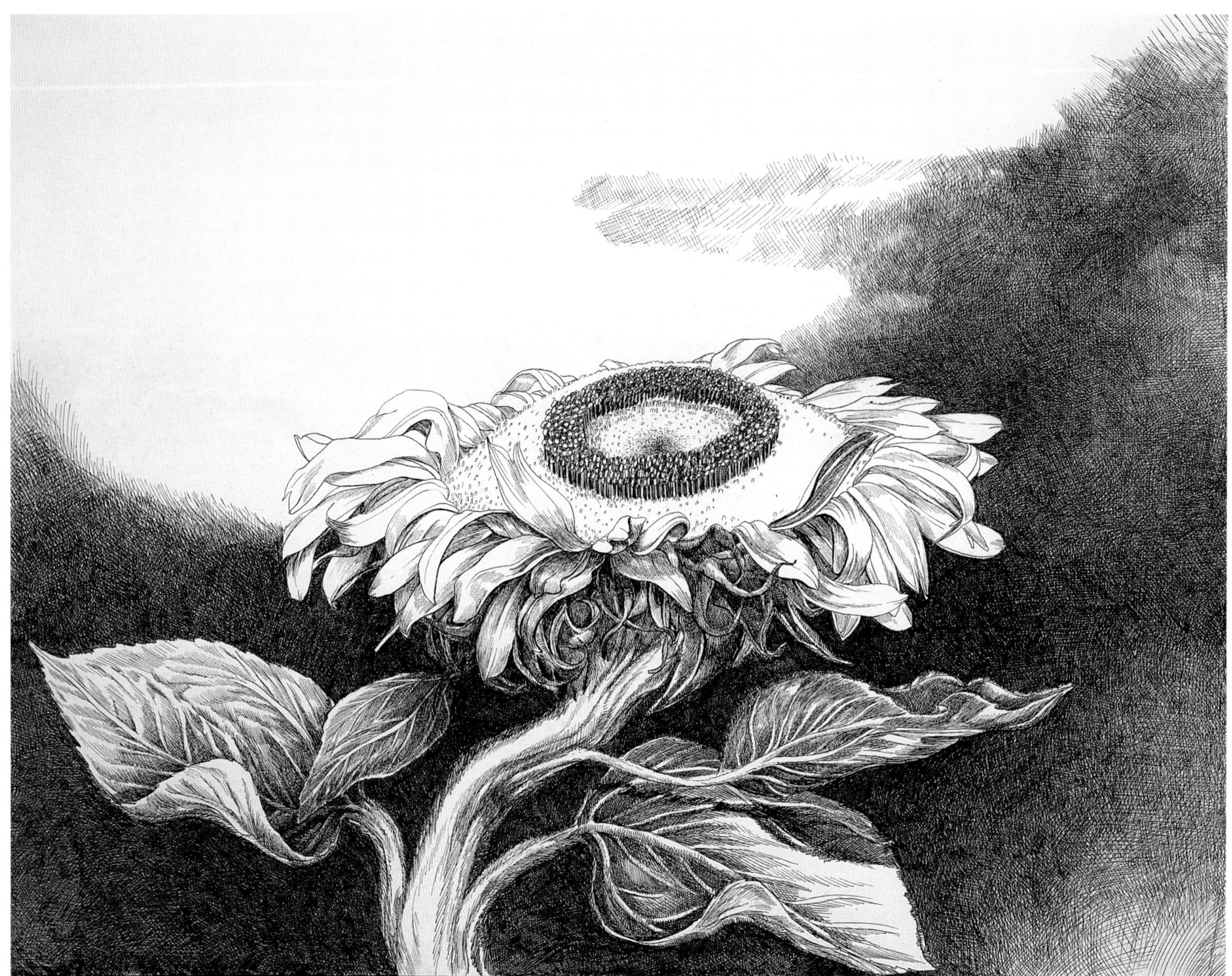

'There is a fleshy, sculptural physicality to these sunflowers that appeals to me. Sunflowers are textural, massive and hefty, really like a vegetable. You can feel their weight, even the pollen is heavy and thick. They come in a variety of colours, forms and shapes and sizes. Their seeds spin out of the centre navel in an elegant design of Fibonacci curves. They lift their faces to the light and hang their heads in death. It's a plant so self-important it is allopathic, but generously will self-seed, shade and feed you. No artist, not even Van Gogh, can do it justice. I am going to keep on adding to the series.'

'After a four-year stint of designing interiors, furniture and gardens for our farm, I am drawing once more, and beginning a new series. Rather than single plant portraits, I want to draw environmental portraits to show the inter-connection of life forms and the dependency of plants on their environment. The soil, the ground, litter, the companion plants, insects and pollinators will be drawn life-size on scratch board on site on our farm and I will attempt to incorporate weather changes as well. Our farm has great diversity; sandy beach, marsh, meadow, forest and gardens. Looking down anywhere, the random design of nature at my feet is breathtakingly beautiful and endlessly fascinating in its complexity. I hope to find a field botanist to help me understand what I see. I believe these drawings will be both botanical illustration and art in the tradition of Dürer's *Das Grosse Rasenstück* (*A Large Piece of Turf*) painted in 1503. In that drawing, the dynamic of the habitat is paramount, but the individual plants are rendered accurately.'

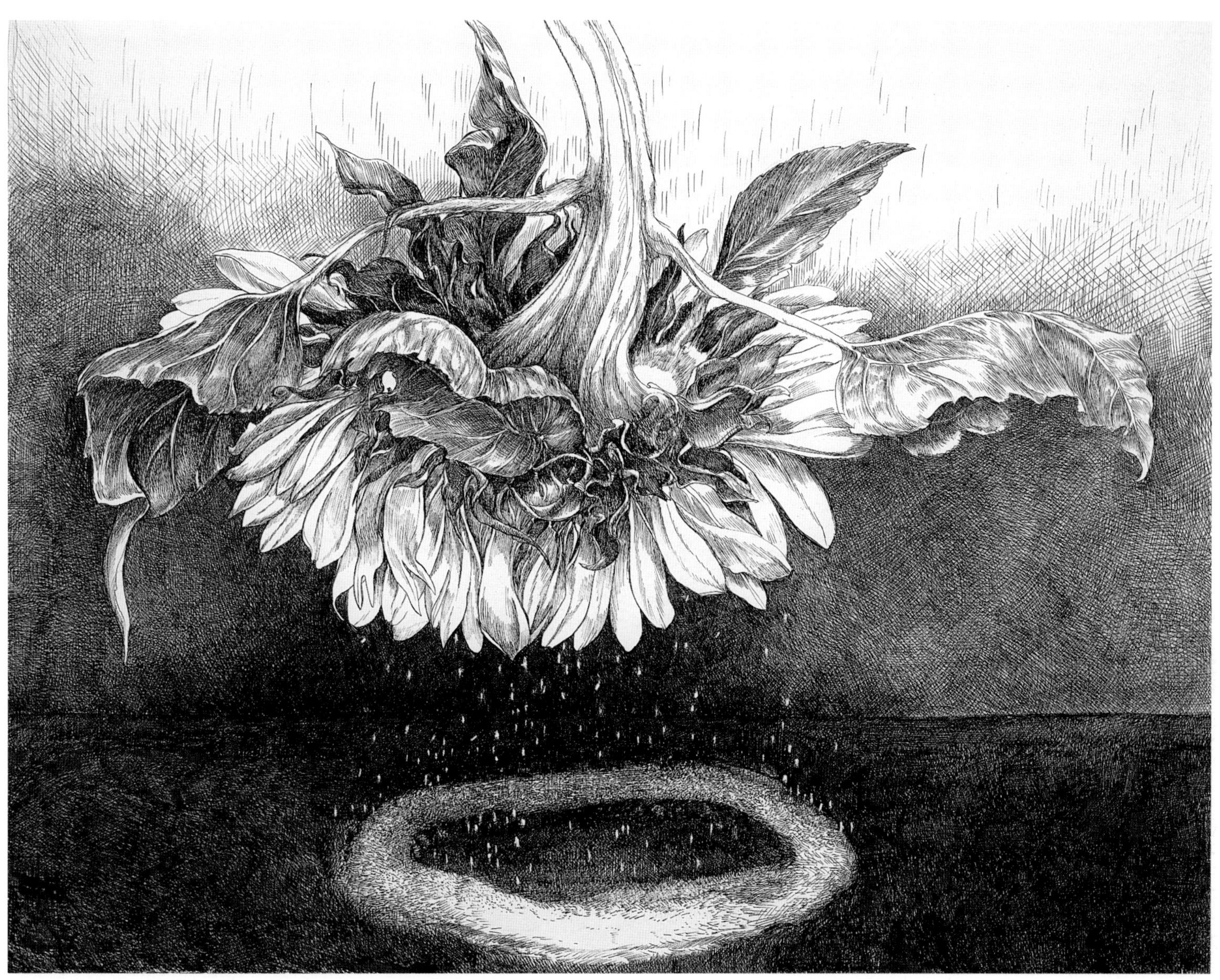

SUNFLOWERS SERIES NO. 2
(Left) Unsigned & undated
Acquired from the artist 1996
Pen & ink
580 × 730 mm

SUNFLOWERS SERIES NO. 5
(Above) Unsigned & undated
Acquired from the artist 1996
Pen & ink
580 × 730 mm

Gillian Barlow

BORN KHARTOUM, SUDAN 1944

Gillian Barlow has always had a career in the arts. She attended the Slade School of Fine Art, University College, London in the early 1960s and obtained a BA and MA in the History of Art at Sussex University. In 1987 she went to India as a visiting professor for the British Council and staged solo exhibitions there during her tenure. During the time she was in India, Gillian Barlow was also having solo exhibitions in the United States, at Vassar College Art Gallery, New York and Hudson View Gallery, New York. In 1988 she became Herald painter for the College of Arms, London and still holds this position, which involves designing and painting coats of arms for newly elevated peers.

She has won a number of awards for her botanical work, with two gold medals from the RHS and has been recording artist for their Orchid Committee since 1995, a position which involves painting new varieties of orchids immediately after they have won awards, in order to register their characteristics and idiosyncrasies.

She also teaches at the English Gardening School at the Chelsea Physic Garden in London. I saw some of her sensitive rose paintings there and felt that her work was in a particularly good period, so I asked her to paint me a rose of her choice. She decided on *Rosa* 'Veilchenblau' and produced an ethereal painting of this delicate China Rose, working fast and furiously before the ephemeral flowers faded.

Her most recent triumph was being awarded 'Best of the Show' at Longwood's 'Flora 2000', an exhibition put on by the American Society of Botanical Artists at the famous gardens in Delaware, USA, formerly part of the Dupont empire. This exhibition generated a great deal of publicity and her entry of a stinking hellebore, *Helleborus foetidus*, was illustrated in the press.

ROSA 'VEILCHENBLAU'
Signed GB '98
Commissioned
Watercolour on paper
540 × 365 mm

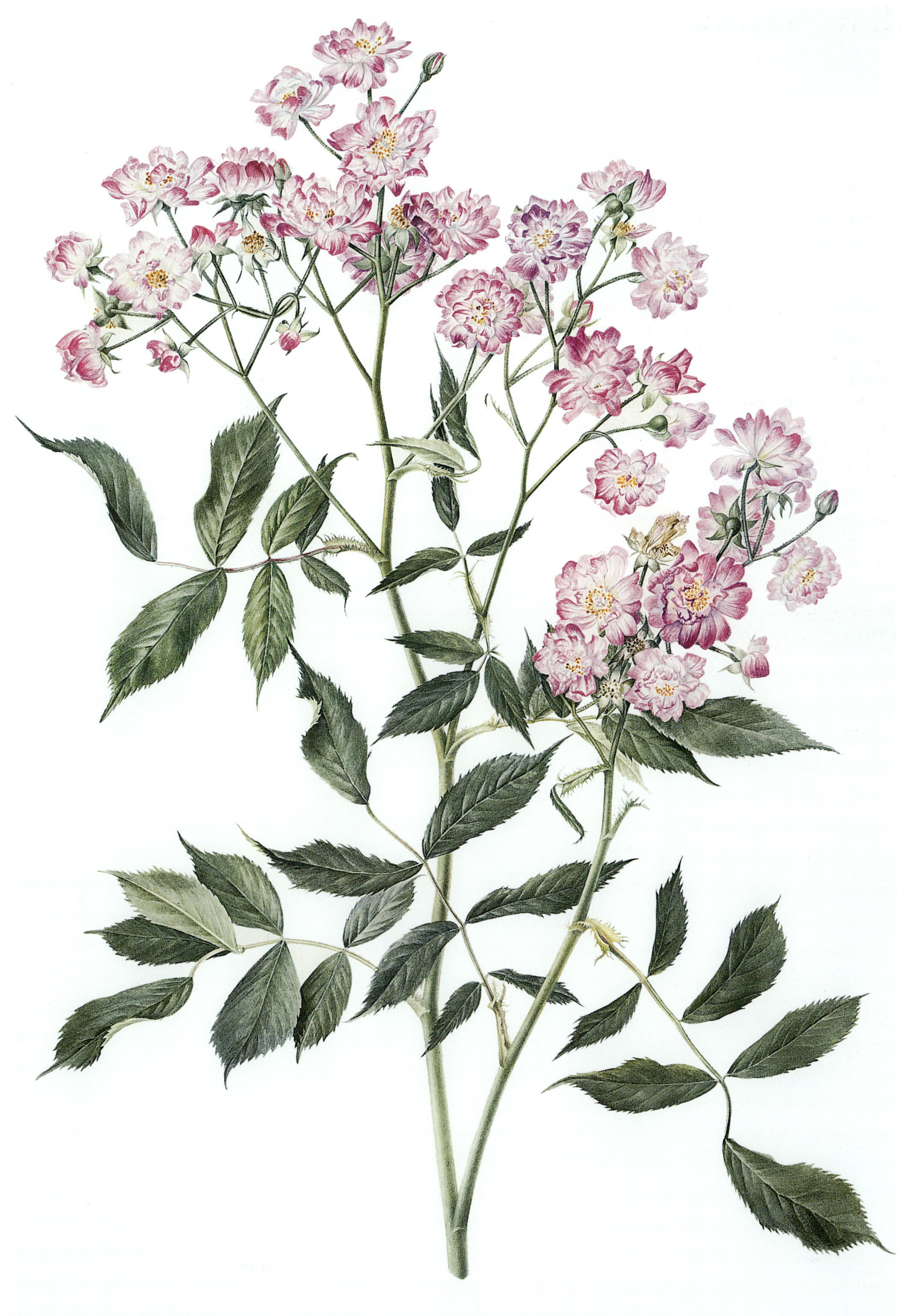

Malena Barretto

Born Rio de Janeiro, Brazil 1952

Malena Barretto is one of those active, intelligent Cariocas that I enjoy seeing in Rio. I have met her on several occasions while I've been there, sometimes in her studio, and sometimes at our hotel, the Copacabana Palace, where she has arrived armed with an interesting portfolio, often containing drawings of bromeliads, a particular favourite of hers.

She has spent a great deal of time travelling and painting on projects all over Brazil. In 1990 she travelled to Britain to study at Kew with Christabel King and took various other courses in England, supported by the Margaret Mee Foundation. She has had a substantial amount of work published, and has most recently been working on a portfolio of rare bromeliads for Banco Boavista. She has been much influenced by Margaret Mee's work, giving her plants a similarly strong outline that fades near the edge of the paper. She loves to paint trees and showed me experimental drawings of flowering trees with landscape backgrounds.

Malena Barretto has taught many workshops and courses at the Rio de Janeiro Botanical Gardens and also in Belem, Fortaleza, Recife and various other botanically interesting places, undoubtedly helping to improve the general standard of painting in Brazil. This has increased in leaps and bounds over the last few years, due in no small part to Margaret Mee scholars who have returned to Brazil and taught there after an inspiring visit to the Royal Botanic Gardens, Kew.

She is currently working on illustrations for a book on Brazilian medicinal herbs which is being produced by Reader's Digest called *Segredos e virtudes das Plantas Medicinais*. She has done most of the research herself and as usual has flung herself into the project with enthusiasm.

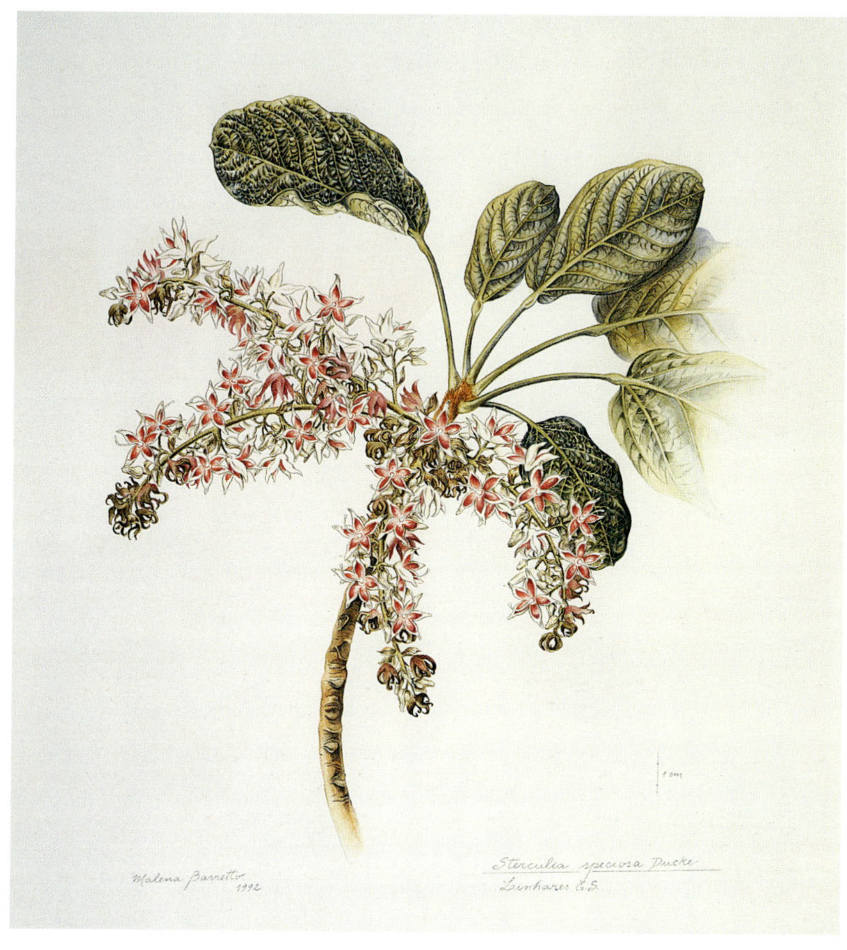

STERCULIA SPECIOSA
(Above)
Signed Malena Barretto 1992
Acquired from the artist 1996
Watercolour on paper
575 × 432 mm

NEOREGELIA SP.
(Right)
Signed Malena Barretto 1997
Acquired from the artist 1999
Watercolour on paper
660 × 480 mm

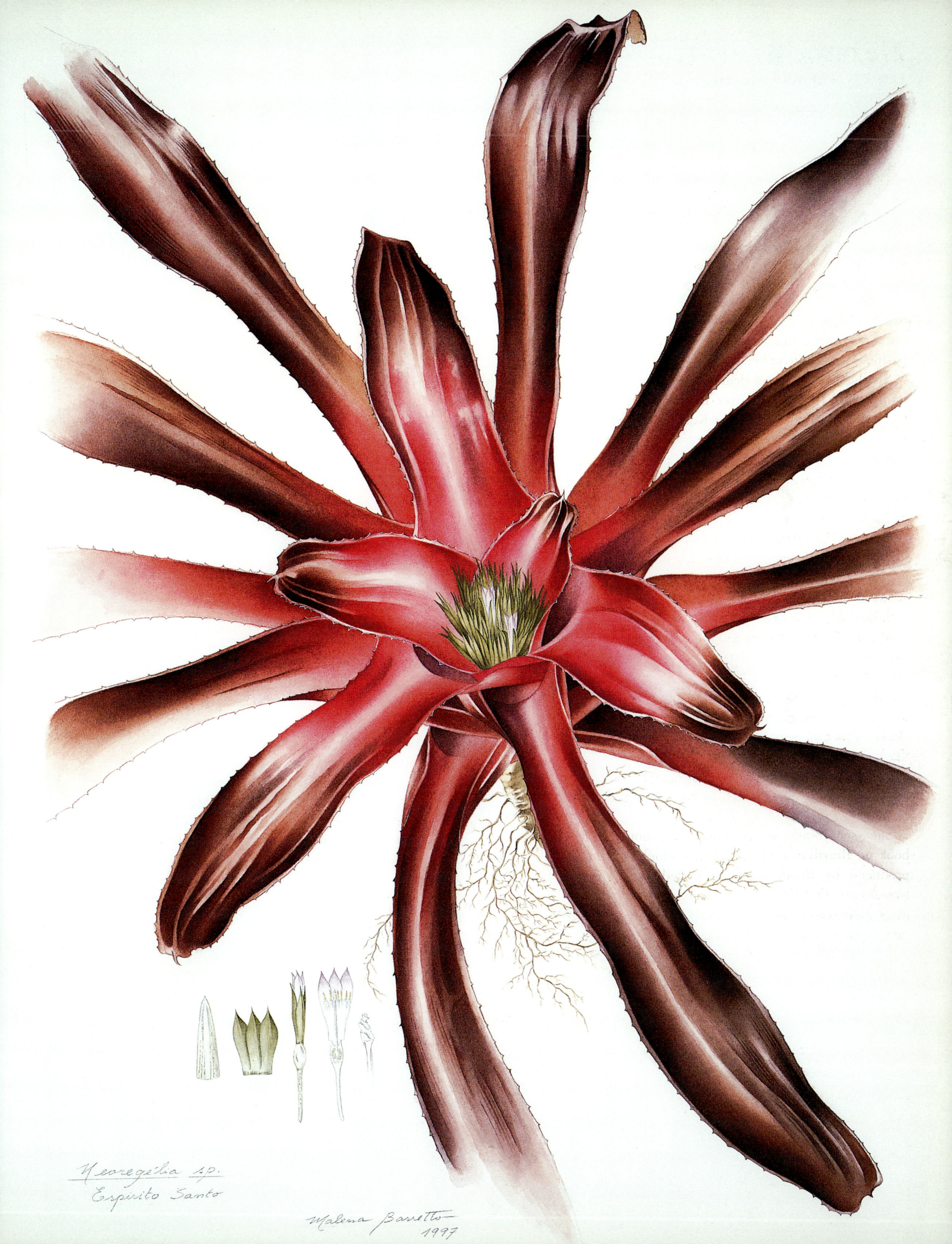
Neoregelia sp.
Espirito Santo
Malena Barretto
1997

Leslie Carol Berge

BORN TAUNTON, MASSACHUSETTES, USA 1959

Leslie Berge was born in the United States but comes from an artistic and musical family originating in France. She lived with her relatives in Paris and Aix-en-Provence while attending the American College in Paris. She obtained her first degree in art history, painting and drawing in 1981 from Bennington College, Vermont, then she spent a couple of years getting a MA in illustration at the Art Institute of Boston, with an emphasis on children's books. She has been a freelance artist since 1981, dividing her time between toy design, illustration and air brush, and her first love which is botanical illustration. Many artists have to split their time like this, since it is hard to survive financially working only as a botanical illustrator.

I first saw her work at the Hunt Institute in 1992 in the 7th International Exhibition. I bought her massive coloured pencil study of a *Colocasia*, drawn with a certainty and pared-down-to-essentials that comes from her background in design.

She attended a course that I had organised in New Orleans, to coincide with an exhibition of my collection at the New Orleans Museum of Art. I wanted the class participants, taught by Katie Lee to use the exhibition as a teaching and learning tool alongside the classes. There had never been any comparable show of contemporary botanical art in the southern United States. One important development as a result of this class was that Leslie decided to try using watercolour, urged on by Katie, and found that it was quicker and the resulting paintings sold well. She wrote to me exuberantly afterwards, delighted with her new approach and progress.

The next time I met her was when I was establishing another botanical painting class at the Mount Nelson, Cape Town, again with Katie Lee as teacher. This time there was a particular emphasis on succulents, borrowed from the huge new glasshouse at Kirstenbosch, with their strange, bizarre shapes and modifications for arid conditions. I encouraged Leslie to join this class as I thought she would enjoy the different South African flora, and in particular the most important collection of cycads in the world, growing on the slopes of Table Mountain in the famous botanical garden. It was love at first sight and she is currently fighting for survival in her apartment in Rhode Island, which is now being overwhelmed with fifteen different species of cycads and their powerfully scented sporophylls.

I invited her to show at the Tryon & Swann Gallery in London when I co-curated an exhibition with Oliver Swann in November 1998. As soon as I saw her dramatic entry of the female cones of the cycad *Encephalartos ferox* I knew that she had made a big move forward. Again she had pared down the fiery red cones and simplified the dense rosette of leaves of this primitive plant to create an enormously arresting painting that was immediately selected for the cover of the brochure. Of course I had to buy it and it is now one of the most exciting pictures in my collection.

She entered *Encephalartos woodii* for Longwood's 'Flora 2000' in Delaware. Her painting looked like a giant nest in which a goose had laid a cluster of golden eggs – a far cry from that elegant garden's normal image, but appropriate nevertheless since Longwood has one of the few specimens of this endangered cycad. All the existing *Encephalartos woodii* come from one male specimen growing in Kirstenbosch, Cape Town, which is 'caged' to prevent cycad enthusiasts from stealing offshoots from the base of the plant. Cycad theft has become so serious in South Africa that rare specimens are being 'microchipped' so they can be tracked by satellite if they are stolen from their desert habitats.

Her bold and exciting picture of *Encephalartos woodii* aroused great interest and was given huge coverage in the press during the Longwood show. It was reproduced in the *Washington Post* and dozens of other newspapers (see page 27).

She hopes to devote more time to her paintings and her plans for the future include visiting Australia to look at the *Macrozamia* cycads along the eastern coast in the tropical rainforest. It is very satisfying to see an established artist adapting and improving in response to the challenge of new botanical subjects.

CYCAD: FEMALE CONES OF
ENCEPHALARTOS FEROX
Signed L C Berge 1998
Acquired from Tryon & Swann Gallery 1998
Watercolour & pencil 700 × 510 mm

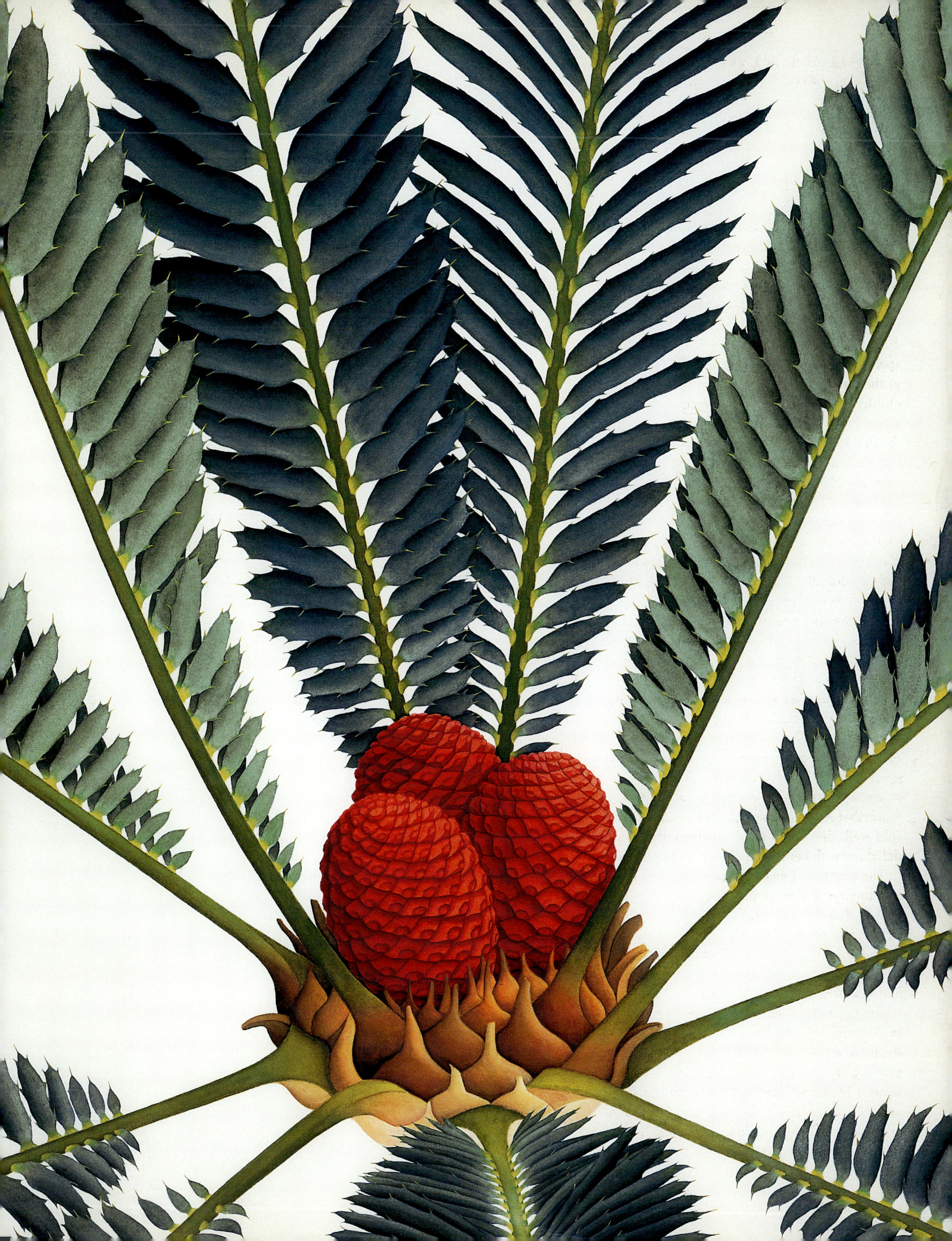

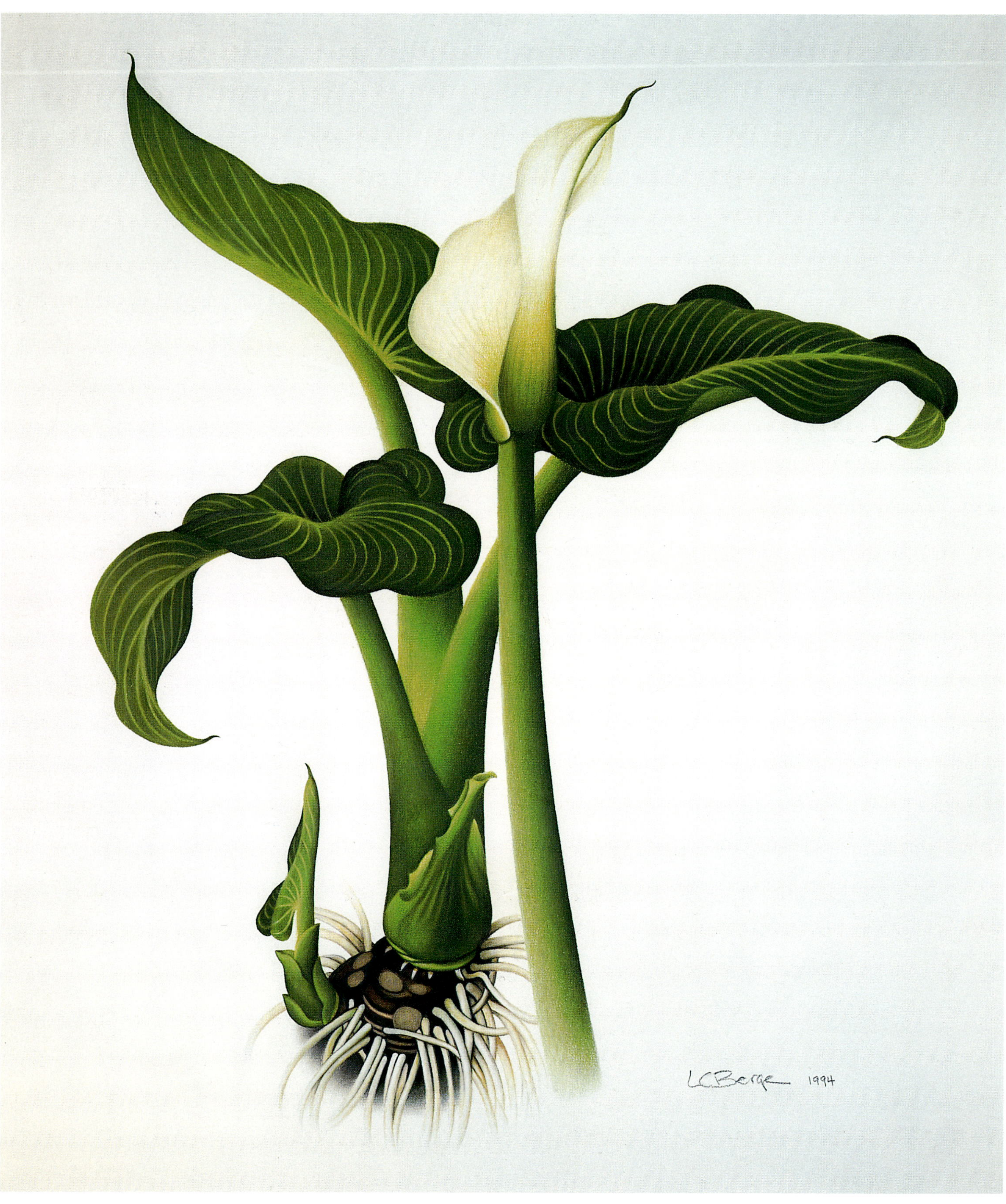
LCBerge 1994

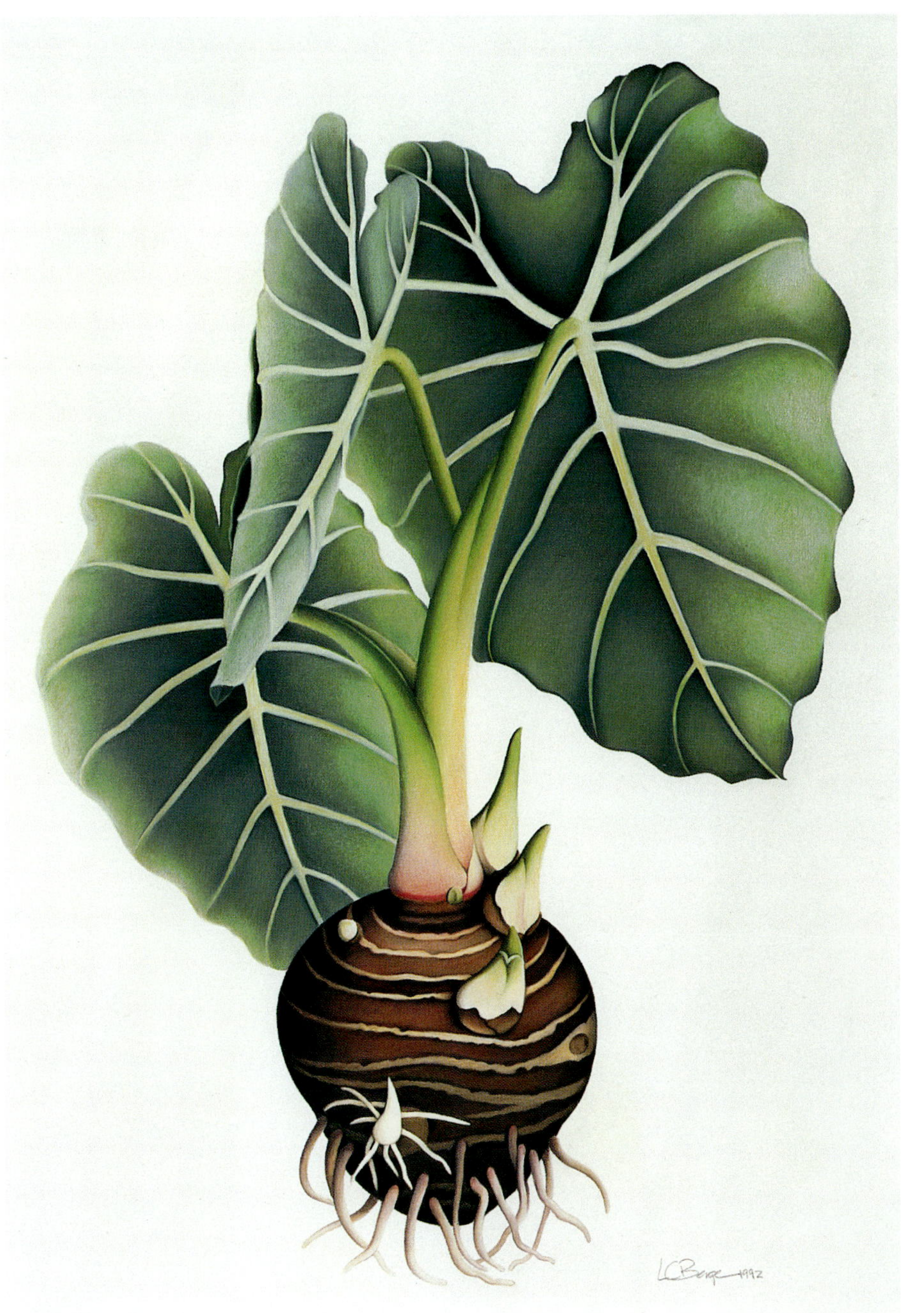

CALLA LILY: *ZANTEDESCHIA AETHIOPICA* 1994
(Left) Signed L C Berge 1994
Gift from the artist 1998
Prismacolor pencil on paper
740 × 590 mm

COLOCASIA
(Above) Signed L C Berge 1992
Acquired from the artist 1992
Coloured pencil on paper
895 × 605 mm

Susannah Blaxill

Born Armidale, New South Wales, Australia 1954

Susannah Blaxill was born in Australia but trained and worked for a period in England and it was at the David Ker Gallery, London that I first saw her work in 1991. She had another sellout exhibition at Spink in 1994 after she had returned to Australia. While she was showing in England I was lucky enough to buy four of her noteworthy paintings. One was a pansy study that I used on the back of the cover of my first book of botanical painting, another was a small, intricate painting of cyclamen, reminding me of a beautiful hieroglyphic. Later at a Spink exhibition in 1994 I bought the most spectacular beetroot which is so notable that virtually every exhibition curator has chosen it when I have shown it around the world, consequently I have never had it hanging on my own walls (see page 17). I can never look at a beetroot again without thinking about it. At that same exhibition at Spink I also bought a study of two superb pomegranates which now form part of my son Simon Sherwood's collection. More recently I have bought a painting of two large, spectacular purple aubergines. Initially I fell in love with their voluptuous texture and gleaming, rich colours, but eventually I bought them because of the exquisitely painted green petioles capping the fruit – they are remarkable in

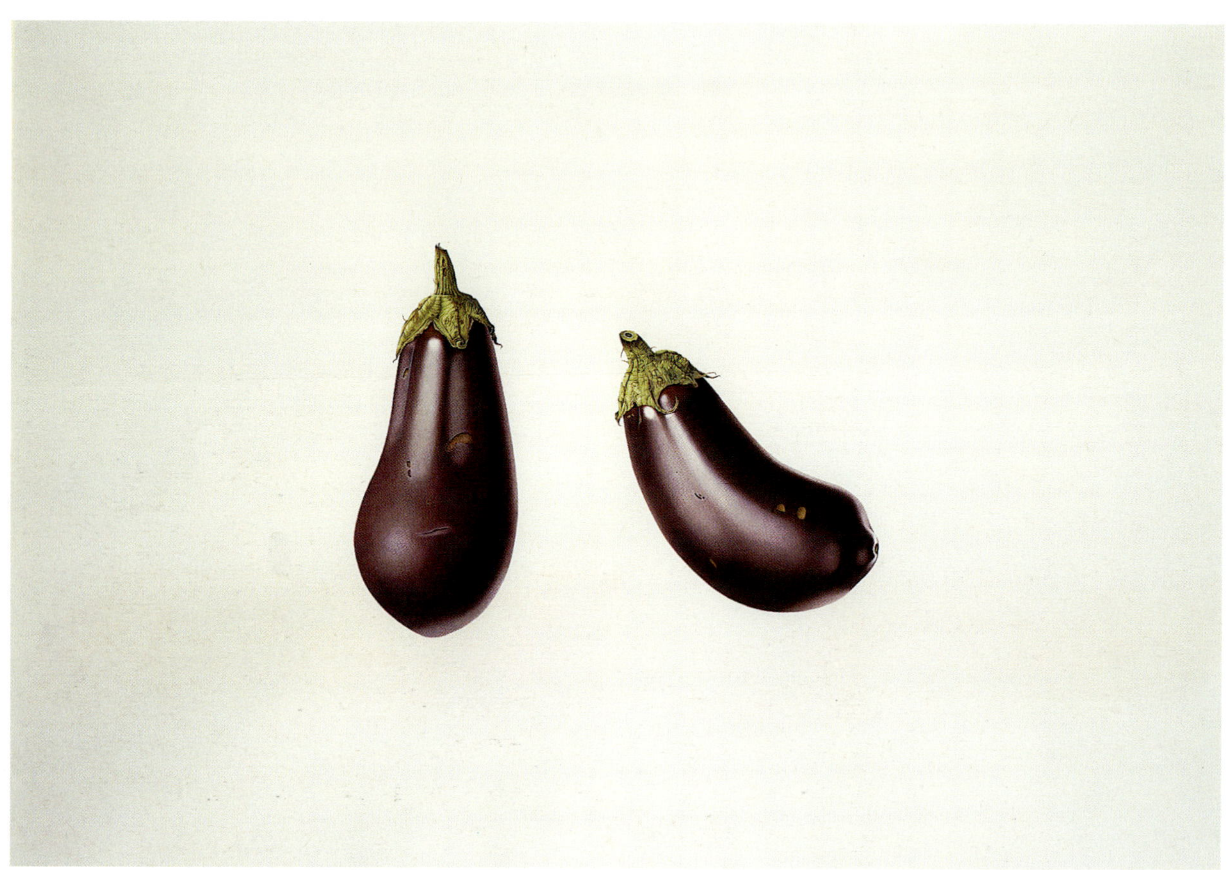

AUBERGINE
(Left & right)
Signed Susannah Blaxill
Acquired from Park Walk Gallery, London 2000
Pencil & watercolour
457 x 622 mm

CYCLAMEN
(Overleaf left)
Signed Susannah Blaxill (undated)
Acquired from David Ker Gallery, London 1991
Watercolour on paper
230 x 200 mm

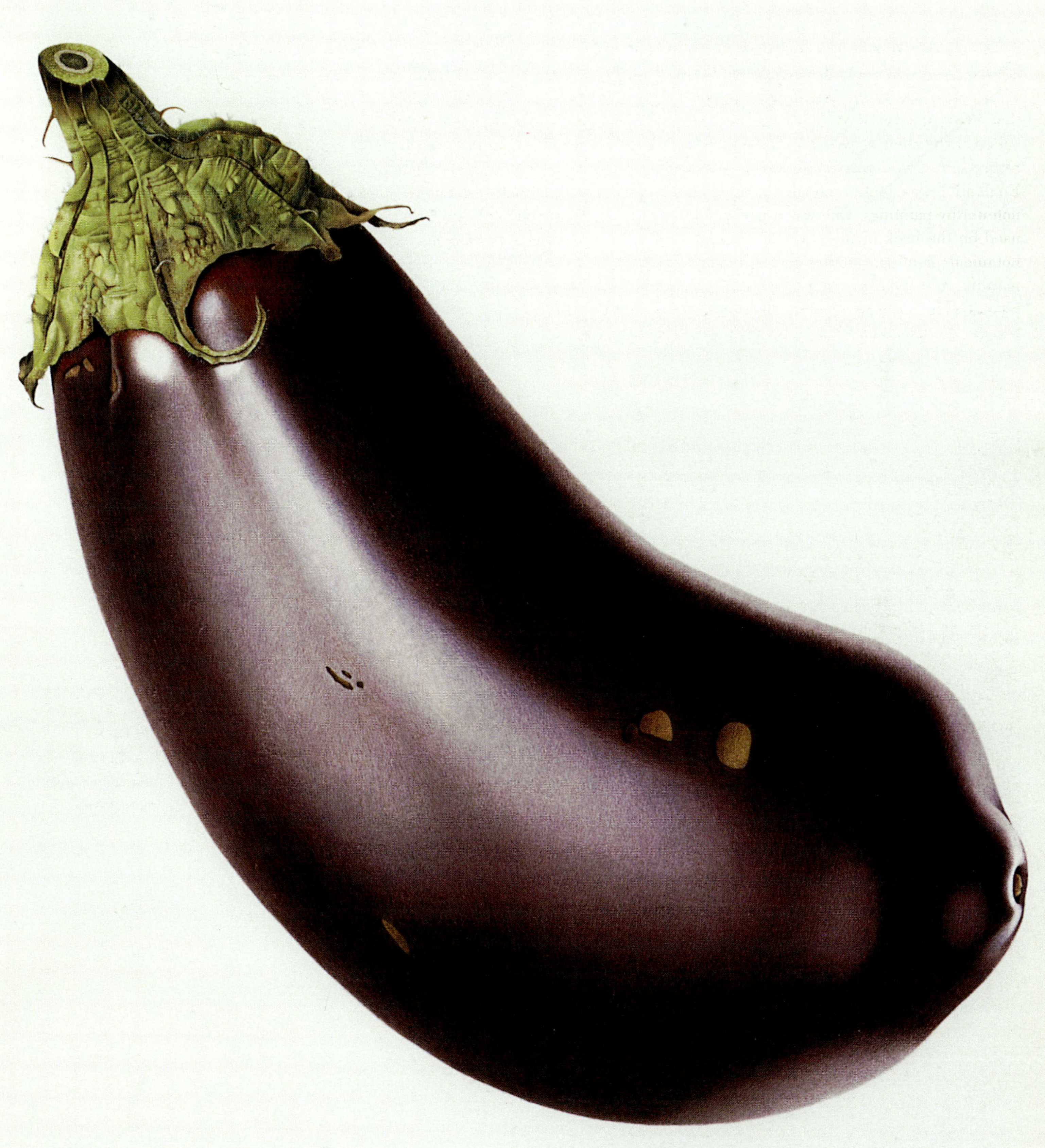

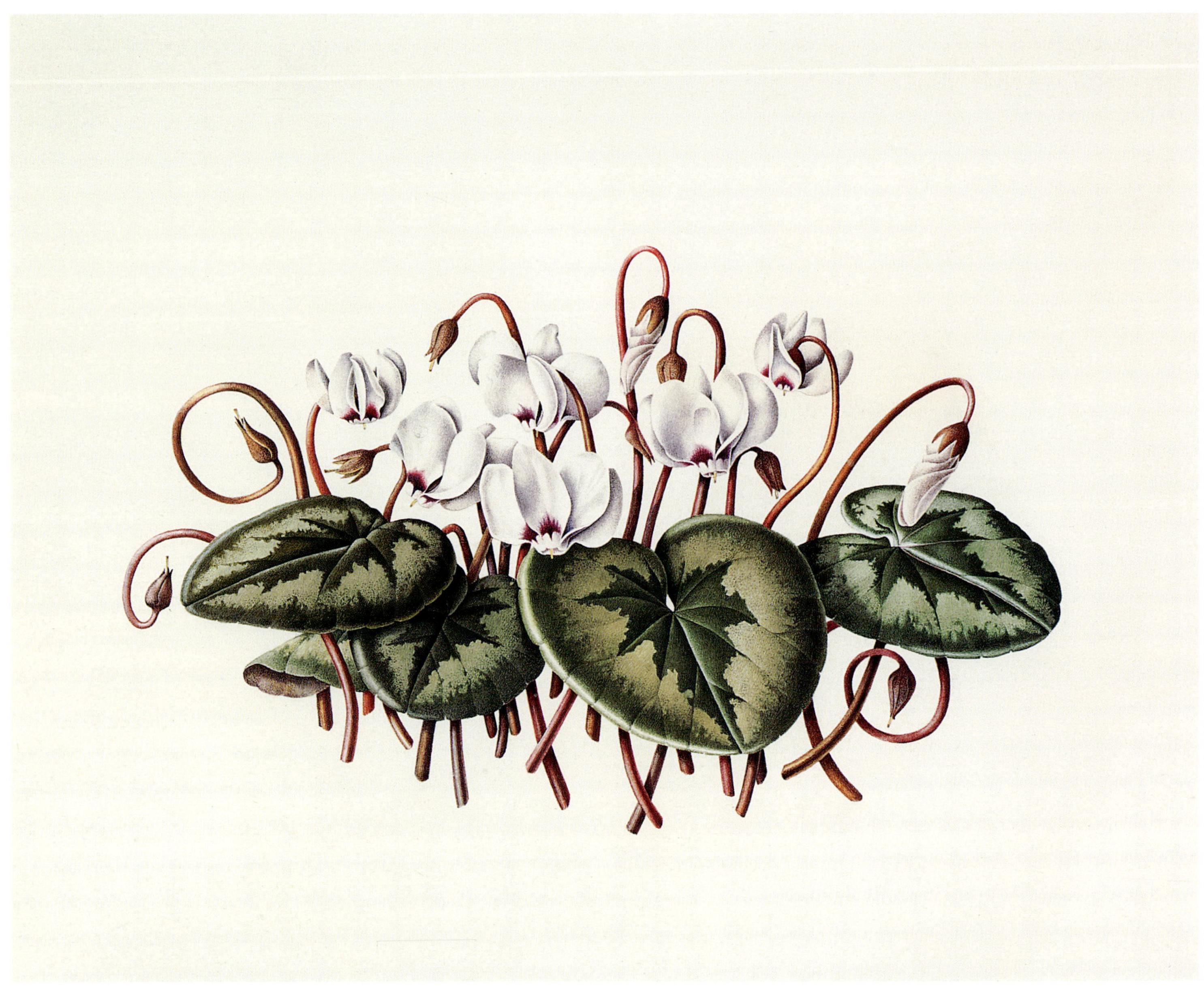

their detailing. The whole painting is a daring, floating composition in which she has made the surrounding space as important as the aubergines themselves.

In 1998 I met Susannah when she came to the opening of my exhibition in Sydney, bringing her husband and two children with her to stay overnight at our hotel. It was the first time we had met and she explained that she had given up painting because of her family commitments. I urged her to start again when she was ready. She tells me she has recently been doing quite a lot of teaching which she thoroughly enjoys but has found it difficult to set aside the long periods necessary for her particularly intense kind of painting and has only recently got back into the swing of things. She likes to set aside twelve to fourteen hours at a stretch, working obsessively until a painting is finished.

Last autumn on a lovely golden day, she found a carpet of mahogany-coloured leaves beneath a magnificent magnolia. She kept some of the dried leaves and later a student brought her one of the magnolia's intricate seed-heads, probably from the previous summer. She felt that she had the right combination and spur to start painting again and this study of a magnolia leaf and fruit is the first major painting she has done in several years. She feels that she has made the next step forward and is now itching to paint again. There is no doubt that she is one of the great contemporary botanical artists and yet another example of the strength of botanical art in Australia.

MAGNOLIA LEAF & FRUIT (right)
Signed Susannah Blaxill March 2000
Acquired from the artist 2000
Watercolour over pencil on paper
228 × 278 mm

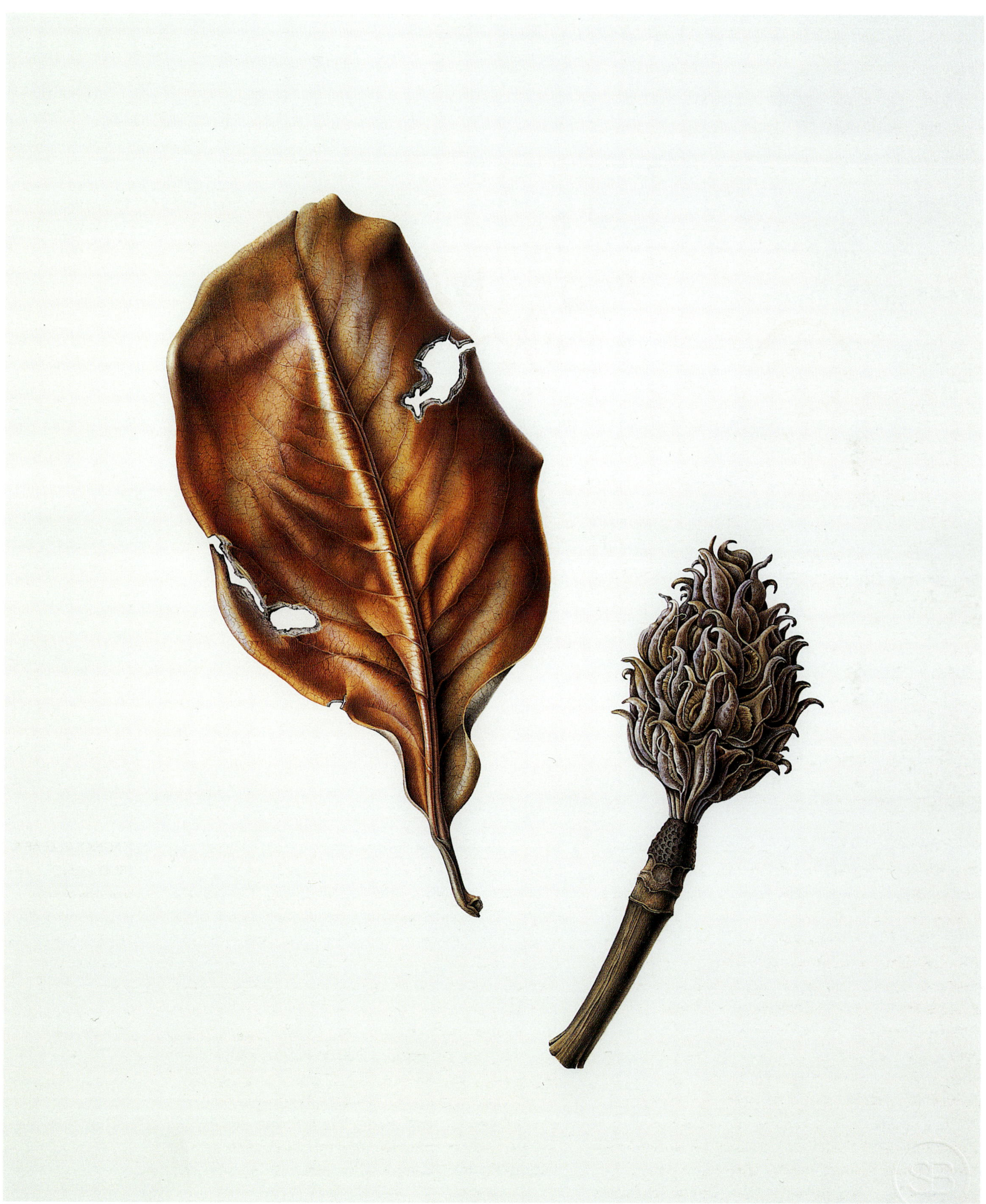

Raymond Booth

BORN LEEDS, ENGLAND 1929

Raymond Booth is considered to be one of the best British painters of plants who, unusually, works in oil on paper. He lives in Yorkshire and is represented in London by the Fine Art Society gallery, Bond Street where he has had four very successful solo shows. This is where I bought the first two works by him in my collection, one of a beautifully observed rose, the other a shower of curious yellow flowers, the toad lily *Tricyrtis macranthopsis*, found growing under waterfalls in Japan.

He went to the Leeds College of Art in 1945, but his training period was interrupted by National Service. His work has appeared in a number of publications such as *The Kew Magazine* and he also produced several plates for the *Camellia* book that Mrs Urquart commissioned in 1956, to which Paul Jones contributed many paintings. However, his most important collection of published paintings is in *Japonica magnifica* written by Don Elick. The original paintings were mounted as a touring show in the United States and I well remember seeing them in the Paine Webber building in New York. They were particularly interesting to me as I had already bought the book and I wanted to compare the originals with the printed reproduction. The book was well presented with good colour printing that was close to the originals.

This more recent acquisition of *Veltheimia bracteata* was in fact painted some time ago, in January 1979, before my other two paintings. I could not resist its masterly composition with the flower and seed detail and the network of roots emanating from the gleaming bulb. I grow this plant in my conservatory and it has flowered faithfully for many years, reminding me of its home in South Africa. It is always interesting to see earlier work from an artist one admires.

VELTHEIMIA BRACTEATA

Signed R. C. Booth

January 1979

Acquired from Park Walk Gallery 1997

Oil on paper

635 × 490 mm

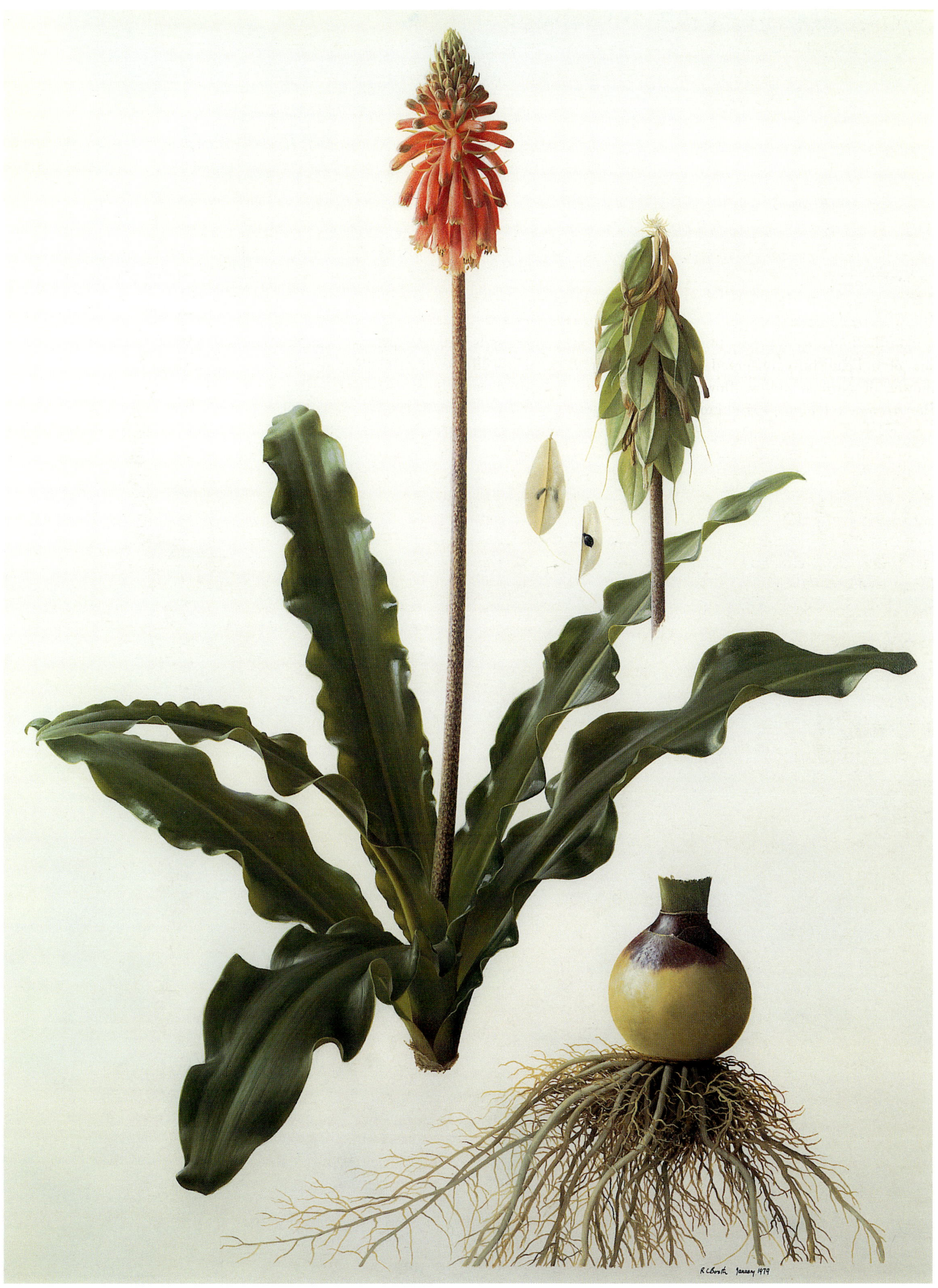
R C Booth January 1979

Anne Muirhead Chambers

Born Dundee, Scotland 1938

Until 1996 Anne Chambers had spent most of her life as a biochemist in the National Health Service in Dundee and Glasgow Royal Infirmaries, after studying biochemistry at St Andrews from 1956 to 1960, followed by an advanced degree. She has been exhibiting more frequently recently and has painted some plates for *The New Plantsman* and received a gold medal from the Scottish Rock Garden Club. Anne Chambers is an intrepid traveller with two great passions – plants and painting. She specialises in growing and illustrating Asiatic species and has trekked extensively in the Himalayas, western China and Tibet. I have two of her paintings, both a result of these expeditions.

I have always loved meconopsis and tried, rather unsuccessfully, to grow them. Their colours seem to have a special purity and the painting of the yellow *Meconopsis integrifolia* particularly appealed to me. Its almost incandescent petals are so beautifully offset by leaves covered with a dense coat of hair. This specimen comes from south-east Tibet. Anne told me she saw a small colony of this plant in June 1995 at an altitude of about 4570 metres below the summit of the Kongbo Pa La, a pass east of Lhasa. The species grows on the high treeless plateaux of Tibet and western China and shows some variation depending on altitude and exposure. This one was growing in a shallow depression and was about 25 cm tall; others with greater exposure can be as little as 15 cm. The whole plant is covered in fine blonde hair.

My second choice is very different – *Rheum nobile*, seen by Anne Chambers on Bimbi La, in 1998. She had painted one version of this for an RHS entry in 1998 for which she was awarded a gold medal. I was intrigued by this curious mound of leaves which she told me had an unusual pink tinge and so she agreed to paint another version for me, which arrived in 1999.

Plants of *Rheum nobile* are quite common at high altitudes throughout the Himalayas, usually growing in the company of dwarf alpines. Since they often grow up to two metres in height on hillsides bare of other tall vegetation, the pale spires are visible from a considerable distance. The lower leaves gradually change upwards into pale bracts that conceal clusters of tiny yellow flowers, that presumably mature in a protective microclimate. The stout central stems are eaten with relish by the local people. This particular plant was growing on the screes of the Bimbi La, a pass in the Tsari area of south-east Tibet near the border with the Indian province of Arumachal Pradesh at an altitude of 4570 metres and was the first that she had seen with a pink flush. Several other specimens in the area were similarly coloured.

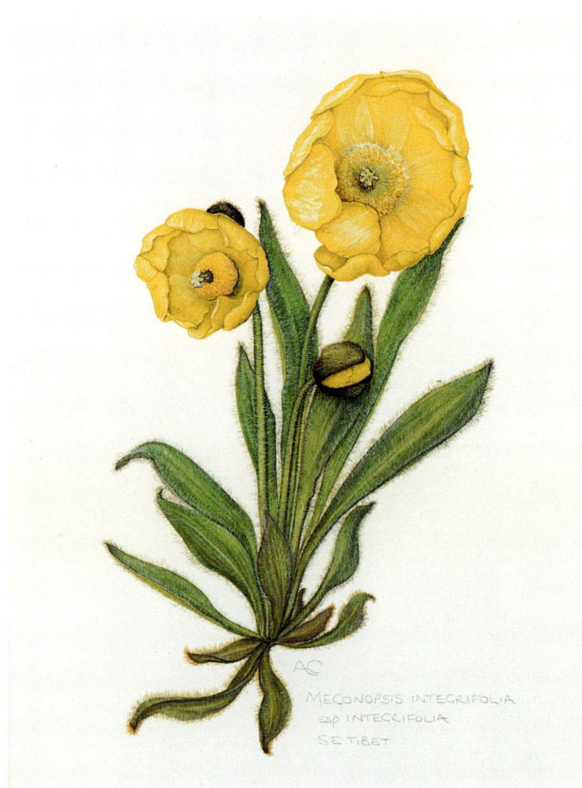

RHEUM NOBILE
(Right) Signed
RHEUM NOBILE
BIMBI LA '98 – AC
Commissioned – received 1999
Watercolour on paper
435 × 350 mm

MECONOPSIS INTEGRIFOLIA
(Left) Signed AC
Meconopsis integrifolia ssp. *integrifolia* SE Tibet
(undated)
Acquired from the RHS Show 1996
Watercolour on paper
300 × 210 mm

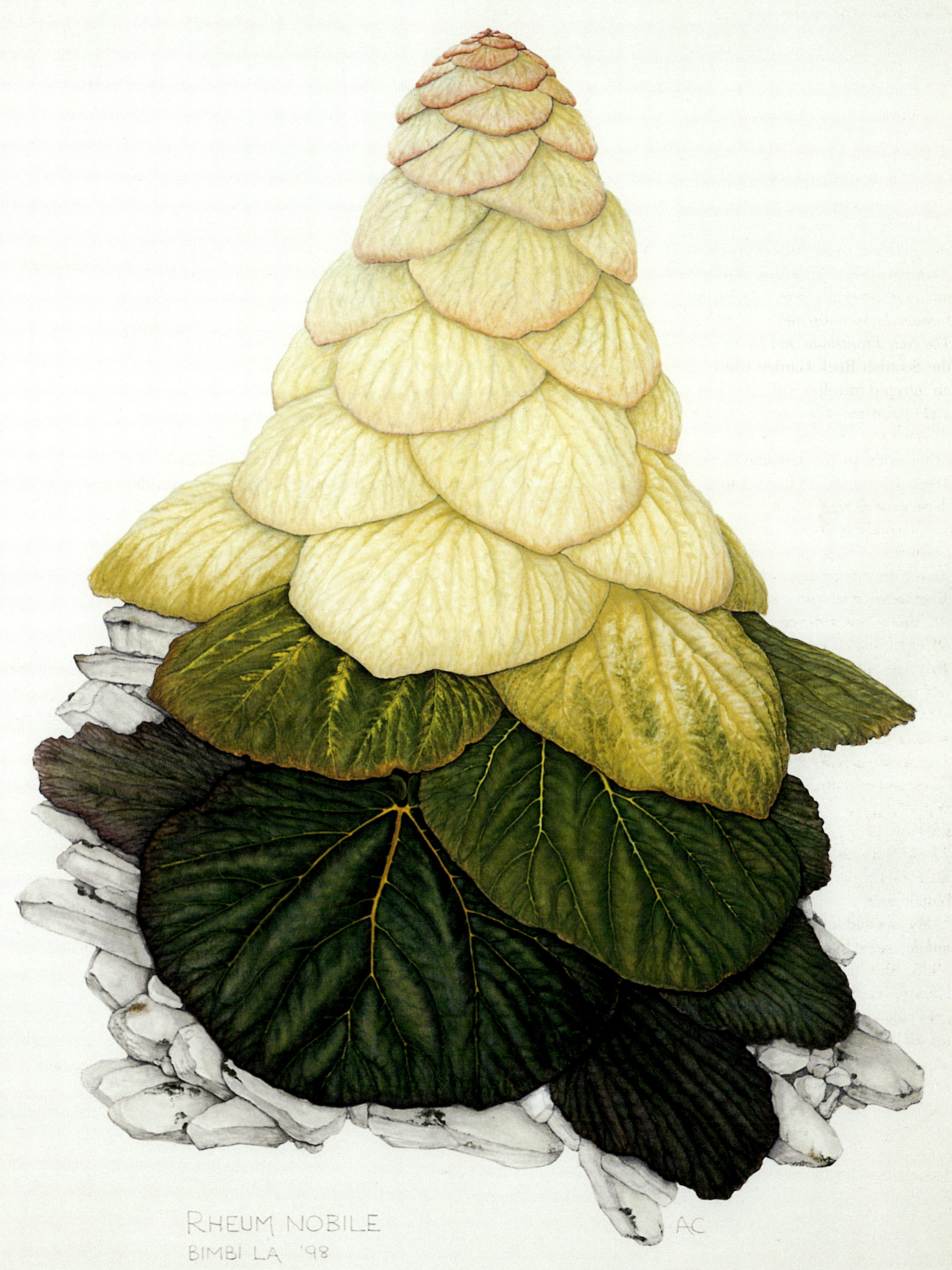
RHEUM NOBILE
BIMBI LA '98
AC

Emmanuel L. Cordova

Born Pasay City, Philippines 1960

In 1996 I visited Manilla and made my usual, hopeful enquiries about botanical artists who might live locally. All my contacts drew blank so I visited a couple of art galleries in town to see if I could find anything for myself. Foraging through various portfolios I came across the work of Emmanuel Cordova. I obtained his address from the gallery and decided to make contact. After some letters to and fro, we settled on a palm as the subject for a commission and a few months later a splendidly informative and charming painting arrived of the Areca nut palm, *Areca catechu.*

Cordova took a Fine Arts Degree in Advertising at the University of Santo Thomas and joined an advertising company for a few years before going freelance in 1990. He has had annual one-person exhibitions called 'Botanicals Elcordova' at the Ayala Museum, Makati City since 1991 and been hung in several group exhibitions. He has executed a number of large commissions for some of the top hotels in Manilla, including murals, botanical paintings and prints. In 1994 he was sponsored by the Amon Trading Corporation to travel widely in Europe to do a modern Grand Tour, visiting museums, galleries and gardens to broaden his experience.

In 1999 he painted the largest botanical paintings he had ever attempted, for a private home. He created eight large panels from floor to ceiling, featuring plants that can be found around Mindoro, where the resthouse was built. He sent me a photograph of this lovely project, with each panel showing different examples of palms, bamboos and ferns, an elegant backdrop of cool green and golden brown plants on a white background.

He has recently completed the illustrations for a republication of a medicinal plant book that was first produced in Madrid in 1892. Called *Plantas Medicinales de Filipinas* by Dr Trinidad H. Pardo de Tavera, the original edition was not illustrated. Emmanuel Cordova was commissioned to produce twenty-six paintings for the new edition by Fr Joey Cruz of the Ateneo University, and it came out in English and Spanish in 2000.

AREGA NUT PALM:
ARECA CATECHU
Signed E. L. Cordova
1997
Acquired from the artist 1997
Watercolour on acid-free paper
500 × 380 mm

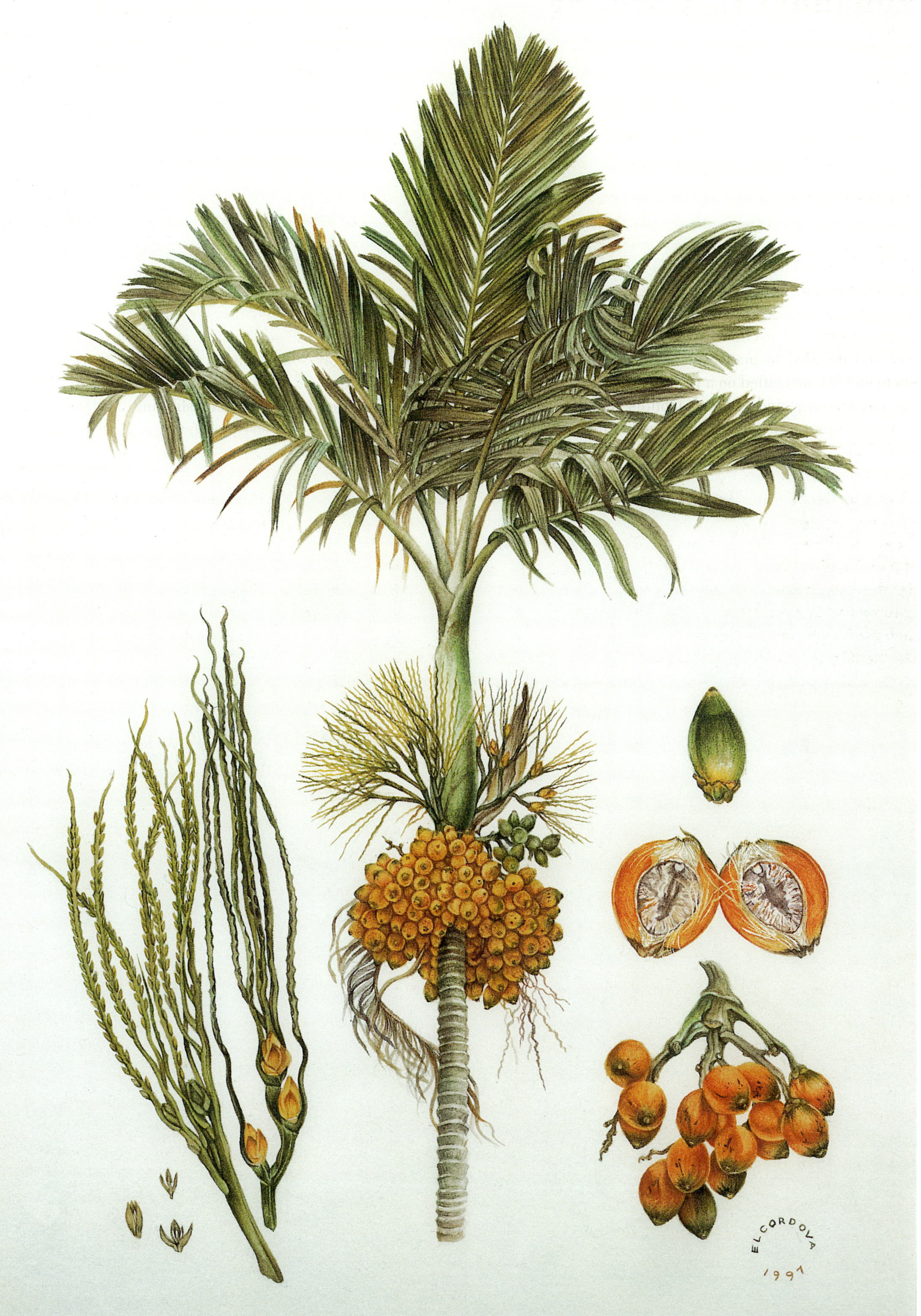
ELCORDOVA
1991

Vicky Cox

BORN YORKSHIRE, ENGLAND 1943–99

I only met Vicky Cox once at an RHS exhibition at Vincent Square in 1998, when she was awarded a gold medal. Sadly she died a year later. I bought two of her coloured pencil drawings of sprouting onions because I thought she had captured their translucent, papery skins to perfection. She had also executed the loose outer skin in the 'White Onion & Skin' with great skill and movement, and the roots were full of character.

She trained as an artist in 1968, gaining first class honours at Maidstone College of Art where her tutors included Patrick Proctor and David Hockney. A couple of years later she completed a post graduate Master's Degree at Birmingham College of Art. From then onwards she was a self-employed artist, doing some teaching and running her workshops for both adults and children.

Her plant drawings were mostly done in coloured pencil and she exhibited steadily from 1968 onwards. She was a founder member of the Society of Botanical Artists and was awarded five silver, one silver gilt and one gold medal at the RHS.

However, she did not only paint or draw plant subjects. She was particularly interested in working from the moving figure in ballet and tai chi, using a very free, loose style in oils, pastels, watercolour and ink. Hopefully there will be a retrospective exhibition of her work in the near future.

WHITE ONION & SKIN
(Far right) Signed Vicky Cox
(undated)
Acquired from the RHS Show 1998
Coloured pencil drawing
350 × 340 mm

SPANISH ONION
(Right) Signed Vicky Cox
(undated)
Acquired from the RHS Show 1998
Coloured pencil drawing
370 × 270 mm

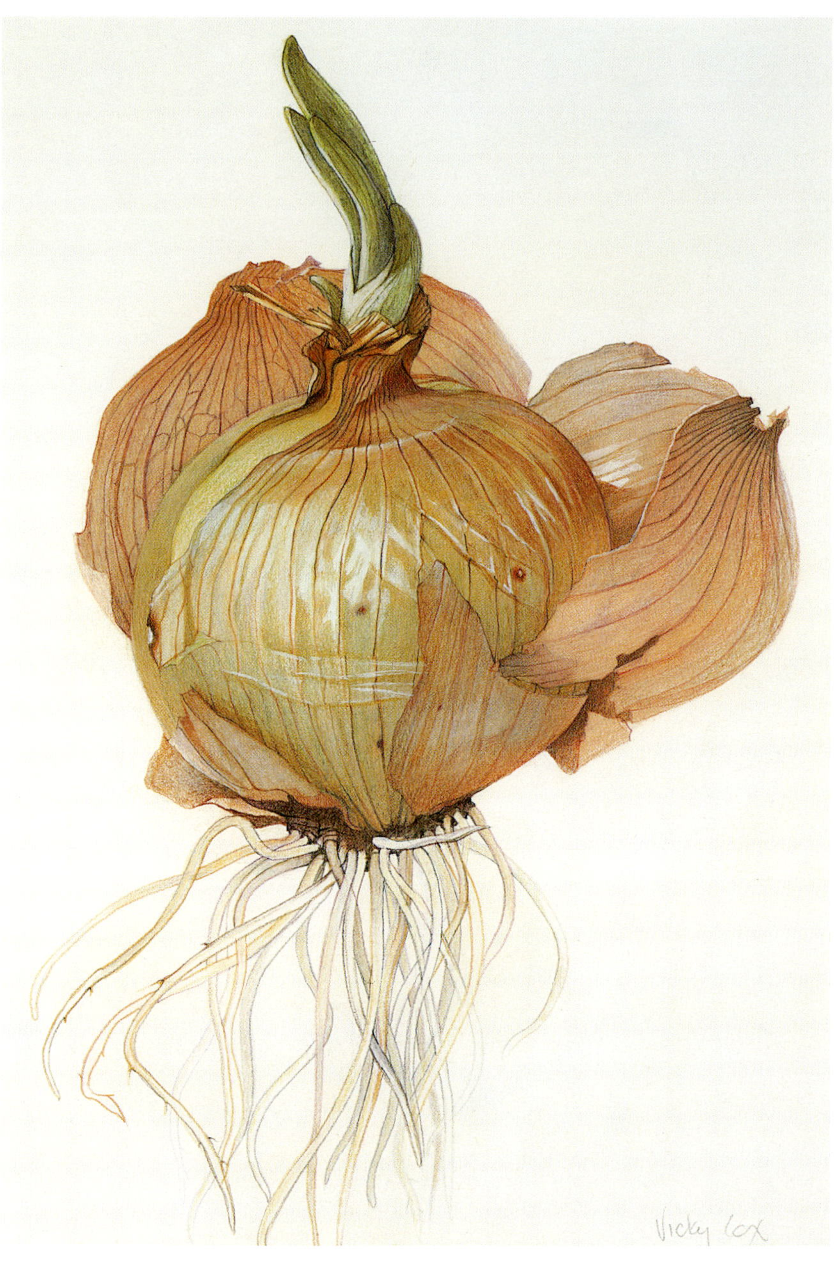

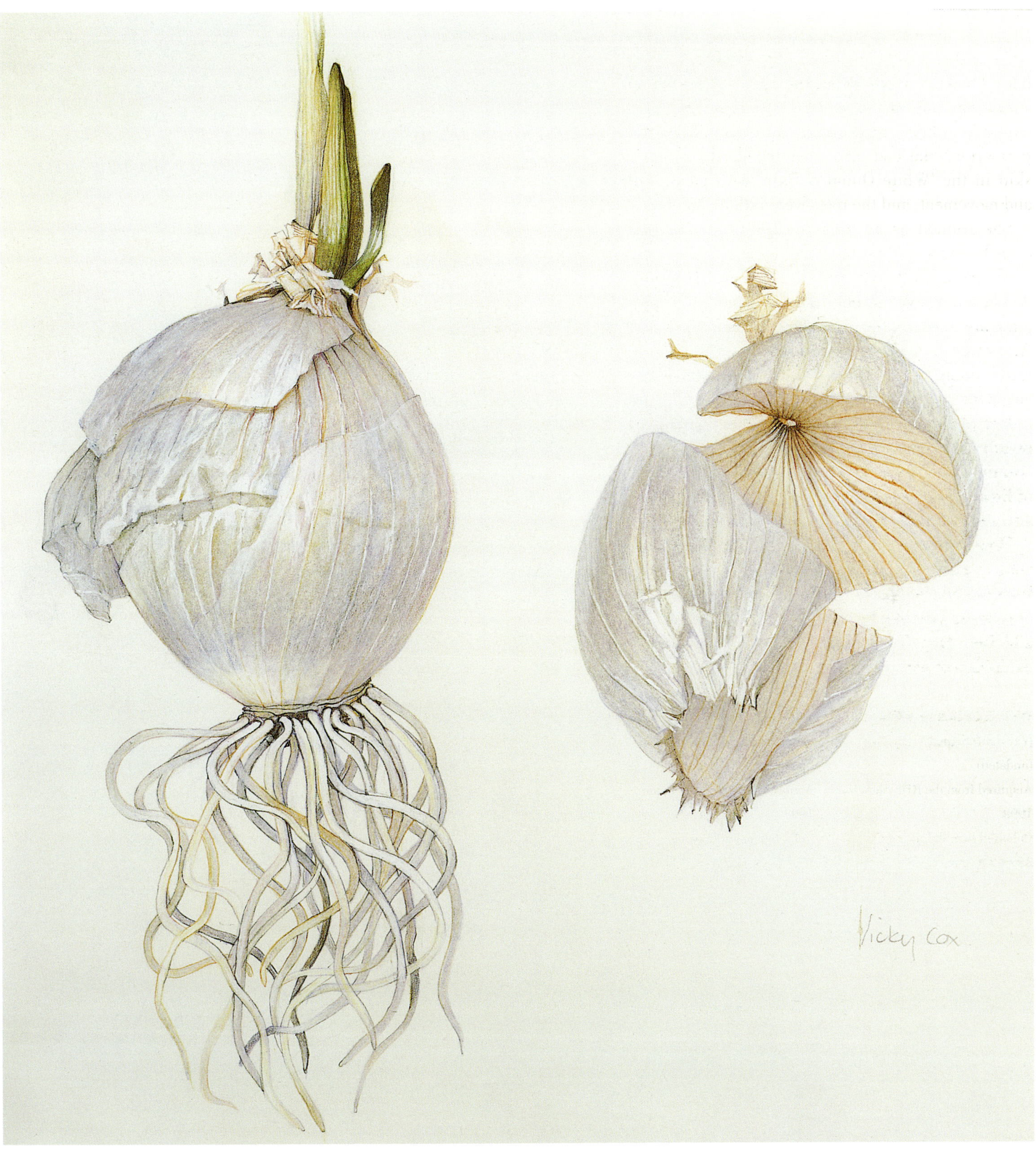
Vicky Cox

Moya Davern

BORN BRIDGEND, WALES 1949

This painting of *Echeveria* 'Paul Bunyan' was one of eight succulents displayed at the RHS in 1998 which gained a silver medal. I liked it for Moya Davern's controlled, yet exciting use of watercolour. Succulents are fascinating plants to paint, not only attractive to the artist because of the different textures of the leaves and stems, but also for the purely practical reason that they do not wilt or experience leaf-drop before the painting is complete. Two of the other paintings in this group have been sent to the Hunt Institute for their exhibition in 2001.

Echeveria 'Paul Bunyan' is a hybrid cross from the species plant *Echeveria gibbiflora* and *Echeveria corunculata*, both native to Mexico. In 1948 Henry Butterfield started hybridising experiments with *Echeveria gibbiflora*, and his work was continued by Dick Wright, a Californian nurseryman. *Echeveria* 'Paul Bunyan' was his truly successful attempt to introduce vivid colours into *Echeveria gibbiflora*. Growing to about 1.4 metres tall including flowering spike, this hybrid is propagated by stem and leaf cuttings, and any offspring thus belong to the same clone.

Moya Davern told me that the technical challenge in painting this plant was to convey the complex colour transitions without muddying the colours, and also to capture the fleshy depth of the leaves with their smooth and sometimes powdery surface. The carbuncle-like excrescencies on the leaves were a challenge to modelling with light and shade. Her particular interest is in achieving surface textures whilst using the flat medium of watercolour.

Moya Davern graduated from Bristol University and worked as an accountant for ten years. In 1989 she started painting murals and hand-painted furniture using enamels, oils and acrylics. As a result of these works she was commissioned to do a number of studies in watercolours. She was also asked to teach courses of botanical painting at Plumpton Agricultural College in 1996 and these proved very popular. Moya Davern now teaches landscape painting and Chinese brush painting as well as botanical studies, and has recently started tutoring two courses on watercolour each year at the English Gardening School at the Chelsea Physic Garden in London. She gained a silver gilt medal for paintings of hippeastrums in 1999 and a gold medal for paintings of fungi in 2000 at the RHS Westminster show.

ECHEVERIA 'PAUL BUNYAN'
Signed MD (undated)
Acquired from the RHS Show 1998
Watercolour on paper
765 × 560 mm

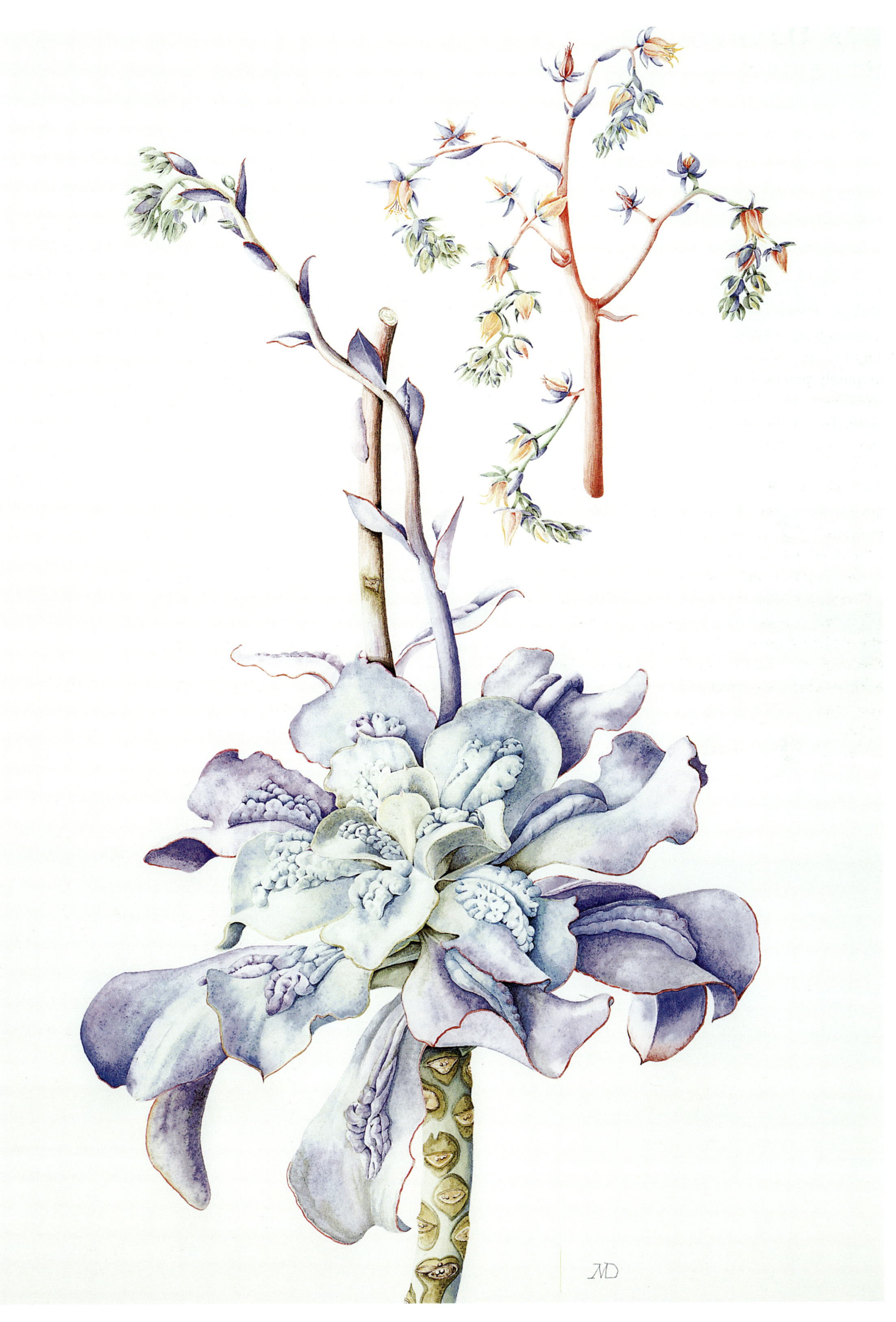
MD

André Demonte

Born Niteroi, Rio De Janeiro, Brazil 1957

André Demonte is a member of the Etelier Demonte created by his father, Etienne, in Petropolis on the edge of the Atlantic rainforest. Together with his brother Rodrigo, they form an enthusiastic family group, united by their passion for the conservation of Brazil's natural heritage. They run classes in their studio and are particularly concentrating on a project to publish the definitive book on South American humming-birds and their role in the pollination of so many tropical flowers.

André started exhibiting his paintings in Brazil in the late 1980s and showed in the United States and England throughout the 1990s, notably at 'Nature in Art' in Gloucester and in the Chris Beetles Gallery in St James, London. In 1998 he exhibited at the Tryon & Swann Gallery, London and at Art Expo, New York. He is trained as a geologist and his work has taken him to the most remote parts of Brazil.

His painting of *Oncidium crispum* shows this splendid epiphytic orchid perched on *Lytocaryum weddelianum*, known as the Petropolis palm or 'Baby cocos palm' when cultivated for horticulture. It is an attractive little feather palm which is found wild in the humid Organ mountains, growing up to a height of two metres with a slender, solitary trunk supporting graceful pinnate fronds. The narrow, stiff segments are a glossy yellow-green and it has small orange fruit.

André found the orchid, which flowers from May to November, on a steep escarpment between his home in Petropolis and Teresopolis. This is an important area of preserved Atlantic rainforest where it is quite common to find epiphytic orchids growing on the trunks of trees and palms. This remnant of rainforest can been seen from the terrify-ingly winding and precipious road between the two towns and is a reservoir of considerable biodiversity. The Atlantic rainforest has been devastated in recent times, leaving only isolated patches of what was once a magnificent swathe of sub-tropical forest along the coast of Brazil. It is endangered now to a far greater extent than the more famous Amazon rainforest. The Demonte family has always been in the vanguard of those trying to preserve the natural treasures of their spectacular country.

ONCIDIUM CRISPUM

Signed André Demonte 1999

Acquired from the artist 2000

Watercolour on paper

728 × 510 mm

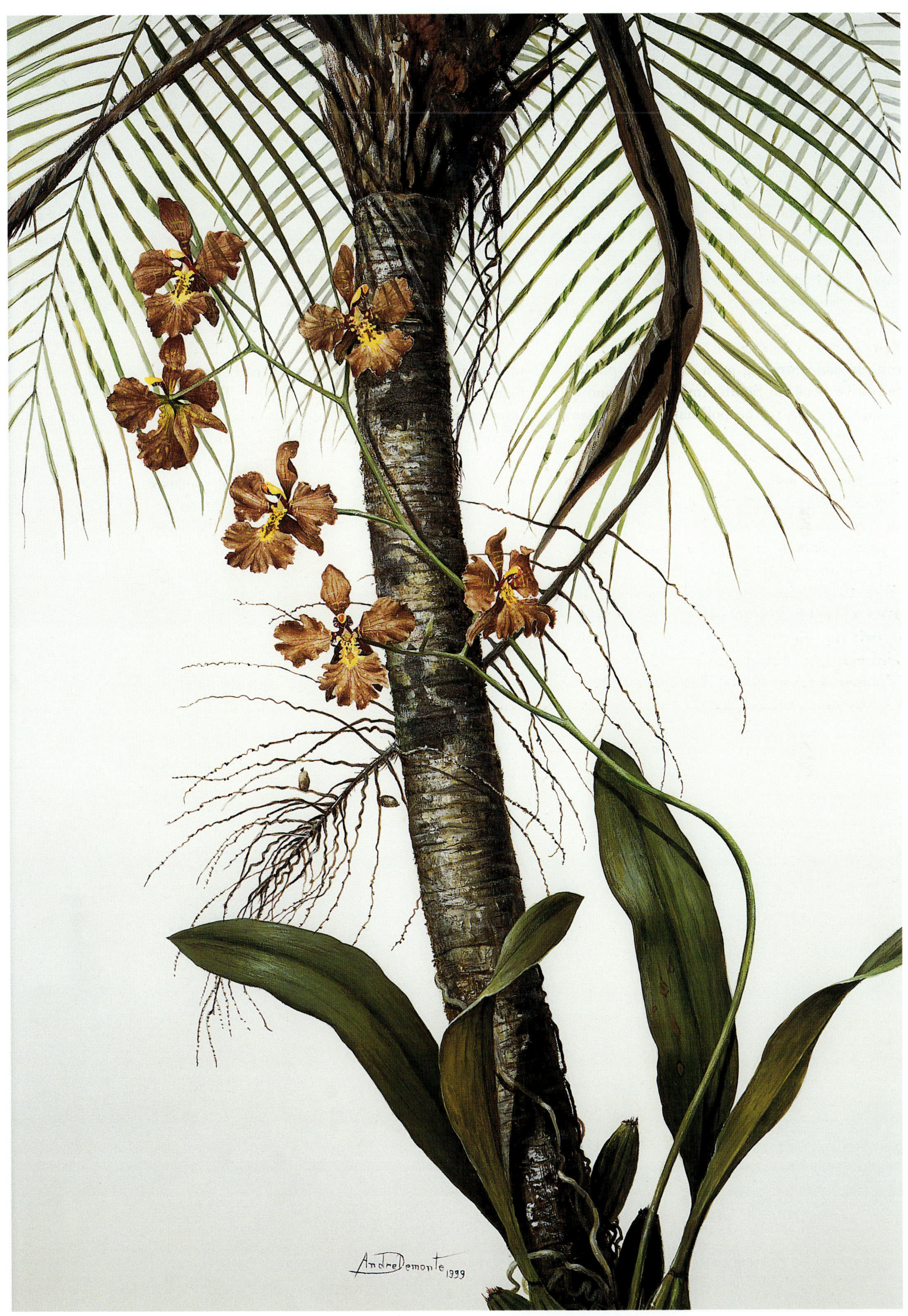
AndreDemonte 1999

Etienne Demonte

BORN NITEROI, RIO DE JANEIRO, BRAZIL 1931

Etienne Demonte has done a great deal to further the cause of botanical art in Brazil, as well as being a famous painter of birds. He lives in Petropolis, a city above Rio in the cooler Atlantic rainforest, where the Brazilian royal family used to spend their summers. He is part of a large family of wildlife painters including his two sisters, Rosalia and Yvonne and Rosalia's daughter Ludmyla. His sons, André and Rodrigo, live nearby and are following his example. They are all passionate about saving the unique environments of Brazil, seeking to trigger conservation through their artistic output and records. In their own words, they 'try to speak for the natural world to call attention to its fragility and harmony'. Etienne's 'etelier' has three or four pupils at any one time, learning the finer points of bird and plant studies.

From the 1960s onwards Etienne has had over two dozen shows in Brazil and he has exhibited internationally in Greece, the UK, Madrid and many other Spanish cities. He has also exhibited in the United States at the Smithsonian in Washington and the Hunt Institute on the Carnegie Mellon campus in Pittsburgh. He and his sisters were featured in a *National Geographic* film for an *Explorer* programme which illuminated his research and painting in the Bahia region in the bay of the San Francisco river.

I asked him to exhibit at the Tryon & Swann Gallery in London in 1998 and this is where I purchased the *Billbergia sanderiana* which he had painted in 1997. Within the work he has included two humming-birds, which pollinate the yellow-green flowers cascading down from the showy pink bracts. It is an elaborate and beautiful composition, with droplets of water condensing on the stiff, serrated leaves, the plant perched high in the canopy, visited by the exquisitely painted *Hylocharis cyanus* humming-birds.

He has recently completed a painting of the orchid *Miltonia cuneata* (which was first described by John Lindley) for the Lindley Library of the RHS. Etienne specially chose this orchid for the Lindley Library for that particular reason. The Library is moving into more spacious quarters and it is hoped that contemporary art will be shown in the new premises, where it will be more accessible. He brought the painting down from Petropolis at the time of our millennium visit to Rio when we were there for the New Year festivities.

Etienne Demonte's next major project is to work with his sons on *The Exotic Tropical Flowers and Their Humming-birds*, a publication which will be composed of original paintings and lithographic watercolour prints, concentrating on several species of South American flowers which depend on humming-birds for their pollination.

BILBERGIA SANDERIANA & HUMMING-BIRDS *HYLOCHARIS CYANUS*
Signed Etienne Demonte 97©
Acquired from Tryon & Swann Gallery 1998
Gouache & watercolour
700 × 480 mm

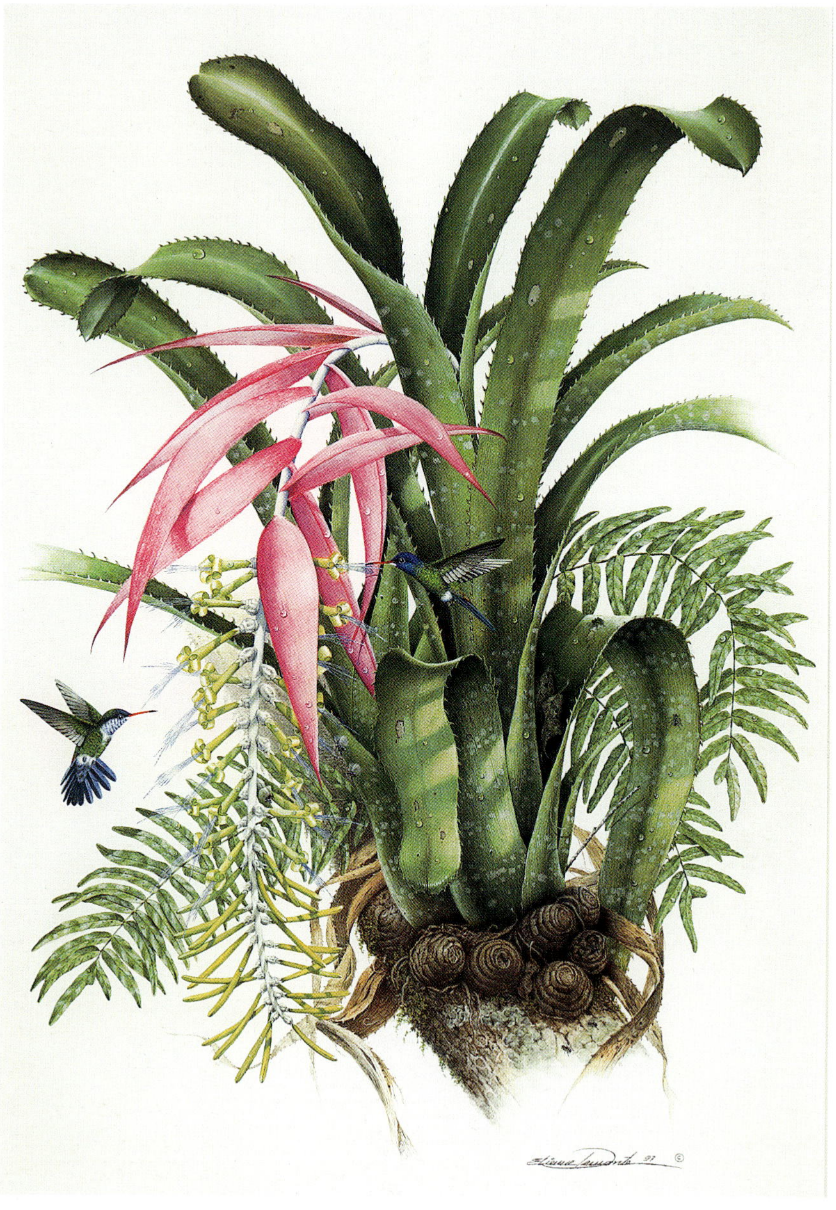

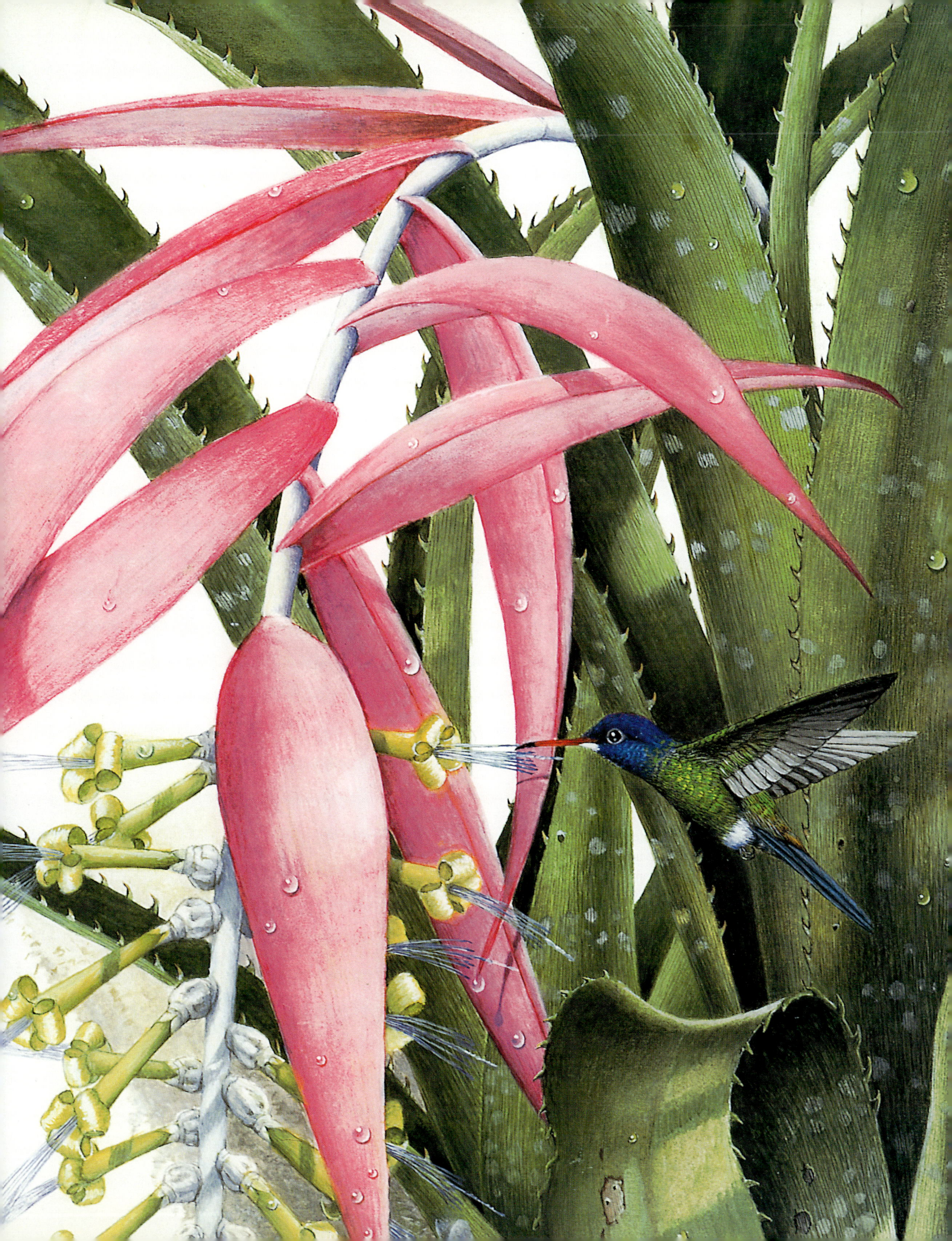

Anne Ophelia Dowden

BORN DENVER, COLORADO, USA 1907

Anne Ophelia Dowden can be considered the 'grandmother' of America's contemporary botanical artists in much the same way that Mary Grierson fills that role in the UK. Both have produced many books and patiently instructed aspiring artists and both continued to paint until very recently.

I met Anne Ophelia Dowden in July 1998 for the first time in her apartment in Boulder, Colorado, close to where she grew up. She enjoys looking out of her windows at the Rockies and has friends who drive her out to see the spring flowers. Her apartment was very organised, with her drawings and notebooks arranged meticulously. She has used these repeatedly as source material over the years when she was writing, illustrating and publishing her many books.

I already had one of her paintings, a beautiful study of squash blossoms which has been shown widely. She told me that she wanted me to have two of her remaining completed paintings, both executed a long time ago. She felt that I had made a contribution to botanical art as a collector and she knew they would be shown rather than stored away. One is a classical botanical painting of a horse chestnut, showing the complete 'candle' inflorescence rising from the large leaves, one isolated flower in exquisite detail and two conkers, one in its prickly shell, the other with its polished autumnal sheen.

The other painting is quite different and one of her favourites. It is a collection of autumn foliage and berries arranged as a casual bouquet. The colours are vibrant and the painting sparkles with life. All the different kinds of leaf are beautifully observed in their autumn colouring and decay and the fruits are quite luscious. She had made a print of it for the same series as another picture of hers that I had bought earlier called 'Squash Blossom 1978' acquired in 1994. She had a print of 'Autumn Foliage and Berries' framed above her bed and I was concerned that she was giving me something she greatly treasured. She was adamant, however, that she wanted me to have the original, which I truly appreciate.

She was worried about her failing eyesight which made it impossible for her to continue painting in the detail that botanical subjects demand. She showed me some abstract paintings she had done long ago and I suggested that she could perhaps return to that genre of painting so that at least she could continue to feel creative.

She has certainly not been forgotten in her later years, as she has recently been given a number of awards. The American Society of Botanical Artists gave her its annual award for her achievements as an illustrator and author in 1996 and she had another award from the Garden Club of America Zone XII in the same year. In January 1999 she was given the Gertrude B. Foster Award for Excellence in Herbal Literature from the Herb Society of America. She appreciates this most recent honour as she often mentions that she values her literary contribution as highly as her paintings.

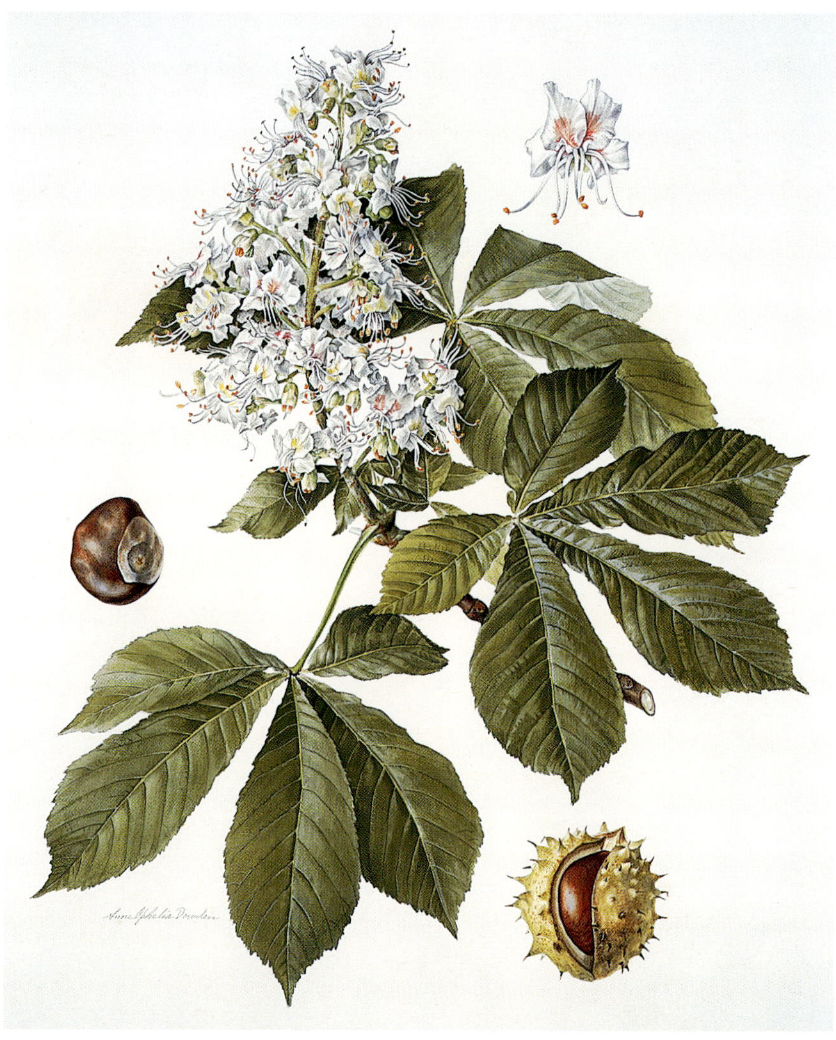

HORSE-CHESTNUT WITH FLOWERS & CONKERS
(Above) Signed Anne Ophelia Dowden
Gift from the artist 1998
Watercolour on paper
415 × 345 mm

AUTUMN FOLIAGE & BERRIES
(Right) Signed Anne Ophelia Dowden
Gift from the artist 1998
Watercolour on paper
500 × 390 mm

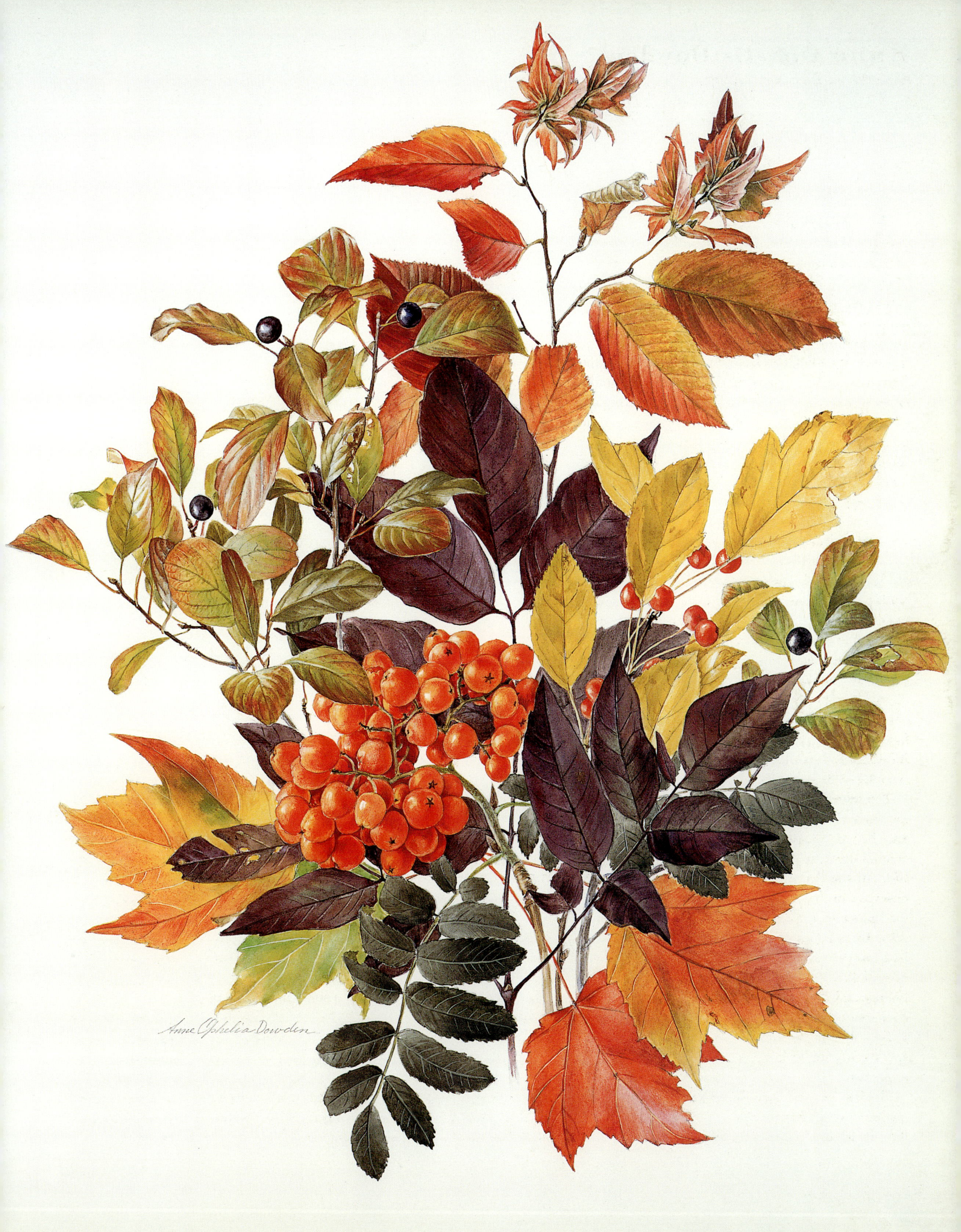
Anne Ophelia Dowden

Elizabeth Dowle

BORN LONDON, ENGLAND 1951

Although Elizabeth Dowle has won seven gold medals at the RHS shows over a period from 1986 to 1998, I had somehow missed her work and only made contact in 1996. I admired her well-researched painting which is meticulous and detailed. She trained by completing a Foundation Course at Croydon College of Art and from then on was self-taught as a botanical artist. She has produced all the plates for an impressive number of books and also contributed some of the illustrations for many more.

She works in watercolour, mainly on paper. She does use vellum occasionally and has some of the late Rory McEwen's vellum stored away for when she has the courage to use it. Rory McEwen had re-introduced the use of vellum and his work has been greatly admired by the cognoscenti in the world of botanical art. He has had a great influence on the work of many of today's painters. Elizabeth Dowle most enjoys painting fruit and crops and she is presently working on a large series of fruit paintings of the National Collection of Fruit Trees at Brogdale. She showed an apple 'Ashmeads's Kernel' at the Hunt Institute in 1998 and is also represented in the Lindley Library (RHS) and at Kensington Palace.

When I first met Elizabeth Dawle she seemed obsessed by pears and showed me as many as ten different varieties. Each of her studies requires at least a year to complete. First she has to find the right specimen and record it when it flowers. Then she has to wait for the pear to develop and paints the fruit as it grows. Finally, she picks the fruit and waits for it to ripen, then paints it all over again. These three stages have to be fitted on to a single piece of paper in a satisfying way. Of course she works on more than one variety of fruit at a time so that there is a great deal of pressure at certain periods of the year when much of the fruit may flower or ripen simultaneously.

We propped her pear paintings around my dining room and eventually I chose two very different ones. The 'Conference' pear is a classic variety, but I have never come across 'Starkrimson' so I chose it as a complete and startling contrast. I had the two paintings framed as a pair and they have since been widely exhibited as parts of my collection have moved around the world. I have acquired a number of her smaller paintings and I am particularly fond of her display of different ivy leaves.

Later I bought two of her paintings of prickly pears, one a preliminary study, the other a painting for a plate for *The New Oxford Book of Food Plants* which also showed the flowers and fruit of the kiwi. I have always found the prickly pear cactus bizarre and the fruit rather disappointing (very like my first bite into watermelon – it looks more interesting than it tastes) but I was intrigued by her immaculate painting. I first saw the kiwi fruit growing in New Zealand years ago, although now it is cultivated all over the world.

Elizabeth Dowle tells me she works full-time from life, seven days a week, until the light fades.

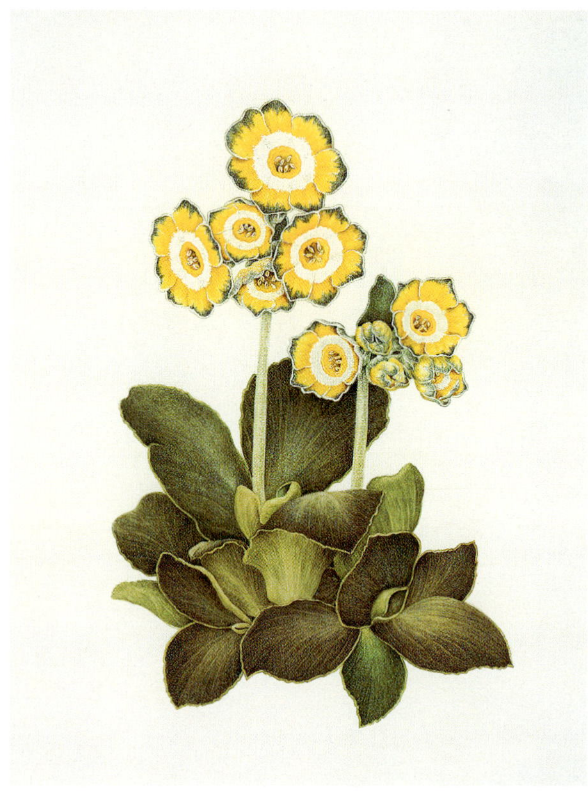

AURICULA 'SWEET PASTURES'
(Left) Unsigned – Painted 1996 (on the back)
Acquired from the artist 1997
Watercolour on paper
237 × 217 mm

KIWI FRUIT & PRICKLY PEAR
(Right) Signed Elizabeth Dowle 1997 (Plate for *The New Oxford Book of Food Plants* by J.G. Vaughan & C. Geissler)
Acquired from the artist 1998
Watercolour on paper
530 × 420 mm

PEAR 'STARKRIMSON'
(Overleaf left)
Unsigned – Painted 1992 (on the back)
Acquired from the artist 1996
Watercolour on paper
435 × 320 mm

PEAR 'CONFERENCE'
(Overleaf right)
Unsigned – Painted 1991 (on the back)
Acquired from the artist 1996
Watercolour on paper
435 × 320 mm

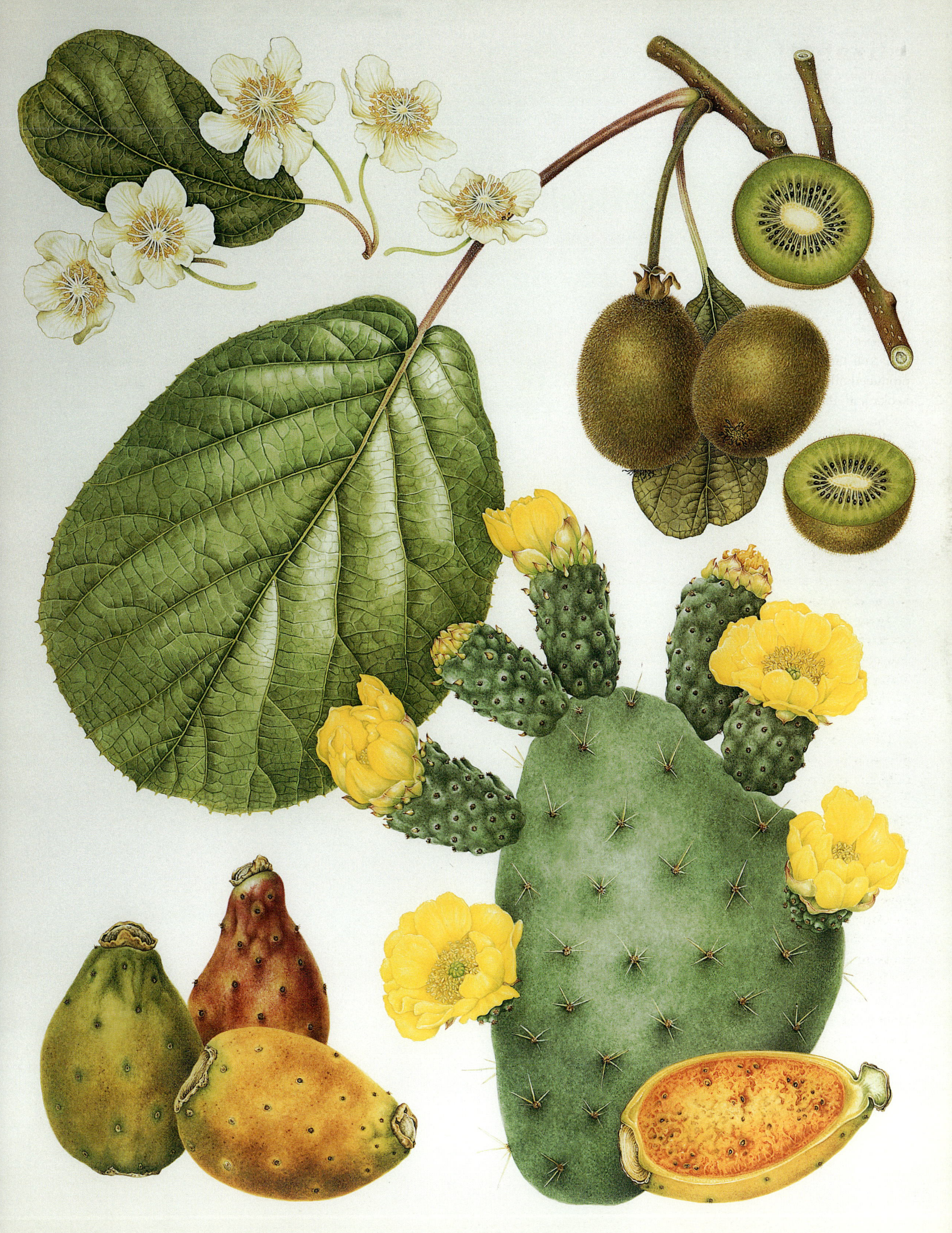

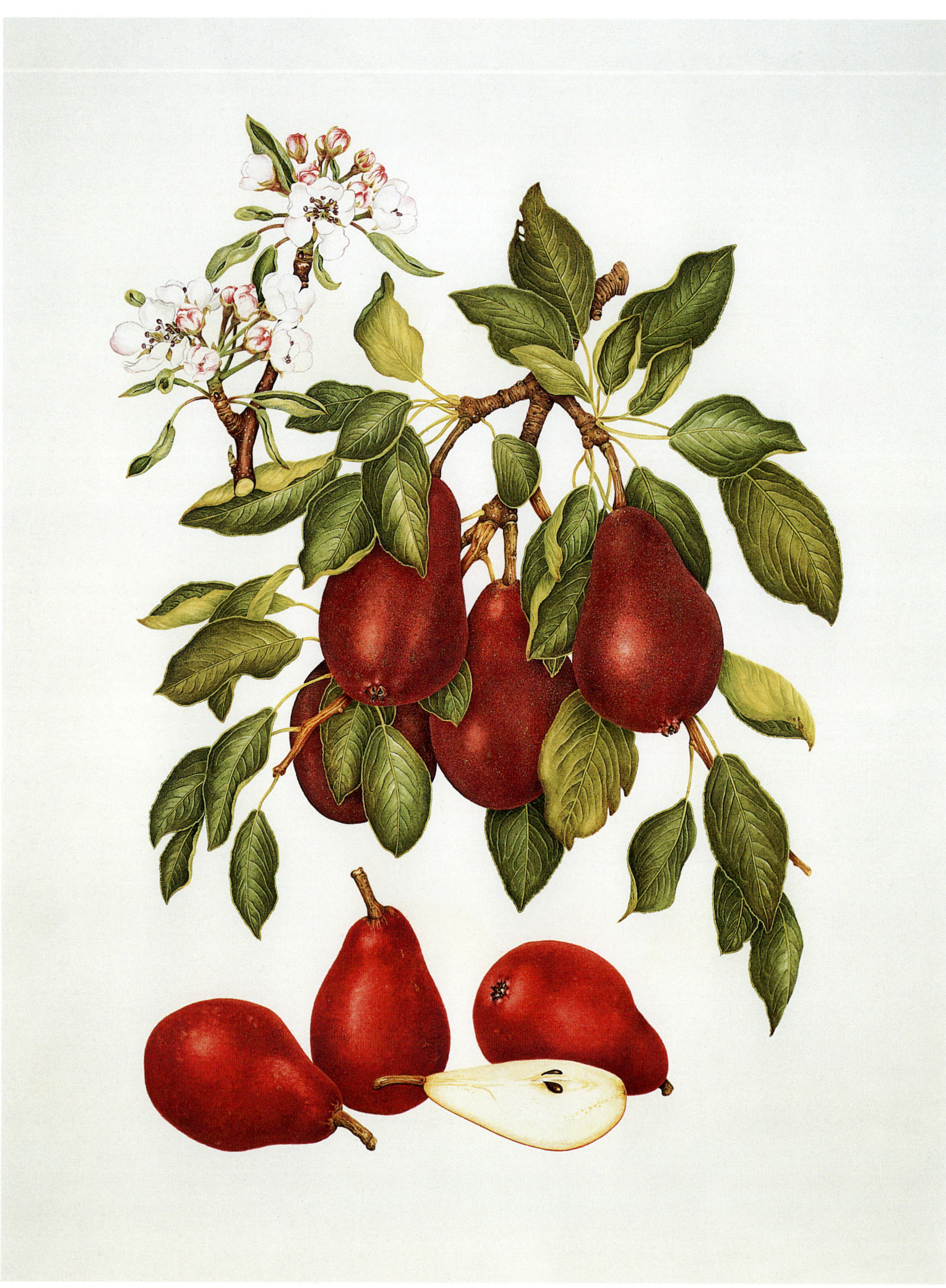

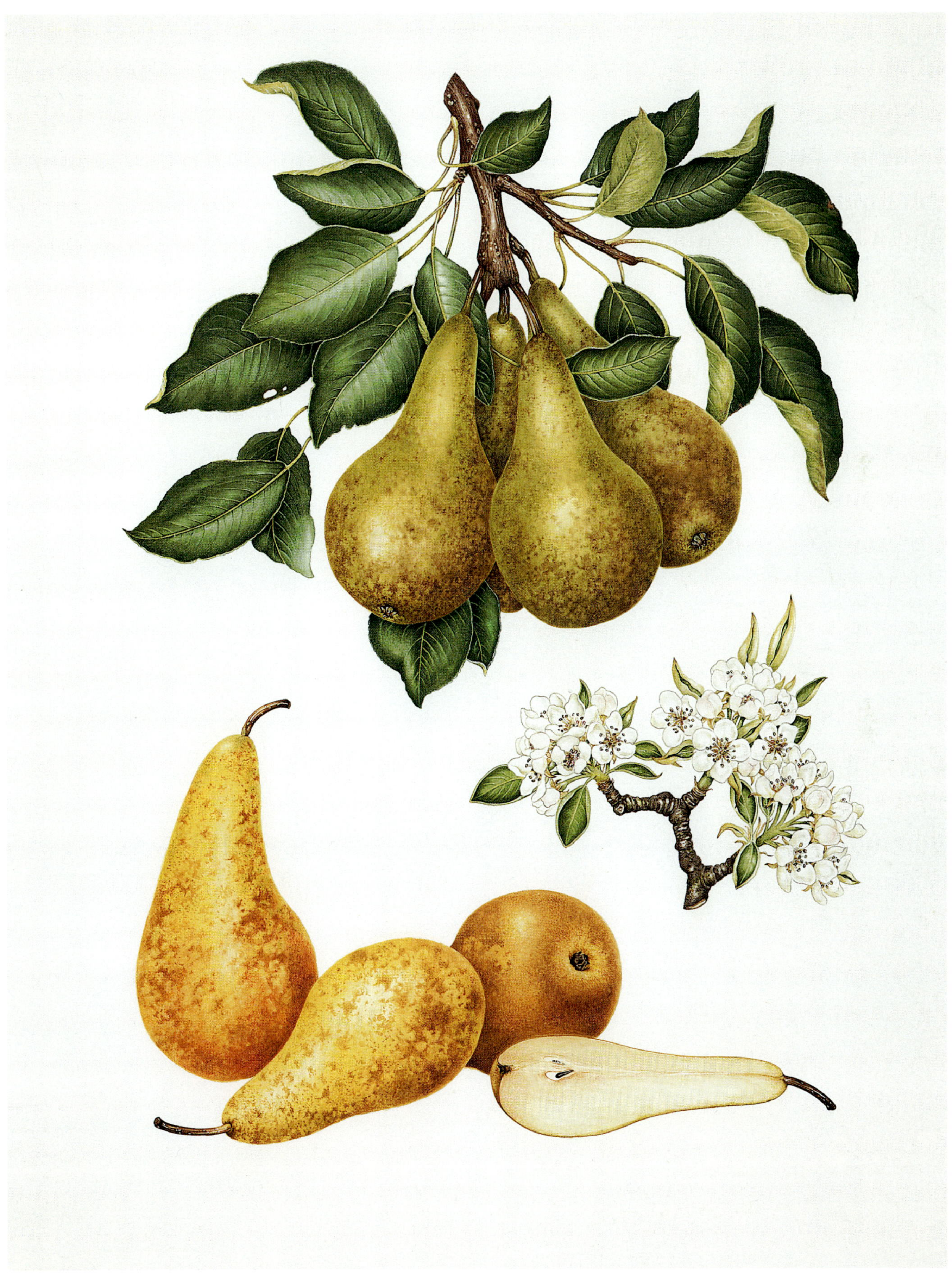

Margaret Ann Eden

BORN LONDON, ENGLAND 1939

I first met Lady Margaret Ann Eden at the English Gardening School in the Chelsea Physic Garden. I had heard that she was one of their most outstanding pupils, working in the botanical art classes first run by Elizabeth Jane Lloyd, later by Anne-Marie Evans. These impressive courses have been fine-tuning some of the best contemporary British botanical artists.

Margaret Ann Eden spent most of her childhood in Canada and Hong Kong. She started painting early, winning an art scholarship at twelve years old to Westonbirt School in Gloucestershire. In 1959 she went to the Byam Shaw School of Art and later studied portrait, life and still-life painting in Bernard Adams' studio. She started painting flowers in watercolours at the end of the 1960s, but she considers that she did not become a botanical artist until 1993. However, this elegant, beautiful woman, like many other artists, has had a double life, and has been the director of her own private school for girls in London since 1977.

I bought her study of tropical fruit from a remarkable solo exhibition she had at Spink & Son Limited, St James, London in 1996. The exhibit was a complete sell-out and a triumph for someone who had only finished her course with Anne-Marie Evans two years previously. She next showed at the 9th International at the Hunt Institute, donating a fine orchid painting to their collection.

Almost immediately after I had added her study of tropical fruit to my collection it was off travelling to exhibitions I had arranged in the United States and elsewhere. It is one of a number of my paintings that has hardly ever been hung on my own walls, a problem collectors have to come to terms with if they lend their pictures.

In 1998 I helped organise a show with Oliver Swann at the Tryon & Swann Gallery in Cork Street, London. Oliver Swann decided to reintroduce top-quality botanical art to the Tryon when he bought the gallery in the mid-1990s. The Tryon used to handle Paul Jones and Margaret Mee in the 1970s but had concentrated on wildlife art since then. Margaret Ann was invited to this show and exhibited an orchid as well as a composite study of a granadilla, kiwano and fig, which was so striking we used it on the catalogue cover.

She has an unerring eye for interesting subjects. Sometimes she can make a mundane object appear in a new, fresh light; an example of this is the bunch of carrots she once painted so memorably for her exhibition at Spink. I was particularly attracted to her study of *Medinilla magnifica*, a spectacular houseplant from the island of Luzon in the Philippines, shown at the new Hortus Gallery in London. It is an epiphytic plant, which perches on tree trunks and likes warmth and humidity but no direct sunlight in the summer months. She has shown each stage of the opening bud and the cascade of flowers, yet it is not a laboured exercise in botanical instruction but a work of art. Her work goes from strength to strength.

TROPICAL BERGAMOT & CHERIMOYA

Signed M. A. Eden

1994

Acquired from Spink, London 1996

Watercolour on paper

330 × 520 mm

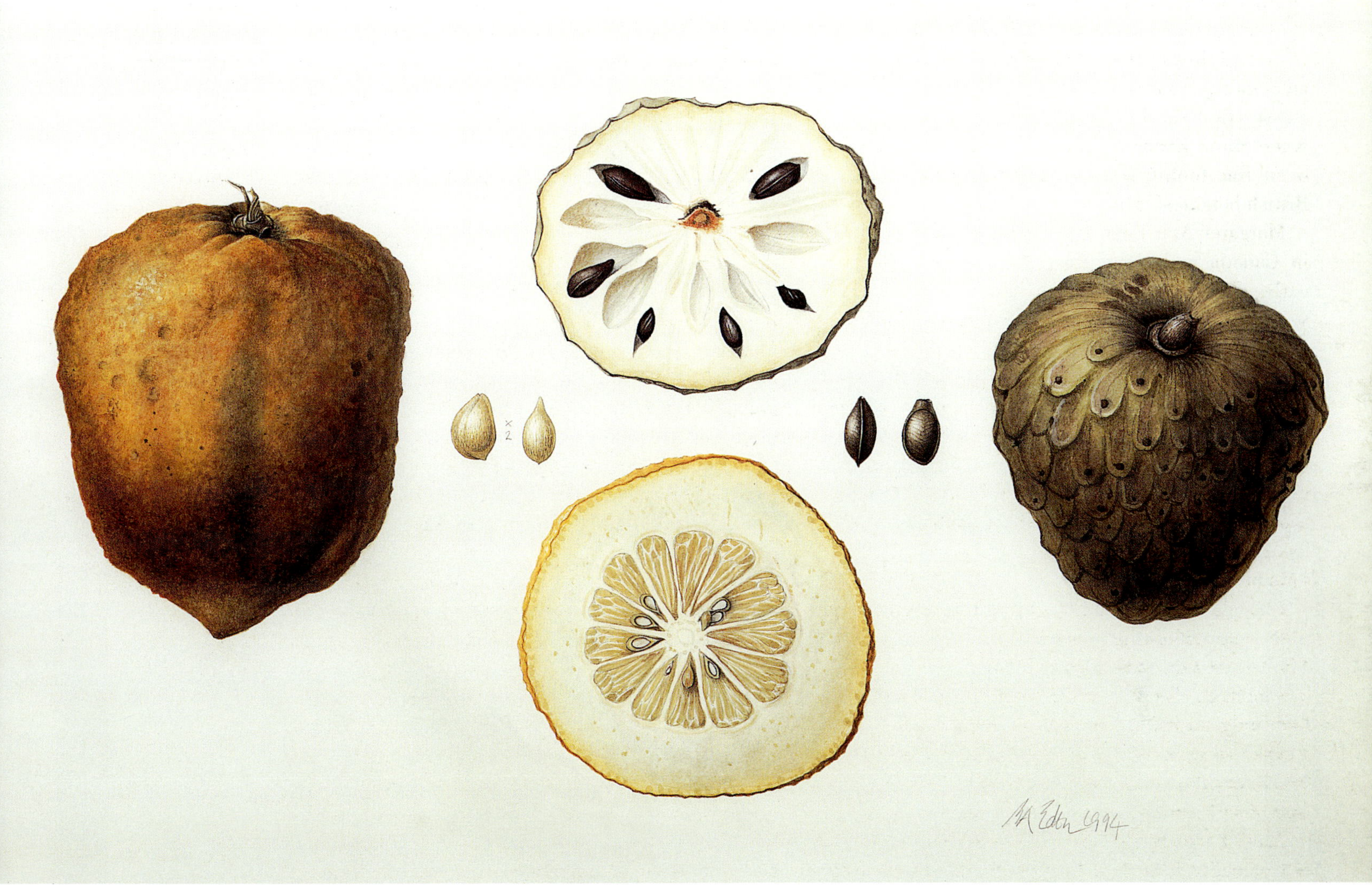

MEDINILLA MAGNIFICA
Signed M. A. Eden 2000
Acquired from Hortus,
London 2000
Watercolour on paper
820 × 1000 mm

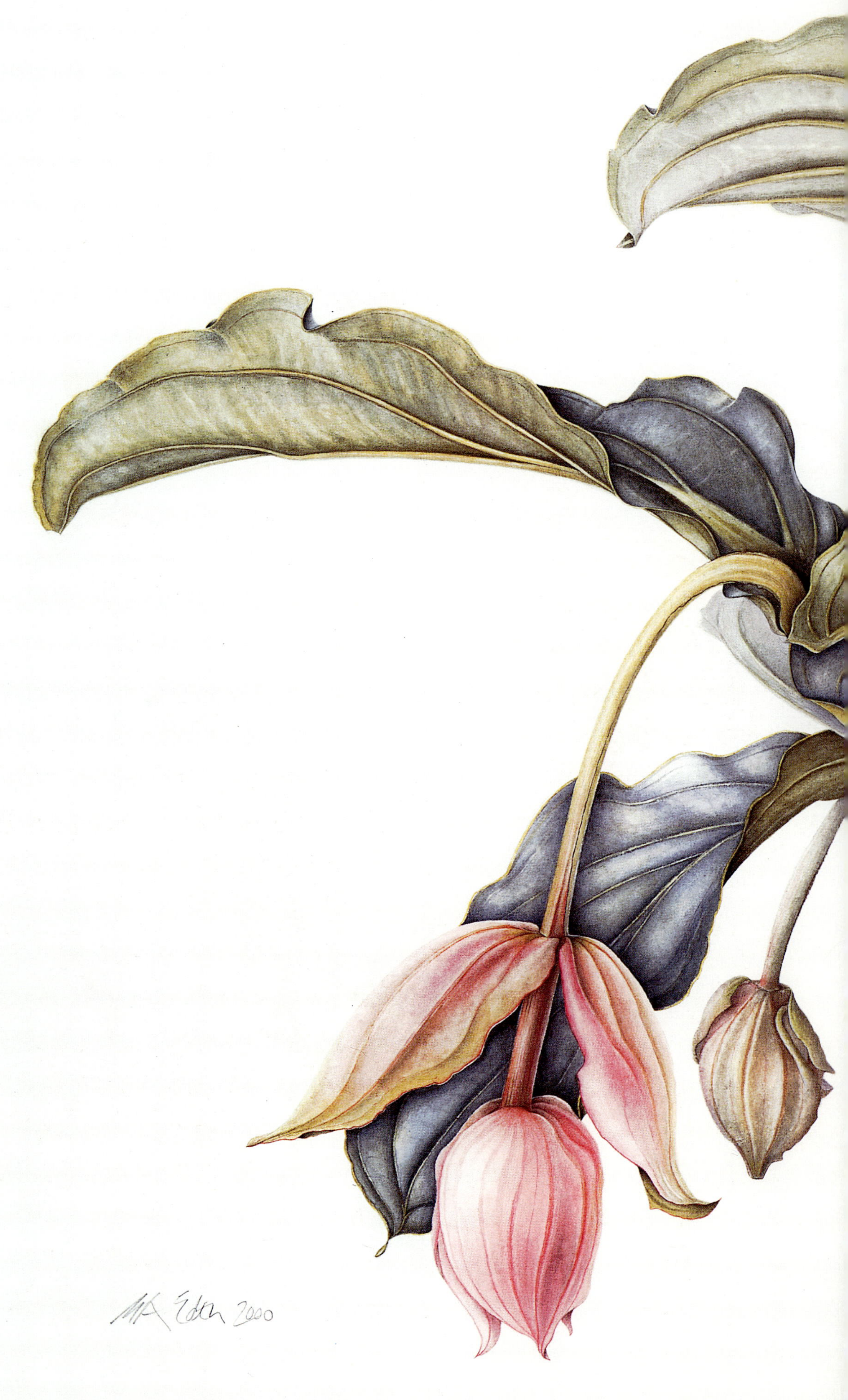

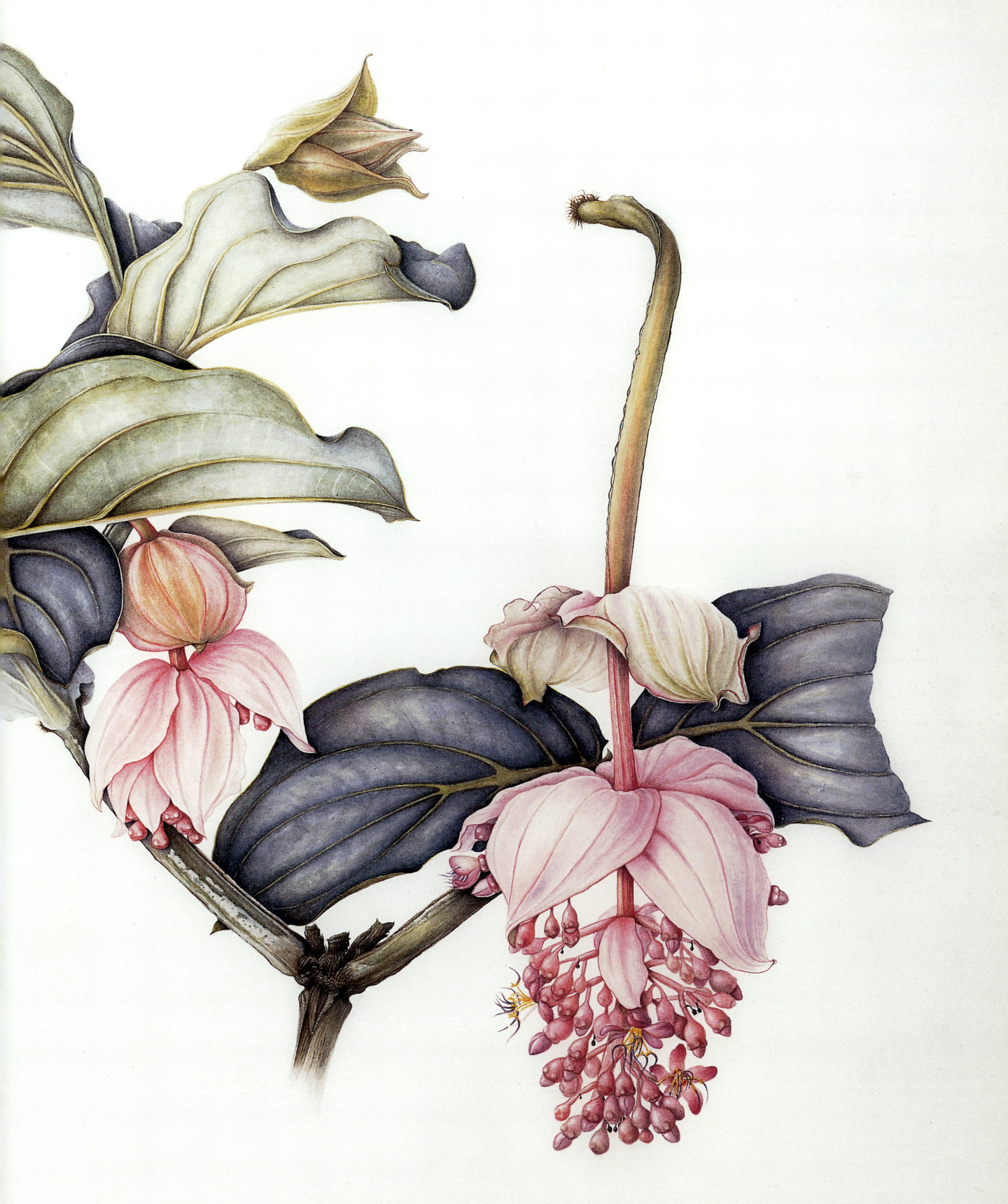

Brigid Edwards

BORN LONDON, ENGLAND 1940

There is no doubt that Brigid Edwards is one of the most important of today's botanical artists. I have always greatly admired her work, from that first moment when I saw her painting of an artichoke on vellum at the Hunt Institute in 1992. She has been a trail-blazer, and a successful one too, with complete sell-outs of her exhibitions at Thomas Gibson Fine Art Gallery, London in 1995 and 1997 even before the gallery doors opened.

She lives near Oxford, quite close to my country home, and I first met her there. I bought two of her paintings: one an artichoke flower on vellum; the other a beautiful study of two magnolia leaves, the mature one separated from an old leaf by a fruit placed between them. This painting was shown at the 1990 Summer Show of the Royal Academy, a regrettably rare honour for botanical artists today. It is quiet, discrete and beautifully painted, contrasting wonderfully with the more powerful artichoke flower. I also commissioned her to paint an onion, which eventually turned out to be two onion bulbs with gleaming, burnished red, scaly skins. Later, in 1995, I bought another red onion study, this time a sprouting bulb with an unopened globe of flower buds. This is a big, vibrant study on a large piece of vellum and a far bolder concept.

In 1994 she participated in a group show at the Kew Gardens Gallery. It was then that I bought one of her primula plates, painted to illustrate *Primulas* by J. Richards published in 1993. I always wish I had acquired more of these plates as they were superbly executed – sadly they were poorly printed in the book, which did not do the originals justice. At the same exhibition I bought an autumnal hydrangea, a memorable study of kohlrabi with a deep purple base complementing its spectacular purple-veined leaves and some sparkling, glowing redcurrants. Two more paintings completed this spending spree, a wonderful study of the Cape gooseberry and another one of a cone of the Douglas fir *Pseudotsuga menziesii*, magnified two and a half times (see page 12). All these paintings have been widely shown and since the publication of my first book, have been both admired and imitated. In the earlier book it was not possible to show them all in a large format for full impact, so I am pleased to show some of them here in a larger size.

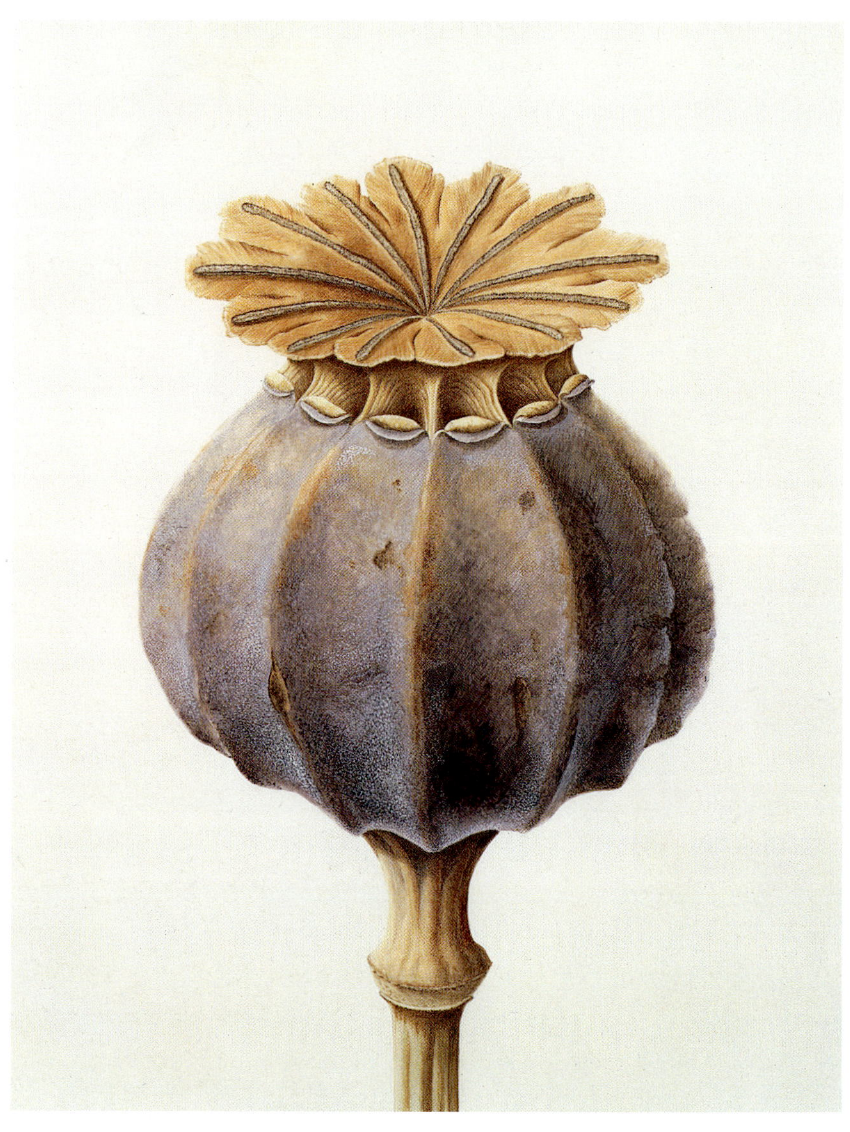

POPPY SEED HEAD
(Above) Unsigned 1999
Acquired from Beadleston Gallery, New York 2000
Watercolour over pencil on vellum
381 × 305 mm

ORIENTAL POPPY: *PAPAVER ORIENTALE*
(Right) Unsigned & undated
Acquired from Thomas Gibson Fine Arts, London 1997
Watercolour over pencil on vellum
530 × 405 mm

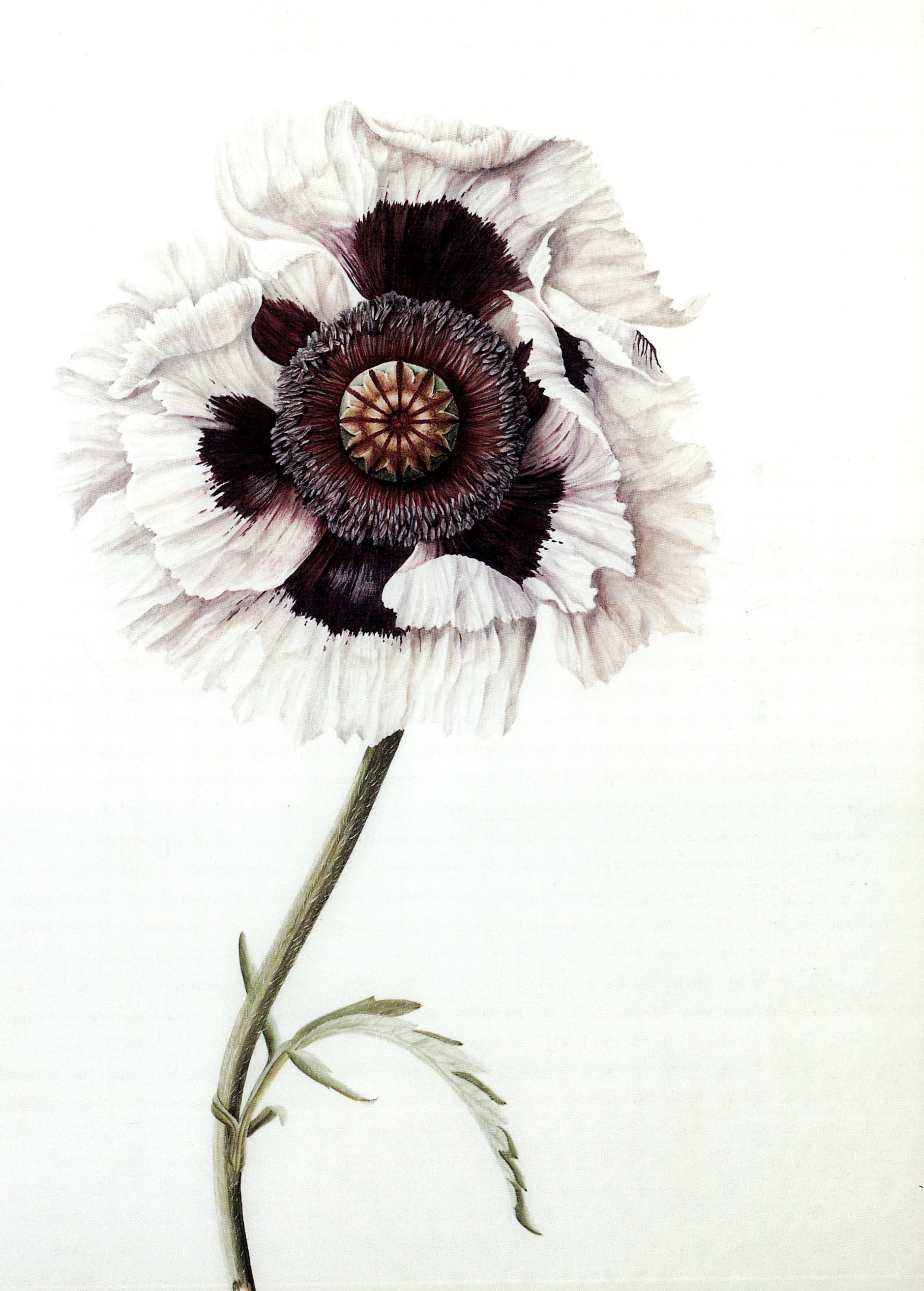

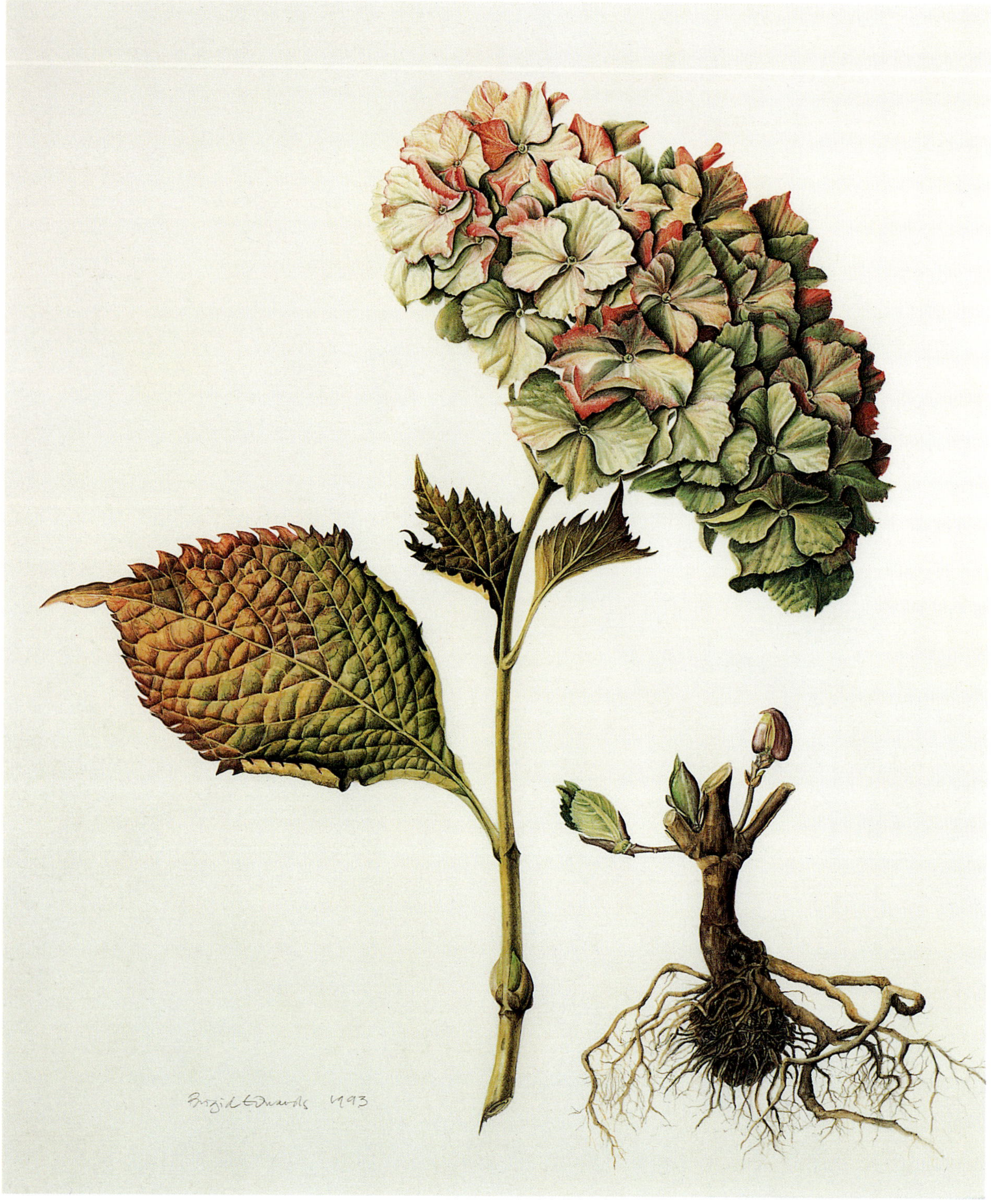

HYDRANGEA
(Left) Signed Brigid Edwards 1993
Acquired from Kew Gardens Gallery 1994
Watercolour over pencil on vellum
330 × 275 mm

RED ONION
(Right) Signed Brigid Edwards 1995
Acquired from Thomas Gibson Fine Arts, London 1995
Watercolour over pencil on vellum
660 × 457 mm

One remarkable study by Brigid Edwards has never failed to have impact when I show visitors around my collection. It is a solitary squash suspended in space and is immensely strong. This must be one of her greatest paintings, a truly powerful portrait, framed for the Thomas Gibson show (1995) in a heavy black wooden frame. One of my latest acquisitions is the rather sinister Oriental poppy *Papaver orientale,* with its black, intricate centre and its pale, crumpled and pleated petals. One of my grandchildren, on her first 'night-away' visit felt it was like a large eye staring at her – something I had not anticipated.

In his introduction to Brigid's second major show at the Thomas Gibson Gallery in 1997, Ian Burton wrote 'The fine painting of the detail on the skin is

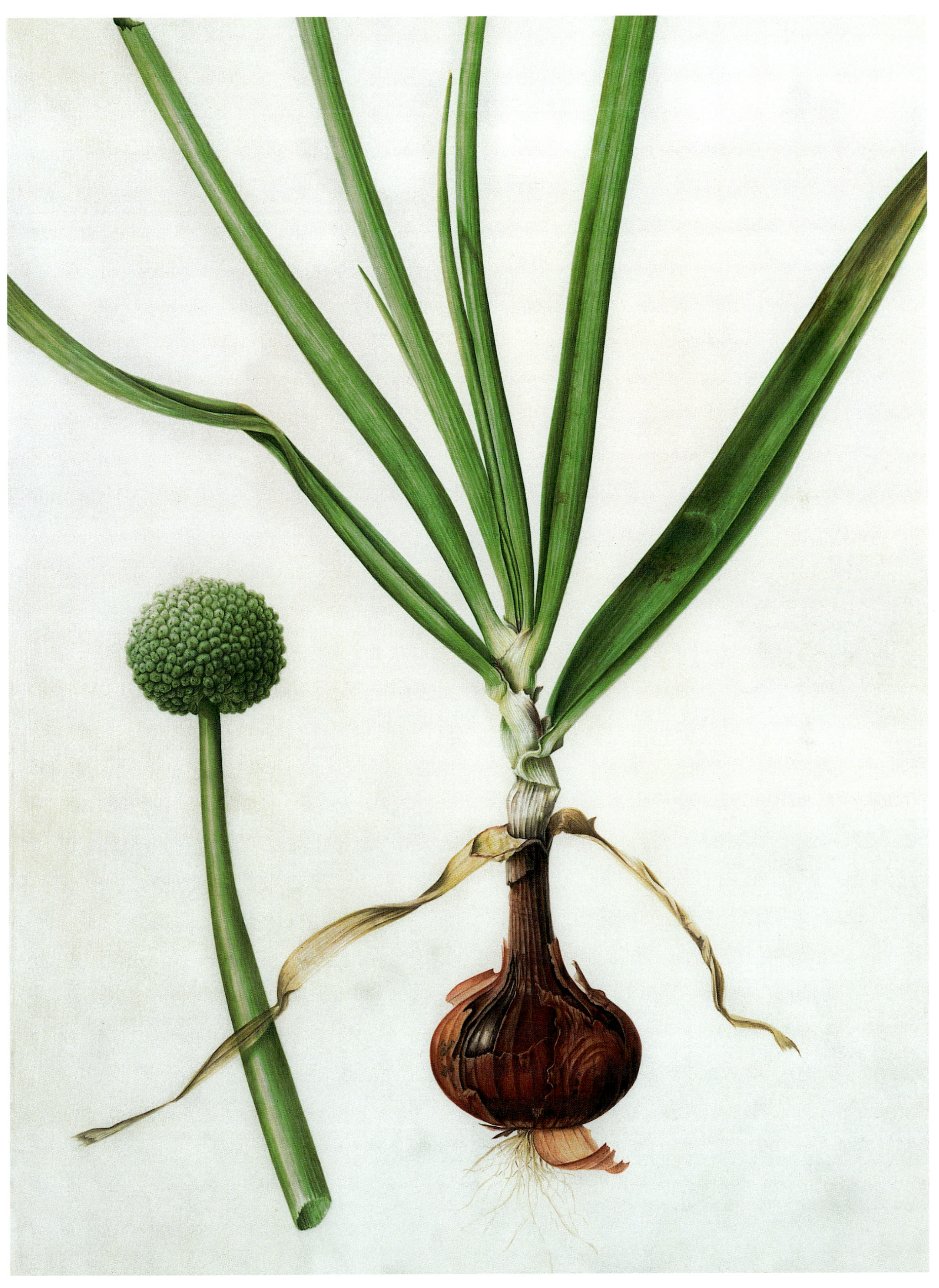

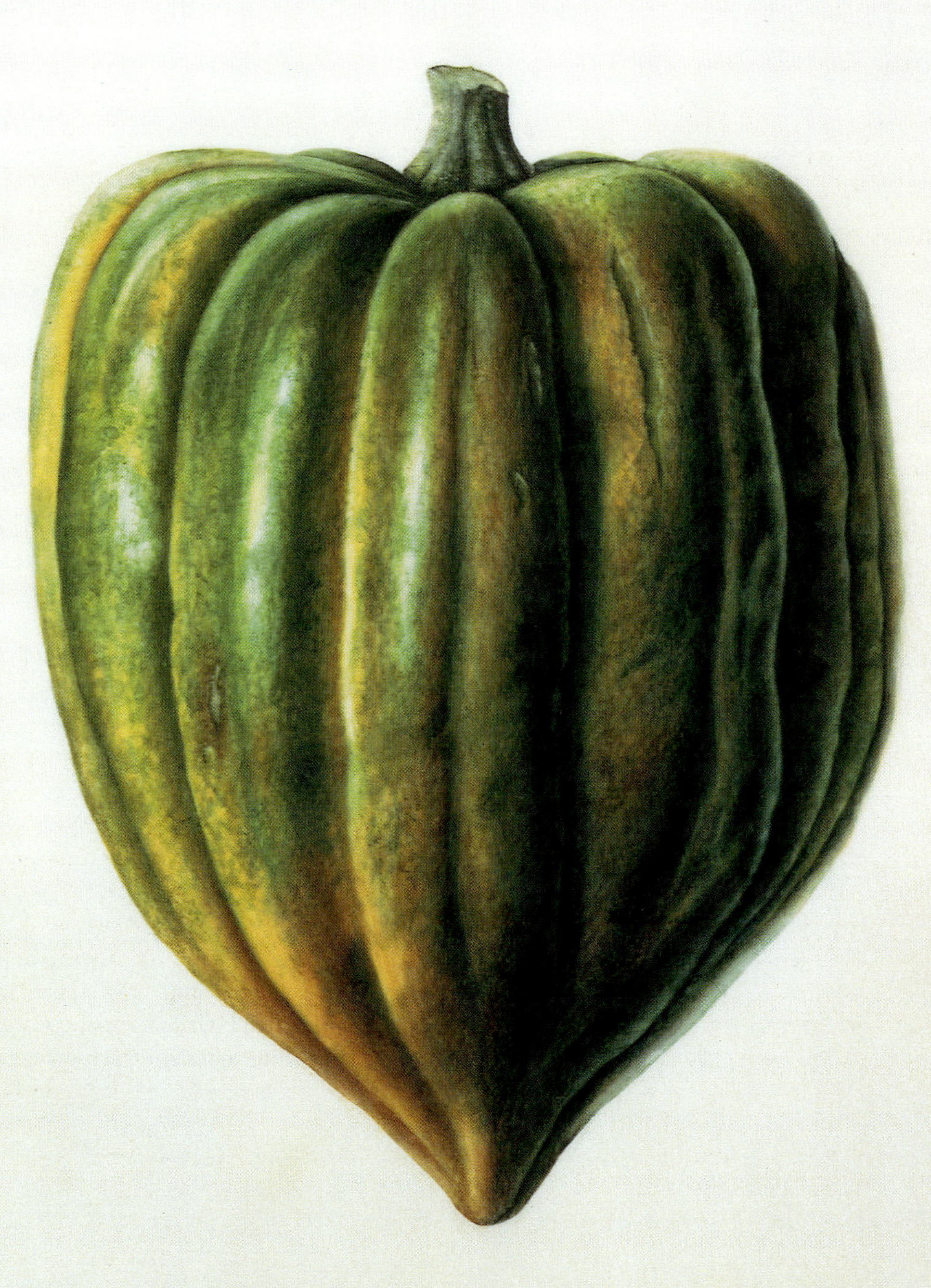

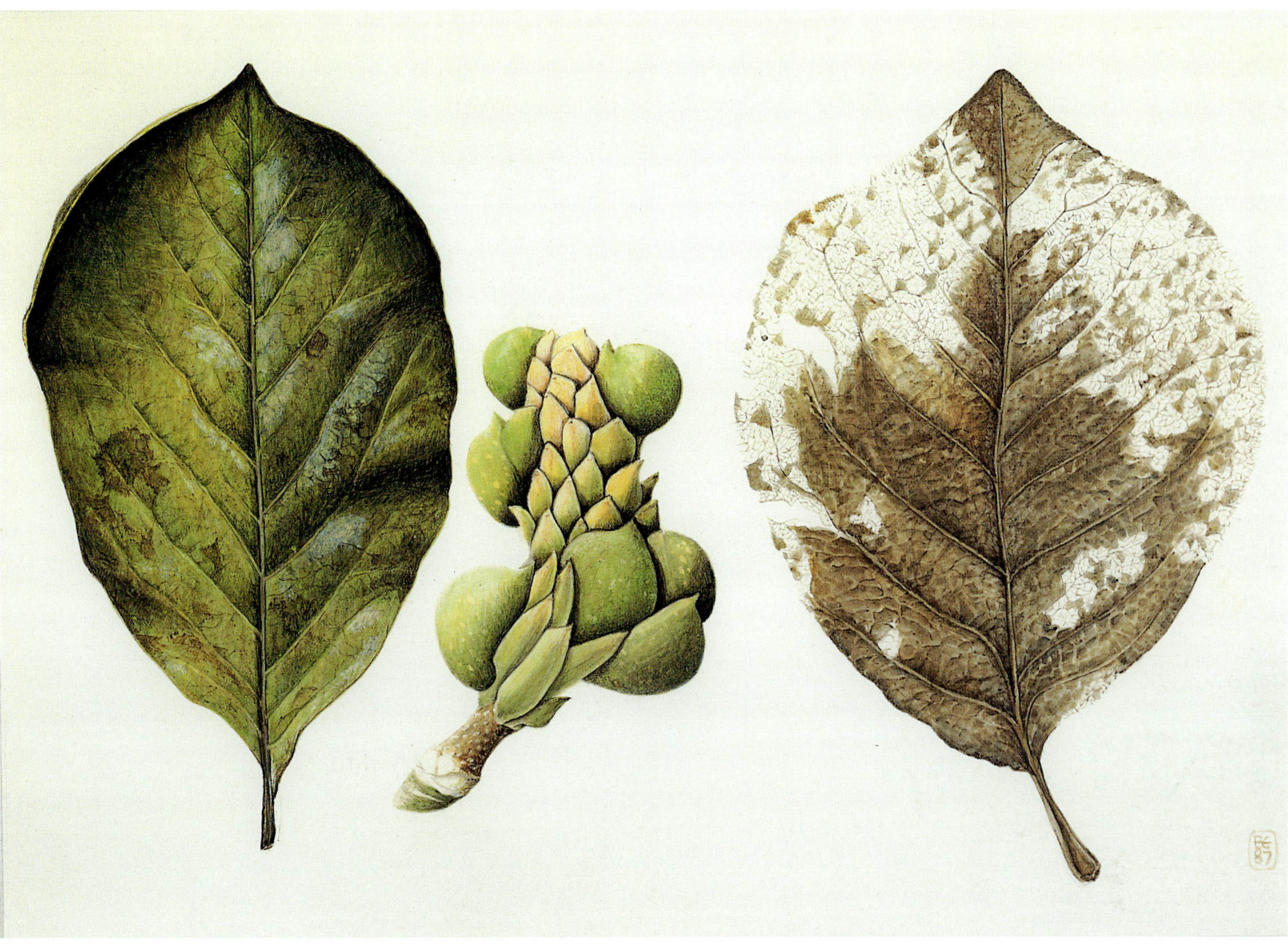

SQUASH
Signed Brigid Edwards 1995
Acquired from Thomas Gibson Fine Arts, London 1995
Watercolour over pencil on vellum
382 × 305 mm

MAGNOLIA LEAVES & FRUIT
(Above) Signed BE 87
Acquired from the artist 1992
Watercolour over pencil on vellum
180 × 250 mm

uncanny, but when these single objects are arranged and suspended in a contemplative space, they achieve their greatest power, and as a result of this creative act of attention, they have an almost religious intensity...there is a gloriously "abandoned" Oriental poppy with papery purple and white petals and hundreds of lovingly counted stamens gathered around a central mandala.'

I am so delighted that Brigid is getting the exposure and recognition that she deserves. The fact that she has shown in a well-known gallery in London with such success has given a great boost to other artists in the field and there are many more galleries now beginning to show botanical art, something vital if today's renaissance is to continue.

Late in 2000 she showed at the William Beadleston Gallery in New York, a move advised by Thomas Gibson, who feels her work should be exposed to another audience. I bought two works from this show: one is an enlarged poppy-seed head which compliments my Oriental poppy and the other a strong and forceful King Protea with a dissection of the floral parts beneath it. I find the seed head particularly interesting as it has a drama and an impact all its own, shown also in Brigid's other magnified subjects, such as the Douglas fir cone.

She showed some of her work in an important exhibition at Harewood House in the autumn of 1999, where a whole range of work was shown – from early Dutch oil painting to Gwen John's *A Vase of Flowers*, David Hockney's *Sunflowers* and Andy Warhol's *Flowers*. As she wryly remarked to me, 'It was interesting they included a botanical artist in an exhibition entitled "The Flower Show".'

I asked Brigid Edwards to describe the way she prepared the vellum for her paintings. She uses vellum stretched smoothly on board. She wrote:

'I get my vellum from William Cowley Parchment and Vellum Works who also mount and stretch the skins on board to my specific dimensions. A white gesso ground is applied which smoothes the surface but inevitably because it is a natural skin there remains an irregularity of texture and pigment. In the past I have made my own boards but it is very time-consuming and expensive if things go wrong. When I did it myself I used organic wallpaper paste to glue the vellum to the board. I think William Cowley use something similar.'

'So far there have been no problems with splitting or cracking. I think I decided to "anchor" them because I found the wavy edges rather distracting. Eighteenth-century vellum was much more fragile as they used the skins from foetuses rather than the hides of calves which I imagine (and hope!) are tougher. I use Winsor & Newton or Rowney & Schmincke watercolours, depending on pigment. I choose vellum rather than paper because I have always found paper too absorbent and difficult to rectify. I use ophthalmic surgical blades to remove paint from vellum where necessary.'

'A large painting (and I mean volume and painted area as opposed to large but unpainted surface) can take up to twelve weeks to complete.'

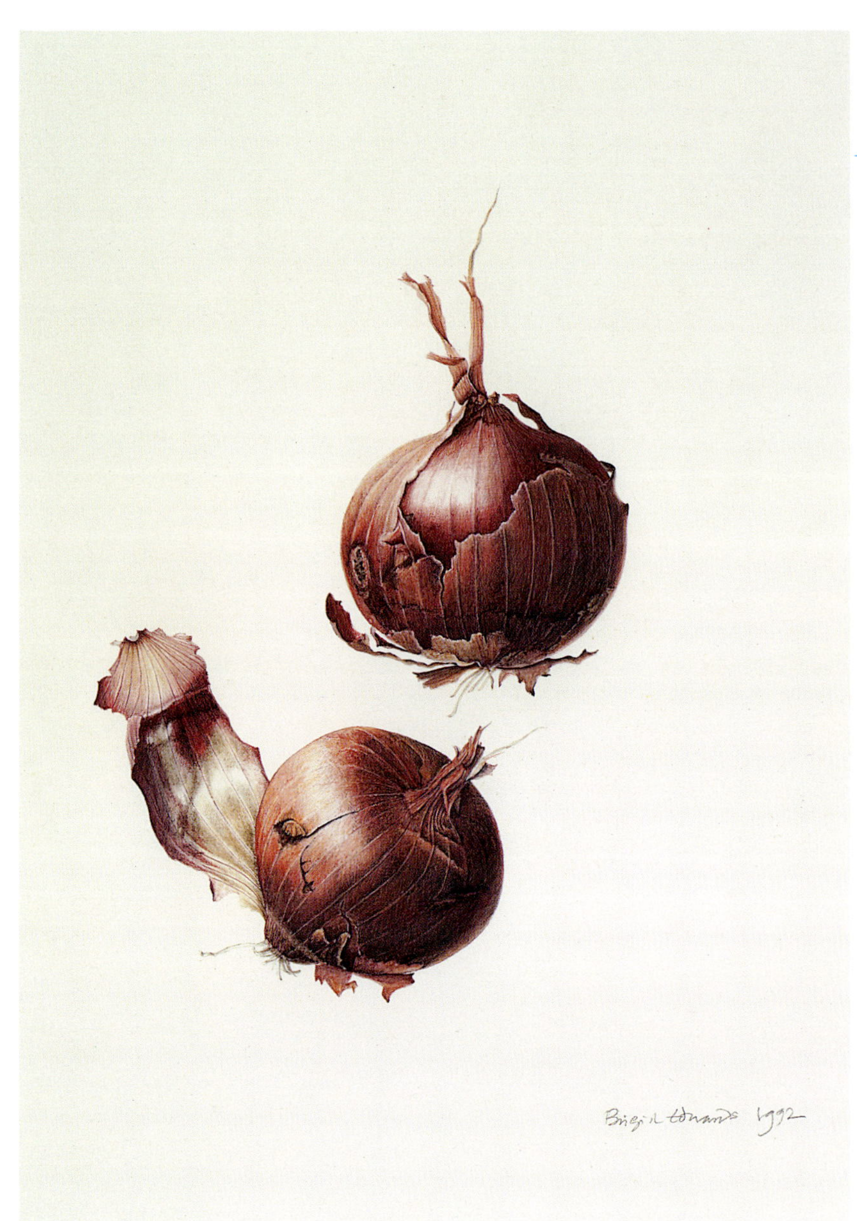

TWO RED ONIONS
Signed Brigid Edwards 1992
Commissioned 1992
Watercolour over pencil on vellum
280 × 220 mm

PROTEA I
(Right) Unsigned 1998
Acquired from Beadleston Gallery, New York 2000
Watercolour & gouache over pencil on vellum
381 × 305 mm

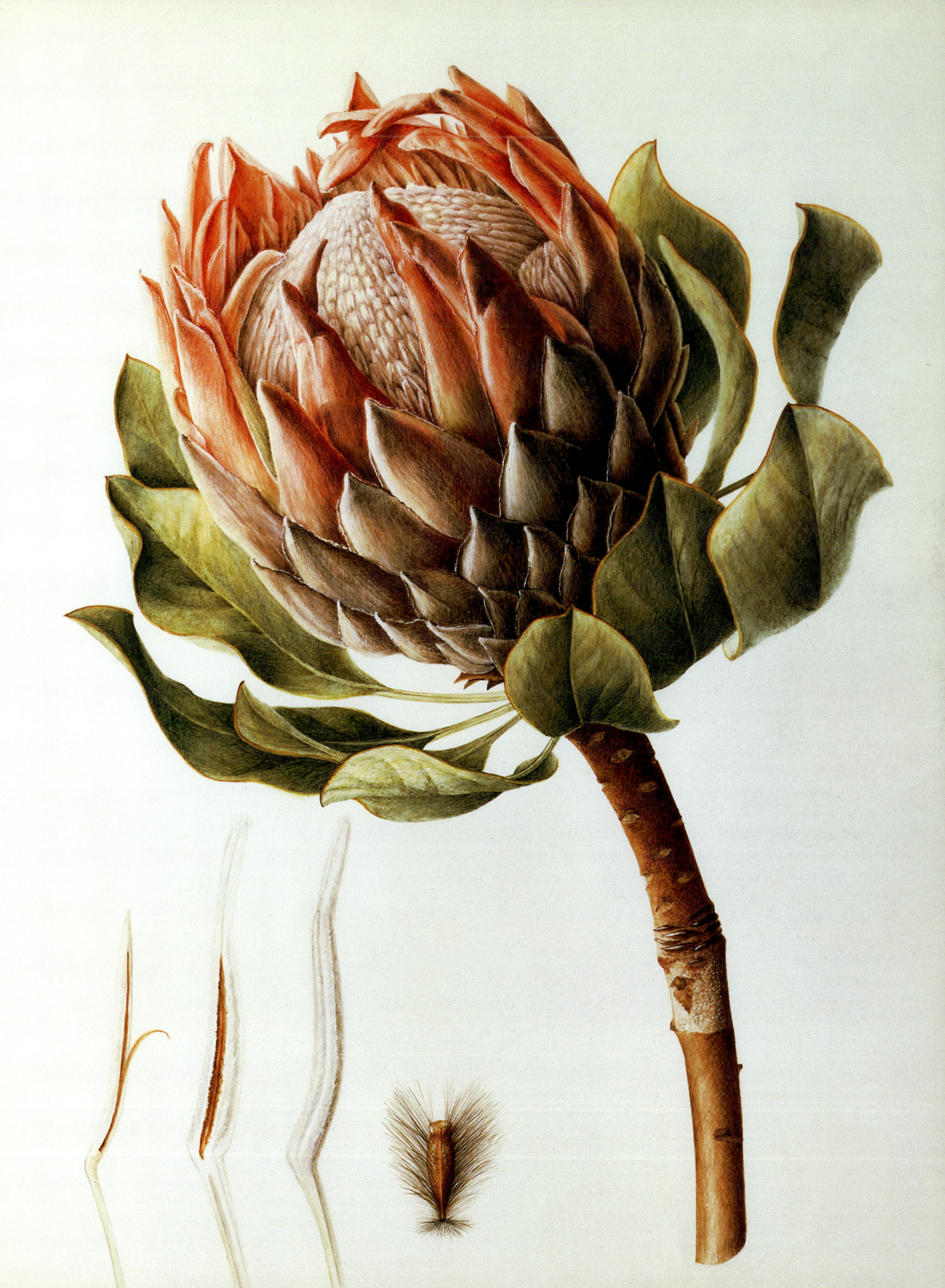

Elvia Esparza

Born Mexico City, Mexico 1944

I first saw Esparza's work in the Hunt Institute, Pittsburgh in 1998 but she made the biggest impression on me with her 1999 entry at the RHS which was of dramatic Mexican cacti and desert plants painted in their natural environment, for which she was awarded a gold medal.

Elvia Esparza has been scientific illustrator at the Institute of Biology and professor at Universidad Nacional Autónoma de México (UNAM), Mexico City. She was founder president of the Mexican Academy of Scientific Illustration from 1991–98 and her work has been reproduced in a number of books and journals. She is especially well-known for her paintings in *The Flora of Veracruz.*

She has had over a dozen solo exhibitions, mostly in Mexico, but also more recently in England at the Linnean Society, at Wisley, at Kew and at the Botanical Department of the Natural History Museum, London in 1999. Her work is held in the Kew Herbarium and in the Hunt Institute as well as at UNAM.

She has taught courses and workshops during the last ten years at UNAM and the Museo de las Ciencias (UNIVERSUM), at the Botanical Gardens in Cuba and in Cordoba, Spain, as well as teaching in Buenos Aires, Argentina. UNIVERSUM is celebrating its first ten years with an exhibition including fifty of her paintings in 2000–01. She paints animals and insects as well as plants in a lively and yet accurate manner and produces a splendid calendar each year for the Botanical Garden at UNAM. I have her calendar for 2000 showing many of the different species of *Dahlia* originating in Mexico.

Echinocereus polyacanthus is a spectacular cactus native to north-central and north-western Mexico and the south-west United States (Arizona and New Mexico). It is probably pollinated by hawkmoths.

ECHINOCEREUS POLYACANTHUS
Signed Elvia Esparza
(undated, painted 2000)
Acquired from Gordon-Craig Gallery,
London 2000
Watercolour on paper
370 × 265 mm

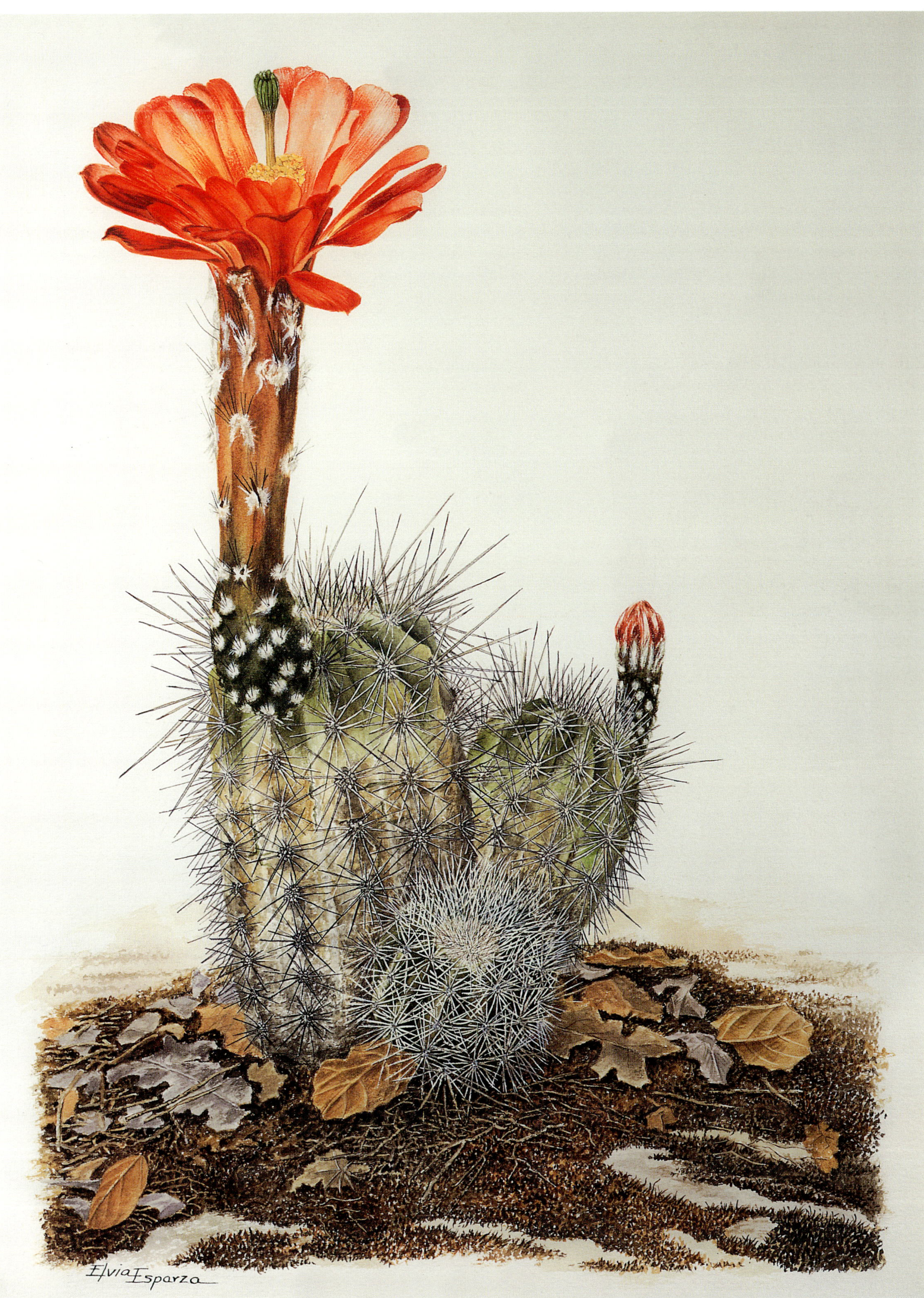
Elvia Esparza

Linda Francis

BORN BRISTOL, ENGLAND 1949

Linda Francis now lives in Kingston, Surrey. She went to art school in Coventry and graduated after a Graphic Design Dip. Ad. course at Maidstone. She followed this by ten years in the publishing world, working for Thames & Hudson, Mitchell Beazley and Marshall Cavendish as a designer, art editor and commissioner of art work and photography. She worked on illustrated books, specialising in architecture, archaeology, history and gardening (which was becoming much more popular at that time).

She felt that this period in the 1970s, was the golden era of publishing and was not going to return. She decided to change careers and went to work for her accountant, where her publishing and artistic background helped him deal with his clients who were mostly artists, designers and photographers. When he emigrated, she took over the practice with a colleague. A few years later she had a health scare and decided that she had to get her priorities straight, started to paint again and now leaves her office promptly at four pm to go home and enjoy the rest of the day.

She took a four-day course with Coral Guest at Kew in 1996 and had some individual tuition with Gillian Barlow (both artists in my collection). She enjoyed it so much she hopes to be painting full-time by 2001. I saw her work for the first time in 1997 at one of the RHS's autumn shows at Vincent Square, London where she was awarded a gold medal. She exhibited eight strong plant portraits, each with a firm sense of design, some shown from an interesting and unusual angle. I felt that here was a new 'voice', an original viewpoint and I bought three of her paintings on the spot.

Recently I have bought two more of her paintings, from another gold medal series at the RHS in 1999, this time particularly focused on leaves. Again, I felt she had a strong sense of design and an appreciation of texture, particularly noticeable in the *Crassula* hybrid (see page 252). The leaf texture in the *Crassula* painting was fascinating, with great depth. I discovered that she achieved this 3-D effect by doing a darkish underpainting, then painted over this with Titanium White mixed with green, trailed over in a cross-hatched style, for layer upon layer. The Lindley Library bought one of her exhibits too, a strong *Vriesea splendens*, as part of their recent policy to collect the best of today's botanical artists.

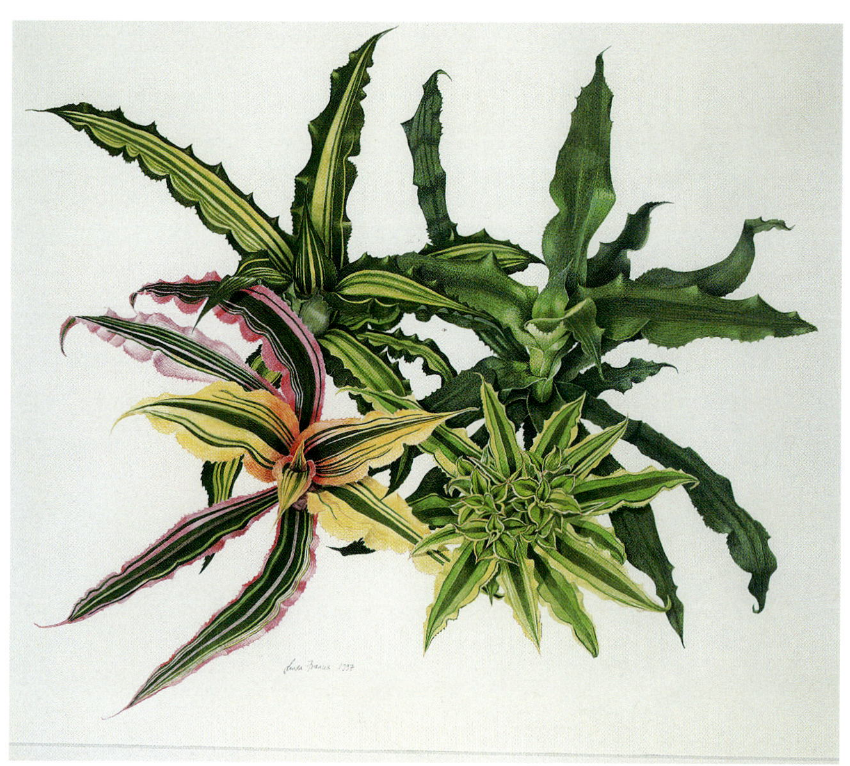

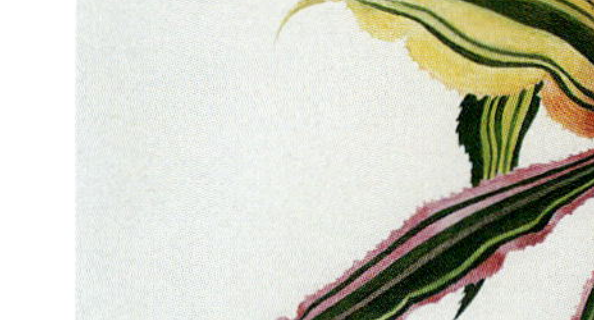

CRYPTANTHUS ZONATUS
Signed Linda Francis 1997
Acquired from the RHS Show 1997
Watercolour on paper
570 × 630 mm

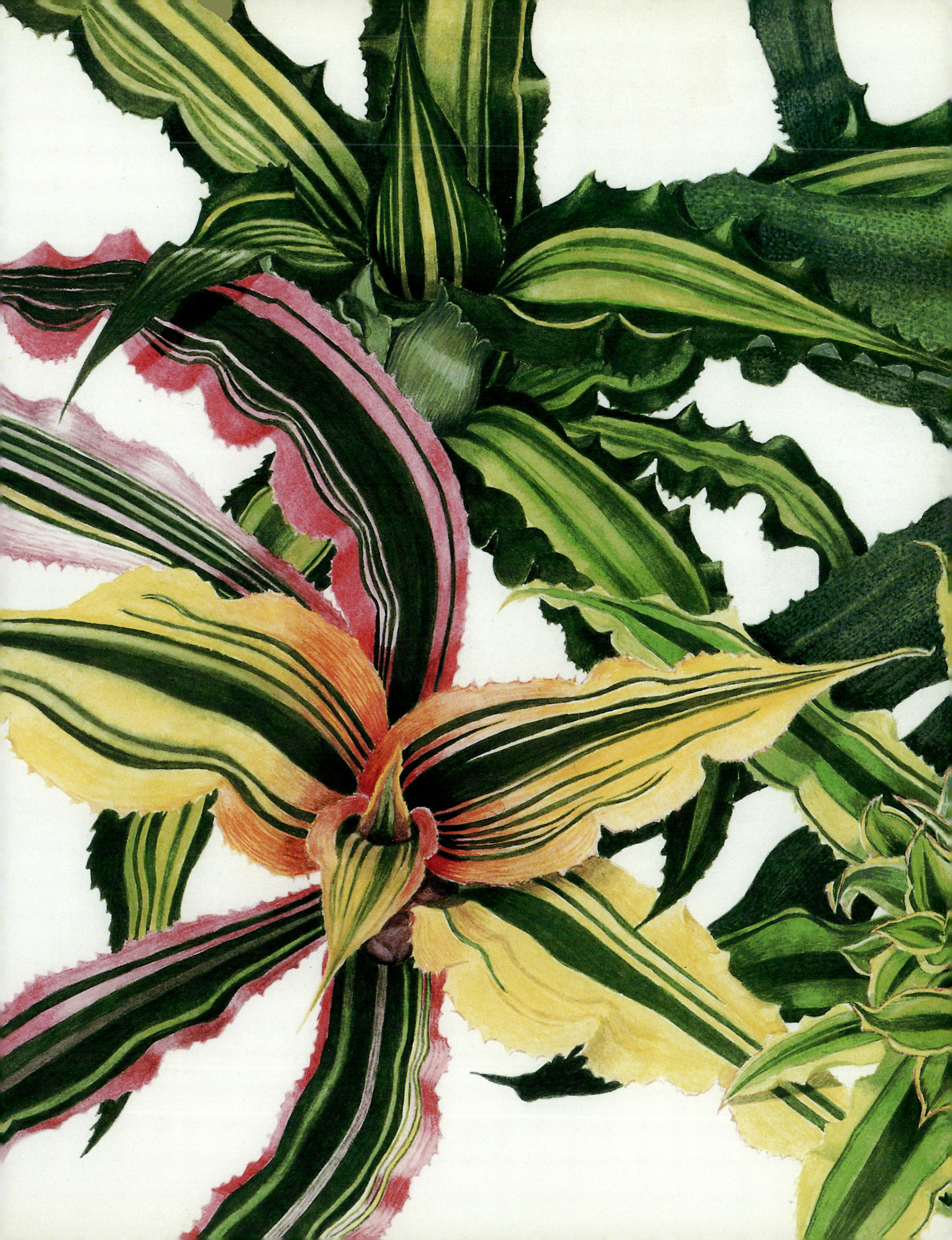

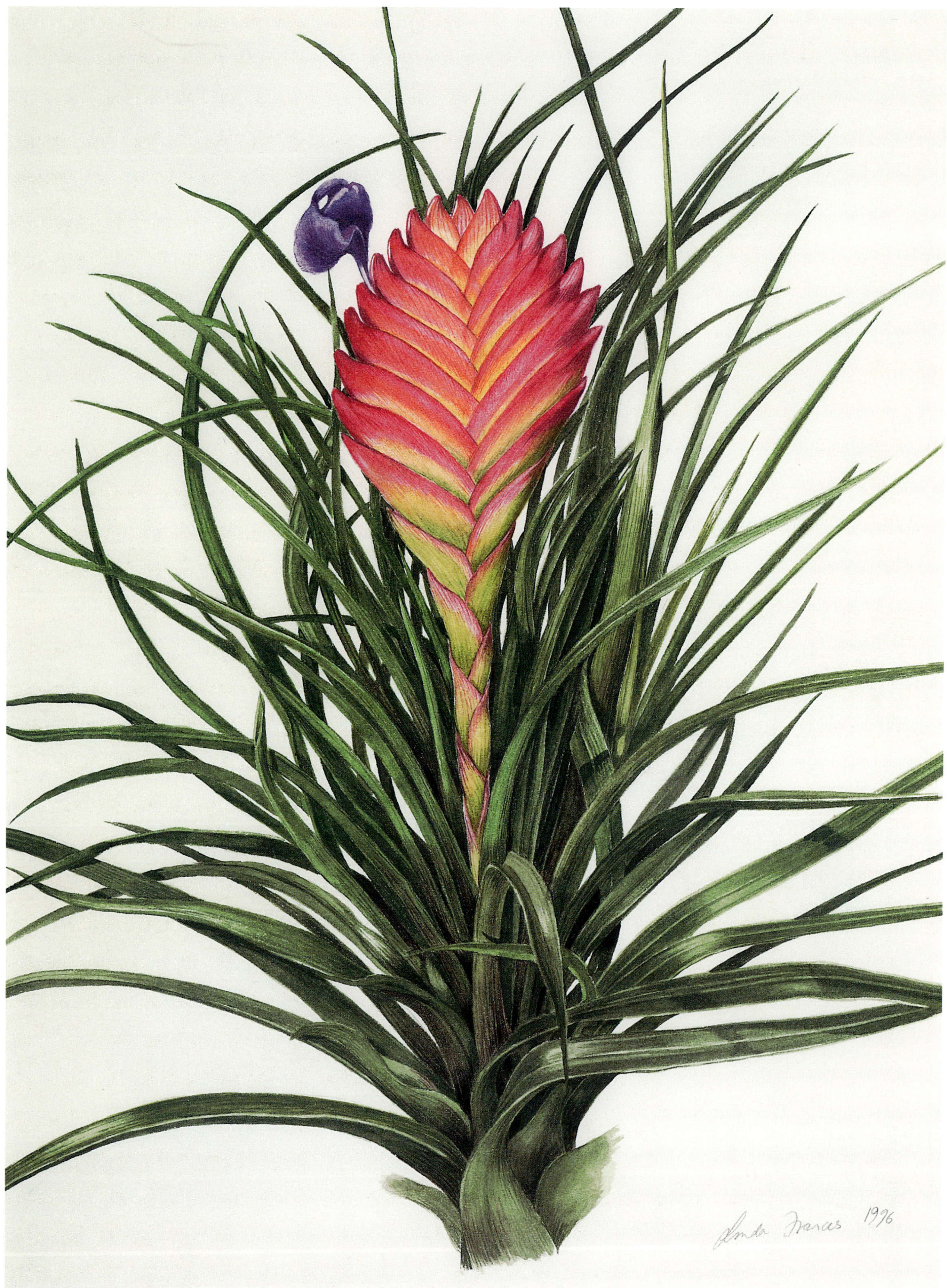
1996

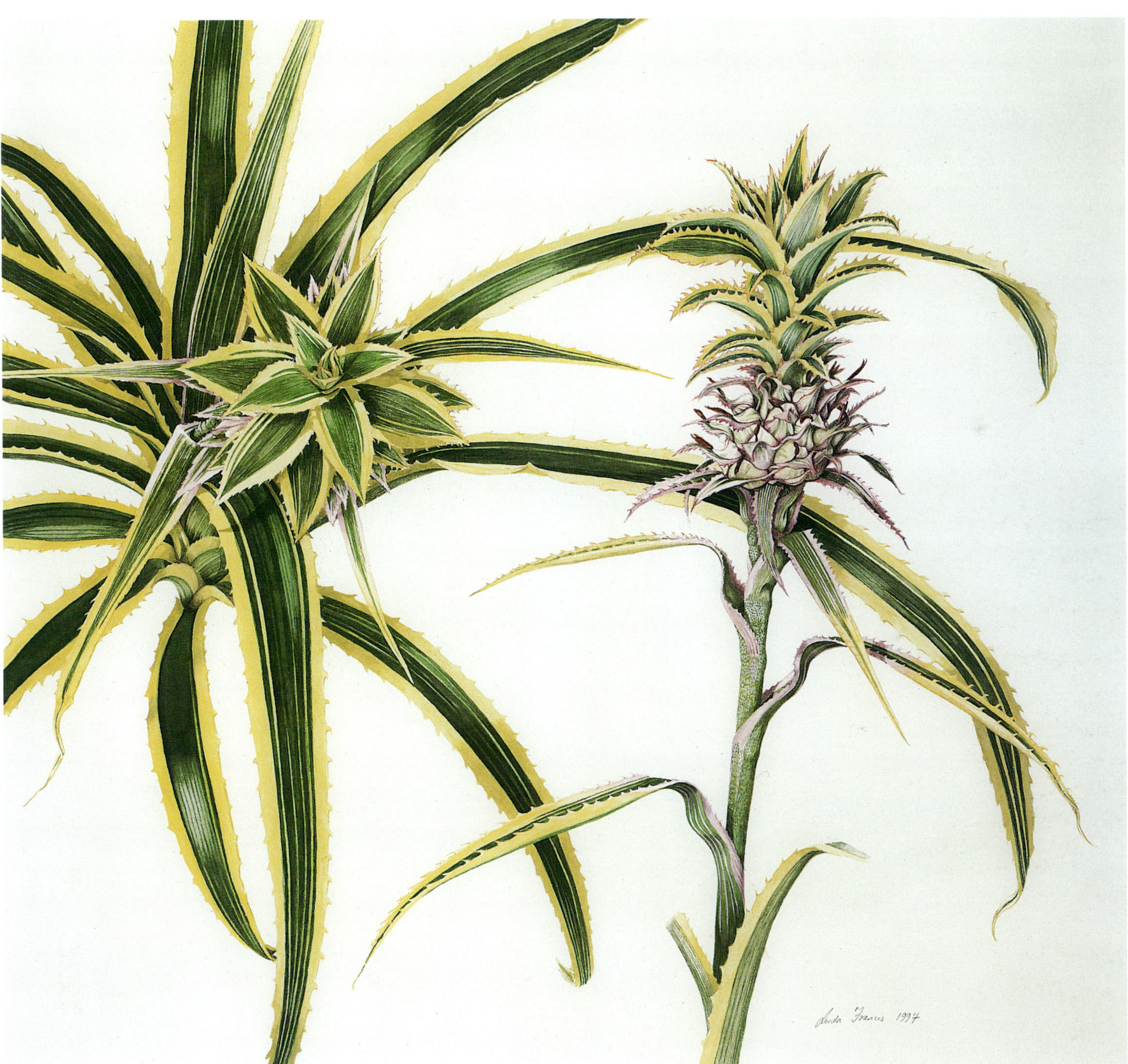

TILLANDSIA LINDENII
(Left) Signed Linda Francis 1996. Acquired from the RHS Show 1997
Watercolour on paper
390 × 300 mm

WILD PINEAPPLE: *ANANAS BRACTEATUS*
(Above) Signed Linda Francis 1997. Acquired from the RHS Show 1997. Watercolour on paper 580 × 600 mm

Coral Guest

BORN LONDON, ENGLAND 1955

Coral Guest has been a very active and productive artist during the last decade of the twentieth century. Already an established artist and teacher by the early 1990s, she has been much influenced by her early training in Japan and at Chelsea School of Art, London. She has been slowly developing her landscape painting as well as her outstanding plant portraits, showing landscapes in some mixed shows as well as a small private solo show in Fuji, Japan at Marubene Villa in 1998.

But her main focus is always plant studies. She has taught at the Royal Botanic Gardens, Kew, giving lectures, courses and workshops, as well as in the Nature in Art Gallery, Gloucestershire, at Monet's garden at Giverny and at Harewood House, Leeds. In 1996 I started planning to hold botanical painting classes in Orient-Express Hotels around the world, sometimes associated with exhibitions of my collection in nearby venues. I wanted to ask the very best teachers and to use the paintings in the exhibitions as teaching tools. The first classes were in Charleston to coincide with the Gibbes Gallery exhibition there, and in the Windsor Court Hotel to coincide with an exhibition in the New Orleans Museum of Art.

Later I realised that it was not essential to have a simultaneous exhibition as a teaching tool, so I arranged a class at Reid's Palace Hotel on Madeira, an island famed for its wonderful range of flowers, an excellent botanical garden and many well-tended and interesting private gardens. I asked Coral to teach the first class there in 1997. She was a great choice, captivating her audience with her command of watercolour techniques and artistic skill. She explained how she created her washes and had everyone practising their breathing while trying to emulate her. Later she quietly showed slides of her own work, demonstrating the results of her techniques in one superb painting after another. With her long blonde hair and serious approach she captivated her group, giving generously of her time during the week and delivering a thoughtful lecture on eighteenth-century fruit painters.

Since the class at Reid's she has taught two courses in Venice at the Cipriani Hotel. As they were held in October we concentrated on autumn fruit and foliage, with Coral preparing some potent

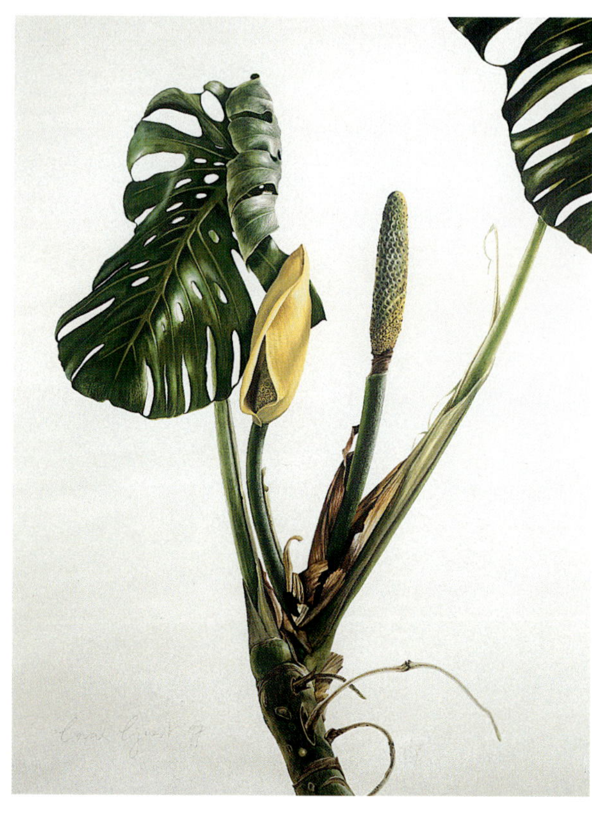

MONSTERA DELICIOSA
Signed Coral Guest '97
Acquired from the artist 1997
Watercolour on paper
750 × 550 mm

pictures and sketches as teaching aids. Early on the second day of the five-day course the entire class went to purchase their painting subjects from Venice's famous local fruit and vegetable market, returning laden with Turk's-cap gourds, sweet chestnuts, rosy pomegranates, bunches of garlic and huge green artichokes. The studio looked out over the lagoon and rapidly became redolent with delicious, fruity smells. One great advantage of using these kinds of subjects is that they stay fresh for longer than some other plant material. On another day the class went to Padua to visit the world's oldest botanical garden and Coral discussed and demonstrated the problems of sketching away from the studio. These classes have appealed to a wide audience with participants flying into Venice from as far afield as Japan and California.

Coral Guest is one of the most important artists that I have collected, starting in 1994 with a magnificent, deep red peony. Later I commissioned her to paint a white lily, a remarkable composition most subtly painted (see page 12 where I have compared it with a lily by the Bauer brothers). I knew

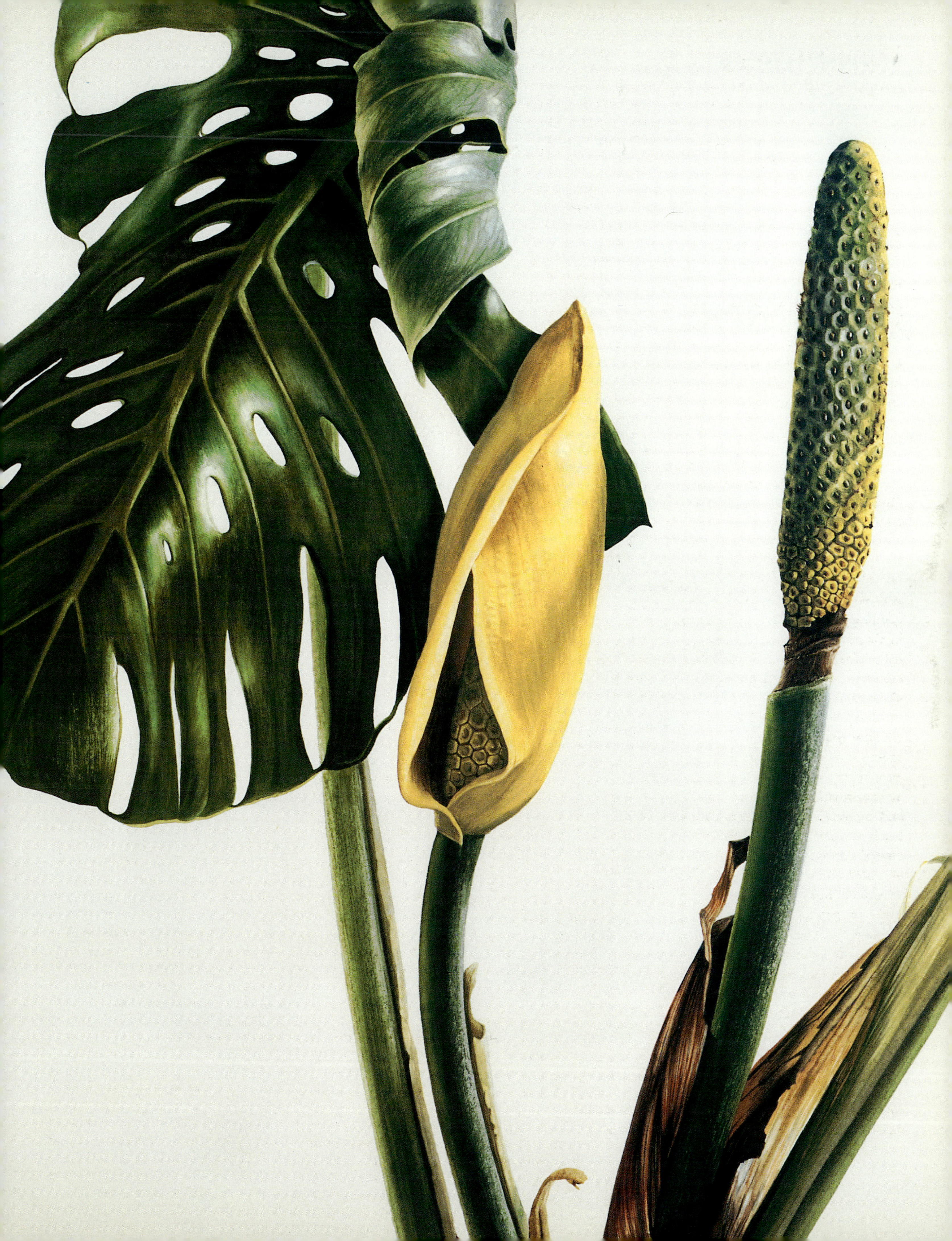

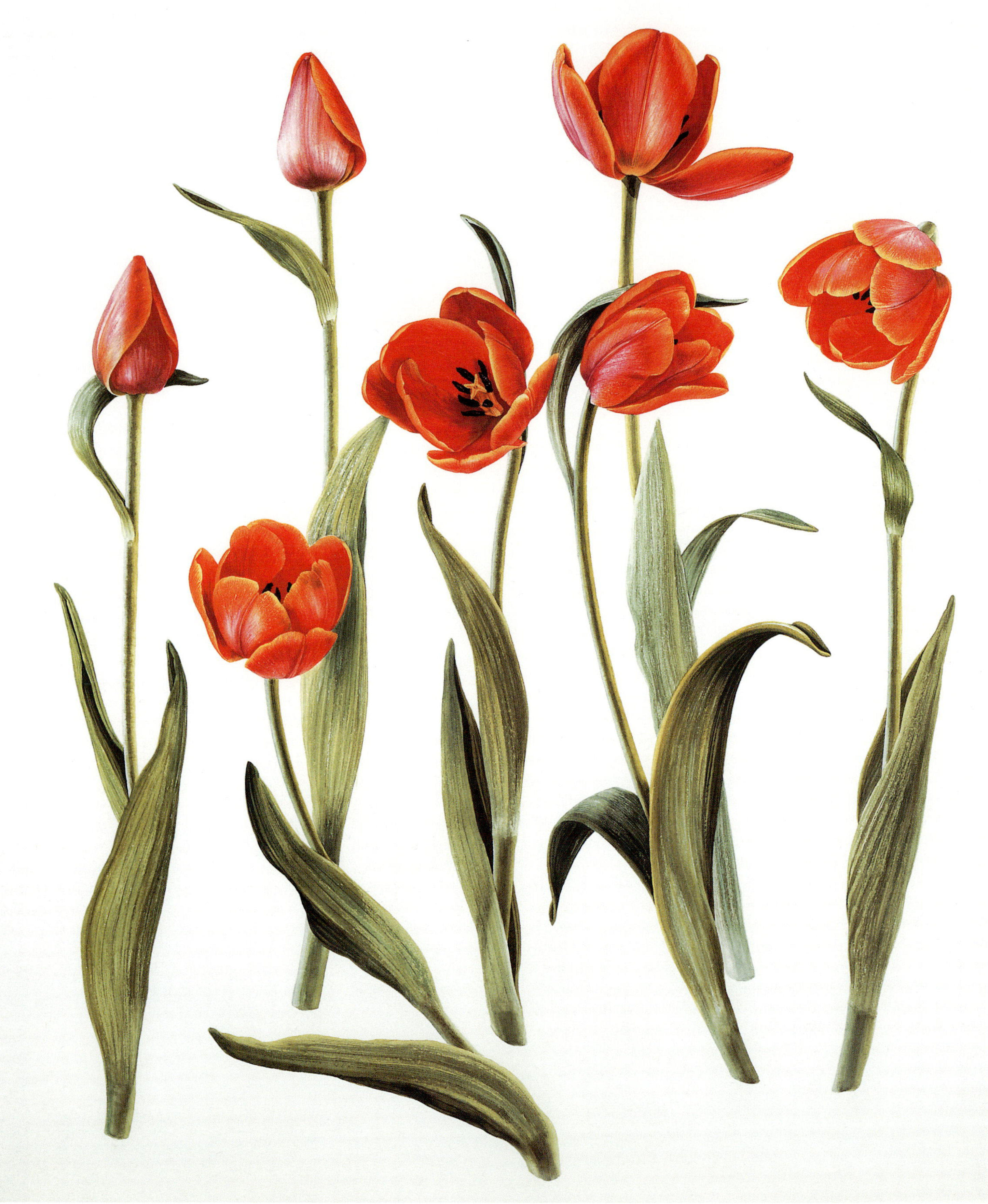

SCREWPINE NUT, BORNEO
PANDANUS SP.
Signed C.G. '95
Acquired from the artist 1996
Watercolour on paper
230 × 180 mm

TULIPA 'DE MOLEN'
Signed Coral Guest '96
Commissioned 1996
Watercolour on paper
689 × 565 mm

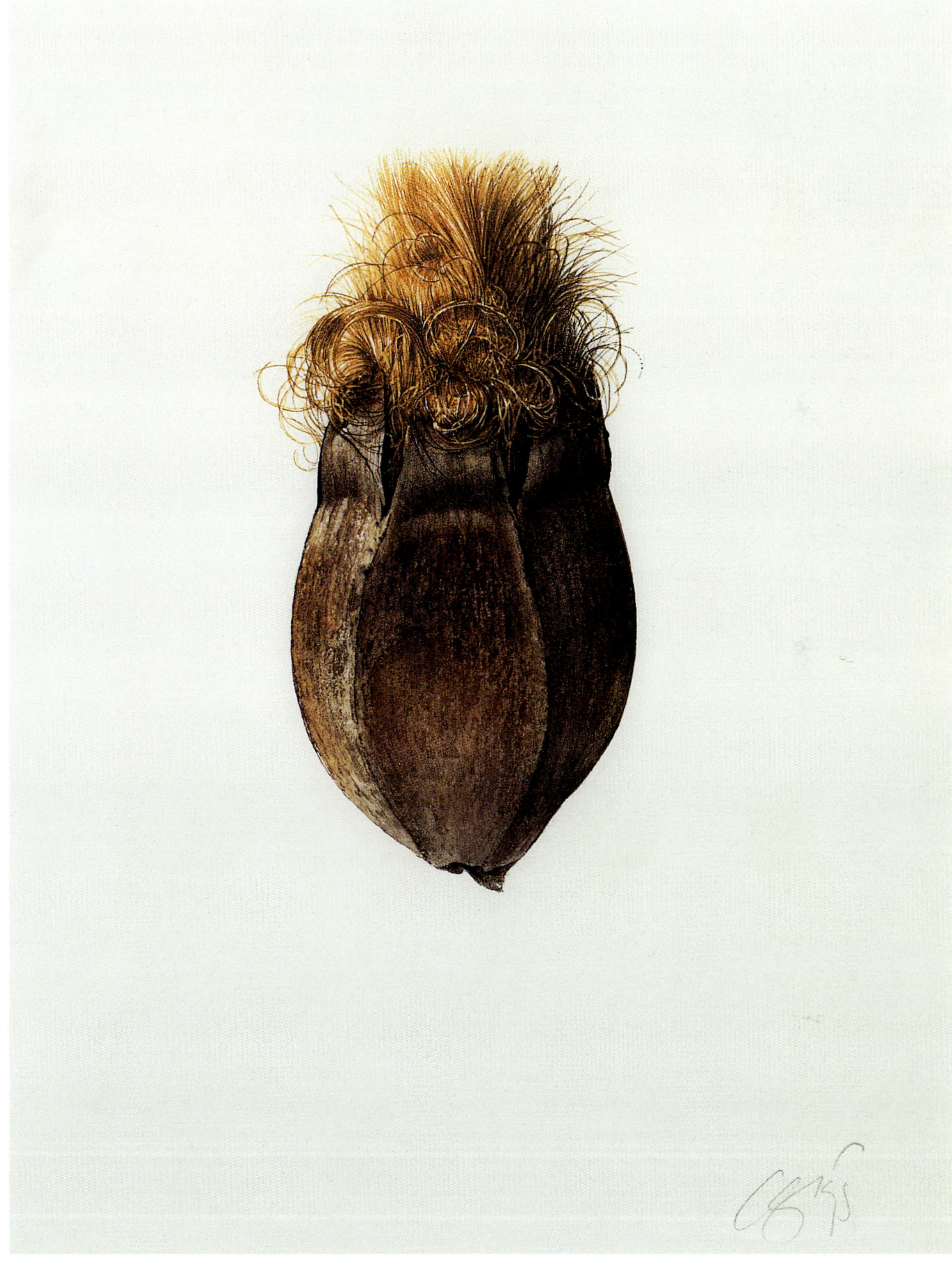

she liked painting tulips, so in 1996 I asked her to paint me something spectacular. Her watercolour of Tulip 'de Molen' was the result. She told me that as the buds opened they had followed the light, twisting and turning as the scarlet petals expanded.

Another commission was of a plant I had grown in my orangery at Hinton. *Lapageria rosea* is known as the Chilean bell flower and is the national flower of Chile. Surprisingly little grown in Europe, it is a spectacular climber which will grow outside in a very sheltered spot in southern England. It has beautiful, bell-shaped flowers with thick, waxy petals which cascade from the trailing stems. It is tricky to germinate and has only recently appeared in seed catalogues. Many years ago I obtained five seeds and managed to get three to germinate. One of these seedlings died but the others struggled on, growing incredibly slowly, putting out a substantial root growth but almost no further development above ground. I discovered that they were extremely lime-sensitive and that an accidental watering with my local tap water was enough to set them back for months, with a very characteristic browning of the leaf tips showing up immediately. Years passed. After nearly a decade they started to flower, just about the time I was threatening to toss them out. By great good fortune one plant turned out to be the usual pink *Lapageria rosea* while the other was a shining, pure white with just the faintest trace of green or pinky green (*Lapageria rosea var. alba*). Terrified that after all this effort they would die on me, I alerted Coral, took photographs and clipped off some hanging cascades of flowers. She kept them in the glass tubes used by orchid growers for their cut specimens and the flowers lasted perfectly for several weeks, although the leaves fell off. The resulting picture is a wonderful record of one of my favourite horticultural triumphs.

Since she painted it we have managed to grow seed from the only seed pod the pink *Lapageria* has produced so far. We have a dozen seedlings slowly developing in ericaceous potting mix and will not know the flower colour for many years – but gardening is like that. The first two plants continue to flower, most prolifically in the winter, sometimes with as many as fifty blooms at a time, a truly spectacular sight. The great plant photographer and gardener, Peter Smithers, told me it was possible to import rooted plants from Chile, but I have never been able to organise this on trips there.

Once when I visited Carol's apartment in north London, I saw a pencil drawing of an interesting fruit which she had left suspended in the centre of the white space of a large piece of paper, lonely yet intriguing. Later in 1996 she showed me a painting of this strange, large nut which had been collected in Borneo on a recent expedition by Sir Charles Burrell. He is one of the old-fashioned freelance explorers who has collected an extraordinary array of trophies from expeditions to far-flung places. He keeps these specimens on display in his baronial hall, Knept Castle, in East Grinstead. This specimen had a fuzz of stiff, curly hairs and was used as a scrubbing brush by the local people. I asked Dr Brinsley Burbidge to help me identify it when I visited the Fairchild Tropical Garden in Miami. Bending down and picking a similar nut from the lawn he told me it was fruit from the Screw Pine *Pandanus*. The specimen he showed me was only a fifth of the size of the nut that Coral had painted life-size but there are some 600 *Pandanus* species exhibiting a huge range of fruit size. I hope that we have the correct identification. Whatever it is, I find the painting very beautiful, with the golden strength of the nut and the bizarre fuzz of the 'top-knot' that Coral enjoyed painting so much.

The most recent commission I have given Coral was to paint *Monstera deliciosa*, the cheese plant, which grows very successfully in my orangery. It had produced a couple of fine spathes which I longed to have captured in paint. The stem beneath the flower was sawn off and the whole upper part of the plant transported to London. Unfortunately, in transit the spathe was knocked off and Coral had to wait for about six weeks for the second one to develop – one of the problems of plant portraiture. This very powerful painting never fails to arouse comment from visitors.

She has recently published a number of articles in *The Artist Magazine* and her *Painting Flowers in Watercolour – a Naturalistic Approach* (A & C Black) is being published in March 2001. To the dismay of her dedicated followers she cut down on her teaching for two years while preparing the plates and text for this book.

LAPAGERIA ROSEA & LAPAGERIA ROSEA VAR. ALBA
Signed Coral Guest '96
Commissioned 1996
Watercolour on paper
770 × 570 mm

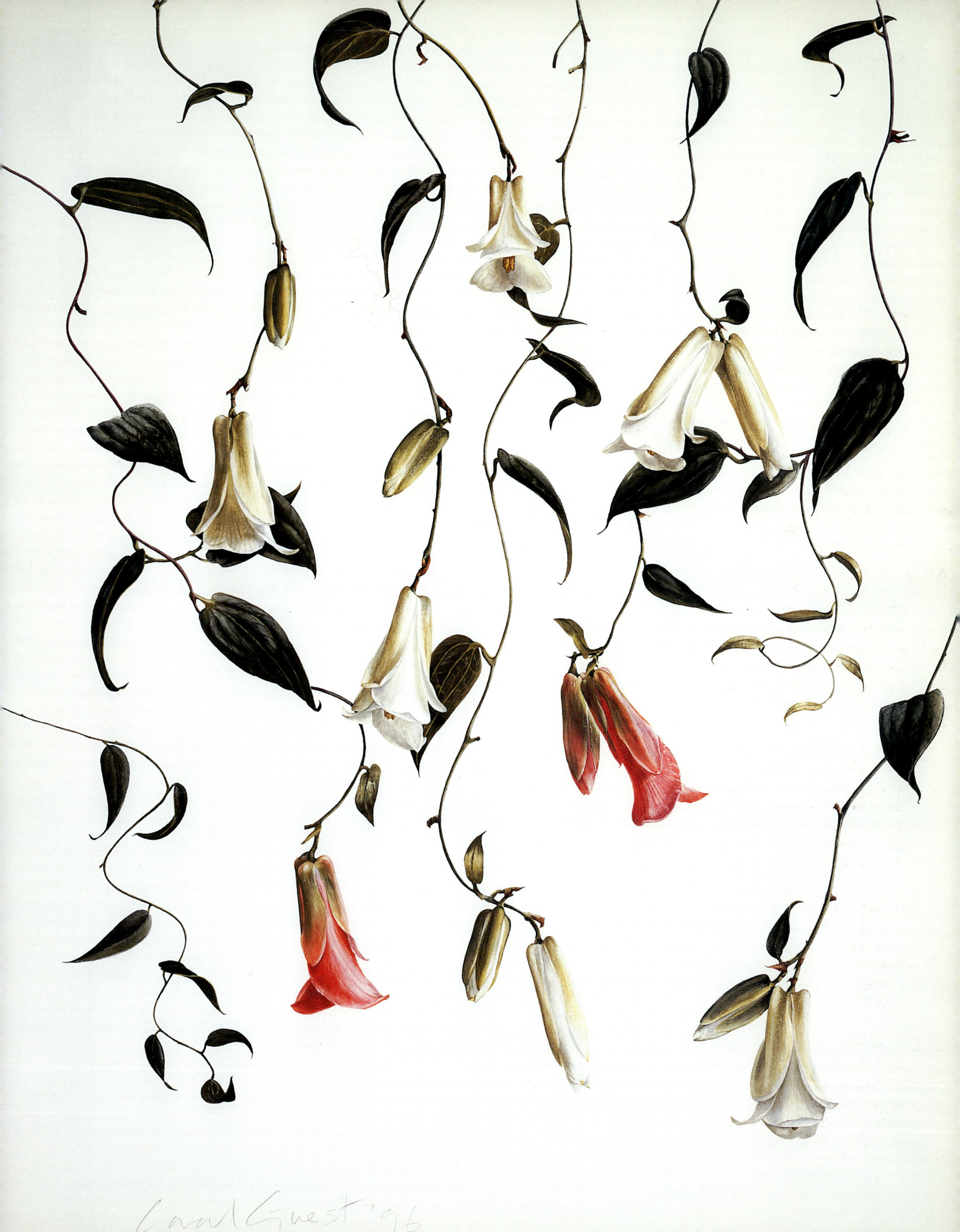
Carol Guest '96

Damodar Lal Gurjar

Born Nahira, Rajastan, India 1958

Damodar Gurjar comes from a farming family living in a village east of Jaipur. His father wanted him to go into the army – a safer choice than becoming an artist – but he showed considerable ability at school and started taking art classes in high school and winning prizes in painting and drawing. He had two years of training at a government art college in Jaipur. The area abounds with artisans, miniaturists and extremely skilled craftsmen who can copy a photograph or painting. Gurjar reproduced the traditional eighteenth- and nineteenth-century Jaipur-style paintings and produced botanical works influenced by the 'Company' type of study (colonialists working for the East India Company would commission local painters to draw exotic flora for them).

I first saw Gurjar's work in 1992 at the Hunt Institute for Botanical Documentation in the 7th International Exhibition, where he showed two paintings of bonsai, a Japanese black pine and a Japanese white pine, both grown in shallow bowls. In style and subject matter his work seemed almost identical to that of V. K. Sharma who had been commissioned to illustrate bonsai trees in 1987 for an American patron, and who also showed in the same exhibition.

In 1994 the Hunt Institute put on another exhibition entitled 'Natural History Paintings from Rajastan' which had been collected by James White of the Hunt Institute as a result of several visits to India. I saw a lovely study of onions by Gurjar and mentioned that I might be interested in acquiring something of his. This small painting of a vivid orange nasturtium (*Tropaeolum*) on a blue background is the result, brought to me from Jaipur by James White.

Recently Damodar Gurjar has taken part in a number of exhibitions in India and abroad. He paints in watercolour, gouache and tempera on a wide variety of materials such as handmade paper, marble, silk, wood, leather and canvas. He is a superb craftsman in the Jaipur tradition.

NASTURTIUM:
TROPAEOLUM MAJUS
Signed Damodar Gurjar (undated)
Acquired from the Hunt Institute, Pittsburgh 1998
Gouache on paper
160 × 125 mm

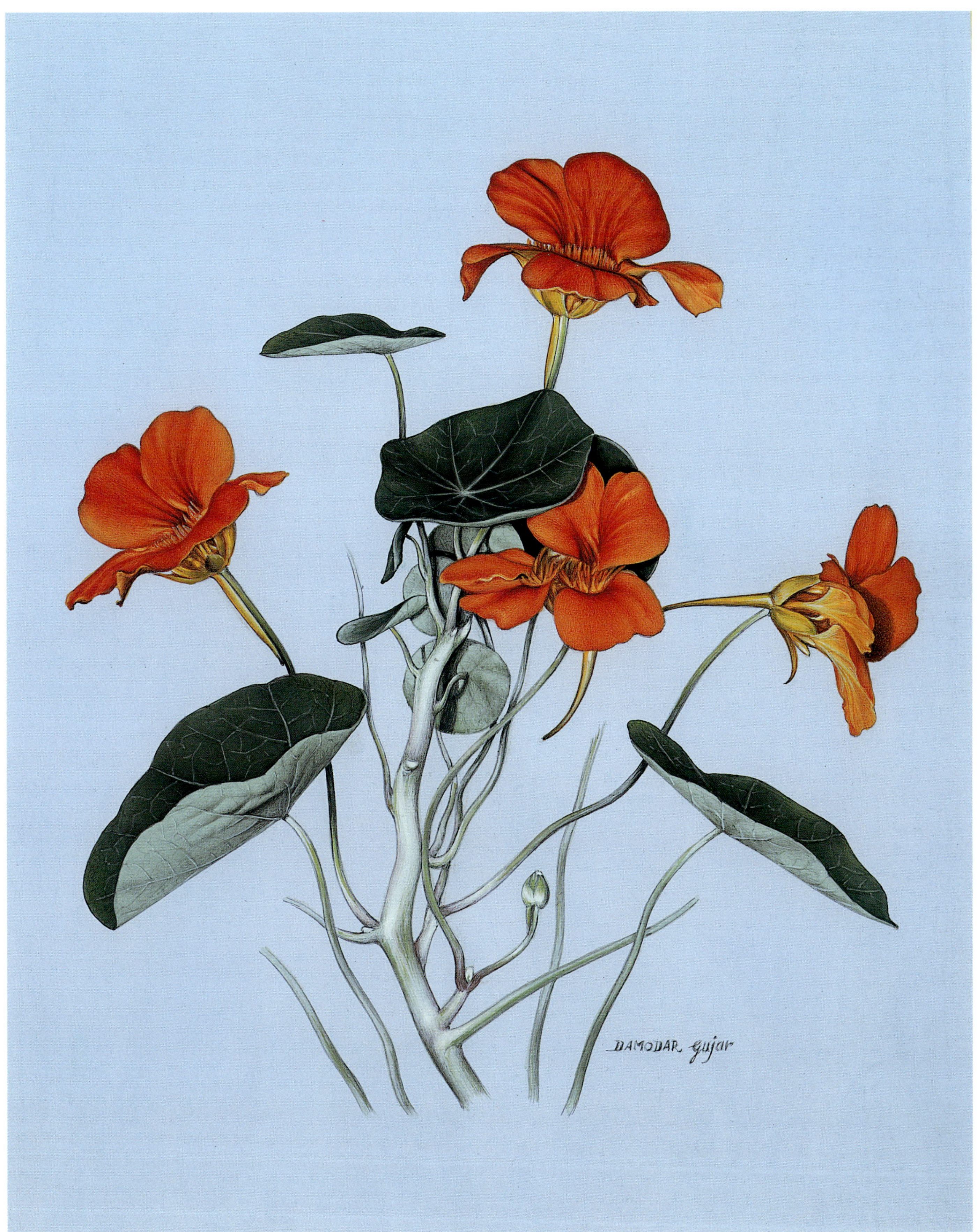
DAMODAR Gujar

Regine Hagerdorn

Born Gottingen, Germany 1952

Somehow I had missed Regine Hagerdorn's paintings at the RHS in 1998 and 1999 but I liked her work as soon as I saw it in February 2000, when she was awarded her second gold medal. Her tight, meticulous studies of thorns, stems, rose hips and tree buds were laid out almost like a child's exercise in neat rows, so exquisitely painted that they could be best appreciated under a magnifying glass. Each was labelled in minute, delicate pencil script, an essential element in her composition which gives an added dimension to her work. These watercolours have an intense, introspective quality that is hard to convey in reproduction.

Although a German citizen, she has lived in France for many years, and now works from Villes. She was educated in Switzerland and France and decided to study design and jewellery at the Ecole des Arts Décoratifs in Geneva, although at the time she had been tempted to study horticulture instead.

For some years she designed contemporary jewellery and in the early 1980s she teamed up with Florent Etienne to establish a graphic design studio. For ten years they were commissioned to draw wine labels, covers for magazines and advertisements. During this period she started to do more and more botanical paintings, and also designed a private garden near Geneva.

She is a passionate gardener, admiring a range of styles from Islamic symbolic gardens through to humble vegetable plots to the Alhambra gardens in Granada, Spain. She is particularly addicted to hybrid roses and cannot stop buying new ones to add to her collection of over a hundred varieties. She admires the work of avant-garde gardeners like G. Clément and J. Wirtz and feels that gardening is one of the most important art forms, perhaps because it is so ephemeral and uncontrollable.

ROSIERS
Rosa – Rosacées
R. inermis morletii
R. macrocarpa
R. pimpinellifolia
R. roxburghii normalis
R. californica
R. pendulina
Hybride de *R. moschata*
R. 'Queen of Musk'
Rameaux de L'Été
récédent
Representés en Janvier
2000 en Taille Réelle
Signed RH 15.1.2000
Acquired from the RHS
Show 2000
Watercolour on paper
497 × 357 mm

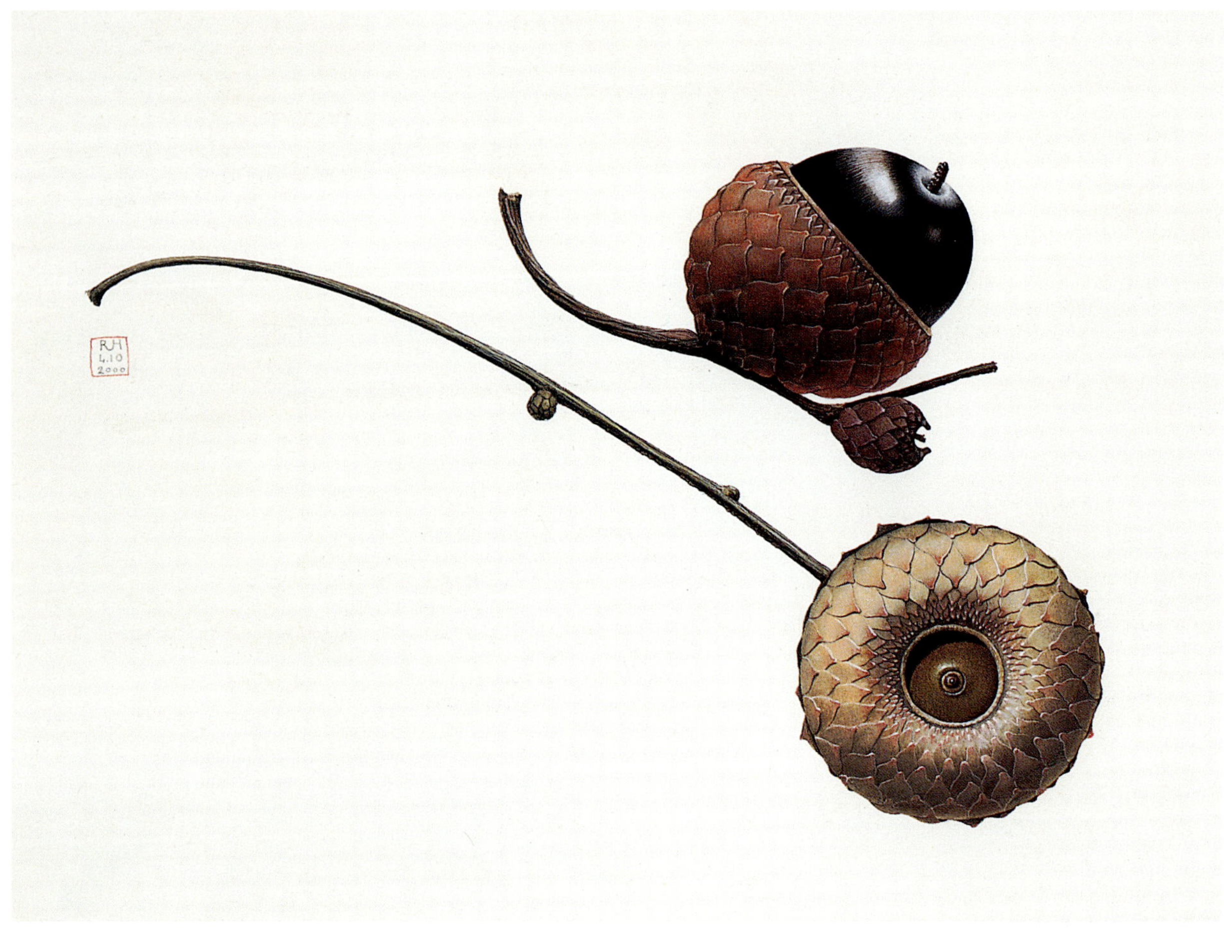

QUERCUS ROBUR:
ACORNS FROM
THE JURA
Signed RH 4.10.2000
Watercolour on paper
345 × 390 mm
Magnified × 3.5

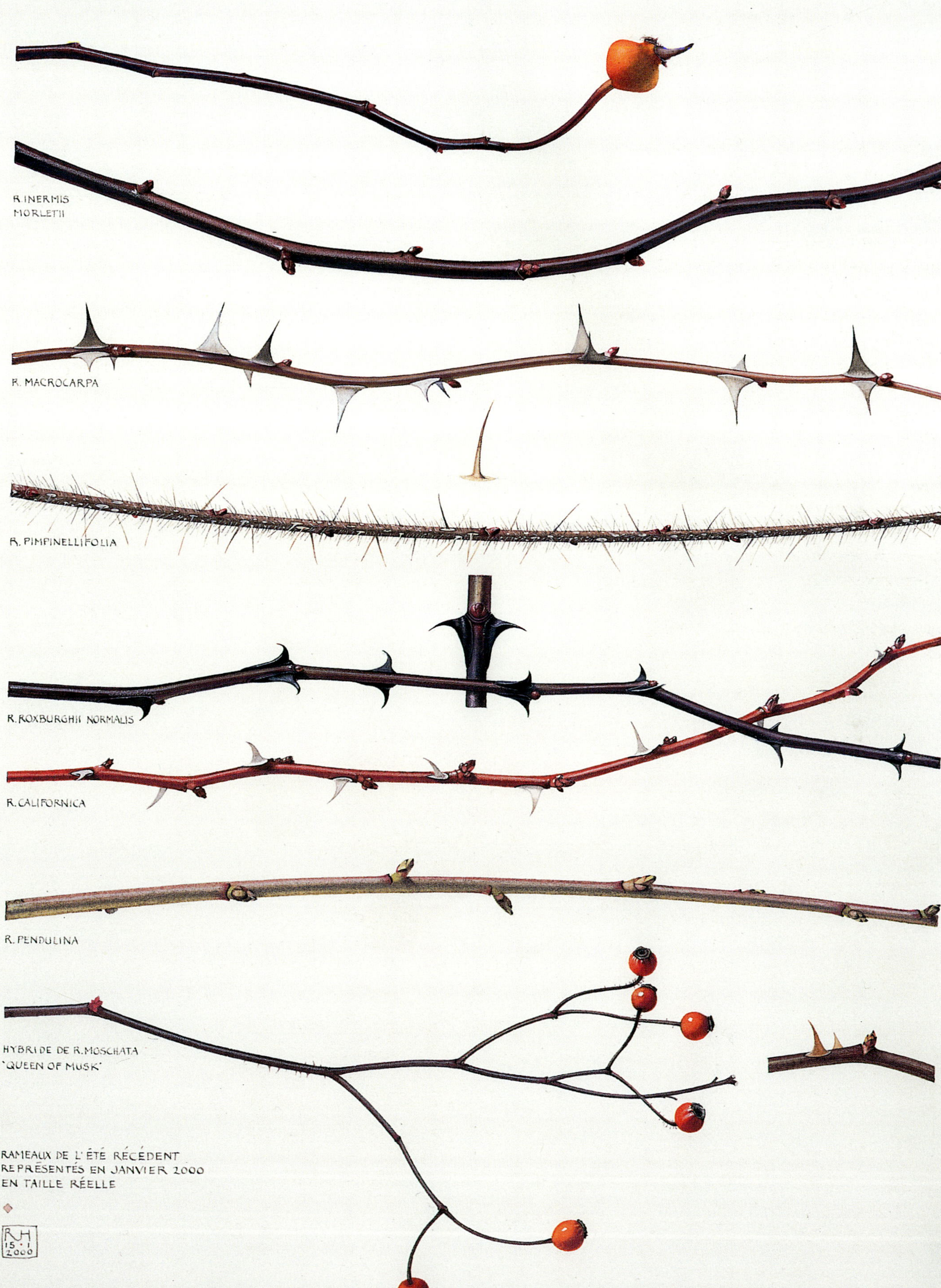

ROSIERS
ROSA · ROSACÉES
R. INERMIS MORLETII
R. MACROCARPA
R. PIMPINELLIFOLIA
R. ROXBURGHII NORMALIS
R. CALIFORNICA
R. PENDULINA
HYBRIDE DE R. MOSCHATA 'QUEEN OF MUSK'
RAMEAUX DE L'ÉTÉ RÉCÉDENT REPRÉSENTÉS EN JANVIER 2000 EN TAILLE RÉELLE
RH 15·1 2000

Yvonne Glenister Hammond

BORN LONDON, ENGLAND 1943

I met Yvonne Glenister Hammond through the Chelsea Physic Garden Florilegium Society where she is a founder member. This praiseworthy group was founded to record the plants within the famous garden, the oldest botanical garden in London. Each member undertakes to paint a number of specimens and donate the paintings to the library. They meet once a month to compare notes and encourage progress under the watchful eye of Anne-Marie Evans, the inspired teacher who takes the courses at the English Gardening School based in the Chelsea Physic Garden.

Yvonne was educated in London at St Paul's School for Girls and at the Law Society's School of Law. From 1980 onwards she was a writer and researcher, and since 1995 she has worked as a freelance botanical artist, and now lives in Bedfordshire. Her training in botanical art started with a diploma (distinction) from the English Gardening School's course 1995–6. Since then she has shown in a number of shared exhibitions including the RHS, the Society for Botanical Artists and the Department of Plant Sciences, Oxford. She has also exhibited inside and outside London in a number of galleries. She showed two beautiful paintings at the 9th International Exhibition of the Hunt Institute – entitled '*Silene fortunei*' and 'Wild Plums' – in 1998.

I bought two paintings from her in 1999. Both are meticulously painted, showing flower and fruits of cherry and bullace (wild plum). The texture and glow of the dark cherries compliments the delicate white flowers above and this contrast and balance is also shown with the beautifully executed bullace fruits, which were chosen for the brochure of the Florilegium Society in 1998.

Most recently I acquired an attractive study of a pink tulip, one of a group shown at the RHS where she was awarded a gold medal.

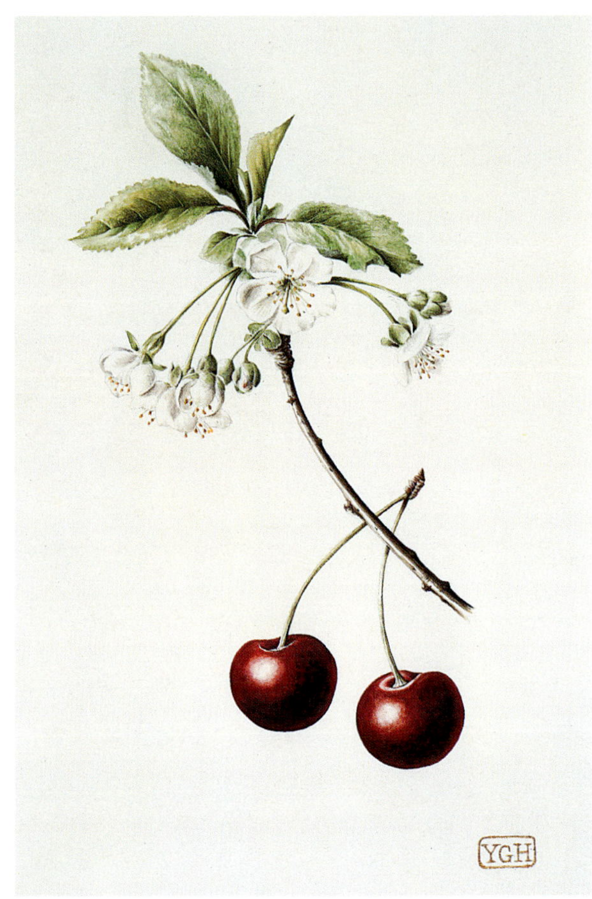

CHERRIES
(Left) Signed YGH
(undated)
Acquired from the artist 1999
Watercolour on vellum
225 × 145 mm

TULIPA 'MARIETTE'
(Right) Signed YGH
(undated)
Acquired from the RHS Show 1999
Watercolour on paper
428 × 325 mm

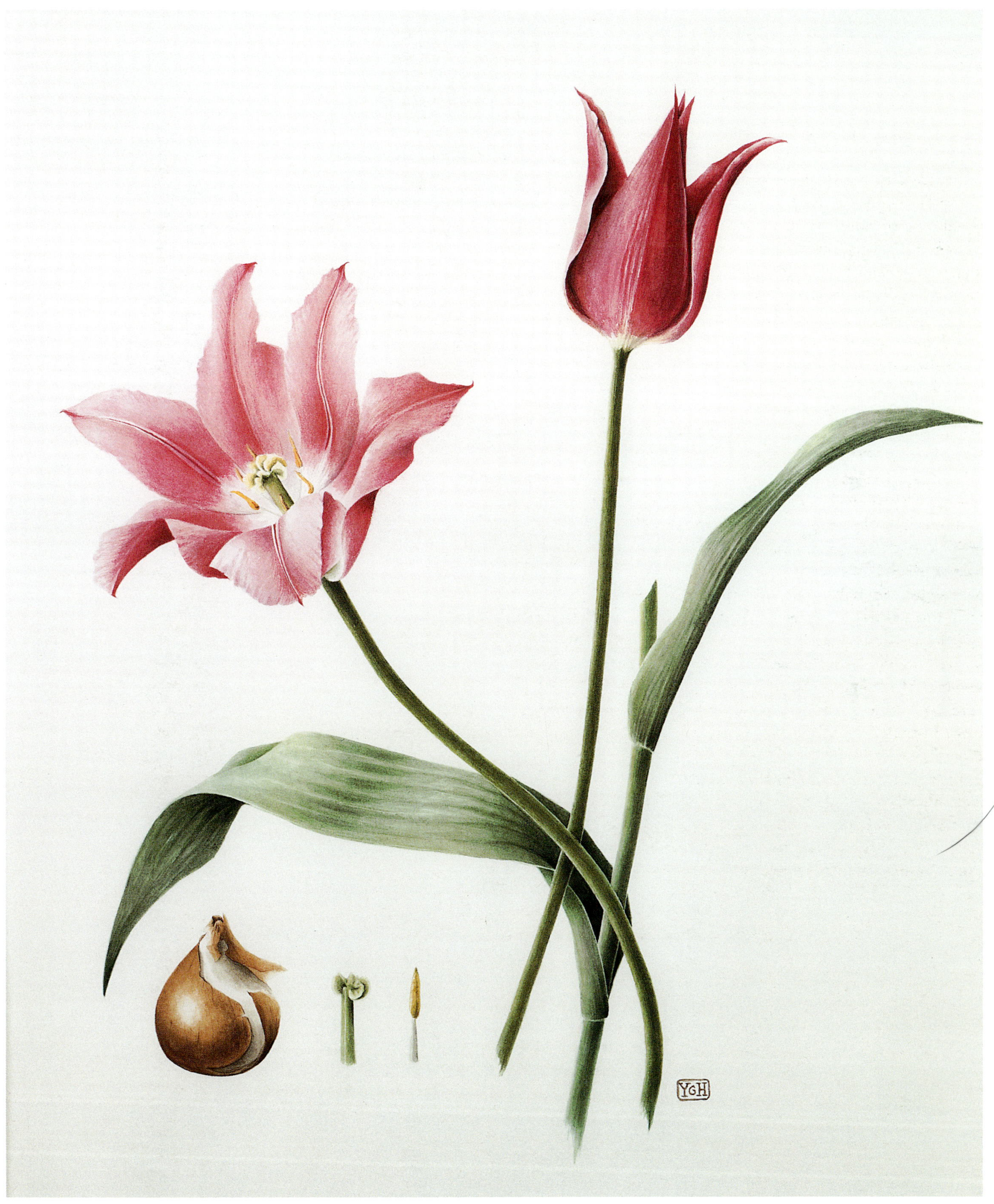
YGH

Toni Hayden

Born Woodbridge, Suffolk, England 1938

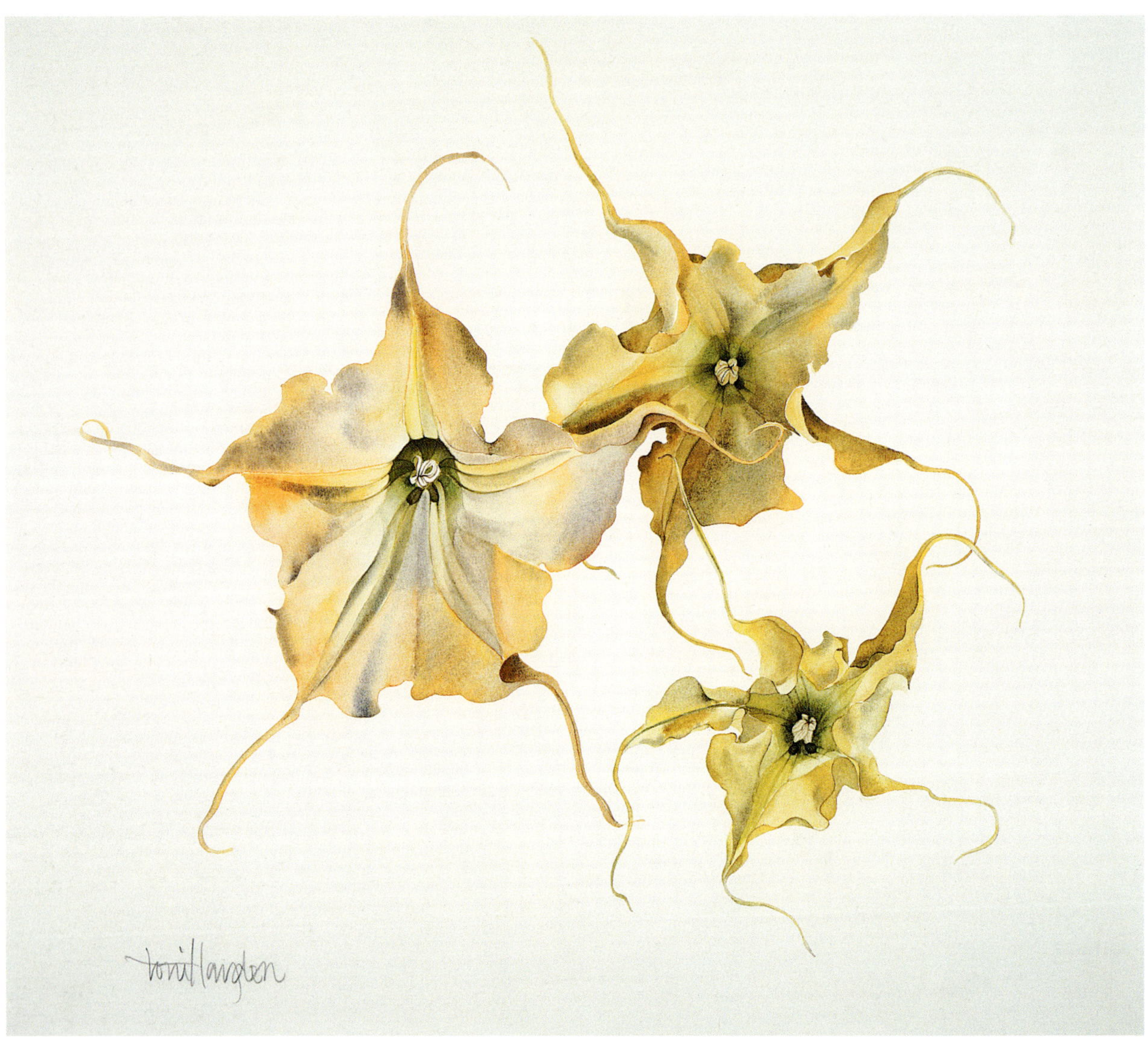

Toni Hayden was educated at the Norwich School of Art, specialising in calligraphy and she has had most of her exhibitions in Norwich or nearby. She was awarded a silver and a silver gilt medal at the RHS and was in the Hunt Institute's 8th International Exhibition in 1995.

I chose two paintings of *Datura* from her portfolio in 1997. They are interesting studies of these strange, rather sculptural poisonous plants which I have often seen in their pendulous splendour in Greek courtyards in late summer. There is a common folk tale in Greece which says that if you want to get rid of your grandmother, you should pop her in the shade of a *Datura* after a good lunch and she might never wake up.

At the same time as I chose the two paintings, Toni Hayden showed me designs she had hand-painted for silk scarves. The one she had drawn of fuchsia was beautiful, intricate and stylish and this is an area where I am sure she could excel. She is also a very good illustrator, with an original approach to book design.

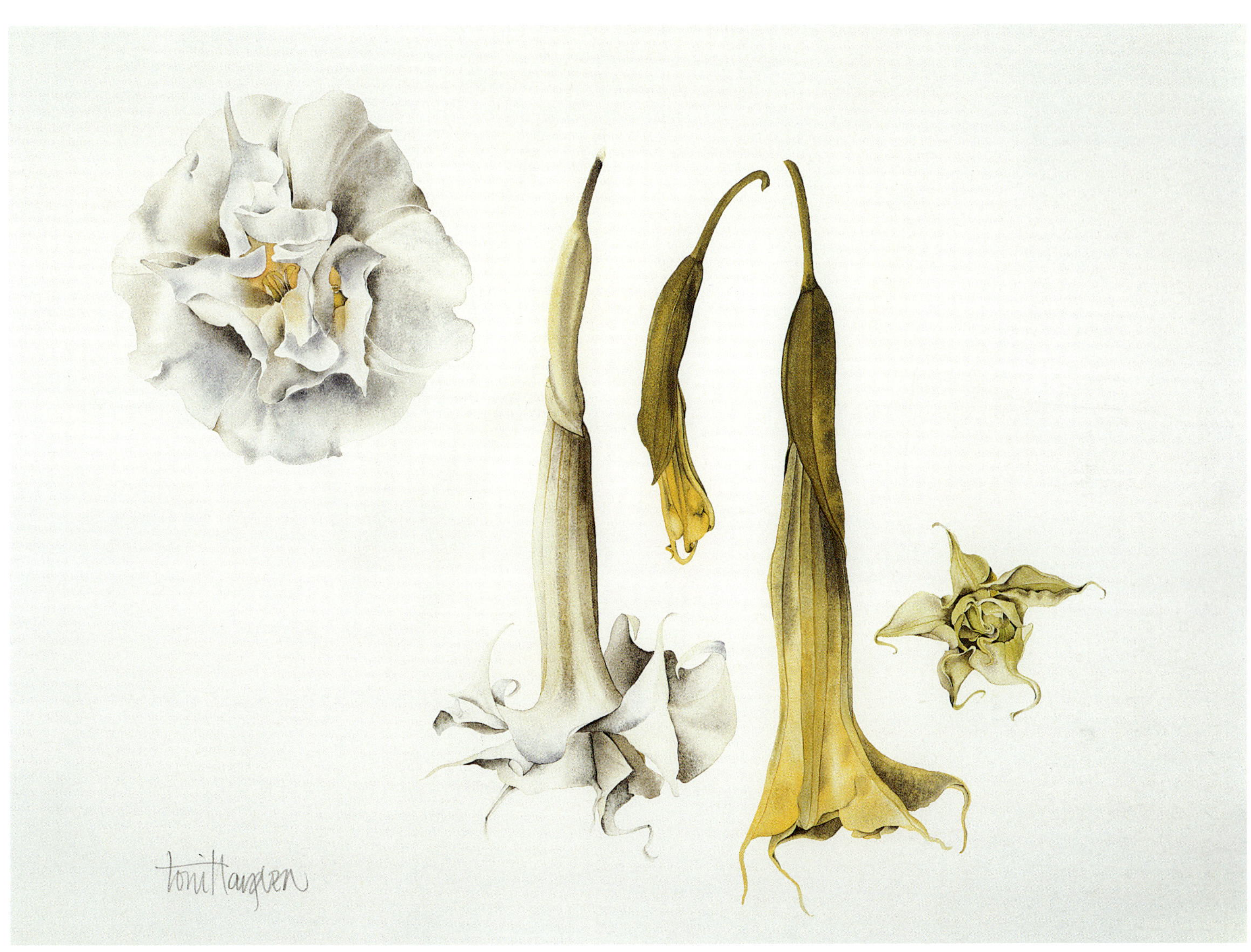

THREE SINGLE DATURAS
(Left) Signed Toni Hayden
(undated)
Acquired from the artist 1997
Watercolour on paper
550 × 630 mm

STUDIES OF DOUBLE DATURA
(Above) Signed Toni Hayden
(undated)
Acquired from the artist 1997
Watercolour on paper
550 × 730 mm

Celia Hegedüs

BORN LONDON, ENGLAND 1949

When she was very young, Celia Hegedüs was taught painting by her mother who was a stage set designer. She went on to train at the Hammersmith School of Art in 1966 and the next year at the City & Guilds, London. She continued to paint while bringing up her family and started showing at the Royal Academy in 1993 and 1995 in the Summer Show. During this time she was also showing at the RHS where she gained a silver gilt medal and three gold medals.

Her first one-person exhibition was at Waterman Fine Art in Jermyn Street, London in November 1995 and she had another most successful exhibition with Offer Waterman at the Park Walk Gallery, London in March/April 1999. She was also invited to show at the Tryon & Swann's international exhibition in November 1998.

In 1996 Celia showed me a selection of her plant portraits. Eventually I chose a trio of iris paintings on vellum which went very splendidly together, *Iris foetidissima*, *Iris pseudacorus* and *Iris sibirica*. The stinking iris (*I. foetidissima*) with its blue and yellow flower and scarlet berries is a robust portrait which contrasts well with the elegant, slender foliage of the Siberian flag (*I. sibirica*). Somehow the yellow flag (*I. pseudacorus*), that lives in my pools in the country, takes a completely satisfying central position between the other two on my walls. In each case she has caught the character and essence of the different irises and has created a wonderful translucence with the light penetrating the vellum. These three splendid paintings are among the best she has ever produced.

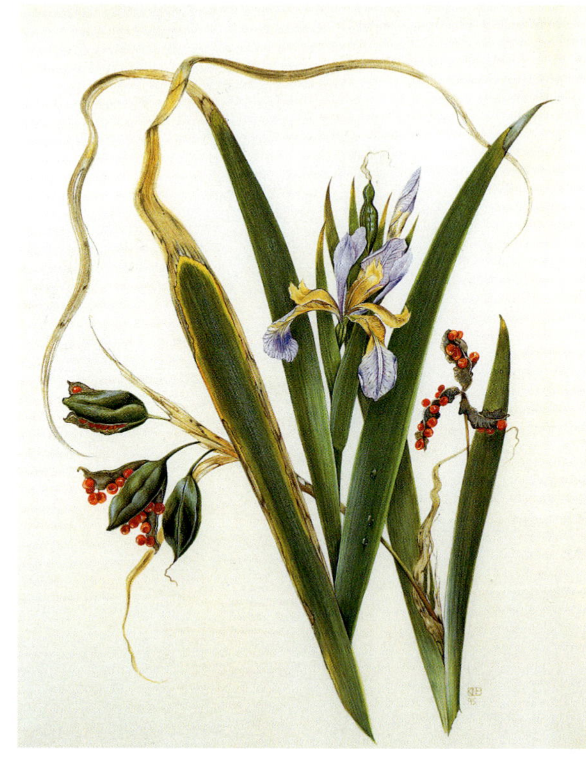

STINKING IRIS:
IRIS FOETIDISSIMA
Signed CNH 95
Acquired from the artist 1996
Watercolour on vellum
540 × 410 mm

YELLOW FLAG:
IRIS PSEUDACORUS
(Overleaf left)
Signed CNH 96
Acquired from the artist 1996
Watercolour on vellum
540 × 410 mm

SIBERIAN FLAG:
IRIS SIBIRICA
(Overleaf right)
Signed CNH 96
Acquired from the artist 1996
Watercolour on vellum
540 × 410 mm

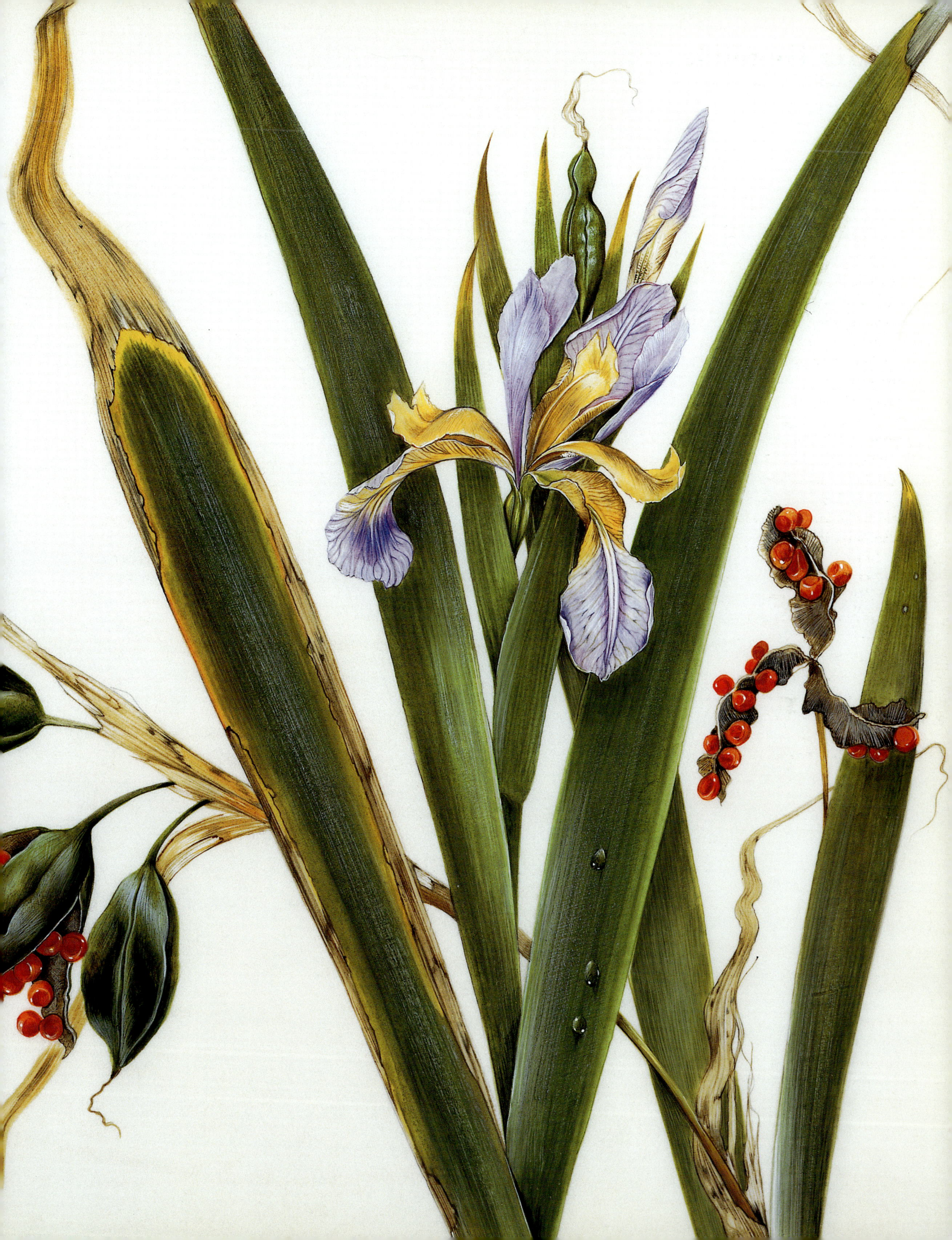

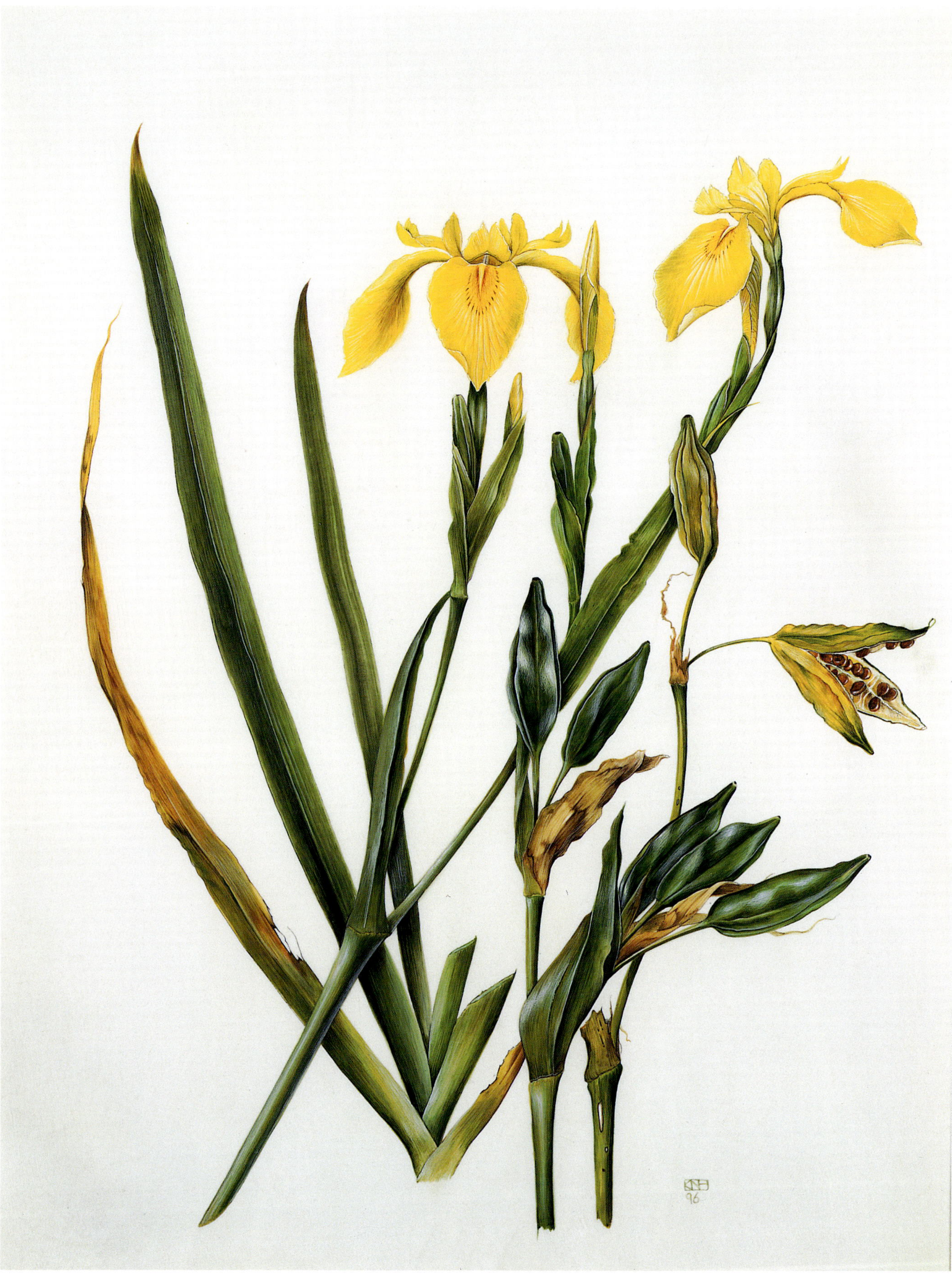

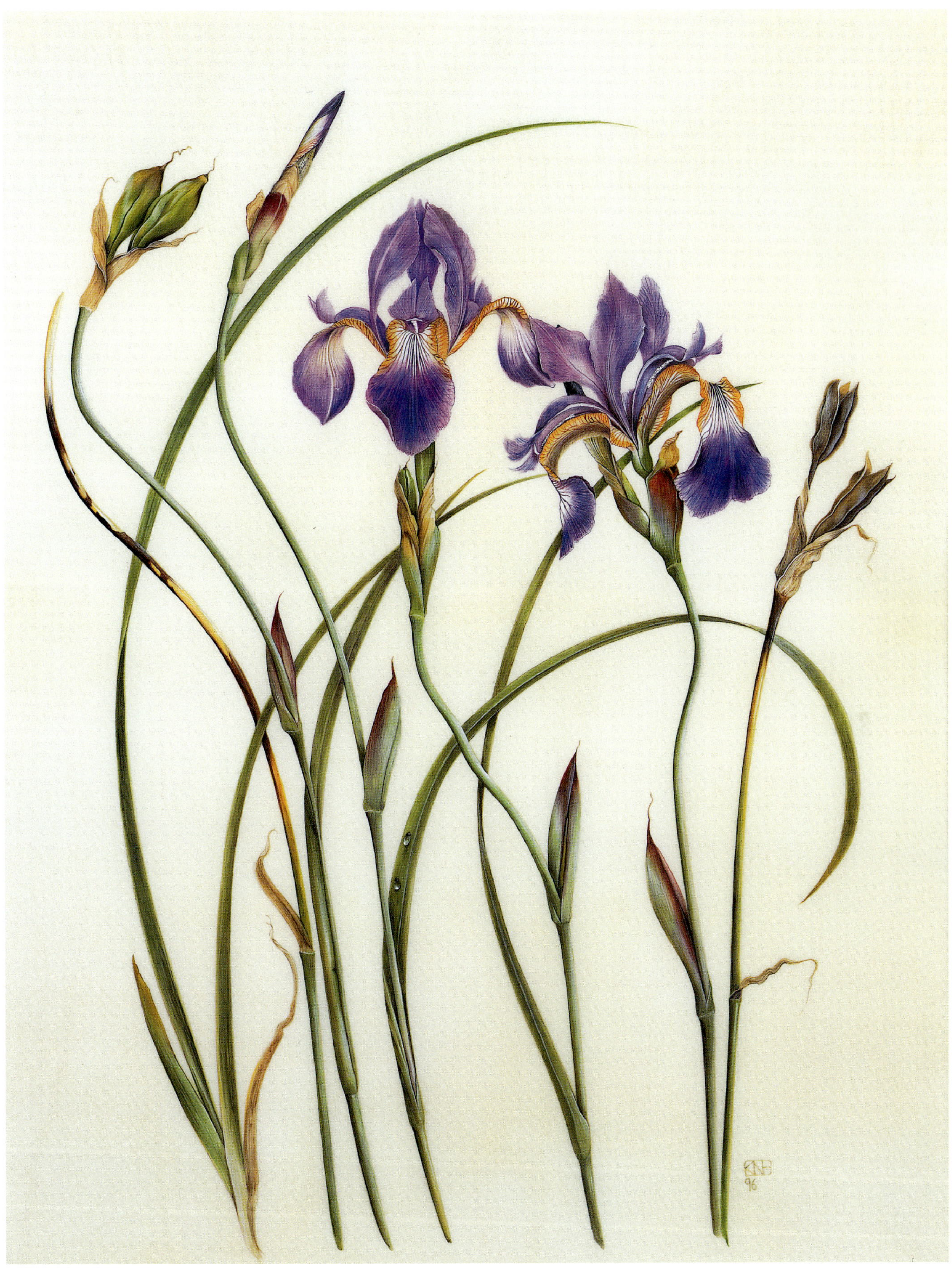

Sue Herbert

BORN DARWEN, ENGLAND 1954

Sue Herbert was trained at Blackpool College of Art & Technology and Sunderland College of Art. She has shown in a number of group exhibitions in London, including the Tryon & Swann Gallery in 1998.

I was first introduced to her work at the Hunt Institute's 7th International Exhibition in 1992, where I saw one of her huge leaf paintings. It was an exciting, arresting picture and I asked her to show me more when I returned to London. Since then I have showed the leaf in my collection in exhibitions all over the world and it is always a focus of admiration and attention.

The next time I saw Sue Herbert's work was at a three-person show at Kew which started in the autumn of 1996. She was showing a number of other large leaf paintings but this time I chose a painting of two fern fronds with a fungus (neither ferns nor fungus were identified by the artist). I liked this fragile, delicate watercolour and bought it to complement and contrast with my first acquisition of her enormous leaf.

SMALL FERNS WITH FUNGUS
Signed Sue Herbert
1996
Acquired from Kew Gardens Gallery 1997
Watercolour on paper
445 x 313 mm

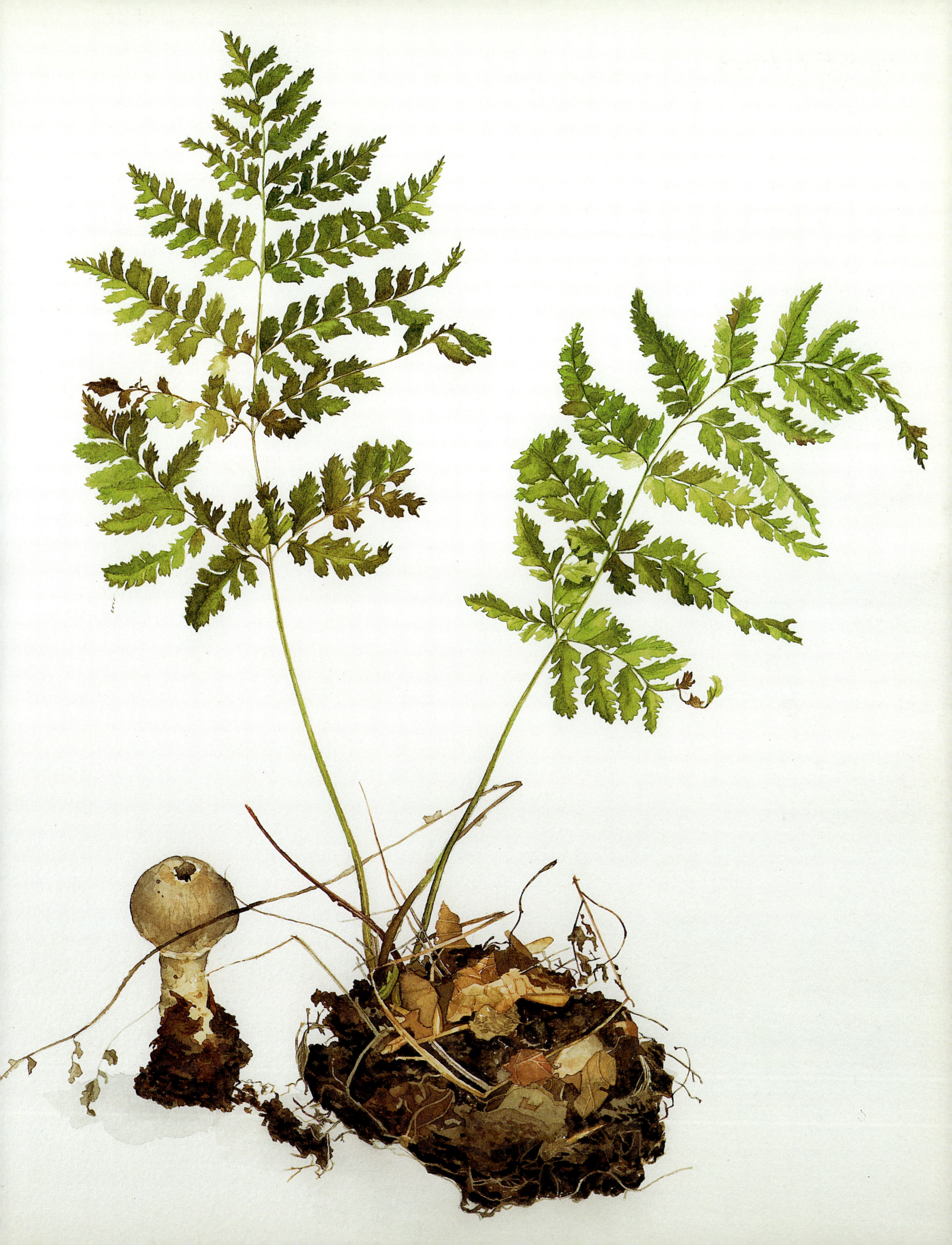

Betty Hinton

BORN GIN GIN, QUEENSLAND, AUSTRALIA 1935

When I first read Betty Hinton's background notes I thought her birthplace, Gin Gin, sounded most entertaining (it is about 150 miles north of Brisbane). She has spent her career in Queensland, beginning as a photographer and then emerging as a painter in the late 1970s. She had no formal training in the arts but received early local recognition with a number of solo exhibitions in the state. In 1980 she was featured in a television documentary entitled *A Big Country* and again in 1990 as a botanical artist in another film entitled *Under Southern Skies*.

In 1992 she embarked on a major project, painting plants from the Daintree Forest Reserve. The tropical rainforest of Daintree (north of Cairns) has a remarkable group of ancient 'plant dinosaurs', remnants left from long ago, most of which are found nowhere else except as fossils. Betty Hinton is producing about forty studies which will eventually be housed in the new library building of James Cook University on Cairns campus. She was invited to the ceremony when the library was opened by the Prime Minister John Howard, on 18 May 2000.

By 1999, when she first wrote to me, she had completed six paintings for the project which is called 'Ancient & Primitive Flowering Plants of Australia'. At that time she was working on several other paintings and, as she always paints from life, she has to wait until she gets the examples of seasonal flowers or fruit. She plans her compositions very carefully and prays that everything does not happen at once. She works with scientific guidance from Dr David Christopher, Senior Lecturer in Paleobotany, Adelaide University, South Australia. Betty Hinton finds her specimens in the rainforests north of the Daintree river which is considered the richest location on earth for relict Gondwanan rainforest plants.

I was interested in her dramatic style and presentation as well as her fascinating and unusual subjects. I was particularly intrigued because I had just been reading *The Future Eaters* by T. T. Flannery, which describes changes wrought by the fauna of Australasia, culminating with the destructive wasting of precious resources by man.

Initially I wanted to commission *Austromeullera trinerva* which I chose as a subject from prints she sent me, showing a lush range of young and mature foliage and catkin-like flowers, but she could not get all the material in time. So I considered Briar Silky Oak (*Musgravea heterophylla*), and Idiot Fruit or Ribbonwood (*Idiospermum australiense*). I finally settled on Idiot Fruit, so-called because the large fruit contains neurotoxins which cause 'madness' and death in cattle.

The Idiot Fruit was first described in the nineteenth century but was 'lost' when forests were cleared for agriculture. Half a century passed before it was rediscovered when some cattle died suddenly and mysteriously. The local aborigines class the fruit as 'very poisonous'. It is a tall tree of 15 metres or more and the only way to look at the flowers is through binoculars or by finding someone to climb the tree. Luckily Betty Hinton had two rock climbers who rigged the tree and returned in triumph after several exhausting hours, carrying flowering branches which she could paint close up.

She hopes that her studies will help promote the rainforest research being done at James Cook University. Some of her work was exhibited beside Sidney Parkinson's paintings which were executed on James Cook's voyage of discovery along the Barrier Reef. Other early paintings of tropical Queensland by Ferdinand Bauer have recently been exhibited in Sydney from the amazing library of the Natural History Museum, London. Bauer accompanied Matthew Flinders on a subsequent voyage and these paintings were the result. Although Betty Hinton's paintings are totally different in style, they reveal a similar intensity of purpose.

IDIOSPERMUM AUSTRALIENSE

Signed Betty Hinton – Leaves 26 Nov 92, Juveniles Sept 98, Fruit Aug 99, Flowers Aug 99

Acquired from the artist 2000

Gouche & watercolour on paper

760 × 560 mm

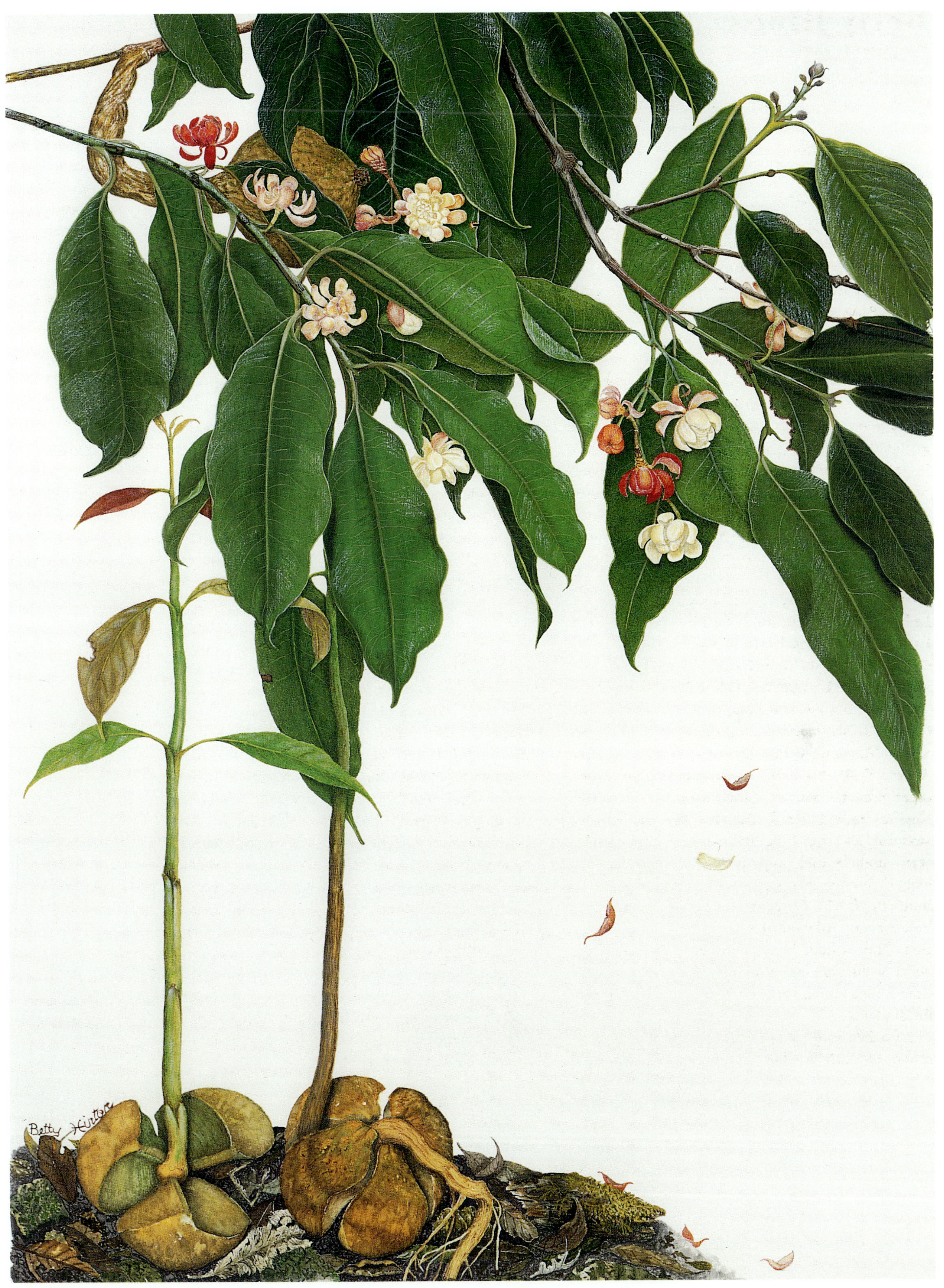
Betty Hinton

Mariko Imai

BORN KANAGAWA, JAPAN 1942

Over the last few years I have been lucky enough to collect nine works by Mariko Imai. She is undoubtedly one of the world's most important botanical artists, working for long, sustained periods on a particular plant family to produce a series of definitive portraits. Her project for the new millennium is to paint species of *Asarum*, concentrating solely on this one group with the hope of producing a book in five years' time.

She has had many exhibitions in Japan and Canada, produced illustrations for several books, some for children, and executed superb covers for the Japanese version of the RHS magazine. In 1996 twenty-five of her botanical paintings were shown at the 5th Exhibition of 'The World's Precious Plants' at Tobu Department Store in Tokyo as part of Mito City's Botanical Gardens contribution to the display. She later sent ten of these to the RHS where they were awarded a gold medal; she eventually donated them to the Lindley Library which is building up a good selection of contemporary botanical art.

Her most recent major contribution is her superb plates in an important multilingual book entitled *Masdevallia and Dracula* by Y. Udagawa. I first met her in Mito in 1994 where she was exhibiting some of these works. It was quite a trek to get there from Tokyo and she was delighted I had made the effort. While I was choosing one of her paintings she mentioned that she would like to give me her very first botanical study, a pencil drawing of *Ipomea* or morning glory. She searched energetically but unsuccessfully through her belongings and eventually posted it to me a couple of years later, together with two other quaintly titled drawings. These three sketches are amongst the best in my whole collection and I have treasured them ever since. They are all drawn larger than life-size and their impact comes from the palpable excitement that artists get when starting to look at plants close up through a microscope or magnifying glass.

The next time we met was at a reception given at the Yasuda Kasai Gallery, Tokyo on the opening of my exhibition there in July 1998. This was a big show with 150 works hung through the large galleries on the top of this distinctive skyscraper. There were huge posters outside and it was advertised widely in the underground and on television. There must have been over a thousand people listening to the opening speeches, one given in fluent Japanese by the British Ambassador, Sir David Wright. All the Japanese works had been hung in the last section, close to the gallery's greatest treasure, Vincent van Gogh's *Sunflowers*. There were as many as a hundred artists there, all excited and delighted at this first major show of contemporary botanical art in Japan. I met every single one and many showed me their work. I think Mariko found it a rather overwhelming experience – I certainly did. There were queues the next morning when the exhibition was opened to the public. Over 40,000 people visited Yasuda Kasai during the six weeks of the show.

Since those heady days I have acquired six more paintings by Imai. Four are large, powerful watercolours of pitcher plants (*Nepenthes*) whose extraordinary leaves trap insects to augment their nutrition. Each study is beautifully designed and placed upon the page. Most were painted for the cover of the magazine of the RHSJ (Royal Horticultural Society, Japan) during 1992 and 1993. She painted the *Nepenthes rafflesiana* in the greenhouses of Mito City Botanical Gardens in Ibaragi. She had to borrow the *Nepenthes maxima* 'Superba' and take it by car to her new home in Yamagata province where she occasionally feeds it grasshoppers and locusts. (She warned me that it was very important not to overfeed it.)

Accompanying the *Nepenthes* were two other plant studies. One, which she sent me as a Christmas card, was the parasitic *Aeginetia indica* which has become a pest in sugar-cane fields in the southeast Asian tropics. She told me she collected it in 1978, when she visited Susukinohara, the name for an area of Japanese pampas grass which used to exist in what is now the suburbs of Yokohama, near Tokyo. The other study is *Sarracenia purpurea*, again a species which traps insects in its modified leaves. They are dissolved in the tubular leaf, to be

SARRACENIA PURPUREA
Signed Imai (hours worked on painting & date in Japanese)
Gift from the artist 1999
Watercolour on paper
360 × 280 mm

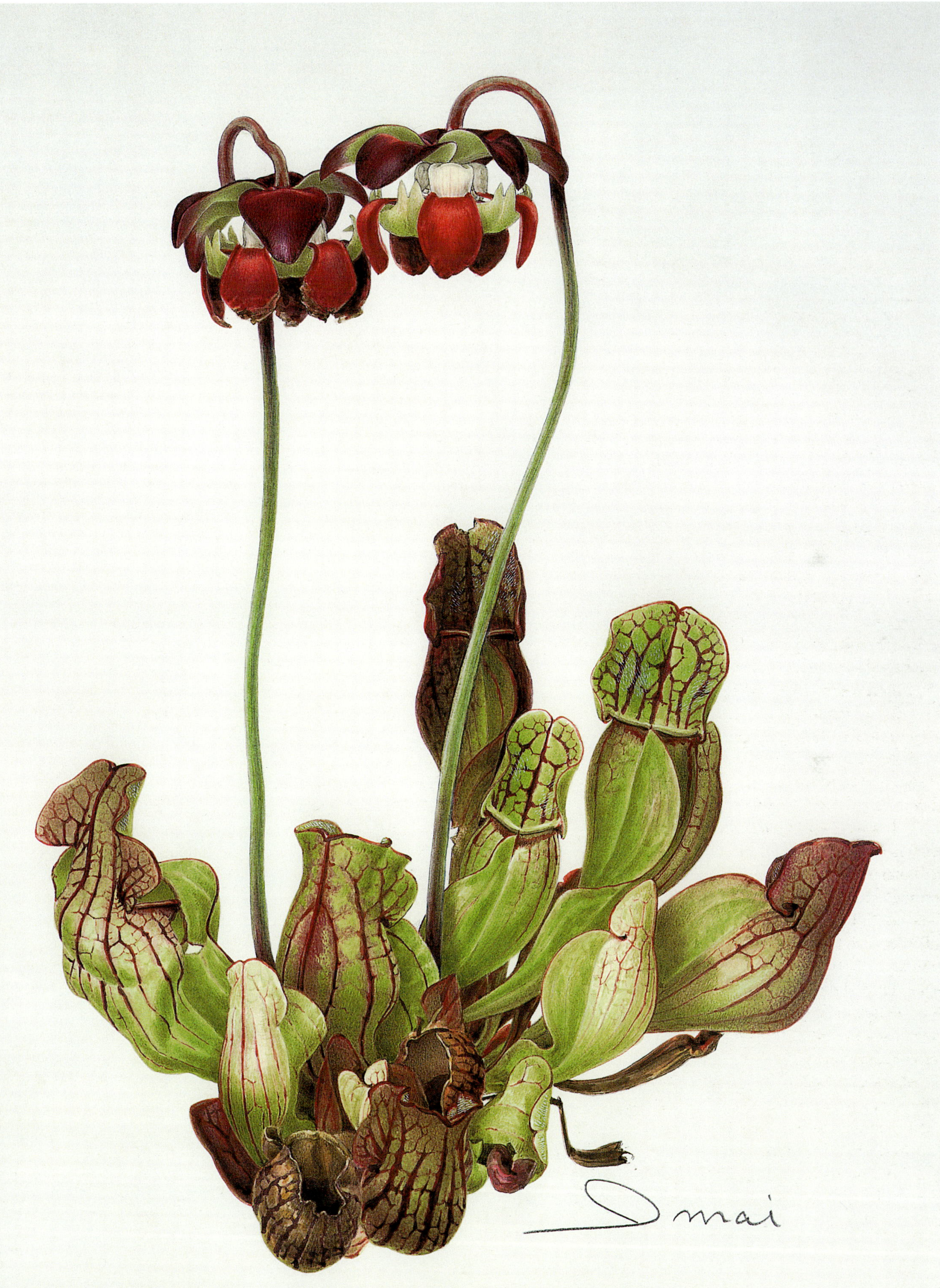
Imai

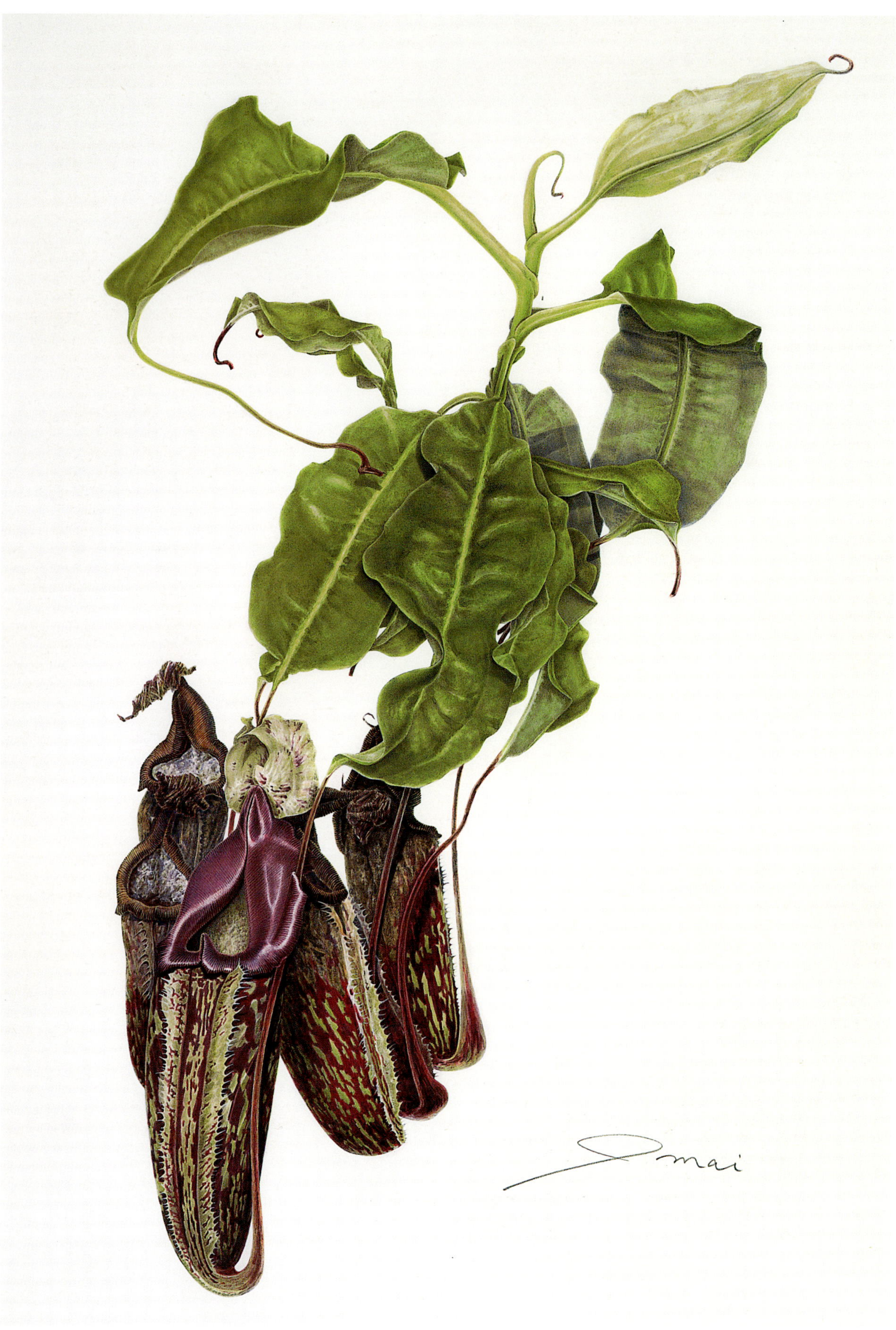

NEPENTHES MAXIMA
'SUPERBA'
(Left) Signed Imai (days worked on painting & date in Japanese)
Acquired from the artist 1999
Watercolour on paper
765 × 585 mm

NEPENTHES
RAFFLESIANA
(Right) Signed Imai (days worked on painting & date in Japanese)
Acquired from the artist 1999
Watercolour on paper
630 × 480 mm

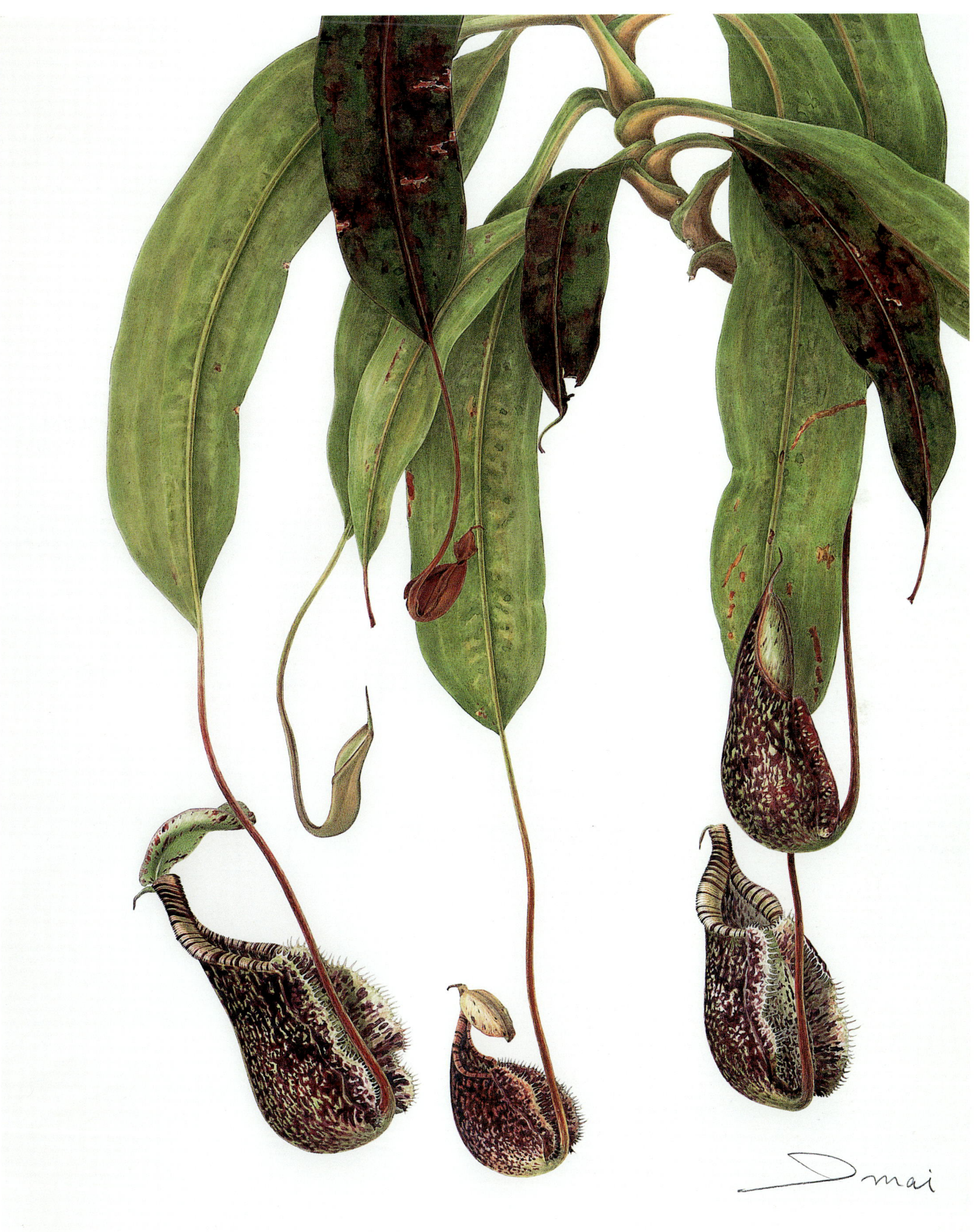
Imai

absorbed as a nutritious brew which supplements the plant's meagre bog habitat with extra nutrients. All but the *Aeginetia indica* were signed with her sprawling signature. Like many artists she notes the number of days she was absorbed with painting each study. The *Sarracenia purpurea* took fifteen concentrated days in May 1992.

She moved to the small village of Yuzamachi, in Yamagata province in 1997 where she lives in a house that her friends describe as a mountain hut. It is in the north of Japan's main island, very remote and snowed in until April. She spends her winters shovelling snow and painting the species of *Asarum* which she grows herself and which flower at that time. In the late spring and summer she sows vegetables and spends a great deal of time out of doors, cultivating her potatoes, carrots and beans. She assures me that she is not a 'cloud-eating sage' but works hard for her living, growing much of her own food.

She has been giving botanical painting classes at Mito Botanical Gardens for over ten years and still goes there about eight times a year, even though the journey from Yuzamachi to Miko now takes as long as the actual two days she teaches there. In 1999 the Gardens produced a special booklet to celebrate her decade of teaching which included fourteen illustrations of her own work followed by paintings executed by her students.

All the watercolours I have by Mariko Imai are of rather strange plants – an obscure orchid, exotic insect-trapping climbers – certainly not ordinary garden flowers. I think she finds these unusual, rather sinister plants satisfying to paint, revelling in their interesting shapes and subtle colours.

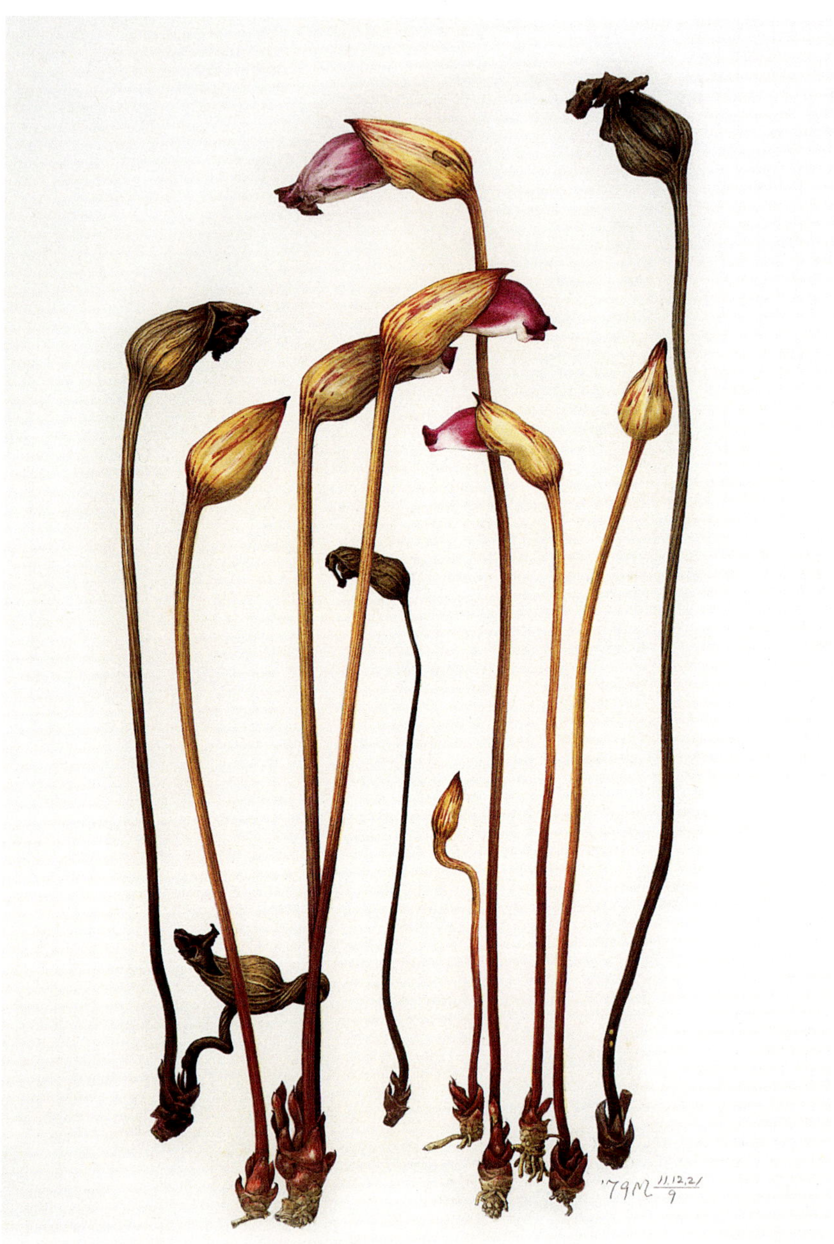

AEGINETIA INDICA

(Above) Signed '79 M. 11.12.2
Christmas Card from the artist 1999
Watercolour on paper
270 × 190 mm

NEPENTHES TRUNCATA

(Right) Signed Imai (days worked on painting & date in Japanese)
Acquired from the artist 1999
Watercolour on paper
540 × 385 mm

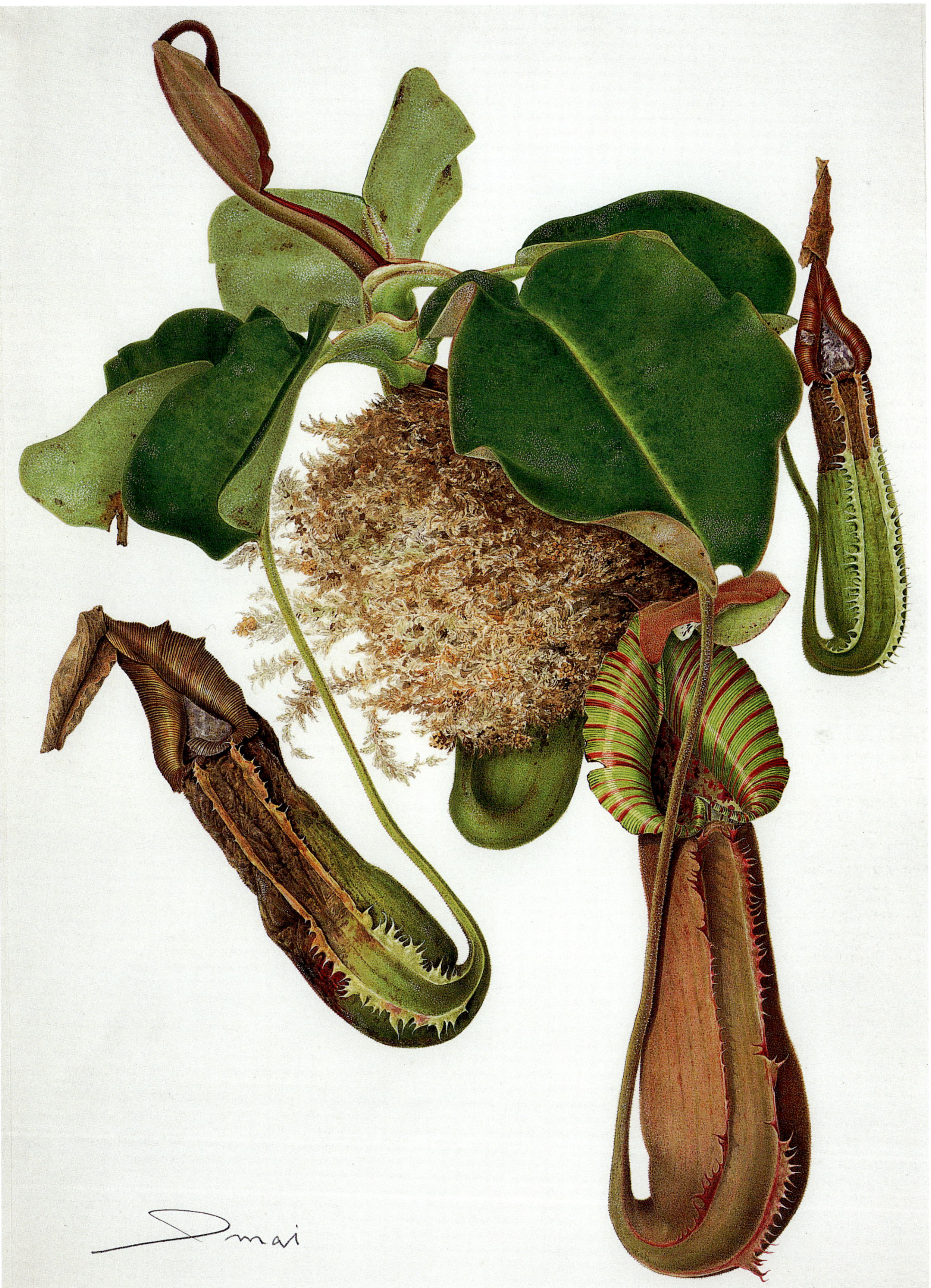

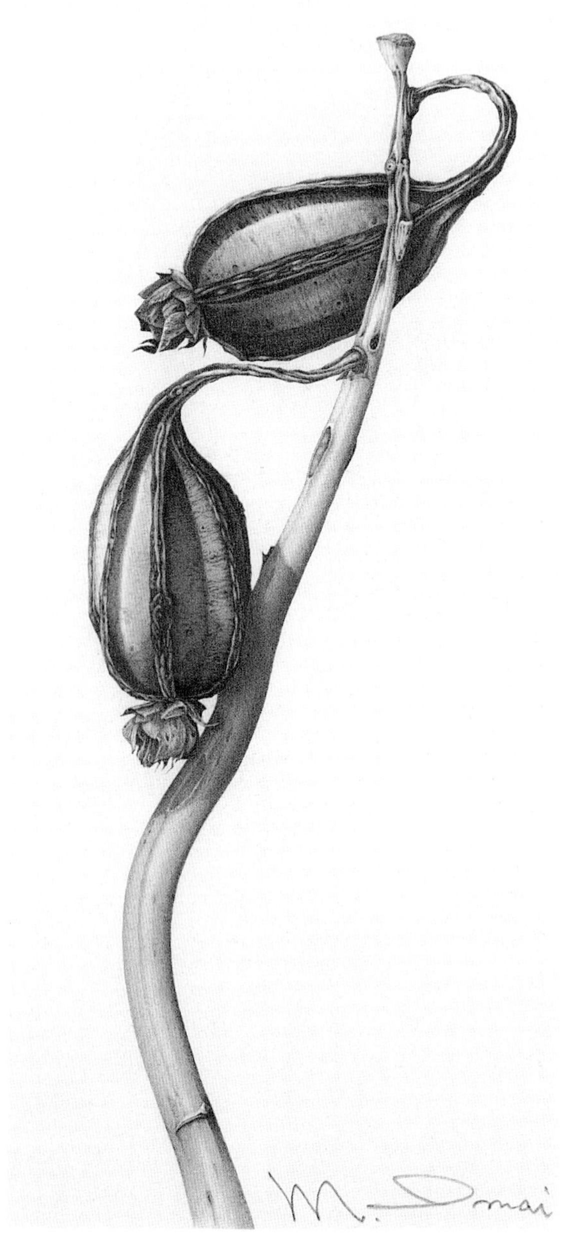

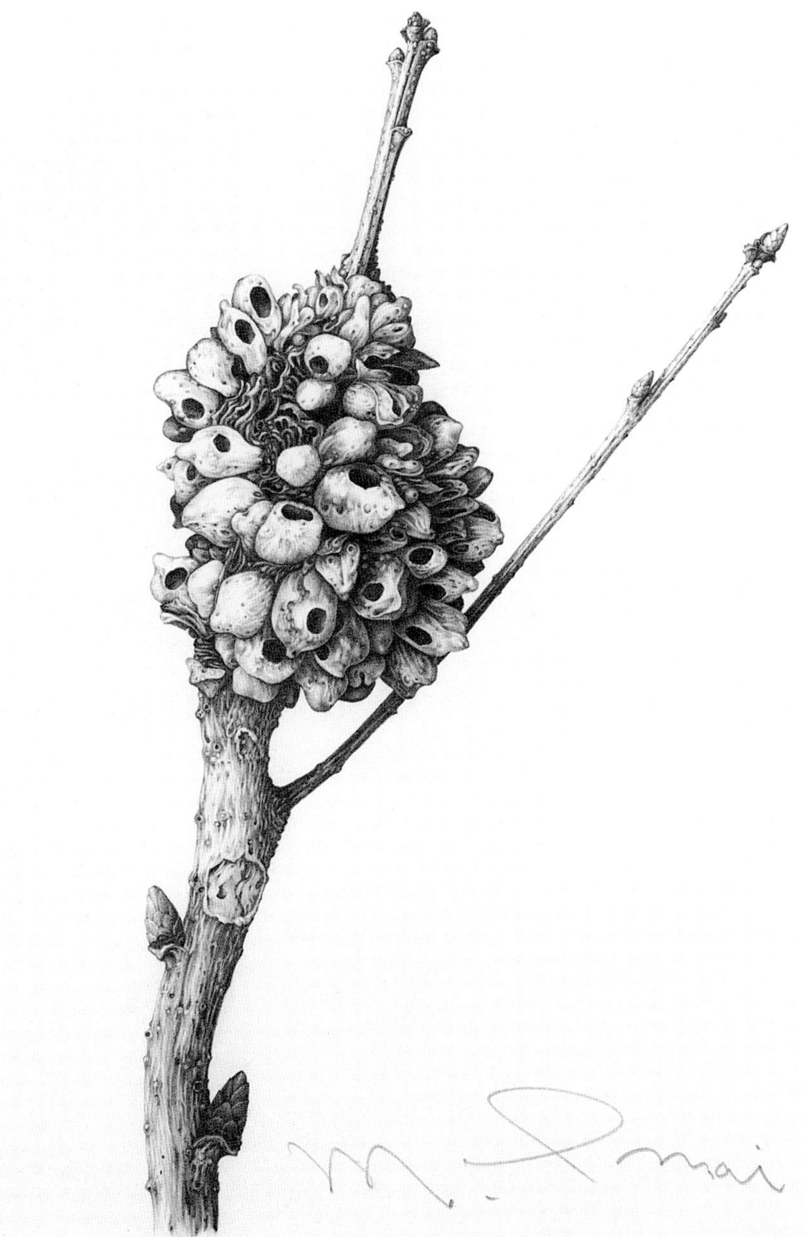

SEEDS OF EBINE OR JAPANESE WILD ORCHID (Left)
TROUBLED TREE OR INSECT BITTEN TREE (Centre)
SEEDS OF MORNING GLORY (Right)
Signed M. Imai (undated)
Gift from the artist 1995
3 early pencil sketches on paper
260 × 120 mm, 240 × 170 mm, 230 × 160 mm

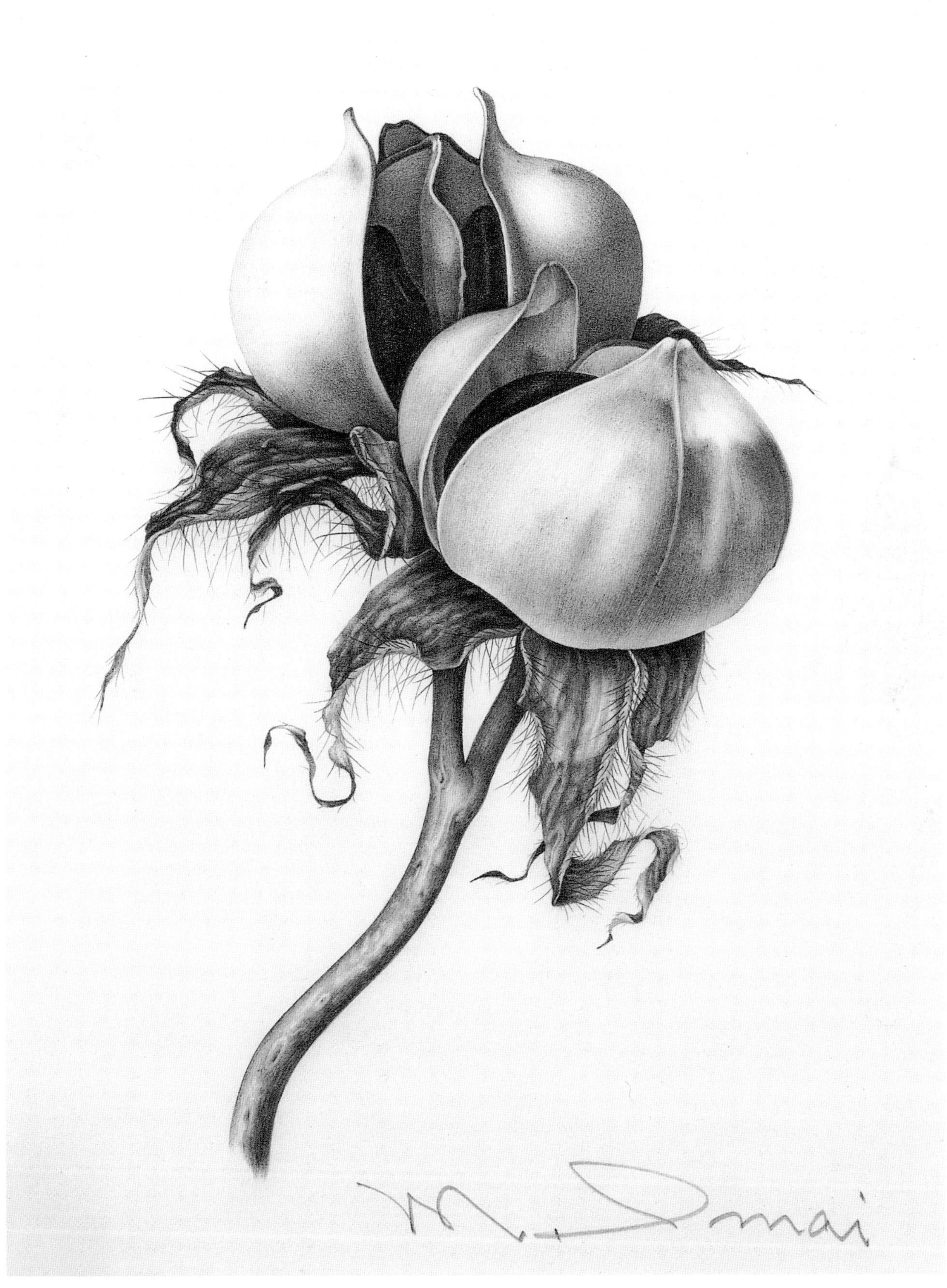

Mieko Ishikawa

BORN TOKYO, JAPAN 1950

Cherry blossom is a time of great celebration in Japan, poets wax lyrical, lovers picnic in the parks and the streets of Tokyo are garlanded with flowers (albeit plastic). Painting the blossoms has become almost a national passion, so I made the assumption that it would be easy to find wonderful paintings of cherries in flower in Japan. But I was wrong. Cherry blossom is so special and revered that it is rare for a botanical artist to sell to a Westerner.

So it is with great pleasure that I can show these two studies of blossom in this book and in my exhibitions. I was introduced to Mieko Ishikawa by Kazunori Kurokawa who held her work in great esteem. We drove to her apartment in Fuchu, Tokyo and I noticed the cluster of flower pots on her doorstep (all botanical artists, world-wide, grow plants whether they have a garden, a farm or a window box). We went up to her studio and study where she showed me some of the many books she has illustrated. She told me she was particularly interested in cherries and was working on a series of paintings, triggered by Junzo Fujishima, her teacher from 1986 to 1989 who was studying cherry blossom. She showed me about a dozen watercolours of different varieties that she eventually wanted to publish. They were very delicate, fresh studies, capturing the ephemeral nature of the flowers while giving due emphasis to the bright young foliage.

Later I met her again when she was showing at the Hunt Institute in Pittsburgh at the 8th International Exhibition. I was fascinated with the study she showed of Japanese acorns. She did a rather similar painting for me after a trip to Borneo, a neat, precise and very satisfying design.

Mieko Ishikawa showed an early interest in painting when she was a child and was working in oils in her teens. She graduated from Musashino Art University, enjoying fantasy and super-realistic subjects. She became a freelance illustrator, working especially on childrens' books and she began to concentrate more and more on plants.

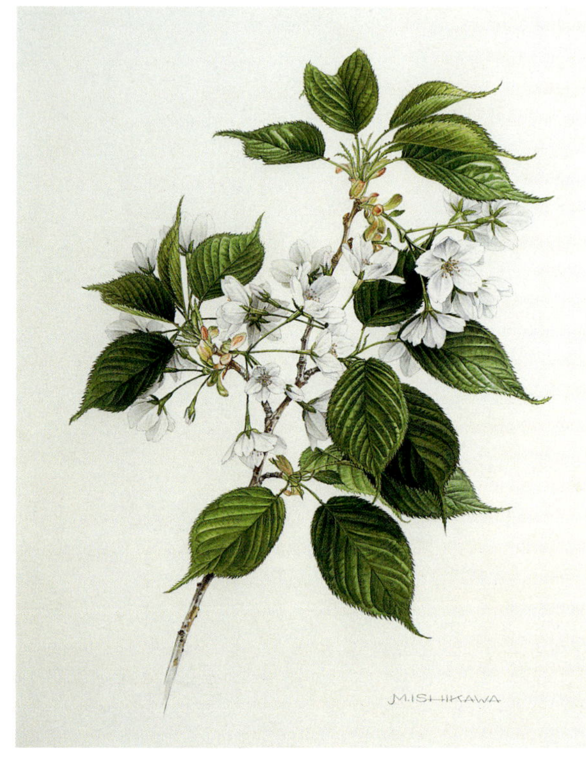

OSHIMA ZAKURA – WHITE CHERRY BLOSSOM: *PRUNUS LANNESIANA* VAR. *SPECIOSA*
Signed M. Ishikawa (undated)
Acquired from the artist 1996
Watercolour on paper
370 × 260 mm

She has done a good deal of teaching, working regularly at the Agahi Cultural Centre, Tachikawa, Tokyo; at Sinjuku, Tokyo; and at several other places including Tokyo Metropolitan Jindai Botanical Park, Chofu, Tokyo.

Mieko has had several one-person exhibitions at the Tama Forest Science Garden, Hachioji, Tokyo and contributed to many group shows in the Okura Gallery and the Jindai Botanical Park, Chofu, Tokyo and her work is held there and in the Hunt Institute, as well as the Flower Museum, Chiba.

Recently she has been concentrating on cherry blossom, conifers and rainforest plants. Every summer she visits rainforests in southeast Asia and she may well concentrate on them for future subjects. Currently she is producing black and white drawings of newly discovered rainforest species for a scientific paper.

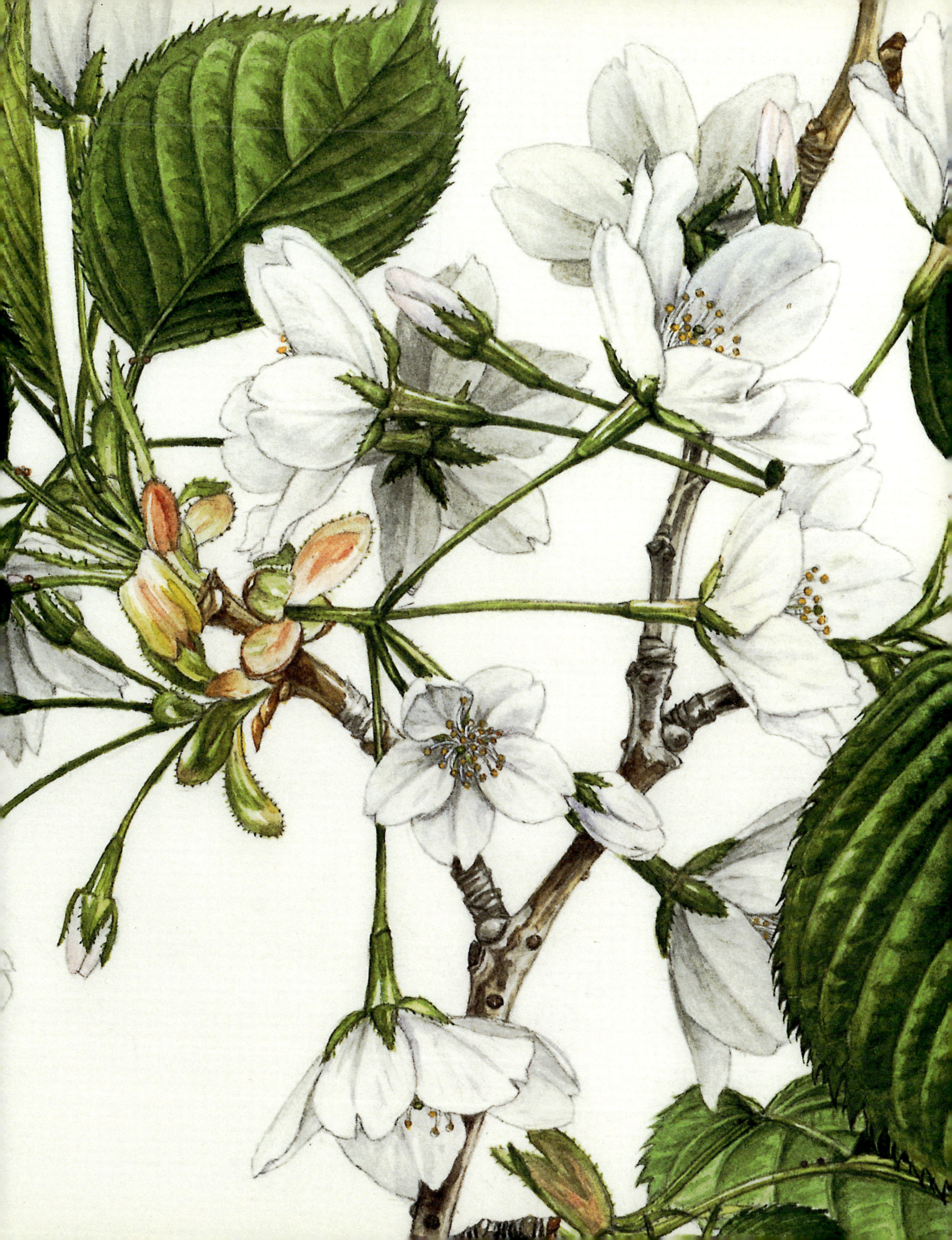

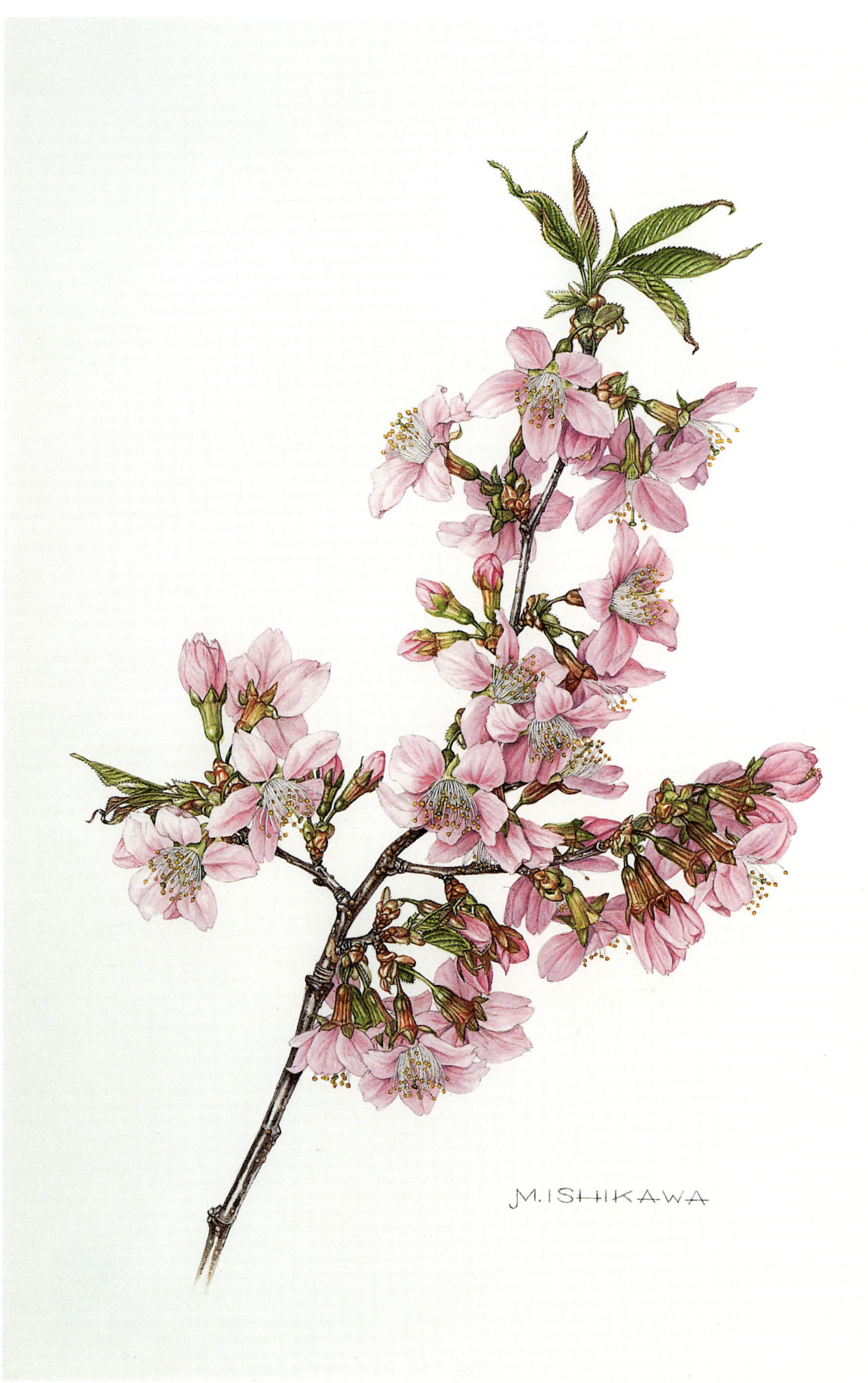

HIMALAYAN CHERRY:
PRUNUS CERASOIDES
(Left) Signed
M. Ishikawa (undated)
Acquired from the
artist 1996
Watercolour on paper
540 × 450 mm

ACORNS FROM
BRUNEI
(Right) Signed
M. Ishikawa (undated)
Acquired from the
artist 1997
Watercolour on paper
200 × 130 mm

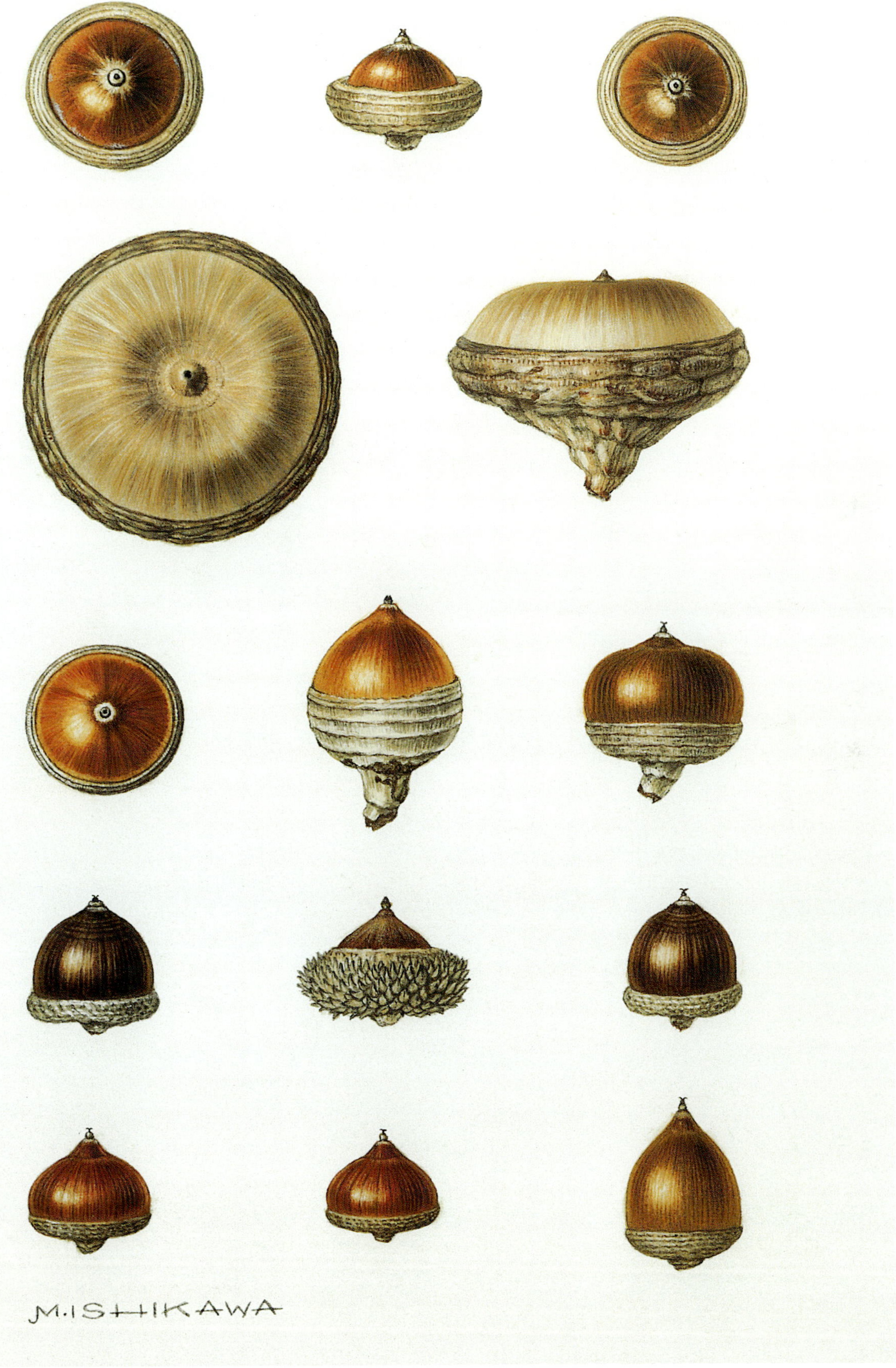
M.ISHIKAWA

Rebecca John

Born London, England 1947

In a masterly introduction to Rebecca John's first solo exhibition of botanical paintings at the Lefevre Gallery no less, Grey Gowrie compared her work with that of the late Rory McEwen. I find parallels with Richard Carroll's still-life studies and Kate Nessler's work on vellum recently seen in Jonathan Cooper's Park Walk Gallery. All these artists have an intense, tightly focused viewpoint, all are conscious of the space around their work.

She was drawn into painting plants by a project she did researching 200 paintings for three books by Elizabeth David. Her meetings with Elizabeth David and their discussions about still-life paintings inspired Rebecca John to pursue her first love, drawing plants. She started painting botanical subjects in 1984 and eventually attended a course at the English Gardening School in 1994, taught by Anne-Marie Evans, where she was awarded a distinction. She interrupted her botanical career in 1996 to curate a magnificent touring exhibition of her grandfather Augustus John's drawings, the culmination of years of research. She also wrote a biography of her father, Admiral Sir Caspar John, which was published in 1987 by Collins.

Rebecca John lives partly in London and partly in a cottage in mid-Wales where she found the subject matter for her recent paintings – twigs and branches of ancient gorse, encrusted with lichen and mosses.

Her first major show, at the Lefevre Gallery, London was a complete sell-out, with the opening night crammed with an excited and admiring crowd. Martin Summers, who had introduced her to the gallery, was delighted with her success, telling me how he visited her remote cottage to encourage her.

Her second show was in New York in April and May 2000 at Davis & Langdale Company, Inc. I received a notice of the show when I was actually in New York and luckily I was able to see the twenty-five paintings before the opening. I was shown the work by Cecily Langdale, an expert on Gwen John, Rebecca's great-aunt. The paintings had a much larger range of subject for, although there was still a number of her lichen-encrusted branches as shown at Lefevre, there were also some delicate studies of thistles, roses and cones, all observed in subdued, quiet tones. Most were watercolour over pencil on paper but there were four works on vellum.

It will be interesting to see how she develops in this expanding and demanding field of painting after such a spectacular start.

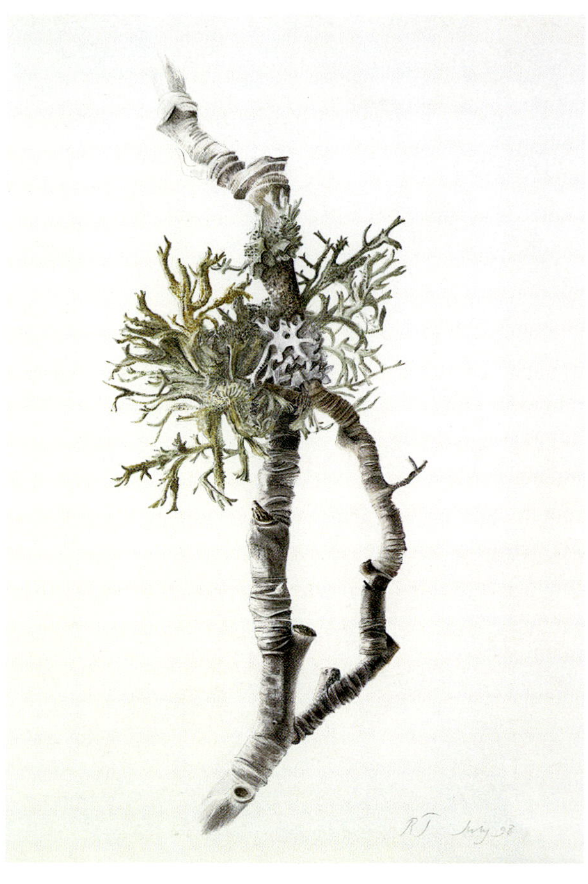

LICHENS ON ROWAN (MAGNIFIED)
(Left) Signed RJ July 98
Acquired from Lefevre Gallery, London 1999
Watercolour over pencil on paper 275 × 185 mm

GRASSES CAUGHT IN BLACKTHORN
(Right) Signed RJ Sep 98
Acquired from Lefevre Gallery, London 1999
Watercolour over pencil on vellum 295 × 210 mm

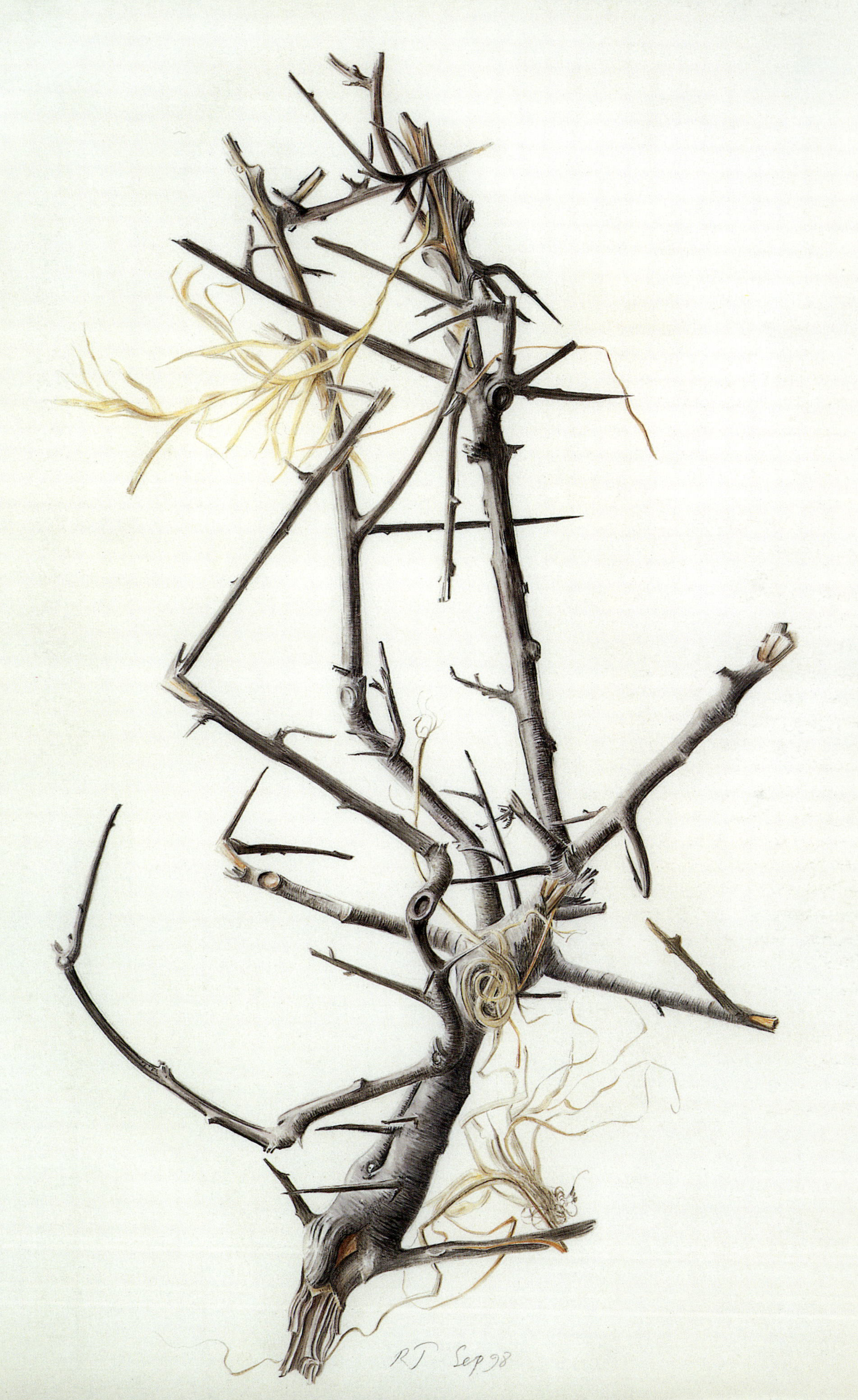
RT Sep 98

Paul Jones

BORN SYDNEY, AUSTRALIA 1921–97

Paul Jones died in Sydney in 1997 after a long battle with illness. He asked me to visit him a couple of years earlier as he wanted me to see the works he had put aside during his active painting periods, and with which he was most satisfied. We had long discussions on flower painting and what distinguishes some as works of art. I asked him to write down his thoughts so I could include them here. At those meetings I looked through a number of his paintings, most executed much earlier, and selected eleven. He wanted to tidy them up and sign them so he sent them to me later. Some were relatively small, delicate watercolours like the violets and camellias shown here; others were large, imposing and dramatic like the sunflower, lilies and magnolia. I also chose *Banksia serrata* and the waratah as characteristic Australian plants.

As we sat in his charming house he told me of his experiences as a young man in England. He had been commissioned to paint camellias by a wealthy enthusiast, Mrs Leslie Urquhart, who lived in a vast manor house in Sussex. Two volumes of the proposed five-volume series were eventually published, with some plates by Raymond Booth. He showed me the two published volumes containing twenty plates in Volume I and sixteen in Volume II, explaining that he had painted enough for the unpublished Volume III as well. He told me that he never discovered what happened to the originals of the remaining works he painted for her. When Mrs Urquhart died the proceedings of her estate went to the RSPCA. Paul Jones was awarded an OBE for his work on camellias.

After I returned to London, Paul sent me a curious footnote to his camellia story. Immediately after he had written me his account of his early work with Mrs Urquhart, he had a letter from the Stark Museum in Texas saying that they had twenty-nine of the original drawings for the camellia books. So after thirty-five years the mystery was partly solved. The Stark Museum had purchased them from an antiquarian bookseller in Chicago, although how they had arrived there is unknown. He was thankful that the drawings were still in existence and would be well preserved.

Paul was very worried that there might be a 'car-boot' sale of his works after he died and I think this

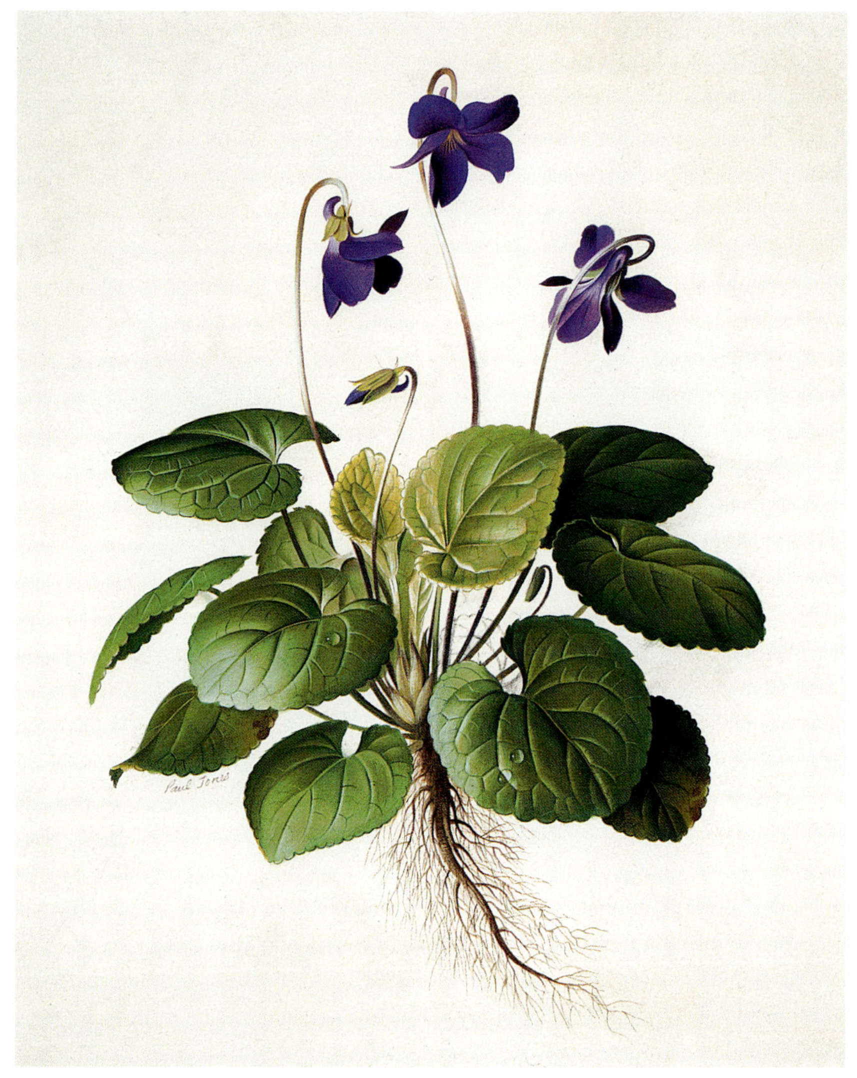

VIOLET PLANT

(Above) Signed Paul Jones
(undated)
Acquired from the artist 1997
Acrylic on paper
245 × 210 mm

FLOWERS OF ERYLDENE

(Right) Signed Paul Jones
(undated)
Acquired from the artist 1997
Watercolour on paper
410 × 310 mm

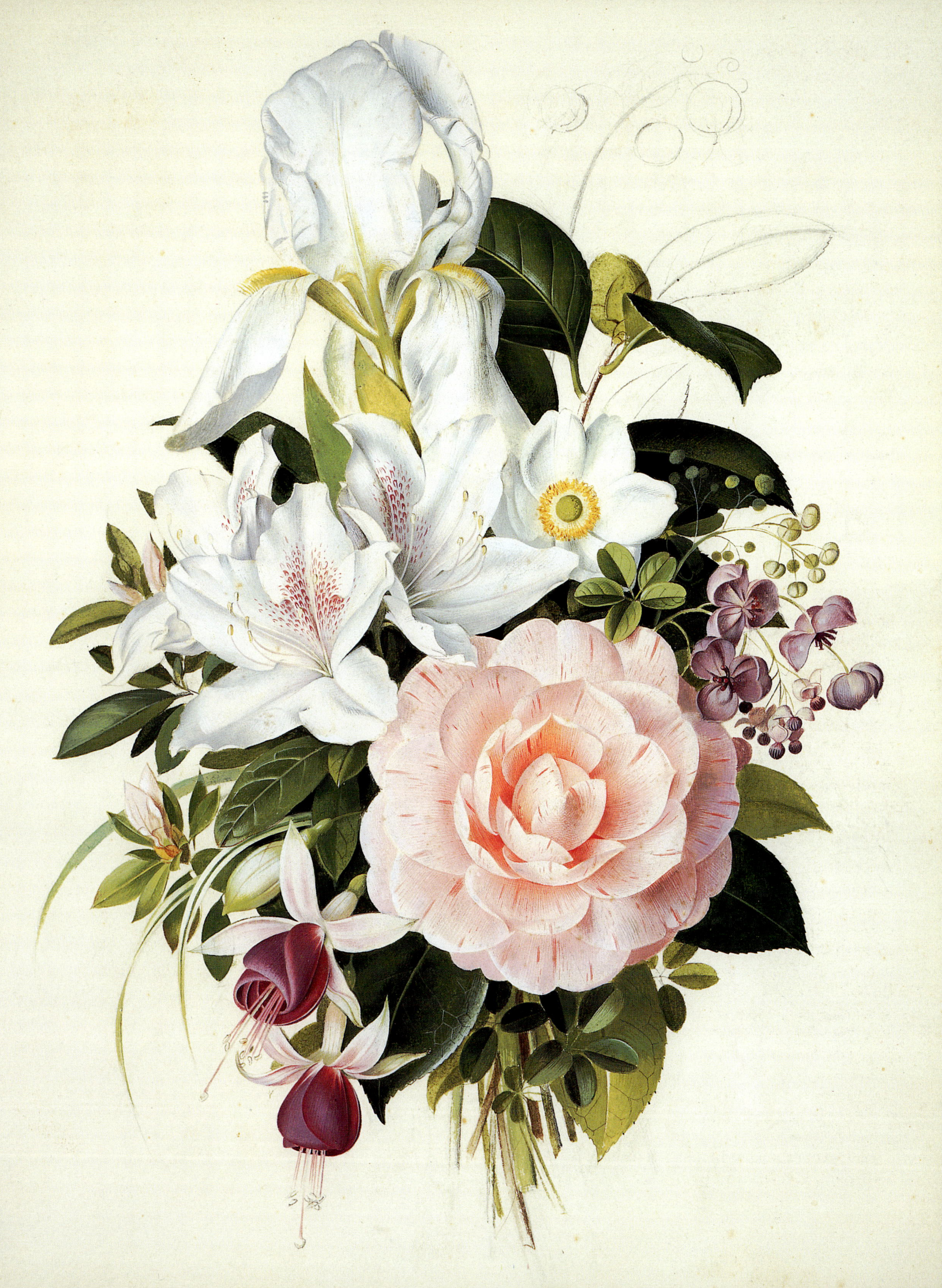

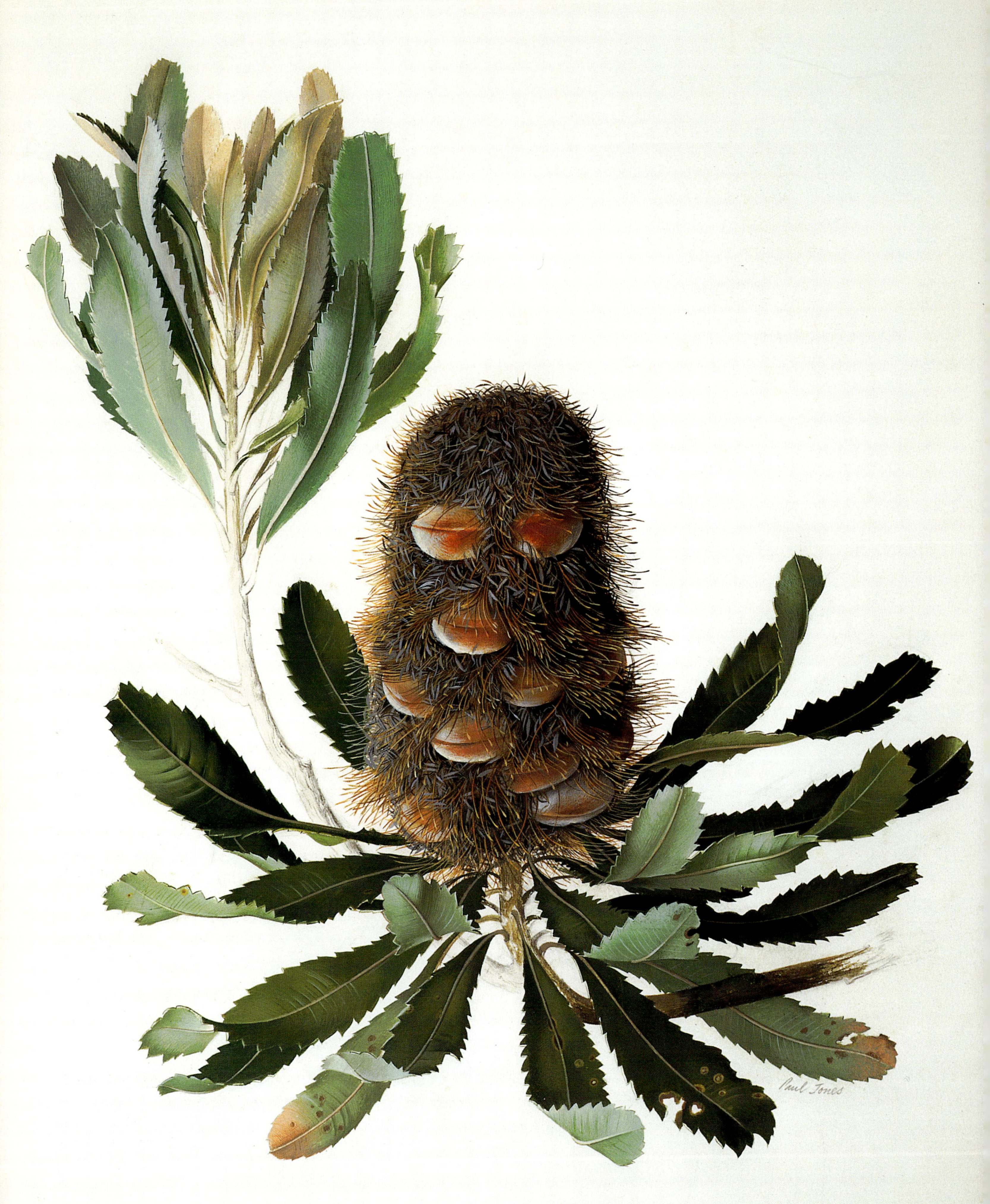
Paul Jones

BANKSIA SERRATA
Signed Paul Jones
(undated)
Acquired from the artist for Charles Sherwood 1997
Acrylic on paper
640 × 500 mm

was one of the reasons he wanted me to see what he considered to be amongst his best work. He need not have been concerned as his sister, Frances Jones, also an artist, arranged an exhibition of his works at the Eddie Glastra Gallery in Sydney in 1998, which turned into a complete sell-out of his remaining sketches and photographs. Shortly after this Frances herself died.

Paul Jones' association with the Tryon Gallery seems to have been much less stressful than his time with the intimidating Mrs Urquhart. He created a series of drawings in the romantic style of Thornton's *Temple of Flora* (1799–1807), published as a new *Flora magnifica* by the Tryon Gallery in 1976. He started by painting his subject in watercolour on plain white paper, then prepared a coloured background of acrylic and painted a second version on top of the acrylic background. My sunflower is the original watercolour painting for the sunflower in the Tryon book, strong and vigorous, in fact so striking that it was chosen for the poster for the exhibition of my collection at Stockholm at Millesgarden Museum in 1999 (see page 8).

My elder son, Charles, has always admired Paul Jones' work and he now has four of his paintings, the two lovely lilies, the powerful waratah and a wonderfully three-dimensional *Banksia*. My younger son, Simon has added the unnamed *Heliconia* that Paul painted in Bougainville, to his small but potent collection. I sent the sunflower around the world on exhibition, but clustered my other new acquisitions together to enjoy them myself. Soon I will send some of them out on exhibition as Paul's work has never failed to draw an admiring audience.

Towards the end of his life Paul experimented with photographic studies of flowers and shells. He only worked in black and white and developed the prints himself. They were of great simplicity and subtlety and certainly rank amongst the best photographic portraits of plants that I have ever seen.

In later years Paul feared for his eyesight and more or less gave up painting. However, he told me that encouraged by my first book *Contemporary Botanical Artists* he found that he could paint in the mornings and so he completed a number of unfinished works that had been sitting in his portfolio for years.

Thoughts on Flower Painting

BY PAUL JONES

There is no one artist who is the supremo of flower painters. Some painters of flowers (and they are indeed, specialists) are more skilful than others, more expert, more observant and have what is called a 'quick eye'. Some have a more emotional approach because of the way they are, some are more poetical, and some more analytical, cerebral and scientific. Sentiment, too, comes into it. One can respond to the style and personality of the flower as we are affected by the personality and presence of people. There are the aristocrats – roses, camellias, iris, lilies and most of the bulbs and peonies. There are the homely cottage flowers – daisies, honeysuckle, nasturtiums. Then there are the strange, unfamiliar and the weird. Of course, there are the sentimental flowers – violets, pansies and forget-me-nots.

Each notable flower painter belongs to his particular period and to spotlight several 'greats', the two most popular and much publicised are, of course, Redouté and Ehret. Redouté belongs very much to his age. His drawings are elegant, perhaps feminine, and certainly much idealised. In my opinion they lack strength and reality. Ehret's drawings are stronger, very Germanic. They are more positive statements, but lack the magic and inspiration of Redouté. There are many other 'greats' of course, but those two spring readily to mind because, perhaps, of over-exposure.

In a more contemporary arena, I must nominate Rory McEwen, whose wonderful paintings I personally find the most original in concept and totally satisfying. His paintings are masculine, have strength and that particular 'something' that cannot be explained. I do believe that if a work of art must be explained, then it is not a work of art. McEwen's concept and appreciation of space contributes such importance to the placement of the subject and is never overpowered by it. The flower takes on a more meaningful dimensional quality and is greatly enhanced by such areas of 'emptiness'.

The painter of flowers must not be intimidated by the presence of the subject. The painter is in control and the flower must do the work. Therefore, take only that which can be of use and ignore that which does not contribute to the drawing as a whole.

What to emphasise, what to eliminate, what to exaggerate? One must be selective and discerning and in total control. There are no short cuts. Adjustments are sometimes necessary. Botanical truth, within reason, is to be observed. How the leaves are placed (nature does not always oblige), the style of the flower, the curve of the stem, how strong to make the foliage; the flower head is, after all, as important as the foliage. The most difficult of all, I suppose is a white flower with strong, dark foliage – a white camellia perhaps. The flower is important, but how to subordinate the leaves so that the bloom dominates? Judicious placement of the foliage dark against white is one way, or tonal contrast, that is, an exaggerated difference between the pale tones and the dark tones. The tones in a white flower are never as dark as they look; they are used only to define the flower, otherwise the flower looks greyish when it should be white. There is nothing as white as the paper unless gouache is used, then, there is nothing as white as white paint.

Generally, the simplest realisations are the most elusive. Important also, are the spaces between the leaves – the voids. These empty spaces should be graceful and of equal value to the overall drawing as are the solids. Clumsy foliage arrangement and awkward foreshortening is usually the cause of such trouble. It is better to avoid difficult foreshortening altogether. It will never be missed. Be aware therefore, of this difficulty and be sure that it will not happen during the initial planning stage. A petal may be plucked out and a leaf altered or removed.

Eliminate, simplify. There is a method of delineation for every flower in terms of making marks on paper with tone and with washes of colour – anything suggesting the third dimension must be explained and with conviction. This can only be achieved with what is called 'shading'. Some flowers, as we know, are less trouble than others. It is essential to thoroughly understand the basic principles of form and how it can be affected by the direction of the light. The five forms upon which all natural objects are based are the sphere, the cube, the cone, the ovoid and the cylinder. There is more strength in a straight line than a curved one – all curved lines can be reduced to angles, therefore

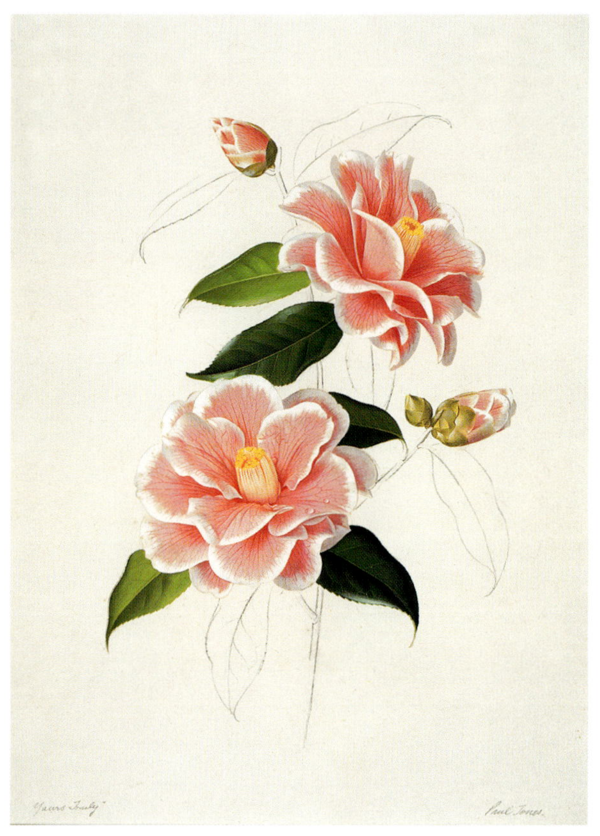

WARATAH
(Right) Unsigned & unfinished
Acquired from the artist for Charles Sherwood 1998
Acrylic on paper
540 × 410 mm

CAMELLIA 'YOURS TRULY'
(Left) Signed Paul Jones 'Yours Truly'
Acquired from the artist 1997
Watercolour on paper
430 × 310 mm

always see in angles, not curves. Also it is very important to understand the principle of the ellipse and how to draw it diagrammatically. A scant knowledge of perspective is useful, too. An awareness of the substance of the subject is essential, whether it is translucent, semi-translucent or opaque. A gardenia, for example, looks as if it was made from white kid or doeskin. It has a dark, shiny foliage. The Australian flannel flower, could well be made of flannel and one has to examine it closely to ensure that it is not! Camellias, generally, are opaque – even leathery – but they can also be translucent.

Remarkable, of course, is the lacquered surface of the buttercup. Peonies are semi-translucent and have the sheen of the finest silk. The daffodil is both opaque and translucent – a good example. Poppies are like crinkled silk. Be mindful of the texture of that which is being painted. The iris is, obviously, translucent, but perhaps the most telling example of translucency, is the sweetpea. Such awareness of all this is so important. If a flower appears fragile or solid, then it must be likewise in the painting. The flower of all the cactus family is absolute satin and

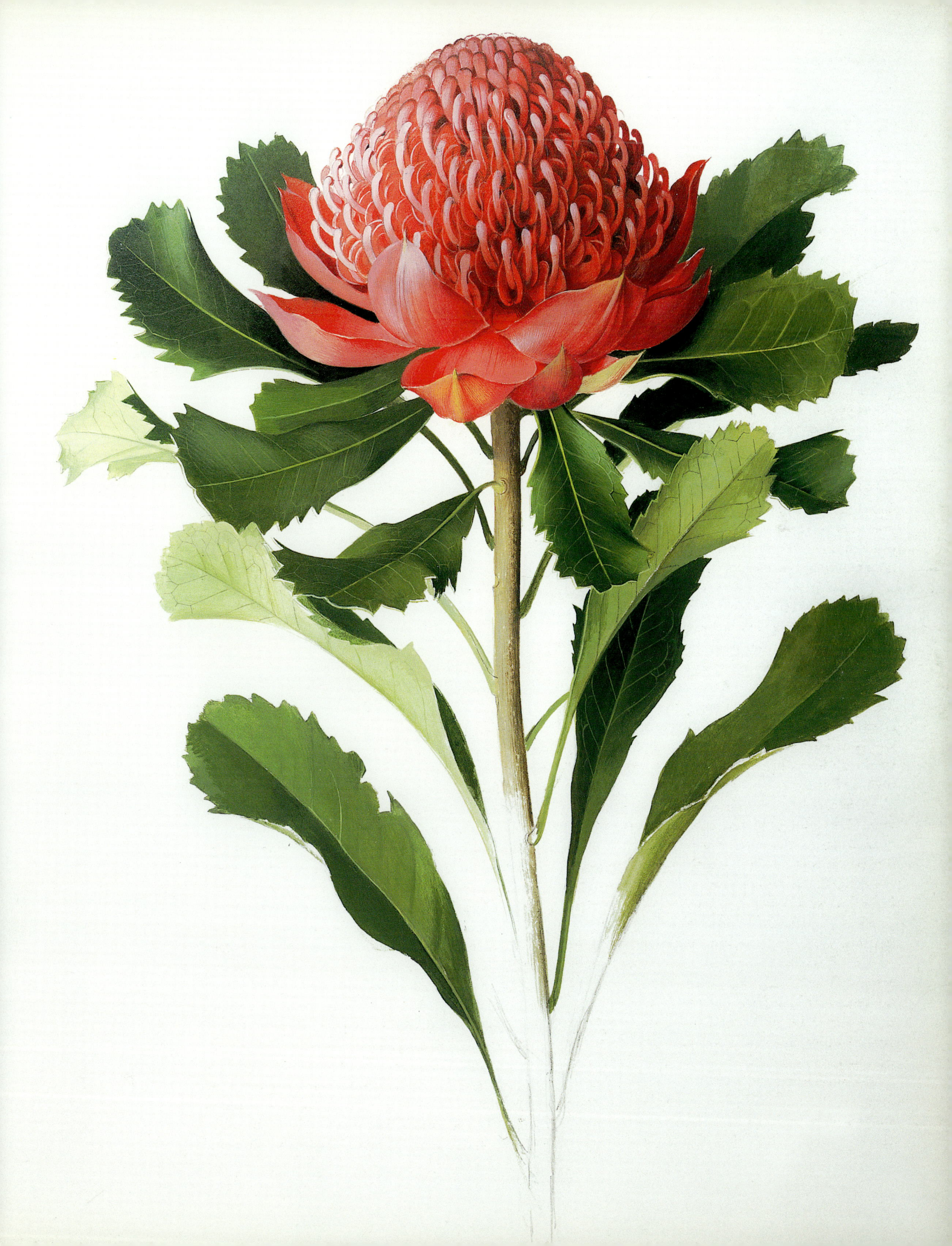

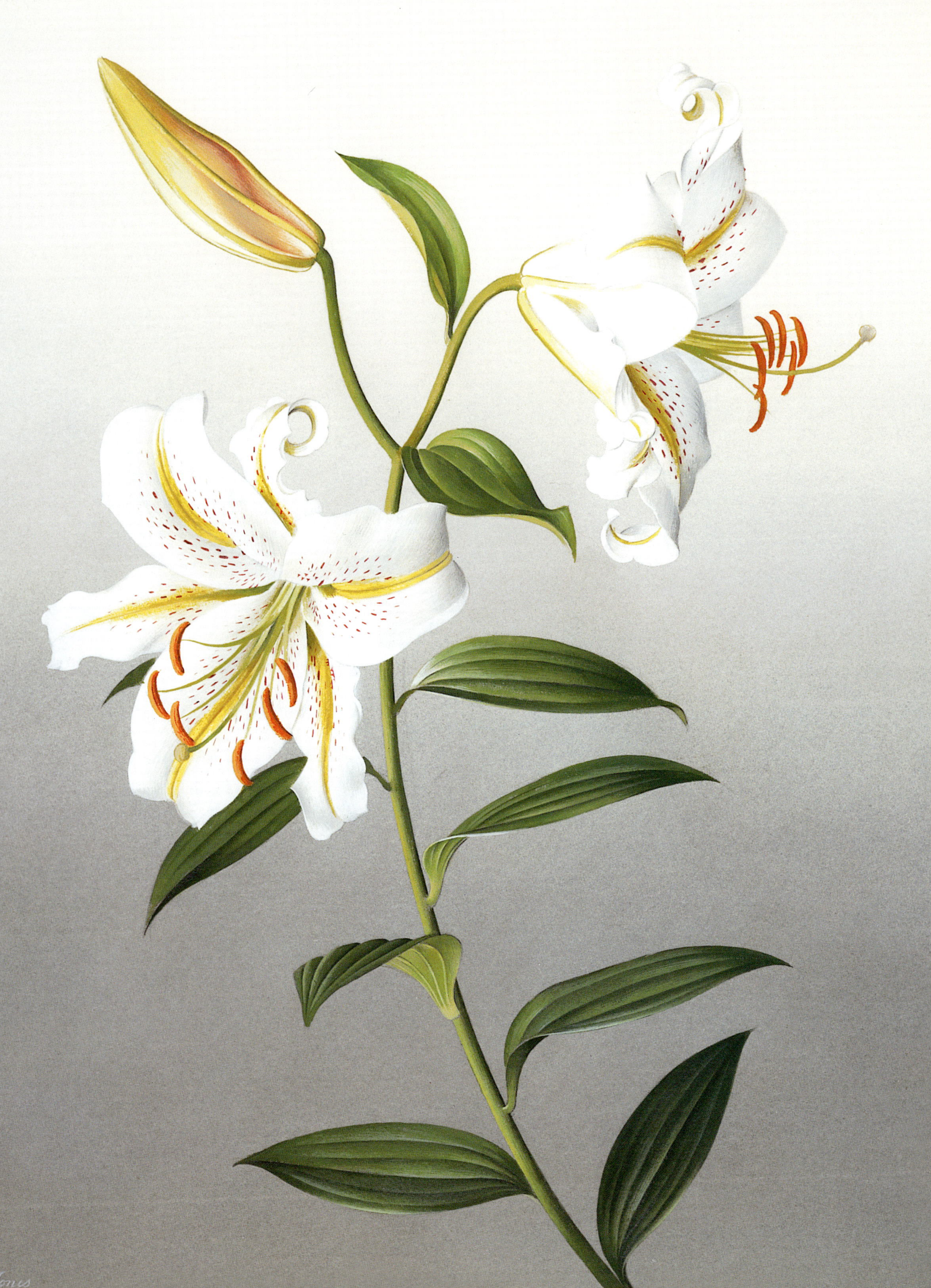
Paul Jones

LILIUM 'LIMELIGHT'
(Left) Signed Paul Jones (undated)
Acquired from the artist for Charles Sherwood 1997
Acrylic on paper
650 × 500 mm

LILIUM AURATUM
(Right) Signed Paul Jones (undated)
Acquired from the artist for Charles Sherwood 1997
Acrylic on paper
680 × 470 mm

not easy to simulate. The gaudy, red anthuriums look more like plastic than plastic itself and the leaves are intensely opaque. In some plants there is this strange resemblance between nature and woven fabrics. The absolute whiteness of the white platycodon has the crispness of starched cotton, as though it has been snipped out of this fabric. The mandevilla, as well, is opaque and resembles fine white linen. Remarkable, too, is the pendulous *Strongylodon*, or jade vine of the tropics. It is so like turquoise plastic, and such an improbable colour in the plant world, that when I saw it for the first time in Lae Botanical Gardens, Papua New Guinea, I thought it was a hoax! Then there is the almost black *Tacca*, which looks quite evil and is known as the devil's tongue. A good example of a flower that is not 'pretty'. The curious black pansy could well be made from black taffeta and the cockscomb or *Amaranthus*, is so like plush that, again, one has to handle it to be convinced that it is real.

Drawing plants is not just a matter of copying shapes and should not be a mere documentation of fact. It must look alive and have a presence. Our response is to this living quality, there are vibrations and the artist must be receptive. There is grace and fine craftsmanship in many of the works of Redouté and in the relaxed groupings of Prévost, which exemplify depth and a third-dimensional quality. This is because of the artists' clever use of tone and strong contrast.

Further to the problem of depicting a white flower on a white background. There are flowers which are well nigh impossible to delineate. The white buddleia on a white background, for example. In reality it has impact, but in a drawing it appears grey as all one has to work with is detail and the overall light and shade. The more detail the worse it becomes. Any white flower projects because it is seen against a normal dark background and all one sees is details and light and shade which defines the overall form. Many tones can be eliminated in order to keep the flower white. Use only the tones which are necessary to describe the form. The whiteness of a flower does not assert itself because the light and shade take over and cause the subject to appear grey. It is not difficult to imagine many Australian wild flowers as being survivors of a primeval forest, such as the Gymea lily,

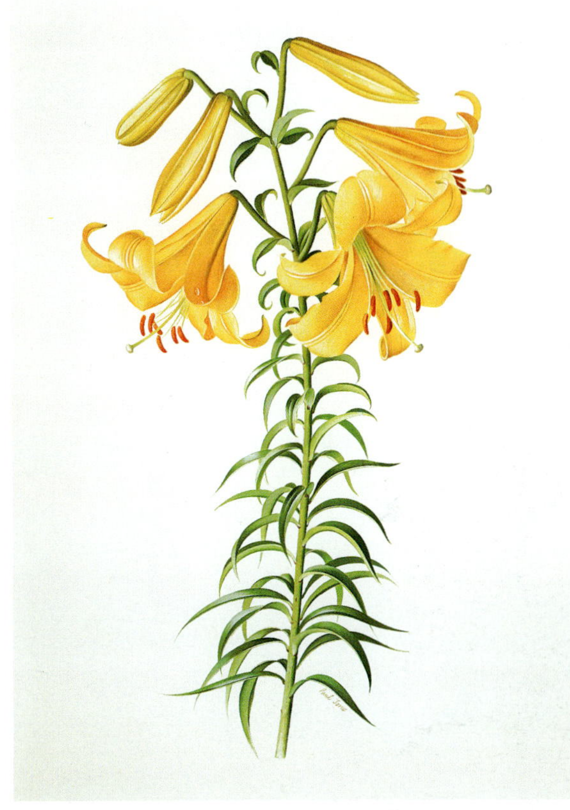

kangaroo paws and many of the heaths and grevilleas. Members of the vast *Protea* family, which includes the Australian banksias, look as though they have come from a primitive forest. Such flowers require strong delineation and can not be portrayed as would the more delicate annuals or bulbs. Be aware, therefore, of the particular character of the subject and adjust the technique accordingly.

As already stated, one must not become intimidated by the presence of the flower – sensitive reaction and practised skill can arrest that presence. But it must also have another element – perhaps the most important – and this is the personal 'something' of the artist that can never be acquired through training. Secure, structural drawing is vital since it is the main support and basis of all refinements and subtleties. Strongly stated pen drawings made directly from the flower are the best exercise one can have. Let yourself go, make mistakes; knowing where you have gone wrong is an achievement. As they say, one learns from one's mistakes. If you get your fingers burnt once you will never let it happen again! Be vigorous and direct – take a flower, disregard detail and draw it over and over again, simply and boldly. Make a mess, it doesn't matter if the result is no good. You are gaining all the time, even though it seems hopeless while you are doing it. Any of the lilies are good to draw in this way. They are simple and structurally interesting forms and lend themselves to direct and simple drawing, especially to pen and ink. Technical achievement is no less remarkable than the ability to register the very essence of the flower – that which makes us respond to these most marvellous and heart-warming miracles of nature. This has become a stimulus and an ongoing interest to the botanist and flower artist alike.

Play around with those scratchy pen and washes. As there are countless discoveries which can only be made during execution, this will be of enormous help. Follow the simple principle of strong and subtle contrasts of pure, clean, sharp and decisive edges. This is a basic principle and is applied to any flower or foliage, however complicated. The lumps, wrinkles, contours, undulations, veining are superimposed, but in a less assertive way, although emphasised where necessary. Avoid overloading with crowded detail, as this can disturb the value of the simple and beautiful form of any flower or leaf. Use only that which is essential for botanical and textural purposes. Above all, be positive and if you are making a statement, make it aloud and not in a whisper.

Sureness of touch comes with unrelenting practice. A blank sheet of paper is very intimidating. There must be perfect co-ordination between the eye which observes, the hand which is directed by the eye, and the brain which makes the decisions. All must work in perfect unison. But the real worth and true quality of a memorable drawing can only come from the heart. Every part of one's being is involved and it is total. Talent raises the drawing from ordinary documentation. Flawless technique can astonish only, but fails to capture that particular 'something' which can only be described as 'magic'.

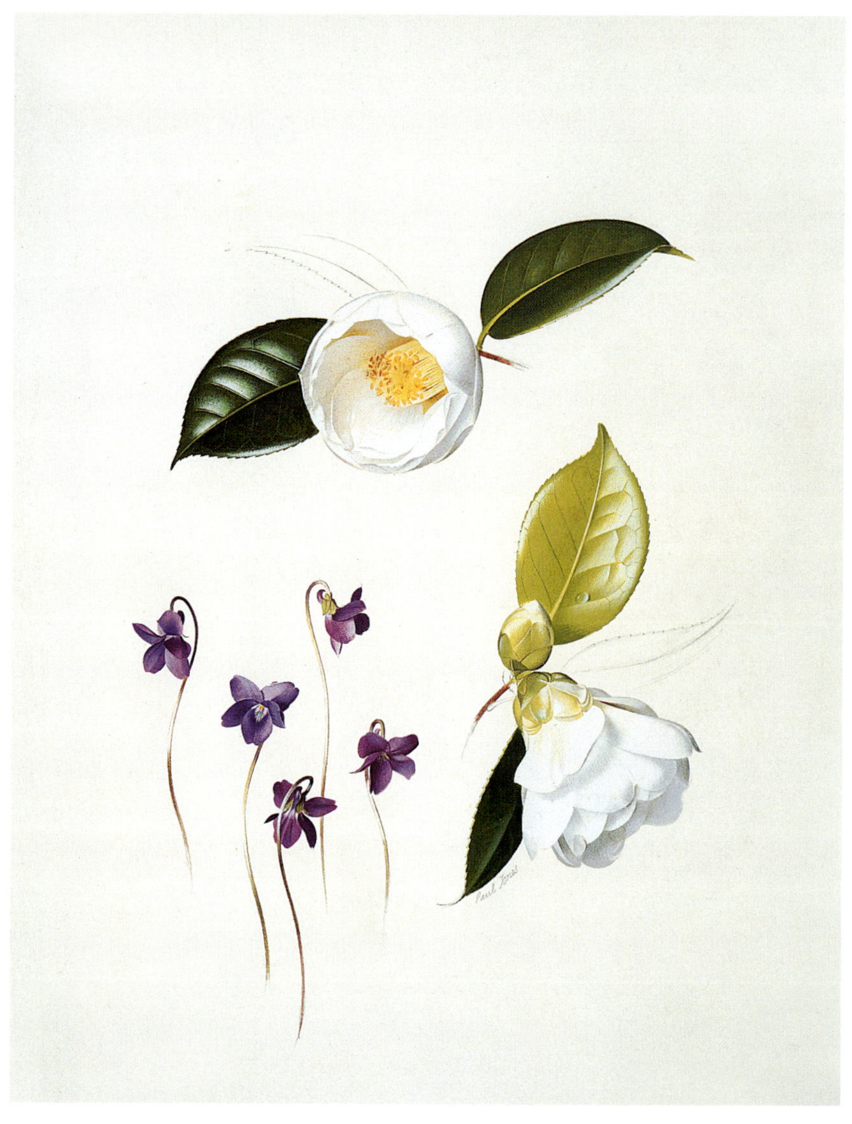

CAMELLIA 'SYLPHIDE' & VIOLETS
(Above) Signed Paul Jones
(undated)
Acquired from the artist 1997
Watercolour on paper
440 × 310 mm

MAGNOLIA
(Right) Signed Paul Jones
(undated)
Acquired from the artist 1997
Acrylic on paper
710 × 540 mm

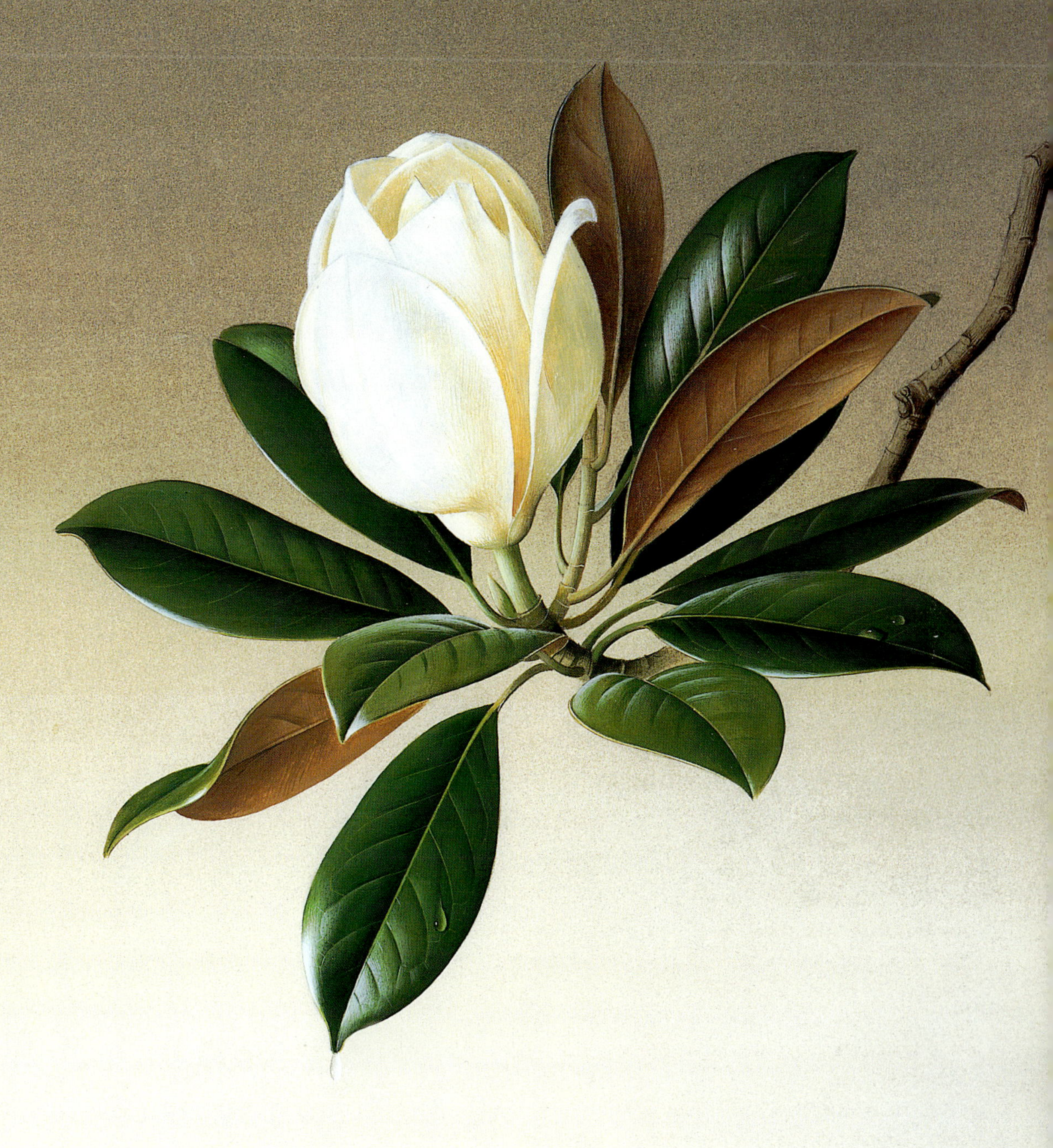

Christabel King

BORN LONDON, ENGLAND 1950

Since 1990, Christabel King has been tutor to many Brazilian students who come to the Royal Botanic Gardens, Kew to work with her under the Margaret Mee Amazon Trust scholarship scheme. She gives them a huge amount of her time and they go back to Brazil enthused and inspired, influenced by her meticulous style and subtle colours, especially with leaves. At the end of each scholar's visit there is a display of their work, showing the most encouraging progress. The work of Margaret Mee scholar, Fatima Zagonel (see page 244 for her entry) was displayed in this manner.

Christabel is a freelance botanical artist although she seems to spend most of her time at Kew. She illustrated a number of books in the 1980s and most recently has painted nineteen plates for *The Genus Galanthus* written by Aaron P. Davis in 1999. She was awarded the prestigious Jill Smythies Award by the Linnean Society of London in 1989.

She is particularly good at cacti, where she achieves a wonderful contrast between their fleshy, succulent, spiny stems and their delicate flowers.

ECHINOCEREUS TRIGLOCHIDIATUS VAR. *PAUCISPINUS*
Signed C F King, *Echinocereus triglochidiatus* var. *paucispinus*, Cult CFK, 17 May 1998
Acquired from the Tryon & Swann Gallery 1998
Watercolour & gouache
290 × 225 mm

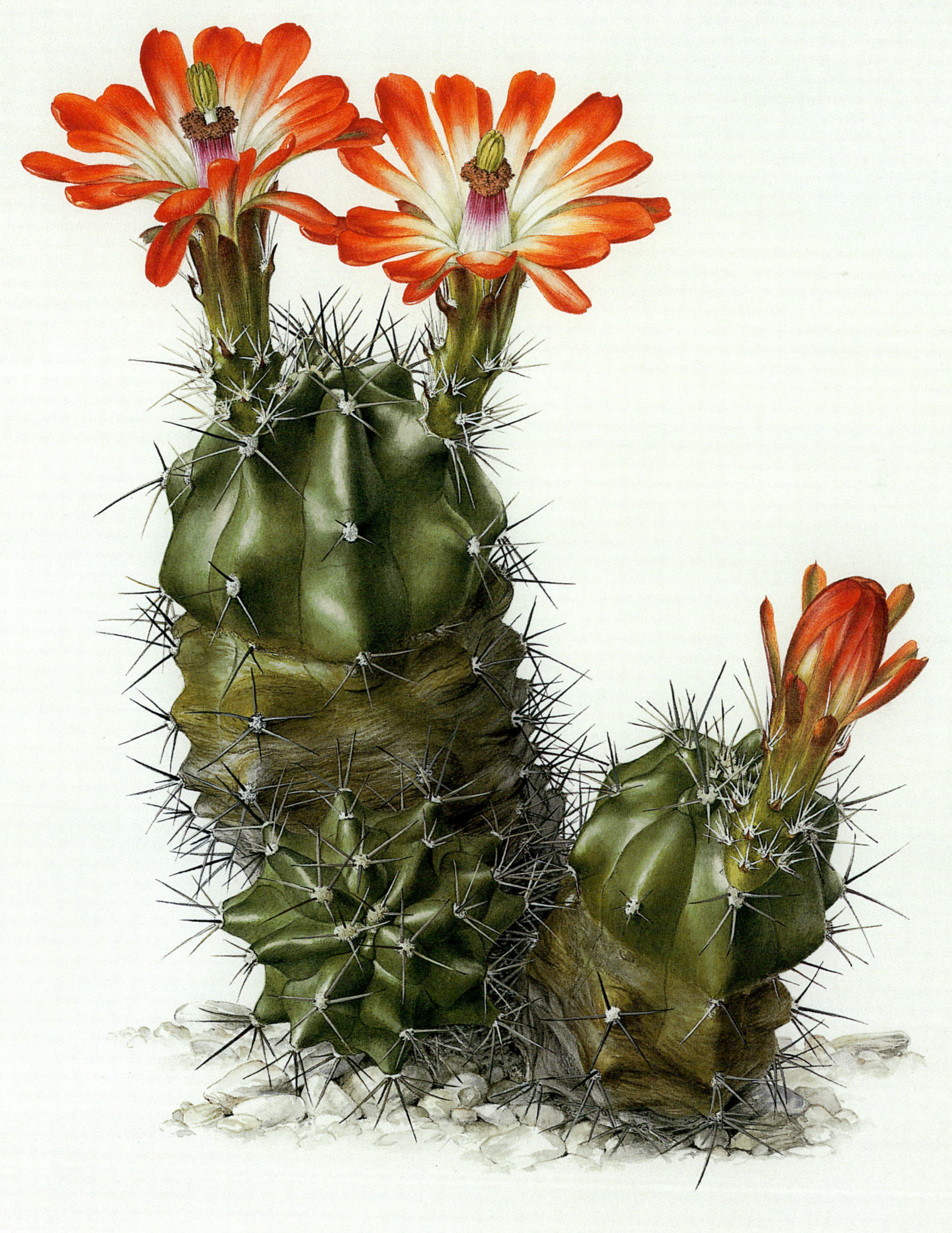

Echinocereus triglochidiatus var. paucispinus

Cult. CFK, 17 May 1998

CF King

Katie Lee

BORN ELDORET, KENYA 1942

Katie Lee's life has been packed with botanical activity over the last few years. She started training as a botanical artist at New York Botanical Gardens in 1989 and swiftly moved into a teaching role there. In 1997 I began an experimental series of classes in Orient-Express Hotels and Katie taught the first one in Charleston Place, South Carolina and the second in the Windsor Court in New Orleans. In both cases the teaching coincided with exhibitions of my collection nearby, in the Gibbes Gallery and the New Orleans Museum of Art. Since then she has taught in Cape Town at the Mount Nelson, the Cipriani Hotel in Venice and visited Gametrackers in Botswana to show artists how to create a Safari Sketchbook. She is particularly qualified to initiate such a sketching course as she has already led groups to the Galapagos, up the Amazon and to Trinidad.

She is now involved with new workshops in Tucson, Arizona, where scientists and artists can study together. This new school called 'Drawing from Nature' will open at the Desert Museum in Tucson, Arizona in 2001. The initial focus will be on pollinators and the flowers they visit and there will be funding for artists-in-residence. Katie will be an advisor, after having helped to set it up. She has illustrated three recent publications: *Underwater with Ogden Nash*, *Undersea City* and *Monarch of Aster Way*.

In 1996 I added another painting of Katie's to my collection of six, a wisteria which she did at Kew on a visit a few years earlier. I have always loved wisteria and have it growing up walls in both my London and country gardens.

She has given a number of solo exhibitions, most recently in the New London Art Society Gallery, Connecticut in 1999. She came to London for the excellent group show at the Tryon & Swann Gallery in 1998 where work from invited artists from all over the world combined to make an exceptional exhibition of the highest calibre.

She is an excellent teacher with a devoted following in the United States. She has reached the point where she is having to pace herself in order to make time for her own painting – always a conflict with professional artists who also enjoy teaching.

WISTERIA AT KEW
WISTERIA FLORIBUNDA
'MULTIJUGA'
Signed KT© 1993
Acquired from the artist 1996
Gouache on Arches 140 lb. Hot Press
720 × 520 mm

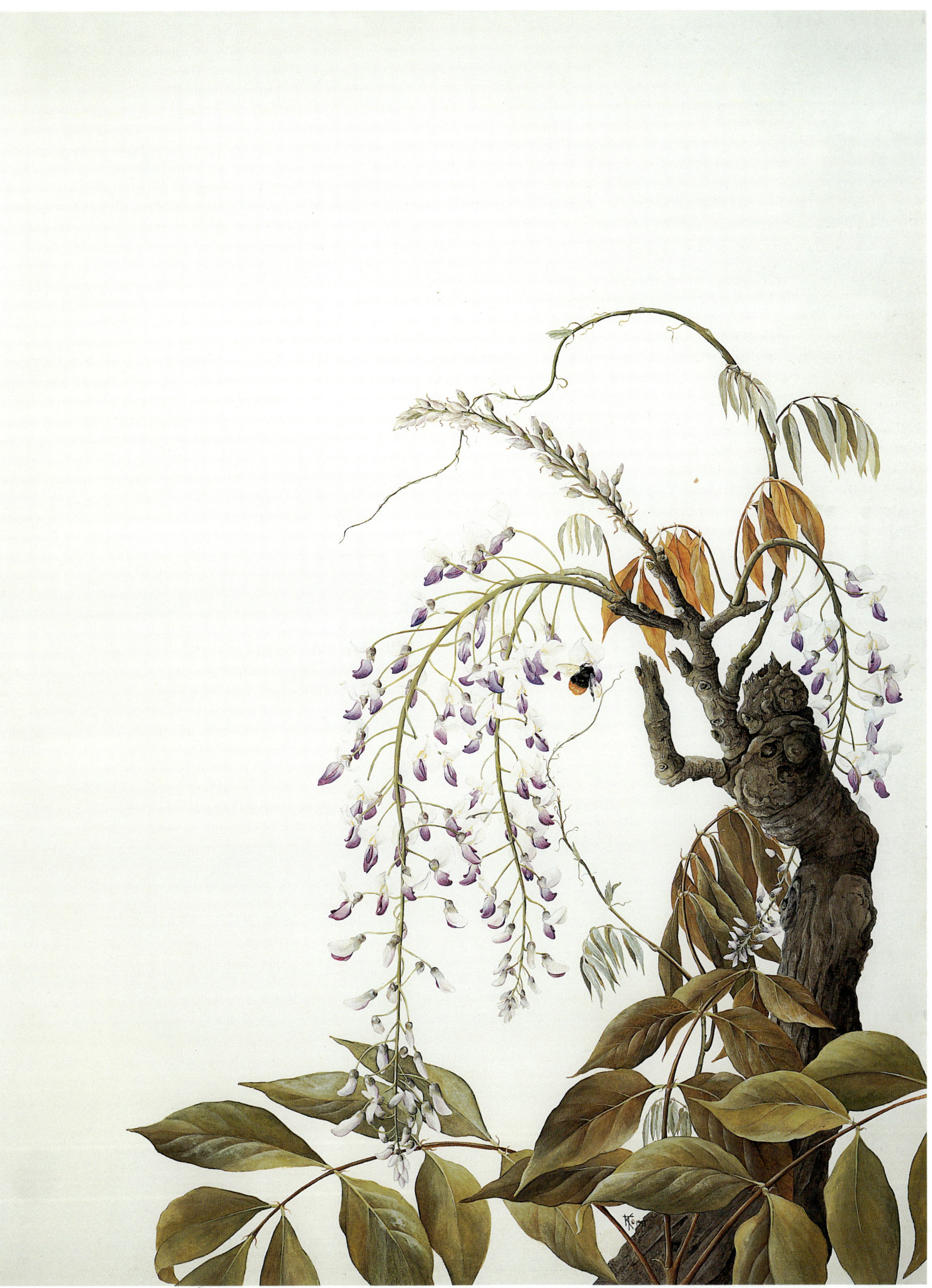

Rory McEwen

Born Scotland 1932–82

Rory McEwen was one of the most important influences in the development of the current renaissance of botanical art. Many artists in my collection saw his retrospective in 1988 and its catalogue has become a treasured record. He inspired some of them to think anew about painting flowers as a serious and worthy subject.

He was a man of many talents; as well as being an outstanding painter he was also a musician and appeared on television in the 1960s. He started painting while still at Eton. and his teacher, Wilfrid Blunt, felt that McEwen was the best artist that had come his way during his long period as art master there.

I have collected four of his paintings over the years, all on vellum, which he reintroduced as his favourite surface and which is being used more frequently today. Some artists are using sheets of vellum that McEwen selected, which were passed on to the Hunt Institute after his death and have been given out by James White since then. One of his paintings is shown in the introduction where works by the established masters of the past are compared with today's outstanding studies (pages 24–5).

I have acquired his painting of an 'Old English Florist Tulip' recently and was amused by the note on the back of the vellum which explains that it came from the Wakefield and North of England Tulip Society, the high command of the tulip-fanciers' world which jealously guards its specialised striped tulips and is the ultimate authority in this area. It is a lovely painting with its curved stem and quietly gleaming 'broken petals'. I noticed before framing it that he had originally drawn the stem much more stiffly; he must have scraped it off to give it a curve, an alteration that is possible on vellum.

Reading Anna Pavord's account of tulip classification, this tulip should be called a 'bizarre' because it has a yellow base colour, marked with red brown, and 'flamed' because the tulip is 'broken' by the tulip virus giving petals with a stripe down the centre which merges with a feathering of colour all around the edge of the petal. The Wakefield and North of England Tulip Society was founded in 1836 and at their shows the tulips are traditionally displayed in brown beer bottles, carried in a beer crate. The society is the only survivor from a long history of tulip-fanciers' competitions, dating back to 'florists' who bred their own special varieties in the seventeenth century.

Another recent acquisition is the 'Ginkgo Leaf' which he apparently picked up in a New York street and probably painted in 1979. He painted a number of 'found' objects at that period and he has deliberately placed it off-centre, conscious as always, of the space around his work.

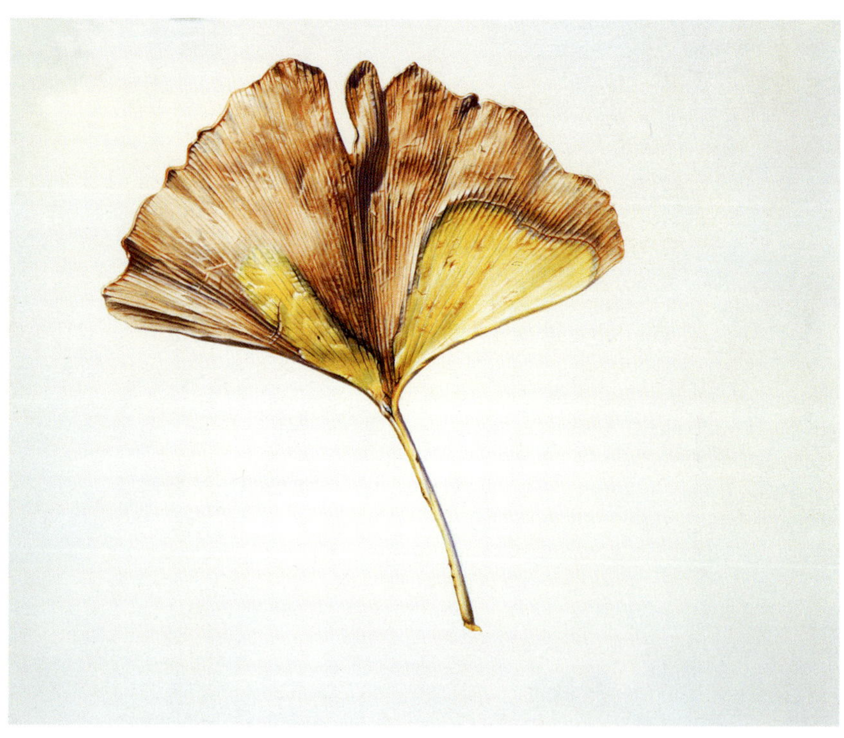

GINKGO LEAF, EAST 61st STREET, NEW YORK
Probably painted 1979 (Romana McEwen) Acquired from Offer Waterman & Co, London 2000 Watercolour on vellum 190 × 230 mm

OLD ENGLISH TULIP 'SIR JOSEPH PAXTON'
Signed Rory McEwen.Old English Florist Tulip Sir Joseph Paxton. From the Wakefield & North of England Florist Tulip Growers Assocation, Mr. Calvert (sec) Started May 29th, 1962. Finished September 29th, 1962. Acquired from Offer Waterman & Co, London 2000. Watercolour on vellum 380 × 260 mm

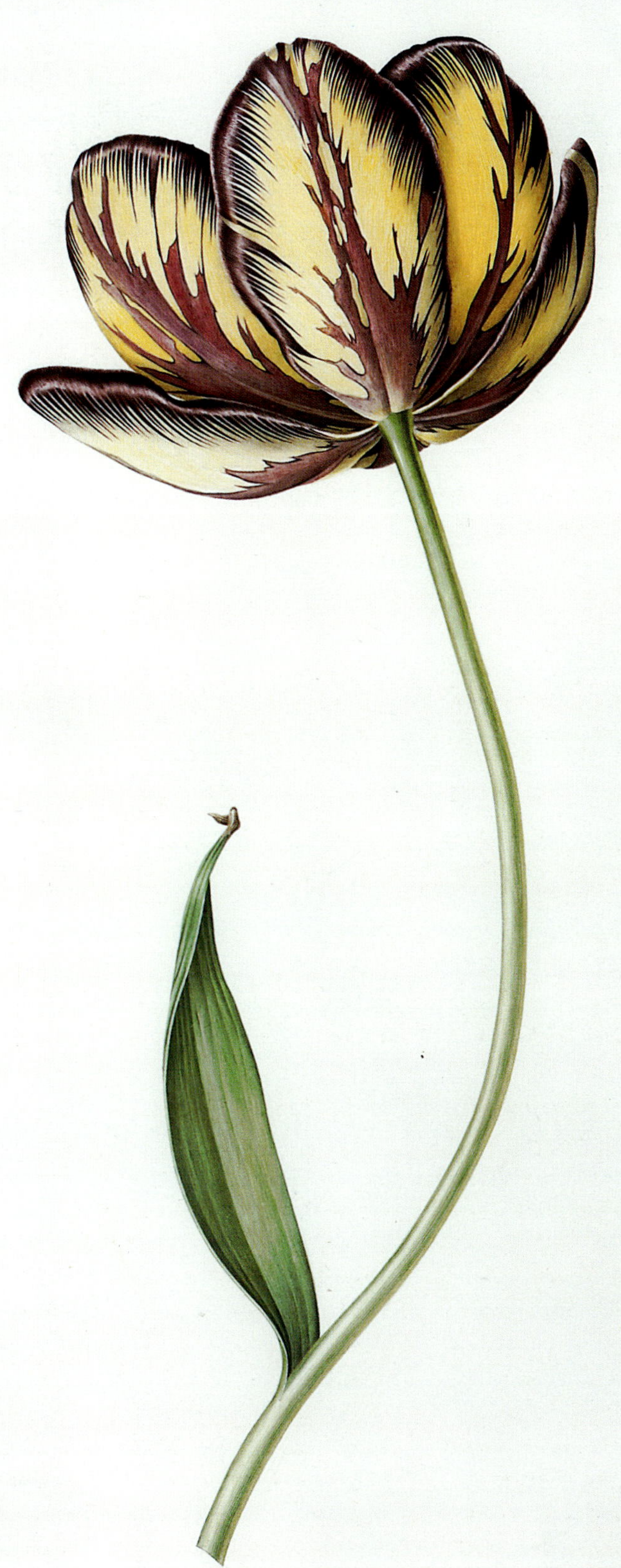
Rory McEwen

David Mackay

Born Hornsby, New South Wales, Australia 1958

David Mackay began his professional career in the 1970s by preparing botanical illustrations for the Papua New Guinea National Botanic Gardens in his school holidays. Since then he has worked at a number of botanic gardens and universities in Australia and overseas, including over ten years at the Royal Botanic Gardens Sydney as a botanical illustrator. During that period he took a B.Sc. (Hons) at the University of Sydney.

His work has received much acclaim and is represented in public and private collections in Australia, Great Britain and the United States. He began exhibiting in 1989 and has since made major contributions to numerous group shows in Sydney (including the Art Gallery of New South Wales), Adelaide and elsewhere in New South Wales and northern Queensland. Thousands of his drawings and paintings have been published in well over a hundred books and scientific papers as well as calendars, magazines, greeting cards and other media. He honed his skills under a family friend, the well-known wildlife artist William T. Cooper. He now works freelance from his home and studio in Armidale, New South Wales.

Margot Child invited me to visit an interesting exhibition hung at the Lion Gate Lodge of the Royal Botanic Gardens Sydney early in 2000. She is very interested in botanical art and had masterminded an excellent show of artists from New South Wales. This is where I saw David Mackay's striking acrylics. He had five paintings in the show, comprising three large, strong studies, one of a *Banksia serrata*, another a scarlet waratah (the state flower of New South Wales) and a huge mottlecah (an unusual eucalyptus). Besides these he showed two quietly elegant hellebores.

I bought his *Eucalyptus macrocarpa* or mottlecah which is a spreading glaucous scrub eucalyptus growing as tall as 5 metres, restricted to southern Western Australia on undulating heathland south from Enneabba and in remnant vegetation in the wheatbelt near inland Corrigin. The large solitary flowers are very showy, the largest in the genus and indeed of any Australian Myrtaceae. The rare, relatively small-fruited form illustrated here is recognised by some botanists as a distinct subspecies, *E. macrocarpa* subsp. *elechantha*.

Mackay studied the species in 1998 in a small population south-west of Enneabba on a highway north of Perth, growing in the low heathland. His subject was a small, straggly tree, only standing 2 metres tall, but he told me that nevertheless it stood out dramatically with its striking blue-green leaves and huge scarlet blooms. He wanted to capture this drama and this is why he painted it twice life-size. Apparently some specimens do grow as large as the flowers in the paintings. It is difficult to grow outside Western Australia although it is cultivated in California where it forms a showy ornamental plant. He considers this project to have been one of his most challenging to date, as the texture and strongly glaucous character of the leaves, stems and fruits was a complex and difficult effect to achieve.

He learned to paint using watercolours and continued to develop his skills as a botanical artist in this medium for many years. Some years ago, however, he tried adapting acrylic paints to the classic style of botanical art and now uses them exclusively, mixed with acrylic 'watercolour medium'. He prefers the greater range of pure, bright colours and the broader scope of applications and techniques possible with acrylics compared with the more restricted possibilities available from traditional watercolours. It is interesting to note that Paul Jones, another Australian painter, also often used acrylics.

He sometimes puts a background in his paintings to show the plant's habitat, either the typical habitat of the species or the specific habitat of the individual depicted. Such paintings are obviously quite different from the more formal works with white backgrounds and have a different appeal. He feels that such paintings cannot have separate, enlarged details of the plant as well as the painted background – they just don't work – so it is often quite a challenge to give these paintings the strength of botanical works rather than the appearance of 'flower paintings'. He finds that one important aspect of such paintings is to include the species' identifying morphological details without the use of separate enlargements or dissections. He has recently begun work on a series of paintings of the waratahs

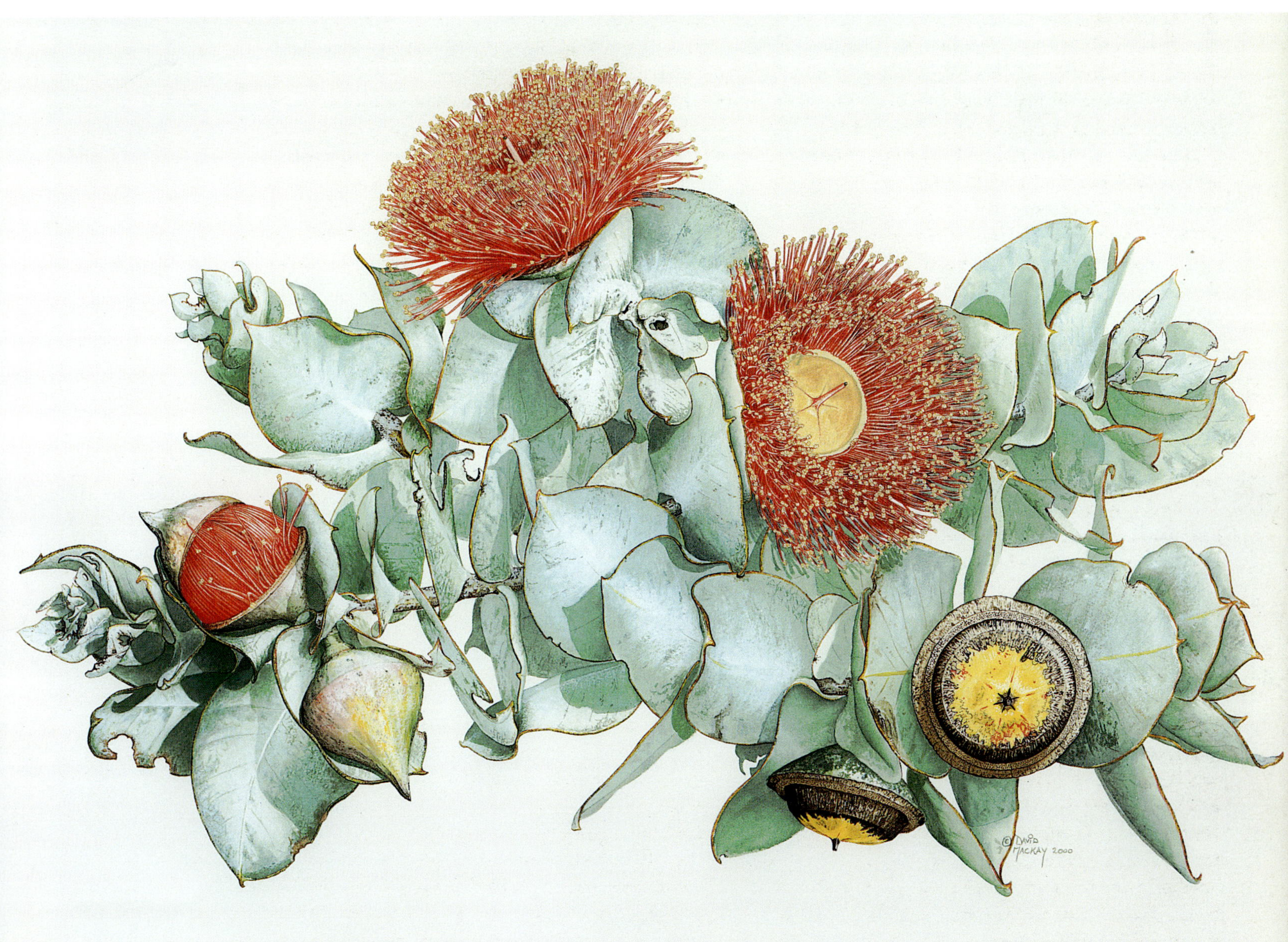

and related species worldwide (the sub-tribe *Embothriinae*, family Proteaceae) in which he will be painting habitat backgrounds. His aim is to produce a limited edition set of prints of these paintings with accompanying text, sketches and field notes (text by Dr Peter Weston). The project will take him some years. He is hoping to see the two South American species of *Oreocallis* in the wild – and possibly the Chilean *Embothrium* as well – in August 2000 when he visits South America for the first time.

MOTTLECAH:
EUCALYPTUS MACROCARPA
Signed © David Mackay 2000
Acquired from Botanica 2000, Australia 2000
Acrylic on paper 750 × 735 mm

Katherine Manisco

Born London, England 1935

Over the years that I have seen Katherine Manisco's work it has changed and developed. I particularly enjoy this robust cabbage which almost seems to be pirouetting on its leaf and root. I bought it in New York at the W. M. Brady Gallery, a venue which had not previously shown paintings of a contemporary artist but had been devoted to eighteenth- and nineteenth-century work. Her one-person show was a great success, with nearly everything sold on the first night. Most encouragingly, it was reviewed at length in the *Wall Street Journal*. It is good news that another gallery is showing this kind of painting in the United States.

She is a graduate of the Slade School of Fine Art, London and studied painting at the Accademia dell'Arte in Florence. She is a member of the American Society of Botanical Artists and the Chelsea Physic Garden Florilegium Society.

Her work is included in the permanent collections of the Victoria & Albert Museum, the Fitzwilliam Museum, Cambridge and the Hunt Institute for Botanical Documentation, Carnegie Mellon University, Pittsburgh.

She finds great satisfaction in her work, stimulated by the brilliant hues and sculptural qualities of the fruits, vegetables and flowers, particularly the bizarre pumpkins and Turk's-cap squash grown in the autumn.

Katherine feels deeply indebted to the Chelsea Physic Garden, that wonderful oasis in the middle of London started by Sir Han Sloane. The Garden's history has been a real inspiration to her, and her involvement with the Florilegium Society has given her an awareness of the continuity of a marvellous tradition. She now divides her time between New York City and Rome.

SAVOY CABBAGE:
BRASSICA OLERACEA
Signed Katherine Manisco '99
Acquired from W. M. Brady & Co., New York 1999
Watercolour on paper
445 x 445 mm

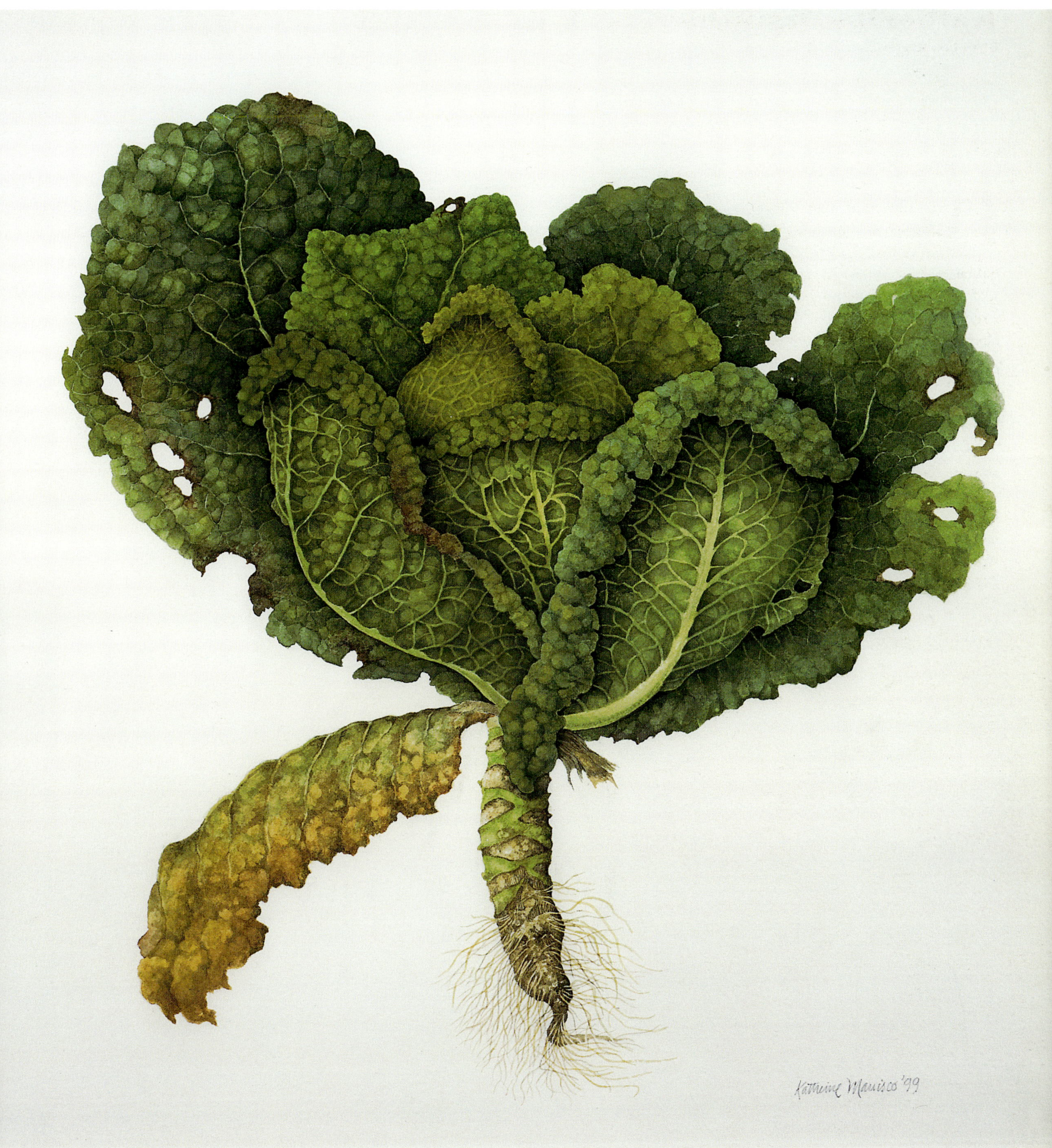

Sheila Mannes-Abbott

BORN HILLINGDON, ENGLAND 1939

I chose Sheila Mannes-Abbott's watercolour painting of *Iris unguicularis* for its assured complexity and as soon as I had decided, she took it away to 'tidy it up'. It came back a few weeks later and I have not regretted my choice. The tangle of leaves almost dominate the subtle blue flowers nestling between them.

She studied at the Ealing School of Art and showed her work at the RHS in the 1970s and again in 1997 when she was awarded a gold medal. She was a founder member of the Society of Botanical Artists and has exhibited there from 1986. She was included in the 9th International Exhibition of the Hunt Institute, showing a fritillary and a lily. Her designs have been reproduced on china for 'collector plates' and on fabrics, cards and puzzles. She produced the illustrations for *The Royal County: a Commemoration of the Silver Jubilee of Her Majesty Queen Elizabeth II* and for *The Four Seasons: the Life of the English Countryside* with Phil Drabble.

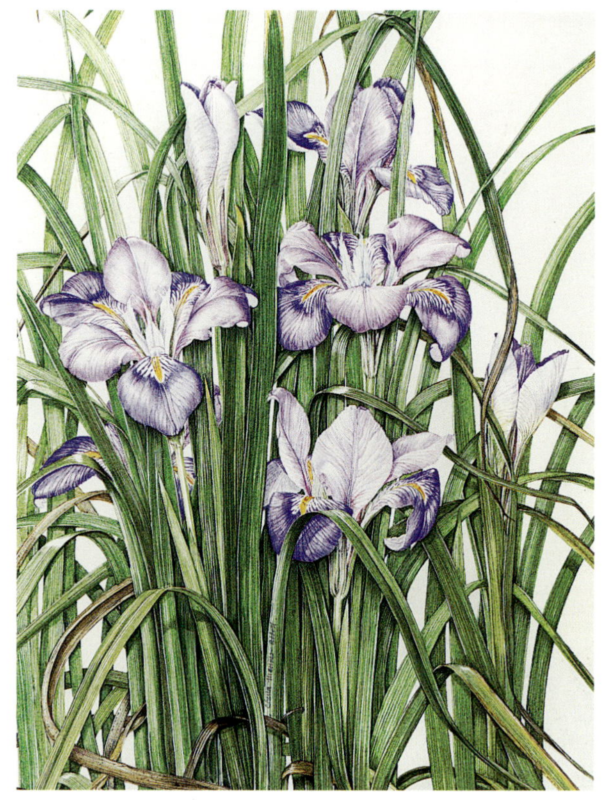

IRIS UNGUICULARIS
Signed Sheila Mannes-Abbott
(undated)
Acquired from the artist 1998
for Simon Sherwood
Watercolour on paper
475 × 335 mm

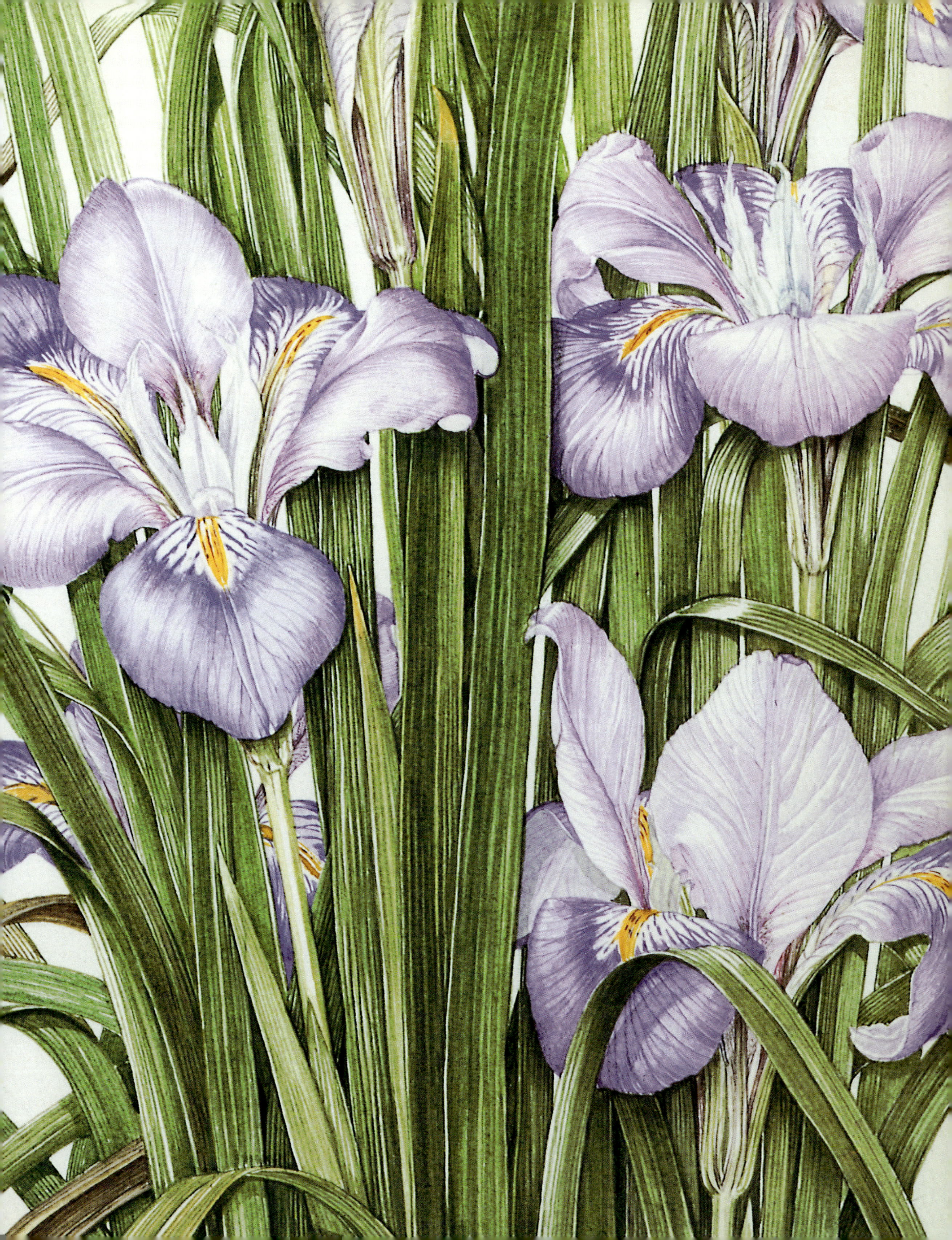

Margaret Mee

Born Chesham, England 1909–88

Over the last few years Margaret Mee's influence has been growing and growing among botanical artists and ecologists. Hers was one of the first voices raised to alert the world to the exploitation of the rainforests. The fifty-eight plates that she painted for her second book *Flores do Amazons – Flowers of the Amazon* were shown at Kew in 1988, shortly before her death in a car accident. These paintings of Brazilian rainforest plants were acquired by Kew in 1995 and became the core of an important travelling exhibition which served to warn visitors of the destruction of the Amazon. This exhibition went to seven venues in the United States and was seen by thousands of people.

Margaret Mee trained as an artist in London at St Martin's School of Art, the Central Art School and Camberwell Art School. She moved to Brazil in the early 1950s, became fascinated with the exotic flora and started organising solo journeys into the Amazonian rainforest, searching for exciting plants to paint. This seemingly frail, petite woman went on fifteen challenging collecting trips into the Amazon, generally with only Indian guides to accompany her. She would sketch specimens *in situ* and then try to bring them back to Rio so that they could be cultivated. She brought back hundreds of valuable plants and four previously unknown species were named after her.

She has inspired many Brazilian artists including members of the Demonte family, Marlena Barretto, Ronaldo Pangella and Alvaro Nunes. The Fundacão Margaret Mee has raised money to facilitate the exchange of dozens of scholars between Kew and Brazil. Each Brazilian artist works with Christabel King at Kew for several months and then goes back to South America with freshly honed skills to teach others there. The Foundation organises exhibitions and competitions in Brazil which have a steadily increasing standard. She has become an icon in South America and her life was chosen as the theme for a samba school for the Rio Carnival, with three thousand eco-friendly dancers parading to a Margaret Mee theme song – there is no greater accolade than that in Brazil.

NIDULARIUM SEIDELII
Signed Margaret Mee
(undated)
Acquired from Greville Mee, Brazil 1993
Watercolour on paper
640 × 470 mm

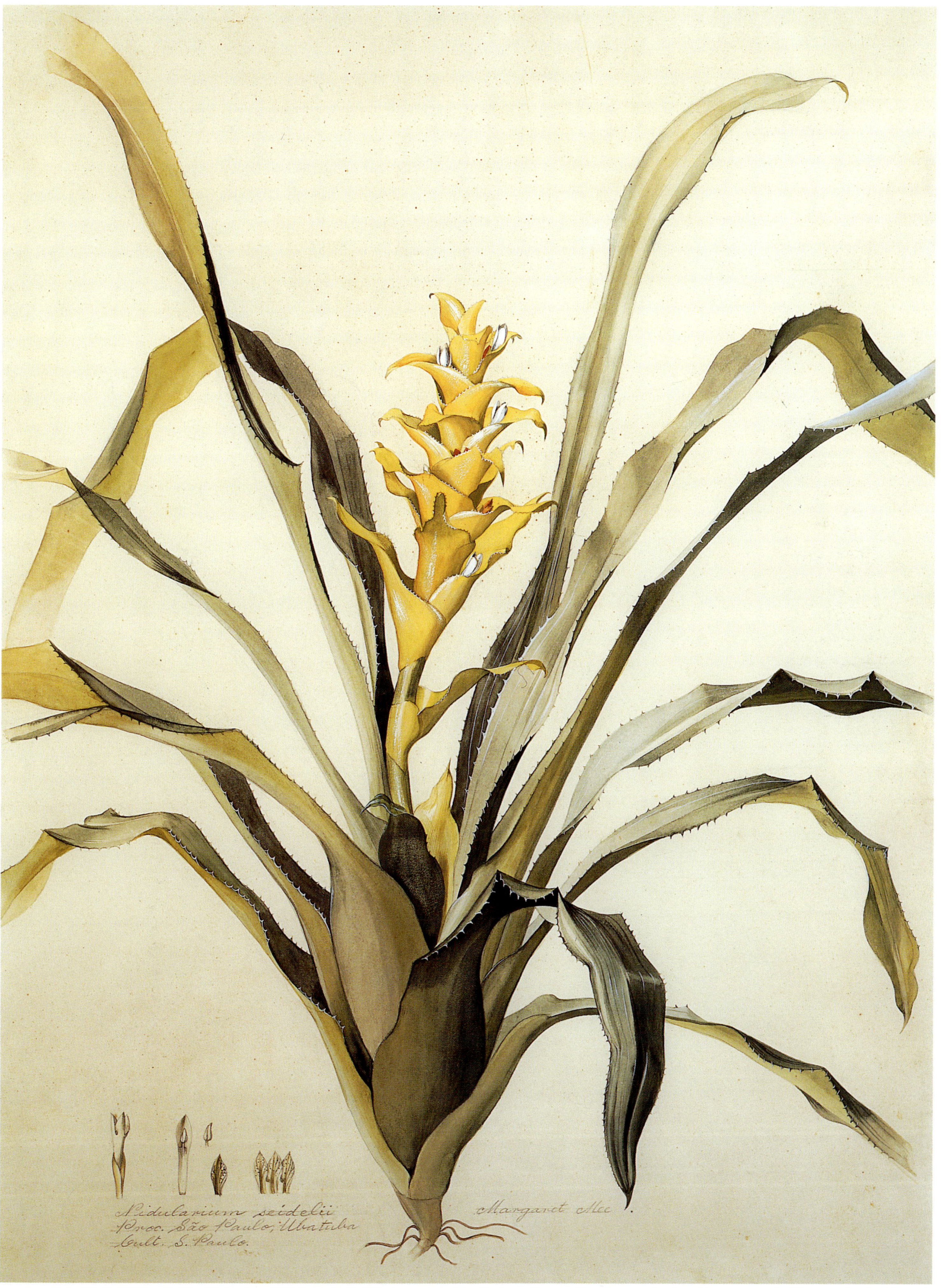
Nidularium seidelii
Proc. São Paulo, Ubatuba
Cult. S. Paulo.
Margaret Mee

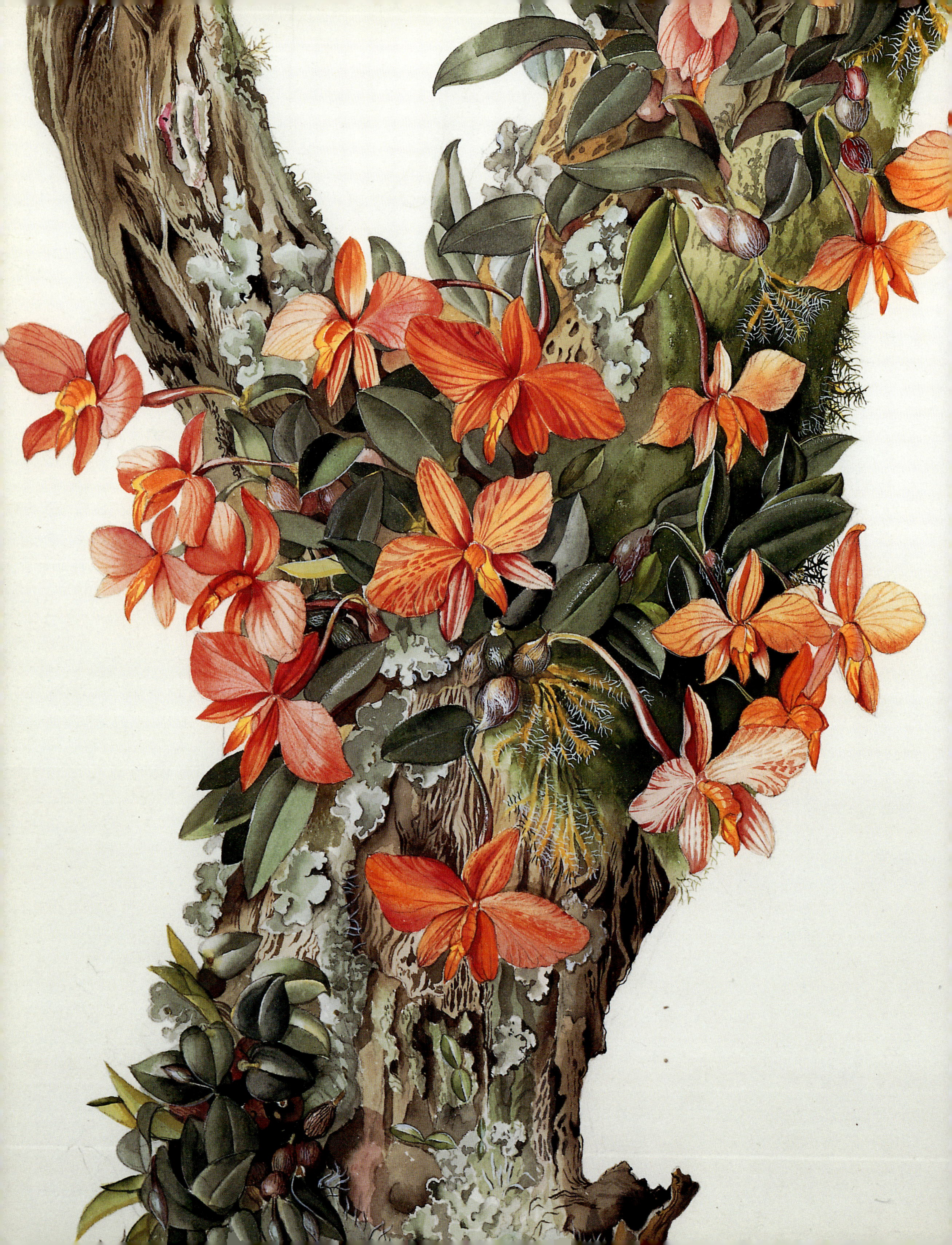

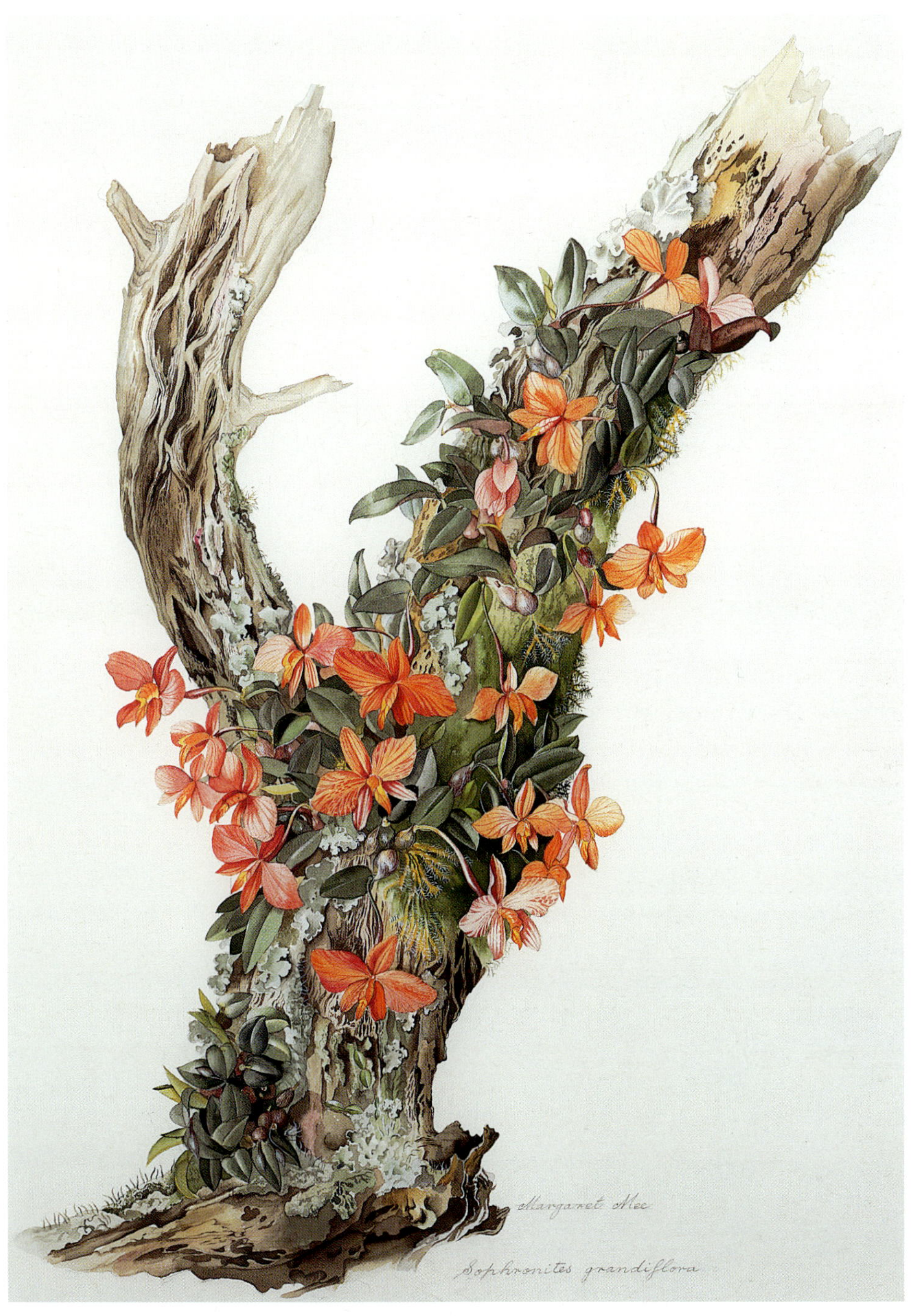

SOPHRONITES GRANDIFLORA

Signed Margaret Mee (undated)

Sophronites grandiflora

Acquired from Tryon Gallery,

London 1992

Watercolour on paper 560 × 390 mm

Carol Ann Morley

BORN KENT, ENGLAND 1942

SENSITIVE FERN:
ONOCLEA SENSIBILIS
Signed CAM 1999
Commissioned 1999
Carbon dust on paper
530 × 275 mm

Although a British citizen, Carol Ann Morley has spent most of her career on the eastern coast of the United States and now lives in New Hampshire. She trained in England, taking the National Diploma in Design in the late 1950s and early 1960s at the Medway College of Art, Rochester, Kent. During the 1970s she was a medical illustrator at Harlem Hospital, New York City and an Associate Professor of Art at Pace University. In 1985 she helped found and co-ordinate the Botanical Art & Illustration certificate programme at the New York Botanical Garden and has taught there since then. She has been involved with many different workshops as a science illustrator in Connecticut, Vermont and New York, has had four one-person exhibitions in New York and has illustrated a number of publications for the Brooklyn Botanic Garden.

She showed at the Hunt Institute in 1998, which is when I first saw her work. She had drawn the mysterious skunk cabbage emerging from a mass of roots, with wonderful gradations of soft grey and black tones. It had been done using a carbon dust technique which was new to me. She sent me some preliminary pencil sketches and we decided on an autumnal study of the elegant *Onoclea sensibilis*, known as the sensitive fern. She used a microscope to make accurate drawings of the globular pinnules and the sporangia which are shown magnified on the final work. The fronds are drawn dried and curled up, distorted in their wintry desiccation.

I had no idea when I agreed on this commission that the carbon dust technique was so difficult and demanding. Carol Ann Morley told me that it was originally developed by the illustrator Max Brödel (1870–1941), who wanted to achieve a photographic realism in his medical drawing. When he came to America in 1894 he established the first art school in the world connected with medical drawing at Johns Hopkins University. He used clay-coated paper known as 'Ross stipple board' for his carbon dust studies, but this is no longer available. However, the *Guild Handbook of Scientific Illustration* has produced a chart of opaque-surfaced papers for guidance, which gives some idea of how effectively carbon dust can be applied, shaded and highlighted. Morley selected Color-Aid paper for my drawing from the types of paper available now.

She starts by making some highly detailed sketches on regular drawing paper with a graphite pencil. This drawing is traced on to tracing paper, which is then placed image-side down on the coated paper. The tracing is transferred onto the coated paper by gentle smoothing. She then brushes carbon-dust rubbed from a 3B carbon pencil onto large areas of shadow. Apparently the first sweeps of the brush leave no obvious darkening, it is only after a number of applications that the shaded area begins to show up. If she wants an area sharply defined she uses a stencil, as the dust is messy and she has to be careful not to rub the coated surface with her hand. She also wears a mask so that she does not inhale the dust. She uses a 'workable fixative' at intervals throughout the application of the carbon particles to prevent the layers of dust falling off. Finally she creates highlights with an eraser or a razor blade.

It all sounds very fiddly and tedious to me, but it is possible to get wonderful subtle greys in a continuous tone drawing, grading through to deep, rich blacks and Carol Ann Morley finds this a very satisfying medium.

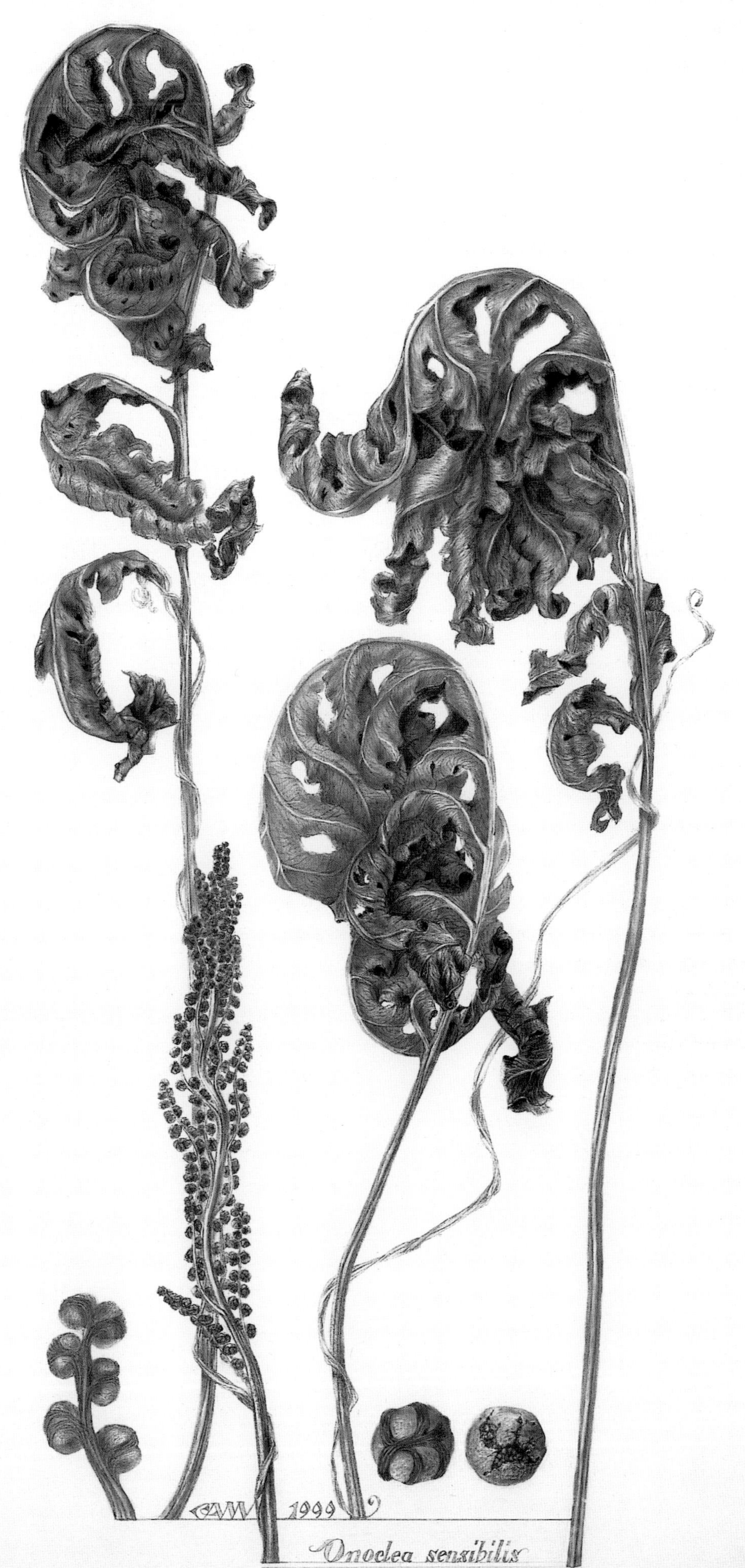
1999
Onoclea sensibilis

Kate Nessler

Born St Louis, Missouri, USA 1950

CLAMSHELL ORCHID: *ENCYCLIA COCHLEATA*
Signed Nessler
(undated)
Acquired from Park Walk Gallery, London 1995
Watercolour on paper
845 × 685 mm

With her most recent exhibition in the Park Walk Gallery, London, Kate Nessler has confirmed her position as one of today's most important botanical artists. Jonathan Cooper has put on three one-person shows of her work at his gallery in 1995, 1997 and 1999, all of them most successful. I now have eight Nessler paintings, collected since our first meeting at the RHS in 1993. The four most recent are all on vellum which has had quite an impact on her style, making her more introspective and detailed. Although she was still showing some classical portraits of garden flowers in her latest show in 1999, she seemed to be moving into more intense studies of plants in their natural surroundings, with snowdrops breaking through a covering of dried, dead leaves, a clump of bird's foot violet nestling on sticks and stones, and a brilliant study of rose hips, oak leaves and an acorn withered at the onset of winter. The largest painting in the show was a spectacular, yet almost microscopically detailed painting on honey-coloured vellum of a fallen bough with fungi, lichen and autumn debris, very much in the spirit of Dürer's *A Large Piece of Turf – Das Grosse Rasenstück*.

Always an admirer of the late Rory McEwen's work, she came to see one of his paintings in my home (on one of the rare occasions it has not been away on exhibition somewhere in the world). It was the first original of his that she had seen and she was entranced. Some of the paintings in her show had been on McEwen's unused vellum, given to the Hunt Institute for distribution to artists after his death. She had been given some of these precious sheets by James White, the discerning curator of the Hunt Institute.

Her last few years have been packed with achievements. Apart from her solo exhibitions in London she has been represented in 'Celebrating Orchids', one of the last proper exhibitions of new work shown at the Kew Gardens Gallery, Royal Botanic Gardens Kew, and in the American Society of Botanical Artists' exhibition in Chicago Botanic Gardens in 1997. The next year she exhibited in three shows; 'Botanical Art in the Arboretum', at the University of California, Davis; in the American Society of Botanical Artists' international exhibition in Wilmington, Delaware, and in London in 'Botanical Artists of the World' at the Tryon & Swann Gallery, a show I helped to curate. She was involved with the American Society of Botanical Artists from its onset, becoming its president and she received their most important accolade, the American Society of Botanical Artists' award of excellence in 1997. She has paintings in the Hunt Institute and the Lindley Library, RHS, London; and her exhibition 'The Baker Prairie Wild Flower Collection' has travelled in Arkansas in cooperation with the Arkansas Natural Heritage Commission, helping to teach children about their local plants.

I wanted to know how she had tackled painting on vellum, a skin that many artists are now starting to use. Used well it can be a wonderful surface, giving an added jewel-tone translucency to watercolour. The following is Kate Nessler's own description of the technique she uses for painting on vellum:

Painting on Vellum

by Kate Nessler

Throughout the year I have experimented with various types of vellum. While there is a general similarity in vellum, each type seems to handle slightly differently. I found the Kelmscott vellum to be the finest and most consistent to work on, especially when the specimen required extremely detailed work (such as the webbing and veining on dried leaves). It is very smooth, hard and without any visual texture. However, I have been able to locate it in only small cut pieces (5 × 7 × 9 inches). A remarkable vellum. Dutch vellum, while a most beautiful surface in terms of colour and visual texture, was the most difficult and challenging to paint on. The surface is extremely slick, the paint difficult to adhere. The Rory McEwen vellum is treated and has a very smooth, fine, hard and consistent surface. Cowley's English Vellum ranges from classic (ivory-coloured) to natural (honey to darker coloured). The surface texture seems to range in each skin, from light visual texture to heavily marked and almost 'tobacco-stained' and very old looking. The surface texture in terms of 'feel' also seems to have ranges. I found some very hard, some slightly softer. Some

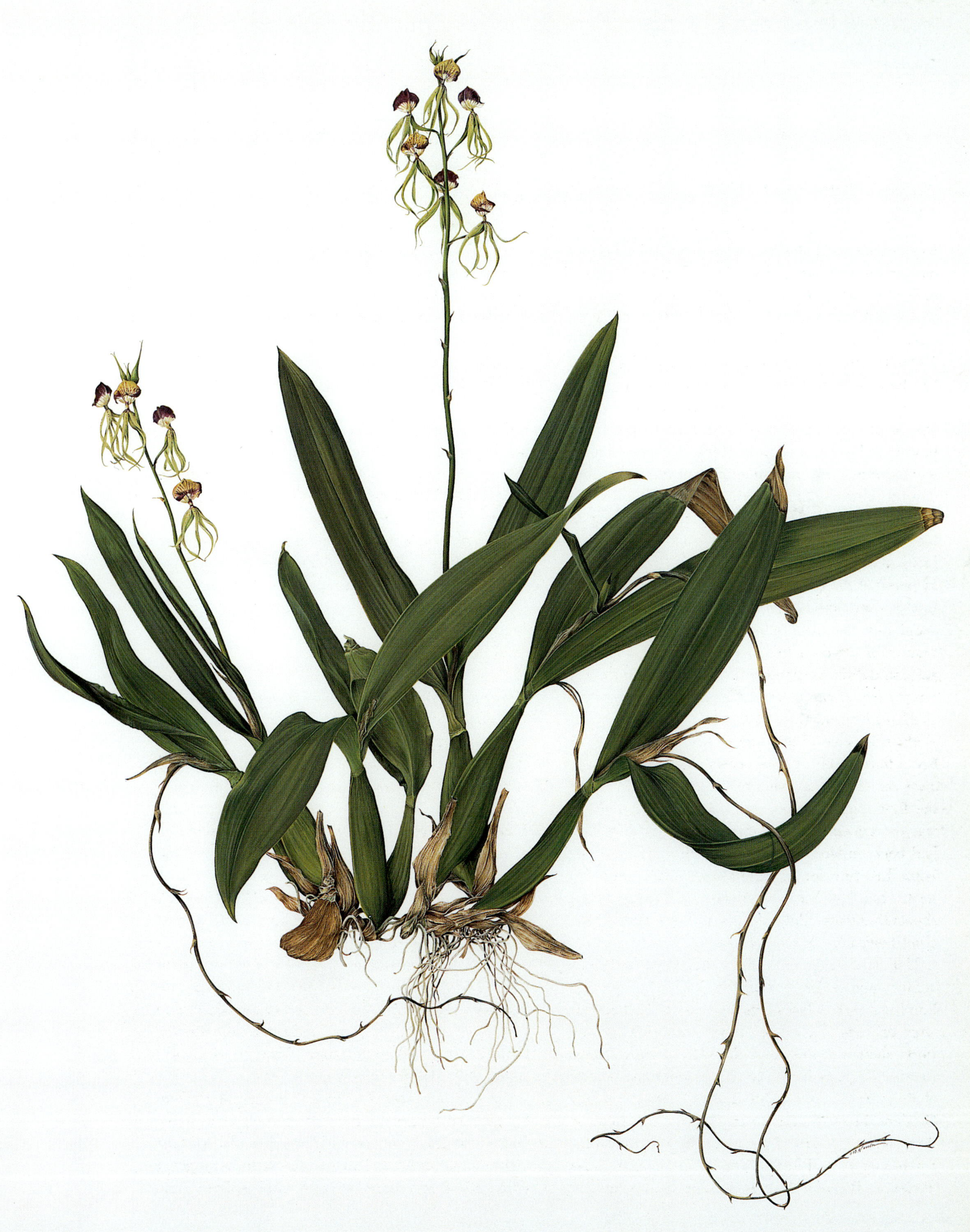

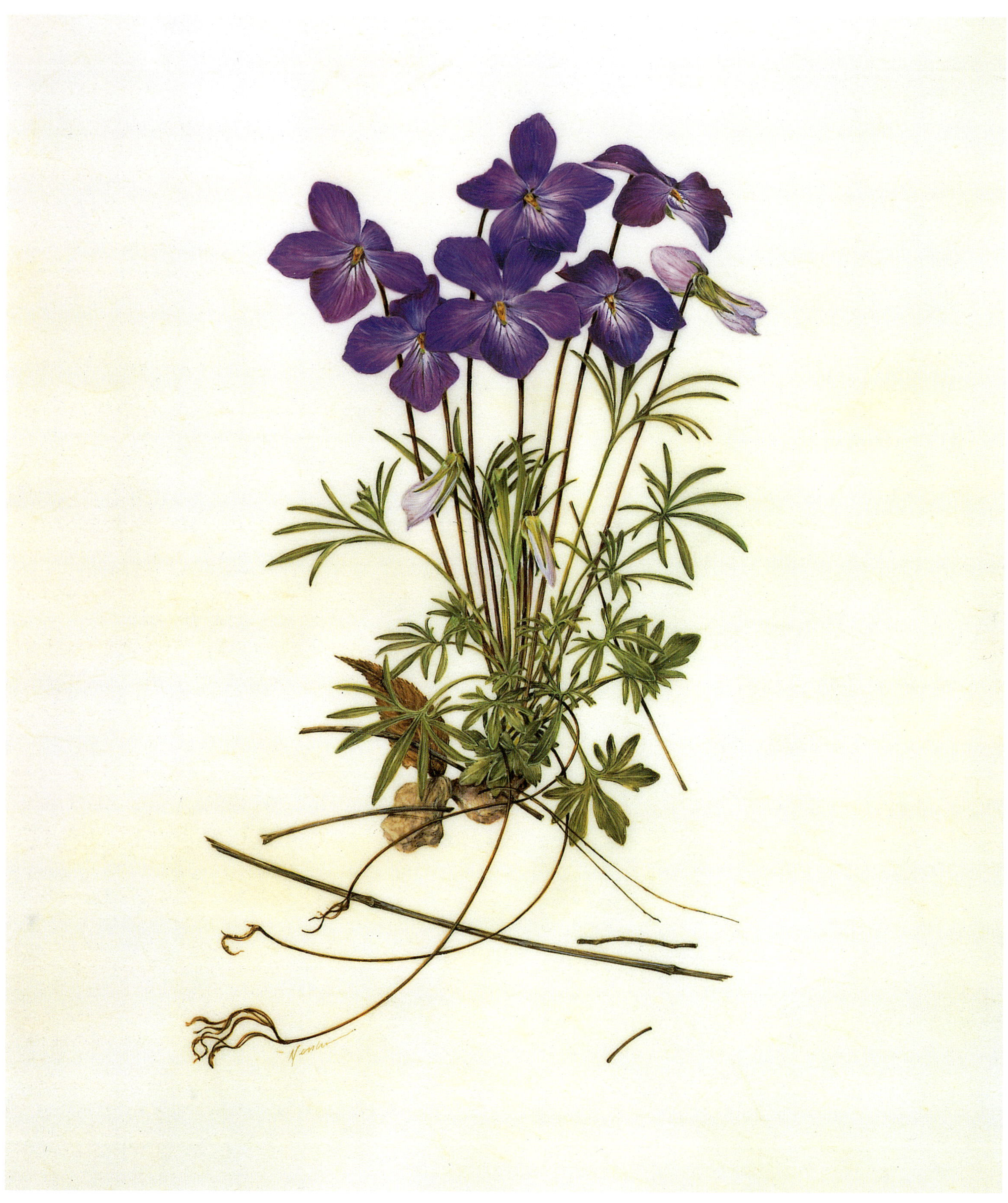

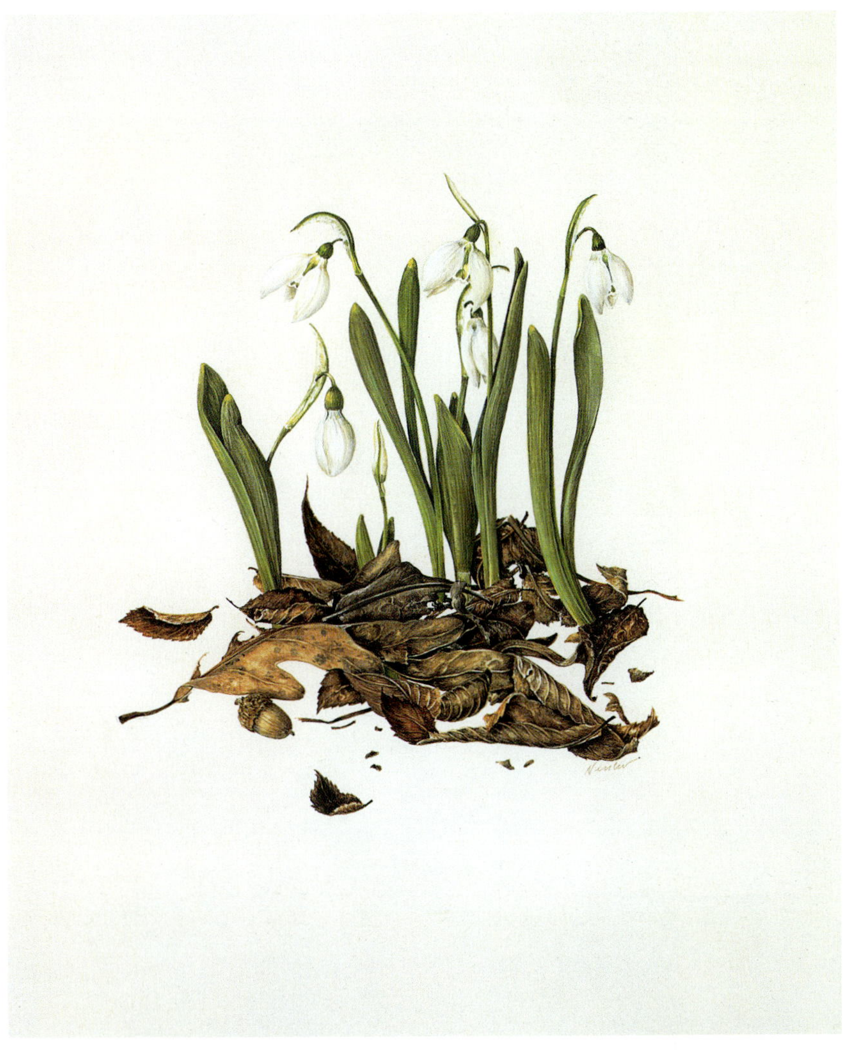

BIRD'S FOOT VIOLET
(Left) Signed Nessler (undated)
Acquired from Park Walk Gallery, London 1999
Watercolour & body colour on vellum
320 × 230 mm

SNOWDROPS & LEAVES
(Above) Signed Nessler (undated)
Acquired from Park Walk Gallery, London 1999
Watercolour & body colour on vellum
270 × 220 mm

areas smoother, some rougher. Before painting on any vellum (exception – Rory McEwen vellum) I treat the surface with a light buffing of pumice powder to rough up the surface slightly for better paint adherence. The excess is brushed off, then lightly wiped off with a soft rag to remove any remaining powder. Care must be used in handling the pumice powder, as it is unhealthy to ingest.

Beginning

The skin can become an integral part of the painting, not just a vehicle on which to display a specimen. I spend a lot of time simply looking at the vellum and the specimen: Is there a gradation of colour or surface texture in the skin? How would the specimen be best placed on the skin to use that component? This is the most critical point. This is where the painting begins – visualisation of the completed work.

I believe that along with the creative process, problem-solving and an acute awareness of what is happening in the painting at all times is essential. While I go into the painting with a clear idea of an end result, I must keep an open mind and a clear eye attuned to the changes and problems and alterations that happen along the way. That uncertainty is the challenge and the joy.

Technique

Once the specimen is selected, I begin with a quick gestural sketch on tissue to determine size and placement. After that determination and vellum selection, I draw directly on the vellum in pencil. The drawing is detailed and complete. Excess lead is removed by pressing a kneaded eraser on the drawing. Any other excessive or unnecessary drawing is carefully removed. I am left with a precise, very light impression. At completion of the painting any visible and unnecessary pencil will be removed.

The first layer of paint (transparent watercolour) is very light to provide a base of colour. I do not wash in the entire specimen and the selection of the starting area is random or instinctive. Often I will choose a small area to begin with to give myself the confidence and visual impression of the whole work. The starting point is whatever area that allows me to enter the work. That first layer is a very thin wash (just enough water to move the paint). Vellum holds paint differently from paper, depending on the hardness of the skin, but mostly it sits more on the surface rather than being absorbed as it would be into paper.

Next is the layering of the finished colour. It is somewhat like fine drawing. A good paint brush with a very fine point is important. I use small, light strokes with a minimal amount of colour or water – just enough paint to move it on the surface. From then it is simply a slow, meticulous, continuous process of building colour – working from light to dark, creating shape and form and shadow. I do occasionally use body colour (Chinese White) for highlighting or opacity when the specimen requires it, although it must be used sparingly to avoid flat colour or a heavy, dull look.

Mostly I try to complete similar areas (such as all the leaves or all the flowers) within the painting at one time. This way I am able to maintain a consistency of colour and feel throughout. Probably one of the biggest dangers to a painting is heavy handedness. If I find myself labouring over a selection, I will move to another or step out entirely. Vellum does require a light, fine touch. The beauty of vellum is the way the colour glows on the surface, but with overworking, one can kill that.

One benefit of vellum is the ability to remove applied paint. Again, each skin seems slightly different, but you can usually lift small areas of colour with light scraping of a razor blade.

Vellum must be kept dry and flat. I have had some problems with buckling, but chose not to mount the skin permanently, but rather to allow the natural tendencies to be present. When not in use, I keep the skins in an acid-free environment, under weights.

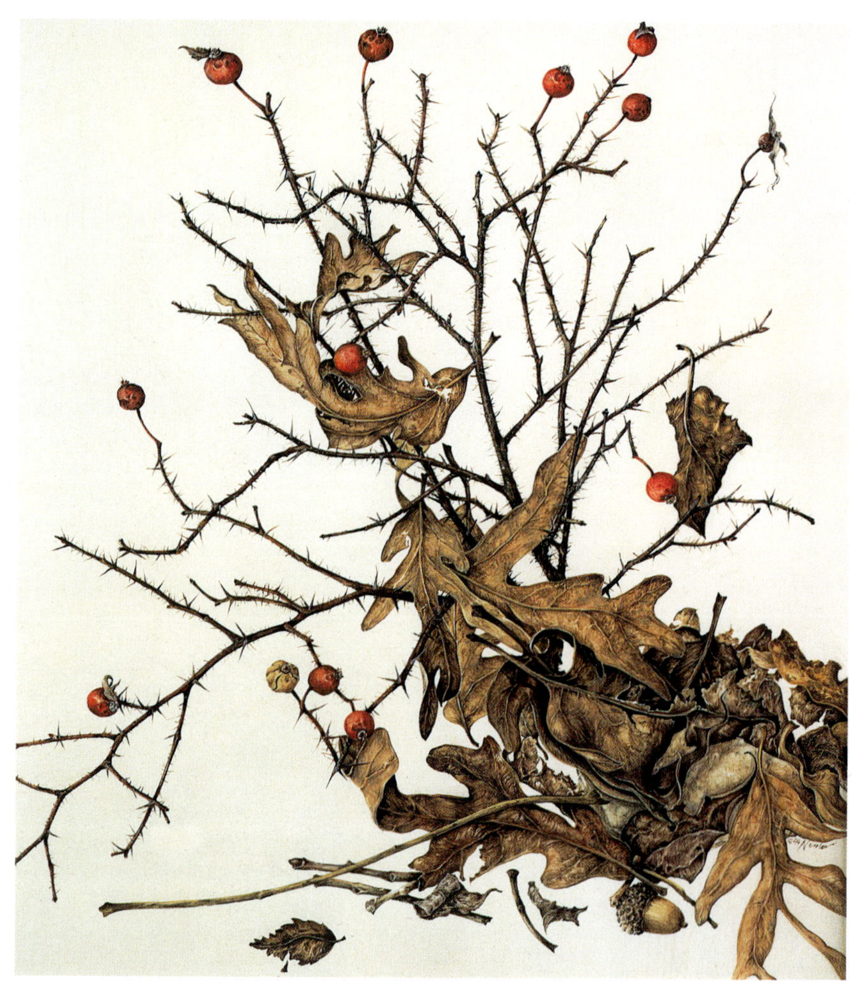

ROSE HIPS & OAK LEAVES
Signed Nessler (undated)
Acquired from Park Walk
Gallery, London 1999
Watercolour on vellum
270 × 220 mm

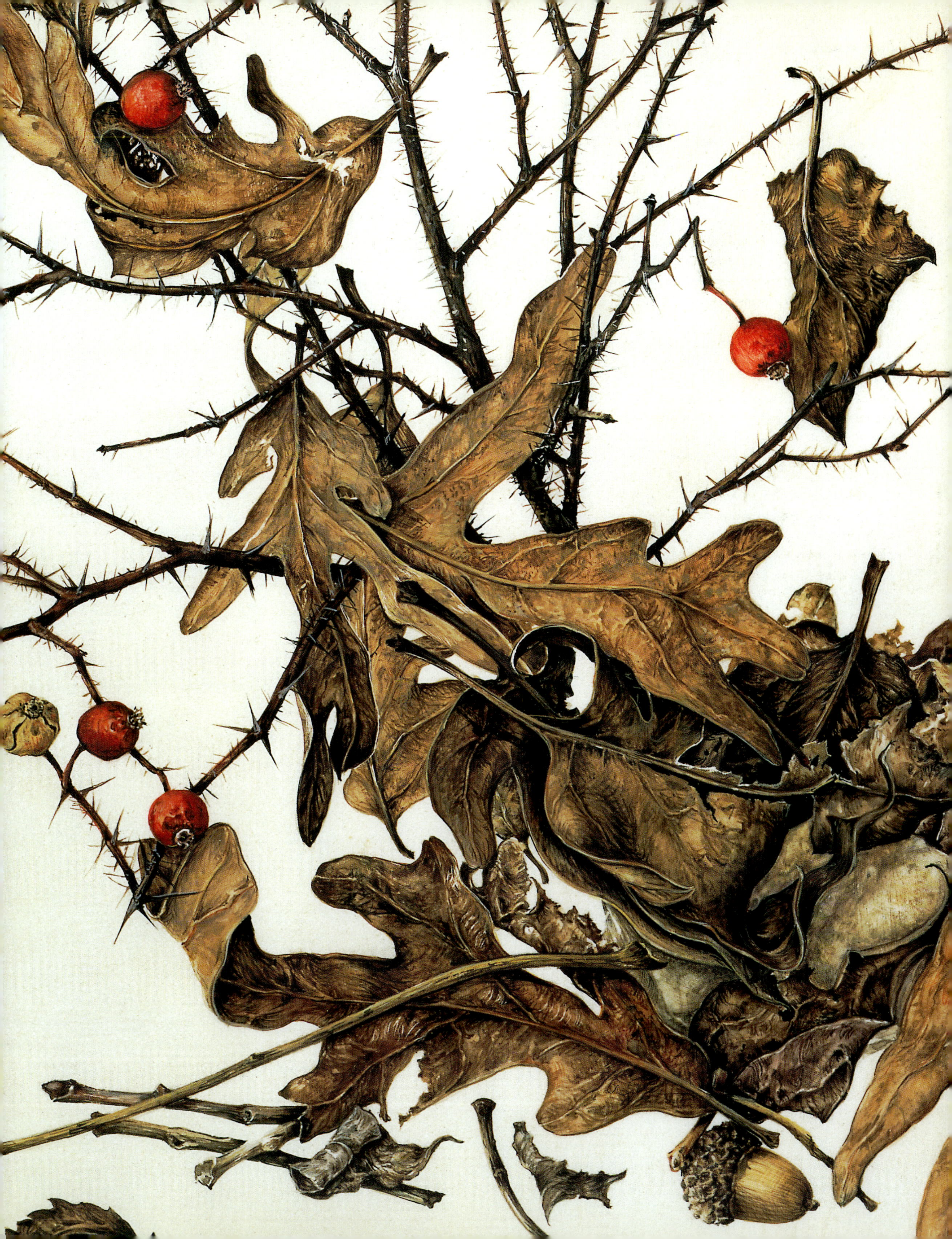

Alvaro Evando Xavier Nunes

BORN ANÁPOLIS, GOIÁS, BRAZIL 1945

Alvaro Nunes is still based in his birthplace Anápolis in the state of Goiás but spends long periods away, working in remote areas of Brazil. He is particularly interested in the Brazilian savannah and has painted many of the fruits of native trees from the savannah, Amazonia and the Pantanal. Finding the specimens has involved long journeys of up to eight months to these isolated parts of the country.

He qualified as an architect at the Federal University of Brasilia in 1971 and then worked for the government of Brasilia on local urban projects until 1981. His botanical studies started with a six-month internship in the botanical department of Brasilia Federal University in 1989 where he focused on the flora of the Brazilian savannah. He also attended a painting course taught by Christabel King at São Paulo Botanical Institute in 1993.

He participated in botanical drawing workshops in the Federal Universities of Brasilia; Juiz de Fora, Minas Gerais, Goiás; and at the 'Swamp-land campus' of the University of Matto Grosso do Sul. His drawings have been published in a number of books including *Fruiteras da Amazonia* (*Fruit Trees from the Amazon*), *Peixes do Pantanal* (*Fishes of the Brazilian Swampland*) and a series of books *Plantar* and *Frutex* all published by Embrapa, the Brazilian Institute for Rural Research.

He has had six one-person exhibitions during the last ten years and shown in several group shows including the 9th International Exhibition at the Hunt Institute for Botanical Documentation in 1998, which is where I first saw his paintings. I was impressed by the superb quality of his workmanship and the intriguing and unusual subject matter. As I was going to Brazil early in 1999 I made contact

THEOBROMA SUBINCANUM
(Right) Signed Alvaro Nunes (undated)
Acquired from the artist 1999
Watercolour on paper
560 × 355 mm

FRUITS OF SAVANNAH
(Left) Signed Alvaro Nunes (undated)
Acquired from the artist 1999
Watercolour on paper
330 × 440 mm

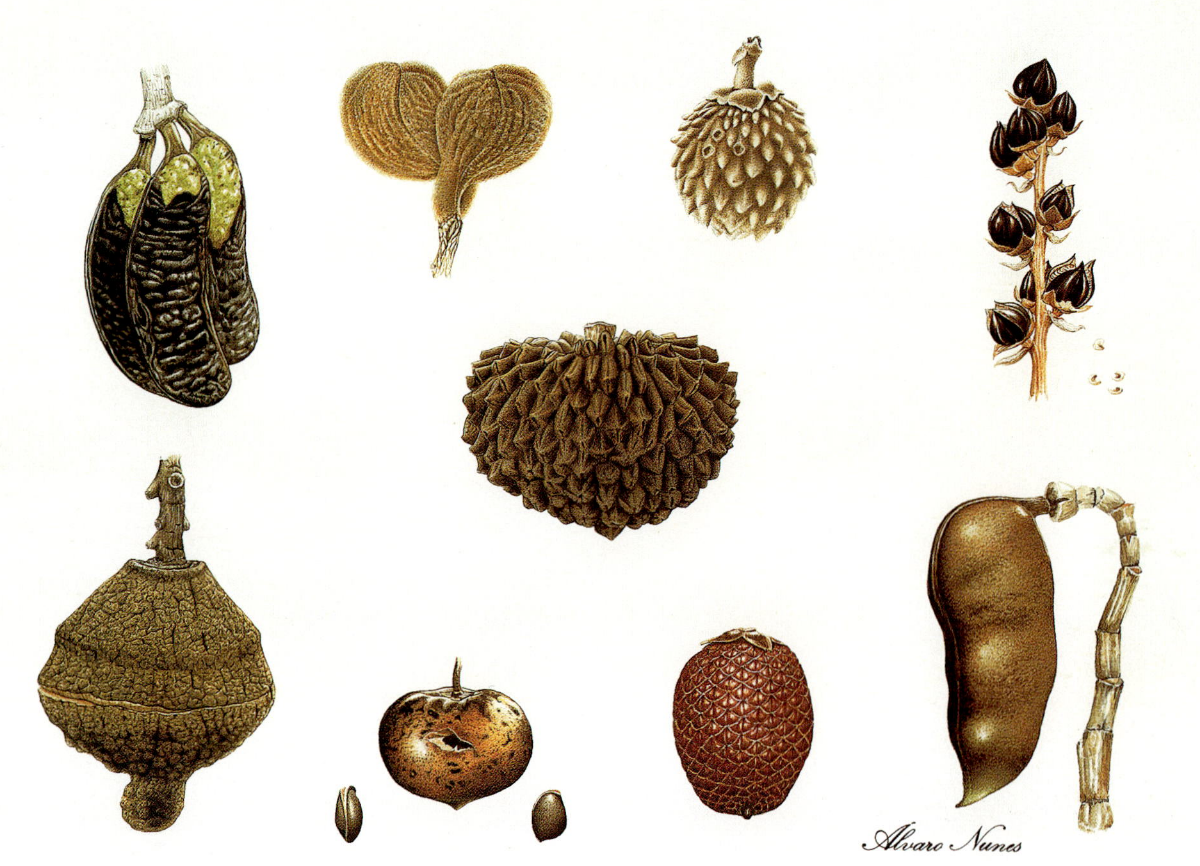

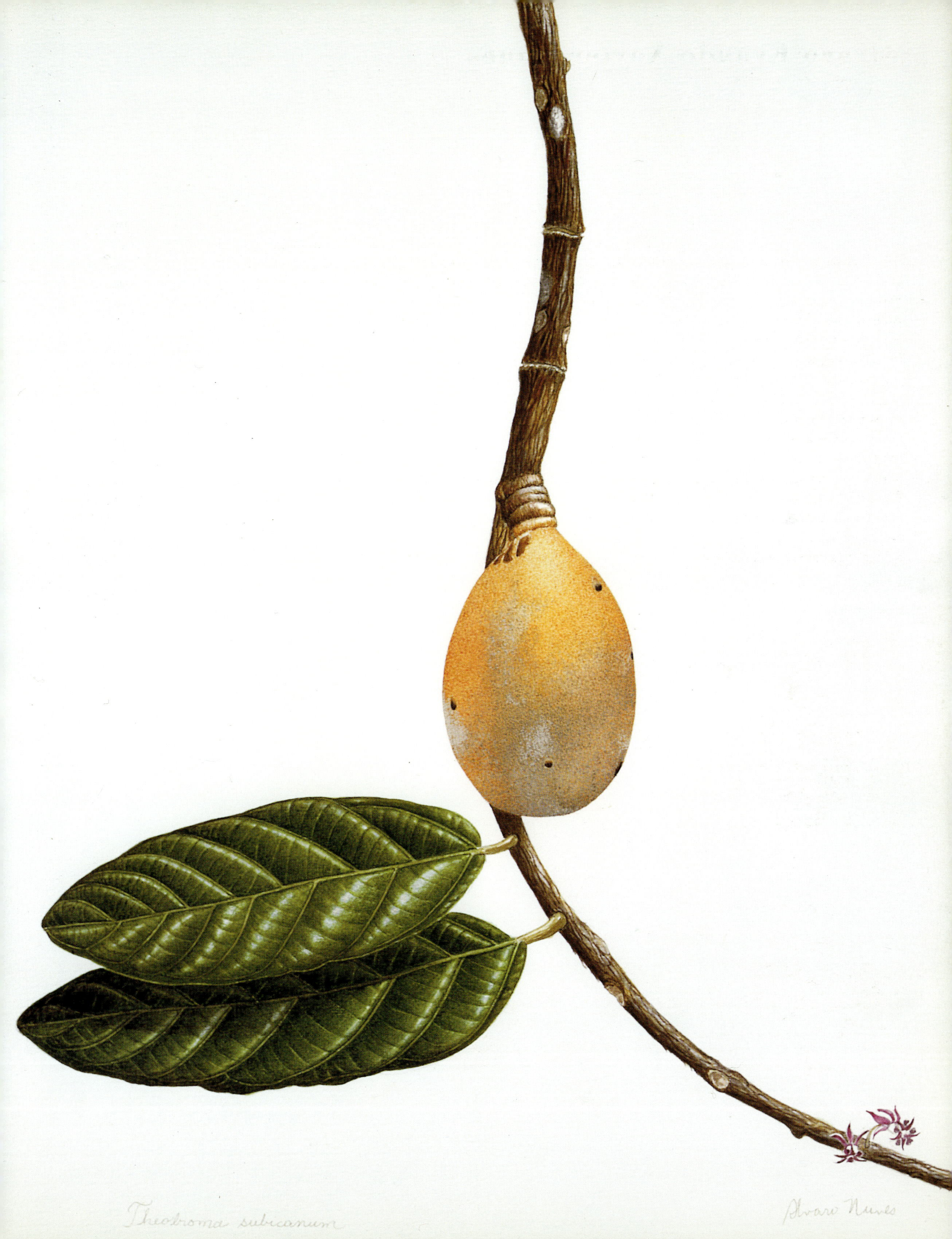
Theobroma subicanum
Alvaro Nunes

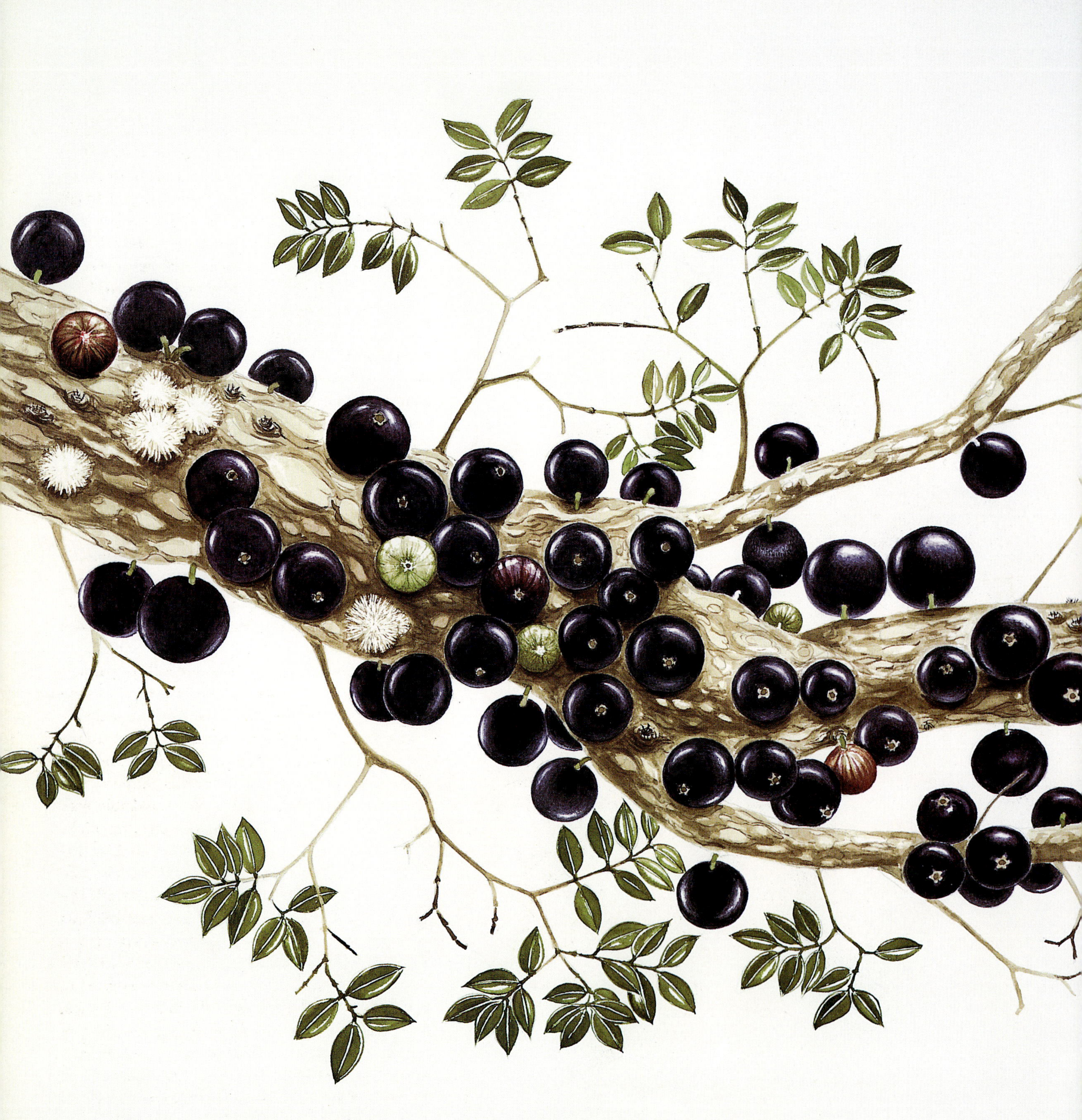

Myrciaria cauliflora ALVARO NUNES 97

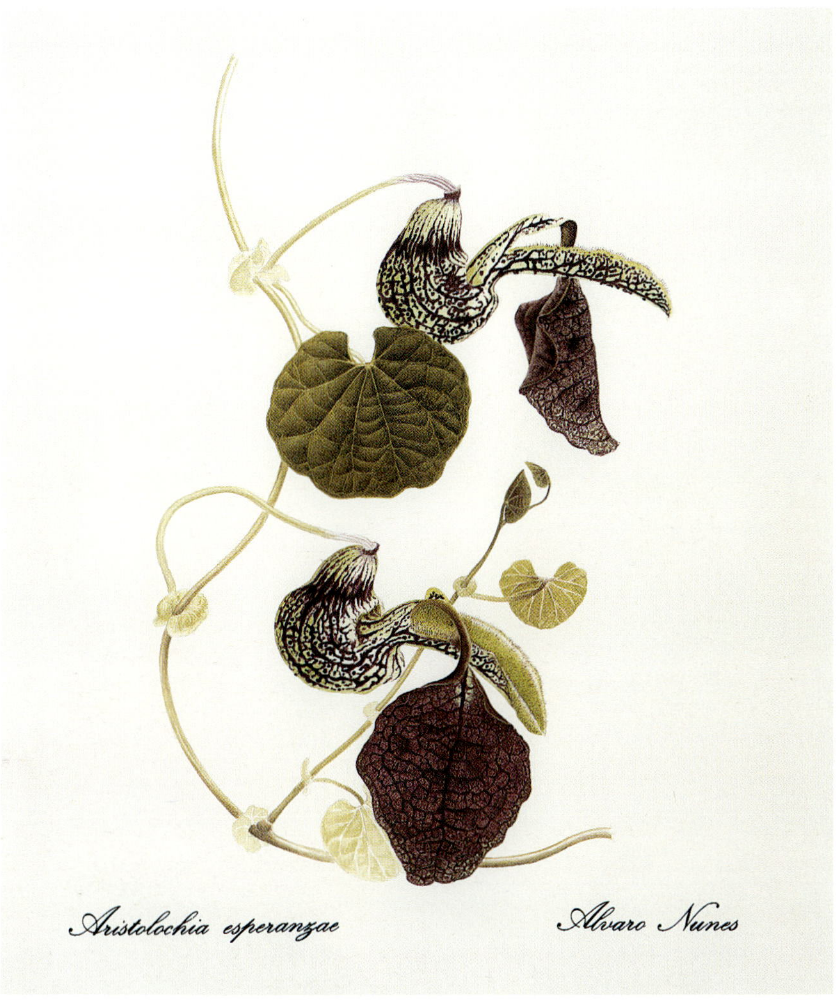

ARISTOLOCHIA ESPERANZAE

(Above) Signed *Aristolochia esperanzae* Alvaro Nunes (in Letraset)
Acquired from the artist 2000
Watercolour on paper
510 × 380 mm

MYRCIARIA CAULIFLORA

(Left) Signed Alvaro Nunes 97
Acquired from the artist 1999
Watercolour on paper
415 × 305 mm

with Alvaro Nunes, hoping to see more of his *oeuvre*. He was available in Rio and brought his fascinating portfolio there to show me. He told me of his long, arduous and lonely trips to the wilder parts of Brazil and showed me paintings of the fruit he had collected from the native trees. After a great deal of indecision, I chose four from different areas of Brazil, a difficult choice as they were all so good.

Myrciaria cauliflora, Jaboticaba is a large shrub (about 4–5 metres tall) which produces its fluffy, white flowers tight up against the trunk, followed by shiny, black berries (rather like blueberries). I had seen this plant only a few days earlier, in Rosalia Demonte's garden in Petropolis, producing flowers and fruit simultaneously. The flowers smell delicious and the fruit is used for liqueurs and jelly. It is cultivated in gardens in central and southern Brazil, as well as other tropical and subtropical parts of the New World.

The 'Fruits of Savannah' is a group of beautifully painted and detailed seed-cases, shown in sombre, dried-up hues which compared in an interesting way with his drawing of the fruits of the more lustrous *Orbygnia speciosa,* used to produce most of the palm oil for cooking, soaps and perfume. This palm is cultivated in Brazil from the Amazon region to the states of Bahia and the Mato Grosso (see page 257).

The most elegant of these paintings is the striking *Theobroma subincanum*, again with flower and fruit on the same stem, like the *Myrciaria cauliflora*. The execution of this painting is quite remarkable with the voluptuous fruit, angled leaves and tiny, pink-mauve flower at the end of the stem, making the design perfectly complete and satisfying. The tree comes from the Amazon and is 6–12 metres tall. The ripe fruit has a hard, rigid rind and can weigh as much as 250 gm. The sweetish pulp is eaten raw and the seeds are used in the preparation of household chocolate. He told me he was most interested in painting fruit and seeds from the Brazilian forests, but later sent me a delicate painting of an *Aristolochia esperanzae* which proved that he was equally comfortable with flowers. Most recently, at the time of my family's millennium visit to Rio, I acquired another *Aristolochia* complete with leaves and stem (see page 257).

Susan Ogilvy

BORN KENT, ENGLAND 1948

Susan Ogilvy qualified as an occupational therapist in 1969 and completed a foundation course at Luton School of Art one year later. She went to work at a mental hospital just north of London and found it both fascinating and rewarding, but left upon her marriage because her husband, who was in the Fleet Air Arm, was posted to Scotland. Fifteen years later they moved to Muscat with their three sons. She started painting again, portraying the exotic flowers in the gardens around the British Embassy during their three-year appointment. She returned to domesticity until her sons were grown up and resumed painting when she was given a birthday present of a weekend course in botanical illustration in 1994.

As soon as I saw her work at the RHS in 1995 I felt that here was an artist with a different viewpoint. I bought her three precariously balanced apples immediately. The next year she had a lively show at Jonathan Cooper's Park Walk Gallery in London where I acquired her delightful string of dancing cherries which was used on the cover of her catalogue. In 1997 she exhibited again at the RHS and was awarded a gold medal.

In 1998 she had another show with Jonathan Cooper where I bought 'Taurus Moulding', a beautifully painted pattern of laurel leaves 'reclaimed'

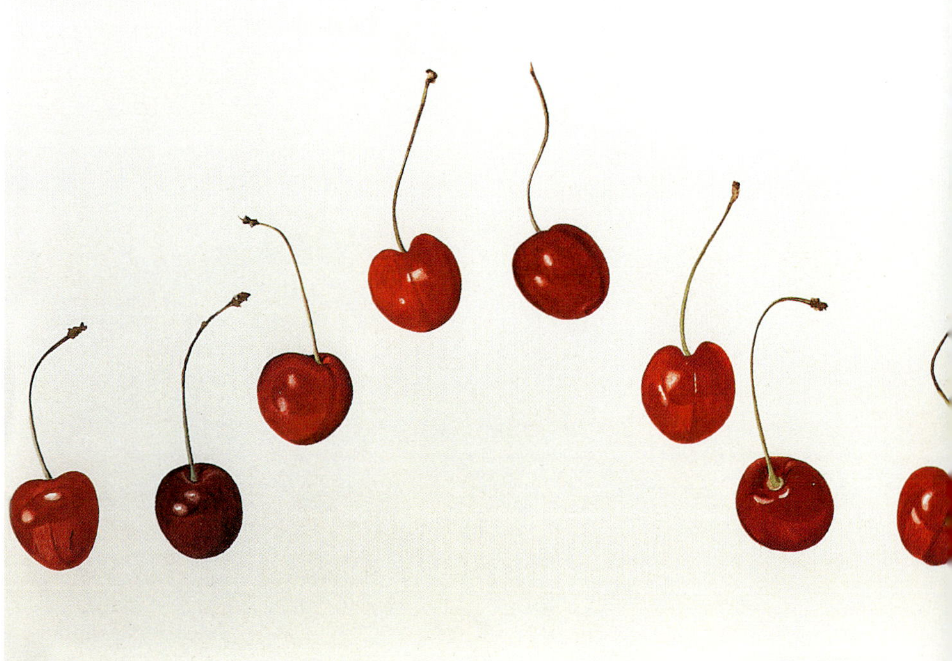

CHERRIES

Signed Susan Ogilvy 1995

Acquired from Park Walk Gallery, London 1996

Watercolour on paper

150 × 520 mm

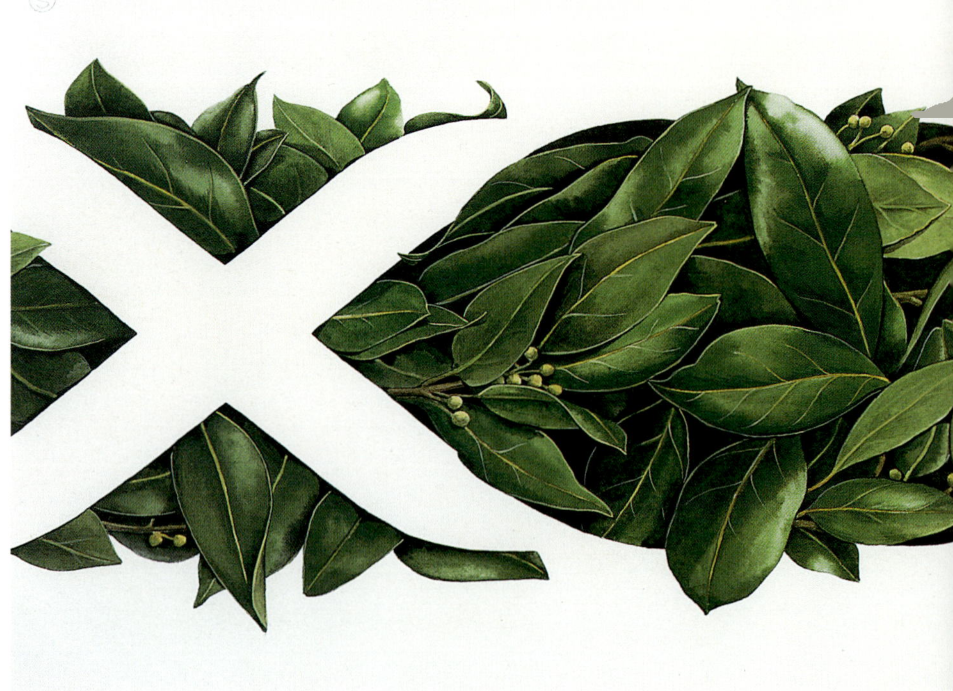

TAURUS MOULDING

(Right) Signed S (undated)

Acquired from Park Walk Gallery, London 1998

Watercolour on paper

200 × 730 mm

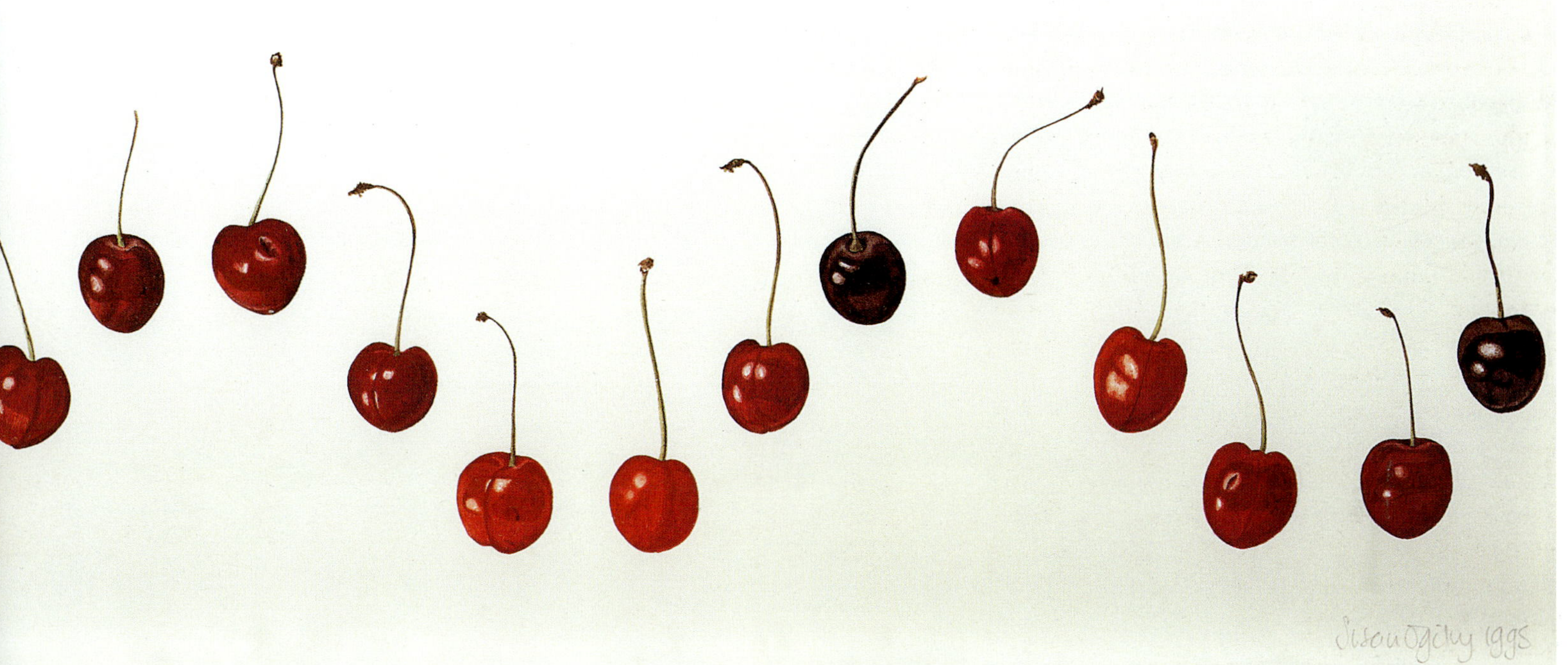
Susan Ogilvy 1995

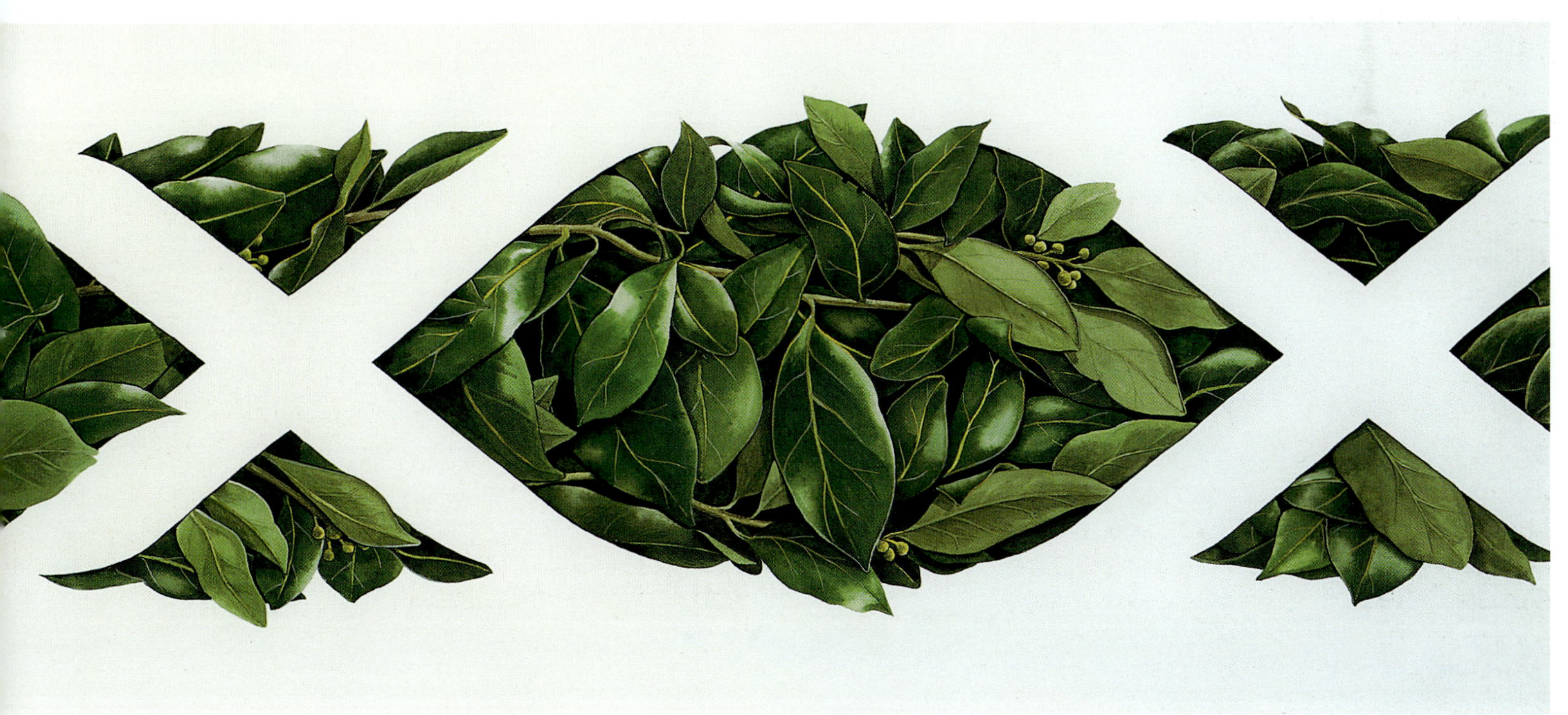

from being used over the centuries as the model for ceiling mouldings. I could not resist hanging this painting above a large door in my country house as a *faux* moulding.

From the same show I also purchased 'Green Leaves', a remarkable study of different kinds of leaves, the shapes and colour tones so varied and cunningly balanced. There is something curious and fascinating about this painting which is difficult to define.

She was invited to show at the Tryon & Swann gallery in the 'Botanical Artists of the World' exhibition I helped curate in 1998, with considerable success.

This lively, attractive painter has a profound sense of design combined with superb technique and a refreshingly original viewpoint. Whenever I give a talk on botanical art I find that I select the transparency of her cherries to end on a fresh and lively note. They are irresistible.

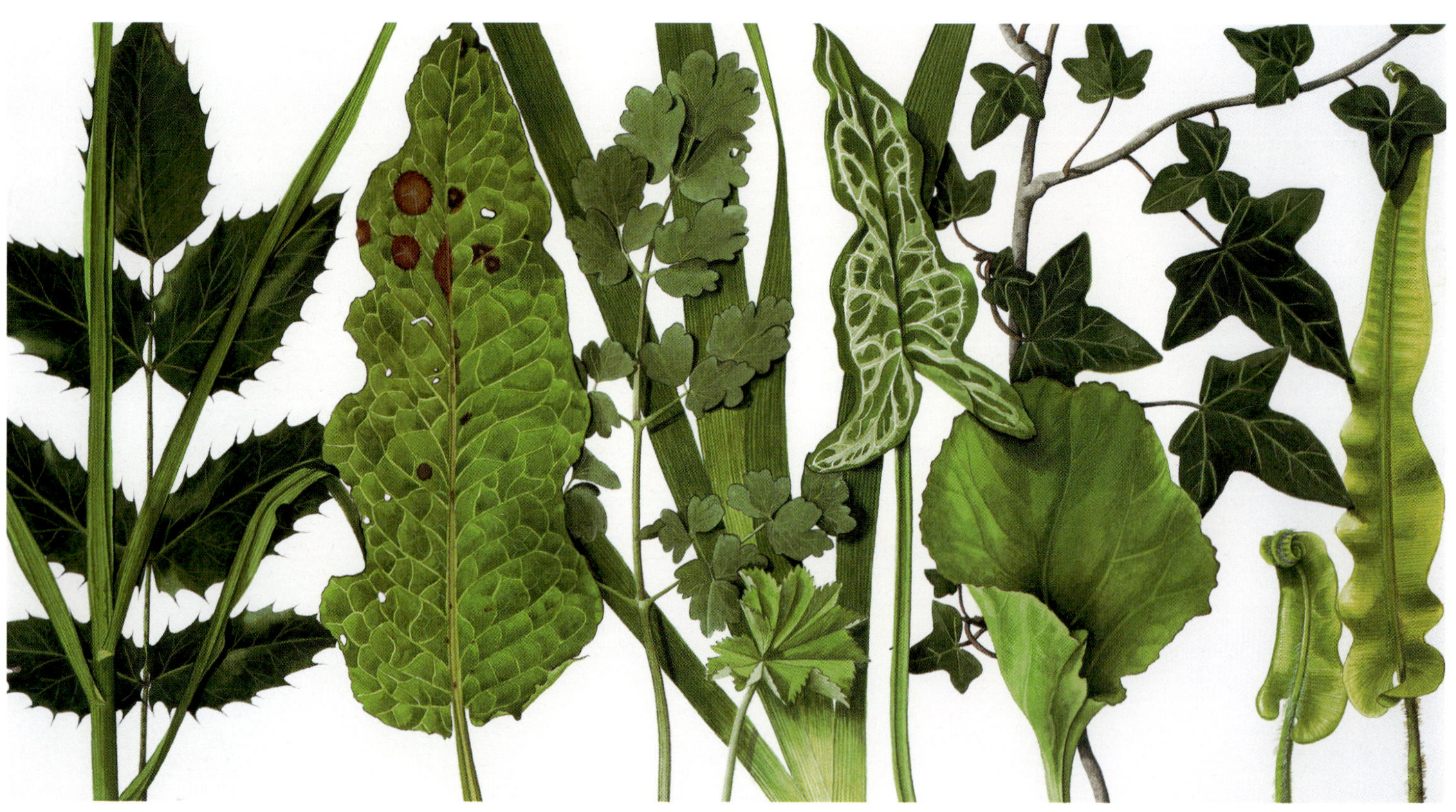

GREEN LEAVES
Signed S (undated)
Acquired from Park Walk Gallery, London 1998
Watercolour on paper
210 × 390 mm

THREE APPLES
Signed Susan Ogilvy 1995
Acquired from the RHS Show 1995
Watercolour on paper
175 × 167 mm

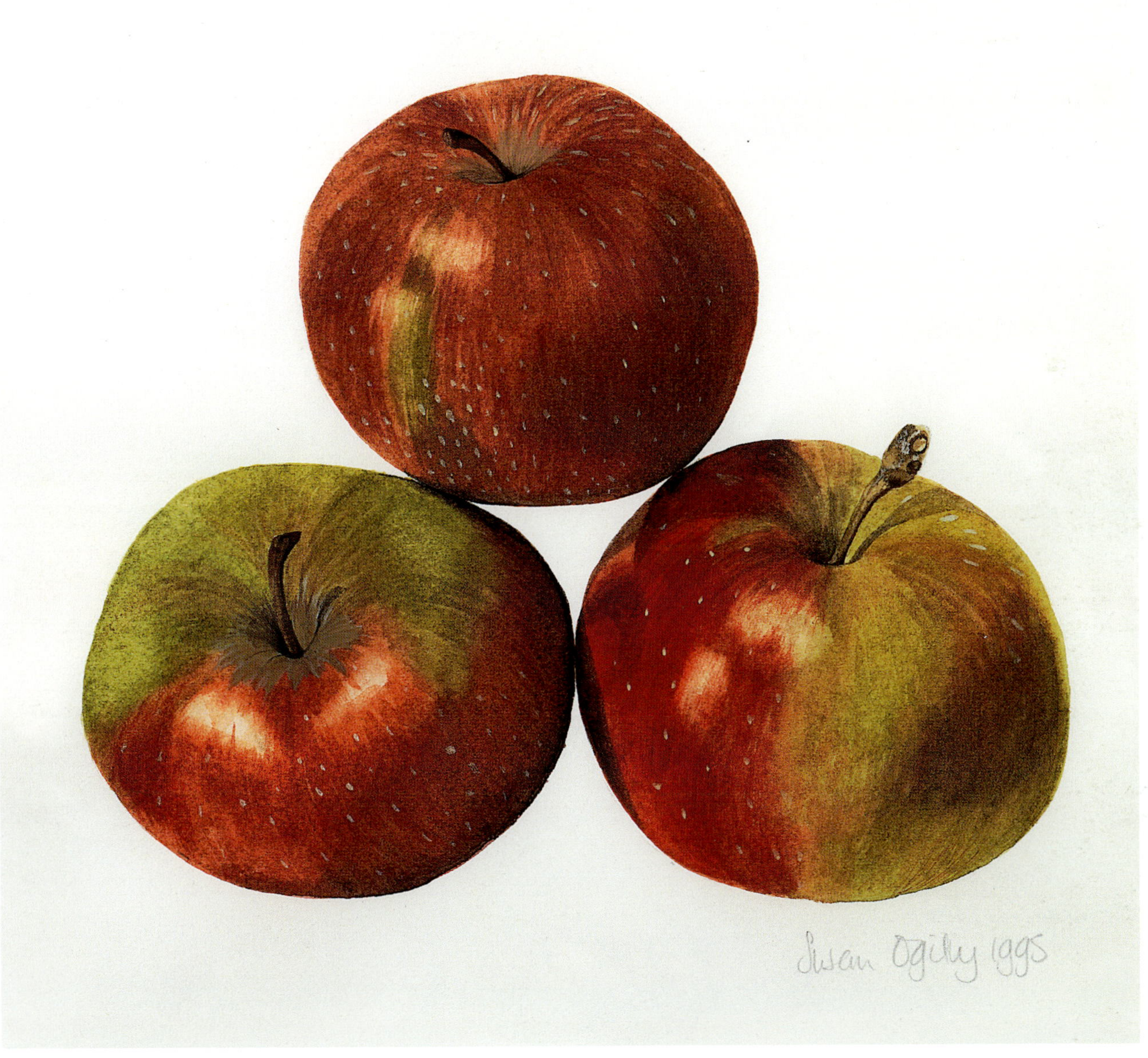
Susan Ogilvy 1995

Barbara Oozeerally

Born Poland, 1953

Barbara Oozeerally is an energetic, lively person with a glowing passion for flower painting. She trained as an architect in Warsaw and worked there from 1976 to 1979. Then she became a fashion designer and has only been painting full-time since 1996. She has shown several times at the RHS, being awarded silver gilt medals, and at the Graphic Fine Art and the Chelsea Society.

I saw her entry of poppies at the RHS and thought they were excellently composed and painted. She had caught the still-crumpled, expanding poppy petals so well, with their fragile, ephemeral and startling beauty.

Another of her paintings is a wonderful magnolia which was painted at Kew, the result of many visits. Here the texture is quite different from the poppies, with the thick outsides of the rather coarse petals shown as a lustrous deep pink, with the palest shell-pink inside. Without labouring the point, she has shown all the stages of flowering from a young furry bud through the opening and expanding of the petals, to the newly developing fruit. It is a beautiful portrait, lovingly observed, painted by an artist with great control of her medium.

More recently I bought a lively yellow gourd, the kind that is widely grown in the United States to decorate the festive table at Thanksgiving. This pear-shaped squash had a warty, corrugated surface that obviously fascinated Barbara, who had painted the ornamental skin with loving and meticulous intensity.

She is a painter who impresses me not only with her work but also with her determination to make her way as an artist, putting in many hours each day, trying to improve, not cutting corners, excited by what she is doing.

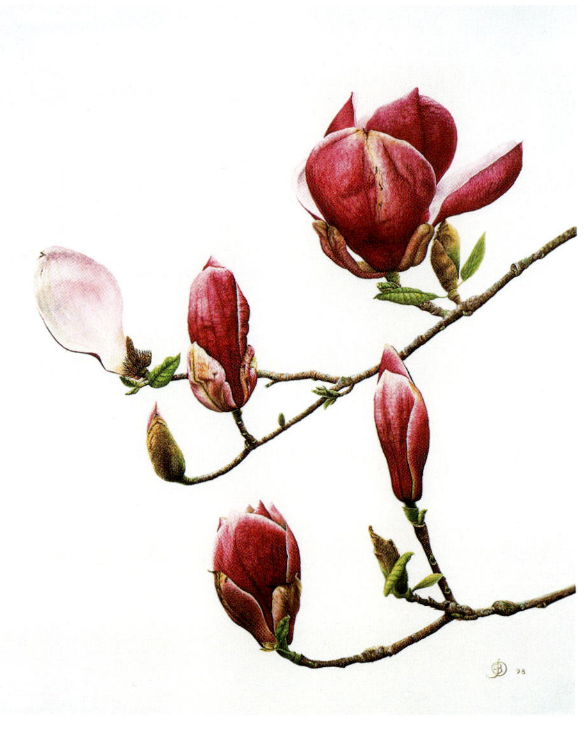

MAGNOLIA X SOULANGEANA
Signed BO 98
Acquired from the RHS Show 1998
Watercolour on paper
430 × 350 mm

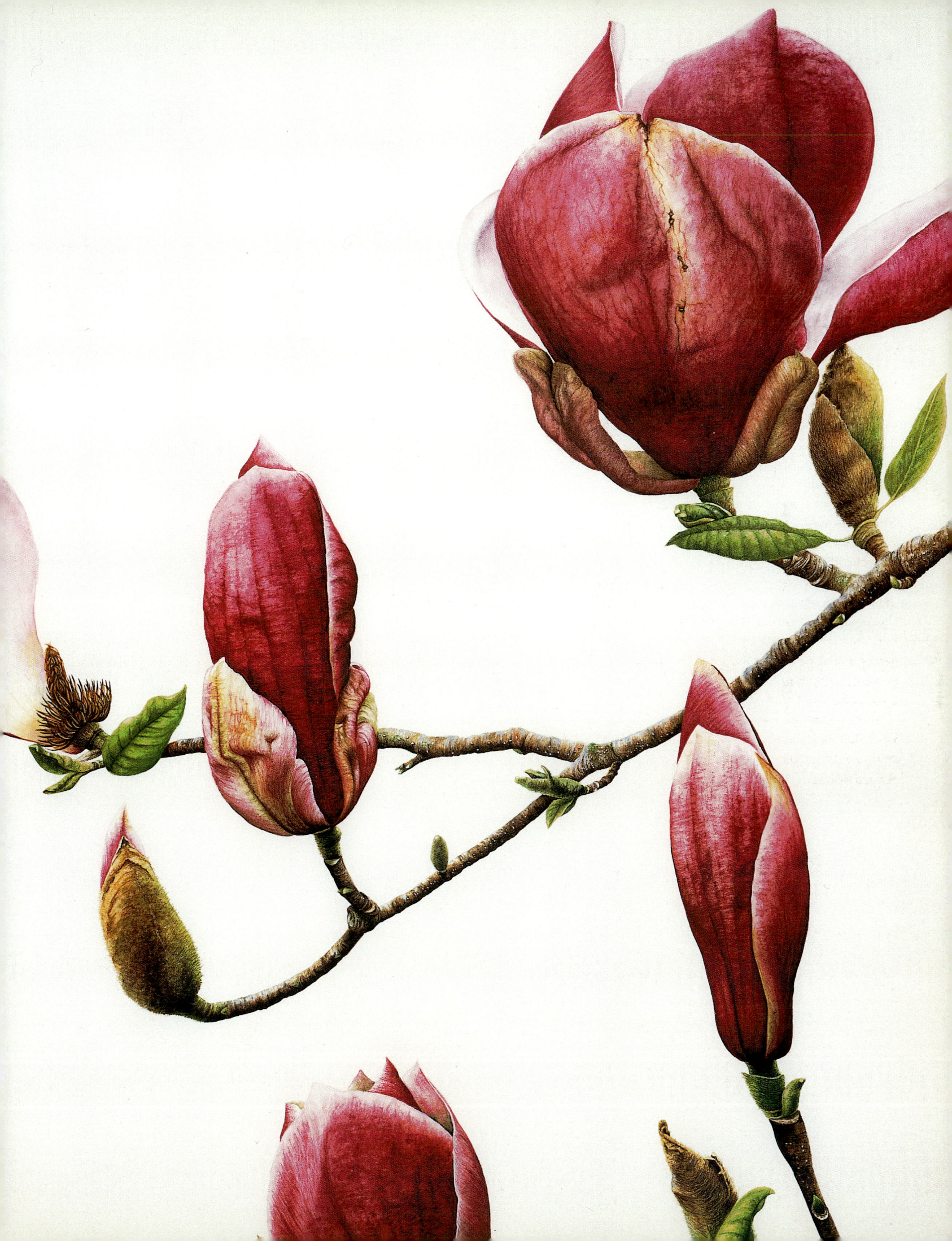

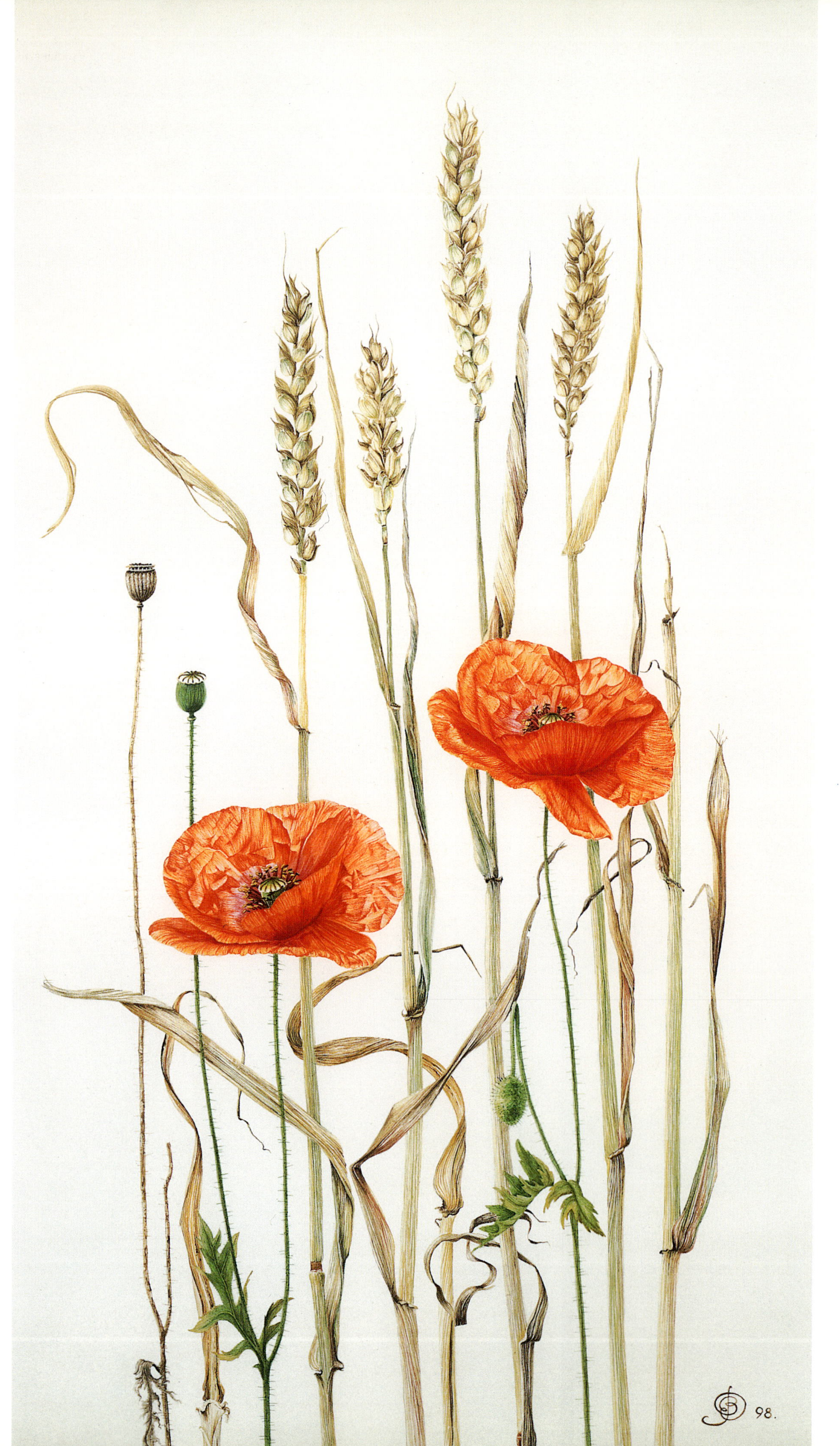
98.

HARVEST POPPIES
(Left) Signed BO 98
Acquired from the
RHS Show 1998
Watercolour on paper
430 × 240 mm

PEAR-SHAPED
YELLOW WARTED
ORNAMENTAL
GOURD
Signed BO 99
Acquired at the RHS
Show 2000
Watercolour on paper
195 × 155 mm

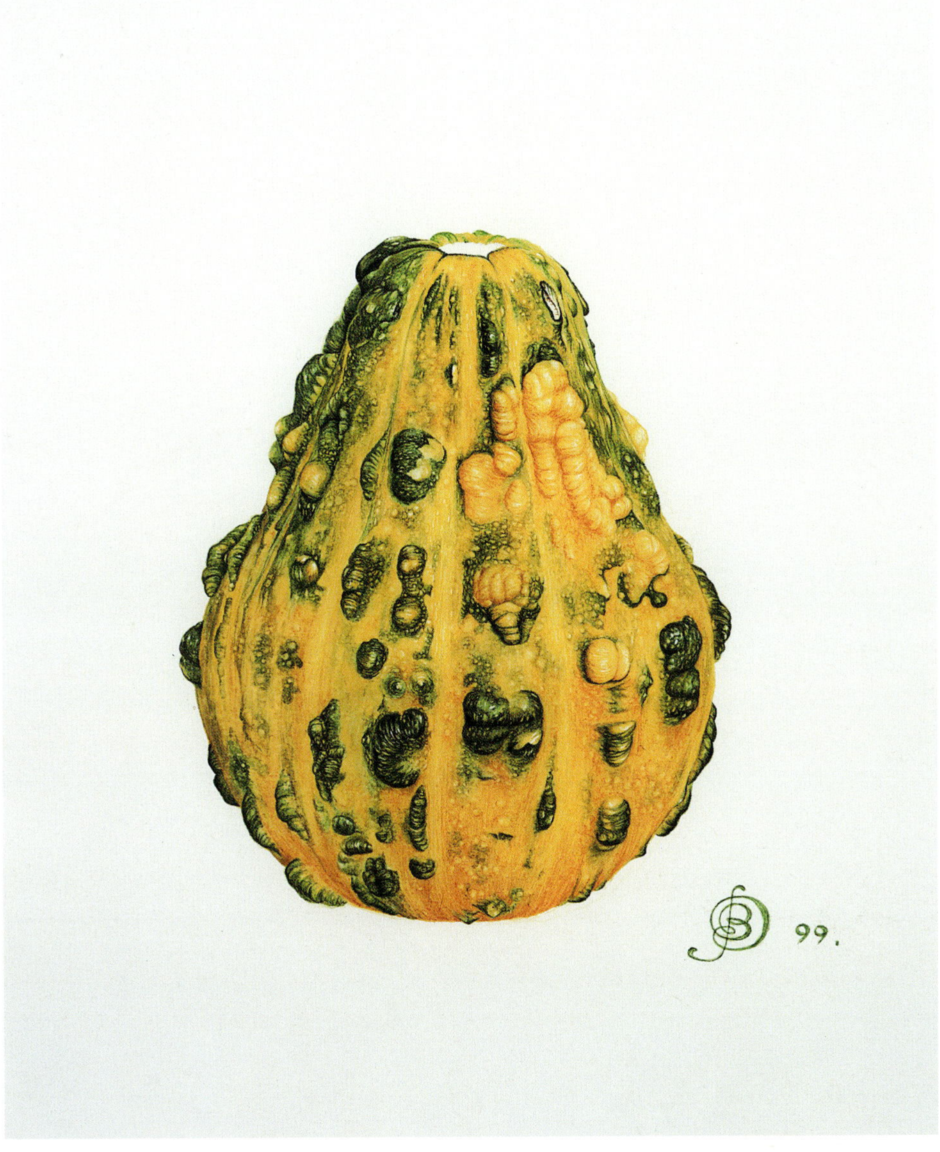

Jenny Phillips

BORN BOORT, VICTORIA, AUSTRALIA 1949

I first met Jenny Phillips at the RHS in 1993 when she was visiting from Melbourne. She showed eight examples of *Euphorbia* and was awarded a gold medal. At the time she was rather uncertain which way she should go with her painting and had spent some months studying in Europe, looking at the Old Masters stored in the rich libraries and collections of the Italian, English and French museums.

Shortly after this she established her Botanical Art School of Melbourne which I visited in 1995. Since then she and her husband Robert Crompton have created a purpose-designed studio there. She has trained several teachers to work with the classes while she is travelling and the School is an undoubted success with students not only from Melbourne, but from Europe, the United States and Japan. She has proved an inspired and influential force with hundreds of devoted pupils.

When I initiated botanical painting classes in Orient-Express Hotels in 1997 I asked Jenny to become one of the teachers. Since 1998 she has given master classes in the Observatory Hotel, Sydney, the Mount Nelson Hotel, Cape Town, and Charleston Place, Charleston. We aim for about sixteen students, maximum twenty, and recently Jenny has been teaching up to four classes each January in Sydney, often with waiting lists.

The first of Jenny's classes in the Observatory Hotel, Sydney was planned to coincide with the opening in January 1998 of my collection in the S. H. Ervin Gallery. It was a splendid surprise that there was a Ferdinand Bauer exhibition in the Sydney Museum at the same time. It was the first time most of the Bauer paintings had been shown and Jenny and I took the class to see his paintings executed on the Flinders expedition which circumnavigated Australia between 1801 and 1803. An elated and yet daunted class emerged later, overwhelmed by the visual feast of these rarely displayed treasures from the Natural History Museum, London. As we walked outside I challenged Jenny to paint something comparable.

She set to work on her return to Melbourne, choosing a tremendously complex flower to paint on vellum which was Bauer's material. This pink gum tree has a close 'look-a-like' called *Eucalyptus calophylla* which can only be distinguished by a spur on one of the petals. As Jenny had painted the flowers and fruit in the meticulous style of Ferdinand Bauer, it was indeed possible to identify this specimen as *Corymbia ficifolia*. Now, with DNA analysis, it should be possible to see how close these almost identical but apparently unrelated trees prove to be using the new taxonomic techniques.

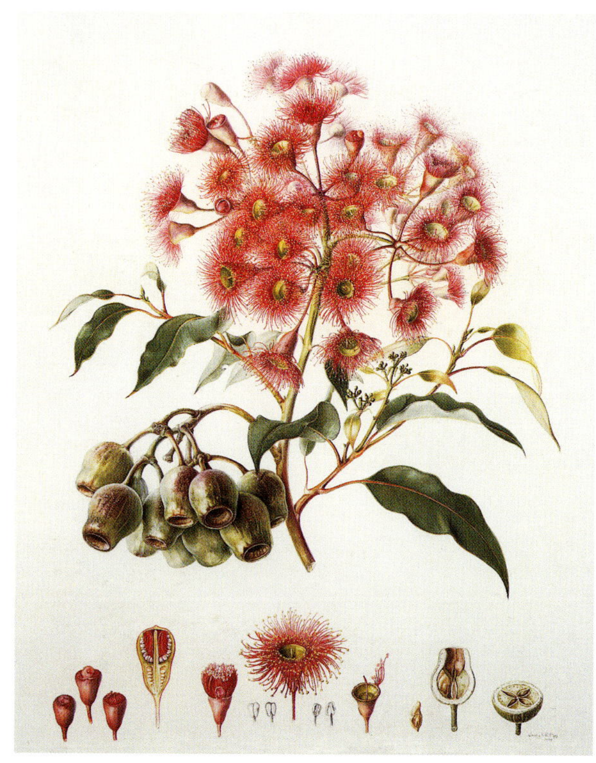

CORYMBIA FICIFOLIA
Signed Jenny K. Phillips 1998
Acquired from the Tryon & Swann Gallery, London 1998
Watercolour on vellum
530 × 390 mm

I had been keen to show botanical art in the UK and when Oliver Swann approached me to co-curate an exhibition in the Tryon & Swann Gallery in London I leapt at the opportunity. One of the three paintings Jenny sent in was the pink gum and we selected it for the cover of the brochure. It is now part of my collection. Another was a spectacular *Agapanthus*, the third a subtle and sophisticated watercolour of *Protea grandiceps*.

All artists who are also teachers find a conflict of interest. It is hard to find time for one's own painting in a demanding schedule of teaching. But Jenny has managed to balance her time very well and still has energy for her own work, which is so important because it keeps her painting and teaching fresh.

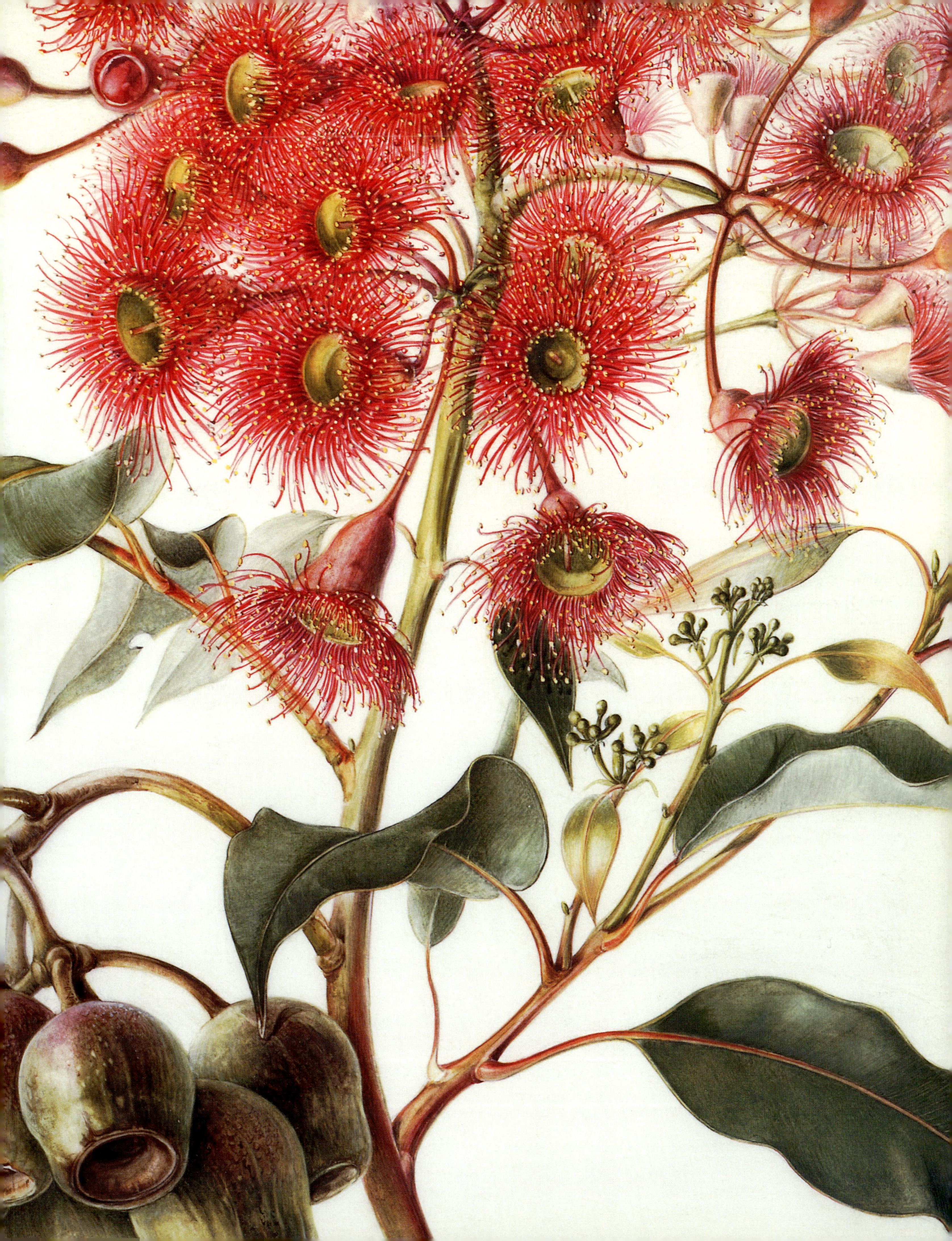

Barbara Pike

BORN JOHANNESBURG, SOUTH AFRICA 1933

I met Barbara Pike in Cape Town, at Kirstenbosch Botanical Gardens where her work was included in a small exhibition by South African artists in 1998. They had come together for a discussion group initiated by Gillian Condy of the National Botanical Institute in Pretoria and were revelling in the inter-reaction that occurs between artists who spend most of their working life in a rather solitary state. I had given a talk on contemporary botanical art earlier and went in to see their show.

I was immediately struck by Barbara Pike's arresting watercolour of *Strelitzia nicolai*, an extraordinary outsize flower with a wild extravaganza of white and blue petals bursting out of deep purple bracts, shaped like spiky boats. It grows as a large, untidy bush, best looked down upon from above, and I have seen it flourishing as far afield as Madeira, Lisbon and Cape Town with equal enthusiasm. The painting is powerful and she has handled a vulgar, slightly grotesque subject with practised skill.

Barbara Pike became a biochemist and medical artist after graduating from the University of Witwaterstrand. After a couple of years she moved to the University's botany department as a botanical artist and became freelance in 1959. She has shown in many exhibitions in South Africa, particularly at the Everard Read Gallery in Johannesburg and in congresses devoted to succulents. She has completed many commissions and painted *Clivia miniata* and *Rothmannia capensis* for the restored and redecorated Blue Train.

Her artworks have been published in many local magazines and newspapers and she has produced the illustrations for all three editions of *A Natural History of Inchaca Island, Moçambique* by W. McNae and M. Kalk as well as producing plates illustrating the flora of the veld and Witwaterstrand.

In February 2000 I was asked to open the Inaugural Kirstenbosch Exhibition of Botanical Art where she was awarded a silver Kirstenbosch medal. She showed six strong works and amongst them a relatively low-key watercolour of *Nymania capensis*, commonly known as Chinese lantern or klapperboo. This is an unusual shrub or small tree, belonging to the *Meliaceae*, that is found in semi-desert areas such as the Little Karoo in Cape Province, South Africa. It is quite a bleak area notable for its ostrich farms, the desert studded with cactus and mimetes, where the bright reddish pink 'lanterns' of the balloon-shaped fruits stand out. Buds, flowers and fruit in different stages of maturity can appear together on the same branch. The flowers first appear in the winter and mature to greenish-pink and then deeper pink bells in the spring. However, this specimen of klapperboo was painted from a plant growing in a garden in Johannesburg where it is grown for its charming decorative quality.

STRELITZIA NICOLAI
(Right) Signed Barbara Pike '96
Acquired from the artist 1998
Watercolour on paper
502 × 304 mm

NYMANIA CAPENSIS
(Left) Signed Barbara Pike (undated)
Acquired from the Kirstenbosch Exhibition of Botanical Art 2000
Watercolour on paper
430 × 330 mm

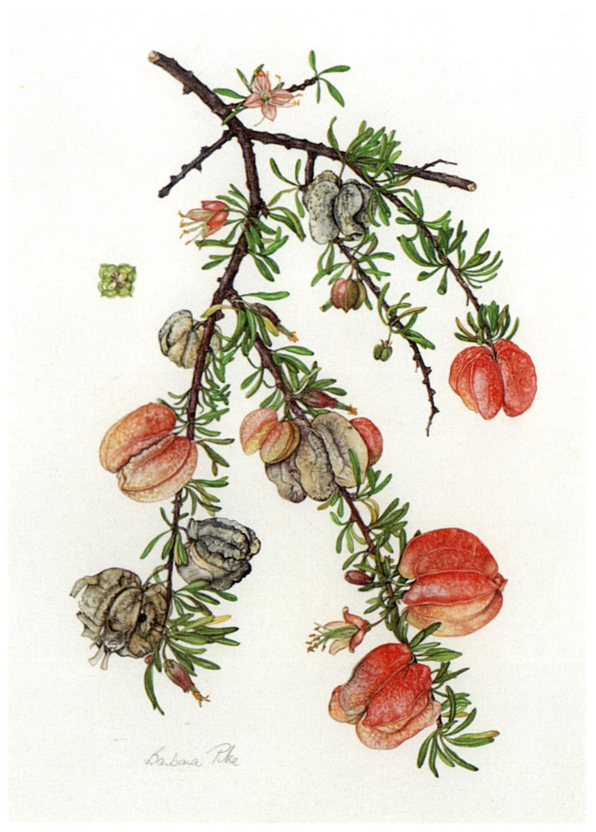

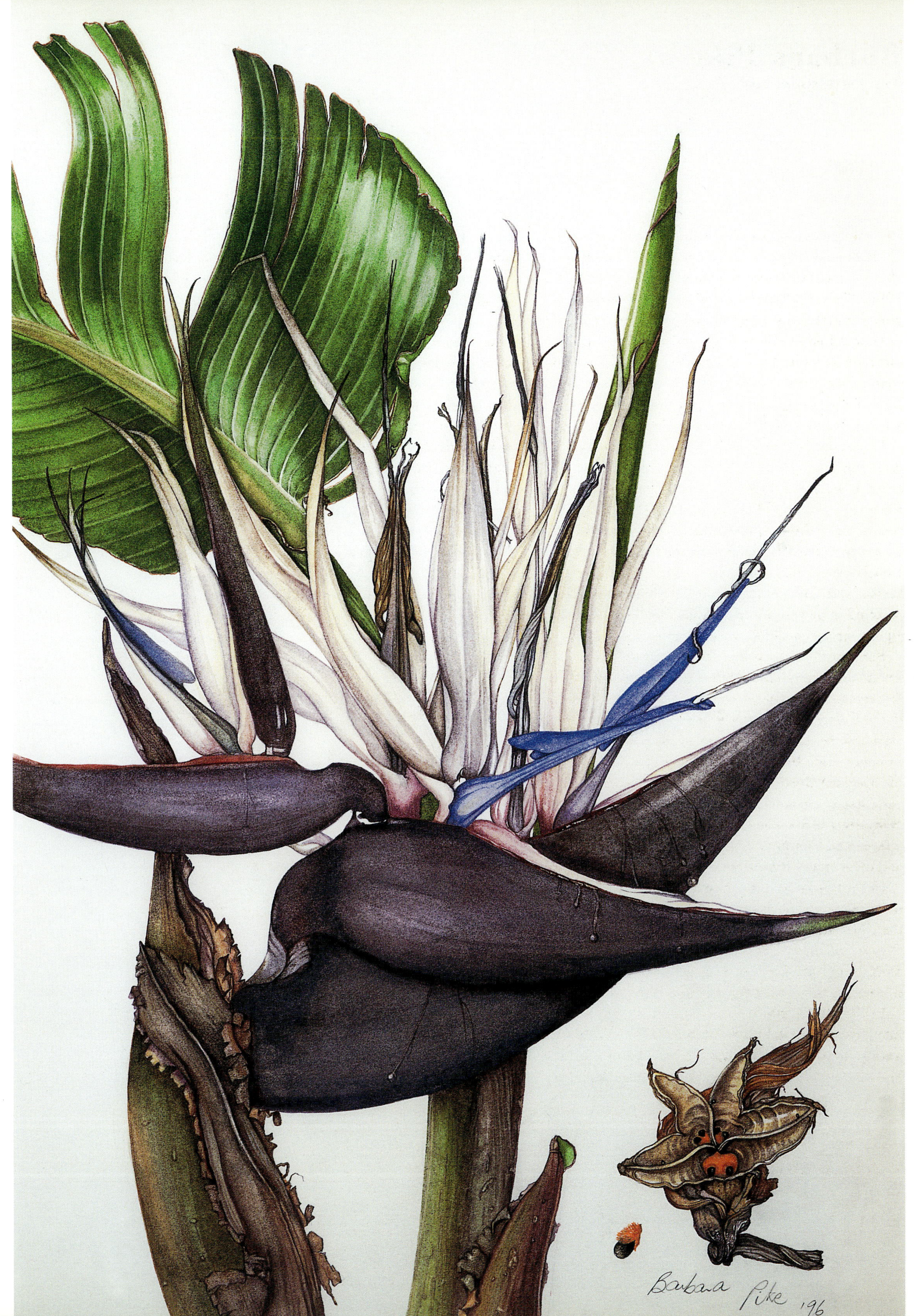
Barbara Pike '96

Rodella Purves

BORN PAISLEY, RENFREWSHIRE, SCOTLAND 1945

Rodella Purves has had a long career in the botanical world. Educated in Edinburgh, she took a diploma in agricultural botany followed by another in seed testing. She went briefly to New Zealand before returning to Scotland to work on exhibitions at the Royal Botanic Garden, Edinburgh. She made her first attempt at portraying plants when she was helping to put up a large introductory panel for an exhibition, featuring a pansy. Other displays followed and eventually she was introduced to the refinements of botanical painting in 1971 with an illustration course at Flatford Mill with John Nash R.A. and an interpretative course at Edinburgh College of Art by Robin Phillipson, tutored by Edward Gage. Since 1976 she has been a freelance artist producing work for both private and public collections.

She has published work in *The Kew Magazine* (incorporating *Curtis's Botanical Magazine*) and *The Plantsman*, as well as more general magazine titles. Her work has appeared in *The Orchid Book* by James Cullen, 1992, in *The Rhododendron Species* by H. H. Davidian, Volumes 1–4, and *The New Royal Horticultural Society Dictionary of Gardening* and she is included in *The Flower Artists of Kew* by W. T. Stearn (1990).

She has exhibited regularly since 1975 and was represented in the Hunt Institute's 4th International Exhibition in 1976, but probably her most important show has been a retrospective of twenty years' work in 1996 at the City Art Centre, Edinburgh for which she was able to borrow back many commissions from far afield to provide an impressive display of sixty-nine watercolours.

Having wanted to add one of her paintings to my collection, I had to wait several years before Rodella Purves could fulfil my commission. We decided on a blue *Meconopsis*, a wonderful azure poppy that blooms briefly in May and flourishes in the Royal Botanic Garden, Edinburgh. At last it arrived, a composition with the hairy leaves as beautifully observed as the opening buds and the striking, spectacular flowers. It has made me renew my efforts to grow it in my own garden where I already have a yellow *Meconopsis cambrica*, the Welsh poppy, but have so far failed with blue ones.

MECONOPSIS X SHELDONII (M. BETONICIFOLIA X GRANDIS)
RBG EDIN. JUNE 1999
Signed Rodella
(undated)
Commissioned 1998,
Acquired 1999 (154 painting hours listed on edge)
Watercolour on paper
720 × 540 mm

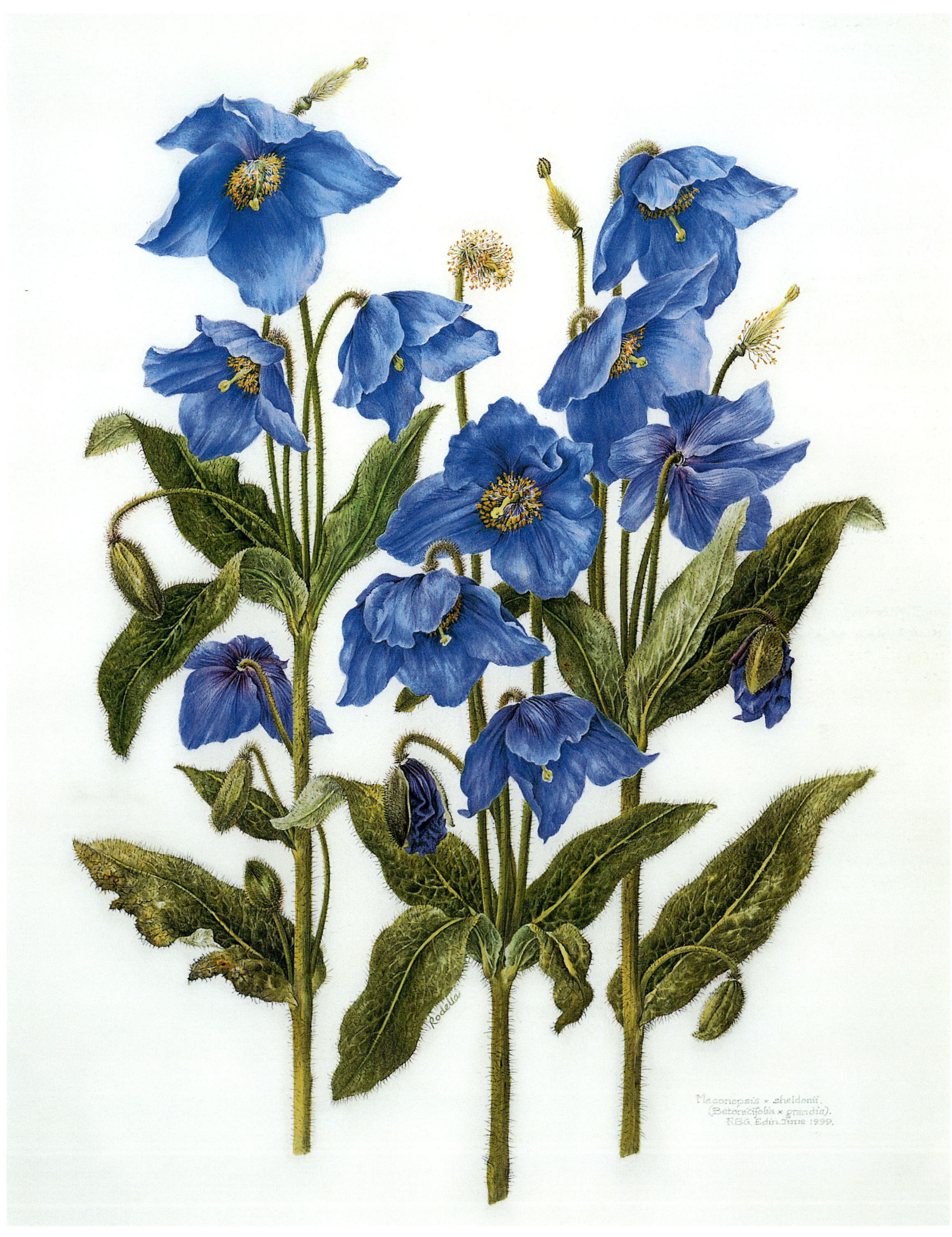
Rodella
Meconopsis × sheldonii.
(Betonicifolia × grandis).
RBG. Edin. June 1999.

Celia Rosser

Born Melbourne, Australia 1930

Celia Rosser can certainly claim her place in history as one of the world's most important botanical illustrators through her remarkable work on the Australian genus *Banksia*. These paintings have been reproduced in three volumes by Monash University: Volume I published in 1981, Volume II in 1988 and the long anticipated Volume III in 2000. She became Science Faculty Artist at Monash University, Melbourne, Australia in 1970, started her monumental work there on the banksias in 1974 and has been painting them ever since. Every time the end was in sight another new species was found, so the last volume contains the portraits and descriptions of four extra species, bringing the total in all three volumes to seventy-six. This is the first time there has been such a comprehensive study of an entire genus and each life-size portrait is magnificent in its design, colour and elaborate detail of the complex cones, varied leaves and spectacular blooms.

The text for the three volumes has been written by Alex George, known throughout Australia as the 'Banksia man'. George and Rosser travelled all over the country for rare specimens and George's unrivalled knowledge meant that they could collect specimens at the right time of flowering or fruiting.

Some species of banksia are widely distributed and easy to track down, but some examples are only found in remote and inaccessible areas. On one occasion George and Rosser had to get special permission to collection *Banksia oligantha* from a distant Aboriginal sacred site.

They deliberately selected aesthetically pleasing examples of each plant, which displayed the major stages of growth, flowering and fruiting, but would look 'in character' on the page. Celia Rosser took notes on leaf and cone colour in the field and then

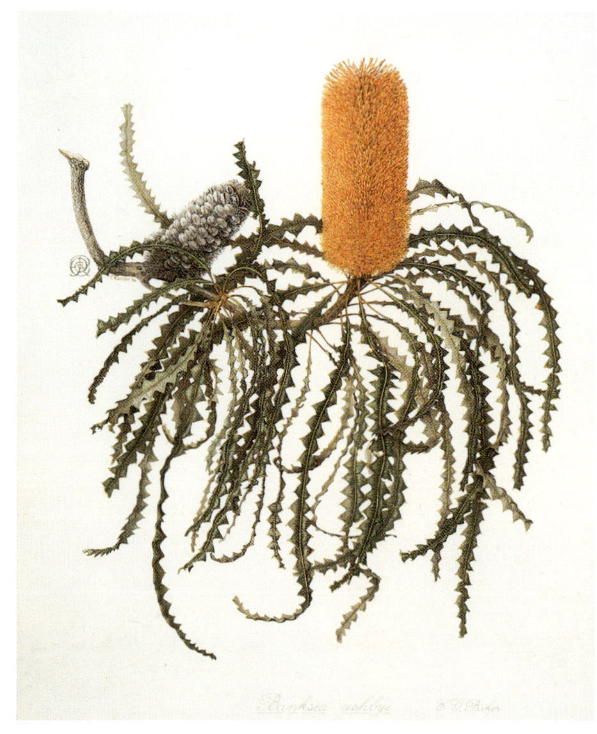

BANKSIA ASHBYI
Signed C. Rosser '94
From an original transparency
from *The Banksias* Volume III
by Celia E. Rosser &
Alexander S. George, Monash
University, Published 2000
Watercolour on paper
760 × 530 mm

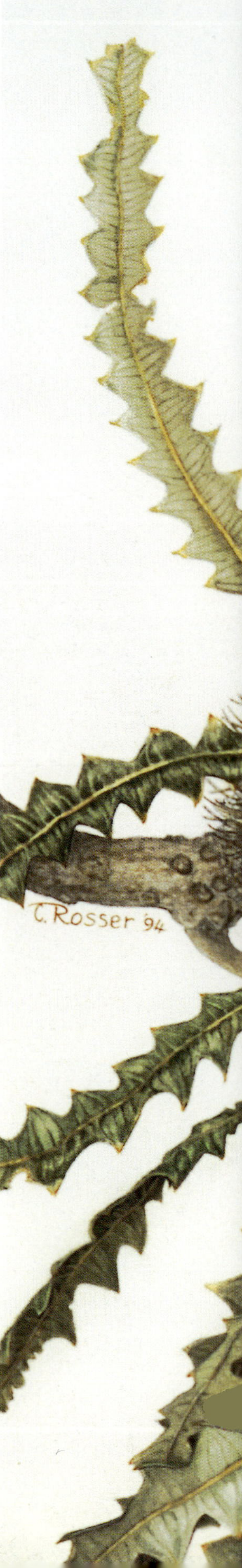

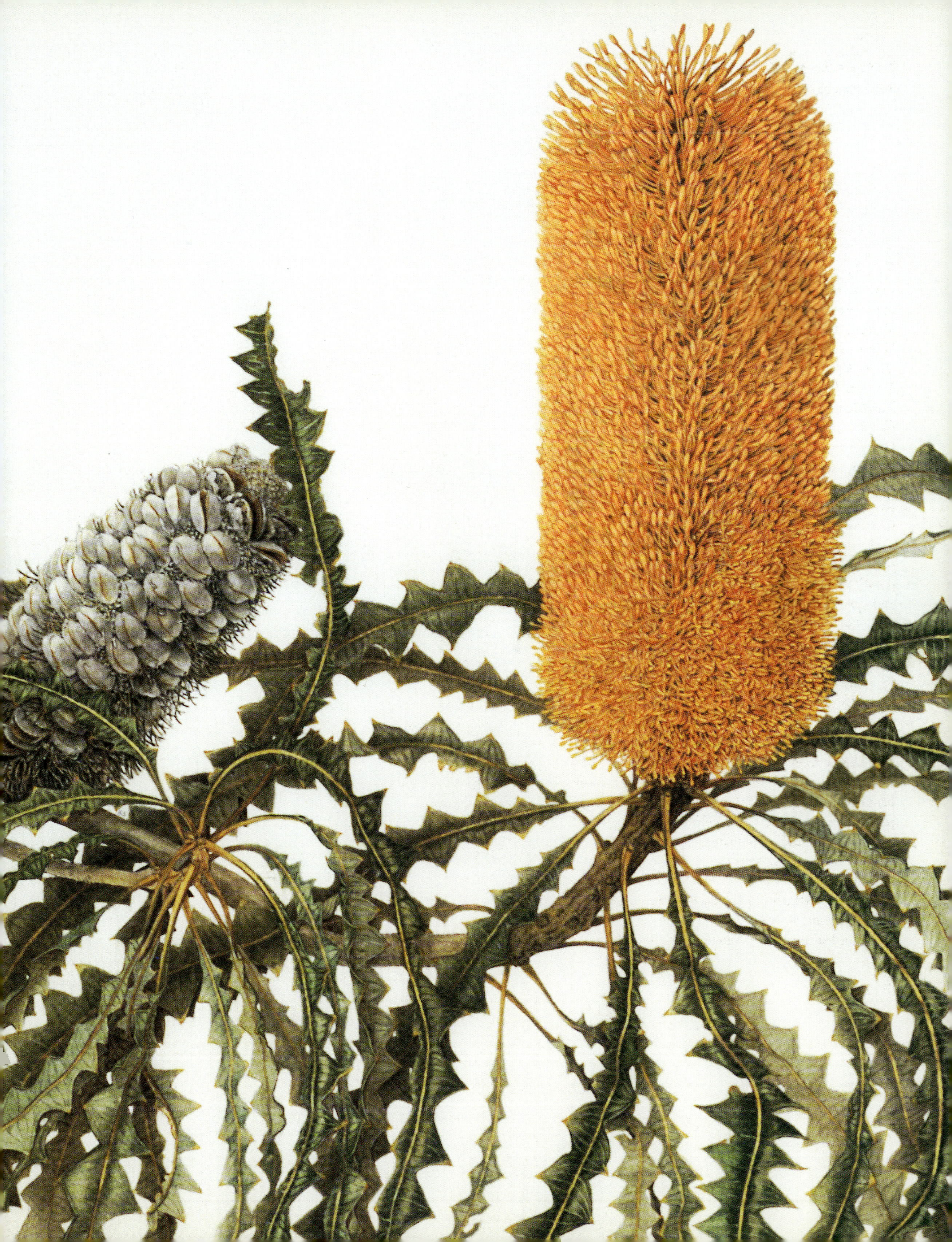

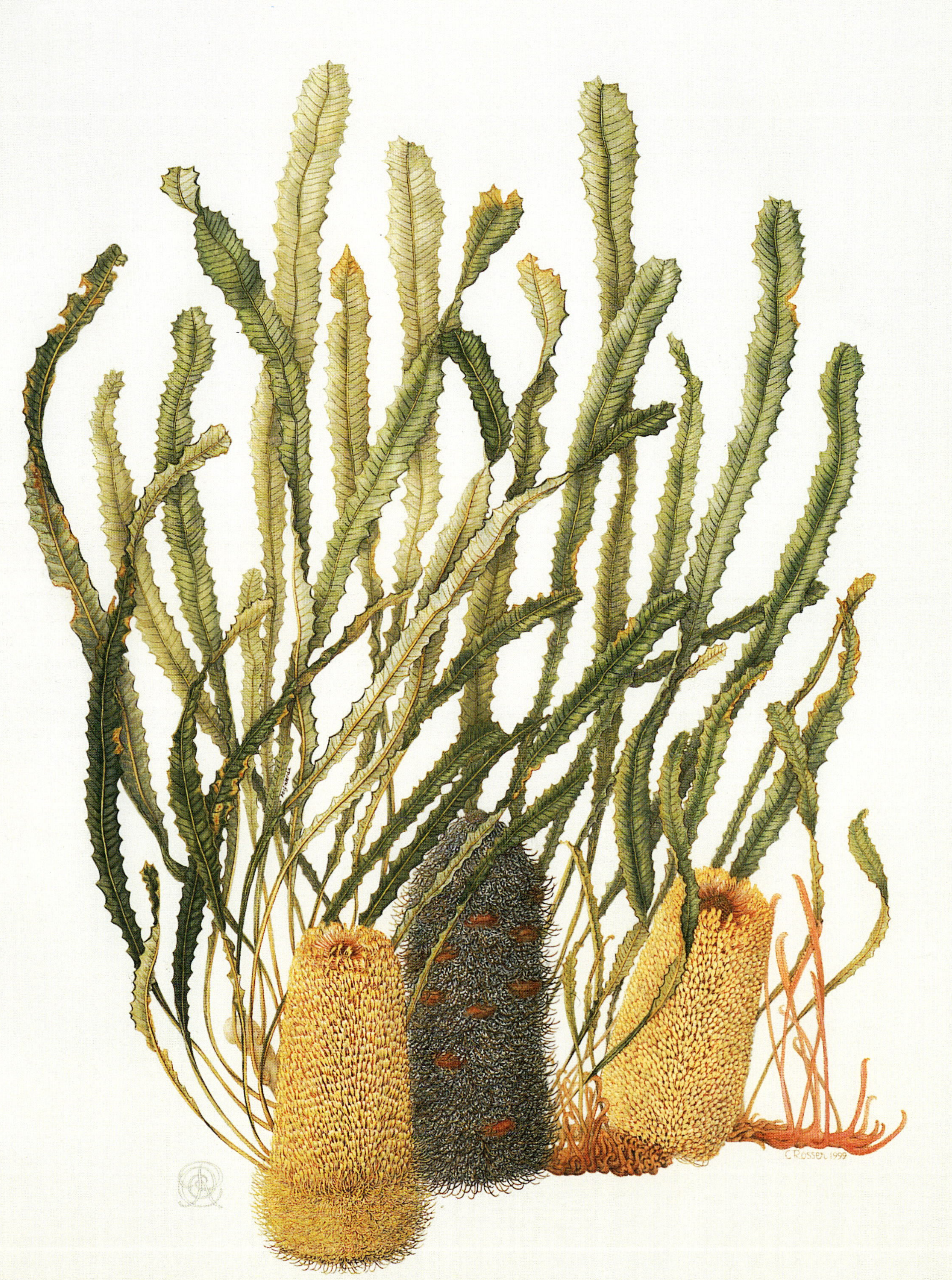
C Rosser 1999

BANKSIA PETIOLARIS
Signed C. Rosser
1999
From an original transparency from *The Banksias* Volume III by Celia E. Rosser & Alexander S. George, Monash University, Published 2000
Watercolour on paper
760 × 530 mm

kept the specimens in the fridge for constant reference while she was building up the watercolour layers in her studio. She learned the defining details of each species and made sure these were clearly yet subtly shown in each portrait. Her design and execution are quite wonderful and how she kept going for twenty-five years, working with enthusiasm on such a detailed genus, is a mystery to me. She had obviously fallen in love with these strange, complicated plants that are quintessentially Australian.

I consider the three volumes of *The Banksias* one of the very best publications in any field produced in the twentieth century, or indeed, in any century and it represents a truly colossal achievement. They are beautifully printed, compare faultlessly with the original watercolours, have authoritative text – in fact every page is magnificent. Less than a thousand copies of each volume have been printed, all on the same batch of archival rag paper from the Inveresk Paper Company which matches the textured 100 percent rag paper from Arches that Celia Rosser used for her original paintings. Because of their large size and weight the three volumes are mostly to be found in specialist libraries but they are bound to be collector's items in the future. The Queen was given a set on a recent visit to Australia, to add to her remarkable royal library at Windsor and they can certainly take their place with pride alongside the volumes by Catesby and Audubon.

Monash University owns all but one of Rosser's original watercolours and showed them at Kew and some venues in the United States in the 1990s. I remember seeing them at the Kew Gallery when I was starting to collect. There was a recent plan to tour the originals making up the third volume in 2001 and 2002 in a similar way, but sadly I understand this has been cancelled.

Celia Rosser has received a number of accolades for this mighty work, including the Jill Smythies Award for Botanical Illustration from the Linnean Society of London in 1997 and an Honorary Master of Science and PhD from Monash University. Her painting of *Banksia serrata* in my collection has been shown all over the world, from Kew to Tokyo and from Sydney to Stockholm, including the Museum of Modern Art in Edinburgh, part of the National Galleries of Scotland. Celia came to the opening in Edinburgh, which happily coincided with her Linnean Society award. Soon it will be on exhibition at the Ashmolean Museum, Oxford in 'The Renaissance of Botanical Art', a show comparing the older masters with today's artists.

Graham Rust

Born Hertfordshire, England 1942

Graham Rust is best known for his murals and his ceiling paintings which he has painted in houses all over the world. Perhaps the most remarkable is *The Temptation*, his spectacular mural at Ragley Hall, Warwickshire, which took him over ten years to finish. But besides his skills as a muralist he is a wonderfully accomplished painter of flowers and a prolific illustrator of books. He put many of his mural designs together to produce *The Painted House*, a best-selling book now published in four languages. He is doing a sequel, *The Painted Ceiling*, to be published in the autumn of 2001. I well remember my delight in finding, by chance, his *The Secret Garden* which became a treasured Christmas present for one of my grandchildren. His flower paintings were used to illustrate a very successful edition of Vita Sackville-West's essays, *Some Flowers*, in 1996.

He was trained in art schools in London and New York and has had an amazing number of solo exhibitions in cities ranging from Panama to Chicago, New York, San Francisco and London. One of the first of his works I acquired was a rich, dark *Iris* 'Spartan', painted with a lush, velvety texture, so beautifully executed that one was tempted to stroke it. It has been greatly admired whenever it has been shown in exhibitions around the world.

I bought this elegant, striking tulip petal at his twenty-second one-man exhibition, which was held in London for the charity Sight Savers International. He has always been most generous in supporting worthy causes (I remember that the first picture I bought of his was at an auction for Gardens at a gala charity ball). Some of the subjects were plants, others were the original illustrations for his most recent books *Decorative Designs* and *Needlepoint Designs*. He showed two very well produced tulip prints there, with the graceful bulbs growing in ornamental Chinese bowls. Some excellent prints of his work have been produced over the years, which are always much in demand as they are both decorative and beautiful. He has always been quite hard to contact because painting murals requires a great deal of travelling and time, but he tells me he is now living and working for longer periods at his home in Suffolk.

'BLACK PARROT' TULIP PETAL
Signed Graham Rust
(undated)
Acquired from the artist's exhibition in aid of Sight Savers International 1999
Watercolour on paper
225 × 170 mm

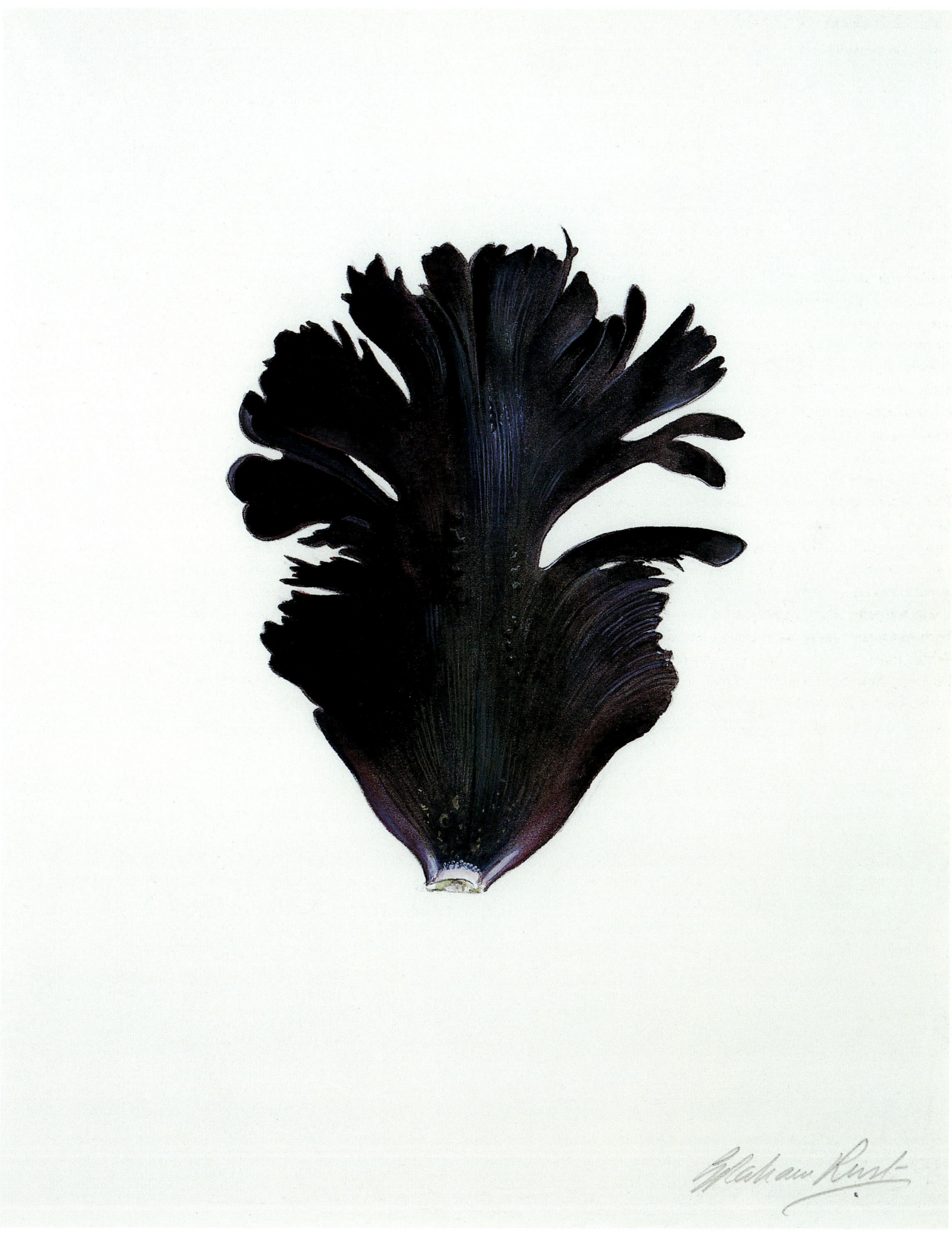

Manabu Saito

Born Tokyo, Japan 1929

Although Manabu Saito was born in Japan, he has spent most of his life in the United States and became an American citizen in 1968. He now lives in Stillwater, New Jersey and has recently been spending his winters in Tucson, Arizona painting a series of Sonoran Desert flora, mostly cacti, in their winter (non-flowering) forms.

Saito has just visited Zimbabwe for the Malilangwe Conservation Trust to record some of the local flora. There are 650 square miles of low veld in south-eastern Zimbabwe in the reserve and although it was mid-winter, he found some good examples of the Sabi star (*Adenium multiflorum*) to paint. He sent me a clipping from a local newspaper explaining his role as a painter there.

He went to school in Tokyo and studied English literature at St Paul's University there. Between 1953 and 1957 he took a degree in industrial design at the Pratt Institute, Brooklyn, New York where he was awarded two scholarships, one by the Pratt Institute Art School and the other by General Motors. For ten years he worked as an industrial designer in New York, then became a freelance botanical artist in 1971.

But long before 1971 he had started contributing black and white illustrations and colour plates to a variety of books, and his work became more and more focused on plant subjects. He has an impressive list of titles, having produced all the 127 plates showing 1563 species for *Wildflowers of North America, a Guide to Field Identification* by Frank D. Venning (1984) and another massive project of colour plates of 230 species of cacti, again authored by Frank D. Venning (*Cacti, a Golden Guide*, 1974). In 1989 he painted the cover and twenty-seven plates for a new edition of *How to Know Wildflowers* by Mrs William Starr Dana, a book originally published in 1893, a project which gave him particular pleasure. He sent me a copy of this delightful small book, with the plates executed in a Victorian style, with faintly coloured backgrounds.

In the 1970s and 1980s he produced plates for *Audubon*, *Horticulture* and the *National Geographic*. During the same period he made many signed and numbered collector prints, principally with the Frame House Gallery. His first one-man exhibition was in 1968 and he has had an annual show at the Zyt Gallery, Los Altos, California since 1980. He showed at the Hunt Institute in 1977 at the 4th International Exhibition.

He has done a certain amount of teaching, most recently at annual workshops at Brooklyn Botanic Gardens, New York, instructing on watercolour techniques. He was introduced to me by Elizabeth Scholtz, a former director of the Gardens who is a great enthusiast of botanical art and Saito's work. As a result of her introduction, Manabu Saito brought a portfolio of paintings and prints to show me in New York. I bought two paintings and a recent print he had made of hydrangeas.

The ginkgo has always interested me and I had actually seen people picking up the fruit from under the large trees in Brooklyn Botanic Gardens when I was shown round by Elizabeth Scholtz. I have a ginkgo avenue of my own, planted about fifteen years ago, which was meant to make a wonderful arching vista. The result is not quite as I planned because the trees have grown slowly and unevenly. Nevertheless, I love the fresh young leaves with their elegant, simple and distinctive shapes and the

MOURERA FLUVIATILIS:
'KOEMAROE-NJANNJAN'
Signed Manabu Saito Aug '68
Acquired from the artist 1996
Watercolour on paper
612 × 460 mm

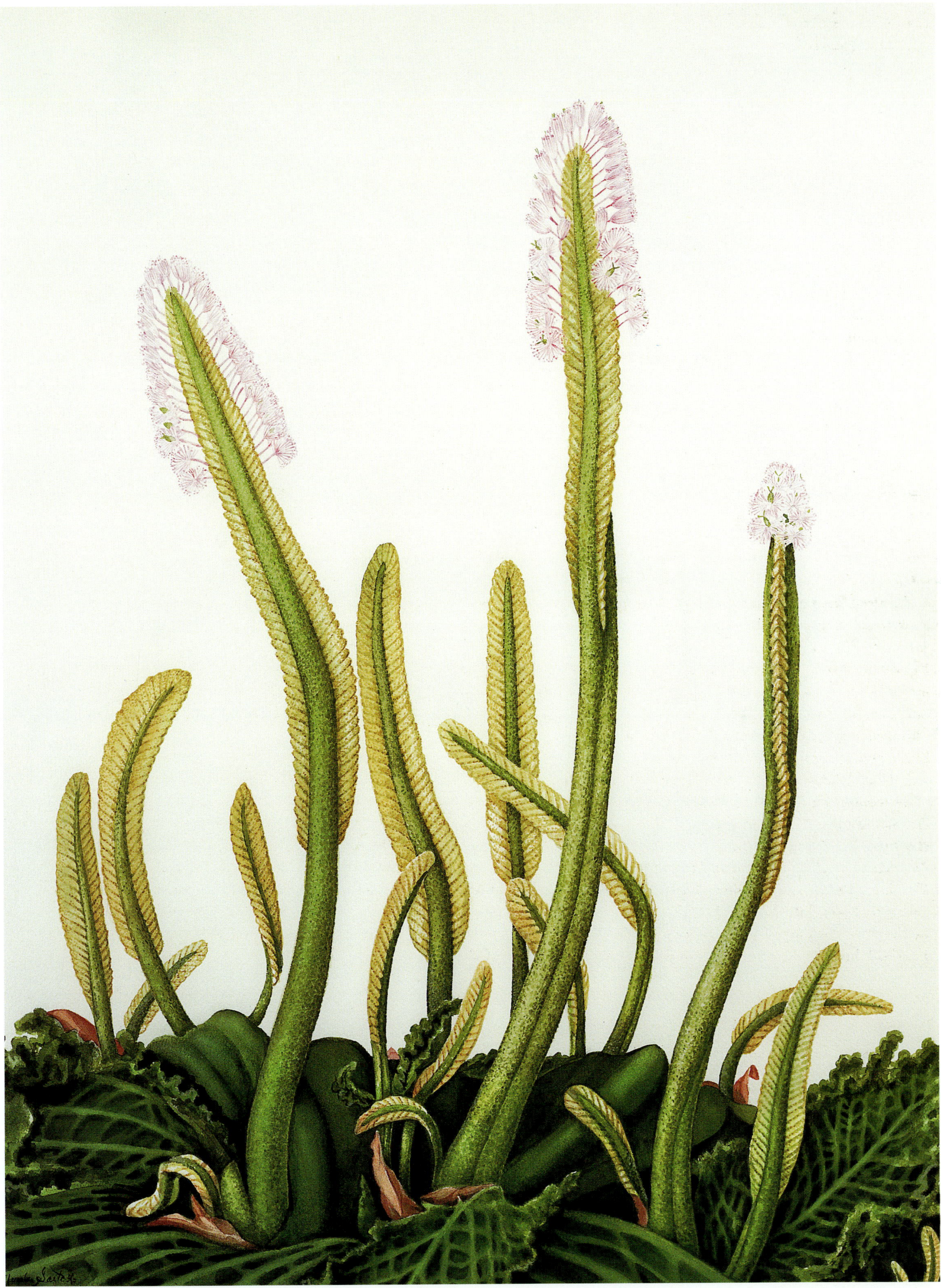

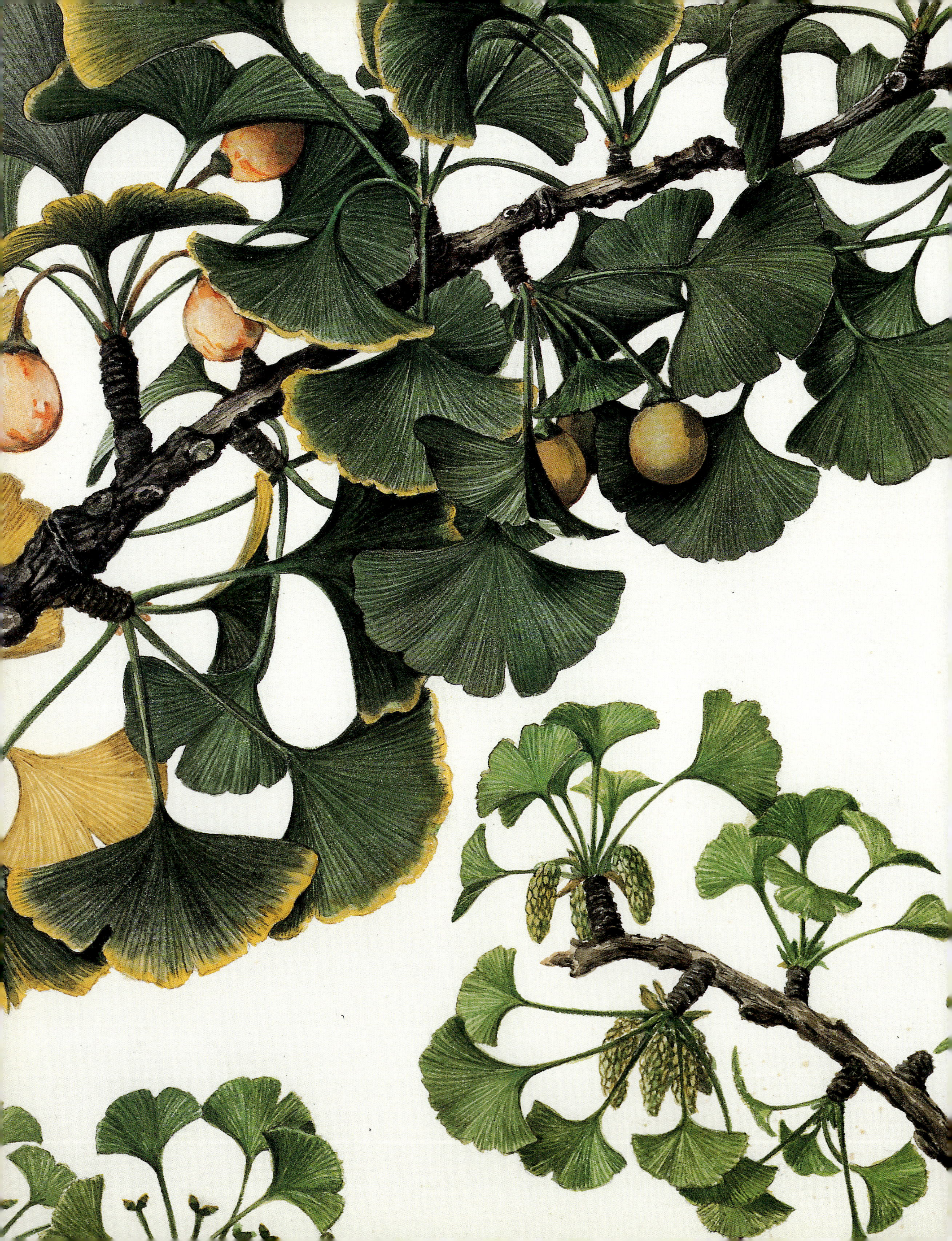

glowing gold of their autumn foliage after the first cold snap. Saito shows all the stages in his painting.

The second work is of *Mourera fluviatilis*. This is a strange and intriguing painting and always rouses the curiosity of visitors because it is so unusual and dramatic. Since I acquired it in 1996, it has been widely exhibited at the Museum of Modern Art, National Galleries of Scotland; the New Orleans Museum of Art; the S. H. Ervin Gallery in Sydney, Australia; the Yasuda Kasai Museum of Art, Tokyo; the Kirstenbosch Botanic Gardens, Cape Town and at the Millesgarden Museum in Stockholm.

He painted it in August 1968 near Stoelman's Island, Surinam, on the north-east coast of South America. The plants were growing on rocks in the rapids of a tributary of the Morowijne River north of Stoelman's Island. He was on an expedition with Dr John Craig who took several photographs of Manabu crouched sketching, perched precariously on partially submerged rocks surrounded by a fast-flowing river. Dr Craig sent me other slides of close-ups of this rather weird plant with its lichen-like thallus and mossy leaves. Apparently the leaves can be up to 2 metres long and it is known locally as *kumaru-nyam-nyam* or 'food-for-fish'. Dr Luis Diego Gomez, director of the Robert & Catherine Wilson Botanical Garden, Coto Brus, Costa Rica recently wrote to Dr. Craig:

'*Mourera fluviatilis* is a member of Podostemaceae, the river moss family. Locals in South America use this and other related plants to obtain much needed salt. They harvest it, dry it and reduce it to ashes, then extract the salt with water and evaporate to obtain crystals. Of course it has other uses: it is used to fight diarrhoea, some tribes use it to restore menstruation. Applied to wounds it seems to expedite healing, especially burns. Found from Colombia to Bolivia, not terribly common in collections mostly because it is overlooked, or botanists are afraid of going into the water.'

When I look at the photographs of Manabu Saito in the middle of this raging torrent I can well understand that botanists might be too nervous to collect it, let alone attempt to paint it *in situ*.

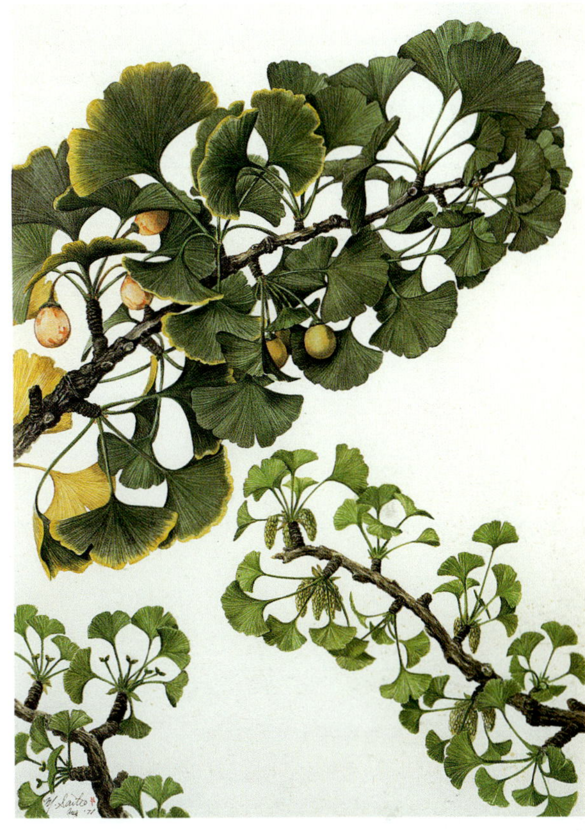

GINKGO BILOBA
Signed M. Saito Aug '71
Acquired from the artist 1996
Watercolour on paper
510 × 357 mm

Lizzie Sanders

BORN LONDON, ENGLAND 1950

Although Lizzie Sanders was born in London she considers herself to be Scottish, as her family is Scottish and she lives in Edinburgh. She is a founder partner and director of a graphic design consultancy and was a former Scottish Designer of the Year. She has been a judge for several design awards and involved in projects for the National Museums of Scotland, British Waterways, Scottish Ballet and the Scottish Tourist Board, among much other creative work. She has lectured widely in Scotland at art schools in Edinburgh, Dundee and Glasgow and has been particularly involved with the Duncan of Jordanstone College of Art, Dundee where she herself qualified.

She showed at the 14th World Orchid Show with other students of the Royal Botanic Gardens, Edinburgh in 1993, at the Royal Society of Arts, Edinburgh and in a touring exhibition organised by Inverness Museum of Art Gallery where she won an award in 1998. Most recently she has shown in the Royal Botanic Gardens, Edinburgh and at the RHS, where she was awarded a gold medal for her paintings of an interesting group of plants from Socotra. This is where I saw her portraits of these rather weird and wonderful specimens.

These paintings were of plants from the remote, cloud-enveloped island of Socotra, that were collected by a team of botanists led by Tony Miller from the Royal Botanic Gardens, Edinburgh and which are now cultivated at the Gardens. Dr Miller has organised eight expeditions there, the most recent in 1999. Socotra is in the Indian Ocean at a latitude of 24°N, 240 km north-east of Somalia and is part of the Republic of Yemen, having been a British Protectorate for a hundred years from 1866.

It is possible that Marco Polo visited Socotra in the thirteenth century, where he collected the magical 'dragon's blood' resin – cinnabar. In 1880, Isaac Bayley Balfour, then Regius Professor of Botany at Glasgow University, led the pioneering botanical expedition to Socotra, eventually publishing *Botany of Socotra* in 1887.

Although relatively small (3650 km square) Socotra has a very diverse climate and terrain, with two monsoons each year. The central mountains (1500 metres) are shrouded in cloud for most of the time and summer temperatures rise to over 40ºC. At lower altitudes the bizarre landscape is dominated by plants with succulent stems. Dense woodlands of the dragon's blood tree are unique to Socotra. Higher up, micro niches support plants such as begonias, which thrive in crevices in the rocks, sustained by moisture from mists and fog.

I acquired Lizzie's portrait of *Begonia socotrana*, partly because this plant has given rise to all the winter-flowering begonias in cultivation and partly because it was such a good drawing. She has painted the almost circular, rather domed leaves with wonderful texture and colour tones. It is low-growing with shocking pink flowers, and each plant has male and female flowers, as do all species of *Begonia*.

Begonia socotrana was discovered in 1880 by Balfour on his pioneering expedition to the island. It was described and published by Joseph Hooker of Kew soon afterwards, who stated 'Socotra is one of the last places in the world in which a Begonia could have been expected to occur'. This is because the island suffers a prolonged and severe dry season and is very different from the forest habitats preferred by most other *Begonia* species. The plant was an immediate horticultural success as it flowers in the winter and is easily propagated from bulbils. *Begonia socotrana* was thought to be on the verge of

TRICHODESMA SCOTTII
Signed Lizzie Sanders
1995
Acquired from the RHS Show 2000
Watercolour on paper
552 × 368 mm

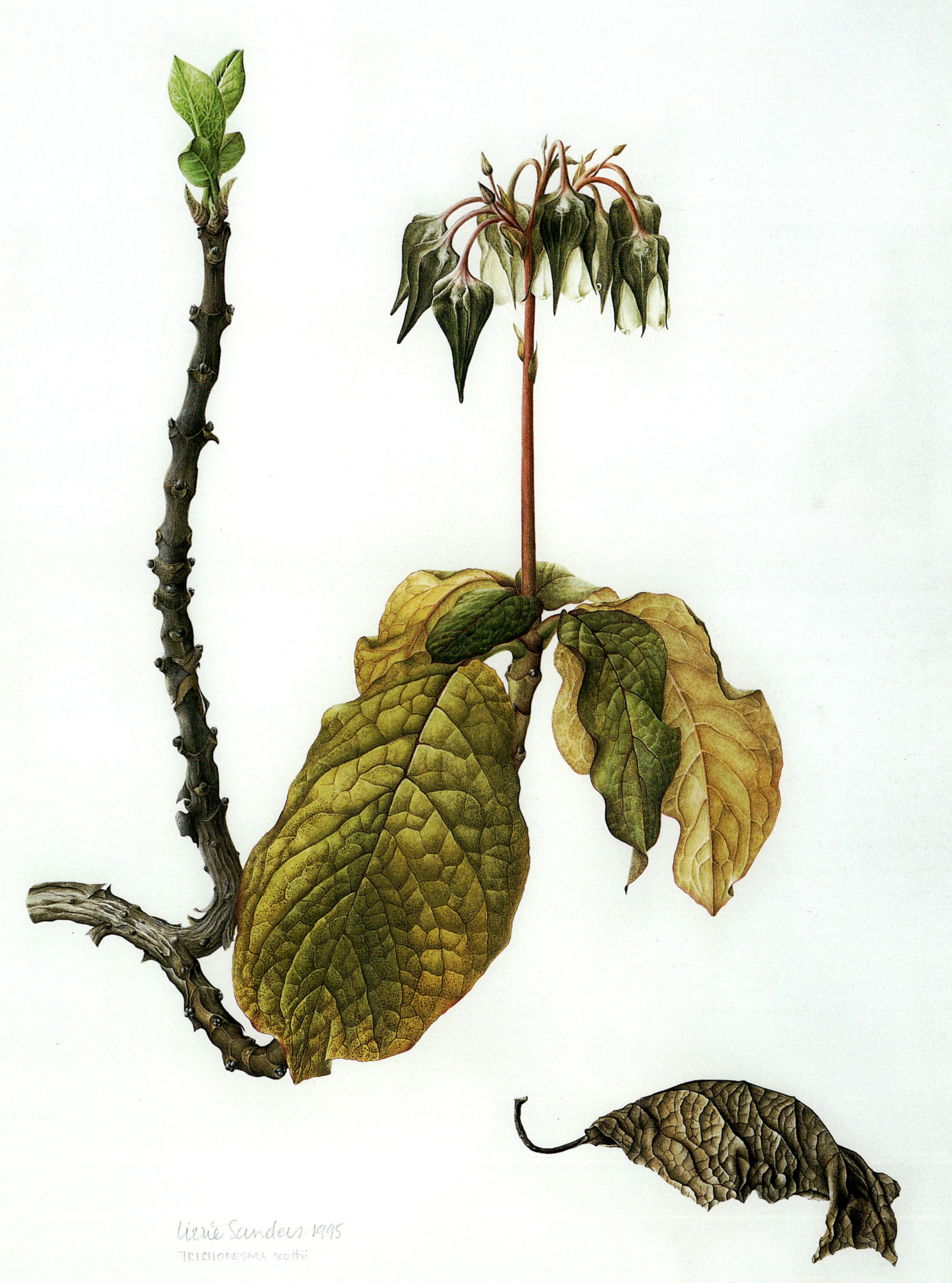
Lizzie Sanders 1995
TRICHODESMA scottii

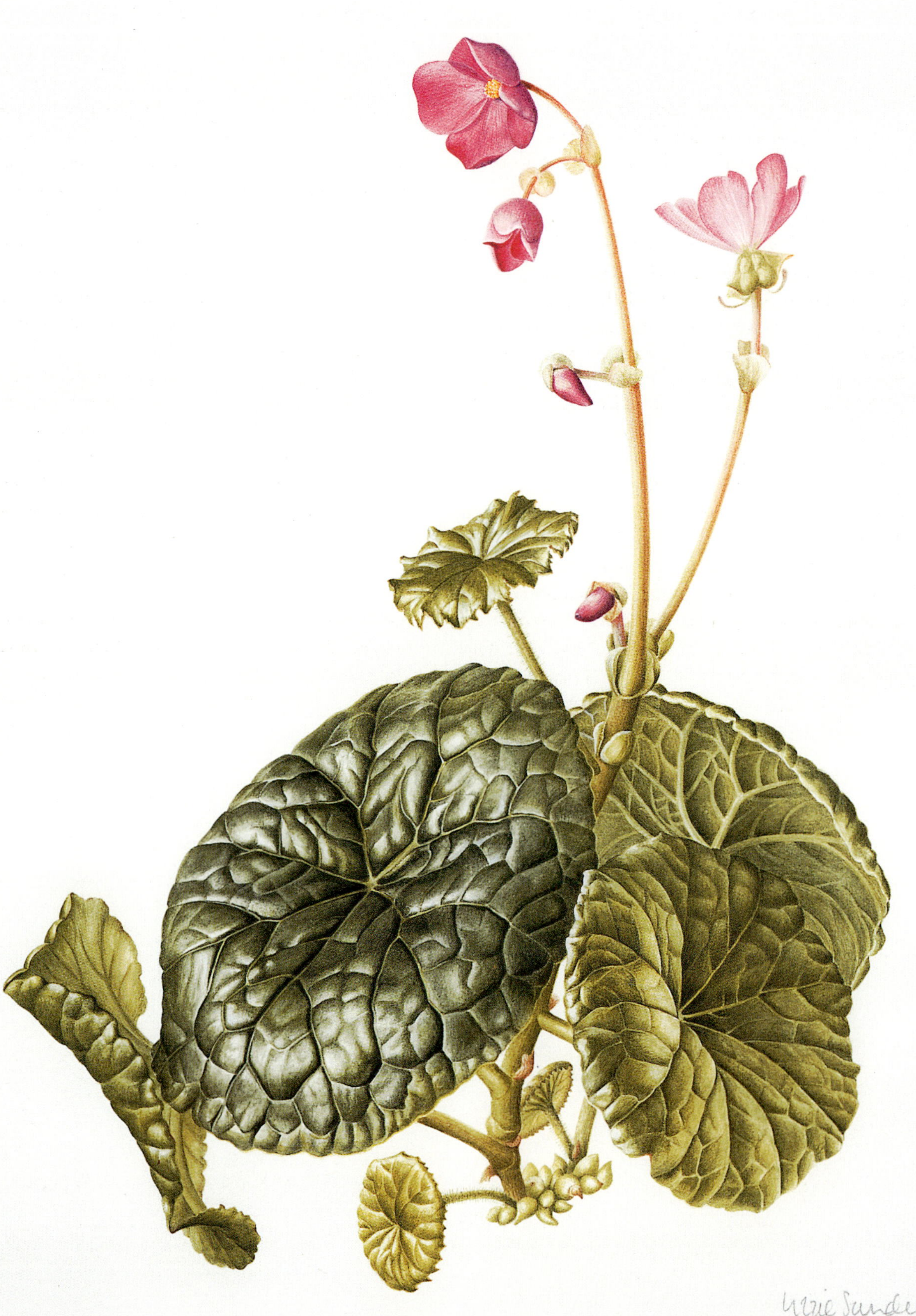
2000
BEGONIA socotrana

BEGONIA SOCOTRANA
Signed Lizzie Sanders
2000
Acquired from the
RHS Show 2000
Watercolour on paper
350 × 276 mm

extinction in its native habitat, due to excessive grazing, however in 1999 the Royal Botanic Gardens, Edinburgh expedition found it was still thriving in high areas.

The other painting I bought at the RHS show was of *Trichodesma scottii* which is a small tree with wide-spreading branches. The leaves and flowers grow in clusters at the ends of the branches. The flowers are strikingly large drooping bells. It was one of three species of *Trichodesma* found only in Socotra and was named *Trichodesma scottii* by Balfour after it was collected by Scott in 1880. Lizzie Sanders has just been told that the specimen grown in the glasshouse at the Royal Botanic Gardens, Edinburgh has produced seed heads – the first time this has been recorded in cultivation. Again, she has handled the speckly leaves well and the flower head is beautifully composed.

Socotra has a relatively small population of about 40,000 and the islanders are generally farmers. It has been famous for its frankincense and bitter aloes and now grows dates and myrrh. Its isolation has meant that its unusual flora has survived relatively intact, something very rare in these days. The island supports about 850 different plant species, of which 300 are endemic. However, large scale development is threatening Socotra's future and this is where the Royal Botanic Gardens, Edinburgh has an important role. It is currently involved in a large conservation programme for the sustainable development of Socotra, funded by the Darwin Initiative and the Global Environmental Facility. *

Lizzie Sanders has been portraying these rare plants which are skilfully propagated by the Royal Botanic Gardens, Edinburgh far from their remote island home in the Indian Ocean. It is hoped that more work will be published on Socotra's strange plants and it will be illustrated by her meticulous, skilful and beautiful paintings.

* Much of the information about Socotra and its unusual flora was extracted from Lizzie Sanders' notes for the RHS show, supplied by Mark Hughes from the Royal Botanic Gardens, Edinburgh.

Rosanne Sanders

Born Stoke Poges, Buckinghamshire, England 1944

I suppose that Rosanne Sanders is best known for her superlative studies of fruit, but for apples in particular. She lives in Devonshire, in cider country, and has devoted much of her time to painting old varieties, culminating in her book *The English Apple*, published in 1988. I bought two apple paintings from her in 1992 which have since been widely exhibited.

She went to High Wycombe College of Art and started as a freelance botanical artist in 1974. She has been awarded four RHS gold medals and received the Royal Academy Miniature Award in 1985. Her work has been exhibited in Britain, and appeared in the 7th International Exhibition at the Hunt Institute in 1992. Her commissions include paintings for HM Queen Elizabeth II, HM the Queen Mother, the RHS, the Royal National Rose Society and designs for a set of wild plant stamps for the island of Barbados.

She is not only interested in fruit studies but has been involved in a number of crafts as well, particularly print-making. She was made a member of the Devon Guild of Craftsmen in 1997 and in the same year was involved in the compilation of *A Printmakers Flora*. There were only thirty-five copies made of this hard-bound and hand-printed volume. In it her subtle, fragile dandelion 'clocks' seem to float from page to page and her print of rose hips was a delight.

In 1998 I asked her to send some paintings for Tryon & Swann's International Exhibition 'Botanical Artists of the World' which I co-curated with Oliver Swann. She produced an outstanding pear study and another of golden quince.

Recently she came up from Devon to show me her portfolio. It is always a pleasure to have such an attractive, lively artist visiting my home and I bought a study of a striking string of garlic which she said she could not resist painting when she hung it in her kitchen. It is a memorable watercolour and she was pleased that I acquired it, as she felt it was one of the best things she had done.

STRING OF GARLIC
Signed Rosanne Sanders (undated)
Acquired from the artist 1999
Watercolour on paper
590 × 805 mm

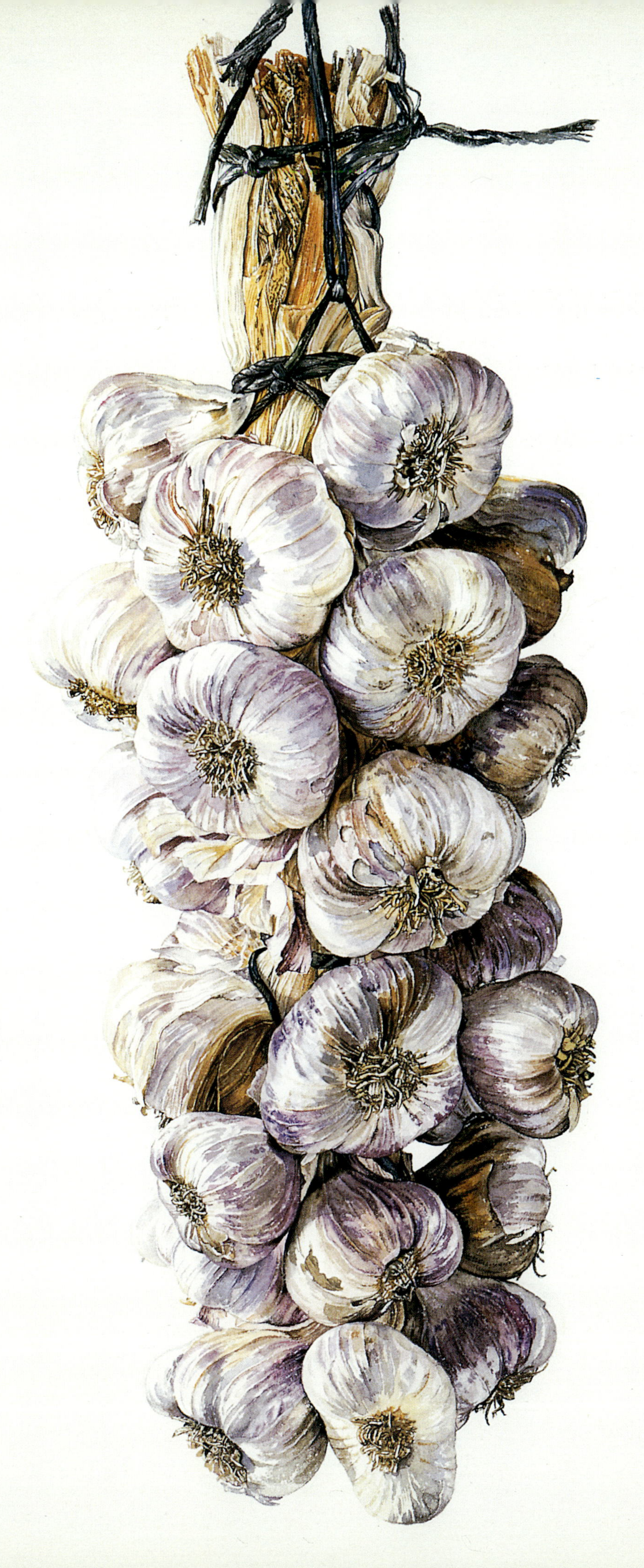

Masako Sasaki

BORN JAPAN 1939

While she lived in Japan, Masako Sasaki worked as an artist, metal carver and enamelist. But since 1988 she has been based in England because her husband's job keeps her here. She returns home twice a year for visits and she tries to make one of these visits coincide with cherry-blossom time, something very important to the Japanese.

She joined a class at Sutton College of Liberal Art near her home in Surrey in 1989. She told me she loved the English way of teaching which she found very positive when compared with the stylised and rather rigid Japanese methods. Later she studied at Juniper Hall with Michael Hickey and took a course at Kew with Annie Farrer.

Masako started sending in work to the RHS and received a number of awards, including a gold medal in 1994 and this is where I saw her exhibit an interesting group of paintings of *Streptocarpus*, a favourite plant of mine. I liked her relaxed, assured yet disciplined style and eventually I bought one for my collection. In the beginning she did not want to part with any of her RHS entries, while she savoured her gold medal but eventually she decided she would enjoy having one of her *Streptocarpus* in my collection. I liked the way she had handled the flowers, but I especially admired her treatment of the long, strappy leaf and narrow, characteristic seed-pod.

Later she showed at the 9th International Exhibition at the Hunt Institute, and she was awarded two Certificates of Botanical Merit at the Society of Botanical Artists.

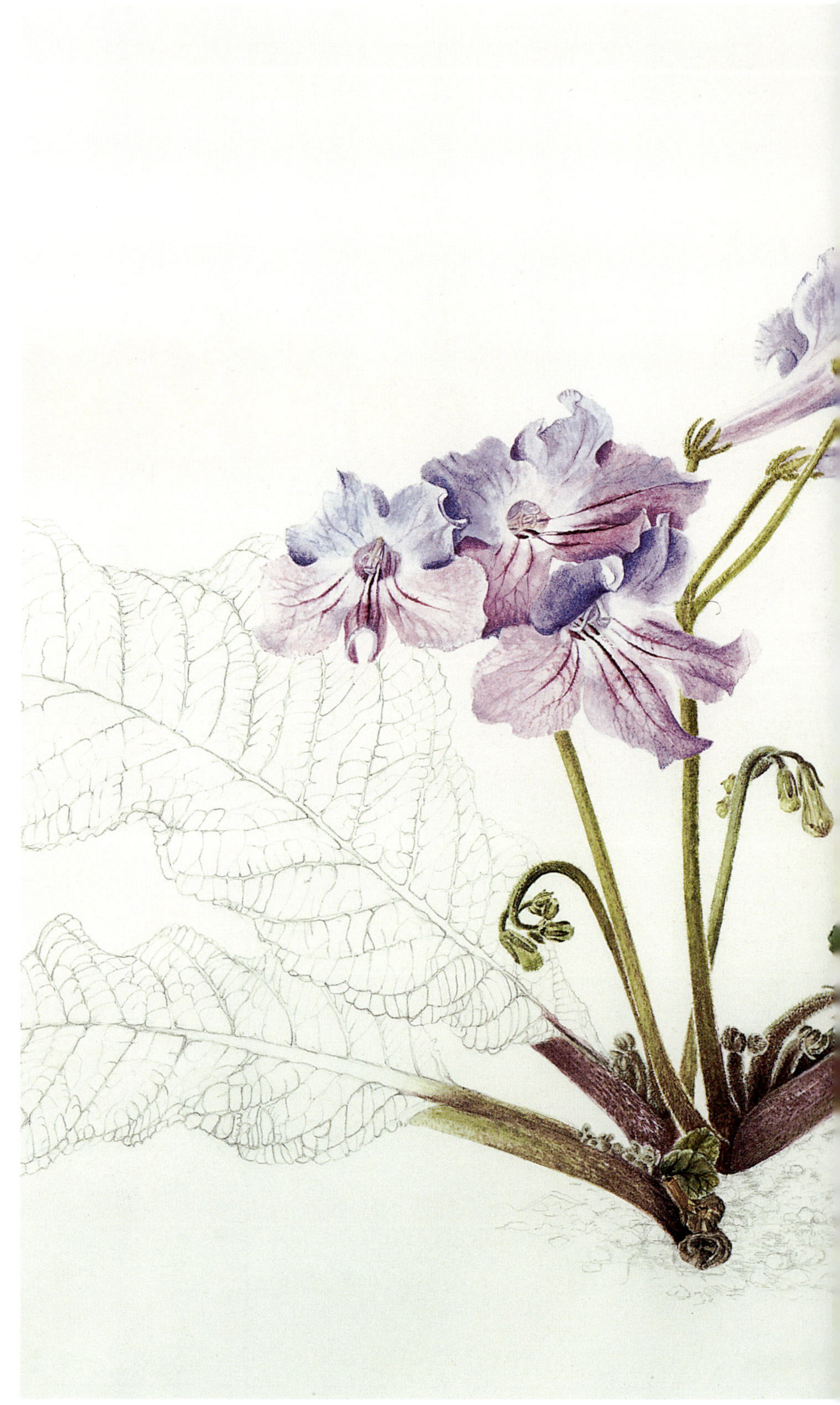

STREPTOCARPUS
Signed Masako Sasaki 1994
Acquired from the artist 1997
Watercolour on paper
320 × 520 mm

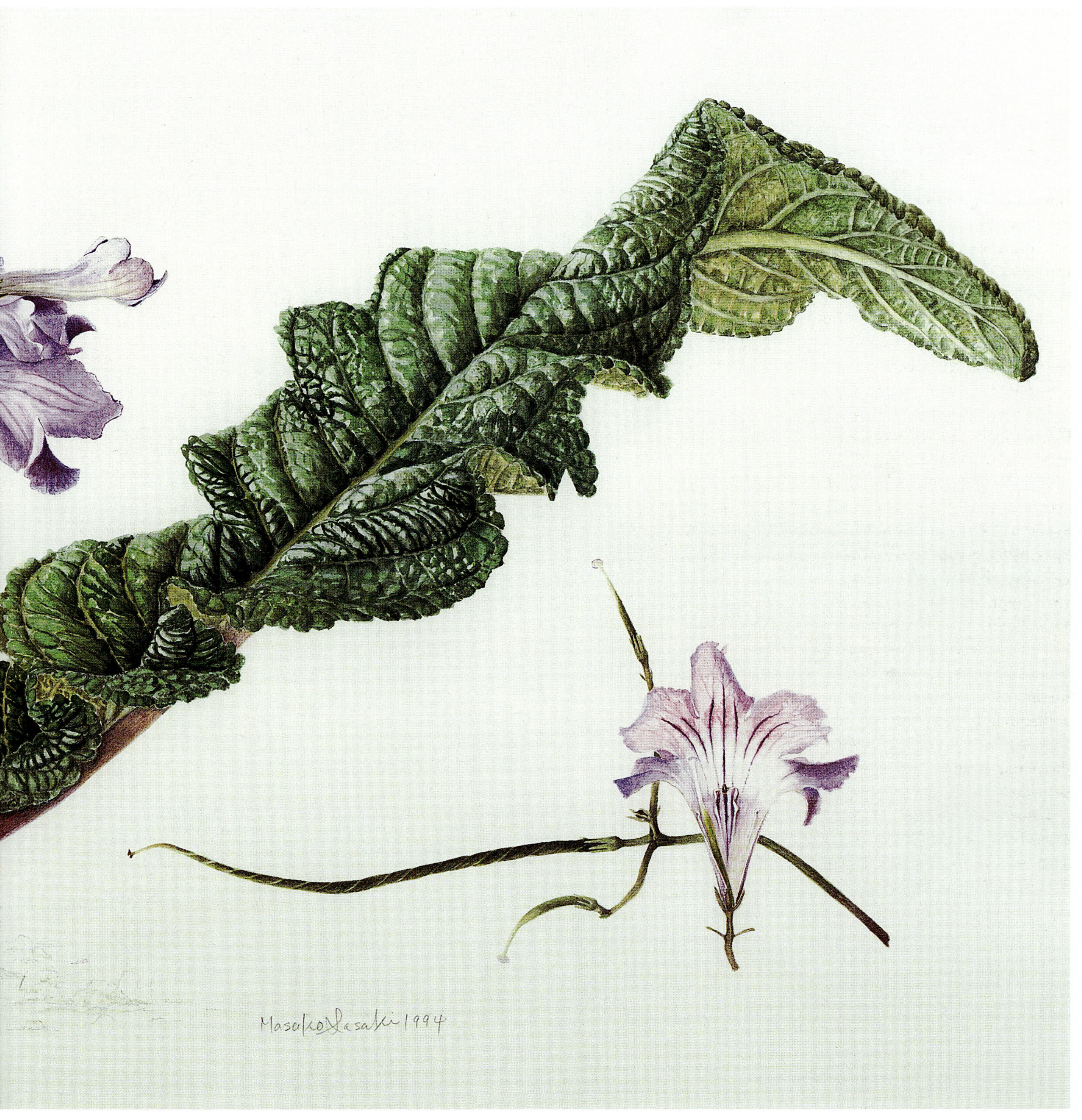
Masako Sasaki 1994

Hiroki Sato

BORN KANAGAWA, JAPAN 1925–98

Hiroki Sato was considered to have been one of the best of Japan's contemporary botanical flower painters. I met him at a gathering of botanical artists organised by Kazunori Kurokawa in Tokyo, when I was first trying to get a feel for what was happening in the field in Japan. I entertained them all in the Hotel Okura and looked at their portfolios. Hiro, as he always signed himself, brought along some lovely watercolours and I particularly admired his paintings of cherry blossom. He was reluctant to part with any of them, giving me two books and a calendar instead.

One book was a 'how to paint flowers' which was skilfully presented. The text is entirely in Japanese script, but even I can understand the techniques he advocates through the diagrams and step-by-step drawings. The other book, *The Works of Hiroki Sato*, is a most beautiful series of stunning flower paintings, elegantly arranged across two or sometimes three pages. There I saw again the drawings of cherry blossom that I had admired at the Okura meeting, and many others besides.

He had started his training at Kagawakenritsu Art School, studying architecture. He became a founder member of the Japan Botanical Art Association in 1970 and showed annually at the Odakyu department store in Shinjuku, Tokyo from then onwards, helping to popularise contemporary botanical art. He had one-person exhibitions in Tokyo in Gallery Rei in 1989 and 1990 and in Gallery Shinjubu Takano in 1993 and 1995. He produced other books besides the two he sent me, one called *The World of Botanical Art* and another *Illustrated Book of Japanese Trees*. He was given the International Art Culture award by the Japanese Culture Promotion Society.

Eventually, several years later, I did manage to buy a painting by Hiro, from the most unlikely venue, the Society of Botanical Artists show in London which shows Brisith artists almost exclusively. Unfortunately, it was too late to include it in the exhibition of my collection shown at Yasuda Kasai, Tokyo in 1998. When I saw him at the reception for the opening, he was in a wheelchair and was obviously terribly ill. However, we had our photograph taken together and he seemed thrilled with the show which was hung throughout all the galleries on the top floor of the Yasuda skyscraper. Sadly, he died only a month later.

The painting of *Adonis amurensis* is a skilfully composed drawing of an early spring flower called 'Fukujusou' in Japanese. Kazunori Kurakawa tells me that it means 'Happy New Year' and is used as a buttonhole at that time of year. The yellow flower is similar to the English colt's foot, except that it has beautiful feathery leaves poking out of the scaly bracts. The painting is a most accomplished plant portrait and was well worth waiting for.

ADONIS
Signed Hiro (undated)
Acquired from the Society of Botanical Artists' Westminster Show 1998
Watercolour on paper
315 × 235 mm

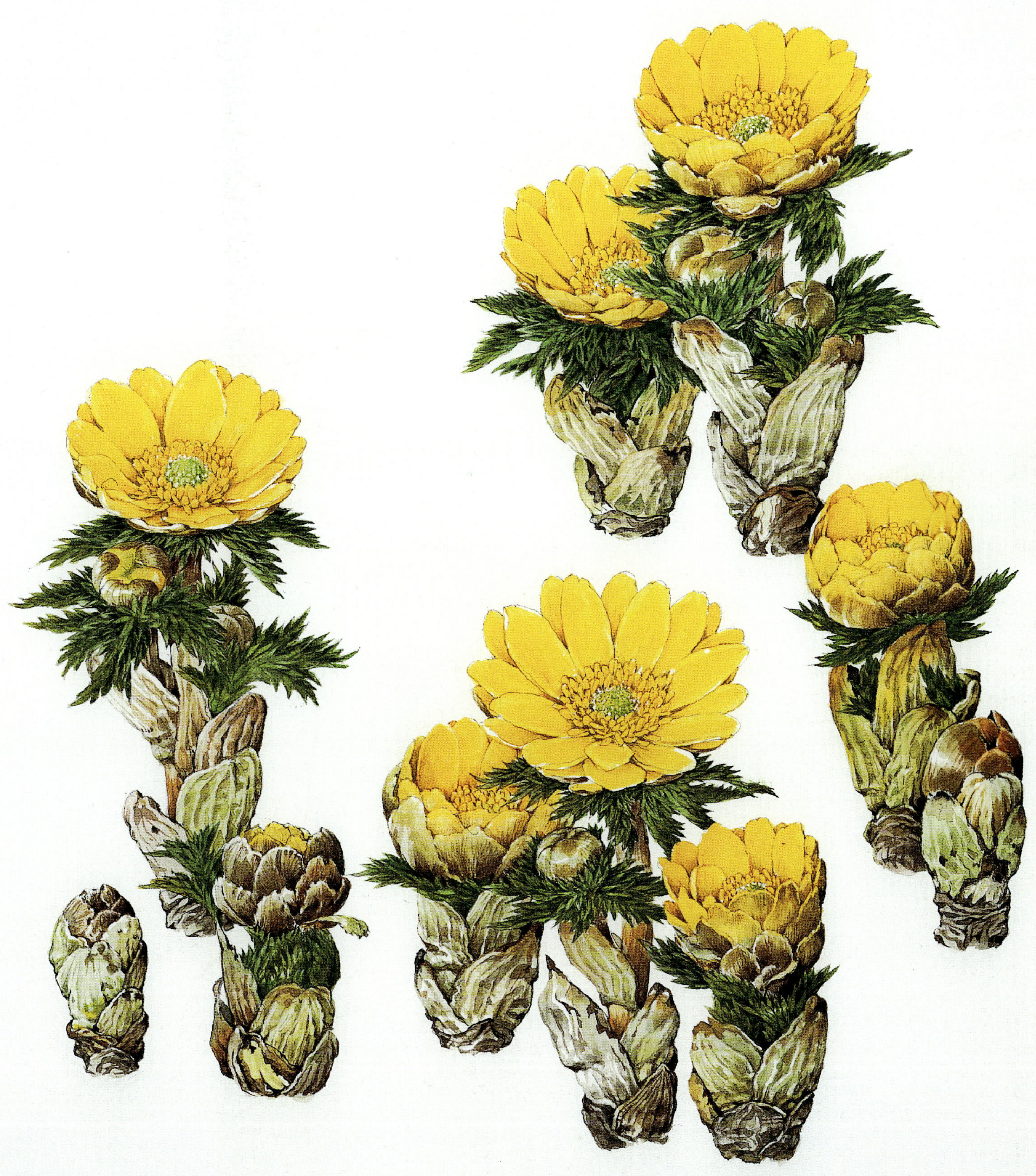
HIRO

Margaret Saul

BORN BRISBANE, AUSTRALIA 1951

When I unpacked the first painting I had commissioned from Margaret Saul in 1995 I knew immediately that I would like to see more of her work. She had sent me a splendid portrait of the locally named 'Peanut Tree', *Sterculia quadrifida*, with lovely leaf texture, vibrant colours and excellent composition. It has been widely exhibited ever since as my collection has been shown around the world. I commissioned her again and this time she decided on another tree native to Queensland, the blue quandong, *Eleocarpus angustifolius*. The composition, colour tones of the leaves and luminous, glowing blue fruit are quite wonderfully depicted in this splendid three-dimensional watercolour. This is a subtle, sensitive painting and like its predecessor, it has been widely shown in exhibitions of my collection.

I met Margaret in Brisbane a year or so later and she showed me the strange, almost unnaturally blue berries of the blue quandong. I photographed them together with the gaily coloured leaves of this interesting shrub. Her family home in Brisbane was buzzing with activity as we leafed through her notebooks and preliminary sketches and she explained her teaching programmes to me. She originally started teaching at Brisbane Botanical Gardens, Mount Coot-tha in 1988 and then began her own school in 1997. The Margaret Saul School of Botanic Art & Illustrations has introduced a more structured programme, based on traditional art teaching and it has become a real success. At the time of my visit the school had just opened and she gave me copies of her class notes, all most sensibly set out. Currently (in 2000) she has about eighty students enrolled in the various courses and workshops and has assistant teachers to ease her work load.

Despite her hectic schedule she finds time to accept commissions for a variety of publications including the *Flora of Australia* and paintings for a public collection 'Aridland Flora of the Barcaldine Region'. She is a founding member of the Botanic Artists Group Queensland (1994) and the Australian Botanical Society which started in 1999, triggered by two exhibitions in Sydney: 'An Exquisite Eye', a show of Ferdinand Bauer's work; and my collection shown simultaneously in 1998 at the S. H. Ervin Gallery. The same year Jenny Phillips started teaching master classes at the Observatory Hotel. We all met for the opening of my show and the initiation of the classes, which have continued annually in January with as many as eighty participants.

Recently Margaret and her husband, Dr Allan Saul, have decided to leave Australia for a period to go to the United States. Dr Saul will work in the National Institute of Health in Bethesda, Maryland with a group of specialists working on the development of a malaria vaccine. Margaret will continue to keep her classes running in Brisbane and return at frequent intervals to liaise with her two teachers. I called her just before she left for the United States and she told me she was hoping to have more time for her own painting again, once they had found somewhere to live.

BLUE QUANDONG: *ELAEOCARPUS ANGUSTIFOLIUS*
Signed Margaret A. Saul 1996
Acquired from the artist 1996
Watercolour, gouache & colour pencil on paper 690 × 570 mm

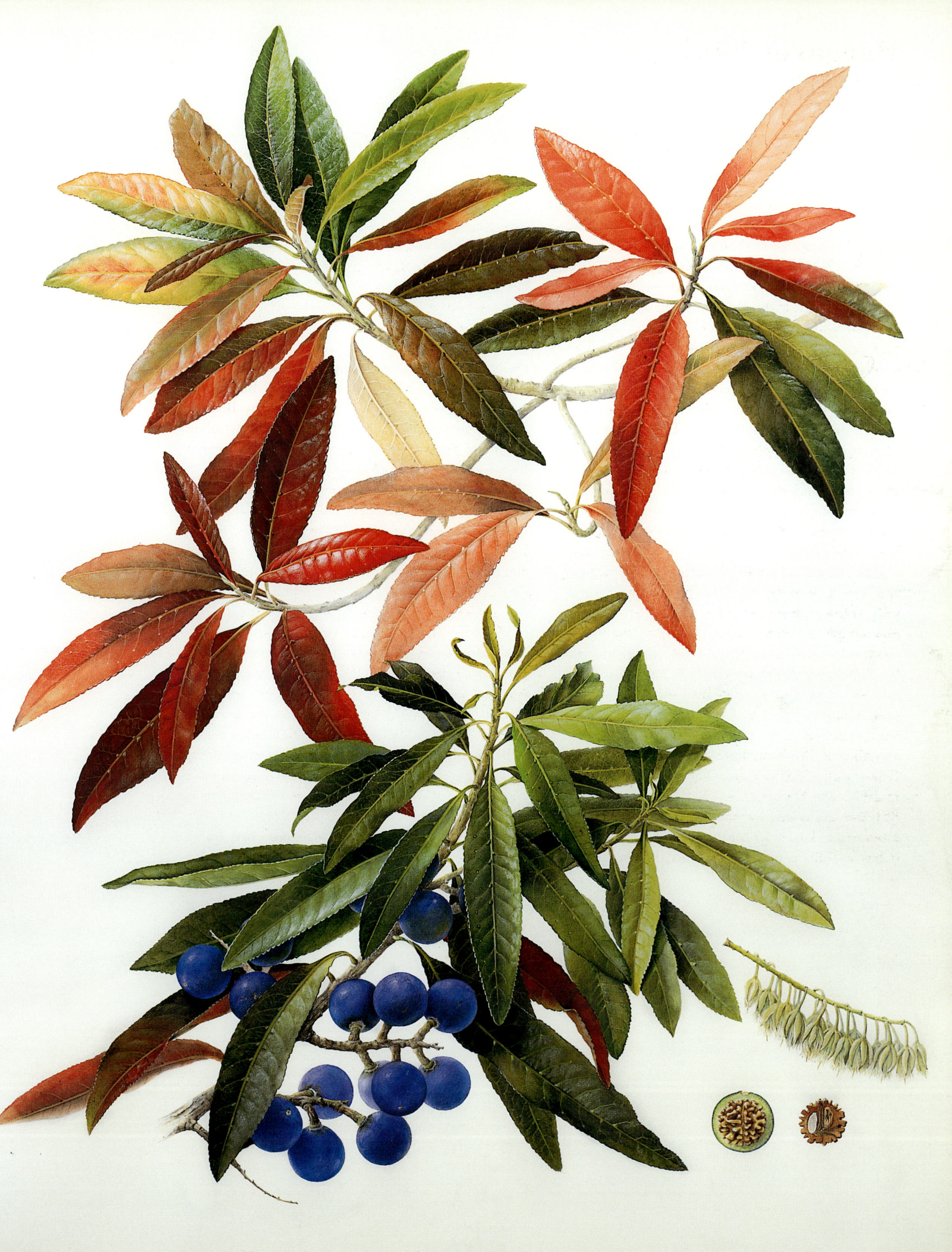

BLUE QUANDONG *Elaeocarpus angustifolius* Margaret A. Saul. 1996.

Sara Anne Schofield

BORN TWICKENHAM, ENGLAND 1937

Best known for her compositions of seasonal flowers, Sara Anne Schofield also does some delightful studies of isolated specimens. Recently she has completed a commission of eight elaborate plate designs called 'Bouquet for the Queen Mother' executed by Royal Doulton.

Sara Anne Schofield studied at Twickenham College of Art, worked at Kew and has had many exhibitions in London and elsewhere in the United Kingdom. She holds two gold medals from the RHS and is a founder member of the Society of Botanical Artists, having shown in all their annual exhibitions. Her work is in the Hunt Institute's collection and she had a solo show at the Tradescant Trust Museum of Garden History, London shortly after it opened.

I acquired these paintings of hers in 1997. Her composition of black and mauve parrot tulips and pink honeysuckle is a lovely example of her flower painting, fresh and spring-like. Her more traditional bog bean, *Menyanthes trifoliata*, is a quiet, elegant little study of this pretty water plant. The beautifully shadowed cactus flower *Epiphyllum*, against a dark green background, was her first attempt at working with acrylic paints – and I certainly hope she tries it again, as it gives me a great deal of pleasure.

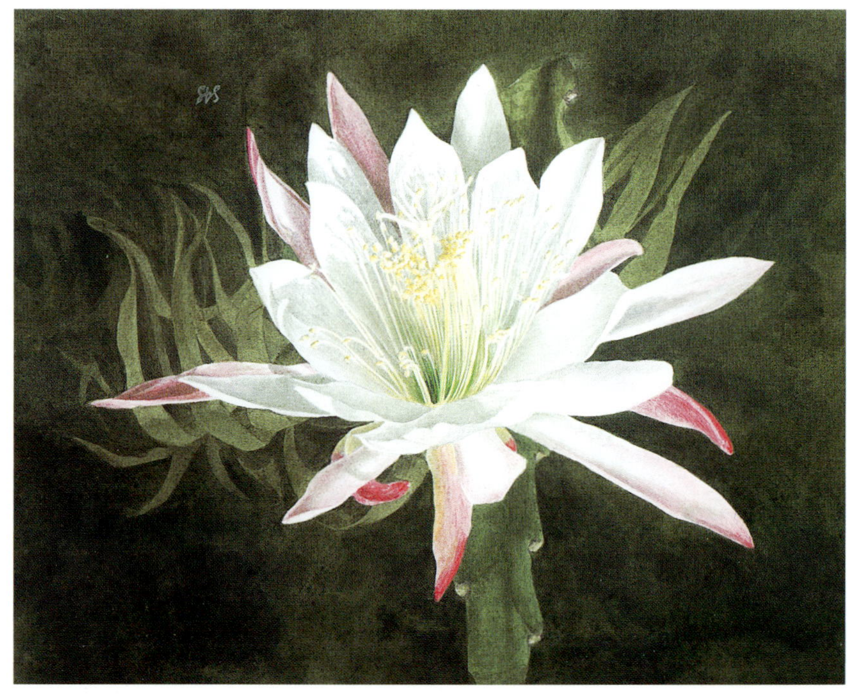

PINK *EPIPHYLLUM* '96
(Above) Signed SAS (undated)
Acquired from the artist 1997
Chromacolour on paper
130 × 170 mm

TULIPS & HONEYSUCKLE
(Right) Signed Sara Anne Schofield (undated)
Acquired from the artist 1997
Watercolour on paper
610 × 420 mm

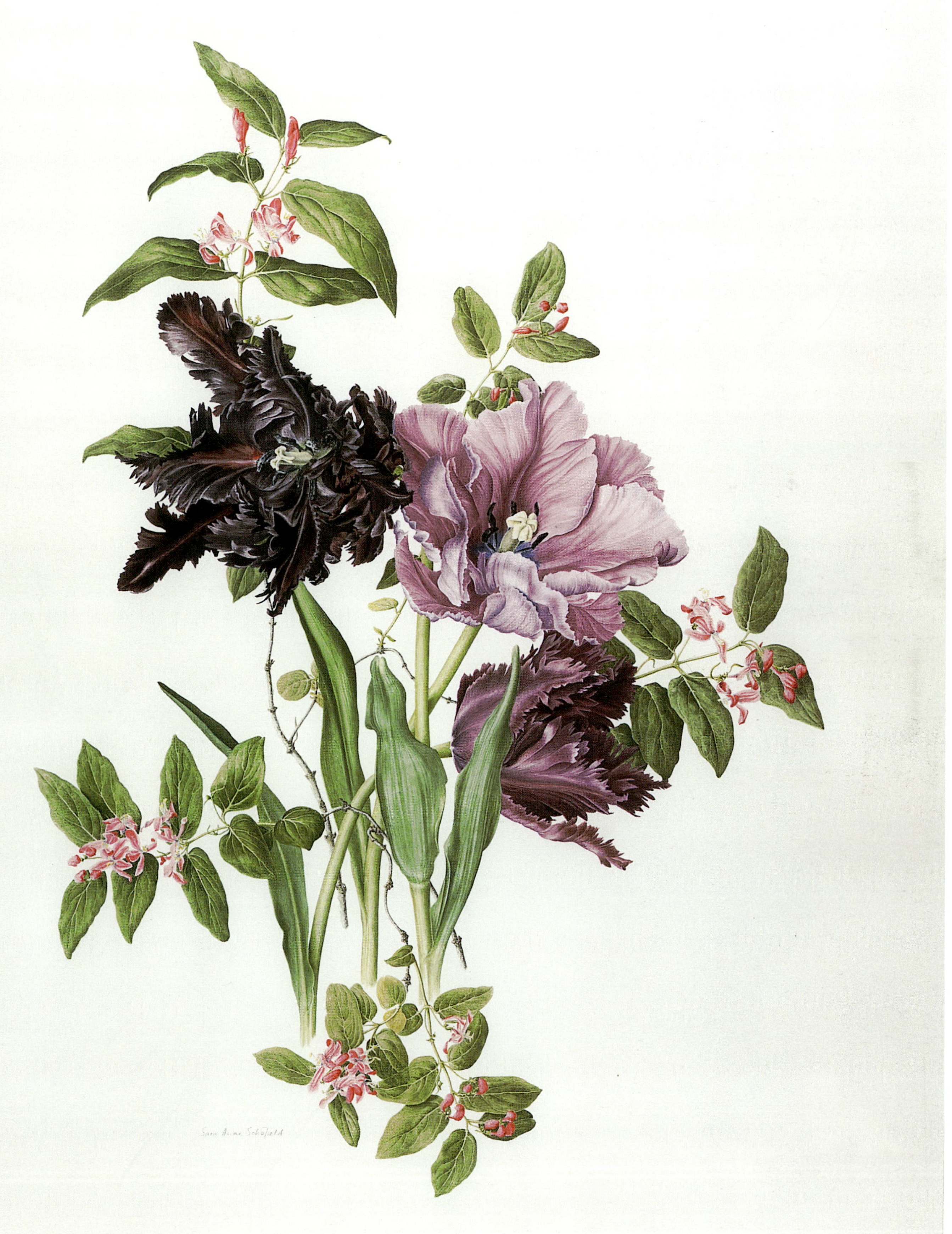
Sara Anne Schofield

Ann Schweizer

BORN CAPE TOWN, SOUTH AFRICA 1930

As soon as I entered Kirstenbosch's new conference centre to judge the 'Inaugural Exhibition of Botanical Art' in February 2000 I knew that I had seen Ann Schweizer's work before. Later, I realised that I had seen a reproduction in a catalogue some eight years earlier, when I was starting to collect botanical art and I had tried unsuccessfully to track the artist down at that time.

All six of her exhibition entries were outstanding and she was awarded a gold medal. Perhaps the most prominent work was a striking watercolour of *Strelitzia nicolai* in full sail. The huge, purple, boat-like carapace was crammed with pale, untidy petals. Another *Strelitzia*, this time a dried version, painted in sepia tones, was hung above. Both the pictures were chosen for Kirstenbosch, as the *Strelitzia* is their emblem and logo.

I selected two very different works for my own collection. One is a cascade of figs, in varying stages of ripeness. The subtle range of colour tones enchanted me and I am filled with admiration by her masterly use of watercolour. Ann Schweizer painted these from a Cape fig (*Ficus sur*) tree in her garden in Cape Town which attracts birds, insects and beautiful fruit bats. My second choice was a much more 'academic' study of *Thamnocalamus tessellata*, the only indigenous bamboo so far recorded in South Africa. It grows in damp mountain ravines from Table Mountain to the Drakensberg, but the example here was found in a local park in suburban Cape Town where it grows abundantly. Apparently this bamboo was used by Zulu warriors for constructing the framework of their hide-covered shields.

Ann Schweizer has had a wide range of academic interests. Her first degree was in art and languages from Rhodes University, Grahamstown and she studied Fine Art Practical Studies under Maurice van Essche. Later she took another degree at the University of Cape Town in archaeology, followed by further courses in botany and geography. She became a scene painter at the Hofmeyr Theatre, Cape Town for a year and then was resident artist at the South African Museum. From 1963 to the present she had been freelance, producing botanical and plant painting; archaeological and ethnological drawing; book illustration and posters; designs for silk-screen printing and – perhaps most unusual of all – drawing a cartoon strip entitled *Travels of William Burchell* for the Botanical Society of South Africa.

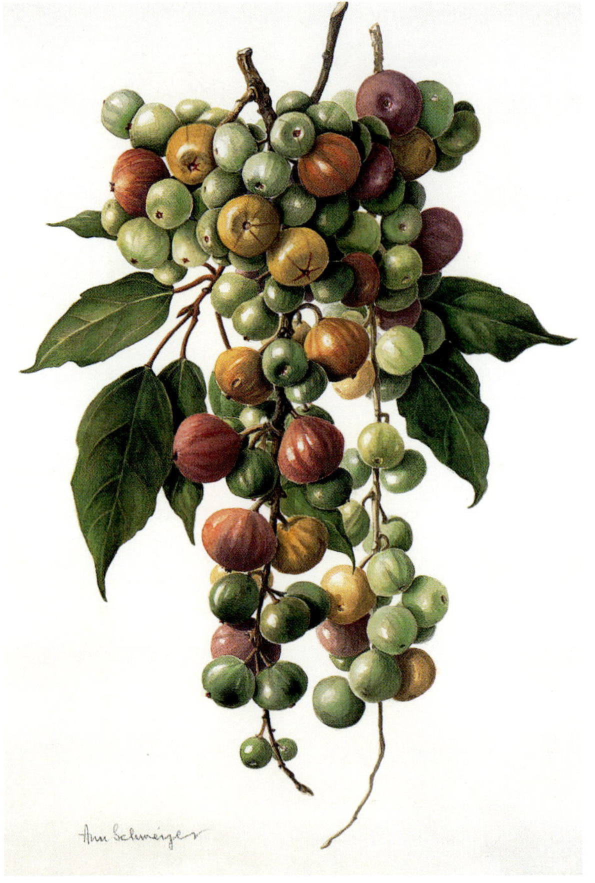

FICUS SUR

(Left) Signed Ann Schweizer (undated)
Acquired from the Kirstenbosch Exhibition of Botanical Art 2000
Watercolour on paper
550 × 380 mm

THAMNOCALAMUS TESSELLATA

(Right) Signed Ann Schweizer (undated)
Acquired from the Kirstenbosch Exhibition of Botanical Art 2000
Watercolour on paper
650 × 450 mm

She had a solo exhibition in the Forum Gallery, Claremont, Cape Town in 1982 and has participated in a couple of shows at the Everard Read Gallery, Johannesburg. I think it must have been in one of their catalogues that I first saw her work, a splendid painting of *Monstera deliciosa*, the cheese plant, that has stayed in my mind ever since. Recently she has shown in several galleries near Cape Town, mostly showing botanical subjects.

I am very impressed by her sure touch and flowing control of watercolour. I intend to send her work out in future exhibitions of my collection as it has both 'wall-appeal' and great integrity and should be more widely appreciated.

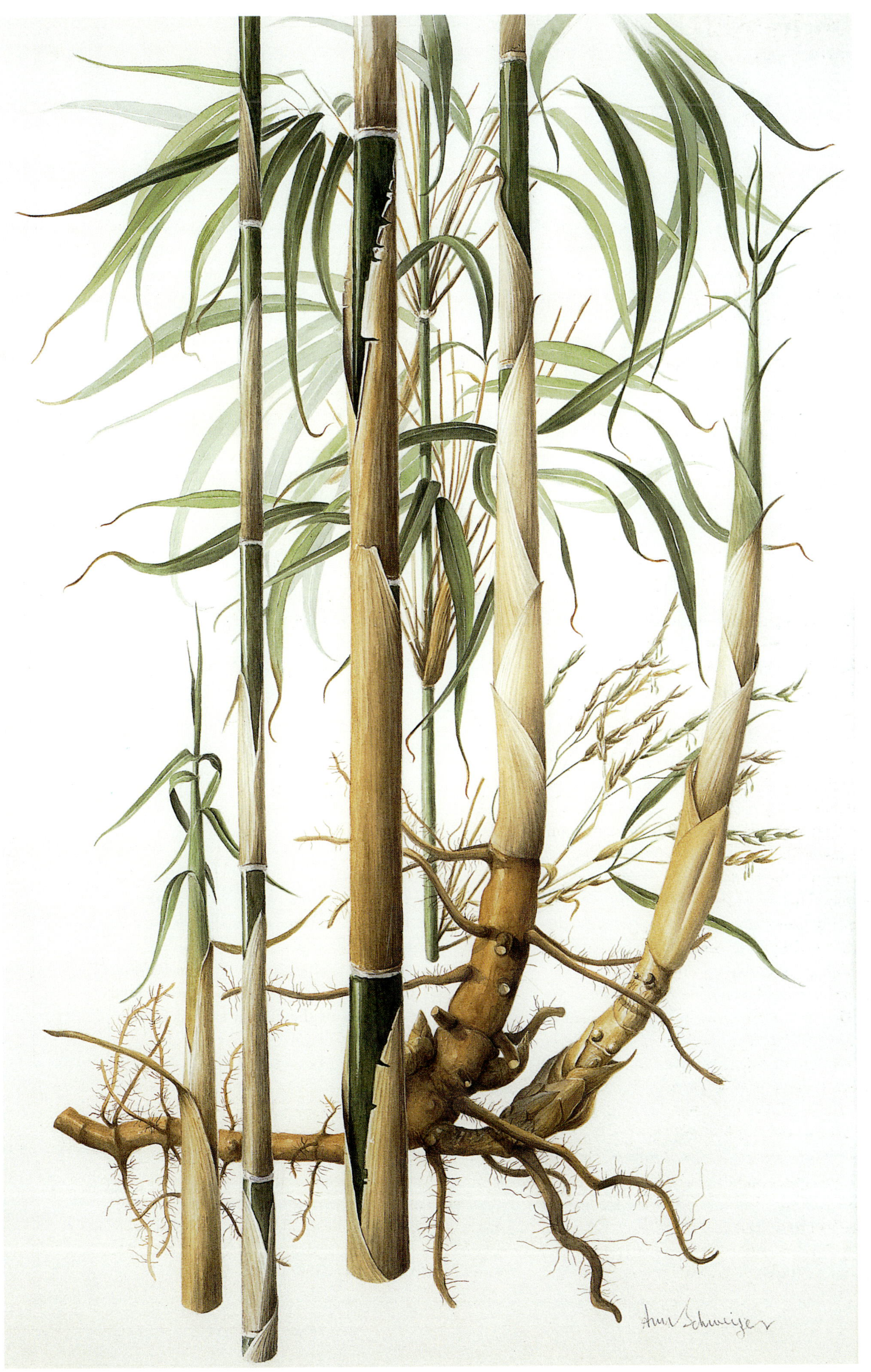

Pandora Sellars

BORN HERTFORD, ENGLAND 1936

When Dr Brinsley Burbidge asked Pandora Sellars to exhibit at the Kew Gardens Gallery in 1990 he could hardly have guessed that he would trigger the start of my botanical art collection. He called Pandora's work 'Botanical Theatre' and it certainly has had a dramatic effect on my life during the last ten years. I had become involved with the Royal Botanic Gardens, Kew, initially with the start-up of the 'Friends of Kew', later as a Trustee of the Kew Foundation, raising money for major projects, of which the World Seed Bank became the most prominent. I was a frequent visitor to Kew and quickly succumbed to buying an important painting by Pandora Sellars of a pink and brown orchid, *Laelia tenebrosa*, growing through a tangled mass of tropical foliage. This became the first painting of a collection that has now grown to over 400.

I now have nine of Pandora Sellars' paintings, most of which have been almost continuously out on loan in exhibitions world wide.

The earliest of Pandora's paintings I have is another orchid, *Paphiopedilum parishii*, painted in 1983. This is a wonderfully composed work, showing her early training as a designer. Each green-gold slipper orchid flower trails a pair of extravagantly twisted brown petals, and the painting is executed with almost unnerving perfection down to the finest hairs on the stem which are hardly visible except under a magnifying glass. The flower's waxy, slipper-shaped lip forms a trap for insects which can only escape by way of a chute to the rear of the lip. This forces them to brush against the pollen masses which they then carry to another flower.

Paphiopedilum parishii is a lovely orchid named after the Reverend Charles Parish (1822–97) who collected it near Moulmein and illustrated it during his time as a chaplain in Burma. He sent many orchids to Kew and when he eventually returned to England, he gave Kew a complete set of 350 beautiful drawings. They are now preserved in the Orchid Herbarium in two folio volumes, part of Kew's unique and unrivalled library of orchid books and drawings which complement its living collection of over 20,000 orchid plants.

I commissioned a number of paintings from Pandora during the 1990s, the most recent being a collection of three different species in the family *Araceae*. This restrained, yet spectacular painting shows the three types of spathe nestling under glossy leaves, with the scarlet fruit showing through from the rear. She has sectioned two of the spathes, one to show the encircling mass of down-pointing hairs that trap unwitting insects inside the vase-shaped base until pollination has been achieved, the third section showing the rather different anatomy of *Arisarum proboscideum* (mouseplant). These finely executed scientific details add to my satisfaction with this wonderful composition and its superbly executed leaves and spathes. She has done a number of studies of *Arum* species and I know it became one of her favourite genera when she illustrated a *Kew Magazine* monograph on *The Genus Arum* (1993).

Most recently I have acquired two interesting smaller studies. *Pontederia cordata*, known as pickerel weed, is a delightful North American water plant that I intend to grow in my water garden at Hinton. I am always tempted by plant subjects that I want to cultivate. It is as much a study of the spathe-like leaves as a portrait of the small blue flowers.

The last painting shown here is another of her striking collections of plants arranged against a back-drop, this time of a purple *Bergenia* leaf. She has placed dark purple hellebores together with a couple of vivid pink cyclamen against this sombre background. In many ways this is reminiscent of one of my favourite paintings of water-lilies, where she had ranged the flowers against their upturned leaves. I selected the water-lilies for the cover of my first book and it was used as a poster for the first exhibition at Kew in 1996.

I know that I am not alone in considering Pandora Sellars one of the most important botanical artists of all time. It goes without saying that her work is scientifically accurate, but it is much more. Here is an artist who has transcended the pedantic plant study to paint true works of art. Hers is a subtle approach, restrained and yet surprising. Her paintings have an immediately recognisable stamp and probably her leaves are amongst the most beautiful yet accurate that have ever been painted.

PAPHIOPEDILUM PARISHII

Signed Pandora Sellars '83

Acquired from A. J. Gassner, South Africa 1999

Watercolour on paper

430 × 300 mm

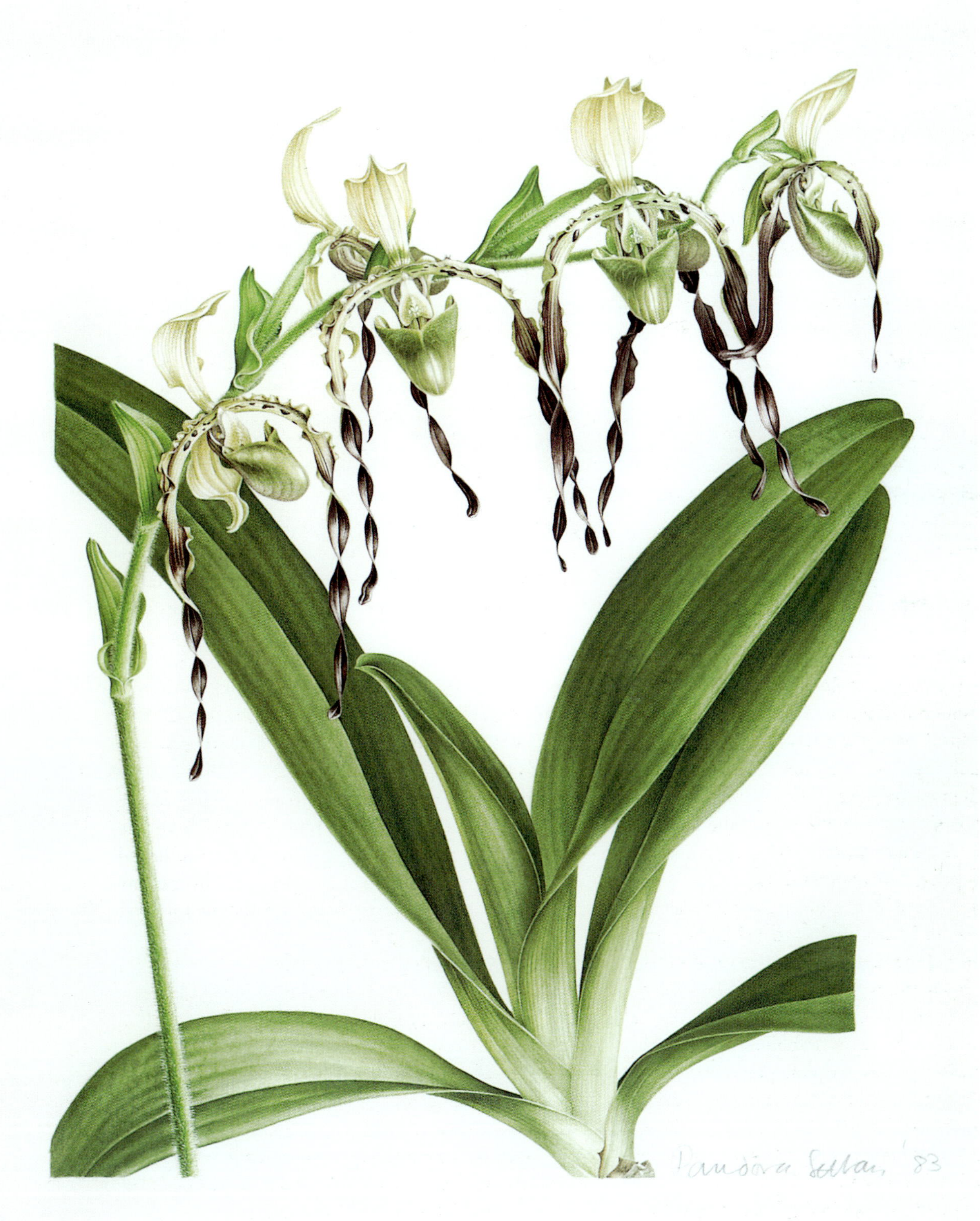
Pandora Sellars '83

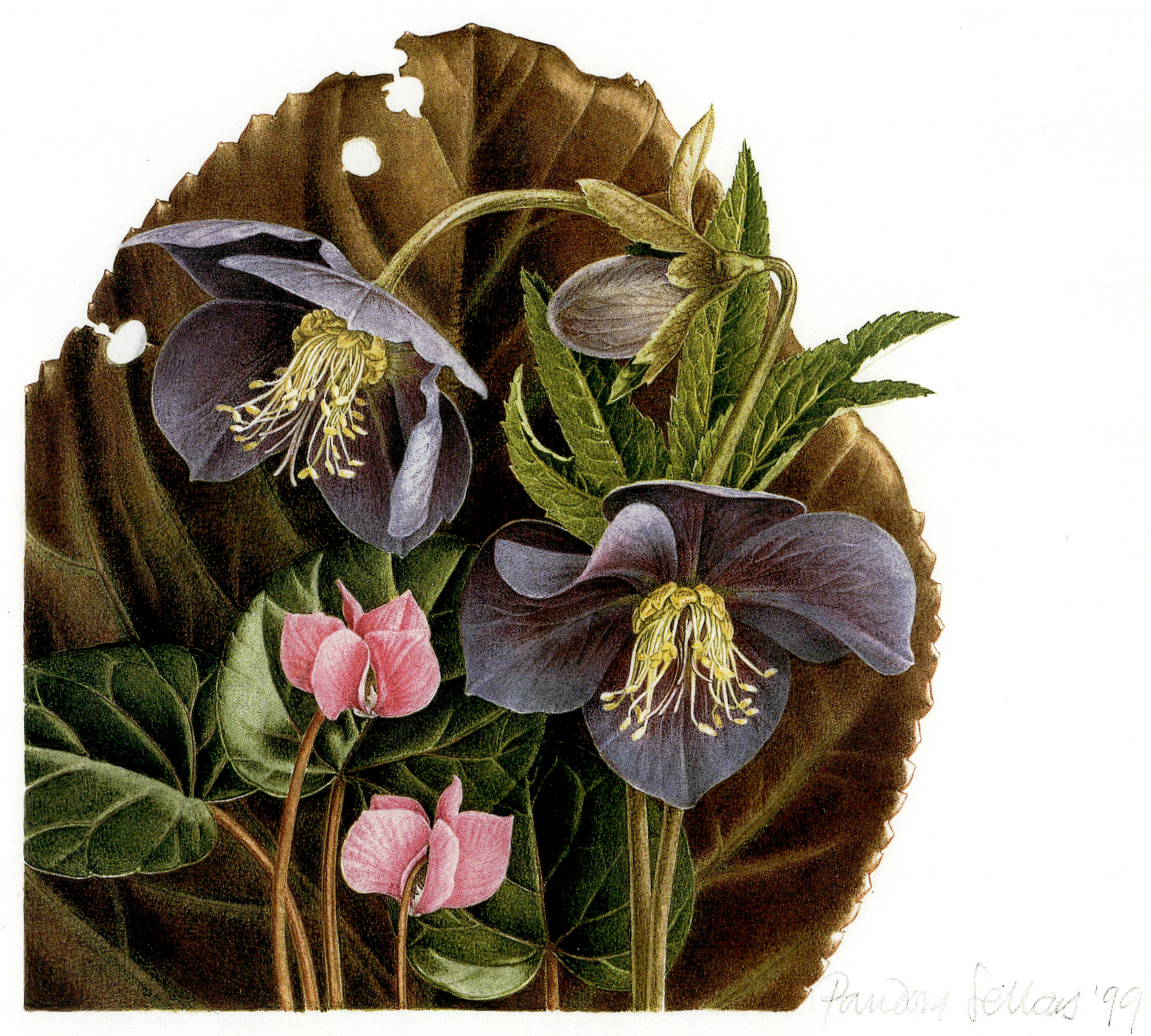

Helleborus orientalis 'pluto' with Cyclamen coum and a Bergenia hybrid.

HELLEBORUS ORIENTALIS 'PLUTO' WITH *CYCLAMEN COUM* AND A *BERGENIA* HYBRID
(Left) Signed
Pandora Sellars '99
Acquired from
Waterman Fine Art,
London 1999
Watercolour on paper
220 × 215 mm

PONTEDERIA CORDATA
(Right) Signed
Pandora Sellars '98
Acquired from
Waterman Fine Art,
London 1999
Watercolour on paper
340 × 205 mm

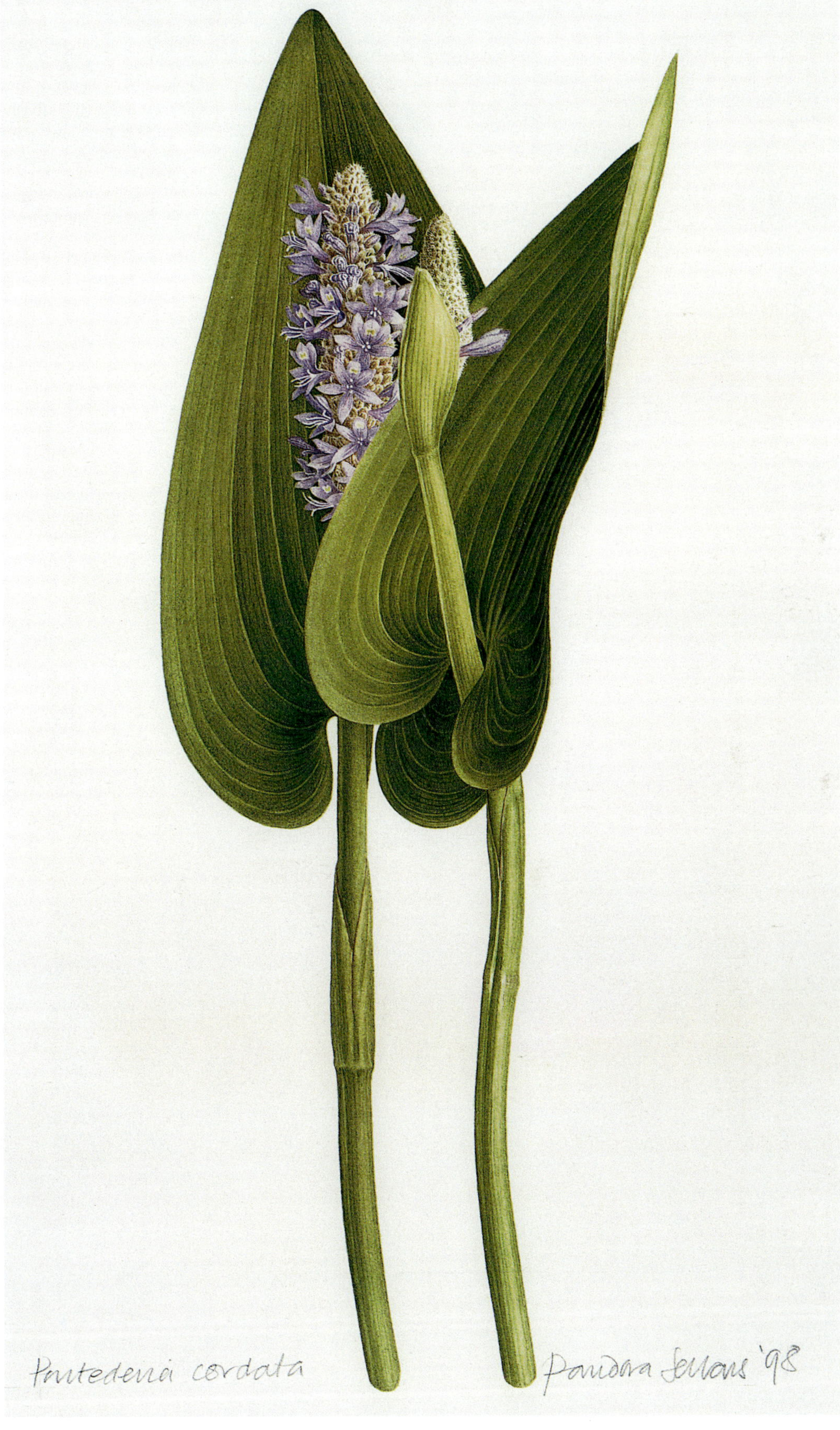

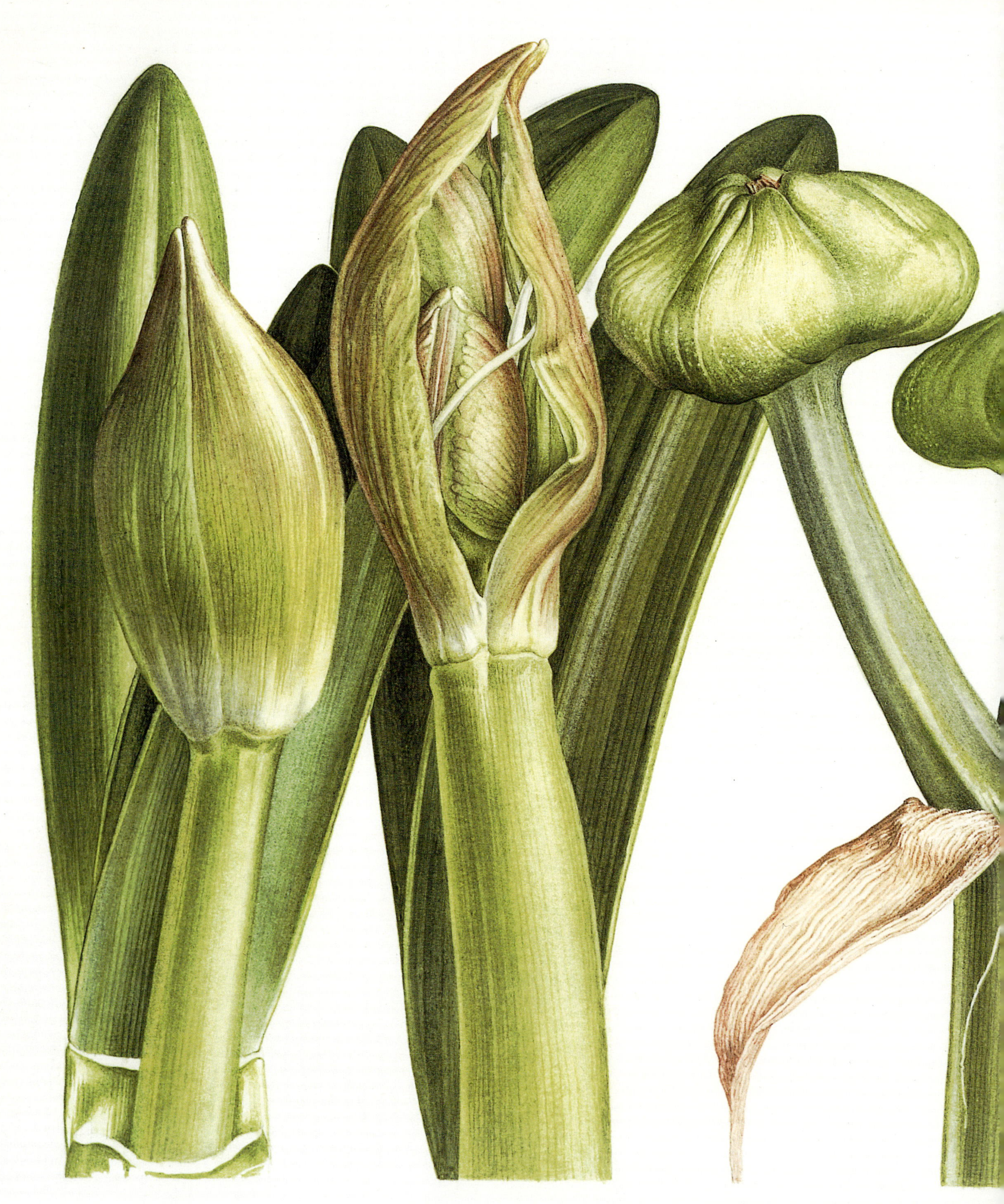

Hippeastrum buds and seed capsule

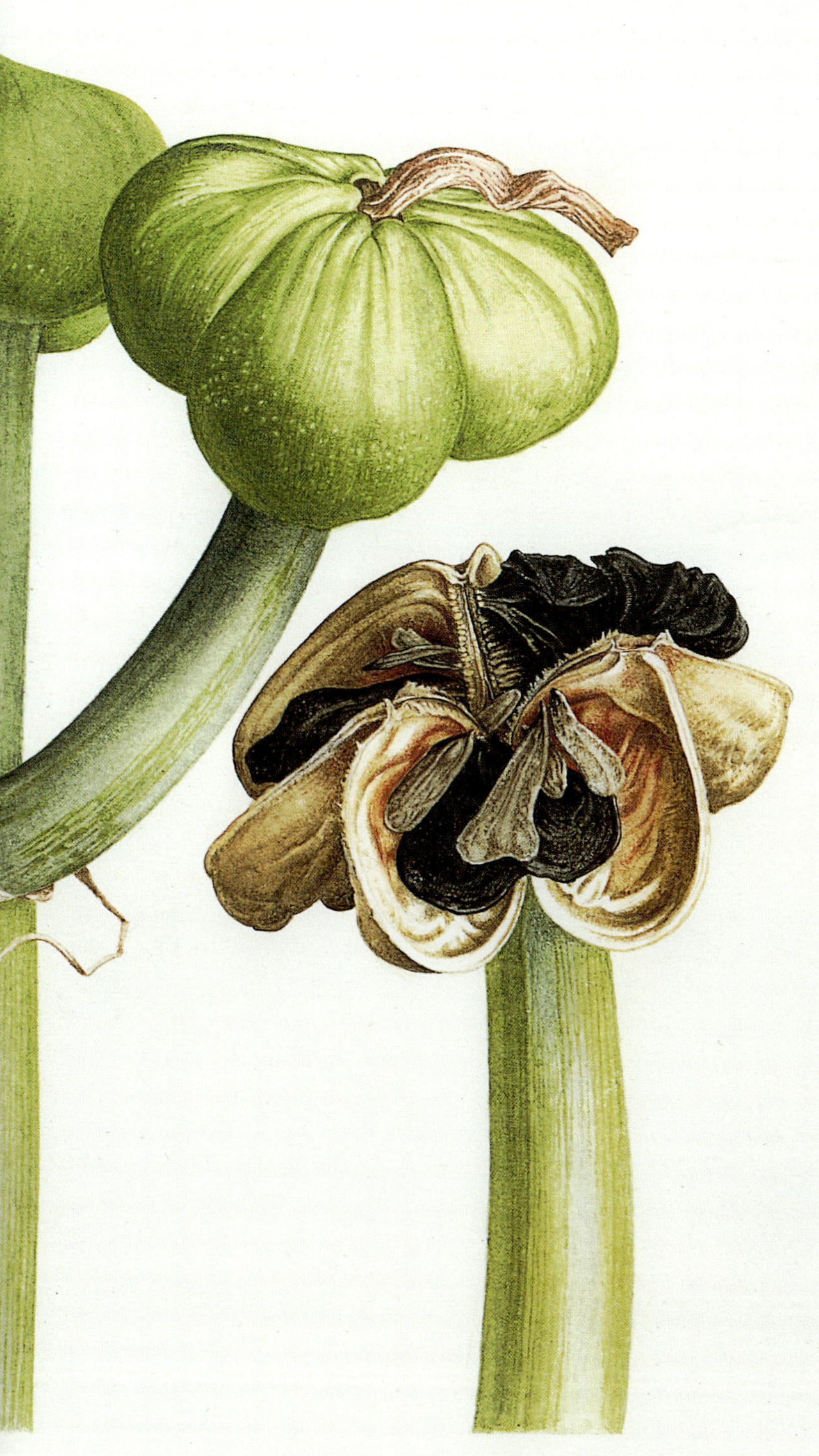

HIPPEASTRUM BUDS AND SEED CAPSULE
Named & signed
Pandora Sellars '99
Acquired from the
Gordon-Craig Gallery,
London 2000
Watercolour on paper
170 × 225 mm

Siriol Sherlock

BORN NANTWICH, ENGLAND 1954

I have known Siriol Sherlock since I first started collecting botanical art and she has taught several of the master classes in Orient-Express Hotels that I initiated when I started exhibiting my collection around the world.

I have a number of her beautiful, free watercolours, impressive for their design, translucent colour and fresh, crisp detail. She rarely uses pencil and teaches her pupils how to plunge in straight away with watercolour and achieve astonishingly good results far more swiftly than the average botanical artist. But this is not with a loss of detail, as she teaches how this can be achieved as well as retaining and capturing the original fluidity that comes with speed. She has put her teaching experience to good use in producing her book *Exploring Flowers in Watercolour*. This is an excellent book for beginners and for experienced artists who have got too 'tight' and long to loosen up. It won the Art Instruction Book of the Year award in 1998. She notes the time it takes her to do a painting, as she says it is always a question she is asked.

She has had a tremendous amount of experience in teaching, painting and, more recently, judging. She has been a member of the RHS Picture Committee since 1997 and often speaks as an artist to the contributors at the RHS shows, explaining the reasons for a particular medal award – a difficult job she is able to perform most sympathetically, as she herself is an artist.

She studied textile design at the Winchester School of Art and then worked in the textile industry producing floral furnishing designs. She began exhibiting in 1986 and has continued ever since. She has shown with the Society of Botanical Artists annually since 1988 and had a solo show at Kew in 1992. She was the organiser of a very big exhibition for the Society of Floral Painters in Sofiero Castle, Helsingborg, Sweden in 1998, a huge logistical undertaking, that was a great success. She has painted detailed botanical studies for *Curtis's Botanical Magazine* and *The New Plantsman* and has undertaken numerous other commissions.

I added to my holding of her work with a delightful set of pansy studies that she had showed at the RHS. I bought this particular painting to celebrate the birth of Saskia Sherwood, one of my grandchildren, and it will be the starting point, I hope, of Saskia's own interest in this subject.

HYBRID PANSIES – BLUES & MAUVES
Signed Siriol Sherlock (undated)
Acquired from the RHS for Saskia Sherwood 1998
Watercolour on paper
155 × 490 mm

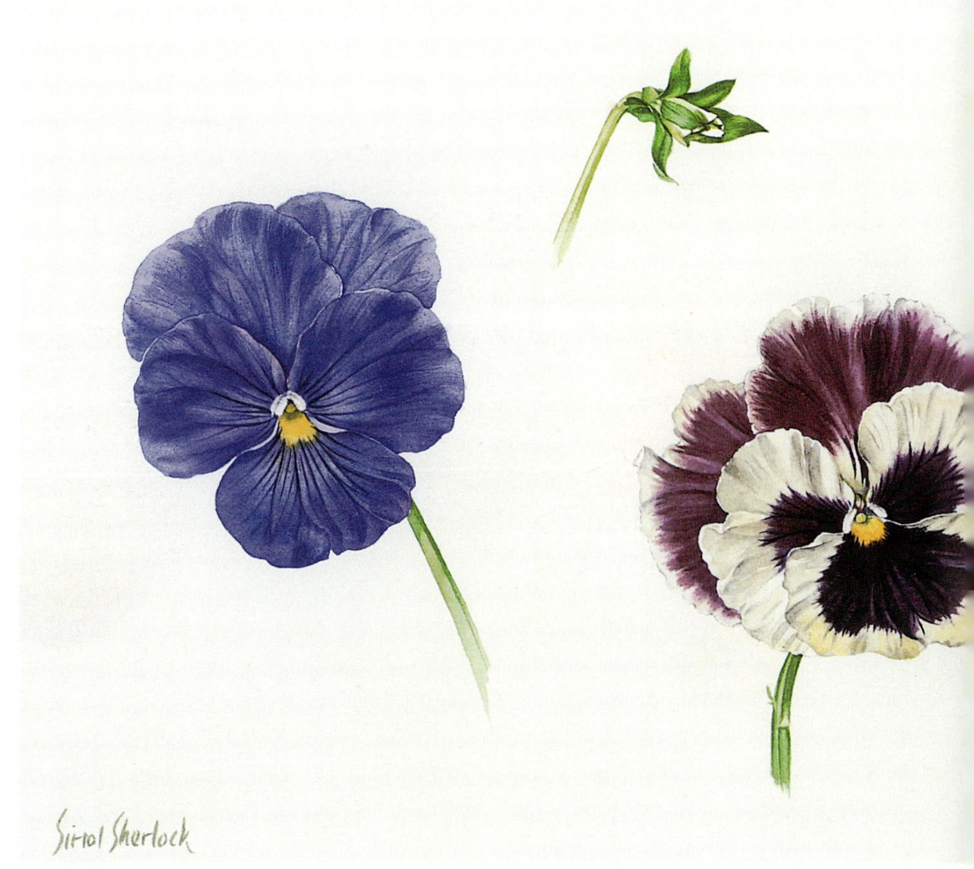

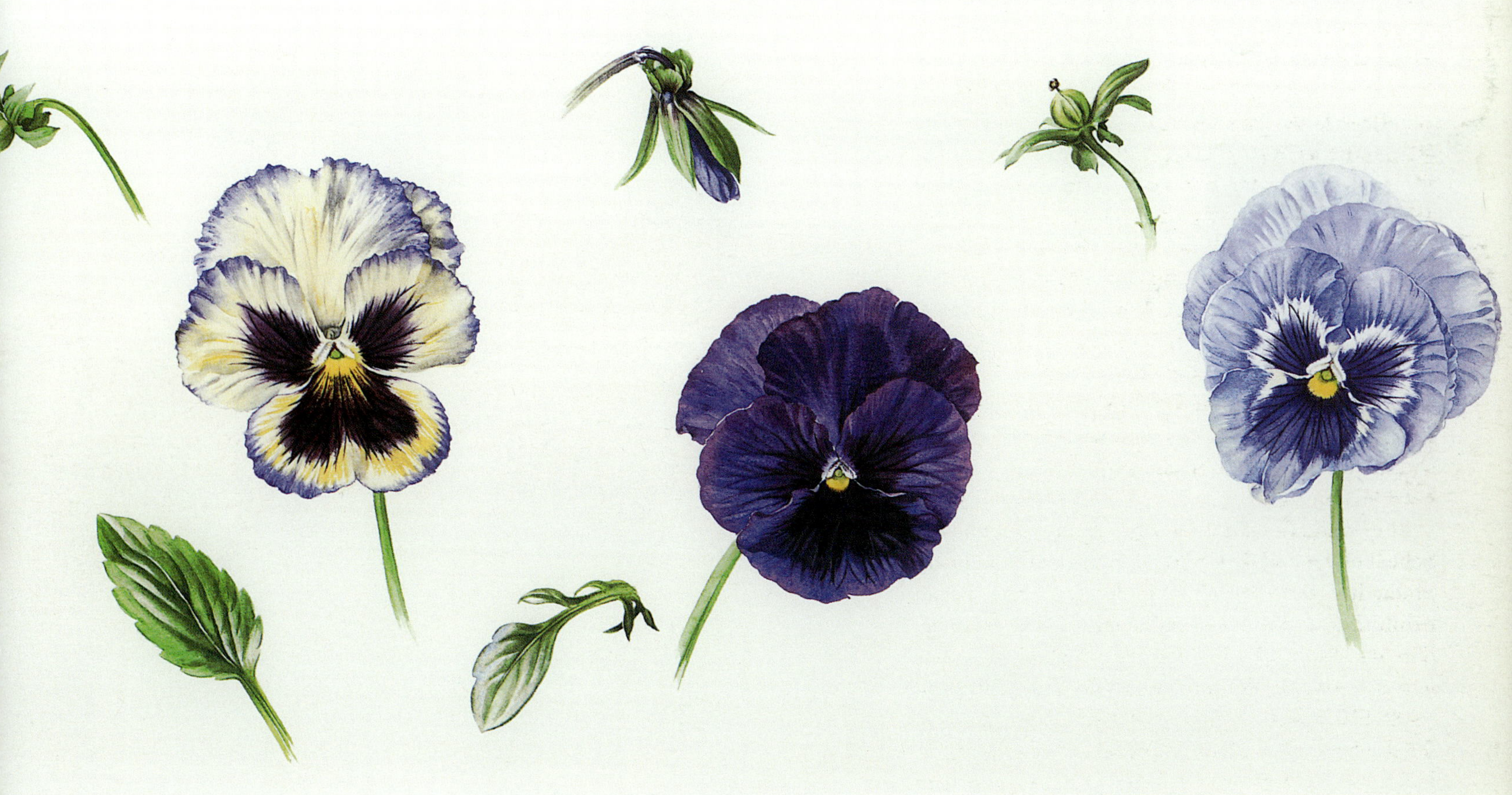

Elisabeth Sherras Clark

BORN KINGSTON UPON THAMES, ENGLAND 1936

Elisabeth Sherras Clark (known as Liz) now spends her time chasing the sun, spending one half of the year in her home in a village near Guildford, in Surrey, England, and the other half in Australia and New Zealand. She is involved with botanical and flower painting in both hemispheres as well as teaching and lecturing. She was trained at the Ruskin School of Fine Art and at the Westminster School of Education at Oxford. She taught Art & Design at Tiffin Girls School and Tolworth Girls School, both in Kingston Upon Thames, as well as running short courses at West Dean College, Chichester and Denman College, Oxford in botanical and flower painting. She retired from teaching full-time in 1996 and began her present peripatetic existence.

She showed at the Royal Academy and elsewhere in the UK in the 1960s. During the 1990s she exhibited in group shows at Nature in Art, Gloucestershire, the Flagstaff Galleries in Auckland, twice in the RHS, and in the Cuppacumbalong Gallery, Canberra. Her recent exhibitions have been at the Royal Geographical Society, the Pumphouse Gallery, Auckland, Denham College and the Showcase Gallery, Guildford.

In 1998 she became a founder member of the Wildlife and Botanical Artists Society in Canberra, which she tells me was started after a number of artists attended courses that I initiated in Sydney, taught by Jenny Phillips.

This Peruvian cactus can be found at high altitudes on the western side of the Andes, in the mountains' rain shadow. I have seen it from the train going between Cusco and Machu Picchu in the arid terrain along the track, where the pale flowers look very striking.

PERUVIAN CACTUS:
CEREUS PERUVIANA
Signed Sherras Clark
(undated)
Acquired from the
artist 1998
Watercolour on paper
660 × 475 mm

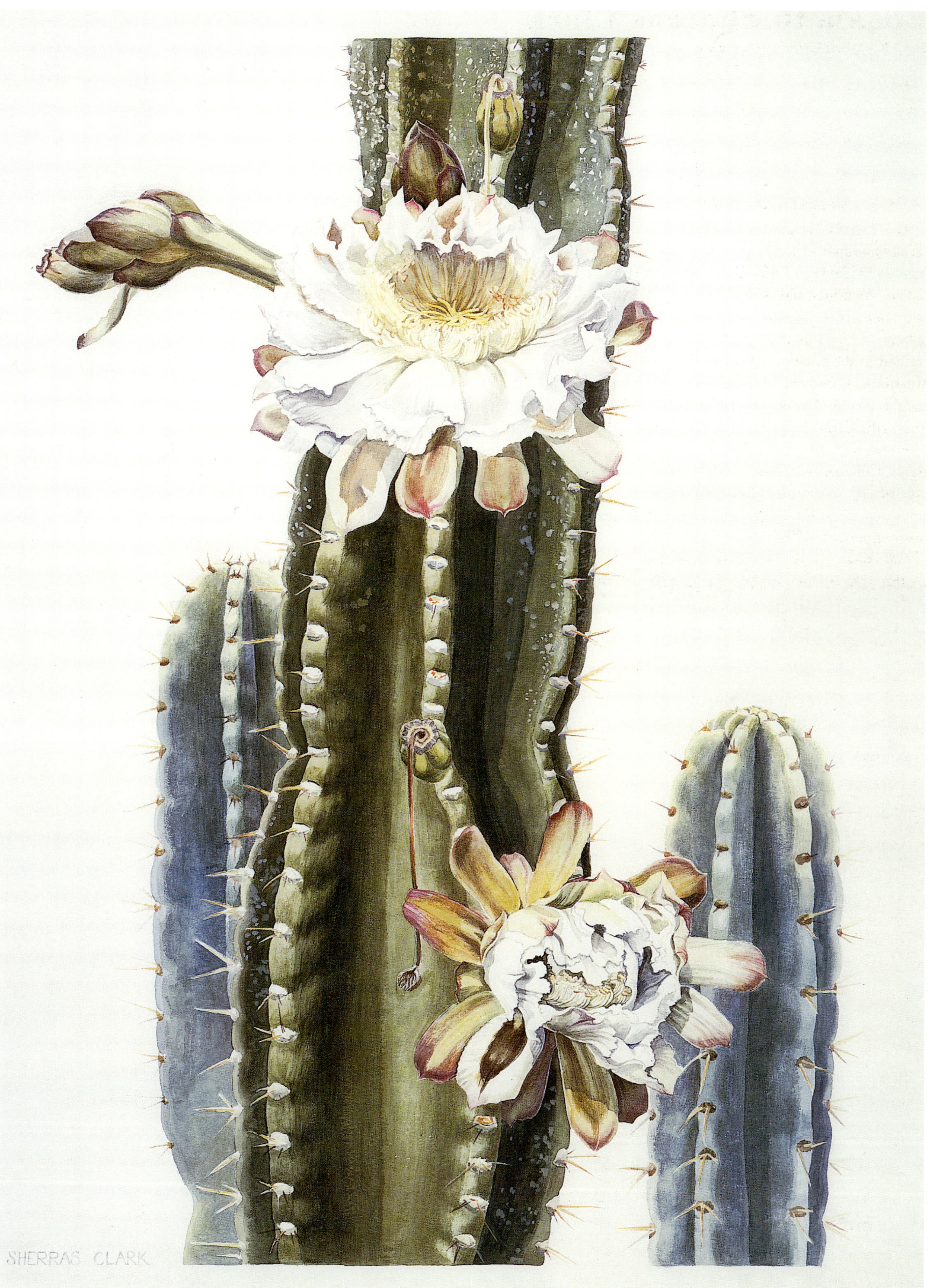
SHERRAS CLARK

Sheila Siegerman

BORN KAMLOOPS, BC, CANADA 1931

Sheila Siegerman's career was dominated by design work until the late 1980s. She was a jewellery designer in Vancouver, a graphic artist in Hamilton, Ontario and from 1957 she lived in Toronto as a theatrical scenic designer. It was in the late 1980s that she started concentrating on botanical art and had a number of solo exhibitions in the McLaren-Barnes Gallery, Oakville, Ontario and also in 1993 she had a show at the Niagara Parks Botanical Gardens. She had a number of exhibitions at the RHS, and was awarded gold and silver gilt medals. I acquired my first painting from her in 1993, a magnificent and showy orchid which she had grown herself and painted several times. It has been widely exhibited around the world and she has had other orchids exhibited by the Hunt Institute and the Greater New York Orchid Society.

Recently I received a letter from her telling me she wanted to give me a very elegant painting of the litchi including its leaves, fruit and seed which had been in an exhibition, 'Flora 2000', at Longwood Gardens near Philadelphia. She wanted to send it to me because she felt that her botanical life had been improved by the publicity I have been able to give over the last few years to botanical art through my book and exhibitions. She had also been to one of the classes I initiated in Charleston, taught by Katie Lee. Like many artists she had felt very isolated and she welcomed the chance to make friends and contacts with other people working in the same area. I was particularly delighted to receive this painting which is very different in tone from my first orchid painting. It has appeared widely in the American press, from the *Washington Post* to the *International Herald Tribune*, reflecting the increased interest amongst the public which has resulted in newspapers and magazines beginning to cover exhibitions of botanical art far more frequently.

She has always been particularly interested in orchids, but it is good to see her trying another subject and succeeding so well.

LITCHI CHINENSIS
Signed Sheila Siegerman (undated)
Gift from the artist 2000
Watercolour on paper
370 × 290 mm

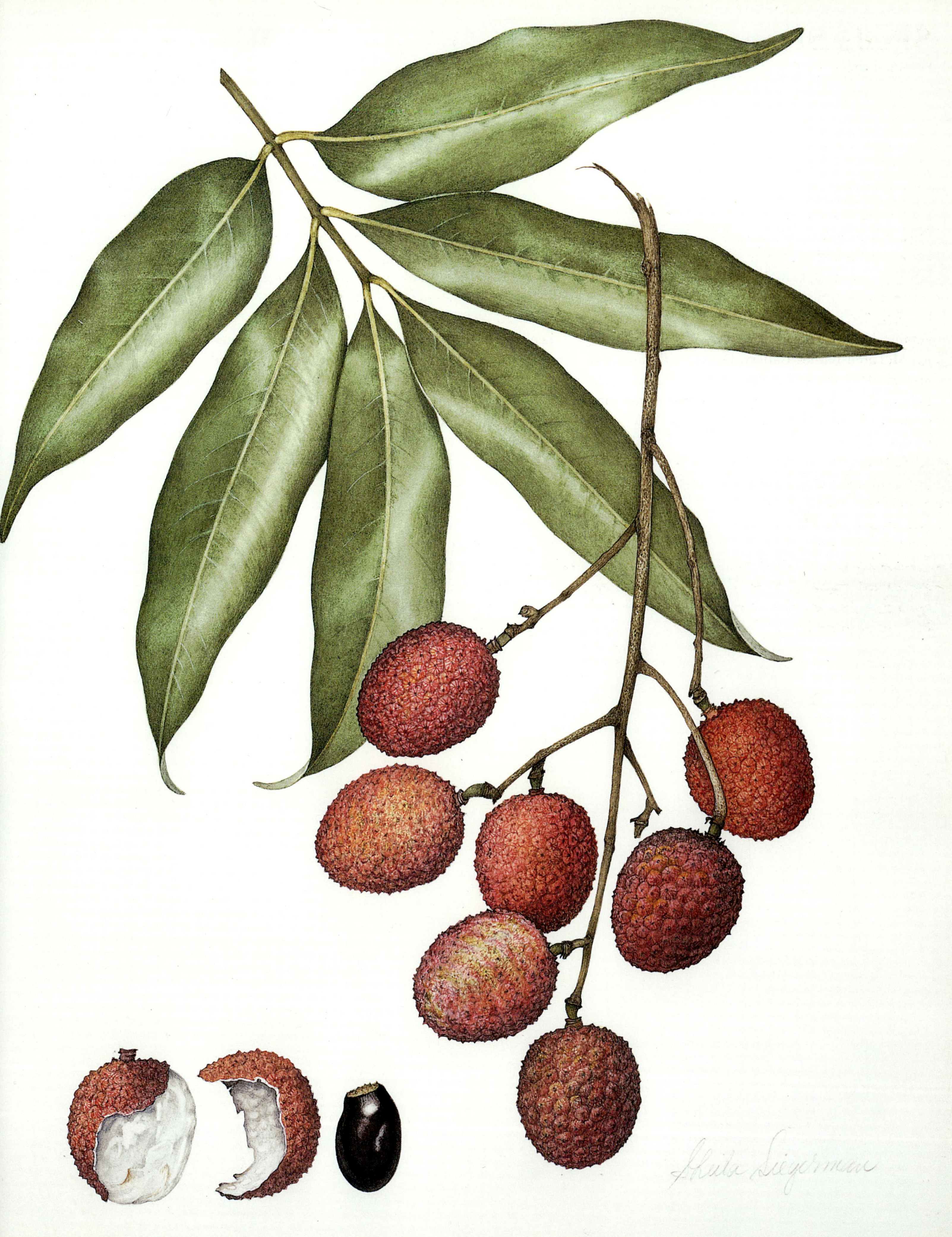
Sheila Siegerman

Thakur Ganga (Rai Sahib) Singh

Born India 1895–1970

Thakur Ganga Singh was made Rai Sahib for his contribution to the arts after thirty years of painting at Dehra Dun Forest Research Institute, India. During that time he and his colleague, P. N. Sharma (see page 258) painted 188 watercolours and made many ink drawings which are still held at the Institute.

In 1931 he was awarded a scholarship to the Slade in London and travelled to England overland by train. Ten years later Singh was commissioned by the Maharajah Yadhavindra Singh of Patiala to record the flowers of the Simla Hills in Kashmir for a book. This most beautiful part of the Himalayas has a spectacular flora and Singh completed over 400 watercolours. He died in 1970 and the Maharajah died two years later with his book unfinished, although the paintings were complete. Since then, the Maharajah's son has taken on the task of preparing the work for publication.

When I was a schoolgirl I visited Pakistan just after partition and spent some wonderful months exploring the Himalayas of the North West Frontier Province, close to the border of Kashmir. I will never forget the spectacular drifts of delphiniums flowing down the mountains, the alpine streams and high valleys dotted with orchids and lilies. As a budding botanist I scrambled up the mountains with my pony, collecting and pressing plants which I eventually took to Kew.

I bought this lovely lily in London, when there was an exhibition of about seventy of Singh's paintings commissioned by the Maharajah. I am not sure of its date but it seems that the works on display were painted between 1942 and 1962, with five being dated 1947, so it may be the oldest painting in my collection of contemporary botanical art. It has a charming, old fashioned 'Company' style, reminiscent of the kind of work commissioned by officials of the East India Company in the days of the Raj and it reminds me of that exciting time when I was first bitten by the travel bug and set my heart on becoming a botanist.

LILIUM
Unsigned & undated
Acquired from
Mallett, London 1999
Watercolour on paper
370 × 285 mm

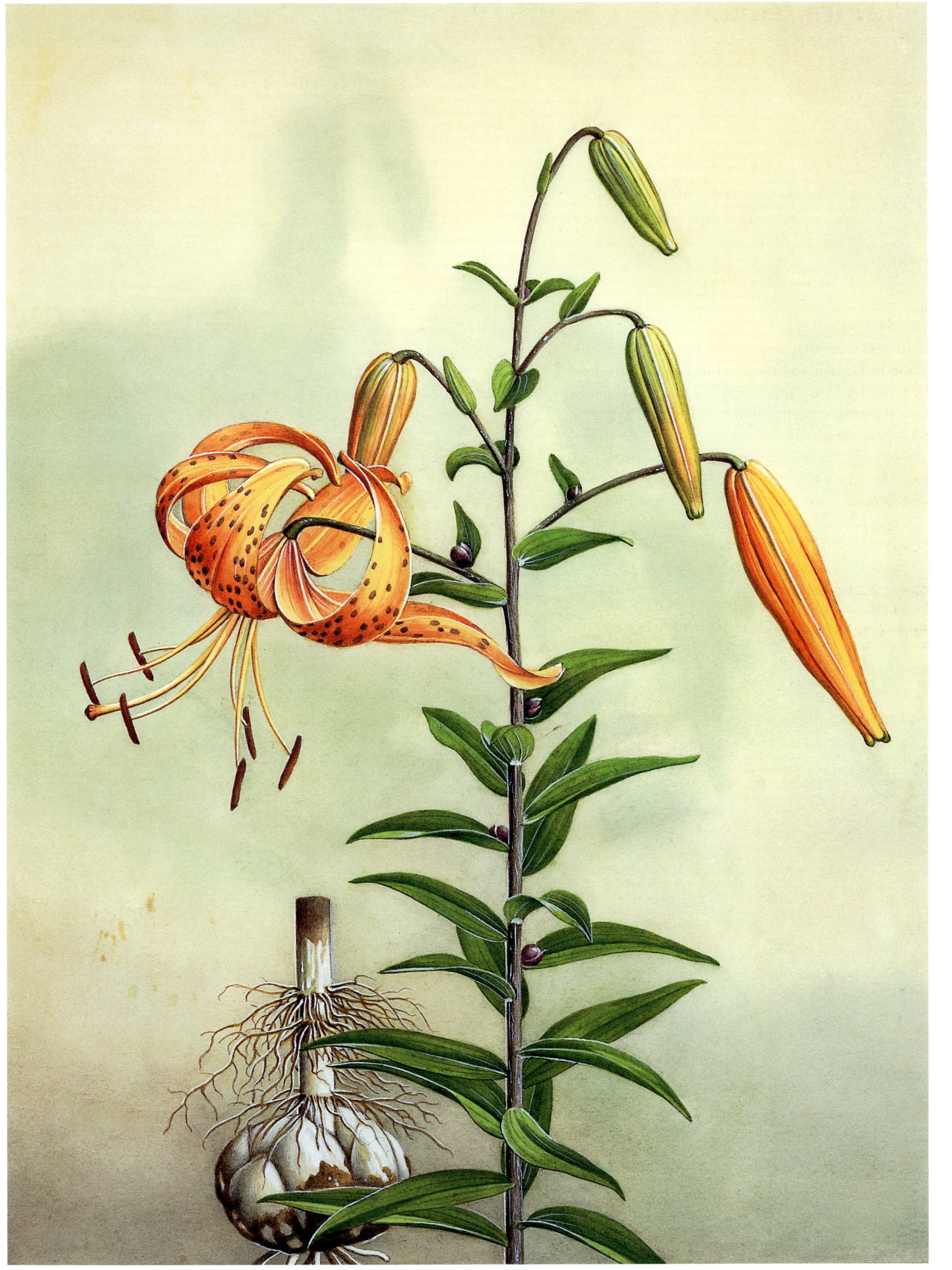

Camilla Speight

BORN OXFORD, ENGLAND 1974

Hating her first year of tuition at Camberwell College of Art in 1992–3, Camilla Speight launched herself as a freelance botanical artist when she was only twenty years old. Her draughtsmanship is quite remarkable and for the last few years she has contented herself with exquisite line drawings in pen and ink although she has been experimenting with colour recently.

Initially she worked freelance, but full-time for Macmillan, and produced many line drawings for a series of RHS manuals and dictionaries published by them. These covered climbers and wall plants, grasses, orchids and bulbs. They were masterminded by Mark Griffiths and horticultural experts in the relevant fields. From 1995 she prepared illustrations for *The Royal Horticultural Society Concise Gardener's Dictionary* by Mark Griffiths and Michael Pollock (published 1997), and worked on drawings of *Anguloa* species for Dr Henry Oakley, who holds the British National Collection of *Anguloa* and *Lycaste*.

She started showing plates of line drawings from 1995 onwards at the RHS, winning a gold medal each time and was awarded the Garden Writers Guild special award for the *Royal Horticultural Society Manual of Orchids*.

Since 1997 she has been working at the Royal Botanic Gardens Kew. She was introduced to me by Gordon Rae, the former director general of the RHS, just after she had started working there. He has done much to encourage young artists and he thought very highly of her work. Clearly her professional work was immaculate but there is a danger that artists who only work to produce plates for publication can become too tight, trying to pack yet another species into a crowded drawing. I advised her to do a few drawings each year that were just for herself, where she could experience some spontaneity. I bought three drawings at that first meeting. The *Dioscorea elephantipes* and the *Dioscorea discolor* (1994) were crowded into the

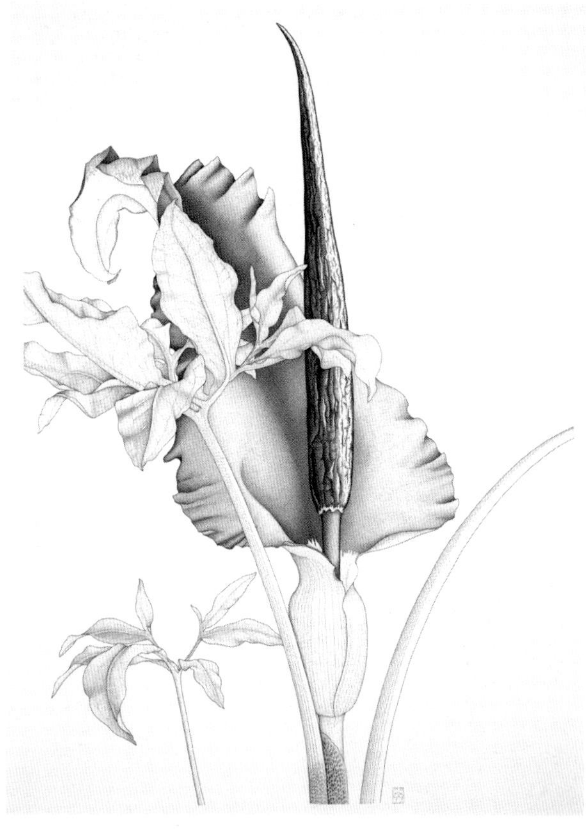

DRAGON ARUM: *DRACUNCULUS VULGARIS*
Signed CS 99
Acquired from Waterman Fine Art Gallery, London 1999
Pen & ink drawing
450 × 320 mm

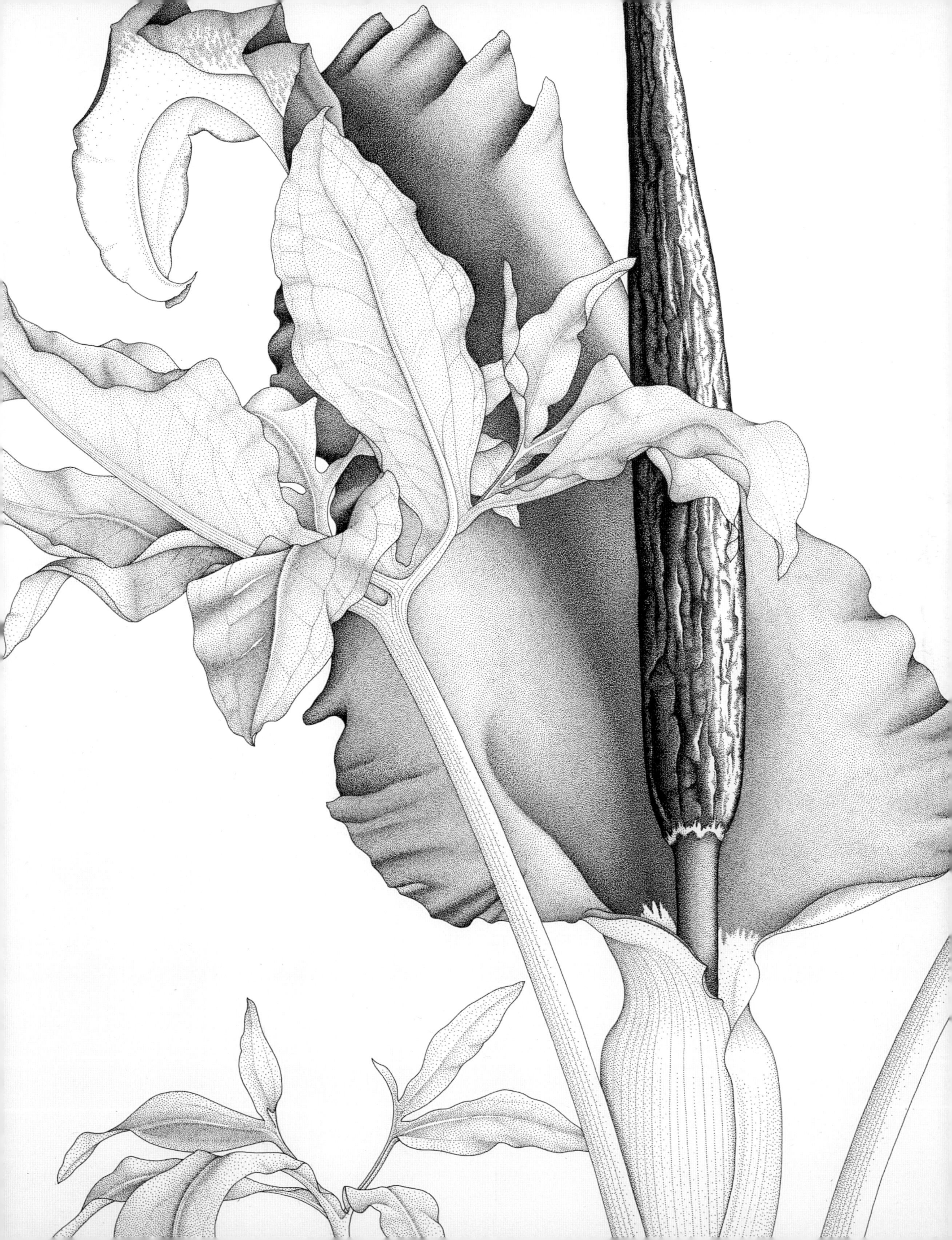

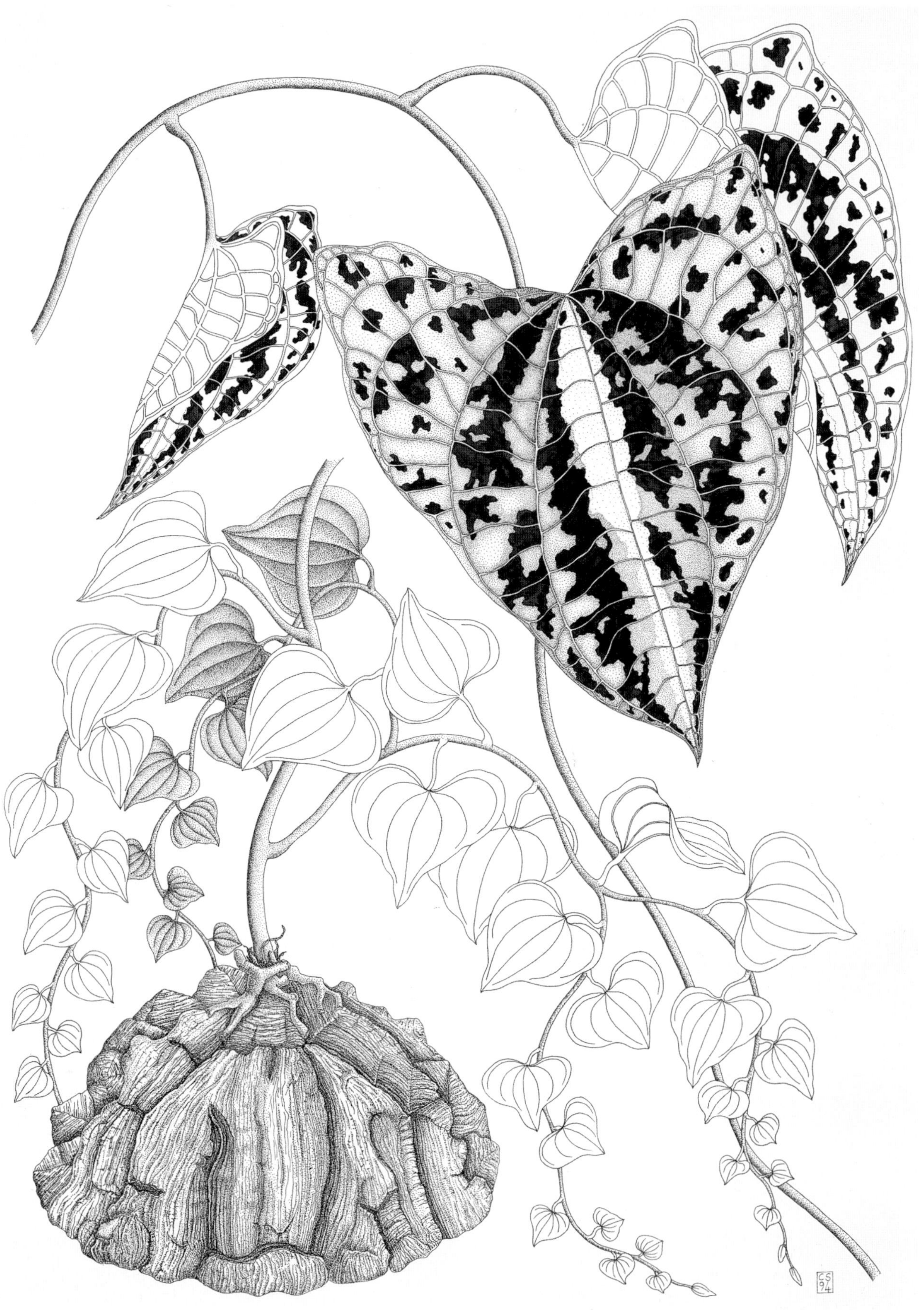
CS
94

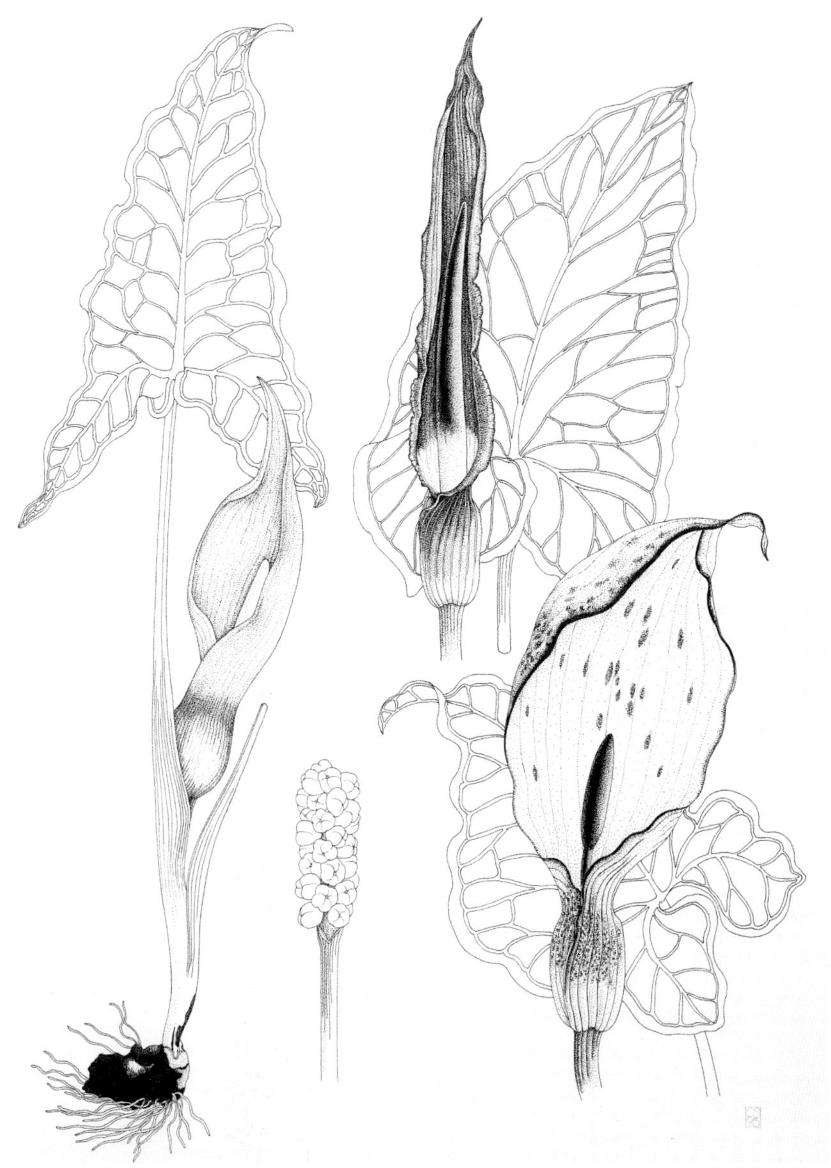

DIOSCOREA ELEPHANTIPES & DIOSCOREA DISCOLOR
(Left) Signed CS 94
Acquired from the artist 1997
Line drawing 295 × 418 mm

ARUMS: *A. ITALICUM, A. RUPICOLA, A. MACULATUM*
(Above) Signed CS 94
Acquired from the artist 1997
Line drawing 295 × 418 mm

plate but I enjoyed them as I had seen them in all their strangeness at Kirstenbosch. The jade vine, *Strongylodon macrobotrys* (1994) is a particular favourite of mine, native to the Philippines, now climbing in the garden of Reid's Hotel, Madeira and in the Caribbean – a plant I would like to introduce far more widely in the sub-tropics and have longed to grow in my conservatory (see page 259). The third drawing of arums I liked for the treatment of the spathes. I acquired a firm, tough little drawing of *Banksia coccinea* in 1997 after I saw it in a show at the RHS, because I admired her masterly treatment of the complex flower.

In 1999 I saw the remarkable *Dracunculus vulgaris* in an excellent Waterman Fine Art exhibition. Camilla has managed to convey the sinister spathe in all its strength and drama in one of the best pen and ink studies I have seen. She did another remarkable study in the same show, of *Hosta* leaves, somehow conjuring up the subtleties of their texture using only pen and ink. Both these drawings are outstanding and I was torn with indecision, trying to decide which one I would acquire for my collection.

Pamela Stagg

Born Nottingham, England 1949

I first saw Pamela Stagg's work at the Hunt Institute in 1992 and then followed her one-person exhibitions at Jonathan Cooper's Park Walk Gallery in London where I opened her fourth show in 1999. I particularly liked her lively and colourful Turk's-head squash.

A car accident threatened to end her painting career in 1995 but she managed to return to painting six months later and has continued teaching in Toronto. Her pupils have exhibited at the RHS and four of her students showed at the 9th International Exhibition at the Hunt Institute in Pittsburgh.

This watercolour of a variegated squash and two vivid orange pumpkins was painted with great finesse and skill and I find the texture and colours are particularly pleasing. The painting has been widely shown around the world in exhibitions of my collection since I acquired it in 1996.

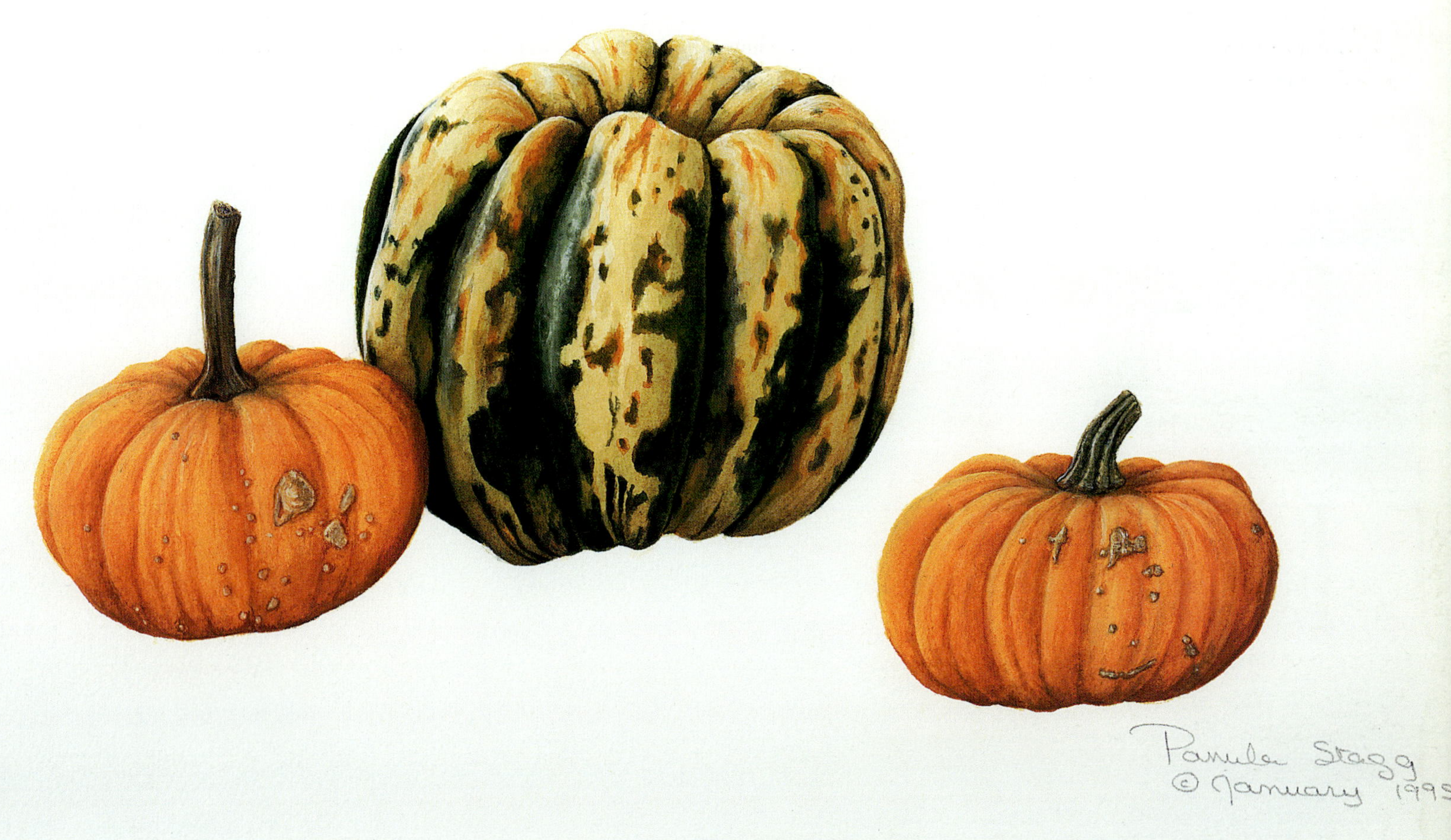

VARIEGATED SQUASH &
PUMPKINS
Signed Pamela Stagg
January 1995
Acquired from Park Walk
Gallery, London 1996
Watercolour on paper
230 × 380 mm

Ann Swan

Born England 1949

Ann Swan is celebrated for her elegant drawings in pencil and conté or pastel. They are very detailed, fine and precise, sometimes with glowing colour tones.

She qualified in textile design in the 1960s at the Manchester College of Art and Design and worked for many years in advertising and industry. She began to exhibit her drawings in 1990 and has since shown her work widely in England. She has received two gold medals from the RHS and was awarded a silver medal at the 14th World Orchid Conference. Most of her very detailed drawings are in pencil, but she sometimes uses conté pencil or pastel to apply small areas of colour. She showed a superb drawing of celeriac (*Apium graveolens* var. *rapaceum*) in the Hunt Institute's 8th International Exhibition in 1995 which has stayed in my mind ever since.

I usually call in to her stall at the Chelsea Flower Show and in 1998 I was tempted by her outstanding original drawing of a Brussels sprout plant. Just before I arrived HRH Prince Philip had bought a print of the same work. Her prints are of superb quality, barely distinguishable from the original and we have used them to decorate rooms in some of our Orient-Express hotels as a welcome relief from the endless repeats of Redouté appearing in every hotel corridor these days.

She is doing a certain amount of teaching at Nature in Art, Twigworth, Gloucestershire and at the RHS at Wisley and Pershore. She also does a day on Anne-Marie Evans' introductory course at the Chelsea Physic Garden (improving drawing skills), but is trying to limit her teaching as she prefers drawing for herself.

BRUSSELS SPROUTS
Signed Ann Swan
(undated)
Acquired from the
artist 1998
Conté pencil with
solvent & graphite
pencil
500 × 330 mm

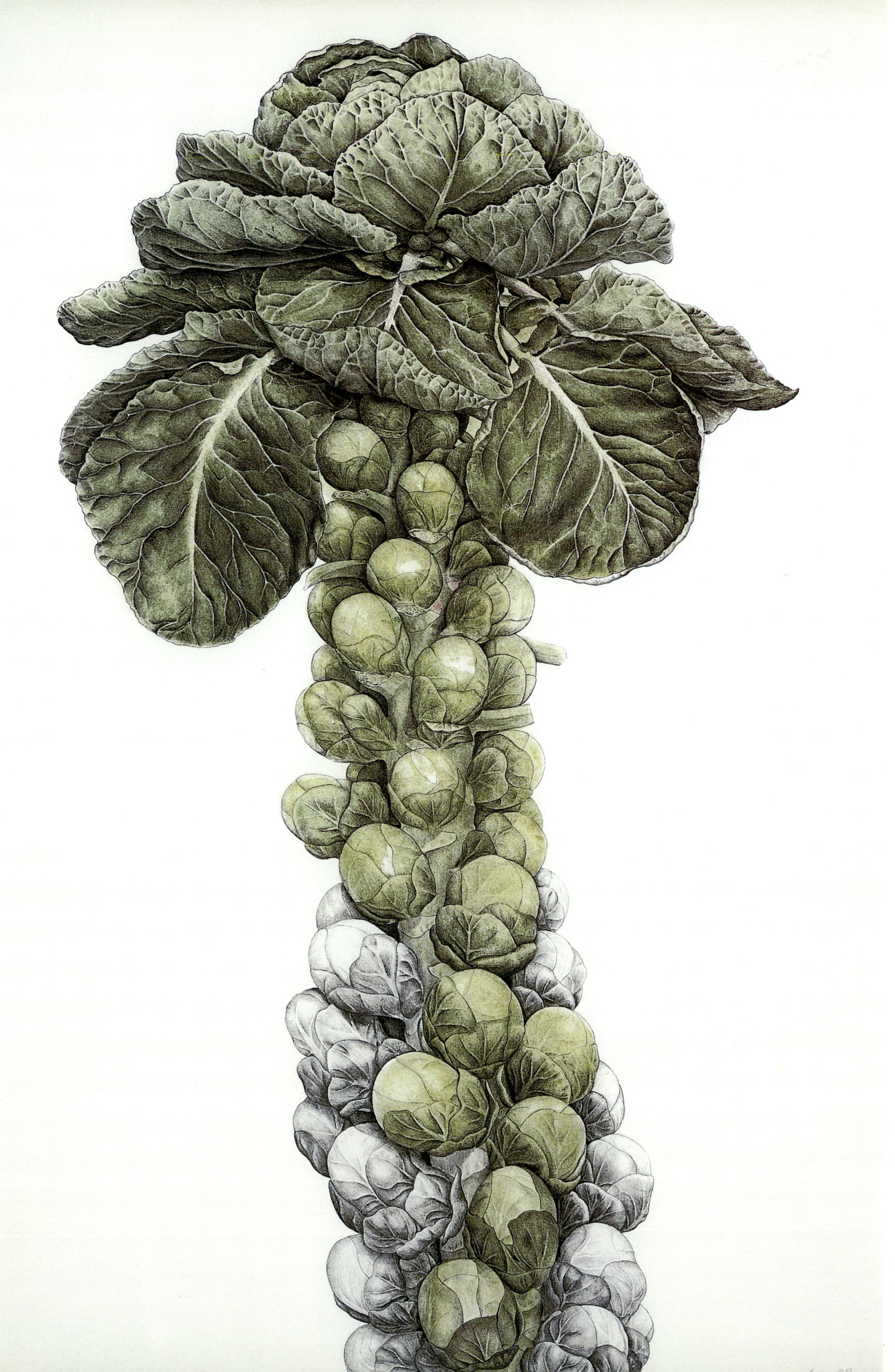

Geraldine King Tam

BORN TORONTO, CANADA 1920

Recently I was asked to review a new book of Hawaiian watercolours – my first proper introduction to the work of Geraldine King Tam. This lovely book, with text by David J. Mabberley, is aptly entitled *Paradisus*. It contains sixty superb plates of flowering and fruiting tropical plants that grow in the Hawaiian islands, some native, but many introduced as food plants by Polynesian settlers, others later by Chinese and European immigrants.

Geraldine King Tam now lives on Kauai, surely one of the most beautiful of the Hawaiian islands. But she was born far away in Toronto and took her first degree in English and French at McMaster University, Hamilton, Ontario. Her father had emigrated from mainland China and brought up seven children. After teaching for two years she took an MA in art education at Columbia University, New York. Like many other botanical artists she had a period as a textile designer, as well as teaching jewellery design. But her main occupation from 1955 to 1976 was teaching art at the Dalton School, New York. During this period she married the celebrated Kauai-born poet and artist Reuben Tam who greatly influenced her later work in Hawaii. While they were based in New York they spent their summers at an artists' colony on Monhegan, an island off the coast of Maine, where she started recording the native plants. She had a solo exhibition of fifty of these drawings in 1968 at Syracuse University. According to David Mabberley her style at that time was rather naive, showing flowers with an inked outline, reminiscent of a textbook illustration.

In 1980 she and her husband moved to Kauai to start a new part of their lives. Reuben wanted to grow the flowers and fruit trees he had known as a child and he encouraged Geraldine to paint them. Her style changed as she was challenged and exhilarated by the exotic tropical flora around her, and her plant portraits becoming striking with their flowing lines, true colours and beautiful designs. Her graceful paintings capture the spirit and essence of her subjects.

I am particularly delighted to have this wonderful drawing of the yellow granadilla (*Passiflora laurifolia*) showing its extraordinarily elaborate purple flower and its glowing orange fruit. Its foliage is reminiscent of a laurel leaf, hence its name. The lilting common name, granadilla, comes from the Spanish for 'little pomegranate'. Geraldine King Tam describes the flowers as 'fragrant, beautiful and delicate, hanging down like an umbrella. Had to do a cross section to show the typical *Passiflora* insides'. The plant is native to north-eastern South America and the West Indies. It arrived in Hawaii before 1871 and now lives in the wetter areas of forest on most of the islands. It only fruits occasionally, in dry conditions and has a pleasant taste, looking very like *Passiflora edulis* when cut in half. It is not so invasive as the banana poka, *P. mollissima* which has rampaged all over Hawaii and Kauai, smothering the native vegetation. I remember seeing it on the road to the Waimea Gorge, enchantingly pretty with its pink, pendulous flowers, but choking everything in its path.

Geraldine King Tam works from fresh plants, growing many in her own garden. Some plant portraits take a very long time to complete, being worked on over several years. She generally used Strathmore three-ply Bristol Board and Winsor & Newton permanent watercolour. She has had to withstand the changeable tropical storms of the region, and had her house and garden wrecked by Hurricane Iniki in 1992. She herself was knocked unconscious and her studio was flooded, but miraculously, none of her work was destroyed. It was after this, in 1994, that she met James White and decided to give thirty-one of her paintings to the Hunt Institute of Botanical Documentation in Pittsburgh so they would be preserved in a museum environment. It is not easy to keep watercolours immaculate in the tropics, as I know from a number of paintings by Margaret Mee in my collection which show rippling and foxing from being painted or stored in damp conditions in Brazil.

She is continuing to paint the remarkable flora of Hawaii, hoping that by drawing attention to its beauty and diversity she will encourage its preservation. I can well understand why she was recently designated as a Living Treasure by the Kauai Museum in Lihue and honoured by McMaster University.

YELLOW GRANADILLA: *PASSIFLORA LAURIFOLIA*
Named & signed Geraldine King Tam 1995
Acquired from the artist 2000
Watercolour on paper
610 × 510 mm

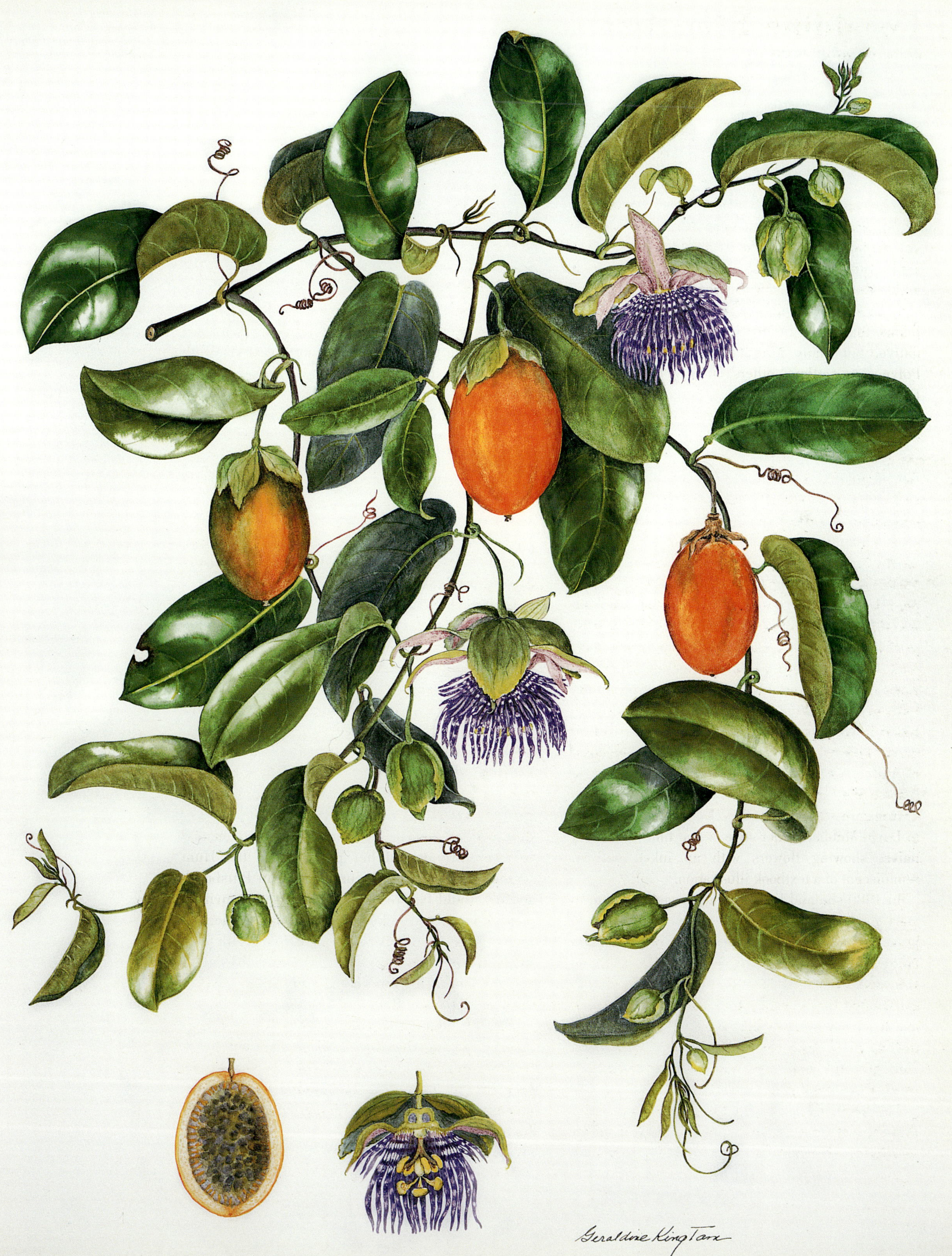
Geraldine King Tam

Vicki Thomas

BORN SOUTH AFRICA 1951

I was asked to open the Inaugural Kirstenbosch Exhibition of Botanical Art by South African artists at the beginning of February 2000. This is where I met Vicki Thomas for the first time and saw her work. This attractive, dynamic woman told me that she was essentially self-taught but had recently attended two of the classes I had initiated in Cape Town in 1998 and 1999, tutored by Katie Lee and Jenny Phillips. I was impressed with the quality of her watercolours and bought two most interesting studies, one of *Mimetes hirtus* and the other of a curious little bush covered with golden fruit called *Adenia hastata*.

Vicki Thomas painted *Mimetes hirtus*, a member of the *Protea* family, from a specimen in cultivation near her home in Betty's Bay. Stands of this species of *Mimetes* occur naturally in marshy places along the coast at Betty's Bay but with the development of holiday homes in the area, the colonies are now regarded as threatened and have been recorded in the Red Data book which lists endangered plants. Vicki's husband has taken cuttings and gathered seed from various plants, in an effort to reintroduce *Mimetes hirtus* back into gardens in the areas where it used to grow. She tells me that there is a magnificent shrub approximately 1 metre tall that flowers prolifically in the Betty's Bay Botanic Gardens. It is a complex inflorescence to paint and I feel she has handled a difficult subject well.

Adenia hastata comes from the northern part of South Africa, and this particular plant was grown from seed collected by the botanist Ernst van Jaarsveld from the banks of the Crocodile River near Nelspruit in 1975. Having nurtured and moved it over the years from the Lowveld, he has established the plant in the magnificent new glass house at the National Botanical Institute, Kirstenbosch where it is thriving, producing the golden but poisonous fruits that Vicki Thomas has painted so beautifully. Its swollen stem allows the plant to survive periodic episodes of drought. There are some paintings that have a 'love-at-first-sight' quality, and for me this study of *Adenia hastata* is one of them. Next time I am in Kirstenbosch I will make sure to visit the original plant.

Vicki Thomas spent most of her youth in Zambia, where she developed her love for wide open spaces. She was brought up on a large property full of tropical plants, with many animal pets, including two small buck and a flock of guinea fowl. She was sent to school in South Africa, a train journey which took four days. At the age of eighteen she travelled alone to Kenya and from there went on to Europe. Her thoughts of further education diminished when she married in Cape Town. Her new mother-in-law was a propagation expert at Kirstenbosch Botanic Gardens and introduced Vicki to flower painting. Surrounded by South Africa's spectacular plants, she fell in love with the rich diversity of the Cape fynbos.

Vicki and her husband designed and built a second home at Betty's Bay, a unique floral area south of Cape Town, rich in endemic species. Her husband is developing a garden full of the interesting and rare plants which grow naturally in the area, cultivating them from cuttings and seeds, to provide Vicki with material to paint. Her studio looks onto majestic mountains and to the sea where the whales are now returning.

Vicki leads a busy life with many interests. She has a black belt in Karate and is learning Tai Chi. She is an avid reader and has run an interior design manufacturing business with her husband for twenty-three years. She is a founder member of the new Botanical Artists' Association of Southern Africa which helped stage the show at Kirstenbosch in early 2000.

MIMETES HIRTUS
Signed V Thomas
(undated)
Acquired from the
Kirstenbosch
Exhibition of
Botanical Art 2000
Watercolour on paper
400 × 270 mm

ADENIA HASTATA
(Overleaf)
Signed V Thomas
(undated)
Acquired from the
Kirstenbosch
Exhibition of
Botanical Art 2000
Watercolour on paper
350 × 650 mm

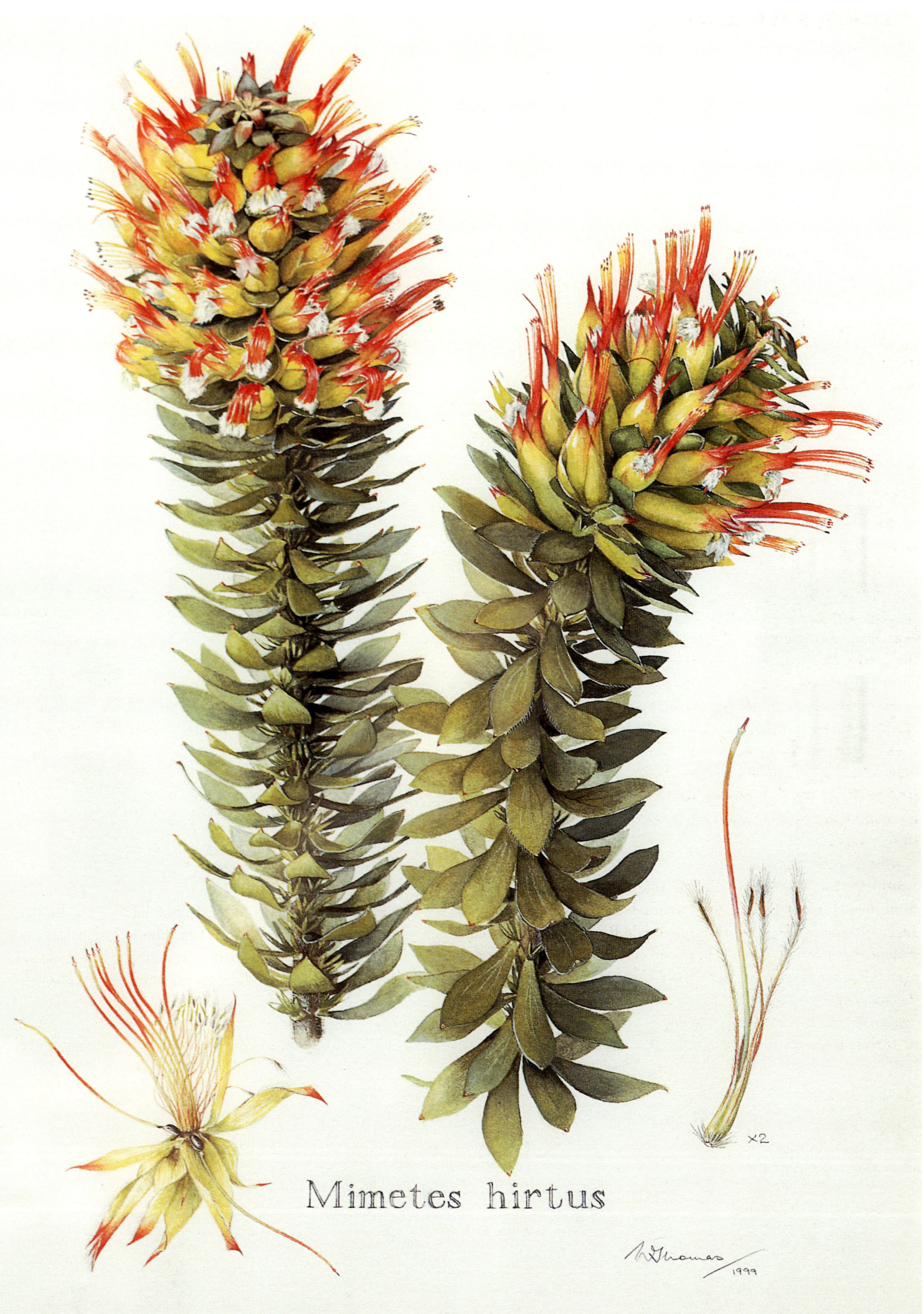
x2
Mimetes hirtus

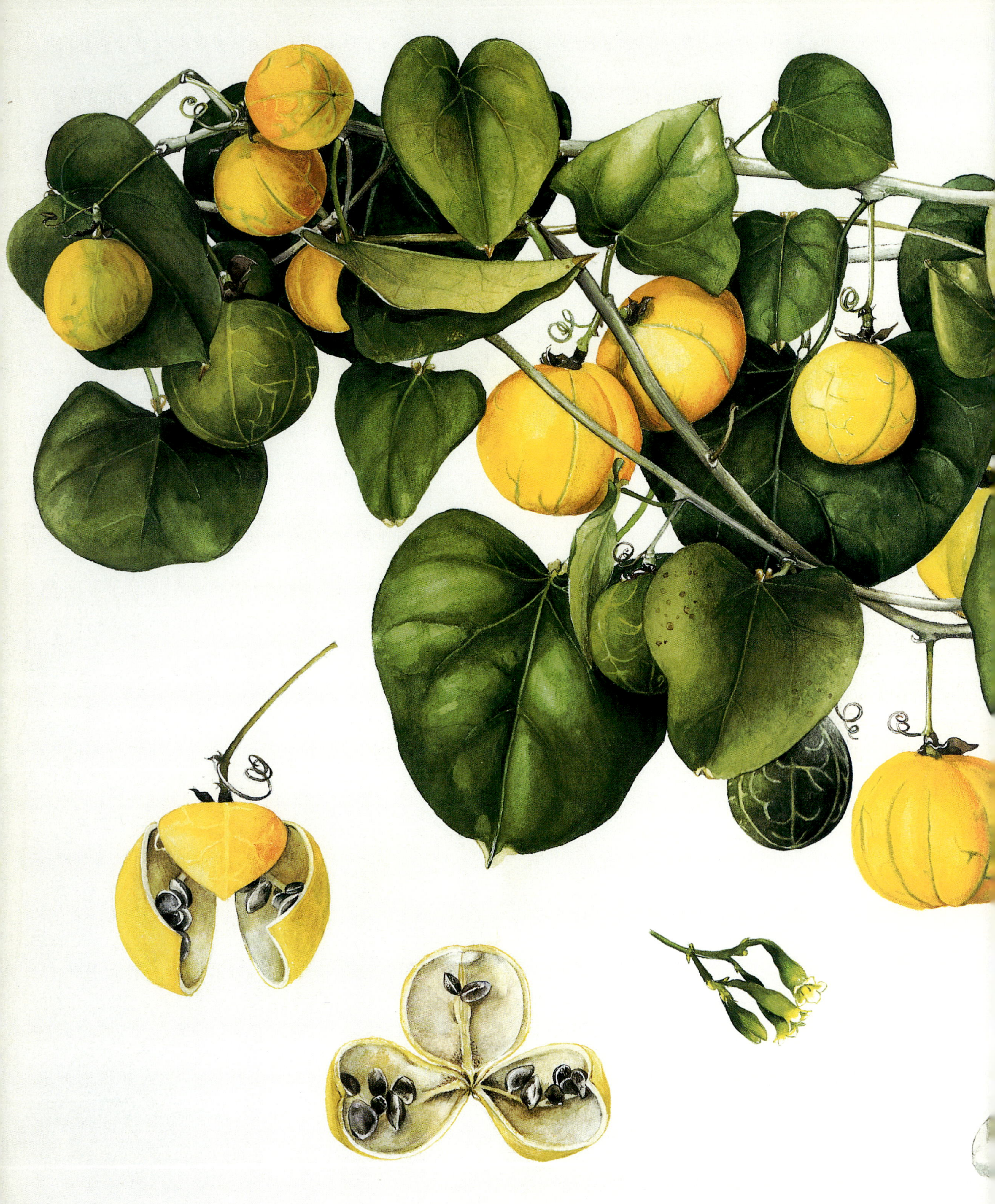

ADENIA HASTATA

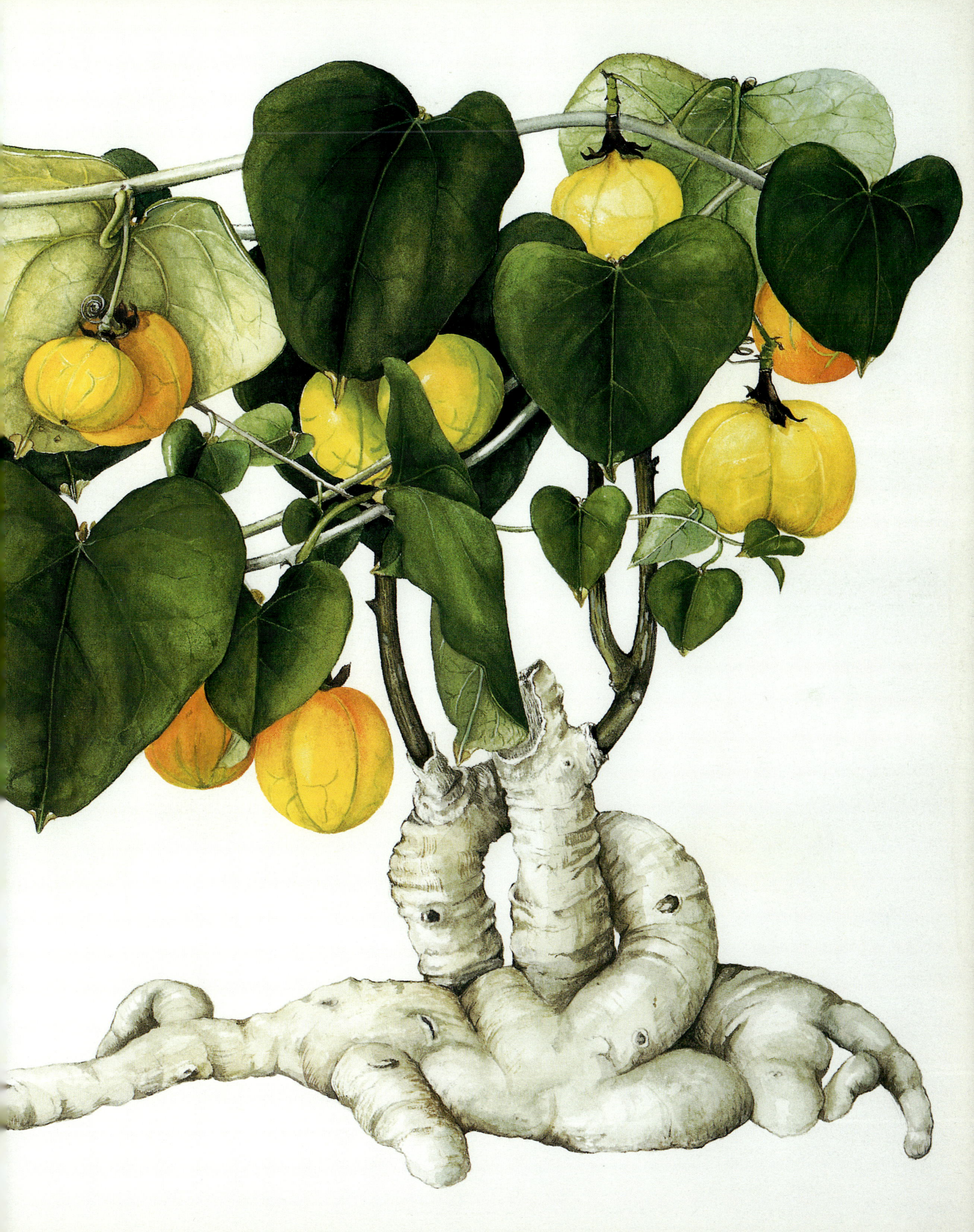

Alexander Viazmensky

Born Leningrad (St Petersburg), Russia 1946

Alexander Viazmensky, known as Sasha, paints both fungi and landscapes. He visited me in London on a rare trip to England and showed me some of his exuberant toadstool studies surrounded by a scattering of the debris of a fungi-hunting expedition. At the end of each summer he ventures deep into the woods near St Petersburg for his specimens, visiting secret spots for his trophies.

His fungi paintings were one of the great successes of the Tryon & Swann International Exhibition in 1998. They were so lively and unusual that they captivated many clients with their 'wall-appeal'.

I had previously bought two studies in 1992, but I noticed a change in his style, which has become more detailed and clearly outlined while still retaining his customary clutter of leaves, pine needles and strands of grass. So I bought four more and encouraged the Lindley Library to add a couple to its collection of contemporary artists.

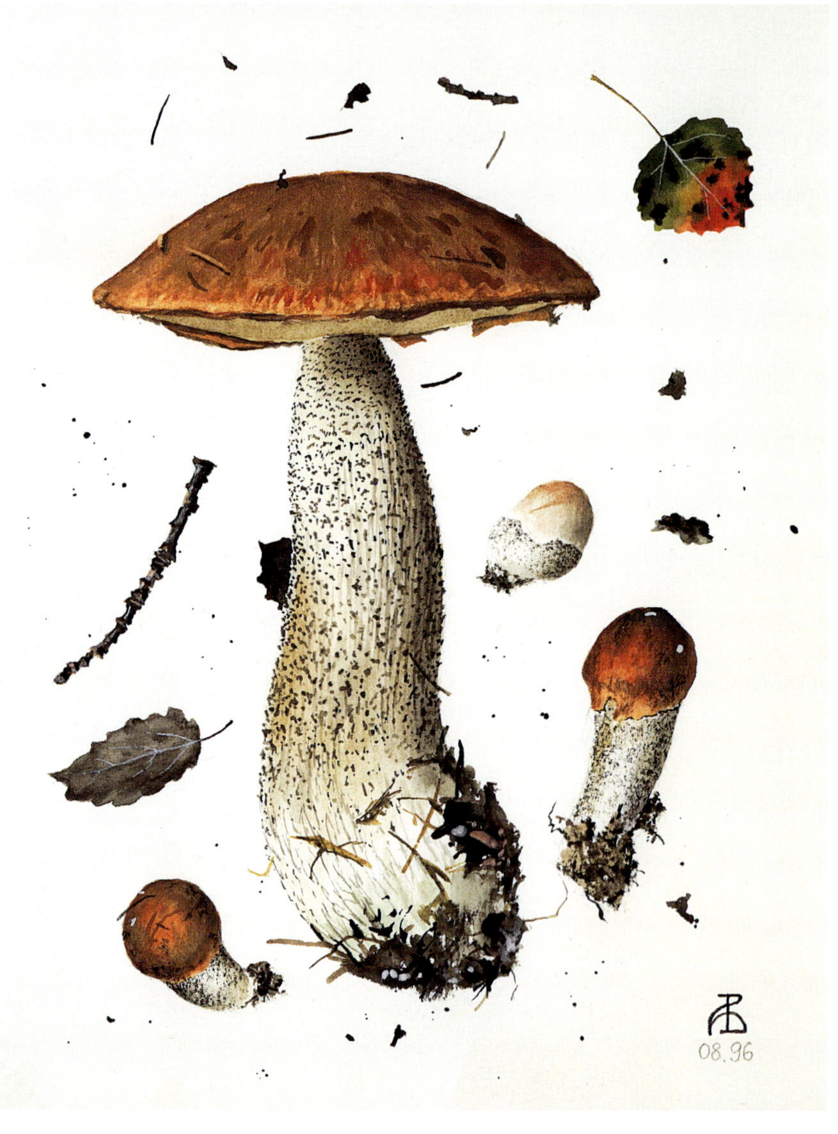

LECCINUM VERSIPELLA
(Above) Signed with
hieroglyphic AV
in old Russion 08.96
Acquired from the artist 1997
Watercolour on paper
235 × 170 mm

LECCINUM VARIICOLOR
(Right) Signed with
hieroglyphic AV
in old Russion 09.96
Acquired from the artist 1997
Watercolour on paper
360 × 245 mm

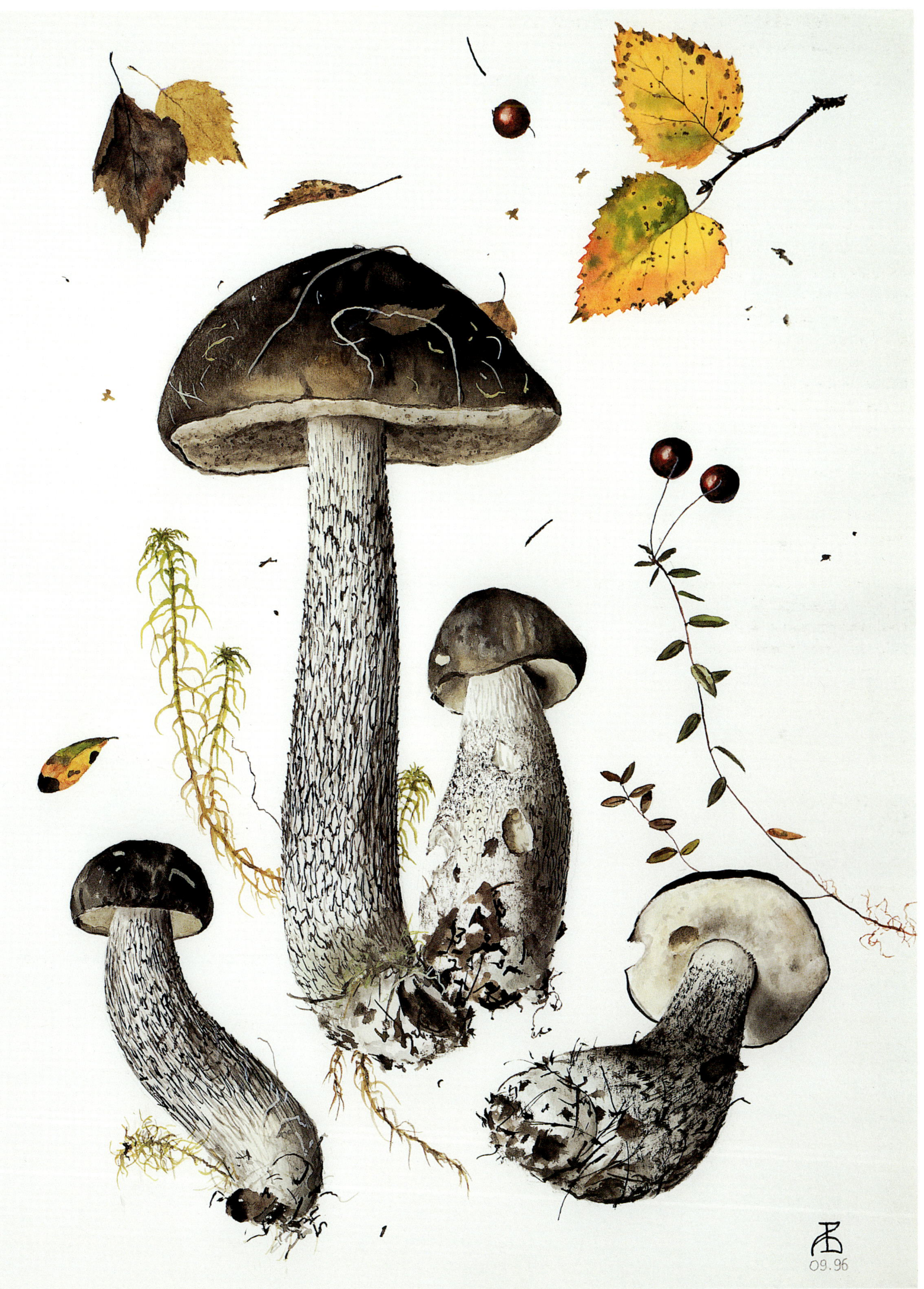
09.96

Marina Virdis

BORN CAGLIARI, SARDINIA, ITALY 1950

Marina Virdis grew up in Sardinia where she obtained her first degree in ceramics at the local School of Art in 1967. After this she went to Rome and continued her studies at the Fine Arts Academy where she obtained a degree in art while also working freelance as a graphic designer in the advertising field.

She created logos and planned campaigns for private companies, public administrations, trade union organisations and cultural societies. As well as graphic design, she taught communication techniques and contributed articles to different papers, among them *Il Corriere della Sera,* Italy's most important daily newspaper. She has played many roles in the field of communication: owner of a graphic and advertising company, a public relations adviser, a journalist and a teacher for eighteen years. She has also been involved in the women's movement in Italy.

In 1989 she completely changed her lifestyle and went to live in Scotland for two years as a member of the Findhorn Foundation, an international spiritual community where she began to work on art and nature themes. Since then Marina has committed herself to botanical painting. She wrote to me that she believes that botanical art paintings have an inherent sense of 'wonder energy' generated by nature and this inspires people to discover in themselves an openness and love for life and beauty in the world around them. Her passion for Gaia, or Mother Earth, has taken her back to live in Sardinia since 1992.

She has had many solo exhibitions in lovely places in Italy, showing two groups of paintings, the first described as 'The Rose Garden', whose subject is old roses. The other group of paintings is 'Gaia's Flowers', watercolours of wild flowers from the Sinis peninsula, near Oristano in her native Sardinia.

Her exhibitions have been supported by FAI, an Italian organisation akin to the National Trust, by the Great Italian Gardens Society and by other similar organisations. In 1999 she was awarded the first prize for paintings at the spring exhibition at Landriana, a beautiful garden near Rome, designed by Russell Page for Marchese Lavinia Taverna. There was a special area devoted to Marina's work. She was also awarded a silver gilt medal at her first showing at the RHS the same year.

I saw her work at the RHS and acquired this *Erythrina crista-galli*, a decorative member of the Leguminosae. Called the coral tree, it comes from South America, but she painted it in Sardinia where it grows very well. One of her other pictures was bought for the Lindley Library of the RHS, which is expanding its collection of contemporary botanical paintings.

ERYTHRINA CRISTA-GALLI
Signed
Marina Virdis '98
Acquired from the RHS Show 1999
Watercolour on paper
400 × 300 mm

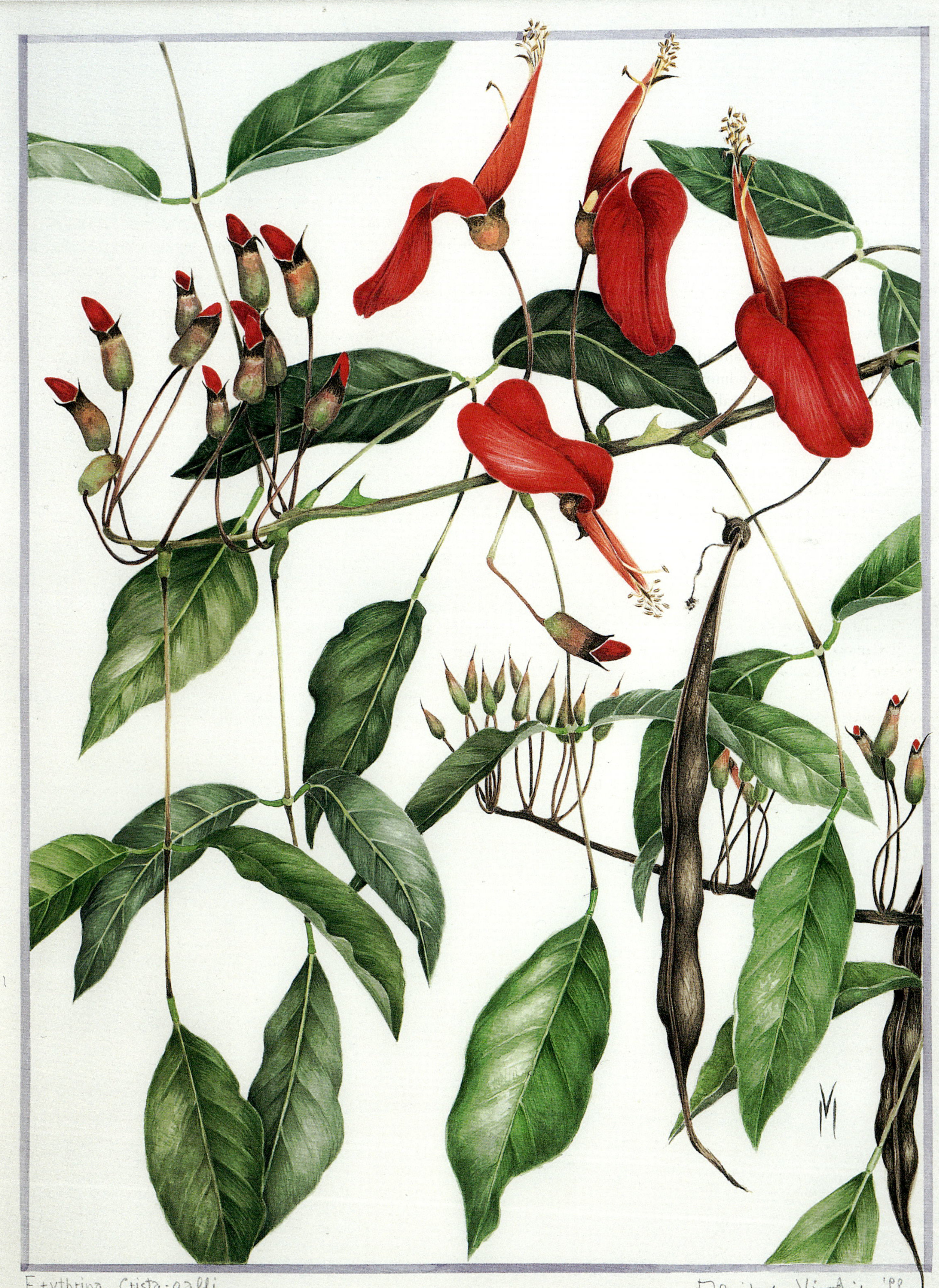
Erythrina Crista-galli

Sarah Wastie

BORN TITCHFIELD, HAMPSHIRE, ENGLAND 1966

This young artist lives in Cornwall and has had a number of solo exhibitions in Trelowarren House Galleries since 1993 and has also shown in group shows in St Ives and Mevagissey. She trained at Cornwall Technical College and at Cambridge College of Arts & Technology for a total of four years. I admired these beautifully painted pears, part of her entry to an RHS Show in 1996 where she was award a silver medal. I think this is a masterly study and it has been widely exhibited. She gained a silver gilt medal in a more recent show which, unfortunately, I missed.

Currently she is concentrating on bringing up her young daughter but hopes to start painting again when her child is a little older. I hope she does, as I feel she has a great deal to offer.

PEARS
Signed Sarah Wastie '94
Acquired from the
RHS Show 1996
Watercolour on paper
250 × 170 mm

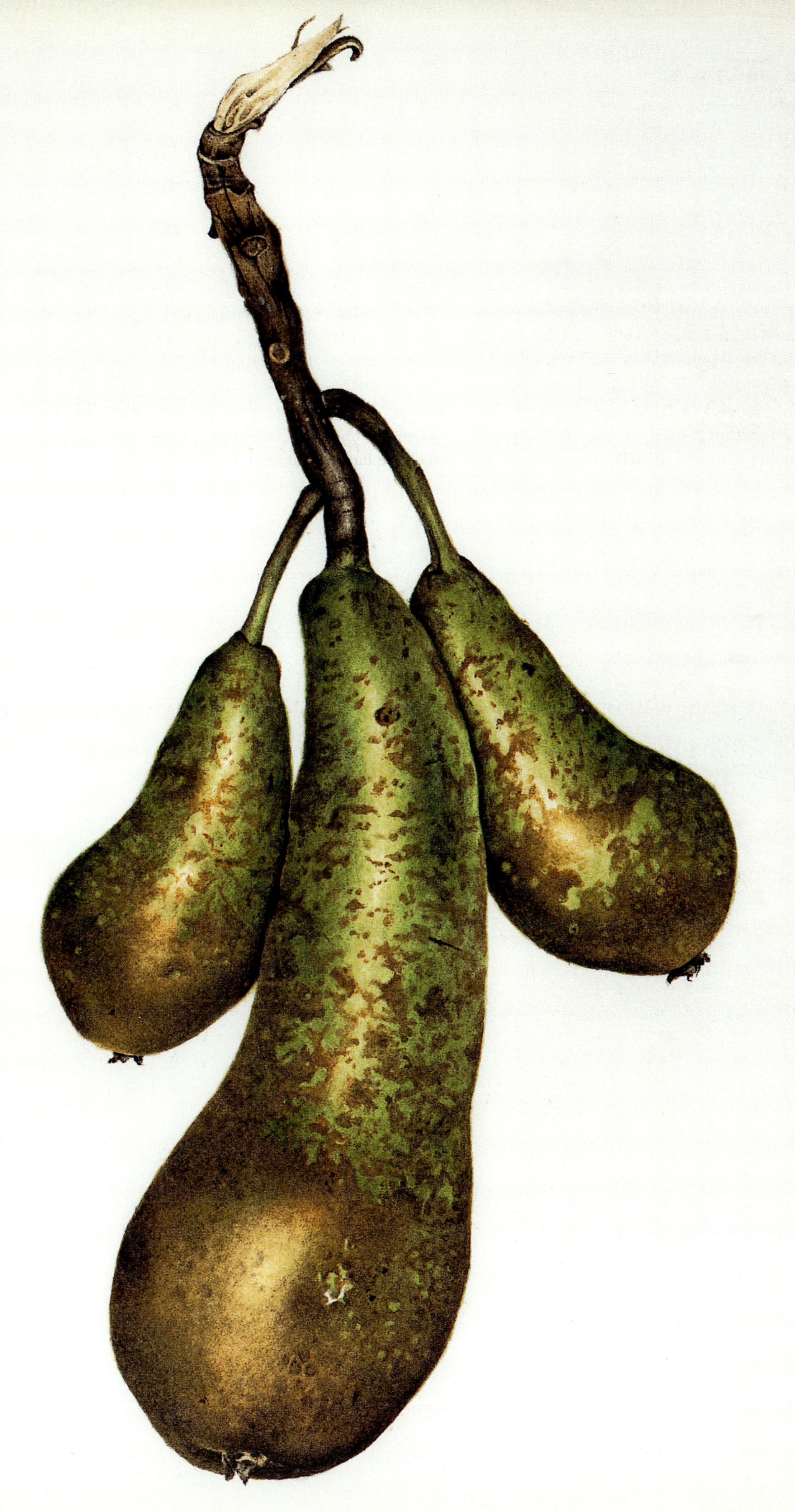

Brenda Watts

BORN ILFORD, ESSEX, ENGLAND 1932

After leaving art college in Essex, Brenda Watts worked in London designing wine labels, work which also involved lettering and calligraphy. After a few years she decided she wanted to see more of the world and eventually arrived in Kenya where she got married. She moved upcountry and raised two boys. After she returned to the UK, she started teaching adults to paint, did a teacher's training course and ended up teaching Art, Craft, Design and Technology for twenty years in the school system.

Following what is quite a familiar pattern, as soon as she retired she immediately plunged into watercolour studies of plants and describes herself as 'in seventh heaven'. Working from her home in Surrey she executes numerous commissions. She paints the most attractive, fresh studies of flowers, fruits and seeds. She has been exhibiting at the Society of Botanical Artists' shows since 1997 when she was awarded the Certificate of Botanical Merit and she also gained the Joyce Cummings award in 1999.

I was attracted to her entry for the RHS Show in February 2000 where she was awarded a silver gilt medal. I particularly liked her fruit studies, but eventually bought a delightful watercolour of a sequence of pussy-willow branches, showing the development from the tight black bud through the silvery, furry stage to the fully opened inflorescence dusted with sparkling golden pollen. It is a lively painting, beautifully executed and now hangs in Tabitha Sherwood's bedroom. I like to give 'proper' birthday presents to my grandchildren rather than plastic ones and I hope this will remind Tabitha of the days when her pockets were full of the furry pussy-willow buds that she would always strip off to stroke, before they had a chance to open properly.

GOAT WILLOW
Signed BW (undated)
Acquired from the RHS Show 2000 for Tabitha Sherwood
Watercolour on paper
315 × 290 mm

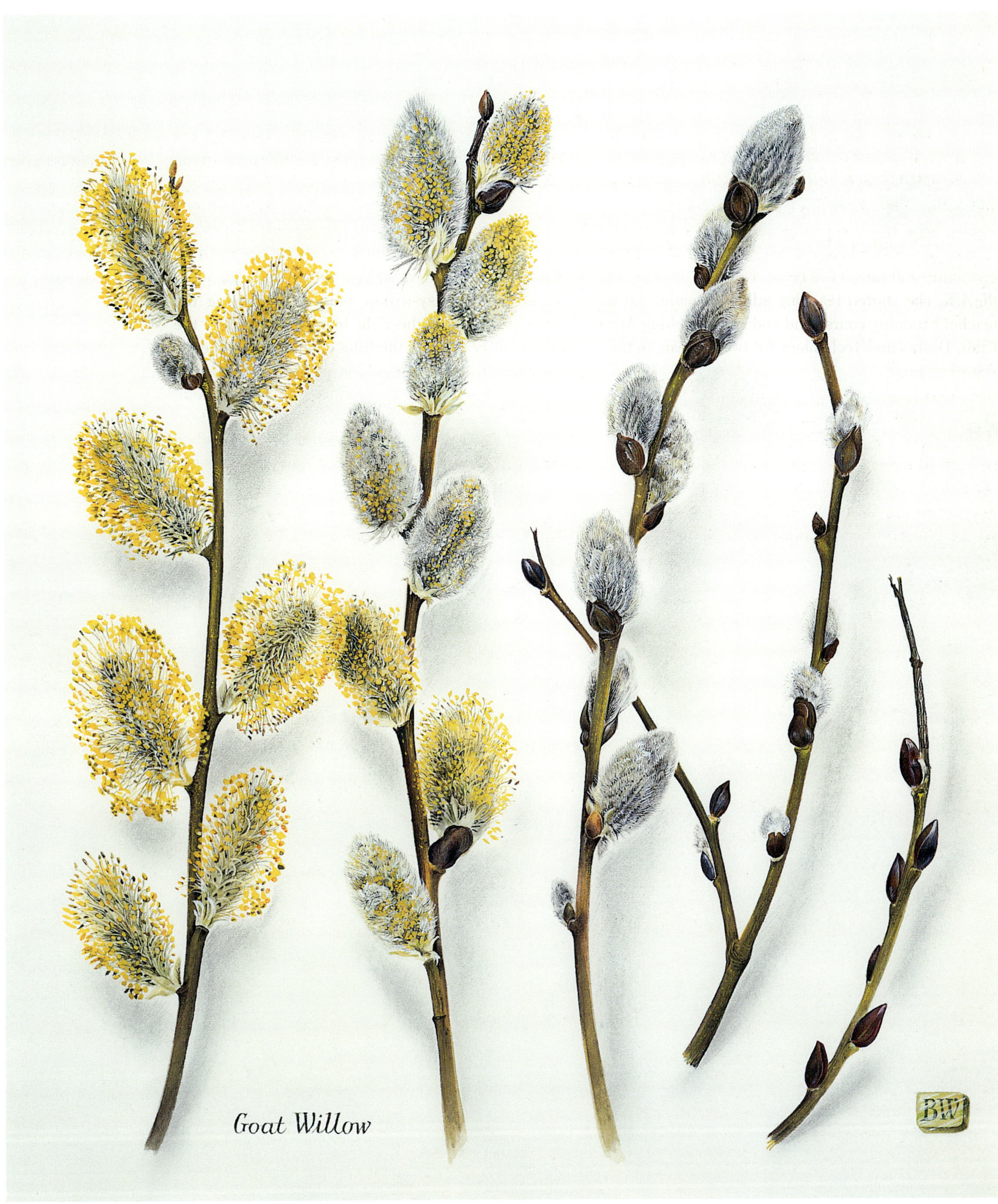
Goat Willow
BW

Marion Westmacott

BORN SYDNEY, AUSTRALIA

Marion Westmacott studied architectural drafting and worked in this field for several years. She also did scientific drafting with the CSIRO, and engineering drafting specialising in civil, geotechnical and environmental work in the late 1970s. She spent sixteen years on cattle and sheep stations in New South Wales, Queensland and the Northern Territories when she began collecting and drawing the local species of grasses and native plants on these properties, learning the art of watercolour and applying it to botanical illustration. She spent a great deal of time observing Australia's different ecosystems from light aircraft and helicopters as part of her work.

She was able to draw on her experiences in the bush when she began illustrating books in 1987 and she has had a huge body of work published including five 'Key' guides to *Australian Wildflowers*; *Trees*; *Palms, Ferns and Allies*; *Australian Mammals*; and the *Australian Flora*. All these guides have recently been updated and were due to be released again in 2000. In 1995 she illustrated a children's book *The Australian Animal Atlas* and four *Environmental Sticker Books*. Her illustrations have been published in the *Flora of Australia*, gardening magazines, *Australian Geographic* and a number of scientific journals.

Currently Marion works at the Royal Botanic Gardens, Sydney, and has been responsible for producing illustrations for interpretive signs for Sydney, Mount Tomah and Mount Annan Gardens. When I visited her studio in the Herbarium of the Royal Botanic Gardens, Sydney, she showed me some exceptionally fine drawings that are being converted into sturdy signs, full of useful information – something I wish botanical gardens elsewhere would copy. She has illustrated posters and designed the floral motifs for the Sundial and Fountain in the Herb Garden. During the past seven years she has run workshops and courses in botanical illustration through the Community Education Unit in Sydney.

She has exhibited her work regularly since 1986 and I bought this *Eucalyptus caesia* from 'Botanica 2000', an exhibition held at the Royal Botanic Gardens, Sydney when I visited in February. This plant, which has large fruits, flowers and leaves and a weeping habit, is widely grown in cultivation under the name 'Silver Princess' and is recognised by some botanists as a distinct subspecies, *E. caesia* subsp. *magna*. It is occasionally found in the wild, growing on granite outcrops in the central wheatbelt near Pingelly and Kellerberrin and further inland in Western Australia.

Marion told me that she had 'observed this species both in a large pot near our garden shop in Sydney Gardens and growing at our Mount Annan Gardens. I had admired it at Mount Annan when visiting with a colleague. A year later at its next flowering season he brought several beautiful pieces back for me. I had not planned to paint it so I had to drop everything and do it immediately. I find this is often a good thing as I start fresh and spontaneously'.

EUCALYPTUS CAESIA SSP. MAGNA
Signed
Marion Westmacott 99
Acquied from
'Botanica 2000'
Australia 2000
Watercolour on paper
1030 × 620 mm

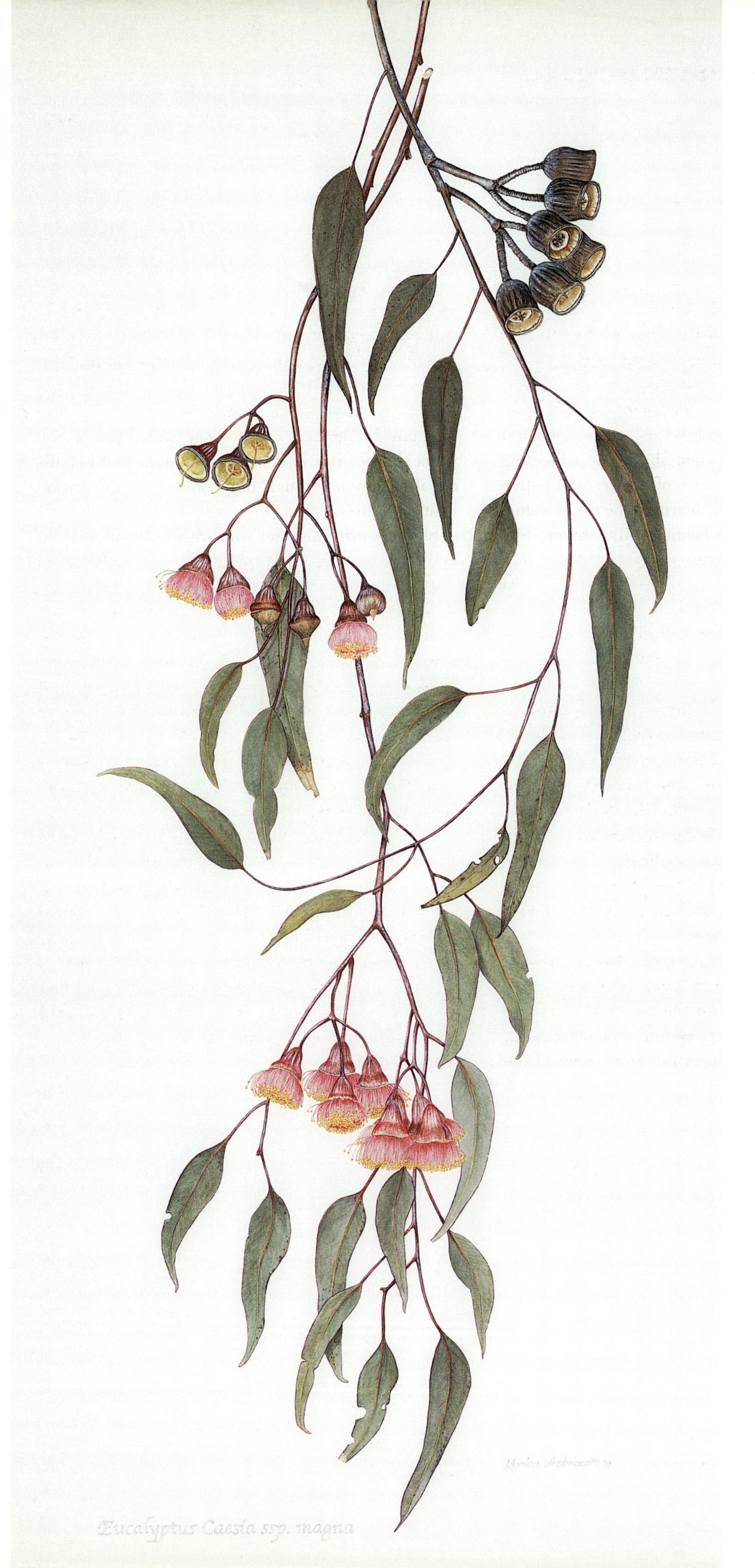
Marion Westmacott 99
Eucalyptus Caesia ssp. magna

John Wilkinson

BORN NORTHAMPTON, ENGLAND 1934

Having been apprenticed as a printer, John Wilkinson worked at a print works in Watford for over twenty years. At the age of forty he changed course and became a painter full-time, working in a variety of media including watercolour, oil, acrylic, egg tempera and pastel.

He illustrated a considerable number of books in the 1980s including *Trees* by Alan Mitchell. I first saw some of his superb plates for this book at the Hunt Institute and John later sent me a copy. I discovered that his work had been shown at the 5th International Exhibition of Botanical Art at the Hunt Institute in the United States in 1983 and I made contact with him through James White, their curator of art, who greatly admired his technical skill and artistry.

He has shown at a number of RHS shows, being awarded two gold medals. In the 1980s he produced many designs for plates and vases for the Franklin Mint and painted the 1987 Chelsea Flower Show plate. He was the founder vice-president of the Society of Botanical Artists in 1986, a group which shows annually in the Westminster Halls, London every April. He has shown in a number of English galleries and currently exhibits at the Bromley Galleries, Bromley, in Kent.

He has just produced the illustrations and text for *The Artist's Guide* (1998) and *The Easy Edible Mushroom Guide* (1999). Besides these he has illustrated books on butterflies and moths, two on trees, two other books on mushrooms and one on the English countryside. Most have been translated into several European languages.

John Wilkinson came to my house in the country with his wife, Elizabeth, whom he'd met when teaching. She is also an artist and they now run summer courses in the New Forest each summer in flower and natural history painting. He brought a number of paintings to show me of iris, roses and other cultivated plants, including *Ligularia clivorum* 'Desdemona'. I particularly liked the more unusual *Ligularia*, a dramatic plant painted against a Chinese backdrop. This is a splendid plant portrait, strong, confident and vibrant with colour, while still retaining subtle leaf-tones and texture. It has been widely exhibited since I added it to my collection.

He told me that some ligularias growing in the hot-coloured garden at Sissinghurst inspired the painting, and although he was unable to find the identical plant, he was able to buy and grow this one instead. Initially the painting had the usual white background, but he felt after a while that it was rather stark and austere because of the shapes of the strongly coloured stems and leaves and so could do with some further additions. He always researches the plants he is painting and found out that most ligularias came from China. He also knew from growing the plant that it liked a lot of water, so he felt that a view of the spectacular, watery and mountainous Guilin district would make a good background, although he has never been to China.

The background was added some time after the main picture was finished. The stems at the bottom were first washed out and extra lower leaves were added which provided a more solid base. The landscape was put in next, with the colours carefully kept to muted greys so as not to disturb the colour scheme. Finally the leaves were adjusted to increase the depth and sheen to their present lustrous texture. The small insects with a brilliant metallic sheen resting on the flower are some of the little beetles that are often associated with bright yellow flowers. Hover-flies are also attracted to the flowers. The moth on the leaf is the common Silver Y, which flies in the daytime. John has always been interested in moths, and many of them feature in his paintings. He feels all plants, real or painted, are more alive with their attendant insects.

LIGULARIA CLIVORUM 'DESDEMONA'
Signed John Wilkinson
On back: *Ligularia clivorum* 'Desdemona'
August 14–27, September 16–21, 1987
A22284
Acquired from the artist 1996
Watercolour on paper
570 × 422 mm

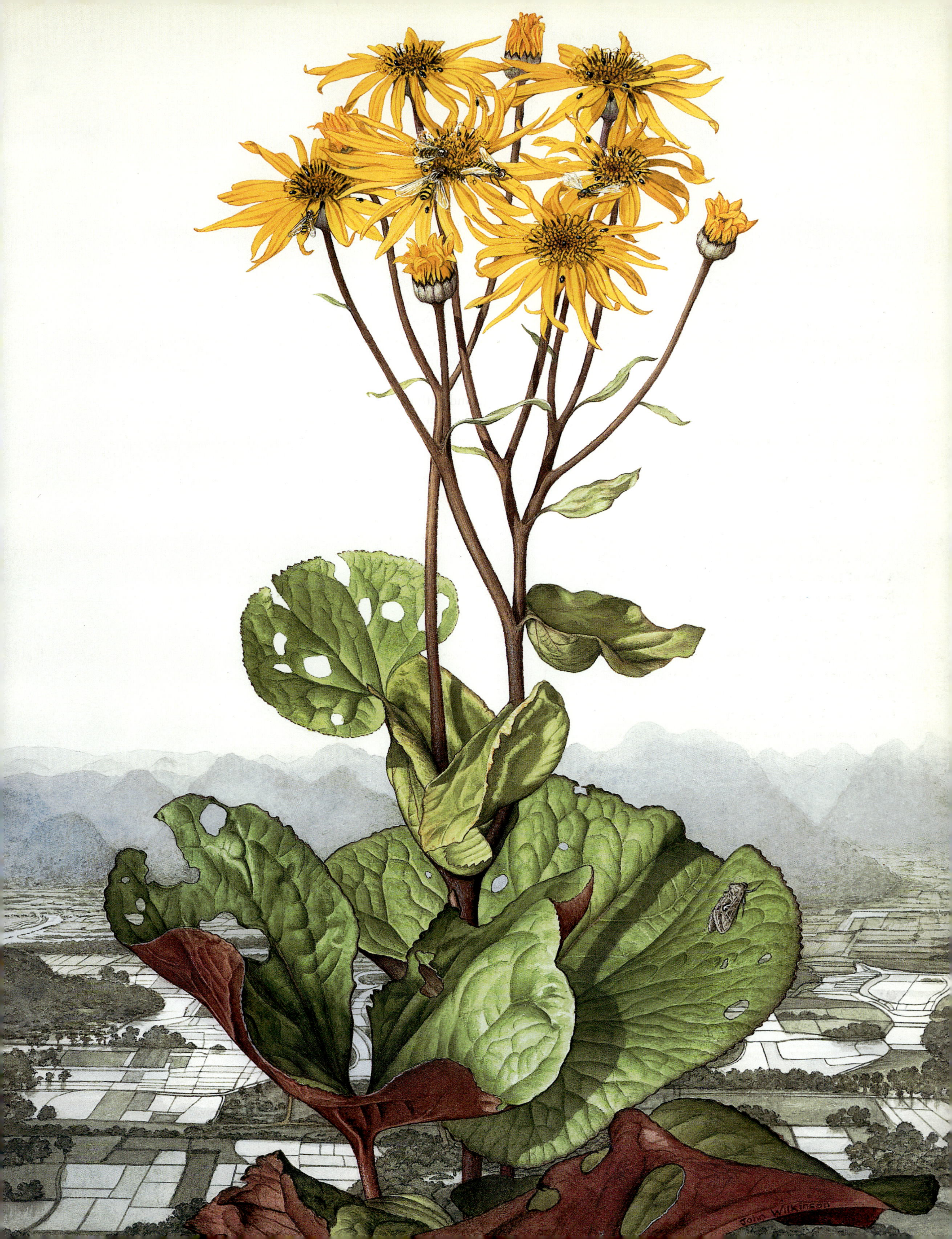
John Wilkinson

Carol Woodin

BORN SALAMANCA, NEW YORK, USA 1956

In recent years Carol Woodin has become one of the most outstanding of the botanical artists working in the United States. She has concentrated on orchids and started working on vellum, a surface where she achieves an astonishing translucency. She has painted a large number of works in the few years since I bought my first painting of hers, showy lady's slipper (*Cypripedium reginae*) in 1991, and I admire the quality and consistency of all she produces. She became a full-time botanical artist in 1990 and has had two one-person exhibitions at the Pennsylvania Horticultural Society, Philadelphia in 1996 and the Buffalo Museum of Science in 1995. She has been involved in many group shows and been awarded a gold medal at the RHS. She won the 1998 Award for Excellence in Botanical Art from the American Society of Botanical Artists, as well as the 'Best of Show' at the National Orchid Society from 1992 to 1996. Her work is held at the Hunt Institute, at Kew and the Niagara Parks Commission, Canada as well as in many private collections.

Currently she is vice-president of exhibits for the American Society of Botanical Artists where she is a very active member. She showed some luminous paintings in the Tryon & Swann International Exhibition in London in 1998 which I helped to curate. Recently she showed at Waterman Fine Arts Limited, London and I was tempted by this beautiful painting on vellum of the most extravagantly patterned orchid, *Paphiopedilum venustum* var. *measuresianum*. She has somehow managed to compose the business of the blotched leaves and the gold and emerald striped flowers into an harmonious and exotic subject. She shows roots, the bud and both full frontal and rear views of the flower. It is like a rather dangerous jewel, suspended in space (see page 22 of the Introduction for the plate of Carol Woodin's *P. venustum*).

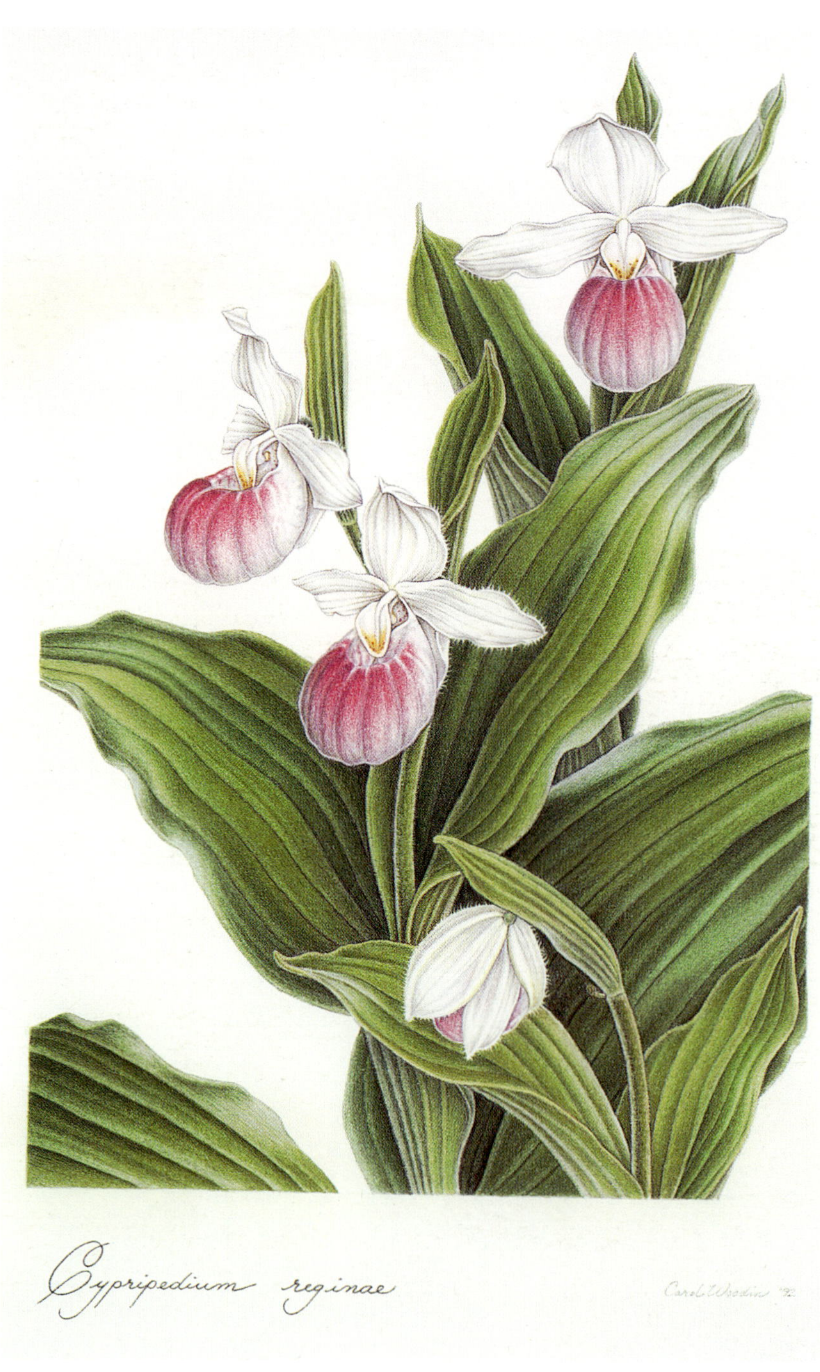

SHOWY LADY'S SLIPPER:
CYPRIPEDIUM REGINAE
Signed Carol Woodin '92
Cypripedium reginae
Acquired from the artist 1994
Watercolour on paper
550 × 420 mm

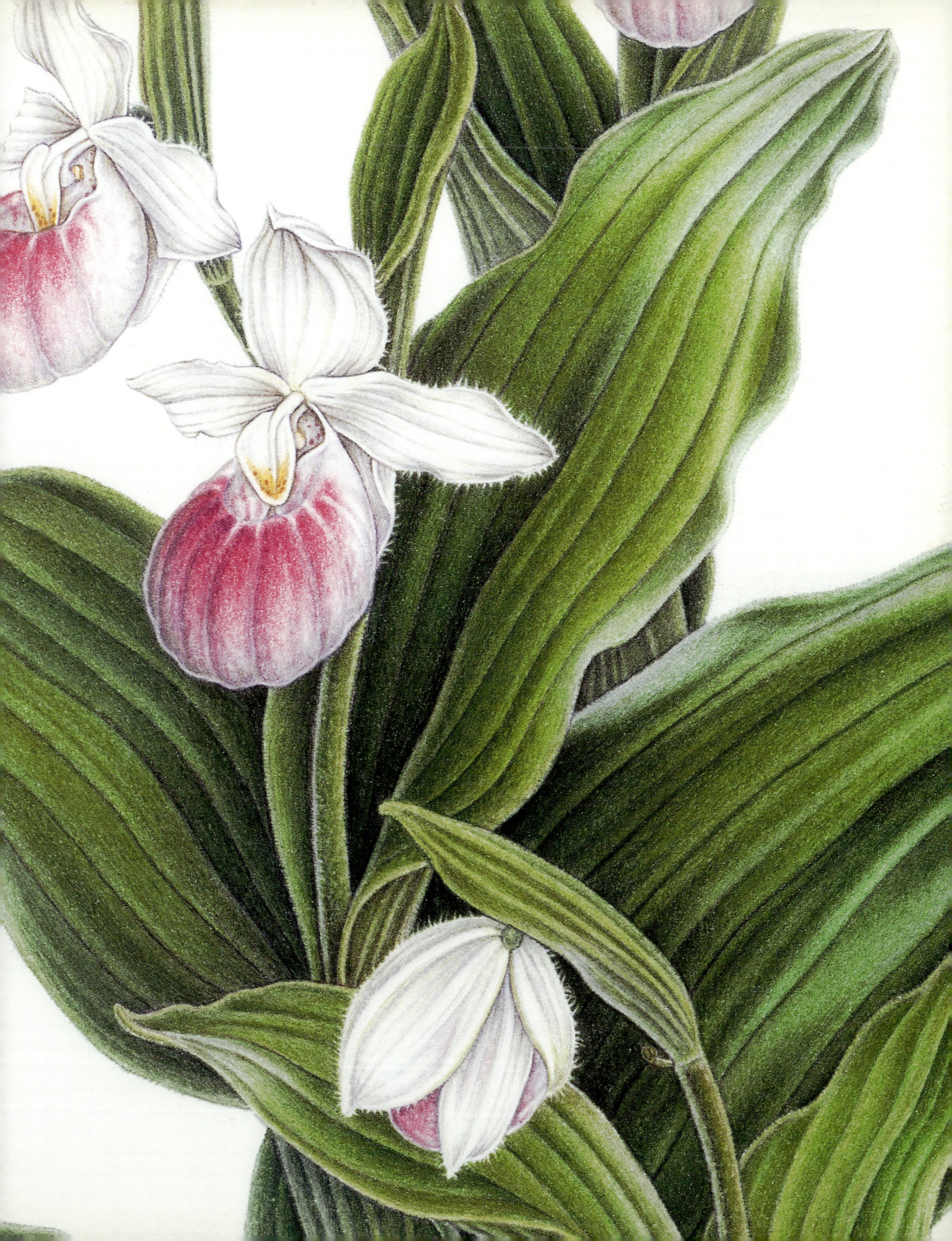

I saw a painting of *Disas* which she painted a few years back and I asked her to do the same subject for me. *Disa uniflora* is a dramatic orchid which lives under waterfalls on the Cape in South Africa. Every year when I visit I have tried to catch a distant glimpse of its vivid scarlet flowers high up on the Cape escarpments through binoculars. Despite its conservation status, it is sometimes collected to the danger of life and limb and every year there are some resultant accidents. Carol Woodin got her specimen of *Disa uniflora* from the well-known orchid breeder, Warren Stoutamire of Ohio.

Carol Woodin feels that botanical painting is somewhat anachronistic. She wrote to me at length describing how she felt:

'It is a painstakingly slow process requiring absolute attention to minute details. It serves as a window into a no longer common way of doing things, in the same way orchids allow a glimpse into a distant past of an increasingly transformed natural world. My first vista into this world occurred on a hillside in western New York State, when I stumbled upon a group of *Cypripedium acaule*. Their exotic and intriguing form in a woodland setting was breathtaking. This serendipitous discovery led to a quest to find others; first native orchids, then orchids of far-flung locales. Orchids are now my only subject, and this is not necessarily a limitation, considering their diversity of form and the tens of thousands of species thus far discovered.'

'While we contemplate the problems of the developing world with rapid growth and habitat loss, we sometimes lose sight of our precious treasures in this country and the pressures they also face. These places are pockets of a primeval past that remarkably still exist. There is nothing more gratifying than spending a warm spring day trying to capture a small measure of this wealth of natural expression in paint. It is an attempt to bridge the traditional art form of botanical painting with the sensibilities of our modern world, and in the process perhaps increase the awareness of all of us of the value of each singular aspect of the natural world, with orchids as catalyst.'

DISA UNIFLORA
Signed C. Woodin
Disa uniflora Berg
(undated)
Commissioned from the artist 2000
Watercolour on vellum
710 × 470 mm

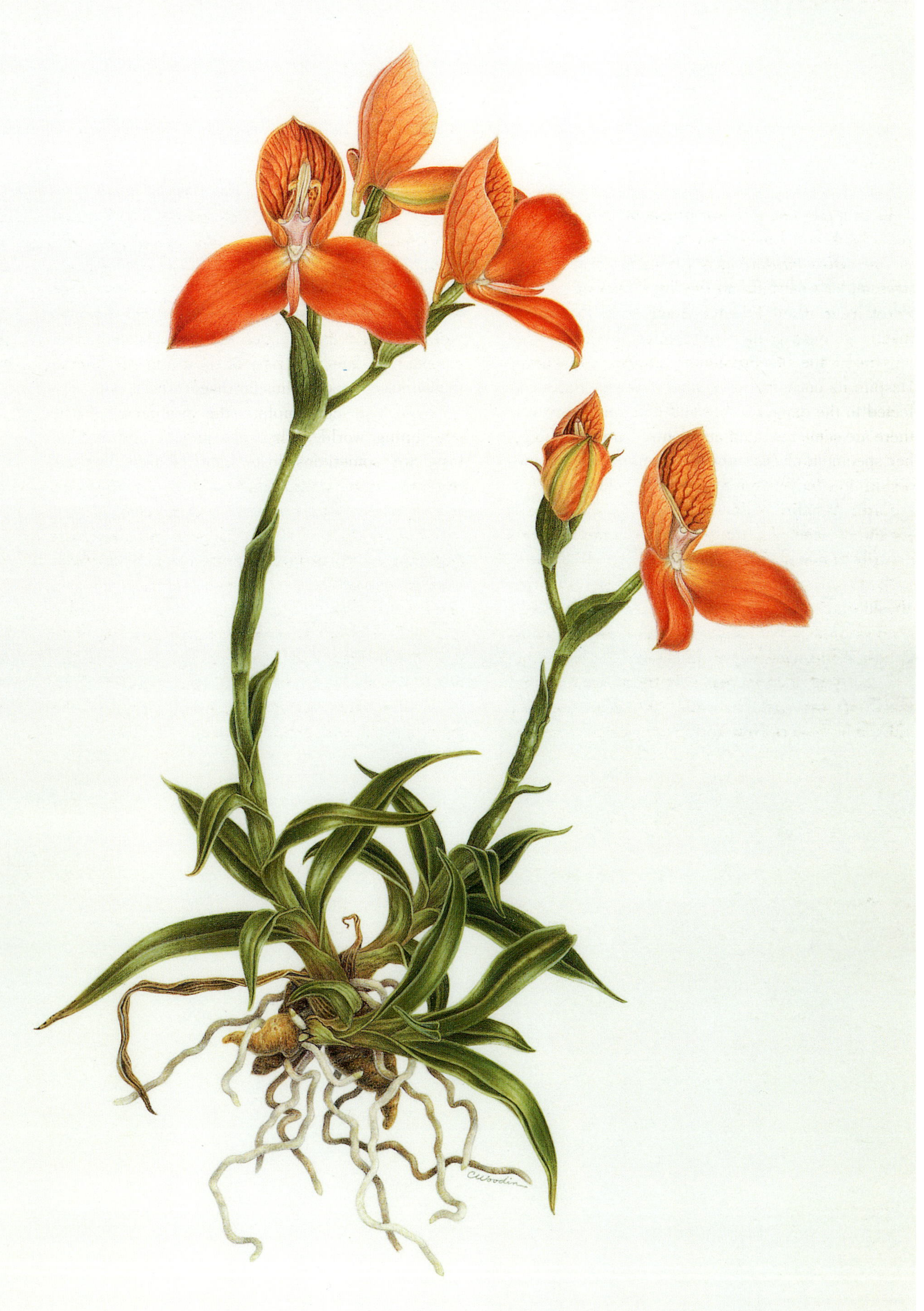

Disa uniflora Berg.

M. Fatima Zagonel

Born Brazil, 1954

Fatima Zagonel lives in Curitiba, Parana in south Brazil. She graduated from the Pontificia Universidale Catolica do Parana in 1976 and in 1993 took a postgraduate degree in publicity and advertisement. She also attended courses in art design and watercolour in the late 1970s. While working as a graphic designer for some twenty years, she became interested in botanical illustration and in 1998 she took a course at Curitiba with Diana Carneiro who had been a Margaret Mee scholar at Kew. In the same year she exhibited some work in a presentation made by the Curitiba Botanical Gardens in Mexico and at another exhibition at her local botanical garden.

In May 1999 Fatima Zagonel was awarded a Margaret Mee Followship to study with Christabel King at the Royal Botanic Gardens, Kew. At the end of her stay she had a small exhibition at Kew of the work she had completed under Christabel's tuition. I always enjoy going along to these shows and seeing how the students' work has developed under Christabel's guidance. I thought Zagonel had produced a very lively, rather luscious study of hawthorn berries (*Crataegus succulenta* var. *macrantha*) that was most attractive. I also purchased a subtle painting of the succulent *Echeveria cante*. Both plants had been cultivated at Kew. As often happens with Christabel's influence, Zagonel's watercolours of leaves were very authentic.

After her intense studies at Kew she has now returned to Brazil where she will be helping other aspiring botanical artists.

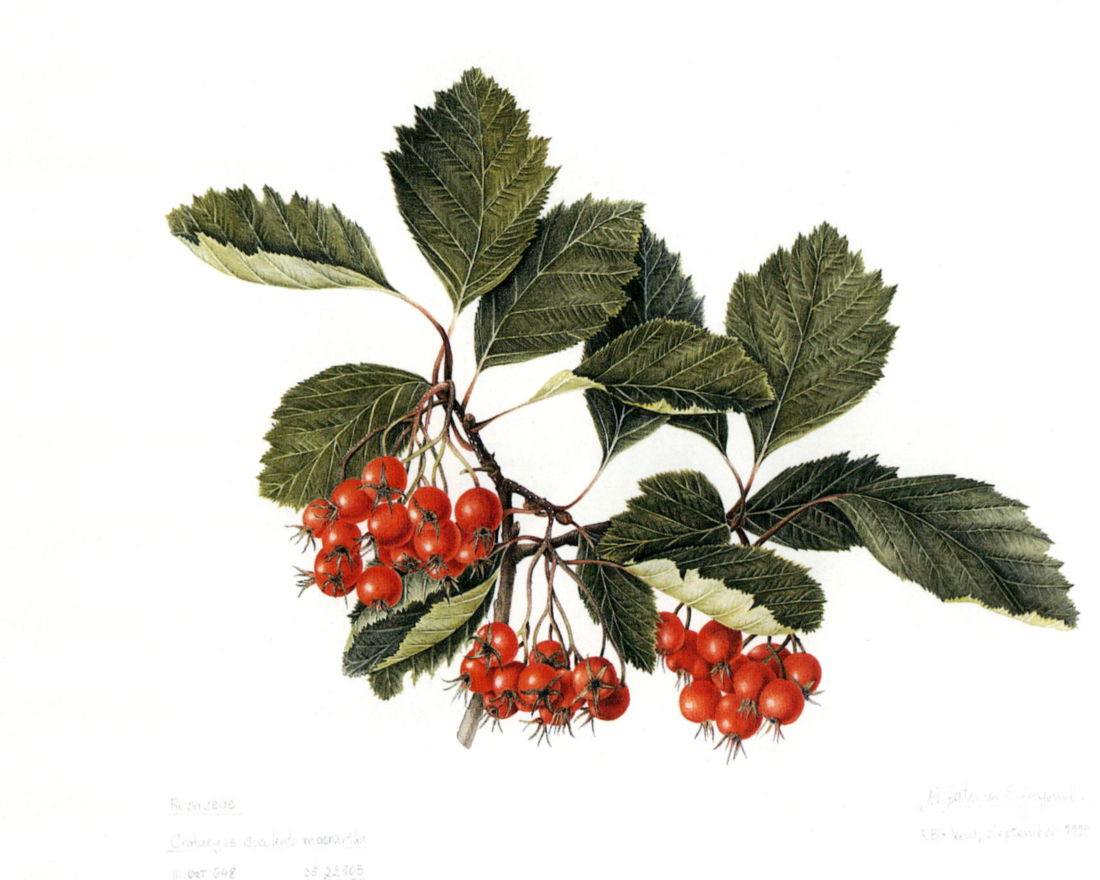

CRATAEGUS SUCCULENTA VAR. *MACRANTHA*
(Left) Signed M. Fatima S. Zagonel, RBG Kew, September 1999
Rosaceae Crataegus succulenta macrantha
M. ORT 648 35.22103
Acquired from Kew Gardens Herbarium 1999
Watercolour on paper
290 × 290 mm

(*CRASSULACEAE*) *ECHEVERIA CANTE*
(Right) Signed M. Fatima S. Zagonel, RBG Kew, October 1999. *Crassulaceae Echeveria cante*
1999–2161 SHDO
Acquired from Kew Gardens Herbarium 1999
Watercolour on paper
705 × 500 mm

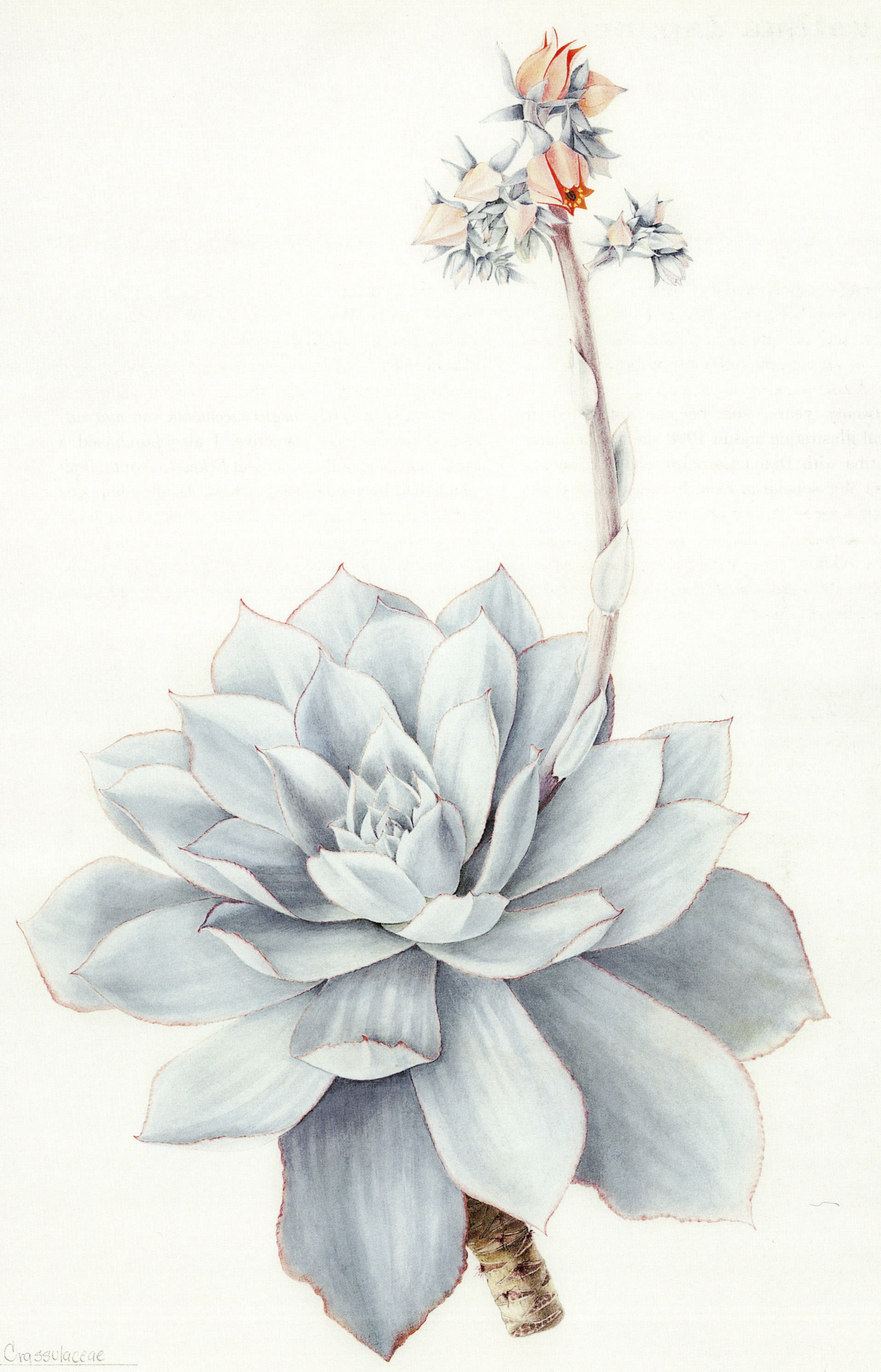

Crassulaceae
Echeveria cante
1999-2161 SHDO
M. Fatima S. Zagonel.
RBG Kew, October 1999.

Harry Zelenko

Born USA 1928

Orchids seem to inspire extremely passionate reactions in horticulturists – sometimes love, sometimes loathing. They are the most varied and complicated plants, with their devotees all over the world. Harry Zelenko is one of their most obsessive admirers, utterly in thrall to *Oncidium* orchids.

He grows his plants high up above his New York house in a two large rooftop greenhouses, one a 'cool' house, the other kept around 21°C. He has been painting oncidiums for thirteen years, working with his wife Betsy Dillard Zelenko and Johanna Warsaw to produce a massive tome edited by the taxonomist Mark Chase. *The Pictorial Encyclopaedia of Oncidium* was published in 1998 and at that time he had an exhibition in New York of some of his orchid watercolours which he had used in the book. This is where I saw his paintings, in the Shepherd Gallery. He produces life-size watercolours of entire orchid plants as well as 'for-the-record' individual flowers showing the wide variation in colour patterns. Some have brown 'tiger' stripes, others are speckled and yet others are subtle shades of green and yellow. He uses Winsor & Newton gouache on smooth drawing paper, applied with very fine sable brushes, exhibiting superb control of his medium.

I met him at his Manhattan brownstone and climbed up several flights of stairs, which gradually got smaller and steeper until we reached his greenhouses on the roof. He grows forty different oncidiums as well as other kinds of orchids in his humid, moisture-laden environments. Some of the flowers were so tiny he had to point them out to me, while others were flamboyant and showy. He has his studio at the top of the house too, so he can paint an orchid when it is in flower without removing it from its humid atmosphere for too long. The conditions attempt to replicate the plants' normal habitats in tropical zones, sometimes as high as 3350 metres in the Ecuadorian rainforest.

He is a graphic designer who founded his own office in 1953. Before that he had been briefly at New York University and then enlisted in the Navy during World War II. He designed the *Encyclopaedia* himself, and very attractively too. It took him thirteen years to gather together the material and draw together all the 800 individual paintings. He has just relocated to Ecuador where he will have wonderful access to his favourite plants in the wild.

FOUR *ONCIDIUM* FLOWERS
Signed Harry Zelenko
Acquired from the Shepherd Gallery, New York 1998
Watercolour on paper
110 × 135 mm,
70 × 75 mm,
70 × 75 mm &
120 × 135 mm

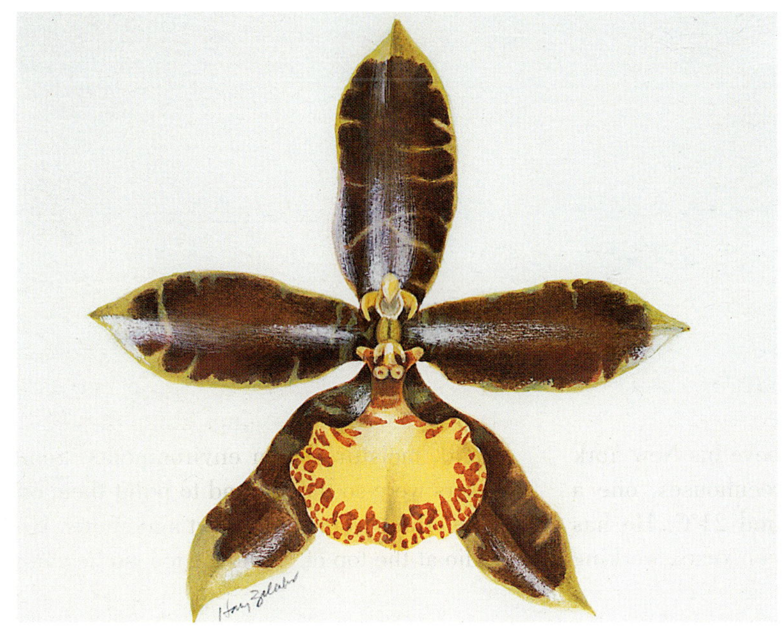

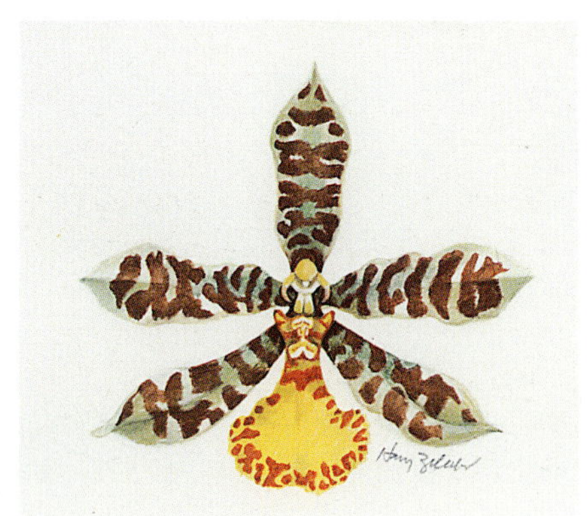

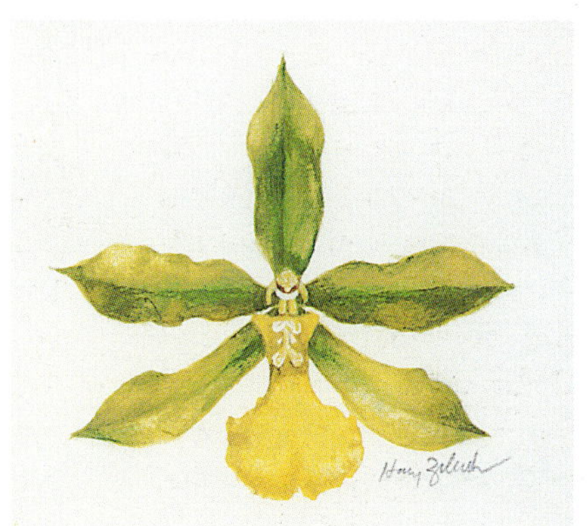

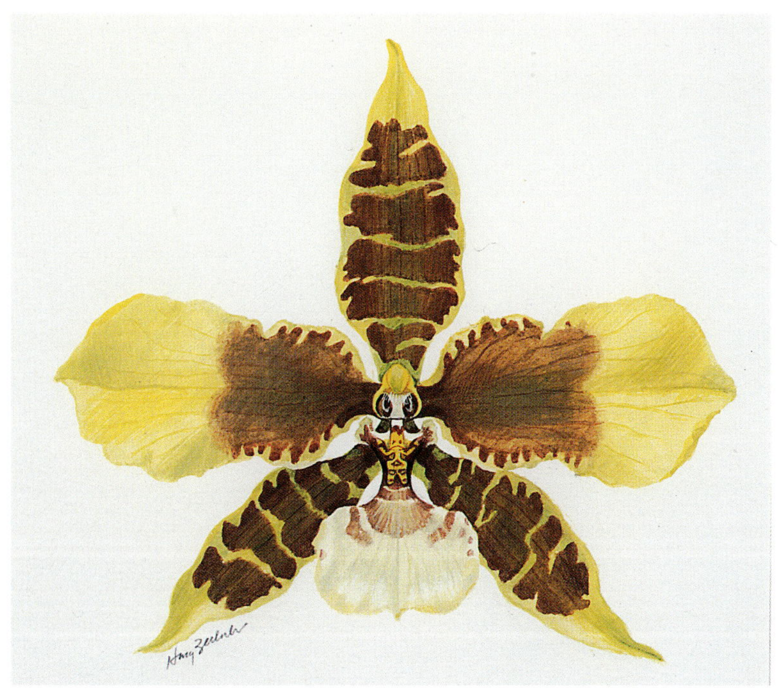

Appendix

It is not possible to illustrate the entire collection in the main body of the book.

Francesca Anderson
See main entry for biographical details

1 SUNFLOWERS SERIES NO. 3
Unsigned & undated. Acquired from the artist 1996. Pen & ink 580 × 730 mm.

2 SUNFLOWERS SERIES NO. 1
Signed August 1993. Acquired from the artist 1996. Pen & ink 730 × 580 mm.

3 SUNFLOWERS SERIES NO. 4
Unsigned & undated. Acquired from the artist 1996. Pen & ink 690 × 580 mm.

4 SUNFLOWERS SERIES NO. 6
Signed Francesca Anderson 1988. Acquired from the artist 1996. Pen & ink 580 × 730 mm.

Isobel Bartholomew
Born Birmingham, England 1943
Since 1989 Isobel Bartholomew has shown regularly at the RHS, where I first saw her work. Early in her career she was involved in teaching food studies at Birmingham College of Food and in St Lucia, where she was lecturer in charge. In 1991 she started teaching botanical illustration courses lasting twenty weeks at Barnfield College, Luton, at the beginners and intermediate level in Adult Education and she now does some full-day seminars. She exhibited at the Daffodil Society during their centennial celebrations and has had an illustration of *Catalpa* published in the *New RHS Dictionary of Gardening*. I acquired a *Dianthus* from the RHS and shortly afterwards a study of spring flowers for one of my grandchildren. I believe children notice the pictures in their bedrooms and need an alternative to dinosaurs.

5 *NARCISSUS ROMIEUXII* WITH *CYCLAMEN COUM*
Signed Isobel Bartholomew (undated)
Acquired from the artist 1999 for Saskia Sherwood's first birthday. Watercolour on paper 265 × 225 mm.

6 *DIANTHUS* 'ISOBEL BARTHOLOMEW'
Signed Isobel Bartholomew (undated)
Acquired from the RHS Show 1999. Watercolour on paper 375 × 255 mm.

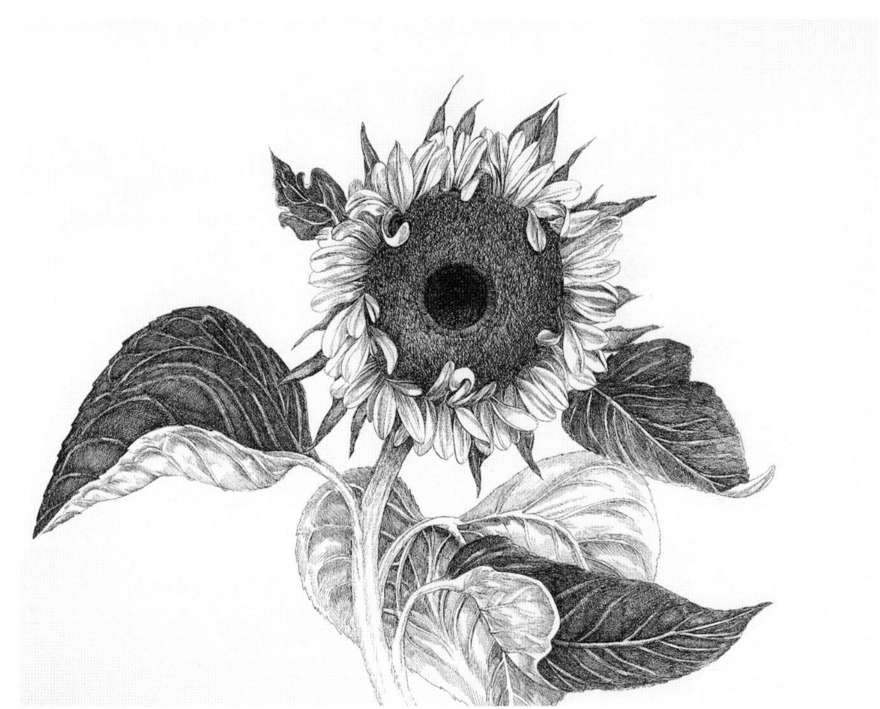

1

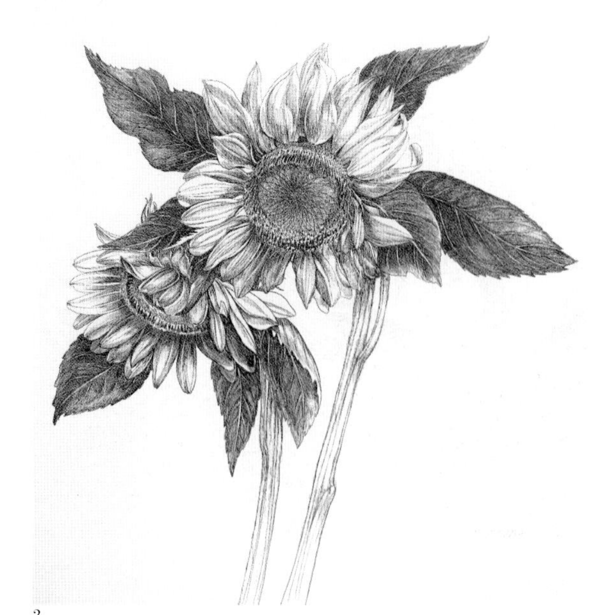

2

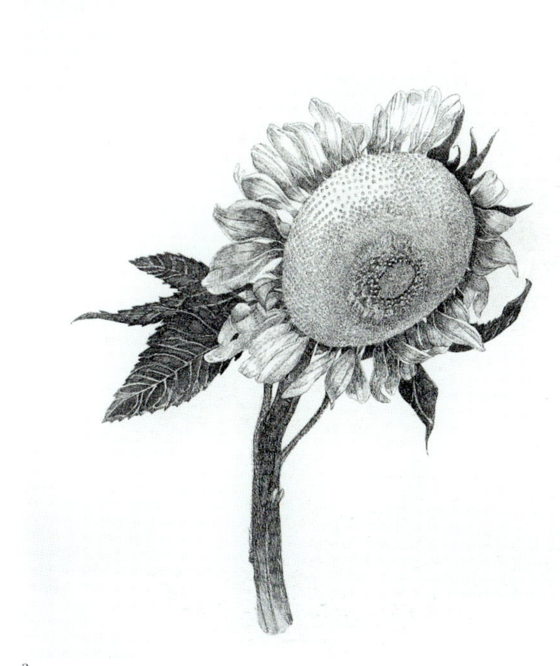
3

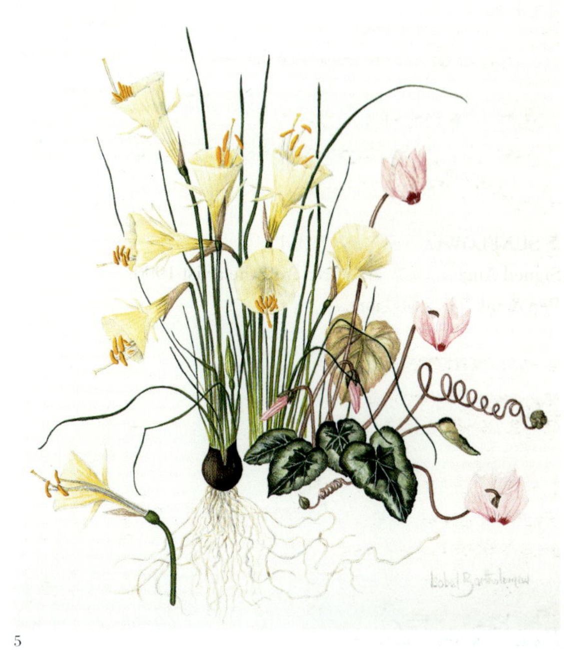

5

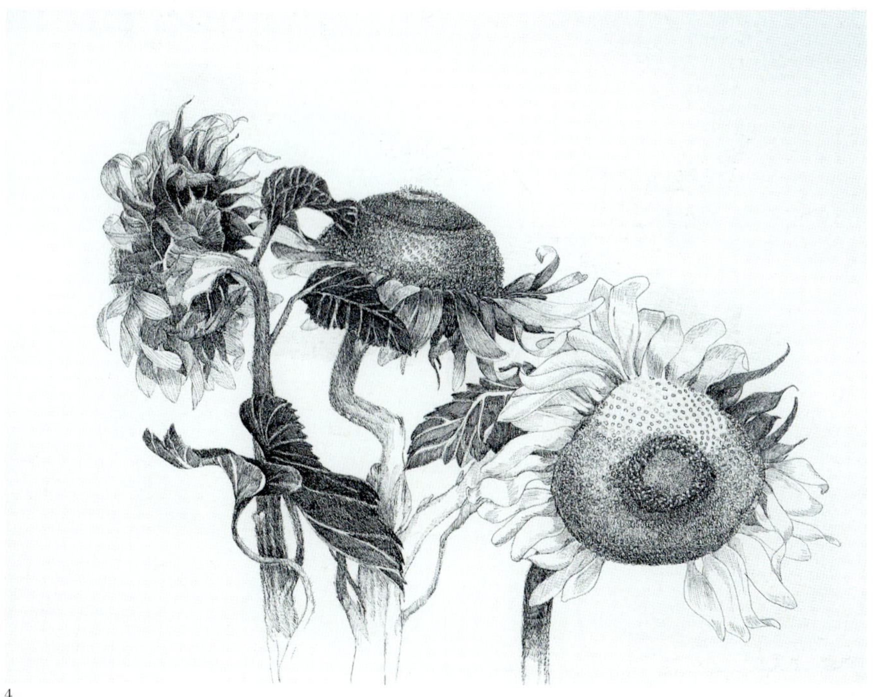
4

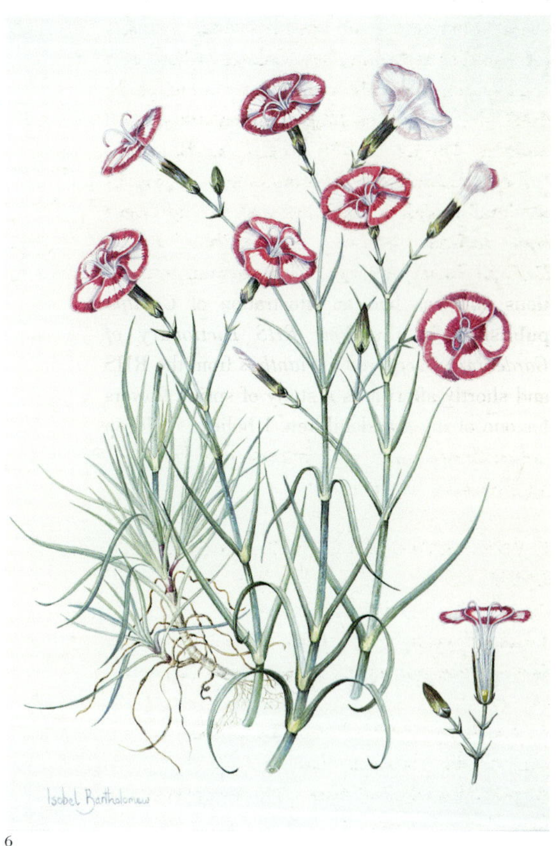

6

Roy Cooney
Born London, England 1935
Roy Cooney lives in Taunton, Devon. He went to Somerset College of Art and spent from 1951 to 1992 in the Hydrographic Office including six years as an engraving apprentice. He also studied copperplate printing under his father who was a master printer. He became a qualified copperplate engraver and cartographer, working in the training and exhibition department of the Hydrographic Office. I first saw his work when I was judging at an RHS show. He exhibited a group of small engravings and I was attracted by the almost medieval quality of this *Saintpaulia*, with its neat habit, formal layout and densely etched leaves. He was awarded a gold medal for a similar exhibition in the year 2000.

7 *SAINTPAULIA*
Signed *Saintpaulia* RJLC Sc A/P I/V Roy Cooney 96. Acquired from the RHS Show 1996. Hand-engraved, hand-printed impression 135 × 76 mm.

Brigitte E. M. Daniel
Born Beaconsfield, England 1959
I first saw Brigitte Daniel's 'Texas Longhorn' fuchsia at the Society of Botanical Artists' exhibition in 1998. The manner in which the paintings at this show are hung can be crowded but I felt this stood out. It is one of the best fuchsia drawings I have seen, capturing that wonderful ballerina pirouette of the suspended flower. Her painting career has been bedevilled by illness. She had to leave University College London, where she was studying botany, because of health problems. However, she has managed to show at the Society of Botanical Artists' exhibitions 1995–98 where she won a Certificate of Botanical Merit in 1997 and she was awarded an RHS medal in 1997 for orchids, a gold medal in 1998 for fuchsias and a silver gilt medal for dianthus in 2000.

8 *FUCHSIA* 'TEXAS LONGHORN'
Signed BEMD (undated). Acquired from the Society of Botanical Artists' Westminster Show 1998. Watercolour on paper 330 × 240 mm

Pierino Delvo
Born Magenta, Italy 1952
Pierino Delvo lives near Milan and has worked as a researcher in holography for twenty years there. He has had no formal training in painting but had been good at drawing from his childhood. He painted a few watercolours in the 1980s but only considered making a more serious effort recently, when encouraged by a friend who gave him a set of watercolour paints. He saw my book and sent me some slides of his work which I thought looked promising, so I bought this small painting of squash blossoms. A year later, in 1998, he was awarded a gold medal at the RHS's spring show. It was a remarkable *tour de force* for someone who had really only been painting for such a short time. Since then he has had an exhibition 'Native Herbs of the Plains of Northern Italy' at the Museo di Scienze Naturali in Brescia, Italy.

9 TWO SQUASH BLOSSOMS
Signed P. Delvo '96. Acquired from the artist 1997. Watercolour on paper 230 × 170 mm.

Rodrigo Demonte
Born Niteroi, Rio de Janeiro, Brazil 1961
Rodrigo Demonte is four years younger than his brother, André, and has followed a very similar path. He is trained as an agronomist specialising in soils and natural resources. He has shown in many exhibitions alongside his brother and his father. He advocates a bold style, painting the flamboyant plants of Brazil in a forceful, colourful way, quite often in oils. All the members of the Demonte family are passionately interested in conserving the natural wonders of Brazil and I generally meet Etienne, André and Rodrigo as a trio, with André doing most of the talking and translating. Most recently we all met in Rio just before the millennium celebrations.

10 *HELICONIA ROSTRATA*
Signed Rodrigo Demonte 98©. Acquired from the artist 2000. Watercolour on paper 728 × 510 mm.

Elizabeth Dowle
See main entry for biographical details

11 PIKES PINK
Signed (on the back) Elizabeth Dowle 1995. Acquired from the artist 1996. Watercolour on paper 222 × 182 mm

12 IVY LEAVES
Signed (on the back) Elizabeth Dowle 1996. Acquired from the artist 1996. Watercolour on paper 300 × 335 mm

13 PRICKLY PEARS
Signed Elizabeth Dowle 1997 (on the back). Acquired from the artist 1997. Watercolour on paper 265 × 430 mm

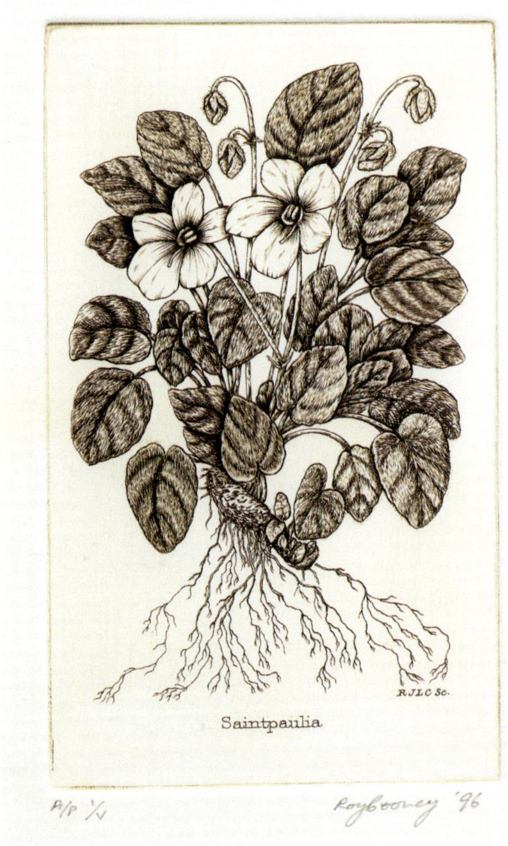

7

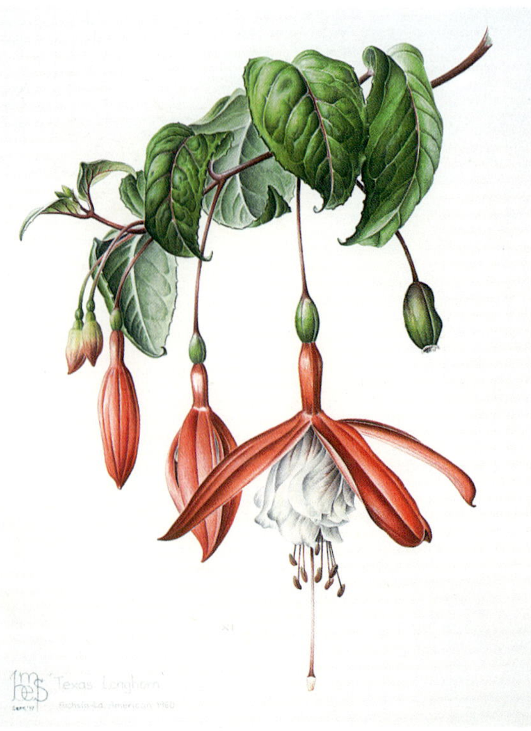

8

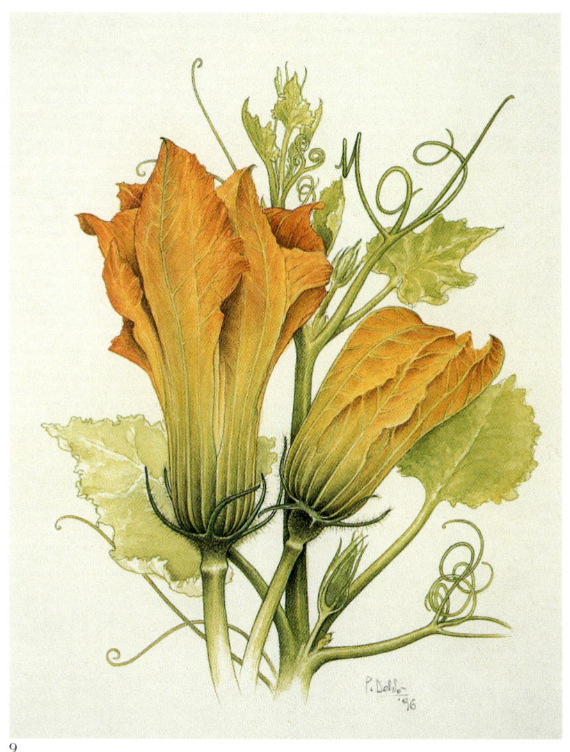

9

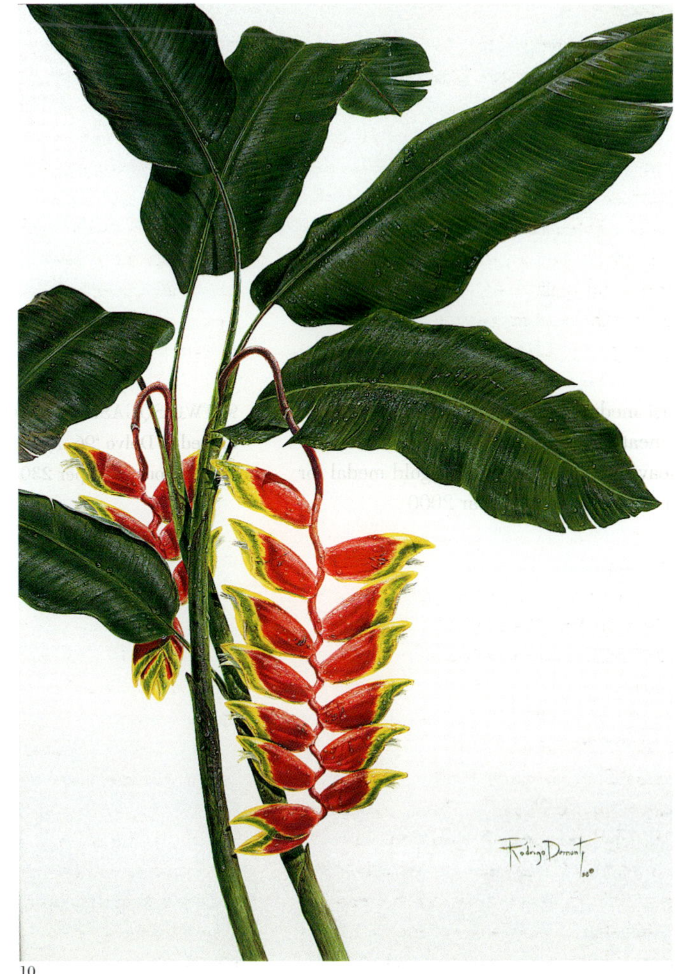

10

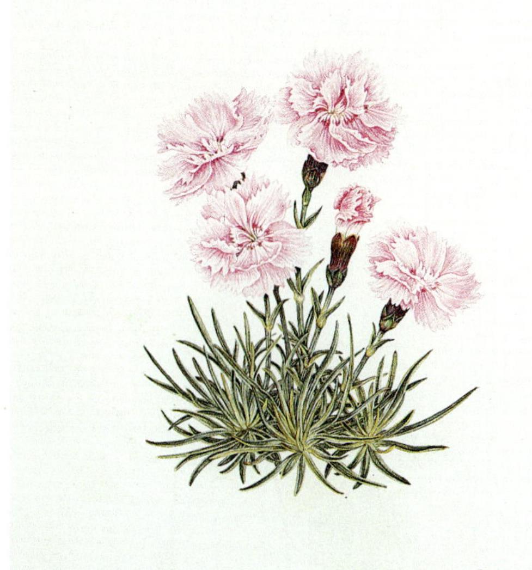

11

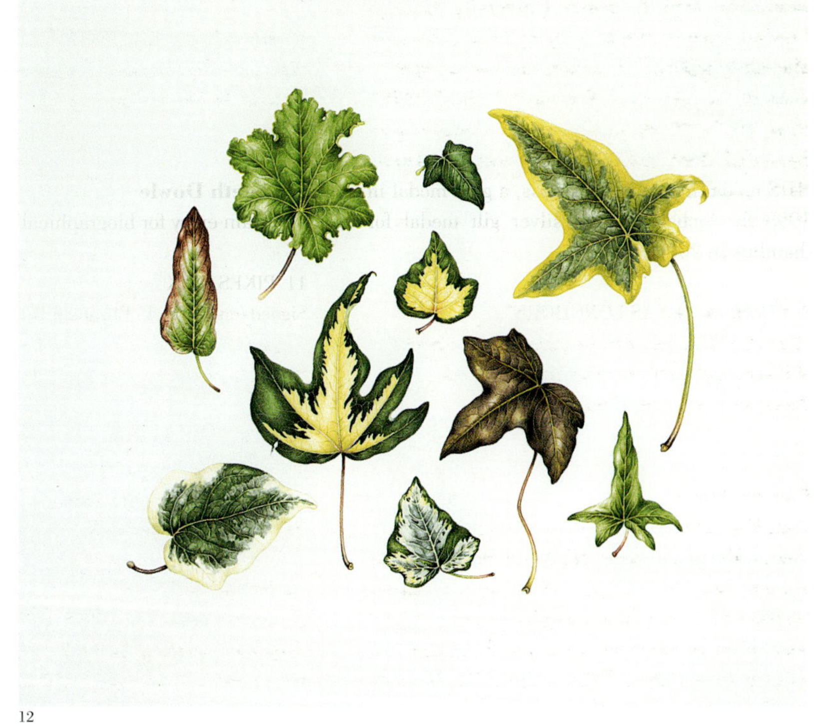

12

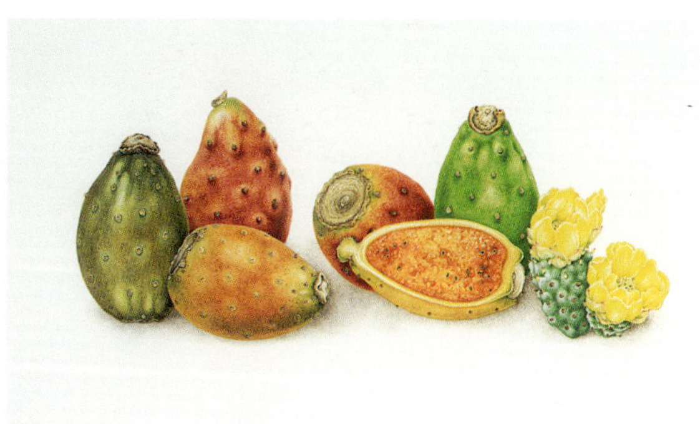

13

Linda Francis
See main entry for biographical details

14 *TILLANDSIA CAPUT-MEDUSAE*
Signed Linda Francis 1999. Acquired from the RHS Show 1999. Watercolour on paper 400 × 300 mm

15 *CRASSULA ARBORESCENS* X *CRASSULA OVATA*
Signed Linda Francis 1999. Acquired from the RHS Show 1999. Watercolour on paper 245 × 210 mm

Lawrence Greenwood
Born Todmorden, England, 1915–98
Lawrence Greenwood was an unusual botanical painter who was able to produce a painting from a photograph provided that the latter was of high quality. He was able to paint plants which are not in cultivation by using transparencies taken by botanists on their plant-hunting travels around the world. This study of *Trillium decumbens* shows the plants *in situ*. He exhibited both the traditional 'botanical illustration' of a plant set against a white background as well as paintings of unusual plants photographed like the *Trillium*, showing at various Alpine Garden Society shows.

16 *TRILLIUM DECUMBENS*
Signed LG. Acquired from the artist 1992. Watercolour on paper 170 × 250 mm.

Regine Hagerdorn
See main entry for biographical details

17 PETIT ARBORETUM
1. *Fagus sylvatica* – Fagacées
2. *Fraxinus exelsior* – Fraxinées
3. *Tilia cordata* – Tiliacées
4. *Carpinus betulus* – Carpinacées
Signed R.H. 5.1.2000
Acquired from the RHS Show 2000. Watercolour on paper 500 × 357 mm.

Yvonne Glenister Hammond
See main entry for biographical details

18 BULLACE: *PRUNUS DOMESTICA* SSP. *INSITITIA*
Signed YGH (undated). Acquired from the artist 1999. Watercolour on paper 375 × 280 mm.

Wayne D. Hand
Born Blackfoot, Idaho, USA 1960
As soon as I entered Wayne Hand's charming house in San Francisco and looked at the paintings on his walls I realised he was a versatile and accomplished artist, seemingly equally happy painting in oils or watercolour. He has attended two of the botanical painting classes that I organised in Orient-Express Hotels, which is where we first met. At one of them he gave me this delightful orchid study.

He has had no formal art training but started teaching calligraphy in the Hebrew University, Jerusalem in 1982 and then became a drawing instructor at the Maryland School of Art in 1993. He began showing botanical art works in the 1990s and has had three solo exhibitions recently in San Francisco. He is a very keen horticulturist and has just acquired a country house nearby with an exceptionally beautiful garden overlooking the sea.

He has been a most supportive member of the Board of Directors of the American Society of Botanical Artists since 1998, leading a group to England which came to Hinton Manor, my country house, to see my collection. Luckily it was a lovely day and the group could enjoy the garden as well as the paintings in the house.

19 *MILTONIA* X *BRASSIA*
Signed Wayne D. Hand (undated).
Gift from the artist 1997. Watercolour on paper 310 × 410 mm

Mariko Imai
See main entry for biographical details

20 *NEPENTHES VENTRICOSA*
Signed Imai (days worked on painting & date in Japanese). Acquired from the artist 1999.
Watercolour on paper 540 × 390 mm

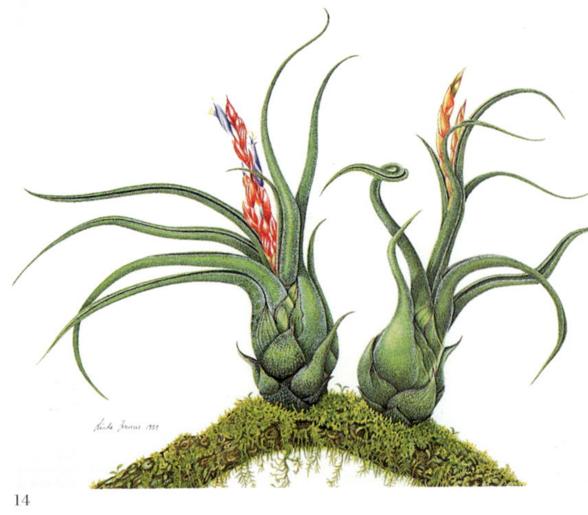
14

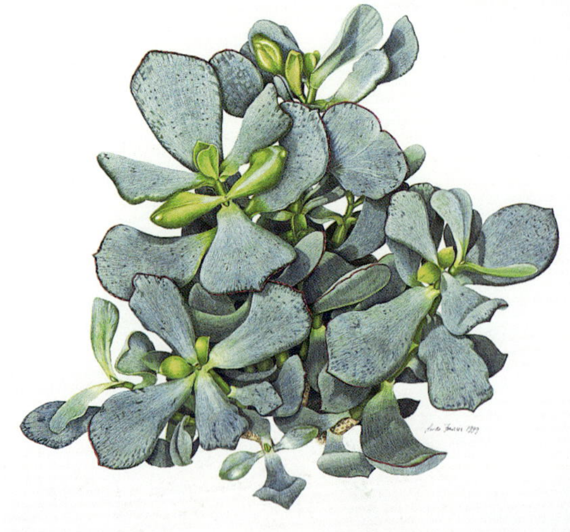
15

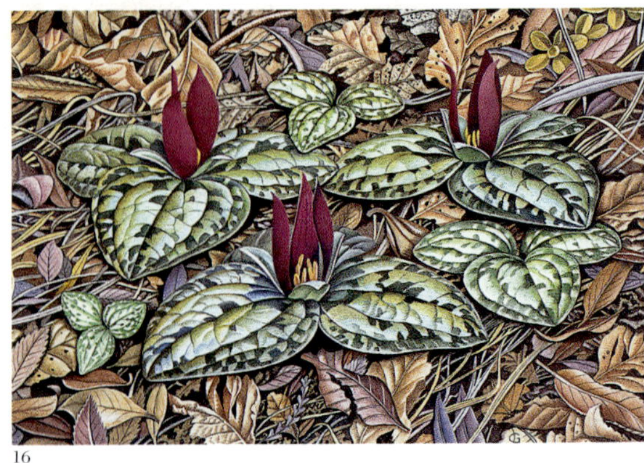
16

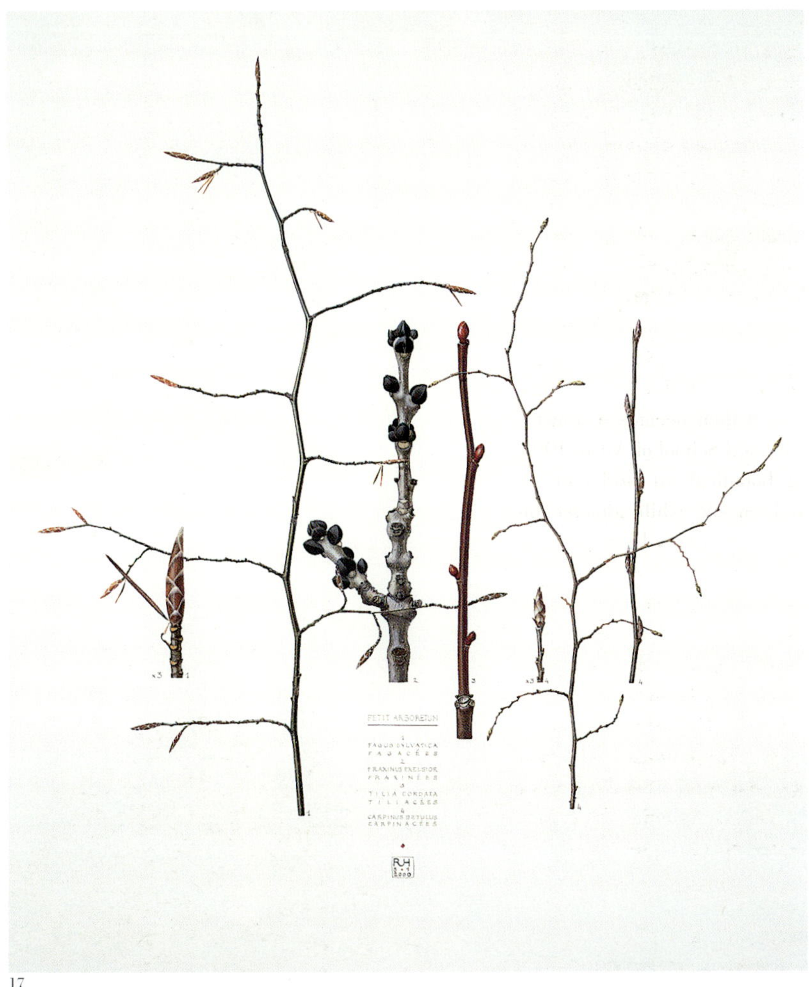

17

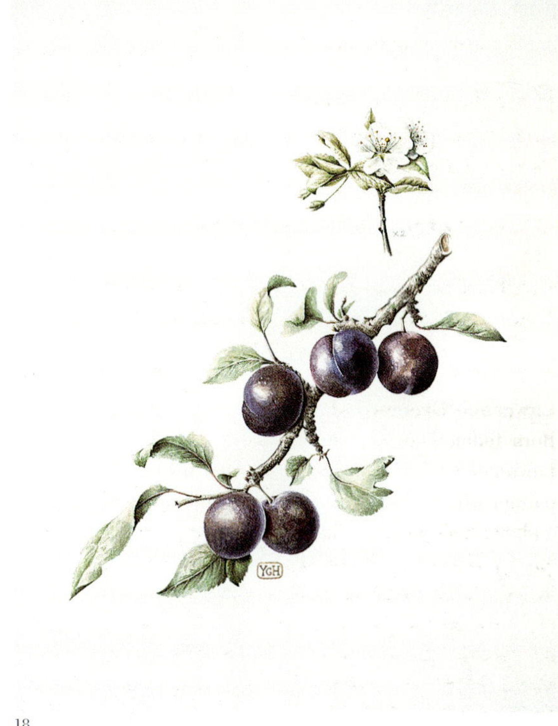

18

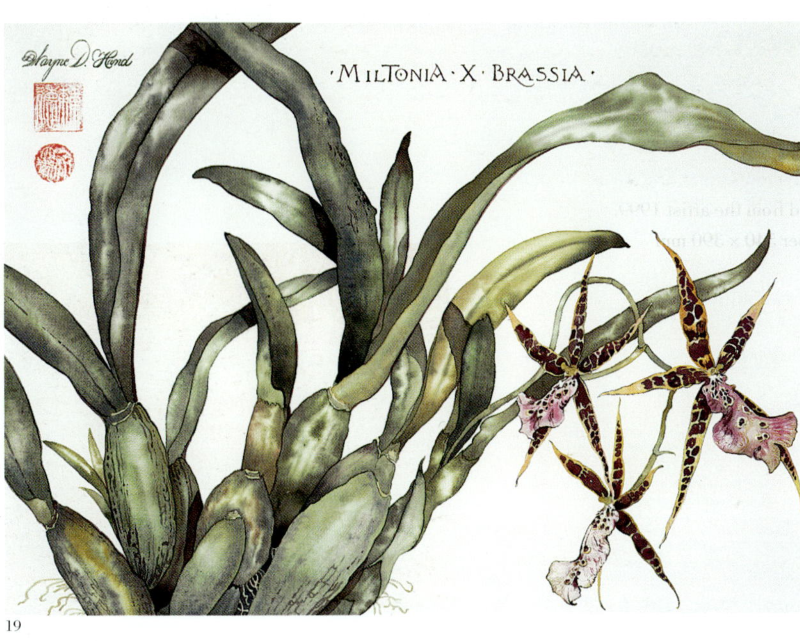

19

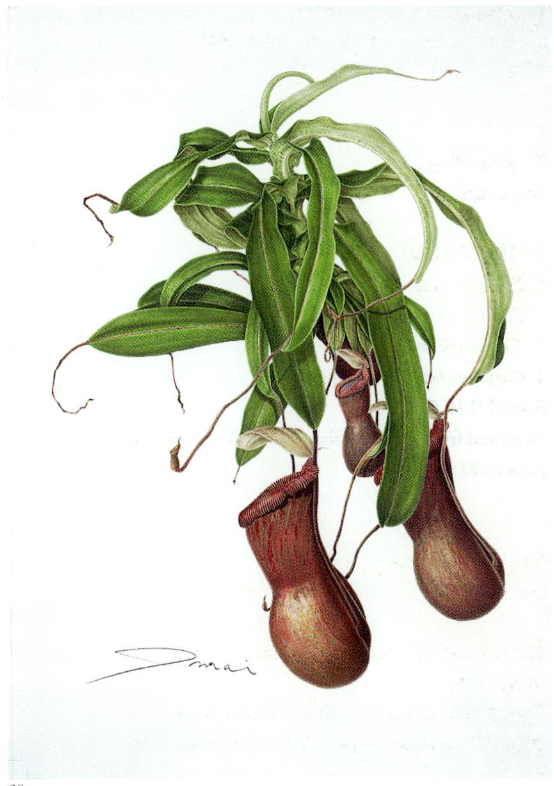

20

Rebecca John
See main entry for biographical details

21 ANCIENT GORSE, BERWYN MOUNTAINS.
Signed RJ August 98. Acquired from Lefevre Gallery, London 1999. Watercolour over pencil on paper 380 × 270 mm.

Paul Jones
See main entry for biographical details

22 PINEAPPLE
Signed Paul Jones (undated). Gift from the artist 1997. Acrylic on paper 240 × 160 mm.

23 *HELICONIA*
Signed Paul Jones – *Heliconia*, Bougainville, 1977. Acquired from the artist for Simon Sherwood 1997 Acrylic on paper 740 × 510 mm.

Andrew Kamiti
Born Nairobi, Kenya 1970
This young Kenyan artist made an impressive debut at Kirstenbosch Botanical Gardens in 1999 with an exhibition of paintings of butterflies associated with plants. Merle Huntley, the curator, felt that his plant paintings were of such a standard that he should be invited to be part of the Inaugural Botanical Exhibition in Kirstenbosch a year later, so she organised his entry. Kamiti gained a bronze medal in some distinguished company.

24 CAPE CHESTNUT: *CALODENDRUM CAPENSE*
Signed Andrew Kamiti © 99. Acquired from Kirstenbosch Exhibition of Botanical Art 2000. Watercolour on paper 300 × 250 mm.

Yasuko Kodaka
Born Tochigi, Japan 1950
Yasuko Kodaka worked as a scientist in the Department of Physiology, Faculty of Medicine in Tokai University, Kanawaga after she had been to graduate school at Ochanomizu University. Later she worked in the biology department of Tokyo University and then became a freelance artist in 1987. She has participated in a number of group shows annually from 1994 onwards at the Art Gallery in Odakyo Department Store, Shinjuki, Tokyo. I asked her to complete an *Hepatica nobilis* var. *japonica*, a small and unassuming plant which she had in an unfinished stage in her portfolio. These plants at the harbingers of spring in Japan and the first flowers are displayed floating on water in an elegant bowl, looking like tiny water-lilies.

25 *HEPATICA NOBILIS* VAR. *JAPONICA*
Signed Kodako 3rd Feb., '96. Acquired from the artist 1996. Watercolour on paper 200 × 190 mm.

Kazuko Miwa
Born Hiroshima, Japan 1943
Kazuko Miwa studied Oriental History at Hiroshima University in the 1960s. During a period living in England she submitted entries to the Society of Botanical Artists' annual show in the Westminster Galleries. She started botanical painting in 1990 when she went to Patricia Foad's class at Sutton College of Liberal Arts. I acquired this elegant drawing of *Datura metel* from the Society of Botanical Artists' show in April 1998. Japanese artists often draw in the outline of the petals with pencil, but here the borders of the petals are very delicately edged with purple watercolour. This curious form of the datura has a double corolla which she has drawn very well in all stages, from the tight bud to the fully opened flowers.

26 *DATURA METEL*
Signed K. M. (undated). Acquired from the Society of Botanical Artists' Westminster Show, 1998. Watercolour on paper 330 × 420 mm.

Yasuko Murakami
Born Tokyo, Japan 1934
I met Murakami Yasuko in Tokyo in the summer of 1997 when I saw the work of a number of Japanese artists who had been gathered together by Kazunori Kurokawa. I had come to Tokyo to try to organise a major exhibition of my collection at the Yasuda Kasai Gallery for the next year and Kurokawa was helping me sort out the details.

I liked the subtle tones of the fruit in her painting of *Ampelopsis brevipedunculata* (a climber native to the Far East), the design of the work and the good greens of the leaves. She had been taught by another of 'my' artists, Yoko Kakuta. Murakami has been painting as a freelance artist since 1996 and had a solo exhibition in Art Space 88, Kunitachi, Tokyo one year later. Before that she had won awards at the Botanic Garden of the Natural Museum of Science in Tsukuba, Ibaragi in three exhibitions.

27 *AMPELOPSIS BREVIPEDUNCULATA*
Signed Y. Murakami (undated).
Acquired from the artist 1997
Watercolour, pencil, pen & ink on paper 450 × 340 mm.

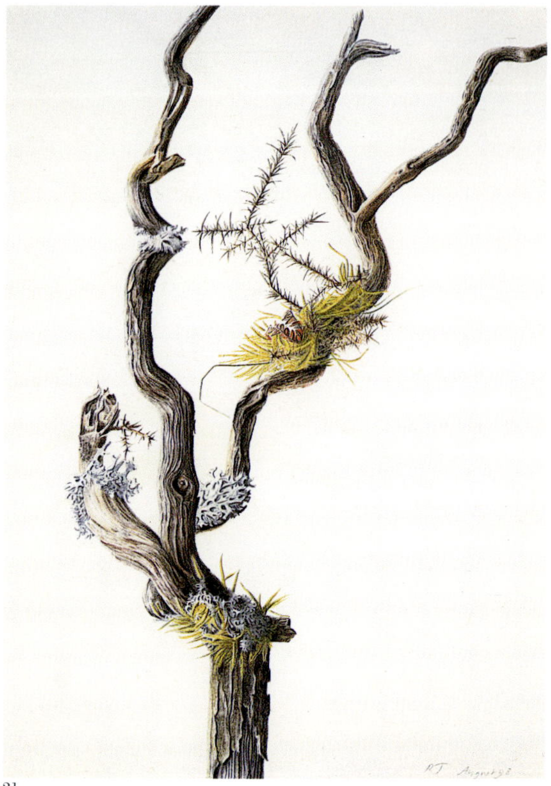
21

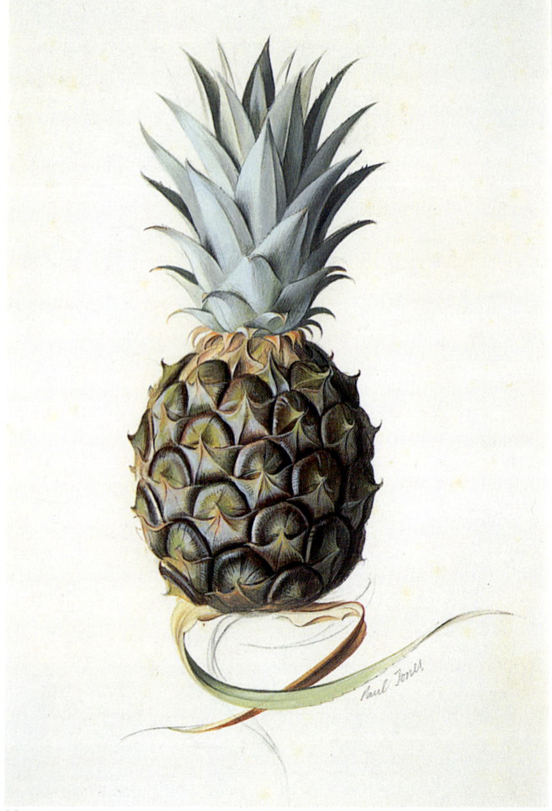
22

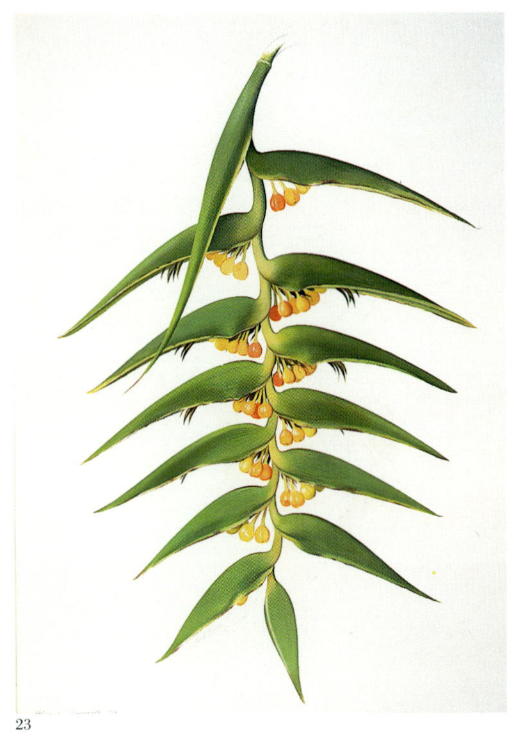
23

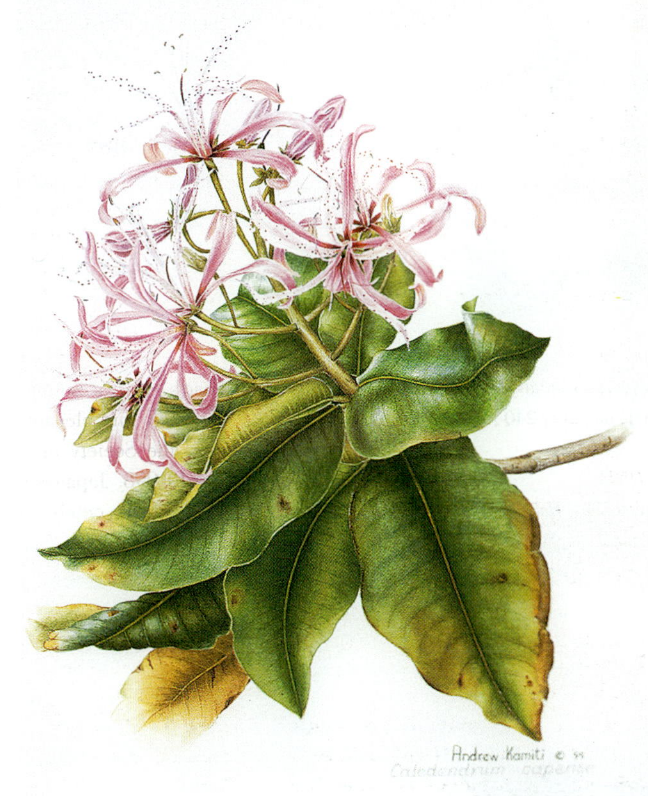

24

25

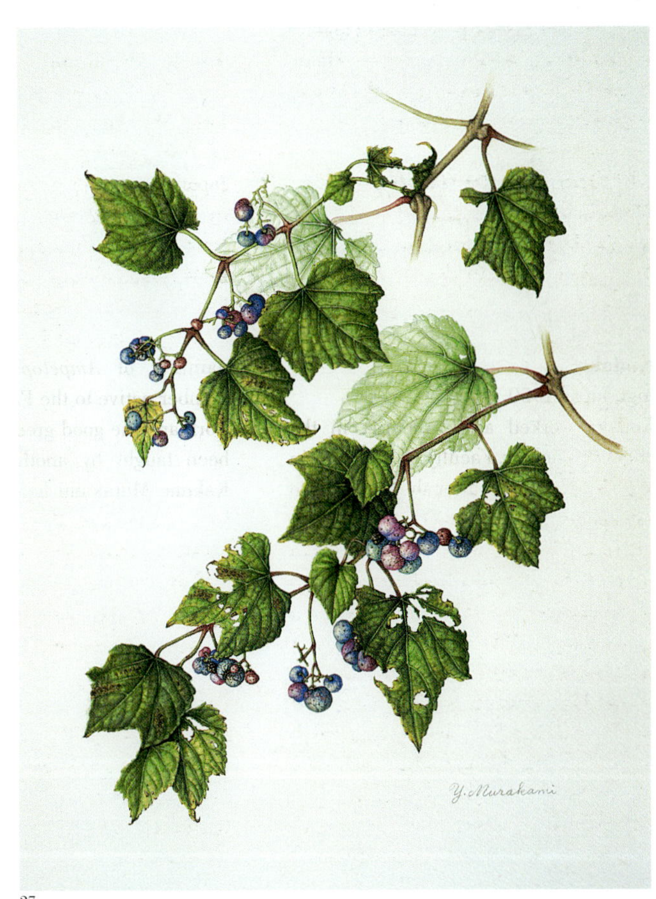

26

27

Kate Nessler
See main entry for biographical details

28 BLACK GUM LEAF
Signed Nessler (undated).
Gift from the artist 1999
Watercolour on vellum 130 × 80 mm.

29 HYACINTH
Signed Nessler 1996.
Acquired from Park Walk Gallery, London 1997
Watercolour on paper 350 × 265 mm.

Alvaro Nunes
See main entry for biographical details

30 *ORBIGNYA SPECIOSA*
Signed *Orbignya speciosa* Alvaro Nunes 94.
Acquired from the artist 1999
Watercolour on paper 395 × 280 mm.

31 *ARISTOLOCHIA* SP.
Signed Alvaro Nunes (undated).
Gift from the artist 1999
Watercolour on paper 201 × 300 mm

Katherine Anne Pickles
Born London, England 1953
Although born in London, Kathy Pickles now lives far north of the Scottish mainland on one of the remote Orkney islands. She read History of Art between 1974 and 1979 at the University of Sussex and became a botanical artist in the early 1980s. She started by having a number of solo exhibitions in small galleries in Orkney and by the mid-1990s was showing in Kew Garden's Gallery and at the Hunt Institute for Botanical Documentation. She was awarded five gold medals at the RHS between 1991 and 1996. I acquired the cyclamen from one of those RHS displays.

She is represented in a number of public collections, including the RHS's Lindley Library, and the Royal Botanic Gardens in both Edinburgh and Kew. She has worked extensively on ceramic designs, including the Franklin Mint's 1997 Chelsea Flower Show Plate. Living so far north does give her some problems with subject matter to paint, as the growing season is relatively short. Her style is very meticulous and precise and she is wonderfully accurate.

32 *CYCLAMEN HEDERIFOLIUM*
Signed Kathy Pickles '96.
Acquired from the RHS Show 1996
Watercolour on paper 205 × 140 mm.

Elizabeth Rice
Born Canterbury, Kent, England 1947
I first saw her work in 1998 at the Hunt Institute's 9th International Exhibition in Pittsburgh where she showed a spectacular collection of citrus fruit that she had painted ten years earlier for a guide book to the crops of Britain and Europe. She trained at Exeter School of Art and Design and then won a bursary to work on wallpaper designs at Arthur Sanderson & Sons. Later she painted heraldic designs for the College of Arms, London, like another of my artists, Gillian Barlow. She has produced the illustrations for nearly a dozen books, particularly concerned with plants, food and wildlife.

She showed extensively in Britain in the 1980s and is held in the Bridgeman Art Library, London, in the National Trust Collection, Sissinghurst Castle, Kent as well as the Hunt Institute. Her commissions include presents for the Queen and the Princess of Wales and the Sultan of Oman on various special occasions, and she has designed cards and calendars.

As she has not been painting much recently she could only show me work for books executed some time ago. Eventually I chose a well presented drawing including comfrey, asparagus and saffron crocus for *A Field Guide to the Crops of Britain and Europe* by G. M. de Rougemont.

33 COMFREY & ASPARAGUS
Signed Elizabeth H. Rice (undated). Acquired from the artist 1998. Watercolour on paper 490 × 320 mm.

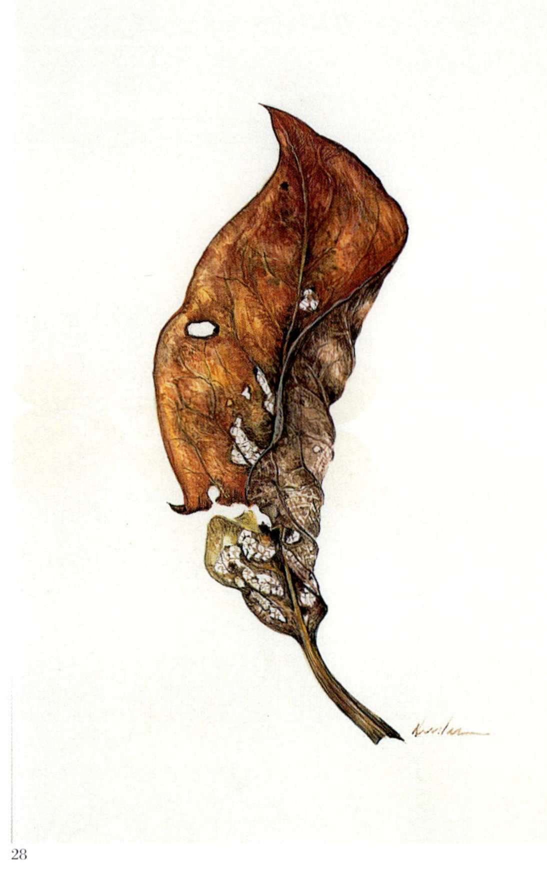
28

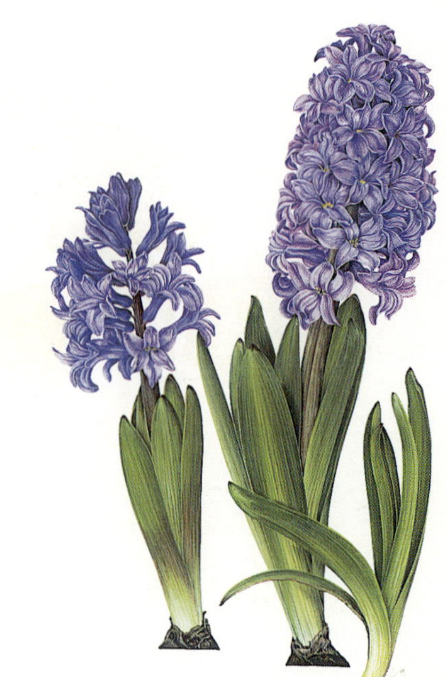
29

Orbignya speciosa
ALVARO NUNES 94

30

Aristolochia sp
Alvaro Nunes

31

32

Elizabeth H. Rice
© ELIZABETH RICE

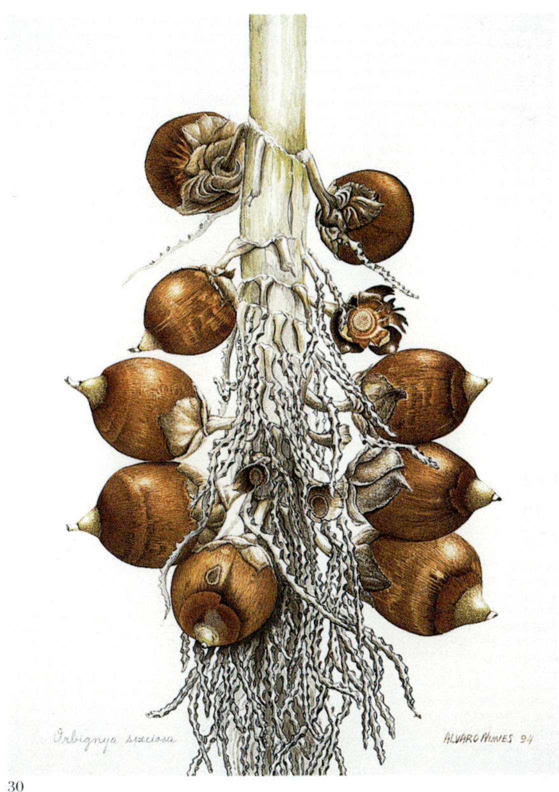

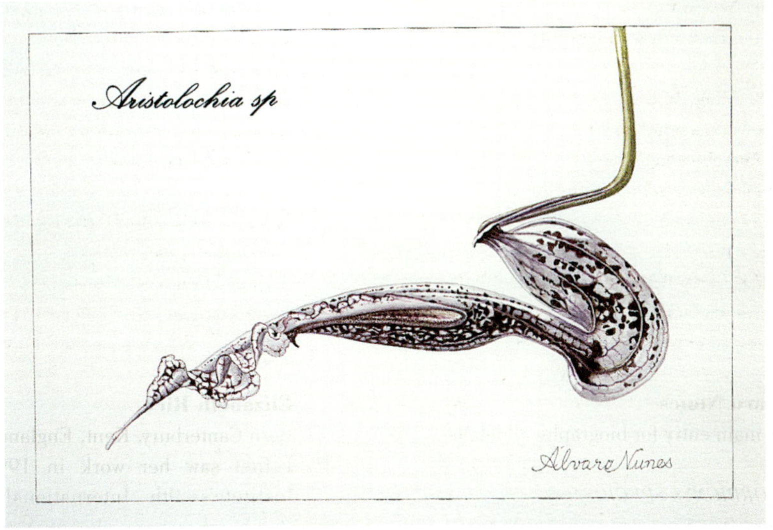

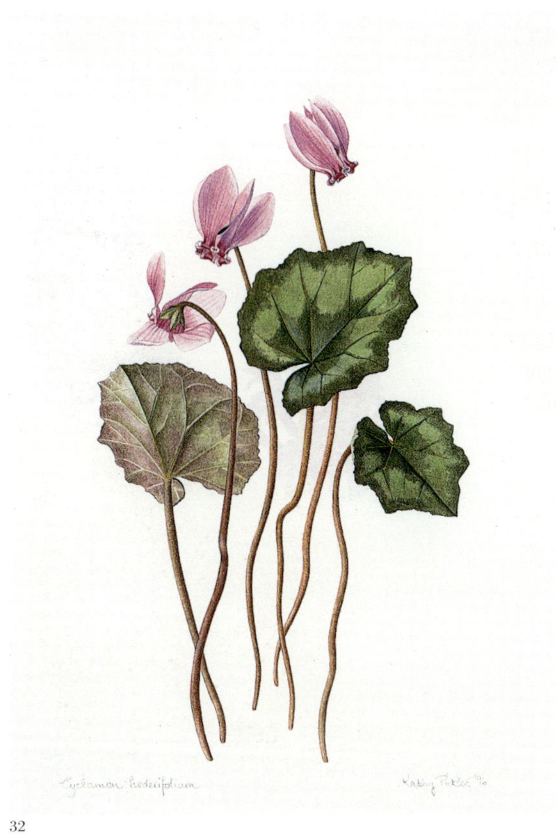

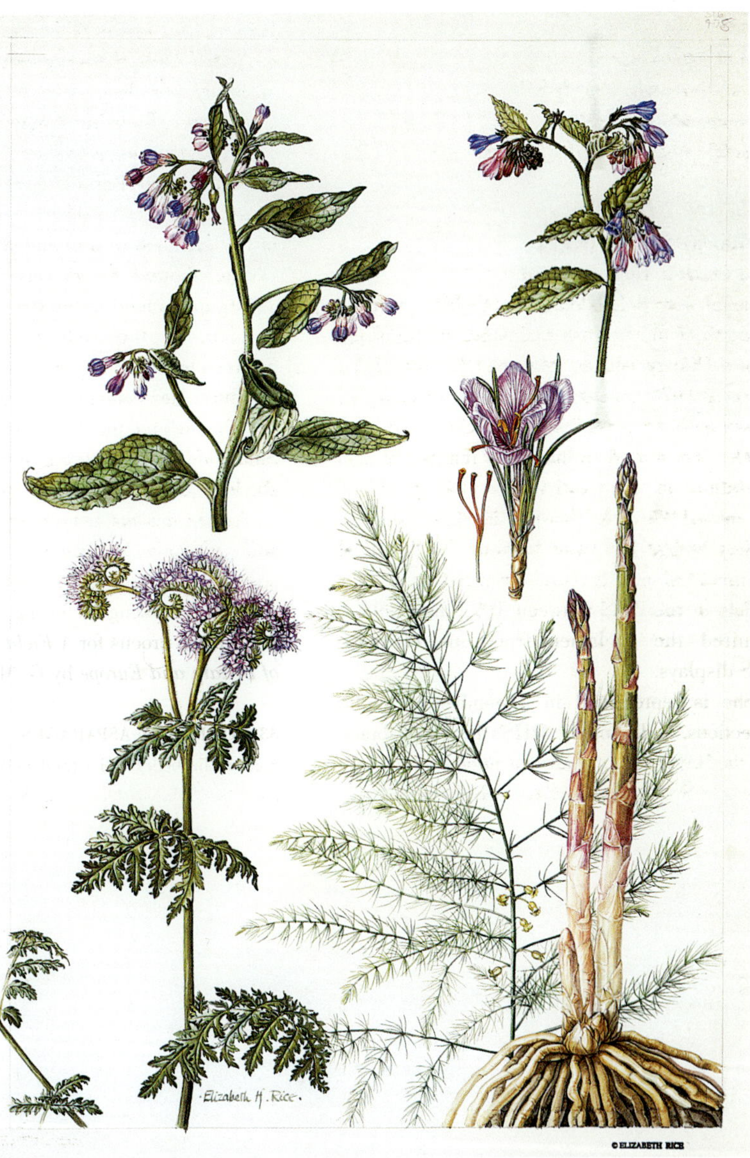

33

Takeko Sagara
Born Fkuoka, Japan 1930
I met Takeko Sagara when I was asked to see the work of a group of Japanese artists, organised by Kazunori Kurokawa. I found her painting of the yellow orchid *Cymbidium ensifolium* very fluid and decorative and more in the Oriental style than many Japanese botanical artists, who prefer a more confined, traditional Western approach.

Her career began as an instructor of nutrition at the Japan Women's University, then she became a botanical artist towards the end of the 1980s. She has had many group exhibitions in Tokyo, in the Metropolitan Art Museum in Okura and the Konoha galleries and in Tokyo Metropolitan Jindai Botanical Park, as well as in Kyoto. She is a particular exponent of Nanga or Suibokuga style. This technique is traditional in the Far East and consists of using black watercolour Sumi-ink on pure white paper to create subtle tones which express the emotions. She has been published in a book about this art form and was included in exhibitions entitled 'Contemporary Japanese Artists' Flower and Bird Paintings' in 1987 and 1993.

34 *CYMBIDIUM ENSIFOLIUM*
Signed TS. Acquired from the artist 1997.
Watercolour on paper 495 × 565 mm.

Sara Anne Schofield
See main entry for biographical details

35 BOG BEAN: *MENYANTHES TRIFOLIATA*
Signed SAS (undated). Gift from the artist 1997
Watercolour on paper 295 × 190 mm.

P. N. Sharma
Born Dehra Dun, India 1922
On one of my many visits to the Hunt Institute for Botanical Documentation on the Carnegie Mellon Campus at Pittsburgh I saw four wonderful drawings of bamboo painted in 1985 by P. N. Sharma. James White, the Curator of Art, explained that he had visited Dehra Dun Forest Research Institute and met the artist at this time. Sharma trained under Thakur Ganga Singh (1895–1970). James White promised that if he revisited Dehra Dun he would see if he could acquire a painting for my collection. Early in 1996, when I was having an exhibition of my collection at the Hunt Institute, James White showed me a substantial portfolio of Sharma's work, this time of rhododendrons. I chose this large, bold work, *Rhododendron wightii*, painted in 1993.

Sharma became a freelance botanical illustrator in 1945 and joined the Botany Branch of the Forest Research Institute at Dehra Dun in 1946. He showed in many exhibitions in India and has paintings in Parliament House, New Delhi and various universities and Indian Embassies abroad. He has illustrated a most impressive list of publications. Jim White describes him as a small, polite man who has retired from his position as senior artist at Dehra Dun Research Institute in 1980 but still continues painting and lives nearby.

36 *RHODODENDRON WIGHTII*
Signed P. Sharma 1993. Acquired from the Hunt Institute 1996. Gouache on paper 845 × 695 mm.

Camilla Speight
See main entry for biographical details

37 JADE VINE: *STRONGYLODON MACROBOTRYS*
Signed CS 94. Acquired from the artist 1997.
Line drawing 295 × 418 mm.

38 *BANKSIA COCCINEA*
Signed CS 96. Acquired from the artist 1997.
Pen & ink illustration 200 × 140 mm.

Alexander Viazmensky
See main entry for biographical details

39 *AMANITA PANTHERINA*
Signed with heiroglyphic AV in old Russian (undated). Acquired from the artist 1996.
Watercolour on paper 245 × 185 mm.

40 *BOLETUS EDULIS*
Signed with heiroglyphic AV in old Russion 01.96
Acquired from the artist 1997.
Watercolour on paper 360 × 245 mm.

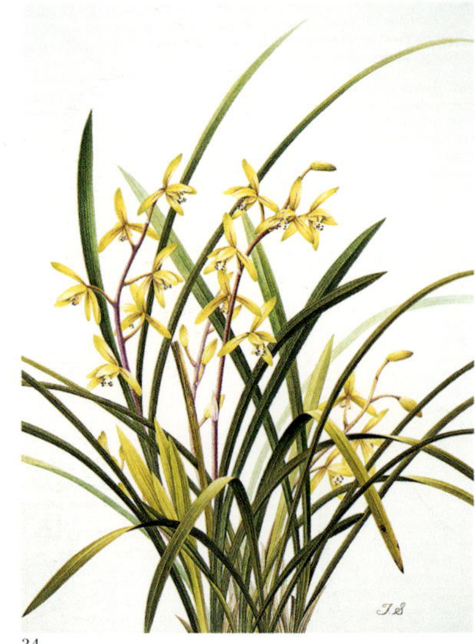
34

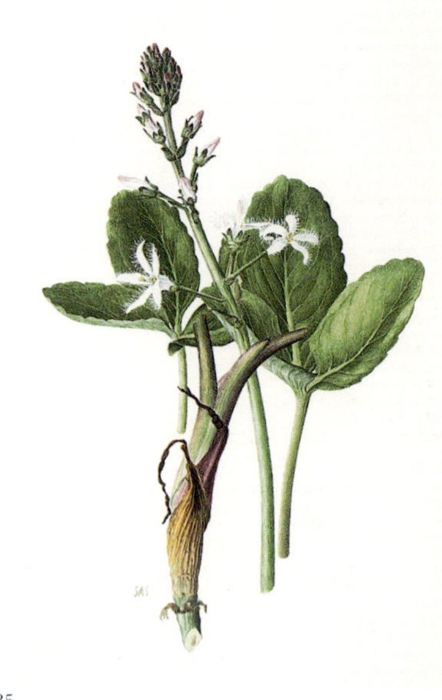
35

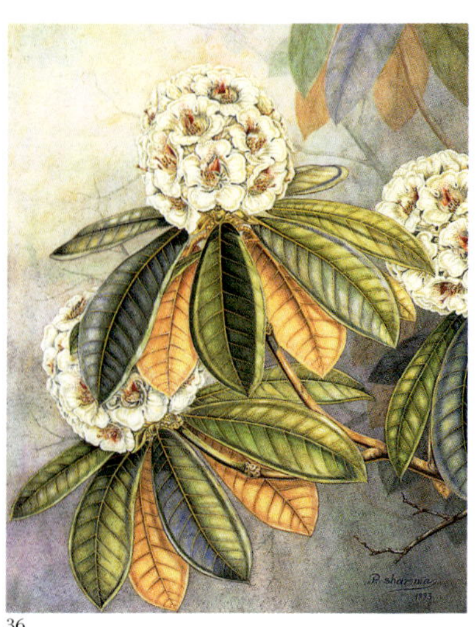
36

Mee, Margaret
Mee, M. 1980. *Flores do Amazonas – Flowers of the Amazon*. Record, Rio de Janeiro.
Mee, M. 1968. *Flowers of the Brazilian Forests*. Tryon Gallery, London.
Mee, M. (ed. T. Morrison). 1988. *In Search of Flowers of the Amazon Forests*. Nonesuch Expeditions, Suffolk.
Palermo, Luca Massenzio
Palermo, L. M. 1998. *Illustratore Botanico – Botanical Painter*. EdUP, Rome.
Purves, Rodella
Davidian. H. H. 1982–95. *The Rhododendron Species*. Vols 1-4. Timber Press, OR.
Rice, Elizabeth
Laessoe, T. 1998. *Mushrooms*. Dorling Kindersley, London.
Rosser, Celia
Rosser, C. E. & George, A. S. *The Banksias*. Volume I (1981) Academic Press, London in association with Monash University, Clayton, Victoria; Volume II (1988) Monash University in asssociation with the State Bank of Victoria; Volume III (2000) Monash University in association with Nokomis Publications.
Rust, Graham
Rust, G. 1996. *Decorative Designs*. Cassell, London and Bulfinch, Boston & NY.
Rust, G. 1998. *Needlepoint Designs*. Ward Lock, London and Harry N. Abrams, NY.
Saito, Manabu
Dana, Mrs William Starr. 1989. *How to Know the Wildflowers*. Houghton Mifflin Co, Boston, MA.
Sato, Hiroki (Hiro)
Sato, H. 1999. *Botanical Art – Works of Hiroki Sato*. Japan Gardening Society, Tokyo.
Sato, H. 1992. *Botanical Text Book – Drawing Flowers in Season*. Japan Gardening Society, Tokyo.
Sellars, Pandora
Cribb, P. 1987. *The Genus Paphiopedilum*. 2nd ed. Natural History Publications (Borneo) in association with the Royal Botanic Gardens, Kew. (Co-artist Carol Woodin.)
Speight, Camilla
Has contributed to many books including recent RHS manuals by Macmillan, London.
Green, P. 1997. *The Flore de la Nouvelle Calédonie et Dépendances*. Muséum National D'Histoire Naturelle, Paris.
Radcliffe-Smith, A. 2001. *Genera Euphorbiacearum*. Royal Botanic Gardens, Kew.
Tam, Geraldine King
Tam, Geraldine King. 1998. *Paradisus: Hawaiian Plant Watercolors*. Honolulu Academy of Arts, Hawaii.
Westmacott, Marion
Cronin, L. 1989, 2000. *Kew Guide to Australian Palms, Ferns & Allies*. Reed Books, Australia.
Cronin, L. 1989, 2000. *Australian Flora*. Reed Books, Australia.
Wilkinson, John
Has contributed illustrations to many books, including the following:
Mitchell, A. 1982. *Trees*. Collins, London.
Pegler, D. 1999. *The Easy Edible Mushroom Guide*. Aurum Press, London.
Zelenko, Harry
Chase, M. (ed.) 1998. *The Pictorial Encyclopedia of Oncidium*. ZAI Publications, NY.

Instructive Books
Evans, A-M. & D. 1993. *An Approach to Botanical Painting in Watercolour*. Hannaford & Evans, Oakham, Rutland, England.
Guest, C. 2001. *Painting Flowers in Watercolour – a Naturalistic Approach*. A & C Black, London.
Sherlock, S. 1998. *Exploring Flowers in Watercolour*. Batsford, London.
West, K. 1993. *How to Draw and Paint Wildflowers*. Herbert Press, London in association with Royal Botanic Gardens, Kew.

Where to Find Botanical Art

Many museums, galleries, libraries and botanical gardens have treasure troves of botanical art stored away in folios (often unpublished), printed in books and occasionally on display. Some commercial galleries represent botanical artists and even if not currently exhibiting, keep some of their work for consideration. Many of the new botanical art societies have newsletters. It is wise to make contact before a visit, if possible listing artists that interest you. Libraries are often understaffed or crowded and access can be difficult. The internet is a further source of information.

Information about the master classes that I have organised in Orient-Express Hotels can be obtained from: Botanical & Flower Painting Master Classes, Orient-Express Hotels, Sea Containers House, 20 Upper Ground, London SE1 9PF, Tel: 44 207 805 5068; Fax 44 207 805 5938. Email christine.martyn@orient-express.com. Teachers: Coral Guest, Katie Lee, Jenny Phillips, Margaret Saul, Siriol Sherlock. 2–6 day classes in Australia, Botswana, South Africa, Italy, and the USA are organised in Orient-Express Hotels.

The following is a non-comprehensive list of places I have visited or heard about from artists or through the teachers of my classes.

LONDON

Commercial Galleries that occasionally show botanical art:

Ebury Galleries
200 Ebury St, London SW1W 8UN

The Fine Art Society
148 New Bond St, London W1S 2JT

Thomas Gibson Fine Art Ltd
44 Old Bond St, London W1X 4HQ

Gordon-Craig Gallery
9a Trevor Place, London SW7 1LA

Daphne Johns Contemporary Art
12 Duke St, St. James's, London SW1Y 6BN

David Ker
85 Bourne St, London SW1W 8HF

Lefevre Gallery
30 Bruton St, London W1J 6LG

Park Walk Gallery (Jonathan Cooper)
20 Park Walk, London SW10 OAQ

Tryon Gallery (incorporating Malcolm Innes Gallery) 7 Bury St, St. James's
London SW1Y 6AL

Offer Waterman
11 Langton St, London SW10 OJL

Offer Waterman Fine Art Ltd.
74a Jermyn St, St. James's
London SW1Y 6NP

Societies, Museums & Botanical Gardens

Royal Botanic Gardens Kew
Richmond, Surrey TW9 3AB

Victoria & Albert Museum
South Kensington
London SW7 2RL

Natural History Museum
Cromwell Road, London SW7 5BD

Lindley Library, The RHS, 80 Vincent Square
London SW1P 2PE

The Royal Horticultural Society (RHS)
80 Vincent Square, London SW1P 2PE

The Linnean Society of London
Burlington House, Piccadilly, London W1V OLQ

The British Museum
Great Russell St, London WC1B 3DG

Fitzwilliam Museum (Broughton Bequest)
Trumpington St, Cambridge CB2 1RB

Radcliffe Science Library, Oxford
Parks Road, Oxford OX1 3QP

Department of Plant Sciences
University of Oxford, South Parks Road,
Oxford OX1 3RB

Royal Botanic Gardens Edinburgh
Edinburgh, Scotland EH3 5LR

The Society of Botanical Artists
c/o Mrs. Pamela Henderson, 1 Knapp Cottages,
Wyke, Gillingham, Dorset SP8 4NQ
(Show at the Westminster Gallery, Westminster
Central Hall, London SW1H 9NH every April).

CLASSES
Royal Botanic Gardens, Kew, Richmond
Surrey TW9 3AB (Teacher – Christabel King)

English Gardening School at the Chelsea Physic
Garden, 66 Royal Hospital Road
London SW3 4HS (Teacher – Anne-Marie Evans)

AUSTRALIA
GALLERIES, BOTANICAL GARDENS & SOCIETIES
Botanical Art Society of Australia
7a Loch Maree Ave, Thornleigh NSW 2120

Botanicart Gallery
1A Shipley St, South Yarra 3141, Victoria

Botanical Illustrators Group
c/o Friends of the Royal Botanic Gardens, Inc,
Birdwood Ave, South Yarra 3141, Victoria

Friends of the Gardens
Cottage 6, Mrs Macquaries Road
Sydney 2000

Wildlife & Botanical Artists, 39 Magrath Cres,
Spence, Canberra, A.C.T. 2615

Australian National Botanical Gardens, Clunies
Ross St, Canberra, A.C.T. 2601

Botanical Artists Society of Australia, 7A Loch
Maree Ave, Thornleigh N.S.W. 2120

CLASSES
Botanical Art School of Melbourne
460 Punt Road, South Yarra 3141, Victoria
(Teacher – Jenny Phillips)

Margaret Saul School of Botanic Art &
Illustration, 14 Dajarra St, The Gap, Brisbane,
Queensland 4061

JAPAN
GALLERIES
Hananoe Museum, 5-234 Oomuro Kougen, Itoshi,
Shizuoka 413-0234, Japan

Orangerie Collections, 1-32-11, Izumihoncho,
Komaeshi Tokyo 201-0003

USA
Many US botanical gardens have galleries where
artists show and sell their work, and run classes

The American Horticultural Society
River Farm, 7931 East Boulevard Drive,
Alexandria, VA 22308

Arizona-Sonora Desert Museum, 2021 N. Kinney
Road, Tucson, Arizona 85743

The Brooklyn Botanic Garden
1000 Washington Ave, Brooklyn, NY 11235

The Chicago Botanic Garden
Lake-Cook Road, Glencoe, Illinois 60022

The Delaware Center for Horticulture
1810 N. Dupont St, Wilmington, Delaware 19806

Denver Botanic Garden, School of Botanical
Illustration, 909 York St, Denver 80206-3799

The Missouri Botanical Garden
4344 Shaw Boulevard, St. Louis, Missouri 63110

The Morton Arboretum
4100 Illinois Route 53, Lisle, Illinois 60532

The New York Botanical Garden
200 St & Kazmiroff Boulevard, Bronx, NY 10458

Wave Hill
675 West 252nd St, Bronx, NY 10471

The New York Horticultural Society
128 West 58th St, New York, NY 10019

The Strybing Arboretum Society Library
9th Ave at Lincoln Way, San Francisco
CA 94122

The United States National Arboretum
3501 New York Ave, NE
Washington DC 20005

COMMERCIAL GALLERIES occasionally showing
botanical art in New York

Beadleston Gallery
724 Fifth Ave, New York, NY 10019

W. M. Brady & Co.
3 East 76th St, New York, NY 10021

Newhouse Galleries
19 East 66th St, New York, NY 10021

Shepherd Gallery
21 East 84th St, New York, NY 10028

Ursus Books & Prints Ltd.
981 Madison Ave, New York, NY 10021

SOCIETIES & LIBRARIES
American Society of Botanical Artists
The Salmagundi Club, 47 Fifth Ave, New York,
NY 10003

The Hunt Institute for Botanical Documentation
Carnegie Mellon University, Pittsburgh
PA 15213-3890

SOUTH AFRICA
The Old Mutual Conference & Exhibition Centre
Kirstenbosch National Botanical Institute
Rhodes Drive, Newlands
Cape Town

Everard Read, 6226 Victoria Wharf
Victoria & Alfred Waterfront, Cape Town

Everard Read, 6 Jellicoe Avenue
Corner Keyes Ave, Rosebank
Johannesburg

The Botanical Artists' Association of Southern
Africa, 1 Marcella Crescent, Newlands 7700
Cape Town

Artists in the Shirley Sherwood Collection

Capitals indicate an artist whose work appears in *A Passion for Plants*, an * after the name indicates an artist whose work appears in *Contemporary Botanical Artists*, while capitals and an * indicate that the artist's work has appeared in both books.

Sergio Allevato, Brazil
FAY ANDERSON* (b. Pakistan), South Africa 30–6, 248
FRANCESCA ANDERSON*, USA 32–5
GILLIAN BARLOW* (b. Sudan), England 36–7
Jeni Barlow*, England
MALENA BARRETTO, Brazil 38–9
ISOBEL BARTHOLOMEW, England 248–9
Helen Batten*, England
June Beckett, Australia
LESLIE CAROL BERGE*, USA 27, 40–3
Elizabeth Blackadder*, Scotland
Marjorie Blamey* (b. Sri Lanka), England
SUSANNAH BLAXILL*, Australia & England 17, 44–7
RAYMOND BOOTH*, England 48–9
Jenny Brasier*, England
Andrew Brown*, England
Jean-Claude Buytaert*, Belgium
Elizabeth Cameron*, Scotland
Richard Carroll*, USA
Jean Cassels, USA
Patricia de Chair*, England
ANNE M. CHAMBERS, Scotland 50–1
Gill Condy* (b. Kenya), South Africa
Jill Coombs*, England
ROY COONEY, England 250
Alison Cooper* (b. Libya), England
EMMANUEL CORDOVA, Philippines 52–3
VICKY COX, England 54–5
Patricia Dale*, England
BRIGITTE E. M. DANIEL, England 250
MOYA DAVERN, (b. Wales), England 56–7
Pauline M. Dean*, England
PIERINO DELVO, Italy 250–1
ANDRÉ DEMONTE, Brazil 58–9
ETIENNE DEMONTE*, Brazil 60–1
Ludmyla Demonte*, Brazil
RODRIGO DEMONTE, Brazil 250–1
Rosalia Demonte*, Brazil
Yvonne Demonte*, Brazil
Jakob Demus*, Austria
ANNE OPHELIA DOWDEN*, USA 62–3
ELIZABETH DOWLE, England 64–7, 250–1
MARGARET ANN EDEN, England 68–71
BRIGID EDWARDS*, England 10, 72–9
ELVIA ESPARZA, Mexico 80–1
Margaret Farr*, USA
Ann Farrer* (b. Australia), England & France
Jinyong Feng*, China
Dasha Fomicheva, Russia & Jordan
LINDA FRANCIS, England 82–5, 252
Ann Fraser* (b. India), Scotland
Linda Funk*, USA
Yoshio Futakuchi*, Japan
LAWRENCE GREENWOOD*, England 252–3
Mary Grierson*, (b. Wales), England
Gillian Griffiths*, (b. Wales), Wales
Noel Grunwaldt*, USA
CORAL GUEST*, England 12, 86–91

DAMODAR LAD GURGAR, India 92–3
REGINE HAGERDORN, (b.Germany), France 94–5, 252–3
Josephine Hague*, England
YVONNE HAMMOND, England 96–7, 252–3
WAYNE D. HAND, USA 252–3
Christine Hart-Davies*, England
TONI HAYDEN, England 98–9
Helen Haywood*, England
CELIA HEGEDUS, England 3, 100–3
SUE HERBERT*, England 104–5
BETTY HINTON, Australia 106–7
Helga Hislop*, England
Jeanne Holgate*, England
Nicole Hornby*, England
MARIKO IMAI*, Japan 108–15, 252–3
J. P. Irani*, India
MEIKO ISHIKAWA, Japan 116–19
REBECCA JOHN, England 120–21, 254
Marilyn Jones*, England
PAUL JONES*, Australia 8, 122–31, 254–5
Annette de Jonquieres*, Denmark
Jenny Jowett*, England
Yoko Kakuta* (b. China), Japan
ANDREW KAMITI, Kenya 254–5
Sally Keir*, UK
Martha G. Kemp*, USA
Patricia Kessler*, USA
Sharon M. Kincheloe*, USA
CHRISTABEL KING*, England 132–3
Charlotte Knox*, England
YASUKO KODAKA, Japan 254–5
Mariko Kojima* (b. China), Japan
Viet Martin Kunz*, Germany
Deborah Lambkin*, Ireland
Joanna Langhorne*, England
KATIE LEE* (b. Kenya), USA 134–5
Thalia Lincoln*, South Africa
Petr Liska*, Czech Republic
Elizabeth Jane Lloyd*, England
RORY MCEWEN* (b. Scotland), England 25, 136–7
DAVID MACKAY, Australia 138–9
KATHERINE MANISCO* (b. England), USA & Italy 140–1
SHEILA MANNES-ABBOTT, England 142–3
Alister Mathews*, England
John Matyas*, USA
MARGARET MEE* (b. England), Brazil 20, 144–7, 258–9
Lindsay Megarrity* (b. Australia), Italy
KAZUKO MIWA, Japan 254–5
Mitsuharu Mishima*, Japan
CAROL ANN MORLEY (b. England), USA 148–9
YASUKO MURAKAMI, Japan 254–5
KATE NESSLER*, USA 150–55, 256–7
ALVARO EVANDO XAVIER NUNES, Brazil 156–9, 256–7
Anne O'Connor, Australia
SUSAN OGILVY, England 5, 160–3
Miyoko Okakura, Japan
George Olson*, USA
BARBARA OOZEERALLY (b. Poland), UK 164–7
Luca Palermo*, Italy
Ronaldo Luis Pangella*, Brazil
Sharon Pedder-Smith, UK
JENNY PHILLIPS*, Australia 19, 168–9
KATHERINE PICKLES*, England 256–7

BARBARA PIKE, South Africa 170–1
Marilena Pistoia*, Italy
Jaggu Prasad*, India
RODELLA PURVES, Scotland 172–3
Reinhild Raistrick* (b. Tanzania), England
Kay Rees-Davies*, England
ELIZABETH RICE, England 256–7
CELIA ROSSER*, Australia 174–7
GRAHAM RUST*, England 178–9
TAKEKO SAGARA, Japan 256–7
MANABU SAITO (b. Japan), USA 180–3
LIZZIE SANDERS, (b. England), Scotland 184–7
ROSANNE SANDERS*, England 188–9
MASAKO SASAKI, Japan 190–1
HIROKO SATO, Japan 192–3
MARGARET A. SAUL*, Australia 194–5
Anelise Scherer de Souza Nunes, Brazil
SARA ANNE SCHOFIELD*, England 196–7, 258–9
ANN SCHWEIZER, South Africa 198–9
Gillian Scott* (b. England), Australia
Jenevora Searight* (b. UK), Brazil
PANDORA SELLARS*, England 14, 200–5
P. SHARMA, India 258–9
Vijay Kumar Sharma*, India
SIRIOL SHERLOCK*, England 206–7
ELISABETH SHERRAS CLARK, England 208–9
SHEILA SIEGERMAN*, Canada 210–11
Annika Silander-Hökerberg*, Sweden
Alan Singer*, USA
Arthur Singer*, USA
THAKUR GANGA SINGH, India 212–3
Julie Small, UK
CAMILLA SPEIGHT, England 214–7, 258–9
PAMELA STAGG* (b. England), Canada 218–9
Penny Stenning*, England
Margaret Stones* (b. Australia), UK
ANN SWAN*, England 220–1
Kazuto Takahashi* (b. China), Japan
GERALDINE KING TAM (b. Canada), Hawaii, USA, 222–3
Mary Tarraway*, England
Jessica Tcherepnine*, USA
VICKI THOMAS, South Africa 224–7
Michiko Toyota*, Japan
Marina Turina, Russia
Yoko Uchijo*, Japan
Arundhati Vartak*, India
ALEXANDER VIAZMENSKY*, Russia 228–9, 258–9
MARINA VIRDIS, Italy 230–1
Ellaphie Ward-Hilhorst*, South Africa
SARAH WASTIE, England 232–3
BRENDA WATTS, England 234–5
MARION WESTMACOTT, Australia 236–7
Joan Wilkinson, UK
JOHN WILKINSON, England 238–9
CAROL WOODIN*, USA 22, 240–3
Jane Wormell, UK
Hedvig Wright Ostern, Norway
Eleanor Wunderlich*, USA
FATIMA ZAGONEL, Brazil 244–5l
HARRY ZELENKO, USA 246–7
Tai-li Zhang*, China

Acknowledgements

First I must thank Jill Thornton who has worked alongside me for over ten years, cataloguing my collection and helping me with the manuscripts of both my books on botanical art. Andrew Donaldson has organised the sorting and packing of my paintings for exhibitions from Oxfordshire, and Pam Seally has similarly helped me in London.

Many have provided valuable help with setting up exhibitions: Dr Brinsley Burbidge, Professor Gren Lucas and Professor Sir Ghillean Prance at the Royal Botanic Gardens, Kew, UK; Timothy Clifford and Richard Calvocoressi at the Museum of Modern Art, National Galleries of Scotland; James White at the Hunt Institute, Pittsburgh; Paul Figueroa at the Gibbs Gallery, Charleston; John Bullard at the New Orleans Museum of Art; Catha Rambusch at Wave Hill, New York; Jay Kamm at the Dixon Gallery, Memphis; Kazunori Kurokawa in Tokyo for the Yasuda Kasai Gallery; Professor Brian Huntley and Merle Huntley at Kirstenbosch, Cape Town; Dr Staffan Carlén at the Museum Millesgarden, Stockholm.

I want to thank HRH Prince Philipp of Liechtenstein for permission to reproduce three of the Bauer brothers' illustrations from the newly published *Codex Liechtenstein* on pages 13, 15 and 16; the Natural History Museum for permission to publish figures on pages 11, 18, 23 and 26; the Royal Collection Picture Library, Windsor for the illustration on page 9 and the RHS Lindley Library for the illustrations on pages 21 and 24. Monash University Gallery, Victoria, Australia allowed me to use transparencies of Celia Rosser's original paintings on pages 174, 175 and 176, used in her recent book *The Banksias* Volume III. Thanks also to Robert Levitt for allowing me to explore his wonderful South African Library and Professor Peter Crane for recent help at Kew.

Classes on botanical art have been taught by inspired teachers: Coral Guest, Katie Lee, Jenny Phillips, Margaret Saul and Siriol Sherlock. These classes could not have been held without the enthusiasm and support of Orient-Express Hotels' managers and staff.

This book would not have been complete without the experienced professional help of my scientific editor, Victoria Matthews in Denver, whose speedy response has been invaluable, while Marilyn Inglis has pulled all the components together in London.

My family have become collectors too and I must particularly thank my husband, James Sherwood, for accompanying me to so many exhibition openings and for carrying home so many paintings by artists from all over the world.

First published in the United Kingdom in 2001 by Cassell & Co
Wellington House, Strand, London, WC2R 0BB

Distributed in the United States of America by Stirling Publishing Co., Inc.,
387 Park Avenue South, New York, NY 10016-8810.

Designed by Harry Green
Art Editor Justin Hunt

Printed and bound in Italy by Printers SRL and LEGO

A CIP catalogue record for this book is available from the British Library.

ISBN 0 304 35828 2